WINGS OF WAR

Now that the United States is the world's only superpower, it is sometimes difficult to recall how woefully unprepared was the nation's military—and especially the U.S. Army Air Forces—for the outbreak of World War II. *They Fought with What They Had,* Walter D. Edmonds's account of the early, dark months of the war in the Pacific, drives the lesson home. In it he tells the story of the U.S. Army Air Forces in the Philippines, describing not only the terrible inadequacy of the training and equipment there in December 1941, but also how the bravery, inventiveness, and downright tenacity of the American fliers and ground crew overcame the deadly shortfall.

Japanese air power was largely discounted by U.S. military leaders, despite warnings from such highly placed and reliable observers as Brigadier General Claire Chennault, who established the American Volunteer Group, better known as the Flying Tigers, in China in the 1930s and headed the U.S. air war there during World War II. American officials regarded Emperor Hirohito's aircraft as poor copies of Western designs and his pilots as physically inadequate and poorly trained. In the American mind, Japan's air force was "bush league."

The author shows in painful detail how tragically wrong these beliefs were. The skill of the aggressors conspired with fate, incompetence, and sheer bad luck to destroy the bulk of the American planes on the ground at Clark Field in the Philippines more than eight hours after word had reached it of the attack on Pearl Harbor. Five months later, by the last days of the battle of Bataan, all U.S. aircraft in the Philippines had been destroyed or evacuated to Australia and American fliers organized into provisional infantry units.

During the entire campaign in the southwest Pacific, U.S. airmen faced impossible odds. The Japanese Zeroes were better than any aircraft in the theater, and their pilots were battle savvy, averaging 800 hours of combat experience. The typical American fighter pilot, by contrast, had as little as 300 hours of flying time

TIME-LIFE BOOKS INC., ALEXANDRIA, VIRGINIA 22314

and no combat experience under his belt. Moreover, the U.S. pilots were flying a handful of obsolete Curtiss P-40 and Seversky P-35 fighters. The Boeing B-17 bombers that had survived the initial Japanese onslaught lacked heavy bombs and armor, and finally did their best work in reconnaissance.

Threaded through this account of a long series of defeats are stories of hundreds of individuals whose acts of heroism set the standard for the entire war: Captain Colin Kelly, who made a sacrificial attack on a Japanese cruiser. Lieutenant Boyd "Buzz" Wagner, who, by the fourth day of the war, had destroyed five enemy planes in combat, the number required to win the airmen's designation as an ace. Or sharp-eyed Lieutenant Grant Mahoney, who excelled in fighting and reconnaissance. Edmonds's meticulous research also details the careers and the achievements of people who were overlooked at the time, such as Captain Paul I. "Pappy" Gunn, who ferried vitally needed supplies throughout the Philippines, taking off in his twin-Beach from a cemetery near Manila. Edmonds praises as well the pilots of the tiny Philippine Air Force, recounting the story of Captain Jesus Villamor, who led six hopelessly obsolete Boeing P-26 Peashooters in an attack on 54 Japanese bombers. *They Fought with What They Had* is an inspiring story of personal bravery with a strong cautionary message about military preparedness for today.

Walter D. Edmonds based *They Fought with What They Had* on interviews with 169 survivors of the long battle, whose accounts he painstakingly checked against official records. Edmonds is the author of more than thirty books, including *Drums Along the Mohawk*, a novel set during the American Revolution, and *The Matchlock Gun*, a Newberry-Award-winning children's book about the French and Indian War.

Walter J. Boyne

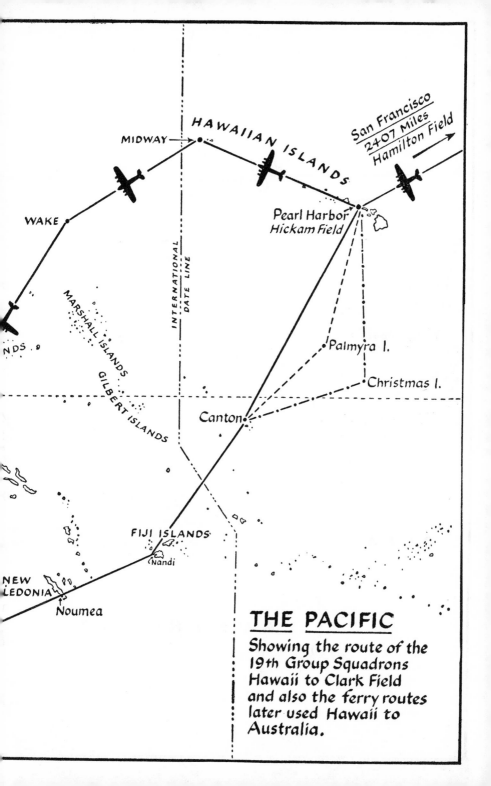

MIDWAY

WAKE

HAWAIIAN ISLANDS

San Francisco
2407 Miles
Hamilton Field

Pearl Harbor
Hickam Field

MARSHALL ISLANDS

GILBERT ISLANDS

INTERNATIONAL DATE LINE

NDS

Palmyra I.

Christmas I.

Canton

FIJI ISLANDS
Nandi

NEW
LEDONIA

Noumea

THE PACIFIC

Showing the route of the
19th Group Squadrons
Hawaii to Clark Field
and also the ferry routes
later used Hawaii to
Australia.

Books by Walter D. Edmonds

THEY FOUGHT
WITH WHAT THEY HAD

THE STORY OF THE ARMY AIR FORCES
IN THE SOUTHWEST PACIFIC, 1941–1942

☆

They Fought
With What They Had

BY WALTER D. EDMONDS

WITH AN INTRODUCTION BY
GENERAL GEORGE C. KENNEY, USAF

MAP SKETCHES BY THE AUTHOR

An Atlantic Monthly Press Book

LITTLE, BROWN AND COMPANY · BOSTON

1951

Grateful acknowledgment is made to the following for permission
to quote briefly:

Doubleday & Company, Inc., for *General Wainwright's Story,* by
General Jonathan M. Wainwright. Copyright 1945, 1946 by Jonathan M. Wainwright. Harper & Brothers for *Global Mission,* by
General of the Air Force H. H. Arnold. J. B. Lippincott Company
for *I Served on Bataan,* by Juanita Redmond. The Macmillan Company for *Bataan: The Judgment Seat,* by Lieutenant Colonel Allison Ind. William Morrow & Company, Inc., for *The Brereton
Diaries,* by Lieutenant General Lewis H. Brereton. Copyright 1946
by Lewis H. Brereton. *The Philadelphia Inquirer* for *The Turn of
the Tide,* by Major Edward C. Teats, as told to John M. McCullough. G. P. Putnam's Sons for *Way of a Fighter,* by Major General
Claire Lee Chennault and for *The Dyess Story,* by Lieutenant
Colonel William E. Dyess. Rinehart & Company, Incorporated, for
Battle Report: Pearl Harbor to Coral Sea, by Commander Walter
Karig, USNR, and Lieutenant Welbourn Kelley, USNR. The Uni-
versity of Chicago Press for *Army Air Forces in World War II,*
Vol. I, edited by W. F. Craven and J. L. Cate.

ATLANTIC-LITTLE, BROWN BOOKS
ARE PUBLISHED BY
LITTLE, BROWN AND COMPANY
IN ASSOCIATION WITH
THE ATLANTIC MONTHLY PRESS

*Published simultaneously
in Canada by McClelland and Stewart Limited*

PRINTED IN THE UNITED STATES OF AMERICA

Introduction

THIS IS a superbly written story of a shoestring war in all its grim and heartbreaking aspects—a story of the War in the Pacific during December 1941 and the early months of 1942 that has up to now been neglected. We have fought wars of this kind since 1775, but it is hard to find a time or place in our history when we were less prepared to withstand an attack than we were to counter the Japanese invasion of the Philippines in the closing days of 1941. A well-planned and skillfully executed surprise air assault on the morning of December 7th had wrecked our Pacific Fleet at Pearl Harbor and stunned the nation with its revelation that the only barrier to the Japanese conquest of the Far East had been removed.

That same day, December 8th Far Eastern Time, bombs rained down on Manila, Hongkong and Singapore, and during the next five months an empire that the white man had held for four centuries was taken over by the Nipponese who boasted that they would organize all Greater East Asia into a "co-prosperity sphere."

In the midst of all the confusion at home and in the Pacific, the heroic defense of the Philippines stood out like a beacon of hope for the future. There we proved that the Japanese soldier was far from invincible. Although his vastly superior forces finally took over the islands, the American and Philippine forces under MacArthur exacted a terrible toll, during their stubborn defense of Bataan and Corregidor, before our half-starved, malaria-ridden garrison was finally forced to capitulate on May 6, 1942.

This story deals primarily with the air operations during those early months of Allied disaster, which have been a source of bitter controversy ever since our small Philippine Air Force was caught on the ground and practically destroyed on the opening day of the war. Various air and ground generals and staff officers have been singled out in an attempt to place the blame. The author has not joined the list of critics. He has presented the facts and backed them up by one of the best research jobs I have ever seen. There was confusion in Manila on that first day of our entry into World War II and for several days afterward. Hawaii had its share of confusion too and so did the West Coast and Washington, D. C. It was an understandable reaction by a nation that suddenly realized that it was in a war for which it was woefully unprepared. All hope of saving the Philippines had vanished. With our Pacific Fleet out of action, we could not send troops to reinforce MacArthur. As a matter of fact we did not have the troops available to send. We did not have the aircraft to replace the losses in the Philippines. Back in the United States we did not have a single fighter or bomber squadron up to full strength in airplanes.

In the Philippines, with the handful of planes remaining, the story becomes one of individual exploits, of gallant sorties against overwhelming odds, of improvisation, of insufficient means, of heroism above and beyond all normal calls of duty. The names of Wagner, Mahony, Marrett, Dyess and Sprague among the fighter pilots, and of Combs, Wheless, O'Donnell, Pease and Kelly, bomber commanders, flash through this saga of brilliant personal heroism. Captain Jesus Villamor of the little Philippine Air Force, who led his antiquated P-26s against the Japanese bombers, and the incomparable Pappy Gunn who fought two wars at the same time, one for the United States and one for himself, are other outstanding figures in a galaxy of individual stars.

The responsibility for the state of unreadiness when the attack came, and for the early confusion, is so widespread that the author has wisely concluded to simply state the facts and let the reader make his own assessment; but one cannot help sympathizing with the inexperienced, insufficiently trained, individually good aviators, who had little but courage to fight with and who lost to the Japanese air force partly because of our own poor staff work.

Let us hope that this story of another case of "too little, too late," will drive home a lesson to the people of this country. We must not again let our defenses down. The next time might be simply—"too late."

GEORGE C. KENNEY
General, USAF

Foreword

THIS ACCOUNT of the United States Air Force units that were sent out to hold the Philippines against the Japanese is not intended as military criticism. It is essentially the story of the men themselves. In a way they are also its authors. For in their interviews, written statements, and their personal, group, and squadron diaries, they have supplied the material from which this book was written.

It is, of course, a story of defeat; and in defeat there is a natural human tendency to hunt for scapegoats. But to do that here would be merely to delude ourselves. The mistakes that were made at the beginning of the Philippine campaign, as well as the defeat that inevitably terminated it, were all implicit in the situation existing there immediately before the war. The poverty in modern weapons, or in more than one case the actual and abject lack of them, had its roots in the situation here at home, and for that situation the people of the United States must hold themselves accountable.

The army of a democratic society like ours belongs to the people, and the people therefore have an obligation to concern themselves in its affairs. If you run a factory or a business or even a farm indefinitely as an absentee owner, the hired management is almost certain to become hidebound in its methods and dictatorial in its defense of them. It then becomes next to impossible for men with more flexible minds to make themselves heard. That is what happened in the United States Army in respect to air power between the two World Wars.

General Billy Mitchell, who tried to take his case to the people over the heads of a reactionary command, was cashiered. The men who supported him and his beliefs within the Army were effectively bottled up. It is strange today to think of the names of a few of them: Arnold, Andrews, Doolittle, Eaker, Kenney, Knerr, Spaatz . . . We had our warning early in Roosevelt's first term, when the Air Corps was asked to carry the U. S. Mail. The resulting accidents and tragic loss of lives were not the fault of the flight crews. Those men simply lacked good airplanes, training, and the bare equipment for such flights. There was an outcry at the time but the whole matter was smothered in the Baker Report.

It is not my purpose to trace here the steps by which the development of air power was stifled. It is enlightening, however, to recall that as late as 1937 the development of long-range bombardment (specifically the B–17) faced powerful opposition within the War Department itself. Not until 1939, when General Marshall became Chief of Staff, were the shackles removed from the exponents of air power and men who had suffered actual or virtual banishment recalled to service. Only then was the Army able to begin preparing itself for what, at least in the Southwest Pacific, was to be primarily an air war.

But it takes time to develop combat planes, just as it takes time to train air crews, and at the end of 1939 little time was left us. When the Japanese struck, the United States Army had only 1157 planes suited for combat service. Of these 913 were based outside the United States on December 7: 61 heavy bombers, 157 medium bombers, 59 light bombers, and 636 fighter planes. But our first-line aircraft even by 1941 standards amounted to less than that. For though, in the case of the Philippines, General Arnold's Report listed a total of 316 planes,[1] there were actually less than 100 first-line planes fit for combat on December 7.*

The situation in the Philippines was a close reflection of the situation here at home. Undeniably there were officers stationed on Luzon during the prewar years who only wanted to let things ride along in the old, familiar, easy grooves. Many of them had completely failed to digest the lessons of the war in Europe, nor were they willing to accept opinions of other men who clearly foresaw what was going to happen when the Japanese chose to strike. But it was the niggardly policy of Congress towards foreign air installations and operations (reflected undoubtedly for

---

* More accurate was the Memorandum to the Chief of Staff, December 1, 1941, which listed 265 combat planes in the Philippines, 153 being modern types, 112 obsolescent. Even that was a somewhat rosy picture of the true status.

many years in the more reactionary members of the General Staff) that lay at the root of their inertia, just as that of Congress derived from the complacent habits of self-advertisement by which we had convinced ourselves of our invincibility. Too often we were willing to elect legislators who were accustomed to bound America by the limits of their own constituencies and pinch pennies at the expense of the national safety. In the last analysis, it was such "economy" that was responsible for the pitiful and desperate lacks that reached their consummation on Bataan, and then Corregidor.

The men sent out to rectify the situation in the final months had neither means nor time. The reinforcements and material rushed to them were not enough, arrived too late, or did not reach the Philippines at all. One convoy, caught at sea by the outbreak of hostilities, had to be diverted to Australia. Among other items, it carried the 52 A–24 dive bombers for the 27th Bombardment Group, which as a result, except for some 28 of its 1200 officers and men, was destined to fight its air war on the ground. This meant that our effective air power in the Philippines amounted to the 35 B–17Cs and Ds of the 19th Bombardment Group, and the planes of the five combat squadrons of the newly organized 24th Pursuit Group.

On the night of December 7, the 24th Pursuit Group's status report showed that each squadron had 18 planes in commission, making a total of 90 planes—54 P–40Es, 18 P–40Bs, and 18 P–35s. But as will be seen in the course of this story, the actual strength of the Group by no means equaled its strength on paper, for one squadron was flying worn-out planes, lightly armed with badly worn guns, outdated to begin with, and overdue for an engine change. Another squadron had received its last plane from the Air Depot on the same evening; none of its planes had finished their slow-timing (a process similar to breaking in a car motor) nor had there been an opportunity to boresight and check all their guns. Only one squadron had had time to become thoroughly familiar with the characteristics of the P–40s it was flying and not one complete squadron had had real gunnery training in P–40s. In fact almost none of the junior pilots in the Group had had a chance to fire their guns at an air target till they encountered their first Jap adversary.[2] Disregarding the matter of training, however, the bare fact remains that the United States had only 54 first-line, combat-worthy fighter planes to throw against the Japanese on the morning of December 8.

There has been a good deal of confusion and some loose writing about the strength of our Air Force in the Philippines at the beginning of the war. The totals vary from 200 planes all the way to 316; 300 seems to be a favorite figure among the commentators who wish to emphasize the way the Army was "surprised" in the Philippines, so it is worth while to list briefly the remaining components of our air power. Besides the three groups already mentioned—the 27th which had no planes at all, the 19th with its 35 B-17Cs and Ds, which had no tail guns and of which 34 were in commission, and the 24th with 90 combat-worthy pursuit ships listed—there was the Philippine Army Air Corps with its 6th Pursuit Squadron, and a light bomber squadron in training. The 6th Squadron was equipped with P-26s that had been turned over to the Philippine Air Corps in October when the already outdated P-35s were being replaced by P-40Es arriving from the States. These P-26s were ready for pasture; they were so old that, as the squadron commander put it, the rivets would pop out when they ran up the engines. The light bomber squadron was doing its training in three discarded B-10s.

Then there was the 2nd Observation Squadron (U. S.), attached to the 24th Pursuit Group, with ten or twelve O-46s that were augmented just before the war by a few O-52s, a completely inadequate plane. At the end of the first two days of war, practically every plane in this squadron had been shot down.

The list of miscellaneous planes included some twelve B-18s that had been relegated to transport service and eight A-27s—dive bombers—but as six of the latter were unable to fly, only two deserve listing here. Altogether, therefore, the Army had about 176 planes in operational shape outside of basic trainers, outmoded observation planes, and oddments such as the old B-3 belonging to the Philippine Army Air Corps. Of these 176 planes not more than 135 could be classed even by the standards of 1941 as first-line aircraft, and 125 of them were combat planes. But this total was our paper strength; actually, our Army entered the war in the Southwest Pacific with under 100 combat planes in tactical commission of a caliber to match the enemy's.*

It is necessary to keep that figure squarely in mind if one is to understand what happened in the Philippines. Seldom in any war has any country asked its men to stand against such odds. In the Battle of Britain, British fighter pilots were at least flying the finest pursuit ship in the world. They had a good system of airfields, good communications; they had replacements. There were no replacements for our men in the Philippines. They had no communication system worth the name; they had an inadequate air warning setup. There weren't enough airfields to permit effective dispersal of their planes. Of the fields they did have, only one possessed anything like real antiaircraft defense,† and in any case, most of the antiaircraft ammunition in the Philippines was of the obsolete powder fuse type that could not reach above 20,000 feet. They had to face shortages—in oxygen, which limited the effective ceiling of pursuit planes to 10,000 or 12,000 feet, or to the individual pilot's reaction to altitude, and in .50-caliber ammunition, which even before the war was so acute that Lieutenant Dyess's squadron were handicapped in their efforts to test and boresight the guns in their P-40s.[3]

These weaknesses were aggravated by similar deficiencies in the Army ground forces and the Navy, though undoubtedly these two services were more directly affected by the weakness of the Air Corps than the Air Corps was by theirs. General Wainwright has made the Army's situation at the beginning of the war abundantly clear.[4] As for the Navy's Asiatic Fleet, it is enough here to recall that its three cruisers were outmatched four for one by the enemy's battleships and its overage destroyers almost three for one by his cruisers.[5]

Finally the Air Corps was called upon to meet an enemy who not only

* The Navy Air Arm, except for a few small observation and utility planes, consisted of the 30 PBYs of Patrol Wing Ten, the "Patwing Ten" whose record makes one of the great stories of the war; but these planes, designed for reconnaissance and patrol, could add little to the offensive or defensive striking force in the Philippines. There were four seaplane tenders in the Asiatic Fleet—but no carrier.

† The antiaircraft defense at Nichols Field, for instance, consisted of a few World War I, drum-fed Lewis machine guns.

possessed an overwhelming numerical superiority in aircraft, but who had had battle experience.

In the light of such odds, it is absurd to try to lay the blame for the Philippine defeat to failures in judgment of any one or more of our commanding officers. There was no opportunity for any exercise of strategy in the air. The Japanese were able to throw a blanket of planes over Luzon. The best chance any small air force has of hurting a vastly more powerful adversary is to strike offensively out of secret bases, and, if possible, to strike first. But our Air Force was denied this chance because as a people we subscribed to principles of national honor and specifically here because the last War Department Directive received at General Headquarters ten days before the war, though warning that attack might be expected at any time, explicitly stated that if hostilities could not be avoided, the United States desired that Japan commit the first overt act.[6] Until Japan struck, therefore, our outnumbered squadrons were limited to purely defensive operations from fields well known to the Japanese, who had been flying night reconnaissance missions over them. The Japanese had only to choose their day.

The events of December 8 and the two succeeding days dictated the pattern that air war in the Southwest Pacific was to follow for the next eight months. By sunset on December 10 only about half of the B-17s were in commission, only a third of the fighter planes. The Observation Squadron was extinct and the remaining P-40s had to be carefully husbanded for reconnaissance. One thing about this opening of the war should be made clear: in the Philippines there was no surprise—in the technical sense, that is, of being caught unawares. (There were surprises over the excellence of Japanese planes and pilots that Intelligence had provided no inkling of.) The Air Force had been on full war alert since November 15. Except for the planes lost in the Japanese attack on Clark Field, the losses in both fighters and bombers were not much higher than the normal attrition rate to be expected when one's fields are under constant attack by superior forces. Of the planes lost at Clark Field, eleven were fighter planes of the 20th Pursuit Squadron, which was in the act of taking off when the Japanese hit the field. There were 17 B-17s, of which two or three were repaired after the attack. The reasons for these planes being caught on the ground by the Japanese have been the source of considerable argument, even recrimination. The fact remains, however, that if they had not been caught there, it would not, in all probability, have made more than a few days' alteration in the course events were to follow on Luzon. To the men at the time and of course to some of our professional witch-hunters, this loss seemed catastrophic; but in the perspective of even ten years it becomes incidental to the general pattern of the war.

After December 10, for a long time to come, the B-17s were the only real offensive weapons left in the hands of the Allied Nations, yet not till August 7 of the following year was the bomber command able to get more than ten of the big ships simultaneously over a target.* There is a legend, probably apocryphal, that General Arnold, in explaining to some men who were fighting out of Australia why they could not expect more support until United States production was able to catch up with the demands from Europe, called the war in the Southwest Pacific a "back yard war." It is a phrase that sticks in the mind, for that is very much how the war was actually fought, by a handful of men with a handful of planes and never enough replacements to let them get ahead of the game. But surely it was the biggest back yard in history.

Take for example the mission flown by the 19th Bombardment Group on December 22. By then they had been forced back to Australia and were operating from Batchelor Field. This mission was to be a major effort. Nine ships took off. They headed north for Davao Harbor and bombed it at sunset through an overcast, so an accurate estimate of results was impossible. That leg of the mission was 1360 miles nonstop. The planes then flew on to Del Monte on the north side of Mindanao,

---

* Three exceptions to this general statement should be noted. On February 11, 1942, in Java, the 7th and 19th Groups between them had 15 B-17s and 4 LB-30s scheduled for a special mission to Palembang. These planes were all forced to take off for air raid precautions and the mission was then canceled. On February 12, the 7th Group contrived to get eleven planes out on a mission against the Jap fleet near Makassar, but one plane had to turn back with engine trouble. Then on February 14, the 7th and 19th Groups put fourteen planes up on a combined mission against a Jap convoy reported off Bandka Island in what was recognized at Bomber Headquarters as a maximum effort. But the convoy was not sighted and the planes were recalled to their bases and ordered to stand by for the same mission next day. On the 15th, however, only eight managed to get off.[7]

landing after dark on the great seamed plateau, and there in the darkness their planes were gassed and loaded with new bombs. They were supposed to go on to attack the Japanese convoy landing troops in Lingayen Gulf 800 miles farther north. But because only six ships could be serviced at once at Del Monte, only that number were ready for the 3 A.M. takeoff. One of these blew a tire, a second had to turn back. Four planes ultimately reached their Luzon objective, two together, two individually, and dropped their bombs among the 80 transports. Only two planes carried 300-pound bombs; the others had to use 100-pounders. With Zeros rising to intercept, they turned about and headed south once more, stopping at Ambon on the way to refuel, and finally coming back to base on Batchelor Field on the afternoon of December 24. Altogether they had covered over 4300 miles to drop those few bombs with unknown results. Later they would fly even longer missions with fewer ships.

At times one wonders what they accomplished or expected to accomplish. At times they wondered about that themselves. They flew missions when and how they could with what they had on hand. A great many of their replacements came to them utterly green, but they used them anyhow. They had to. Unlike the Infantry, who were given months to train in, arriving Air Corps personnel were likely to find themselves in combat within forty-eight hours. Bombers often carried gunners who had never fired machine guns. Some pursuit pilots went into action after only fifteen hours' training in a fighter plane. It was wasteful war. It was disorganized. It reminds one a little of the old Indian wars on our forest frontiers, for the Japanese knew how to use the weather the way the Indians used the woods. It was a matter of ambushes and long hunts. There was no Intelligence worth mentioning. After December 8, 1941, with one exception the first real Intelligence briefing the men ever had came just before the Japanese attacked Milne Bay in August 1942.*

But during those black months our people were gaining experience that later paid off not only in the Southwest Pacific but, through training programs at home, in other theaters as well. They modified planes sent out to them and worked out interceptor and bombing tactics that were

---

* The exception was the talk General Brereton gave the officers of the 19th Group at Batchelor Field, Australia, on December 29, 1941.

to become standard practice. And they gained time. Their accomplishment, little as it may have seemed in that enormous area of island-studded seas, was probably the deciding factor that kept the Japanese from trying to isolate Australia before we were able to prevent him. Together with the work done by the Navy's submarines and her surface ships at Makassar and in the Java Sea, they hurt the enemy and slowed his southward advance. Their long bomber missions made him dissipate his planes among scattered bases, and in their defense of Java, Australia, and New Guinea, they drew some of the sting from his air power. Few American pilots who flew through 1941 and 1942 fail to mention the deterioration in quality of the Japanese pilot.

This book attempts to tell the story of what they did and how they did it. There is not a great deal of glory in it. In victory the tendency is to forget the unhappy times before we started winning, and this is largely true among military men as well as civilians. The emphasis, even in the histories, is all on how we won, not on how close we came to losing; and we read about how unbeatable our men were, how resourceful their leaders, how superb their equipment. All that is true and it is proper that Americans should find a source of lasting pride in its truth. But there is a beginning to any history, and though it is not a pretty story, the beginning of this war should be remembered.

It is not meant as a "glorious chapter" in our history. Glory is mostly a civilian word and unhappily it is too often used to cover up deficiencies. In the beginning of this war we went hero-hunting—if we did not have planes and guns, at least we could have heroes. It helped to make us forget the reasons behind our lack of strength, reasons that came back to ourselves as a people too interested in our prosperity to have time to defend it. It came back to our industrial preoccupation, and to our press that had been fostering it, as well as to our government. But in the end it came back to us. So we had to have heroes and we began to think of Bataan and Corregidor in terms of the courage of our men, and the two names have become symbols in the popular mind for something approaching victory. Emotionally there is a seed of truth in that—both emotionally and strategically the two phases of the war in the Southwest Pacific, the retreat and the return, are keyed to those two names. But actually, for the men involved, the defense was a bitter, ugly, and humiliating business. The men who took part in it will always bear the scars of that humiliation—not only the survivors of the Death March and the prisons, but the very few who managed to get out of the Philippines and tried with the pitifully little they found in the south first to fight back and then merely to delay the Japanese. For all these people, victory may palliate the humiliation but cannot wholly write it off.

Perhaps a word should be said here about how the book was written. Few records were available. In those first weeks of our war men had small time for keeping records. Most of the orders seem to have passed orally. Many of the group and squadron diaries were written up, wholly or in part, after the event. And this of course applies to the men who came out of the Philippines. Those who remained had no reason to keep up and can have had small heart for the paper work of war. So to get the full story it was necessary to go to the men themselves.

This book is therefore based on some 141 interviews with 169 officers and men who fought in the Philippines, the Indies, and Australia. Twenty-seven of these interviews were secured during 1944 and 1945 by two predecessors on this assignment—Mr. Lucien Hubbard and Technical Sergeant George A. McCulloch, whose preliminary work has proved of the greatest value. Forty-two interviews or written statements, including the experiences of 56 men and dating from the autumn of 1942, were drawn from Intelligence Files or the Historical Sections of various commands. The remaining 72 interviews with 86 men were secured by myself all in 1945. Thus a fairly wide coverage has been possible, not only in numbers but in time elapsed since the men had left the theater of war. It is interesting to note that the interviews taken later have proved not only more accurate but more informative.

Besides these sources I have drawn, as stated above, on group and squadron diaries, on some dozen reports by officers, and also on a few personal diaries, and letters written to me, and on several printed books, which are listed elsewhere, and which are, primarily, recitals of personal experience.

But for the most part this history rests on the spoken words and recollections of the men themselves. To rely so heavily on such a source may not make for definitive history in the eyes of military scholars, yet it may come as close to the truth. Newspaper accounts and communiqués and military orders are not always concerned first with the people who are their lifeblood. The average reader following the war in the press would never have heard of the 5th Air Base Unit and its work on Mindanao or the 803rd Aviation Engineers. Nor would he have found in them any reference to Corporal Wiezorek, whose death will provide the closing incident of the second volume of this narrative.

A short and quiet-spoken sergeant, so recently off a torpedoed prison ship that his ruptured ears still drained, took pains to be sure that I had the story straight. He was not quite sure of Wiezorek's name, though he had it near enough, because he had never seen much of him before they left O'Donnell Prison Camp in the same work detail. But he remembered the way Wiezorek faced the Jap firing squad across the little opening in the coconut grove at Lumban, near the schoolhouse. He remembered the words Wiezorek said.

Wiezorek wasn't alone. There were nine men in the line with him that day, besides the other members of the work detail brought out by the Japanese to see ten Americans destroyed. There were many others on Luzon, on the other Islands, and in the Pacific everywhere our war was being fought. It is their kind who fight wars—they may or may not wear stars, they may but probably will not be decorated, but they will surely be called on again to die unless this country has learned at last to keep its defenses strong. We do not want to forget these men because they were defeated.

—W. D. E.

Contents

PART TWO

Java

List of Maps

PART ONE
The Philippines

I

Far East Air Force: Background to History

1. *Pacific Flight*

In ORDINARY TIMES a mass flight like the 19th Bombardment Group's with 26 B-17s, from Hamilton Field just north of San Francisco to Clark Field in the Philippines, would have made one of the great news stories of the year. But by October 1941 the times had ceased to be ordinary. The shadow of Japanese aggression that for years had been gathering over the Central Pacific islands had begun to reach deep into the South China Sea. It made a pattern on the map like fingers of a hand about to close, and though in the United States citizens still hoped to see their country remain at peace, the Army was aware of the urgent need for strengthening their defenses in the Philippines, particularly in the air. But the international tension had risen to a pitch that left no time for dismantling the planes and shipping them. They had to be got out by air, and the flight was to be made under the most stringent secrecy.

These 26 B-17s, together with nine others that had preceded them from Hawaii to Luzon in September, pioneering that leg of the route,* were intended to form the main defensive weapon of our Air Force in the Southwest Pacific. It is hard now to realize that so few years ago we could look upon 35 bombers as a major striking force. Time in man's hands, like distance, has become a variable quantity.

A second group of heavy bombers, the 7th, was expected to join them early in December, but that reinforcement never materialized in the

---

* These nine comprised the 14th Bombardment Squadron, commanded by Maj. Emmett C. O'Donnell, Jr.

Philippines and it was the 19th that for three months had to carry the burden of such air attacks as we were able to produce. A convoy with Naval escort, bearing the ground echelon of the Group, was at this time nearing Manila. Another convoy, which was to depart on the first of November, arrived only eighteen days before war started with two pursuit squadrons and the 27th Bombardment Group (light). The latter's planes, however, were to be shipped on a third convoy that left Hawaii on the morning of November 29 but, being caught at sea by the opening of hostilities, was diverted to Australia. The 19th Group was the largest single Air Force unit to reach the Philippines complete with its equipment.

The flight was under the command of Lieutenant Colonel Eugene L. Eubank, who had had long service with the Group and who was in large measure its creator in its present state. Assigned to him for the mission were the Headquarters Squadron and the 30th and 93rd Combat Squadrons, making a total of 234 officers and men. The remaining squadron, the 32nd, had been left behind at Albuquerque along with the 38th Reconnaissance Squadron, which had been temporarily attached to the 19th Group and one of whose crews was to rejoin it five months later at the other side of the world as a member of the 435th Reconnaissance Squadron. The men were well equipped and trained for such a flight. The 19th was one of the original heavy bomber outfits in our Air Force; for years its essential function had been the training of heavy bombardment pilots and navigators; and at this time it was the first priority group in the United States for personnel, equipment, and training facilities. The fact that it was to be sent to an outpost like the Philippines was evidence of the gravity with which the War Department regarded the international situation.

Over-water flight was not a new experience for the men of the 30th and 93rd Squadrons. In May of the same year they had ferried 21 B-17s to Hawaii, remaining there for two weeks to check off pilots of the 11th Bombardment Group in the new airplanes. They had then returned to the States aboard the transport *Washington,* which on this voyage was evacuating families of Army and Navy personnel from the Philippines, an augury that some of the fliers may have recalled when they entered the operations room at Hamilton Field for their final briefing.

Through the windows they could see their planes drawn up in line along the concrete parking apron. The big ships, sleek in their bright silver finish, dwarfed their crews. Their silhouette was not the same as that of the Flying Fortresses that only a little later were to become almost a symbol for war in the air. These ships lacked the sweeping dorsal fin, the upper and belly turrets, and the cylindrical extension of the fuselage through the tail assembly to provide room for the rear gunner and his guns. But they had the same air of being able to take care of themselves that has stamped every Flying Fortress Boeing ever built, whatever its series, even on the ground.

The men believed their planes to be the best in the world, and in many ways their confidence proved to be justified, for airplanes have seldom stood up under such abuse as these were subjected to, nor, when as badly punished, have still brought home their crews. But there were faults in them. One, which had already been discovered, was the tendency of the skin of the ship to crack from the muzzle blast of the .50-caliber guns above the radio room, and it had been necessary to install reinforcing at the Sacramento Air Depot. Other defects would come to light under combat conditions, but basically, except for the lack of tail guns, the planes were as stanch machines as the crews believed them to be.

The men themselves had little premonition of how close war lay ahead of them, in point of time if not yet of space. Their minds were occupied with thoughts of leaving home and the prospect of the long Pacific flight. In any case they had accepted a large share of the civilian myth of Japanese incompetence. While staging for the flight at Albuquerque, they had been given studies in interrogation and recognition, in the course of which they were told that Japan had only one decent airplane, called the Zero, but that very few were in production. The other Japanese planes were supposed to be definitely no good, with a top speed of about 150 miles per hour and a ceiling of only 15,000 feet.* As a result many of the men had the idea that war against such opposition would be a picnic, and if they had considered the possibility at all, they had not taken it with

---

* It is interesting to note that this belief in the low ceiling of the Japanese planes had become so ingrained that it persisted even after the first attack on Clark Field. On December 9, Lt. John Carpenter was briefed for a photographic mission to Formosa. The pictures were to be taken at 18,000 feet. If he had any trouble, Carpenter was to go to 20,000. "I'm sure nothing can reach you there," he was told.

any seriousness. But now they received a disquieting hint of what might lie in store for them.

The commanding general of the 4th Air Force, Major General Jacob E. Fickel, had come to Hamilton Field to see them off, and at the end of the briefing he spoke to the roomful of pilots and navigators for a few minutes, describing the increasing international pressures in the Pacific and telling them that they and their planes would serve as the United States's "big stick" in future negotiations with Japan. How attentively they listened it is hard to say, but his closing words must have come with sobering abruptness.

"Gentlemen, I wish you straight shooting."

The 30th Squadron was the first element of the flight to take off in the late evening of October 16, with nine planes. Four evenings later, at about 10:30 P.M., the others followed. They took off at intervals of a minute, but each plane flew individually. This avoided the strain of maintaining formation on a night flight of such long range and allowed the pilots to hold each plane to its maximum cruise performance.

They had easy weather. The flight was entirely without incident. The big ships, droning steadily westward among the clouds, seemed in the soft night light above the sea to swing with the turning of the earth, and the crews, except for the pilots at the controls and the navigators at their tables, were able to catch a little sleep. Towards morning they drew in upon the islands and then in the full light of day picked up Diamond Head and came down one by one on Hickam Field.

Here each element of the flight spent five days while the planes were being worked over. There was a good deal more talk in Hawaii about the possibility of war than there had been in the States, and the men became aware of a new kind of tension. Even the chances of a Japanese attack on Pearl Harbor were discussed. Colonel Andrew W. Smith, Surgeon of the Hawaiian Air Force, who had decided to make the flight out to the Philippines with the second element, took pains to inquire of some Navy people what the chances were. He was assured that nothing could penetrate the Navy's cordon of vigilance.

Smith had met the Group when they came in under their Special Orders and asked what their medical setup for the trip was. He found that they had only one man, fresh from civilian life, assigned to the entire Group.* Deciding that there should be at least one surgeon along to cover the second element of the flight, Smith had asked for the assignment for himself. The route needed to be surveyed from a medical angle, for it seemed evident that more and more planes would be going out, and that some regular equipment for the flight should be established. Moreover, the men had had no medical briefing whatever for the tropics. Relatively little was known at the time or thought sufficiently important to tell them. For instance, they had not even been warned of as elementary a fact as that one can get ear fungus from swimming in tropical waters.

The men were beginning to take stock in other ways also. In their briefing for the flight from Hickam to Manila, orders were issued to combat load all armament. "In the event of contact in the air with planes of a possibly belligerent nation, do not hesitate to bring them under immediate and accurate fire." [1] They had now learned the course they were to fly. The first two legs would follow the route of the Clippers to Midway and Wake. But from Wake Island, instead of keeping on to Guam, they would head southwest to Port Moresby in Papuan New Guinea; then westward to Darwin; and, finally, north to Manila.

The purpose of this great southward loop was to avoid having to land on Guam, which the Japanese would be able to pinch off whenever they felt like it. But the hop from Wake to Port Moresby crossed the eastern end of the Carolines in the Japanese mandate and, specifically, passed close to the island of Ponape, which was believed to be one of the strongest Japanese bases. There was no uncertainty about the intent of the orders: what impressed the crews now for the first time was that the ammunition boxes in their B–17s, with a capacity of from 25 to 50 rounds, seemed inadequate, and that there were only 100 rounds provided for each gun, about enough for one good burst of fire. Some of the men ironically recalled General Fickel's parting wish.

But the flight proceeded smoothly. Once more the 30th Squadron led off, to be followed by the rear element on October 27. Both of these next two hops, to Midway and then to Wake, were made in formation with the exception of two planes which were held up at Hickam for repairs

* This was Maj. Luther C. Heidger.

or necessary maintenance, and the squadrons flew in a wide-spaced line at right angles to their course to make sure of picking up their objective. Four hours out of Hickam, the 93rd ran into a severe rain squall and dropped down until the big ships were flying less than 500 feet above the sea; but they came out into the clear again and two hours later picked up the Midway Islands, tiny husks of land caught in the bent hook of a reef.

Two days were spent on Midway and then, on the morning of the 30th, the rear element took off for Wake. At 7:15 that morning they crossed the International Date Line, so that October 30 became October 31. It was a tranquil day with a blue sea shading imperceptibly into a blue sky and broken, white, and sun-filled clouds through which the planes made their approach to Wake early in the afternoon.* Here they found that the reason for the 30th Squadron's being held up was a tropical storm across the course to Moresby. But now time was beginning to run short and their own take-off was set for ten o'clock that same night.

The leg to Moresby, longest of the entire transpacific flight, was to be made at night and at high altitude to minimize the chance of Japanese interference. It had been pioneered in the first week of September by the 14th Bombardment Squadron with nine B-17Ds under Major Emmett C. O'Donnell, Jr., universally known as "Rosie." This squadron had been hastily organized from the 5th and 11th Bombardment Groups of the 7th Air Force in Hawaii while an advance agent was sent out from Manila to New Guinea and Australia to check on airfields and the availability of high octane gas.†

An amusing incident had occurred when the 14th was crossing the Carolines. They were under orders to preserve radio silence until they were well clear of Ponape. About an hour after sunrise, when all members should have been safely past Ponape, O'Donnell began to call for reports from the other planes. He naturally could not know that the

* By coincidence Maj. Gen. Lewis H. Brereton, on his way out to Manila by Pan American Clipper to take command of our air forces in the Philippines, was also held up on Wake by this same bad weather and saw the planes of his future command come in to land.[2]

† This was Capt. Floyd J. Pell, who was later killed over Darwin in the Japanese attack of February 19, 1942.[3]

leader of the second flight, Major William P. Fisher, had had to put back to Wake shortly after take-off for quick repairs to a broken oil line. Consequently he was flying about two hours behind the rest and did not come in when O'Donnell requested reports. Finally O'Donnell called Fisher by name and asked for his position.

"I'd hate to tell you," Fisher replied.

One of the other pilots, describing their reactions, wrote that "every plane in the flight must have echoed to substratospheric chuckles. We knew instantly that Bill was sitting right on top of Ponape at high altitude that very minute in broad daylight!" [4]

No such mischance occurred when the 19th Group made its passage above the Carolines. Each flew alone and for the first eight hours they kept close to 22,000 feet, with the crews on oxygen and dozing fitfully. It was a long night for them, but longer for the navigators. They ran into dirty weather—their first taste of a big tropical front. The overcast was so high, extensive, and heavy that for five of the night hours through which they flew, the navigators could get only a very few glimpses of the sky through their octants. They had none of the usual radio aids and, as one said, he was sweating out the weather, not the Japs, when they went over Ponape at half past three in the morning.

Well after daylight they started letting down. A little before eight, they crossed the Tabar Islands and the spindle shank of New Ireland with Kavieng 50 miles to the west. Then they were over the Bismarck Sea, themselves now west of Rabaul, except for three or four planes that had to go in for gas.* These swung away down over the little town, whose streets, deep in the hollow of framing hills, were laid out along the blue curve of the bay with two volcanoes smoking at the harbor mouth. They landed on one of Rabaul's twin airfields † that later they and many other fliers would seek and find at many times both day and night. But now the town drowsed in the midmorning sun and the sulphurous ribbon of smoke from the peak of Vulcan climbed into a flakless sky.

---

* Among the pilots forced to land at Rabaul were Maj. Birrel Walsh (Operations Officer for the flight), Lt. Walter R. Ford, and Lt. Sam Maddux, Jr.

† Vunakanau—across the harbor from Lakunai drome, and on top of a hill.

At the airdrome the Fortress crews were receiving their first lesson on Southwest Pacific runways. The surface crust had cracked under the unaccustomed weight of the B–17s and, with the help of the Australian ground crews, the planes had to be dug out. But the others continued on their long traverse into the southwest, beyond the scythe blade of Rabaul's western tip, over the Dampier Strait and the dark blue of the Huon Gulf, until they raised the green New Guinea shore.

Buna was on their left, Lae and Salamau on their right, as they crossed it, and for a way the land beneath them lay like a green lowland with deceptive openings in the jungle growth that looked like meadows. But as the ridges lifted southward, the jungle deepened both in color and in the texture of its growth. Behind the ridges the mountain slopes began, knife-edged and fissured, but covered everywhere by the impenetrable green of the jungle. The peaks were lost in towering cumulus clouds, and even at 12,000 feet the men in the planes could look out at peaks still higher. Now and then breaks in the clouds gave them glimpses of the wild upheaval of green-walled cliffs and mountain shoulders under them. There might be a chance sight of a native village of little, lost-looking huts in a precarious clearing. Otherwise there was only the unbroken forest, except where a landslip had laid bare the bone of a mountain, and the jungle fell away in broken folds to valleys and chasms at the bottom of which could be seen the white thread of a river pouring downward in a soundless roaring. To the men looking out from the oil-smelling, metal bodies of the planes, it was like looking into the earth's core.

These were the Owen Stanley Mountains. The planes with a final lift crested the range and started to slide down the southward slopes in their approach to Moresby. There was a haze that day over the seacoast, like the haze that covers Los Angeles at times, and some of the planes had difficulty in locating the field. A few landed with less than forty minutes of gas in their tanks.

The field was known as 7-Mile, because of its distance from Port Moresby, and lay in a circle of brownish, stunted hills. The runway sloped so that there was only one take-off direction for B–17s, regardless of the wind. At that time it had a dirt surface and the ground crews that came out to meet the planes were partly Australians and partly native

Papuans. The Australians were plainly worried by the southward drift of Japanese aggression.

Some of the American fliers were to know this place well, but only one or two of the planes that lifted from it on those mornings in late October and the beginning of November survived to touch wheels down there again. They flew out with good weather westward over the Coral and the Arafura Seas and picked the north Australian shore up beyond the Gulf of Carpentaria. As they passed over the base of the Cobourg Peninsula, they had their first view of Australia's wastelands, where rivers sink entirely into the sand and the scattered trees look less substantial from the air than their own shadows. The planes came out above the sea once more at Van Diemen Gulf and followed the scalloped coastline into Darwin, the last way station on their flight.

This little seaport town of some 1800 souls was supplied entirely by sea. Townsville, the nearest deep-water port, was 1000 miles away. Overland its only link to cities in the south was by 300 miles of narrow-gauge railroad and 600 miles of desert track. But the RAAF men stationed at Darwin brought out stocks of beer they had saved from their rations and threw a party for the Fortress crews. American accounts of this affair are not quite clear, nor is there any reason to suppose the Australian version would be any clearer, for, in the course of their Pacific flight, the Group had become stretched out widely and the leading planes were already in the Philippines by the time the last arrived at Darwin to receive the same Australian welcome. These, except for one that had lost two engines on the hop from Port Moresby,* all took off during the night of November 3-4. There were thunderstorms that had to be flown round and a strong east wind that carried some of the planes nearly 100 miles west of their course; but they had the full moon riding the clouds with them till dawn and they saw it going down just as the sun rose, when they were far out across the Celebes Sea with all the Indies, except

---

* This was Capt. William E. McDonald's plane, which had a hard time getting out of Darwin. It took a week's work to design a special rack for carrying an engine in a B-17 and then the replacement engine was flown down from Clark Field by Lts. Bohnaker and O'Bryan. The change was effected, but as McDonald taxied his plane out, it broke through the crust of the field, damaging two propellers. Replacement propellers were flown down from Clark Field by Lt. Col. Eubank, piloting General Brereton on his survey trip to Australia and New Guinea. The next take-off, however, was successful, and the plane reached Clark Field on November 20.

for Borneo, behind them. Towards 8:30 the tail end planes were raising Zamboanga and heading over the Sulu Sea. They kept well to the left of Negros and Panay, whose mountains were deep shadowed against the morning sunlight. Over the Cuyo Passage they could look down on the myriad islands—small, green-forested bits of land outlined by the thread of their own beaches, with the bright jade water of the shallows ringing them from the darker sea. Here and there were houses, and in the sea the posts of native weirs and now and then men in outrigger canoes.

A weather front had been reported off Mindoro. They saw it hanging in the east as they came abreast of the island; but they kept in the clear and by eleven were approaching Luzon. They came into it from the China Sea, striking for the entrance to Manila Bay, and swept over Corregidor and the round heel of Bataan. Clouds hung low over the Pampanga Plain and the top of Mount Arayat was veiled. But they picked up Clark Field, marked for them by the silver shapes of the planes that had preceded them, and the last one of their own flight came down out of a lowering haze a little before noon. The date was November 4.

They had flown more than 10,000 miles, almost entirely over water, and delivered their planes without loss and on schedule, except for McDonald's, which was waiting for its replacement engine down in Darwin. The American public knew nothing about the flight and in the light of present-day long-distance flights by B–29s it may not seem impressive; but in 1941 it was an achievement of outstanding quality, for which all members of the participating crews were subsequently decorated.

But as they parked their planes along the open borders of Clark Field and turned them over to the ground crews,* they were not thinking of decorations. There was much to be done. Billeting had to be arranged. Training schedules must be worked out. The Group had to be reor-

---

* The ground echelons of the Group had come over under Capt. Cornelius B. Cosgrove, embarking at San Francisco aboard the USAT *Willard H. Holbrook* on October 4. Another transport, the *Tasker H. Bliss,* with the cruiser *Manchester* as escort, accompanied them. They reached the Philippines October 23 and by nine o'clock the same evening were driven out of Manila in busses and up to Clark Field, which they reached about midnight. They were quartered in temporary barracks behind the hangars. These barracks, which later were completely destroyed, had nipa sides and mahogany frames and floors, which impressed some of the men a good deal. Twenty-five or 30 men were assigned to each and they enjoyed the services of Filipino bunk boys and the mess had Filipino KPs. However, for the

ganized to admit O'Donnell's 14th Squadron and also a Medium Bombardment Squadron, the 28th, which had been stationed in the Philippines for years but whose planes—B-10s and B-18s—were completely outdated. This was a strange post for almost all of them. They had a lot to learn about it.

2. *The Philippine Department*

ON ITS ORGANIZATION as a full group with headquarters and four combat squadrons, the 19th became the only bomber group in the Philippines. It was to remain the only bomber group—with planes—to reach the Islands until the Japanese on December 8 flew in across the China Sea. In its equipment and in the experience and training of its personnel, enlisted men equally with the officers, it was rated one of the most valuable groups in the Air Force and considerable opposition had been expressed to its being sent out to such an exposed station.*

For the antiaircraft defenses of Luzon were hardly worth the name. A very sobering scarcity of antiaircraft guns and ammunition was made still more serious by the fact that not a single radar direction finder was then in operation. Communications were primitive, depending largely on ground wires, and Air Force transportation had already been found inadequate for handling the movement of some four squadrons between two fields.†

first few days the 30th Squadron had to mess with the 28th, for the *Holbrook* had sprung a leak and all the 30th's kitchen equipment had come out coated with engine oil. It would have been a good setup for the men if there had been more for them to do in off hours. Some got into town once or twice, but the P-X was about the only diversion they had. Luckily they could get beer there. Most of their spare time was spent sifting the rumors that they were to be moved on, some thought to China. Like the officers, they still weren't sure of the score.

* Among those voicing objections was General Brereton, who was to command the Far East Air Force throughout its disastrous campaign in the Philippines and Netherlands East Indies, December 8, 1941, to February 24, 1942. Events served only to confirm his original conviction. "Prior to my departure from Washington I stated that in the event of war it was almost certain to incur destruction of a bomber force put in the Philippine Islands without providing adequate antiaircraft defense." [1]

† As General Wainwright points out, this shortage was even more serious in the Infantry.[2]

These conditions would have thrown an added burden on even an adequate pursuit force; but the total pursuit protection on Luzon was afforded by the three combat squadrons of the newly activated 24th Pursuit Group [3] and the 6th Pursuit Squadron of the Philippine Air Force. The three American squadrons were the 17th, 3rd, and 20th, and of them only the last had been equipped with first-line planes for any length of time. These were P-40Bs, which had been received in July. The 17th and 3rd Squadrons were still accepting delivery on their new planes from a consignment of about 70 P-40Es.[4] During these same days, the Philippine Army Air Corps's 6th Squadron finally got into the air in something besides their Stearman trainers, when twelve antiquated P-26s were turned over to them.

As these deficiencies became apparent to them, it was natural for the responsible command of the 19th Group to feel increasing uneasiness. They had already discovered that passive measures of antiaircraft defense, such as dispersal and camouflage, were next to impossible. When they landed after their Pacific flight, Clark Field was the one available airdrome for B-17s on Luzon. The only other field in the Islands on which a B-17 supposedly could land was a natural meadow in the Del Monte pineapple plantations on Mindanao, 800 miles to the south. It had not been developed, however, and lacked any servicing facilities. Clark Field itself was turf-surfaced and the ground surrounding it was too wet to carry the weight of a B-17. It had proved impossible to win any appropriation for draining it. All the 19th Group could do in the way of dispersal was to park their planes round the edge of the landing field in such a way that no more than two planes would be in line. But the field lay in the open country well out from the green hills that scarp Mount Pinatubo. Half a mile west was Fort Stotsenburg with its pattern of large white administration buildings, polo field, and neat rows of quarters. Twelve miles to the east the cone of Mount Arayat lifted nearly 4000 feet out of the Pampanga Plain, a solitary and unmistakable landmark. Yet even without these sighting points, the silver of the big planes parked out on the open grass could, in clear weather, be picked up from over 25 miles out by an approaching pilot.*

* As a matter of fact, one pilot speaks of picking up the shine of the planes from over 70 miles out when they were parked on the upland field at Del Monte.[5]

PHILIPPINE
ISLANDS

STATUTE MILES

0 10 50 100 200

BATAN
ISLANDS

Aparri

Vigan

Tuguegarao

San Fernando

Baguio

Rosales

Tarlac • Cabanatuan **LUZON**

Iba

Fort Stotsenburg • Clark Field

Olongapo • S. Fernando

BATAAN • Manila

CORREGIDOR Lamon Bay San Miguel Bay

Legaspi

MINDORO

San Jose

CULION

SAMAR

PANAY

Iloilo Tacloban

CEBU

Cebu

NEGROS

BOHOL

Surigao

SULU SEA

Cagayan

Del Monte
Malaybalay

MINDANAO

Lake Lanao
Cotabato Davao

Zamboanga

JOLO

BORNEO **CELEBES SEA**

PACIFIC OCEAN

CHINA SEA

Lingayen Gulf

PALAWAN

But if the vulnerability of the B-17s at Clark Field troubled Colonel Eubank and his officers, their presence there put new heart into the little Air Force of which they now formed the offensive arm. How much their presence meant, especially to the few men who had seen the issues clearly, can only be understood by tracing the effort to build an air force in the Philippines.

There was a saying out there that when a plane was worn out at home it was sent to Hawaii; and when the people in Hawaii thought it was worn out, they passed the plane on to the Philippines. This was not far from being the truth. The Philippine Department of the United States Army had enjoyed a lower priority rating than the Hawaiian Department, and through 1940 and 1941 the requests of its commanding general, Major General George C. Grunert, for more men, guns, and planes had met with small response. The fundamental reason for this lay in the inability of the United States to arrive at a settled policy for the defense of the Philippines. Ever since our occupation of the Islands in 1898 there had been uncertainty about what the United States ought to do with them. A decision finally was reached in 1934 when the passage of the Tydings-McDuffie Act granted the Philippines full independence to become effective in 1946. Though this clarified our political intentions, it did nothing to settle the military problem. In fact it raised new questions, which in hindsight may seem foolish, but seemed perfectly legitimate then. Was it worth while, for example, to pour money and material into a defense system when the Islands would be out of our hands in a few years? Some thought that doing so not only would offer provocation to the Japanese but would cause ourselves trouble by leading the Filipinos to question the sincerity of our motives. There was a powerful illusion in those days that the Japanese would never attack the United States in any case and all we needed do was sit it out. Running through all arguments was the old materialistic question of whether the Philippines were worth defending, let alone whether they could, or should, be defended.

Like so many other countries through the nineteen-thirties we put over our problems for a vague tomorrow, and in the vacuum of national indecision nothing was done to really strengthen the Philippine Department. It was allowed to remain almost on a Spanish-American War basis, while the Navy's Asiatic Fleet was no more than a skeleton force of one heavy and two light cruisers, a few overage destroyers, and submarines and auxiliary craft.

While the United States was hanging fire, the Philippine Commonwealth embarked on a defense program of its own under the National Defense Act of 1935. This program called for land, sea, and air forces purely for the defense of the Philippine Archipelago, and under the plan the Philippine Army was to meet any invasion force at the beaches with such combat strength that the cost of penetration would be excessive. An air corps, an offshore patrol of motor torpedo boats, one regular and 30 reserve divisions, totaling 250,000 men, were to be developed in the first ten years, and during each of the next two decades 30 additional reserve divisions would be organized.[6]

A brave start was made in 1935, with a budget of $8,000,000 and the appointment of General MacArthur, former Chief of Staff of the United States Army, as commander of the new Philippine Army with the rank of Field Marshal. The Islands were divided into ten military districts and training camps were established in each. But the yearly schedule was never lived up to, nor the necessary funds appropriated. The Philippines were undeveloped industrially and depended for their equipment on what they could get from the United States. By 1941, their offshore patrol totaled only three motor torpedo boats, and their air corps had nothing but a few obsolete planes. Moreover, as Japan's intentions in China and Malaysia became increasingly clear, President Quezon inclined more and more to the position that since the United States alone could decide the question of war or peace for the Philippines, it was her duty to guarantee their defense until 1946.

The development of a Philippine Army, slow though it was, displaced the old established scheme for the defense of the Islands. This was the famous Orange Plan which, conceding that Manila could not be held against a Japanese attack, provided for a delaying action to be fought down through the Lingayen Plain and a withdrawal onto Bataan, where, with water on three sides and the protection of the harbor forts in their rear, a small army could presumably hold out in the dense jungle and mountainous terrain until major reinforcements arrived from Hawaii, and at the same time itself protect the vulnerable flank of Corregidor.

When war came, the Philippine Army was still forming. There were not enough arms for it, and the 90,000 men who filled its one regular and ten reserve divisions and two Constabulary regiments had not received enough training to make their employment in a prolonged open campaign practicable. There seems, moreover, to have been some confusion as to which plan was being followed. General Wainwright in the north, who had been fighting an aggressive battle off the Lingayen beaches, was not notified until the night of December 22-23 that WPO-3 (War Plan Orange) was in effect,[7] though the decision, apparently, had been reached two weeks before by General MacArthur.* In the resulting withdrawal on Bataan, which had been made inevitable by the losses our Air Force had sustained in the first days of the war, an army of almost 90,000 poured onto the peninsula, instead of the few small units contemplated under the original Orange Plan; and this, as will be seen, was one of the primary factors in the desperate shortage of rations that made itself felt almost from the first day.†

It was plain that the success of an open campaign of this nature must very largely depend on control of the air, more especially when the bulk of the defending army was bound to consist of green troops. For if the Japanese did attack, all the key points of Luzon would lie within bomber range of their bases on Formosa, the southern tip of which was only 65 miles beyond the northernmost islet in the Philippines and 500 miles from Manila itself. Unlike Hawaii, Luzon could be brought under attack by land-based planes from the very outbreak of hostilities. And the threat against the Philippines was growing in direct proportion to the Japanese expansion southward. Strategically, the Islands not only dominated the approaches to the South China Sea, they also formed the

---

* According to General Sutherland, the decision was made by General MacArthur after the Pearl Harbor report came in, about 4:00 A.M., and when also a report from a submarine came through that it had sighted 150 Japanese ships heading for Lingayen Gulf. Sutherland gave these reports himself to General MacArthur, who said, "Remove immediately to Bataan." The plan for removal was started the day the Japs landed.

† Some Air Force units reached Bataan well supplied by taking along their own food with them, but all extra stores were confiscated by the first week of January and all Air Force units, like the rest of the troops, went on half rations as of January 5.[8]

geographic center of the great circle that includes the vital areas of Japan, China, Burma, French Indo-China, Thailand, Malaya, the Netherlands East Indies, and the Caroline and Marianas Islands—all territory belonging to Japan, seized by her or, in 1941, beginning to fall recognizably within the scope of her imperial ambition. Already the Philippines were half surrounded, and thoughtful men were coming to realize that it was no longer a question of whether the Japanese would attack the Philippines, but when they would attack. Yet, even up to the final month of peace, few realized how little time was left. Still fewer appreciated the vital importance of air power to the Islands, and the effort of such as did to provide an over-all air defense plan had met small response.

However, the need for a more vigorous air command had become apparent in Washington and in April the War Department sent out Brigadier General Henry B. Clagett, an old-line Army officer of uncertain health, with a long record of peacetime service and a prodigious knowledge of regulations, which had induced conservative habits of thought and a certain inflexibility of imagination. He understood the gravity of his responsibilities; he was seemingly convinced of the imminence of the Japanese threat; he did not spare himself in his work—twice in the crucial months of summer and early fall he was hospitalized; but he lacked the necessary elasticity of mind and body for realistic preparation for total war.[9] In this he was by no means alone, for there were officers at Air Headquarters at Nielson Field who, even two days after the Japanese attack, were still unable to understand how and why they had suffered such heavy losses. Criticism is easy after the event. A man is what he is. General Clagett is less accountable than those responsible for his selection.

With General Clagett, as Chief of Staff, was Colonel Harold H. George, a man who was to leave indelible impressions on the minds of all those who served closely with him on Bataan, and in the hearts of many of them. He had had a long record in military aviation, which included service as a flier in World War I, and it might be said that if General Clagett epitomized the old forces in the Air Corps, Colonel George epitomized the new.

They made a striking contrast as they stepped off the Clipper at Cavite on May 4: the General, tall, erect, with gray eyes and thinning gray hair, the military stamp all over him; and George, short, his broad shoulders making him seem still shorter, dark-haired, with quick brown eyes. People often speak of him as small: he seemed small only in repose.

To their left across the bay lay Bataan, with the long cool outline of Mariveles Mountain that the Filipinos say is like the outline of a sleeping woman. But their interest then must have lain the other way, where, low beyond the water, was the gray and white skyline of Manila, filled, as it often is, with the shadows of moving clouds.

Clagett had been there before, years ago, as a young lieutenant. To George it was all new.

3. *Inventory: May and June*

IT IS DIFFICULT now to realize the extent of this country's military weakness in 1941. About a week before General Clagett and Colonel George landed at Cavite, the Hawaiian Department, which was our bulwark against attack from the Pacific, began to receive its first modern pursuit planes. Captain Allison Ind speaks of the excitement at Wheeler Field when the P-40s flew in from the Naval carrier that had ferried them out.[1]

Ind, who had been assigned to the Philippine Department as Air Intelligence Officer, was on his way out to join Clagett and George aboard the U. S. Army Transport *Washington*. Brigadier General George M. Parker, coming out to an Infantry command, was also on the ship, and the arrival of the P-40s during their brief stopover at Honolulu set them speculating on what they would find in their new station. Their first hint came two days before they docked, when the *Washington* was buzzed by aircraft from Luzon. The Air Corps men on deck must have watched the planes with something close to shock. They were not modern bombers, not B-17s. They were not even the outdated, unsatisfactory, two-engined B-18s. They were utterly obsolete, ancient B-10s, slow, vulnerable as pumpkins in the sky, unarmored, and practically unarmed.

But bomber reinforcements had arrived. They had just come in, and Ind saw the crates containing them in the hangar line at Nichols Field

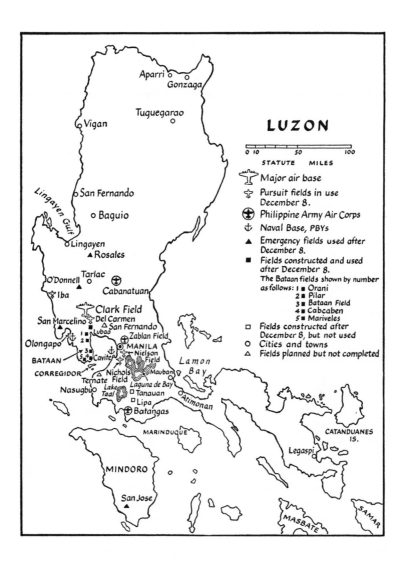

LUZON

0 10   50   100
STATUTE   MILES

✈ Major air base

✿ Pursuit fields in use
December 8.

⊕ Philippine Army Air Corps

⚓ Naval Base, PBYs

▲ Emergency fields used after
December 8.

■ Fields constructed and used
after December 8.
The Bataan fields shown by number
as follows: 1 ■ Orani
2 ■ Pilar
3 ■ Bataan Field
4 ■ Cabcaben
5 ■ Mariveles

□ Fields constructed after
December 8, but not used

○ Cities and towns

△ Fields planned but not completed

Aparri Gonzaga

Tuguegarao

Vigan

San Fernando

Baguio

Lingayen Gulf

Lingayen
▲ Rosales

O'Donnell Tarlac
⊕
☆ Iba   Cabanatuan

Clark Field
Del Carmen
San Marcelino △ San Fernando
Lubao ⊕ Zablan Field
Olongapo 1■ ⚓
2■ MANILA
BATAAN 3■ Nielson
5,4▲ Cavite Field
CORREGIDOR △ Nichols Lamon
Ternate Field Mauban Bay
Nasugbu Lake Laguna de Bay Atimonan
Taal □ Tanauan
⊕ □ Lipa
Batangas

MARINDUQUE

CATANDUANES
IS.

Legaspi

MINDORO

San Jose
▲

MASBATE SAMAR

a few days after the *Washington* docked. They were B–18s. They were never to be used as bombers against the enemy, for as soon as the 19th Group reached Clark Field, the B–18s were relegated to transport work, and by then, since they were not new to begin with, they were in "extremely sad shape." [2] However, the work of assembling them was begun immediately for, though pursuit planes were also waiting in their crates, the possibility of war had become suddenly so actual that it was decided to give the bombers priority. They might be only B–18s, but until the Fortresses arrived they were the only striking weapon the Philippine Department Air Force had.

The decision, of course, was General Clagett's, but it was Colonel George who had been its ardent advocate. From the first he had decided that the one hope of successfully defending the Philippines lay in hitting the Japanese before they came near shore. He wanted bombers, more bombers than were ever sent. Aggressive employment of air power underlay his entire philosophy as a soldier. It formed the heart of his plan for the air defense of the Philippines, which, when finally submitted to Washington, was approved by both General Marshall and General Arnold, though by then in the sudden unfolding of events there remained no time to implement it. It was later also to be evidenced in the defense of Bataan, when he showed that his pitifully small remnant of an Air Force, four broken-down P–40s, could still not only sting, but shatter a Japanese landing force. By then his ability had become recognized and his methods respected, but in the months of summer and early fall, perhaps even up to the actual outbreak of the war, there were men in and out of Air Force Headquarters at Manila who regarded George as something of a radical. Strategic use of air power, though its effectiveness was being demonstrated all over Europe, remained a new and disconcerting idea to minds fossilized by prerogative or sheer inertia. This lack of mental resilience is nothing new in armies.

The decision to give bombers priority was made hurriedly, for both General Clagett and Colonel George were under orders to leave on a tour of China and Burma to scout for possible air bases for American use in the event of war. George even discussed the possibility of war before his return, and he instructed his staff to prepare for sweeping changes. One thing he wanted was objective folders on Formosa and on all enemy-held territory within bomber reach. Captain Ind, starting on the task of gathering data, found that Headquarters had nothing to offer; and he writes of coming back to his office and sitting down at his desk, which had a nail to keep the top drawer locked. He pulled out a blank sheet of paper and wrote "Objective Folder No. 1" at the head of it.[3] Those words represented on that day of May 1941 the sum total of our listed information on Formosa. It seems incredible now. It must have been appalling then.

For that matter there was little enough on the Philippines themselves: a few fairly good files on districts considered militarily important—one on Corregidor, another on Bataan. And there was also a pretty complete series of photographs, obliques and verticals, of the eighty-odd airfields scattered through the Islands. These airfields were almost all mere turfed plots or natural meadows from which major obstacles had been removed, too small and rough for military aircraft.

The Japanese undoubtedly knew nearly as much about the Islands as we knew ourselves. Very likely they knew more. They knew our strong points and our weak ones; they had our fields marked down, radio stations, landing beaches; they had the roads and towns in intimate detail. Their agents were posted all through the Islands, ready and trained for the hour, to cut wires and light beacons and blow roads or bridges. On Mindanao their colony of 25,000 nationals offered cover or refuge for their agents. Their espionage was as effective as the Intelligence Section of the Philippine Department was weak. It was not the fault of the men involved. They were aware of what was going on; but they themselves were only a handful, handicapped everywhere by the lack of funds that had emasculated practically all departments of our overseas installations.

The time was overdue for taking stock.

There was the air warning system, depending on poorly trained Filipino watchers, and the slow relaying of their telephoned messages. It had been a tremendous job merely to organize the personnel. There was no time to teach them plane identification. In air maneuvers they reported any plane they saw and these messages came in over the limited telephone facilities to Fort Santiago and from there were relayed to Headquarters. In a test before the war, in which bombers were sent north far above Clark Field, it was forty-six minutes before the halting reports came in, were relayed to Air Headquarters and up to Clark Field, and the planes there finally took off.

The delays were partly due to the watchers and the telephone operators, who though willing and eager enough were far too inexperienced to handle their assignments with the necessary swiftness, and partly to the old and often obsolete equipment which the Philippines had been hitching along with in perfect peacetime comfort.

Similar limitations of equipment, funds, and personnel reached deep into all sections of the Philippine Department—infantry, coast artillery, antiaircraft, medical department and military hospitals, transportation, even the much advertised harbor forts all suffered in various ways from the parsimony and blindness of the government in Washington. Fort Mills on Corregidor and its three satellite forts, Hughes, Drum, and Frank, sounded impressive with their underground tunnels and their 12- and 14-inch batteries. But these batteries were fixed, basically designed for repelling naval action. Without control of the air or of the flanking shores of Bataan and Ternate, the forts amounted to sitting ducks—rugged ones, perhaps, but requiring only time and sufficient weight of metal to send them under. As they stood in 1941, with inadequate antiaircraft and supporting batteries, their celebrity served chiefly as a kind of Maginot Line behind which men who did not like their ideas shaken or their easy habits changed could take at least conversational refuge.

The Philippine Department Air Force consisted of a single outfit known as the 4th Composite Group. It was made up of one Medium Bombardment Group, the 28th, and the Observation Squadron, the 2nd, both of which were detached at Clark Field, 60 miles north of Manila, and three Pursuit Squadrons, the 3rd, 17th, and 20th, which together with Headquarters and the Headquarters Squadron were all at Nichols Field, just south of the city. In May 1941, the command of the 4th Composite Group changed hands when Colonel L. S. Churchill, who took over Nichols Field, was succeeded as Group Commander by Major J. K. Gregg, who had formerly had the 17th Squadron.[4] This was the beginning of a series of changes in organizations and channels of the higher command that undoubtedly accounted in part for the lack of a cohesive plan of air defense at the outset of the war.[5] It was in some measure inevitable because of the continual reorganization and expansion made necessary by the arrival of reinforcements; and in any case there was little opportunity for group training. But the continual shifting about in the higher echelons was bound to result, among pilots of the individual squadrons, in a loss of confidence in their top command.[6] One happy feature of this particular shuffle in May, however, was that it brought Lieutenant Boyd D. Wagner to command of the 17th Squadron. His name was to become almost a symbol for fighter pilots in the Southwest Pacific, along with those of Ed Dyess, Grant Mahony, Pappy Gunn, and a very few others.

May was a significant month for the pursuit squadrons, for it saw their change-over into P–35s completed. Before this, their standard equipment had been P–26s. The pilots of the 17th and 20th Squadrons, arriving from the States in November 1940, had been surprised, to put it mildly, when they found themselves back in the obsolete type of plane from which they had graduated a year before at Selfridge Field. In fact, when they scratched the paint off a few of these antique numbers, they found some of the identical ships that they had washed out in back in the States.

In January, however, the squadrons began receiving a few P–35As. These little Severskys had originally been consigned to Sweden, but on last-minute orders from Washington the shipment was diverted to the Philippines. Because the plane had been designed for the Swedish Air Force, it was considerably more powerfully armed than the U. S. model, which still carried only two .30-caliber machine guns firing through the propeller. In spite of suggestions by radical Air Force officers, no guns were installed in the wings of our planes; but the Swedes, being practical fellows, had ordered an extra .50-caliber gun in each wing. Some difficulties occurred in assembling the planes and in pilots' transition to them, for they were naturally equipped with Swedish instrumentation and no English version of technical orders was available.* However, by the end of May the transition had been successfully accomplished and all three squadrons were equipped, if not with actual first-line planes, at least with machines that did not threaten to come apart in the fliers' hands.

---

* About this time eleven A–27s (AT–6 type planes), intended for Siam, were also seized at the Manila docks and were eventually distributed among the fighter squadrons for instrument training, with similar language difficulties.[7]

In the meantime, though, all three squadrons suffered from a shortage of pilots. The 17th and 20th, which had arrived with a full complement, were continually losing men through transfers to other organizations more seriously understaffed. Pilot reinforcements began to come in in February, but not until July were the squadrons brought back to strength, when 100 pilots fresh out of training school landed at Manila. As these men all required further training, a unit for that purpose had to be set up at Clark Field.[8] By then the 17th and 20th had lost about 75 per cent of their original personnel, and ultimately the 17th went into the war with only five of the pilots who had come out with the unit and 35 younger pilots who had received their training in the Philippines for periods varying from one to ten months.[9]

Then there were the airfields, or perhaps one might better say, the lack of them. In May there were only four fields on Luzon considered possible for military aircraft. Of these, Clark was the only first-class field—it was, as a matter of fact, the only first-class field in the Philippines, for Del Monte had not yet been developed. As has been stated, it had no hard stand, but was entirely surfaced with turf.

Nielson Field, at which Air Headquarters was to be located, lay just south of Manila, between the city and Fort McKinley. It was classed as a fighter field, but had few facilities and was little used by combat planes then or later. Iba, on the Zambales coast well north of Subic Bay, had been a training camp for the Philippine Constabulary. It was to be used for a few short months by the Air Force as a gunnery training field, but it lacked facilities for extended operations.

This left Nichols as the principal fighter field. It was about six miles south of the heart of Manila and near the shore of Manila Bay, from which it was divided by the constricted, ramshackle barrio of Baclaran and a curve of the Parañaque River. The only approach to the field was down the main road that doubled as Baclaran's village street and then sharp left along a narrow lane that crossed the Parañaque River on a flimsy two-lane bridge. Except by air, there was no other access and a single bomb, rightly placed, could entirely isolate the airdrome.*

---

* Efforts by ranking Air Force officers to have the lane widened and hard-surfaced ran into one of the maddening bottlenecks of resistance and inertia not infrequent in the

The field itself had been placed on the site of a series of rice paddies and over the swampy ground along the river. It had never been properly drained and during the rainy season the north-south runway reverted to its original swampy status and was totally useless. It was unique, however, in being the only hard-surfaced strip in the Philippines.

As for antiaircraft defenses, there were at this time none at all.

This extreme vulnerability disturbed a foreign observer who came at the end of May to make a survey of Philippine airfields in case their use by British and Dutch Air Forces became necessary. He was Group Captain C. Darval of the RAF, at the time Air Officer on Sir John Brooke-Popham's staff at Singapore. On the evening of June 3, a group of officers gathered in Fort Santiago to hear him. He began by saying that in his opinion a sudden air attack, driven home with determination, would practically wipe out our Air Force on Luzon.[10] Lack of dispersal was perhaps our greatest weakness; but also there was our tendency to place air strips close to beaches, and the lack of camouflage, dummy strips, and protection against parachute attack. He hesitated to speak harshly, but he pointed out the dubious value of Nichols and the fact that practically all our air supply was concentrated openly in the Philippine Air Depot, the buildings of which offered easy, obvious, well-known, and inflammable targets.

Later on he embodied his findings in a written report, advocating that there be enough landing fields so that not more than one fighter squadron of 25 planes, or one bomber squadron of 16 planes, be obliged to use the same ground. "It is understood that, provided financial sanction is obtained, the full airdrome project can be finished within 90 days. It will be necessary to push on with this if reinforcing squadrons are to be able to operate. Until this has been done there can be no question of the provision of reinforcing squadrons. *Air defense schemes, denial schemes, and dispersion schemes are vitally necessary and should be pushed on with all speed.*" [11] * There were none in May and June.

Earlier in the report, Darval made clear why, in the event of a Japanese attack, they would strike first against our air power, and the climactic

Philippines, so that the job was still unfinished when the Japanese came. Then a bomb knocked half the bridge into the river, leaving a section barely ten feet wide.

* The italics are mine.—W. D. E.

point of the seven he listed as essential for a defense plan argued that "arrangements must be made to meet the enemy as far from the shore as possible with naval and air forces. . . ." [12] He also indicated that the Philippines must be attacked by Japan. The two points hung on the same reason: that "war experience in Norway, England, Libya, and Crete shows clearly that a satisfactory air situation is necessary if a seaborne expedition is to succeed. . . ." [13]

These points were summarized for the men listening in Fort Santiago on the 3rd of June as quiet boats slid up and down the Pasig River in the growing darkness just beyond the windows. The report, which he wrote after his return to Singapore, was presented to the U. S. Naval Observer there on August 5. It was sent to the Chief of Naval Operations in Washington under a letter of the same date; but it was not until three months later, on November 10, that the report was transmitted to the Army Chief of Staff. Whether its prompt receipt would have materially affected the situation in the Philippines is hard to say, for even in June, as Darval's report itself implied, there was very little time.

How little, a few men came suddenly to realize in that same month of June when Intelligence reported a huge Japanese convoy out in the China Sea. Luzon was alerted and went on blackout. Fighter pilots stood by their planes—they were to stay on alert from that time forward, many nights sleeping beside their planes when trouble threatened. It was as though a still, cold wind had blown across Luzon, and the little groups of military men, waiting for invasion at their stations, must have taken stock of each other and themselves with new eyes. For the insufficiency of what they had was now made obvious to all but those habitually blind.

But the convoy moved on southward to French Indo-China, and in the Philippines we had another breathing spell.

4. Air Forces, USAFFE

GENERAL CLAGETT reported sick on his return to Manila from his Chinese flight and he had to be hospitalized in Sternberg Hospital, which meant that Colonel George was more or less chained to his desk and that, therefore, the problem of finding new airfields, or sites for them, must temporarily be set aside. Dispersal remained very much on his mind, however, and in snatched spare moments he hunted through Manila for possible underground storage sites for Air Corps supplies, even gasoline, which were then concentrated almost entirely in the clustered buildings of the Philippine Air Depot. He found such a place beneath an old Spanish school building, where abandoned waterwork borings formed storage space underground amounting to nearly thirty acres. George was delighted with his find and instructed Captain Harold E. Eads, a junior engineer officer of the Philippine Department, to draw up plans and specifications. These were submitted to General Clagett; but nothing ever came of the proposal, for there was another plan on hand for driving entirely new tunnels under Fort McKinley.[1]

By the third week in July, General Clagett had recovered sufficiently to leave on another strenuous mission, this time to Singapore and the Netherlands East Indies. The orders had been radioed from Washington, for the deepening gravity of our relations with Japan made consultations with our prospective allies imperative. General Clagett took with him Captain Ind, who by then had become his aide, and, through a fortunate last-minute decision, Lieutenant Colonel Lester Maitland, the commanding officer of Clark Field. After stopping briefly at Singapore and Kota Bharu, the mission proceeded to Java, where General Clagett was again taken sick and the work consequently fell on Ind and Maitland and three other officers hastily sent out from Manila and Singapore * with instructions to investigate the Dutch reports on nondelivery of promised munitions. The Dutch concern was well founded; they had ammunition for only a few days of war and an air force that was equipped mostly with B–10s, and Brewster Buffaloes for pursuit ships.† But in the course of their inspection trips, Maitland was powerfully impressed by the thoroughness of air raid precautions, particularly slit trenches and revetments, installed by the Dutch, many of whom were refugees from the German blitz and knew from

---

* Col. H. H. C. Richards and Lt. Fred Walker, Ordnance, from Manila, and Lt. Col. Francis Brink from Singapore.

† The Brewster Buffalo, a converted carrier plane, was tough, heavy, slow, with a top speed of under 190 miles an hour and a rate of climb that required 15 minutes to reach 20,000 feet.

bitter experience what was needed on an open airdrome under air attack. Three months after his return, even in the face of ridicule, Maitland ordered slit trenches dug all round Clark Field.*

During General Clagett's absence, Colonel George made a complete tour of the Islands with Captain Eads, marking down sites for new airfields and investigating the possible development of small existing strips. By the time General Clagett returned—aboard ship, since he was too ill to travel by air—Colonel George had already laid out in his mind a plan for the erection of scattered airfields throughout the Philippines and had begun work with Eads on a comprehensive and unified plan of air defense against a Japanese attack.

But the airfields were slow in building. Military authorities were unwilling to cut corners; owners were reluctant to give up their arable land or rice paddies; no one wanted to accept the fact that war was coming close. It always took a year to lay in an air strip. Of those on Luzon contracted for between July and December not one was properly finished on December 8, and only three were usable at all. Yet after the war began, often with the use solely of native help and hand labor, a strip would be cut out within a single week.

The effort to build new fields was still further handicapped by a shortage of engineer troops. There was one battalion of Aviation Engineers, the 803rd, and it lacked one company until it picked up the 809th to fill out its ranks. The only other unit was the 14th Engineers, which belonged to the Philippine Scouts.

But if the airfield program was difficult to put across, Colonel George's plan for the air defense of the Islands must have seemed a hopeless cause, for in the first place it was essentially offensive in design. This meant that from the start it called for far greater numbers of men and planes than had previously been considered necessary. It called for raids on Hainan, Formosa, and main Japanese islands themselves. Bombs, gasoline loads, attrition losses, service troops, every detail had been worked out. Instead

---

* Some have given credit for the construction of these trenches, without which the loss of life on December 8 would have been literally enormous, to Lt. William A. Cocke, Jr., of the 19th Bombardment Group; but the orders undoubtedly proceeded from Maitland and at the time the trenches were called "Maitland's Folly."

of squadrons, the plan talked in terms of groups—five to eight of them.*
In the light of air war as it developed in the Southwest Pacific, the plan
probably represented minimum forces, but in those prewar days the totals
must have seemed fantastic.

They seemed so to General Clagett, when he studied the plan in his bed
in Sternberg Hospital, to which he had retired on his return from Java.
His experience had prepared him for the explosive effect these figures
might have on the War Department and Congress, and he demanded a
complete revision. It was done at the cost of valuable hours of labor, yet
when it was done the figures varied only slightly from the original totals.
This did not satisfy General Clagett, and he went to work on the plan
himself in his hospital bed, altering and cutting wherever he could. Ind
says that surprisingly enough the General retained most of George's figures, but he had cut out the sustaining evidence and the arguments that
were the core round which George's figures grew.[3]

Time as well as strength was desperately involved. The threat that had
lain over the Islands on those June nights, when Luzon was blacked out
and men stood to their stations with nearly empty hands, might be repeated any day with another convoy heading into the China Sea. It might
follow in the first one's wake to Indo-China, or to Thailand, or Malaya;
or it might turn suddenly against Luzon. And for its air cover and to
prepare its landing, the Japanese had an air strength of 3000 first-line
planes, more or less, to draw on and a completely developed air base less
than 500 miles away. George himself believed that the Japanese had a
minimum of 3000 planes that they could send down from Formosa against
our own tiny force.†

Though the 4th Composite Group had gained strength in planes and
men, it was tactically even less able to defend itself, for in July all air

---

* As the plan has not been made available to the writer, these figures are inferential,
drawn from recollections of Col. George's talks in interviews with his pilots or from
direct quotations, which may not be exact, such as Ind supplies.[2]

† RAAF Intelligence Summary listed a total of 2860 Japanese planes including the
Fleet Air Arm. RAF figures of November 1941 listed 4500 aircraft of first-line strength.[4]
The December 1941 Memorandum to the Chief of Staff estimated 3227 first-line planes.
Interrogations since the war reveal that the Japanese had 2700 first-line planes assigned
to fully trained units.[5]

operations at Nichols Field had to be abandoned. The east-west runway was under construction and the north-south strip had been turned into its customary quagmire with the rains.[6] The entire installation was an island in the midst of flood, connected only by its bridge to solid ground. As a result, the 4th Composite Group had to be moved up to Clark Field, except for the 17th Squadron, which, under Lieutenant Wagner, went to Iba, there to begin an extensive period of gunnery training.

Iba lay on the coast of Zambales Province, north of Subic Bay, and the field itself was directly on the China Sea with beach sand edging half the length of the runway. It was a single, sodded strip. A little winding river flowed along the inland border confining usable land to a minimum, and there was no natural cover for a squadron of planes. They were as open to attacking planes as to the wind from the sea. The 5000-foot comb of a mountain range paralleled the coast and offered constant interference with radio communications. Near the field the mountains came crowding so close to the sea that landings and take-offs after dark had to be made cautiously. The only fair approach was from the south, or from the westward in across the sea.

Here the Squadron went on its own, discovering for the first time the unreliability of communications in the Philippines and experiencing difficulties of transport and supply. But more serious was the defective operation of their guns, due to poor installation and faulty adjustment. All had to be taken out, adjusted, and their mountings modified.[7] Lieutenant Wagner's report on the subject is said to have let its chips fall where they might; but wherever the true responsibility lay, whether in the States or in the Philippines, the fliers continued to be bedeviled by faulty guns, even in combat, and sometimes by guns that refused to fire at all.*

All the rest of our small air forces were concentrated on Clark Field, with the newly arrived pilots to be trained,† and much excitement over the delivery to the 20th Squadron of brand-new P–40Bs. These Curtiss fighters were the first actual front-line aircraft to reach the Philippines,

---

* Careless treatment by the tactical personnel themselves was, however, a contributing factor. Pilots landing after high-altitude flight would leave their planes uncared for. The extremely cold metal of the guns would condense the moist air in the barrels, which quickly became cored with rust.[8]

† A few pilots of the 20th and 3rd Squadrons managed to get in some gunnery practice with the 17th at this time.

but their employment was delayed because the coolant for their engines had been held up on the San Francisco docks.[9] Insufficient quantities of coolant became a source of constant worry, and there was a theory among the pilots of the 24th Group that the shortage was caused by an overzealous supply officer who could not understand why Prestone was needed by planes flying in a hot climate. Until the coolant did arrive, all that could be done with the planes was to put them out on the line, where they sat helpless and naked in the sun.

Meanwhile, construction had been scheduled or was under way on two subsidiary fields—at Rosales nearly 50 miles due north of Clark Field, close to the Agno River, which later became a feature in General Wainwright's action down through the Lingayen Plain; and at Del Carmen about 14 miles south of Clark Field. It was a start towards dispersal, but still only a start. Everything the Air Corps had was in the open and, except for the lone squadron exposed at Iba, was still concentrated in two areas on Luzon. The islands to the south, of course, had nothing, though they lay within bomber reach of Palau, in the Carolines, on which it had been known for the past two years that the Japanese were building fortified bases.[10] Then there were rumors that the Japanese had laid plans for seizing the southwest coast of Palawan, which is the most southwesterly of the Philippines, barring entrance to the Sulu Sea, like a long-boned finger pointing down to Borneo. The Japs had one of their fishing fleets operating there, and they had recently planted a colony of almost three hundred on the small island of Linapacan that sentinels the northern passage into the Sulu Sea.[11] As reinforcements came, if they should come in time, dozens more airfields would be needed, not only in Luzon, but down through all the main Islands.

Oxygen was another thing they needed. George and Eads, together making out their lists of essential stores, figured that it would take six oxygen plants to supply the air fleet they wanted, and it was about this time that they put in a requisition for them. The plants never came.

July, however, proved a turning point in the effort to prepare the Philippines for war. On the 27th, General MacArthur, who had been recalled to active duty, was placed in command of the United States Army Forces in the Far East (USAFFE), relieving General Grunert, and including under his command the untrained and still forming Philippine Army. This did not mean that there was an instant infusion of energy through every channel of what had been the Philippine Department. Habits of long peace are hard to shake. But General MacArthur's appointment was a symptom of the growing interest and concern felt in the States for our farthest Pacific outpost and served to implement the efforts of those men who had been struggling to prepare for war. Requests from the Philippines now carried a new and recognized authority. It was borne in on many more people than had realized it before that the issue of peace or war was balanced on a razor edge, and from this time forward, during the brief remaining months of peace, men and equipment began to reach the Philippines in continually increasing numbers and frequency.

For the Air Forces the new command involved further shifts in organization, and on August 5 they were redesignated Air Forces, USAFFE. Once more the 4th Composite Group changed hands, with Major Grover, formerly of the 20th Squadron, taking over from Major Gregg, who now became A-4 in the new setup. Succeeding Grover in the Squadron command was Lieutenant Joseph H. Moore. Clagett of course continued as Commanding General, with George still his Chief of Staff.

The Air Forces now operated directly under General MacArthur, except for routine administration and supply, which were to continue through the old channels of what had been Headquarters, Philippine Department. To George this meant the ultimate endorsement of his air plan. In working out its details, he had been necessarily in frequent consultation with MacArthur's Chief of Staff, Lieutenant Colonel Richard K. Sutherland.* Several days after General Clagett's milder version was submitted, word came from Headquarters that General MacArthur wished to see the original plans. General Clagett authorized Colonel George to transmit them; and, subject to certain changes indicated from time to time by altered circumstances, this original version was used as the basis for air expansion. The arrival of the 19th Bombardment Group was the first concrete evidence of its effect.

But time had been lost that could never be regained. Even then, late

* On August 19, Sutherland was promoted to Brigadier General.

as the hour was, few men either in Washington or in the Philippines had
yet geared their minds to the swiftness with which time was running out.*

5. *FEAF: October and November*

THE INCREASING STREAM of reinforcements that now began to pour out on
the Manila docks raised continuing problems of reorganization, reloca-
tion, training, and supply. By October, it had become necessary to move
one of the fighter squadrons out of Clark Field to make room for the
expected arrival of the 19th Bombardment Group. The 17th Squadron
was therefore transferred to its old base at Nichols Field, and shortly
afterward, on October 16, the 3rd Squadron took its place at the Iba
camp and began gunnery training. Work on the landing strips at Nichols
Field had not been completed, and their poor condition resulted in a high
accident rate for the 17th Squadron.[1] However, these two squadrons, and
the 20th, which stayed at Clark Field, had now finally reached the fields
on which they were still based when the news of Pearl Harbor came,
near dawn of December 8.

It was now obvious that with the arrival of a bomber group, the old
4th Composite Group would become an unwieldy organization. On
September 26, therefore, the 24th Pursuit Group was created, including
the three squadrons, now at the three separate fields, as well as Headquarters and a Headquarters Squadron, which were based at Clark Field
under command of Major Grover. The 4th Composite Group was to continue a rather shadowy existence at Clark Field for a few weeks more
until the 28th Bombardment Squadron was absorbed by the 19th Group.
This left the 2nd Observation Squadron under Captain J. Y. Parker,
which operated thenceforward under direct orders from Air Head-

---

* The whole reinforcement program still operated on the assumption that the Japanese
would not attack before March or April, 1942. This belief was prevalent in many
quarters and through all ranks in the Philippines, April being the commonly accepted
month. According to General Wainwright, General MacArthur himself held this view
as late as November 25,[12] though General Brereton felt that MacArthur's confidence
in war's not breaking before spring had been severely shaken by November 10.[13]

quarters, and a Tow Target Squadron which ceased to have much use after the 8th of December.[2]

In October the arrival of 35 new pilots from the States brought the pursuit units up to full strength; but the pilots, like the 100 who had arrived in July, required combat training and the program designed for the latter therefore had to be reopened at Clark Field.[3] This completes the long list of shifts and changes in command to which the pursuit force on Luzon was subjected before the war.

During October P-40Es began to arrive, and by the middle of November enough had been assembled to equip completely both the 17th and the 3rd Squadrons, which therefore spent their last few weeks of peace in slow-timing their engines, reinstalling their machine guns, and checking out their pilots in what to most was a new aircraft.

On the 20th of November, two more squadrons, the 21st and the 34th, both from the 35th Pursuit Group, arrived from the States and were attached to the 24th Pursuit Group pending the arrival of the rest of their group, which of course never came.[4] These two squadrons were at only half strength.[5] They came without their planes, for they expected to find new ships ready when they disembarked.[6] Their situation, and that of the 27th Bombardment Group, arriving on the same ship and similarly destitute of its equipment, will be described in the proper place. But their case was only symptomatic of the confusion and lack of correlation in the final efforts to bolster the Philippines. Not only were squadrons and one group sent out without planes, but planes arrived without vital parts, some requisitions were entirely unfilled, and needless muddles were produced that took weeks to unravel.

Changing organization, untrained reinforcements, insufficient, hastily assembled, and poorly installed equipment all played their part in the lack of training as a group that was to prove a grave handicap during the opening moves of the Japanese air attack. Lack of decent communications also contributed and, still more, the sheer inferiority in numbers. But behind these, behind what faults there were of omission and commission, behind all the other factors was the lack of time. During peace too many of our people had forgotten, as they always forget, that the one greatest component of war is time.

The Japanese had not forgotten this. Their bases had long been ready on Formosa; their air groups had been trained for synchronized attacks on specific targets, and the Japanese knew all about those targets. They had an essentially accurate picture of our air strength.* The network of agents they had built up on Luzon had details near every vital point, ready to go into action with the opening gun. These hidden people were watching every move and, as their reports were turned in, it became only a question of how strong the Japanese were prepared to let us grow.

The third and final change in Air Corps organization, and the one that perhaps produced the most profound effect, involved a complete turnover in the top command. On October 7, the War Department assigned Major General Lewis H. Brereton as Air Commander and on October 28 redesignated the Air Force, USAFFE as the Far East Air Force (FEAF), to become effective November 16.[7]

Arriving on November 3, General Brereton brought a number of officers with him, among them a new Chief of Staff, Colonel Francis M. Brady, which meant that Colonel George, as well as General Clagett, was displaced. The Far East Air Force was then organized † with three subsidiary commands: the 5th Interceptor Command, which went to General Clagett; the 5th Bomber Command, which was given to Colonel Eubank, though he also retained command of the 19th Group until December 10;[8] and the Far East Air Service Command (FEASC) under Colonel Lawrence S. Churchill, which here made its beginning with eight officers and 60 enlisted men. The first strength report of the 5th Interceptor Command lists five officers and 15 enlisted men. The 5th Bomber Command was actually a skeleton unit, and though authorized a full T/O strength ‡ had only one officer and 20 enlisted men as late as December 23.[9] These were small beginnings.

Colonel George was made A-4 in the new headquarters, with Major K. J. Gregg as his assistant. It seems to have been understood that the appointment was to be a temporary one, as actually it was, for by De-

---

* The Intelligence Summary used by the Tanaka Force listed U. S. air strength as 130 fighters, 30 bombers, 20 Naval patrol planes.

† Though the effective date of FEAF was November 16 and the headquarters as set up continued till then to be called AF, USAFFE, it was to all intents and purposes the FEAF that existed when war broke.

‡ T/O—Tables of Organization.

cember 8 the Supply Section was headed by Gregg, and George had been made Chief of Staff of the Interceptor Command. But he was now devoting much of his time to the lagging airfield program as well as unsolved problems of supply. Rosales and Del Carmen Fields were nearing completion, though of course they were still nothing but raw dirt strips; and work was in progress or about to start on four other auxiliary airfields: two in the great plain—O'Donnell eleven miles northward and San Fernando 16 miles southeast of Clark Field; the third, San Marcelino, about eight miles northwest of the head of Subic Bay; and the fourth, Ternate, at the mouth of Manila Bay, close to the Cavite shore.

George was disturbed also by the lack of airfields on Bataan. There was still only a single little 2000-foot strip cut out of the jungle uphill from the road on the site of what afterwards became Bataan Field, but in these prewar days it was still known as "Richards's Folly" after the officer who had been largely responsible for having it built.* In Eads's recollection of the Orange Plan, "A. C. was not considered except for one field—'Bataan.' We weren't supposed to be back there." But it was impossible to get anyone to build more fields there until the Japanese struck. Then when the need for dispersal fields on Bataan itself was recognized, they had to be built under fire.

In the meantime the shortage of oxygen had become a matter for concern. None of the six plants requested in the summer had arrived. There was no supply of oxygen in the Philippines that was available to the Air Corps, except for the small amount brought with them by the 19th Group, which was reserved exclusively for their use, and a very little on hand at Nichols Field. Luzon was combed for oxygen plants; but there was only one, located in the northern outskirts of Manila, with an inadequate output that could not be increased. When Eads inspected the plant at the end of October, he found that the Navy shipyard took all the company could produce, except for occasional small surpluses that had been the source of the Nichols Field supply. No fighter squadron at any other base had oxygen,† so when war broke, the ceiling of three

*Col. H. H. C. Richards, who had been Air Officer in the old Philippine Department.
†Col. Eads writes, "I later learned that the oxygen plants we ordered from the States were on the water when war hit us and were diverted to Australia, but I didn't find them there. (However I didn't look too hard because when I got down there, oxygen was not a problem.)" (Letter to the author, dated December 8, 1945.) Col. Churchill

of the five squadrons was automatically limited to the individual pilot's reaction to altitude.

Thus out of constant changes the pattern of the air command that met the Japanese in the Philippines had finally been set. The five leading figures offered some interesting contrasts, both in their past records and in their subsequent careers. Colonel George was the only one to remain in the Philippines after the first sixteen days of war, and of the four who moved south on or before December 24, two, General Brereton and Colonel Brady, had left the Southwest Pacific for the Burma-India theater within two months. Of the other two, General Clagett served as commander of a base section in Townsville, Australia, until his return to the States in March, 1942; and Colonel Eubank continued to head the 5th Bomber Command in Java. He ended his tour of duty in the Southwest Pacific by serving through the month of April, 1942, in his old capacity as commanding officer of the 19th Group.

All five men had long been identified with the Air Service, but George seems to have held the greatest number of active operational commands. Born in Lockport, New York, on September 14, 1892, he entered the National Guard on July 5, 1916, for active duty during the Mexican Border crisis, and served till October 5 of the same year as sergeant in the 3rd Infantry. On April 15, 1917, he returned to the service, attended Flying School, and upon graduation on September 19 was given an emergency commission as 1st lieutenant in the Aviation Section of the Signal Corps. He went overseas the following month and, after nearly a year of serving as an instructor and then receiving advanced flying training and gunnery training, he began his combat career on October 1, 1918, with the 139th Aero Squadron. With them he took part in the St. Mihiel and Meuse-Argonne offensives, shot down five enemy planes, earning the title of Ace, and was awarded the Distinguished Service Cross. After the war he decided to stay in the Army and received a permanent commission as

states, however, that there was no oxygen shortage, that if there was a shortage at any base it was because the Interceptor Command had never requested it, that there were 100 flasks on Corregidor when it surrendered. (Churchill note of October 11, 1950.) It is possible to reconcile these statements only by accepting the view that the Interceptor Command was thinking in terms of a long conflict. In any case the transfer carts required for the low-pressure system with which the P–40s were equipped had not arrived in the Philippines, so no oxygen was available to the pilots.

1st lieutenant, Air Service, Regular Army. From March 1925 to July 1929, he was stationed at Kelly Field as chief instructor of the Pursuit Section of the Advanced Flying School. Then followed two years in the Panama Canal Zone, largely as commander of the 7th Observation Squadron, after which he was transferred to Langley Field, Virginia, as Assistant Executive Officer. He served successively as commanding officer of the 2nd Bombardment Group, the 8th Pursuit Group, and the 33rd Pursuit Squadron. In the winter of 1933-1934 he was with the Civilian Conservation Corps at Camp Weeks in Vermont, and what may have seemed at the time an odd assignment must have been remembered eight years later in the Bataan jungle. When the Army began to operate the Air Mail in February of that year, George was placed in charge of Section III in the Eastern Zone, embracing the routes from Newark, New Jersey, to St. Louis, Washington to Cleveland, and Cleveland to Memphis. He returned to Langley Field in command of the 33rd Pursuit Squadron in January 1935 and in March joined the staff of the 8th Pursuit Group. Between 1936 and 1938 he graduated from the Air Corps Tactical School at Maxwell Field, Alabama, and the Command and General Staff School at Fort Leavenworth, Kansas. He then went to Selfridge Field, Michigan, in command of the 94th Pursuit Squadron and was commanding the 31st Pursuit Group at the same field when he received his assignment to the Philippines. He was then forty-nine years old.

General Clagett, the oldest of the group, was the only West Point graduate among them. His class was 1906, and he was immediately commissioned second lieutenant in the Infantry, in which he served until 1917, including a two-year tour in the Philippines. He transferred to the Air Service, in which he was to hold a wide variety of administrative posts at airdromes, aviation schools, and in Washington, D. C.

Colonel Brady had entered military service through the Officers' Training School at Plattsburg and had had a full and active battle career with the 9th Machine Gun Battalion in the First World War. Like George he decided to remain in the Army and was detailed in the Air Service in 1920. He was a graduate of the Air Corps Tactical School at Langley Field, Virginia, the Command and General Staff School at Leavenworth, and the Army War College. In July 1941 he was named Acting Chief of Staff, 3rd Air Force.

General Brereton had been the first of this group to earn his wings, but his approach to the Air Corps was an oblique one. Graduating from Annapolis on June 2, 1911, he served as an ensign from June 3 to June 5 of the same year, when he resigned for the purpose of transferring to the Army. In August he joined the Coast Artillery Corps, but began flying training in August 1912 and by May 1917 was a captain in the Aviation Section of the Signal Corps. During the First World War he commanded the 12th Aero Squadron in France and Belgium and received the D.S.C., among other awards, for conspicuous gallantry in action. He transferred to the Air Service in 1920 with the permanent rank of major. Between wars, General Brereton held various key positions in the Air Force, directing attack training at Kelly Field and commanding the 2nd Bombardment Group and later the 17th Bombardment Wing. In 1928 he graduated from the Command and General Staff School and was in command of the 3rd Air Force when assigned to FEAF.

Eubank, like George, was primarily a flier. He had been commissioned in the Aviation Section of the Signal Reserve in 1918 and in 1920 received a commission in the Air Service, Regular Army. During the First World War he served as instructor, engineer, and operations officer at various fields and graduated from the Air Service Mechanical School. This was followed by work in various staff capacities and as test pilot and chief of the Flight Test Unit at Wright Field, Ohio. Between 1929 and 1937 he graduated from the Air Corps Engineering School at Wright Field, the Air Corps Tactical School at Langley Field, and the Command and General Staff School at Leavenworth. He then commanded in turn the 32nd and 34th Bombardment Squadrons, and in April 1940 was made commanding officer of the 19th Group. At this time he was rated one of the best all-round heavy bomber men in the service, with an impressive and sound technical mastery of his aircraft. A navigator of the 19th Group has said that Eubank was the best navigator in the outfit. Though most pilots hate the business of navigation and consider it a chore, to Eubank it was both a skill and an art. He was also a good bombardier and gunner. His first demonstration of his ability to organize and lead a long-distance over-water flight came on the night of May 13-14, 1941, when the Group flew 21 B–17Ds to Hawaii. It was a remarkable performance, accomplished without a single mechanical failure, and only one ship reported 20 miles off true course at any time. The 21 aircraft all landed within thirty minutes of each other, and in the order in which they had taken off.

Of these five men, it was George who most measurably increased his stature as a commander during those difficult opening months of the war. In part this was due to the turn of fate that left him on Bataan in circumstances calling forth his native ingenuity and his ability to improvise. For George had his limitations—an impatience with established organization and a stubborn streak that sometimes made it hard to shake him of his preconceptions. But where in many others adversity bred understandable confusion, it tapped in George a gift of personal leadership that sprang from an open but disciplined heart.

The tactics used in fighting the Japanese Zero, as they were worked out by him and his handful of pilots over Luzon, became the basis of our fighter tactics in the Southwest Pacific.* In the darkest hours, the little Bataan Air Force he commanded could still strike back, and though it flew off fields directly under Japanese observation, the enemy were not able to clear the sky as long as four of our planes remained. This came from his ability to draw on the best in others rather than from domineering force. His pilots believed in him.

* Maj. Gen. Wurtsmith, then commanding the 13th Air Force, said in an interview on Leyte, June 28, 1945, that "all our fighter tactics are about 100 per cent Hal George's teaching." They were, of course, similar to those developed by Chennault and his AVG Group in China. For a brief discussion see below, Part Two, Chapter 8.

I I

Approach of War: Reinforcement and
Reconnaissance

6. *Mid-November*

THE 19TH GROUP began preparing for war almost from their first day in the Philippines. Already, during the last of September and all through October, the 14th Squadron had been carrying out intensive unit tactical training in high-altitude formation flying, navigation, bombing, and gunnery, with missions being scheduled at 20,000 to 30,000 feet. When it was decided to absorb all bombardment units into the 19th Group, the 35 planes were divided equally among four squadrons, with three left over for Headquarters Squadron. There was some opposition to this move as it involved shifting round the crews. Captain Combs, among others, felt that it would have been wiser to retain the three fully equipped squadrons with ten planes apiece and five extra as replacements and not tamper with the crews,* but the decision went the other way, and as the Group went into hard training it consisted of the 30th, 93rd, 14th, and 28th Squadrons, each flying eight B-17s.

They were eager for work and ran practice bombing missions nearly every day. Schedules were carried out to determine what the Group would need in extended operations away from base. But for several reasons their operations had to be closely figured. Though they had some B-17 parts, the supply was inadequate, and already they began to feel the shortage of engines that was to prove a continuing problem through

---

* Capt. Cecil E. Combs, CO of the 93rd Squadron. According to Combs the 28th Squadron, commanded by Maj. Fisher, never operated as a squadron in the Philippines.

the first year of the war. The engines in their planes were getting near the 400-hour mark, at which time, according to accepted procedure, they should be changed, but as there were nothing like enough engines for a Group change, it was thought necessary to use the planes as lightly as possible. They were to find out, of course, that their engines would run on longer than they had ever dreamed possible in peacetime, but they did not know that then. As stated earlier, the Group had brought their own oxygen with them, but the supply was limited, and they had to be careful of it. Hangar space at Clark Field, which rated as the only first-class airdrome in the Philippines, was inadequate. There was room for handling only two planes under cover at the same time, and consequently, after it was decided to camouflage the planes, all other maintenance work had to be done in the open. To men accustomed to the sort of facilities the 19th Group had enjoyed at home, these must have seemed strange conditions, but they were merely a gentle foretaste of what lay in store for them.

By the latter part of November the training of the Group had reached an advanced level. Except for one plane,* the equipment was in good order and both ground and air crews had adapted themselves to the requirements of the new station. The skill and efficiency of pilots, navigators, and bombardiers was exceptional for that time and would probably be rated very high today, and there can be no question of the quality of the crew chiefs, who proved able to keep their ships running without facilities of any kind. Without them, the Group could not have kept on operating as it did through the opening months of the war.

Their weakness was in gunnery, which, with a few outstanding exceptions, seems to have been consistently low grade, not only among the crews of the 19th Group, but later among those of the 7th, after it joined the 19th in Java and Australia.† The men had actually to learn

---

* This plane had been damaged in landing when the 14th Squadron came into Clark Field at the end of their Pacific flight in the heel of a typhoon. The ceiling was so low that, as the planes flew in over the mouth of Manila Bay, the men at the side windows looked upwards at the barracks on Corregidor; and Teats wrote that "we flew individually at treetop level, right from sea level to field elevation. The visibility was so low that as I came in to Clark the control tower and hangar line suddenly leaped from the fog and rain directly in front of me. I had to pull up sharply to clear them." [1] The last ship to land hooked into an old plane, invisible in the rain from the control tower, and ripped out its tail section.

† Col. John E. Dougherty, who became Group Operations Officer, recalling his service in Java and Australia, said that the bombardiers and navigators were good. The gunners

their skill in combat. This was due neither to lack of enterprise on the men's part nor to unwillingness to put in practice time, but to sheer lack of training. Why this was so can best be shown by one officer's experience in gunnery training.

"I was a cadet, and we had to qualify as expert aerial gunners before we could be rated as aircraft observers. We were given a lot of skeet shooting, then we went over the Pacific in an old B–18. Once or twice we were allowed to fire the .30-caliber at a tow-target for practice. Then we fired 400 rounds for the record. In order to assure our making an expert's score, they would bring the tow-target ship as close as possible before we fired. . . ."

After that he never fired till he was in combat, nor had he ever fired the .50-caliber except on the ground. The only work he had had with it was to fire about 50 rounds from a truck at a moving target they had rigged up at Muroc Field. Undoubtedly this was due to lack of money and means. "Everyone was eager and willing to fire and to train, and we had detailed training programs. But without the means we merely kept up a front. . . . You can't fly airplanes without gasoline, or practice dropping bombs without the bombs, or fire guns without ammunition."

In their training flights the air crews came to know the mountains of Luzon. At altitude the proportions of the land are changed and the pattern human life has traced on it is less significant. People in the lowlands know the mountains by their vertical faces or the night shadows of their peaks against the sky, but the flier sees them in their true relation to the land. More than two thirds of Luzon is occupied by the mountains. They lie in four main ranges running north and south, but knife-edged ridges extend like ribs from the central vertebrate peaks far out into the lowland. They are entirely green, with either dark forest growth or grass slopes that are far brighter than the variant green of the plains. They have the look of great antiquity, like greening skeletons of an older earth, and in places where a landslide has bitten unduly deep, sometimes the rock shows through as white as bone.

they had were never up to them and "could only hit a plane if it ran up to the gun barrel." Many of these gunners, however, had never, as will be seen, fired a machine gun at an air target till they took off on their first combat mission. Some had never fired a machine gun at all.

The greatest of the ranges is the Cordillera Central, some of whose peaks lift over 9000 feet. Two hundred miles long and 70 wide it runs from a little north of the great Lingayen Plain nearly to the north coast. West of it are the low Illocos Mountains facing the China Sea. East is the Cagayan Valley, which, with Aparri at its mouth, forms one of the main invasion routes from the north. Between the Cagayan Valley and the Pacific are the Sierra Madres. They form a wall down the east coast of Luzon from the northern tip to Mauban in Lamon Bay, well south of Manila. These three ranges are linked by the Caraballo Mountains, a transverse chain that forms the barrier between the great central plain and the Cagayan Valley.

The fourth range, standing alone between the central plain and the China Sea, reaches from the tip of Bataan Peninsula to the Lingayen Gulf. Its major peaks rise from 4000 to nearly 8000 feet. Only two roads cross them, and both of these are on Bataan. In 80 miles there is only a single cart track, and people in the seacoast towns, like Iba, must drive around the mountains to reach the central plain. They are heavily forested, except for the grass slopes of their eastern foothills, and are fissured by steep and dark ravines. Only the Negritoes can live in them. They are called the Zambales Mountains.

Thus it will be seen that the mountains entirely govern the land approaches to the great central plain that is the heart of Luzon, and therefore of all the Philippines. It lies open only in the north, where it meets Lingayen Gulf, but it can be approached from the south below the end of the Sierra Madres from Lamon or Tayabas Bay. Its main features are Mount Arayat, on which the Filipinos believe the Ark was landed, and Manila Bay, whose island forts are like pebbles in its mouth, with the city of Manila on its inner shore, snared in the loops of its rivers. South of the city Laguna de Bay lies in the heel of the flat land like an incredible, three-toed footprint filled with water.

All the plain is under cultivation. Fields, rice paddies, plantations of coconut trees that look from the air like printed rows of asterisks are loosely threaded by the narrow roads, occasional telegraph lines, and the single track of the railroad. The little villages or barrios are brown and blend with the earth; only the larger towns show red or galvanized roofs, or the high white or yellow stucco walls of churches. The plain never rises more than a hundred feet above sea level. It is open everywhere and drowsing under the sun, and life on it moves slowly, even its railroad trains. The only swift thing a flier may see in crossing it will be the shadow of his plane.

To some extent the mountains also influence the air approaches. They are apt to have weather of their own and often by noon the high peaks will have gathered clouds. It is not safe practice anywhere in the Islands to enter a cloud bank if it drops below 5000 feet. In bad weather experienced pilots hold their courses 50 to 100 miles offshore until opposite their objectives, when they head straight in to land underneath the clouds. And then the mountains do strange things to radio reception. The airfield at Iba, for instance, now and then had great difficulty in getting through to Manila. December 8 was one of the worst days. Whether they understood these things or not, the Japanese made good use of the mountains in their first attacks on Luzon.

By mid-November there undoubtedly still were men in the Philippines who clung to the belief that if the Japanese attacked it would not be till spring. But the signs of war were multiplying. During September and October Manila was visited by the Chiefs of Staff of the Dutch commander in the N. E. I. and the British in Singapore, and it had become plain that in the event of war, the lifeline of supply to the Philippines would be up from Australia through the Netherlands Indies. This especially applied to air reinforcements, for by making use of Dutch airfields scattered among the islands, it would be possible to fly fighter planes from Darwin to Manila. The route worked out by the Intelligence Section ran from Darwin to Koepang (in Dutch Timor)—to Kendari (in the Celebes)—to Balikpapan—to Tarakan (both in Dutch Borneo)—to Sandakan (in British North Borneo)—to Del Monte (Mindanao)—to Santa Barbara (Panay)—and finally to Nichols Field. But it had now become obvious that a survey of Australia's possibilities as a base could no longer be put off. If war broke suddenly, Australian military, political, and industrial contacts would be vital necessities. Colonel George had been selected as General MacArthur's representative for the trip, but it

was impossible to spare him, and Captain Pell, who had done the preliminary liaison work for the 19th Group's flight, was assigned in George's
place to accompany General Brereton.[2]

The party was a small one; and they had only days in which to fulfill a mission that in ordinary times would have taken months, certainly
weeks. Colonel Eubank was piloting the plane, and besides Captain Pell
there were Major Charles H. Caldwell, who had come out from the
States with Brereton and for a while doubled on his staff as A-2 and A-3;
Captain Norman L. Llewellyn, Brereton's aide; Captain Eads; and Captain Ind.* They took off from Clark Field in a B-17 before dawn on
November 13 and set course straight for Darwin.

The floodlights were put out behind them. Dust raised by the big ship
in its rush across the field settled unseen through the velvet darkness.
The familiar sounds of the Philippine night took over reassuringly again.
The lizards outside the quarters could be heard uttering their small un-
censored obscenity as they had been doing for centuries before English-
speaking soldiers arrived to understand them. But there were currents
of disquiet that had reached down that night from Headquarters to at
least three points on Luzon. At Clark Field, at Nichols, and at Iba, the
three squadrons of the 24th Pursuit Group had gone on a new and stiffer
alert. From this time forward their planes remained armed, fully loaded,
and in constant readiness with pilots available on thirty minutes' notice.[4]

Though Headquarters in Manila had been warned by Washington during October of increasing tension in our relations with Japan, there was
no need to urge our Far East Command to hurry its preparations for
war. Even if the Japanese were to hold off till April, time was all too
short. The Philippine Division, during late summer and early fall, had
been put through offensive combat training in the field. Now in mid-
November troops were moving north from Fort McKinley for what were
planned by General Wainwright † to be December maneuvers in the
area north of Tarlac.[5] Mobilization was in process, and Filipino Divisions
were being inducted into the United States Army as rapidly as the Fili-

---

* Pell, however, did not make the flight with Brereton and Eubank but went separately
through the N. E. I. and Java. According to Eubank's recollection and Ind's account, the
trip began November 16, but I have here accepted the date given in the Brereton Diaries.[3]

† MacArthur had given Wainwright the command of the North Luzon forces in September, following General Grunert's return to the States.

pino officers could be trained in Divisional Command.[6] Intelligence reports of increasing Japanese activity down through the China Sea were confirmed by reconnaissance by friendly aircraft, which, however, was necessarily of a limited nature. Both Army and Navy Far East Commanders were to recommend taking aggressive action before the Japanese attacked us.[7] But in Washington it had been decided that this country must continue its efforts to achieve peace through diplomatic channels, and this policy was persevered in until the actual beginning of war. Though some felt, as Secretary of War Stimson did on November 28, that the President's warning in August against further moves by Japan towards Thailand justified the United States in attacking without further warning,[8] the idea of doing so was repugnant to our sense of national honor.

The effect of this policy was of course to raise still higher the odds against our slim defenses in the Philippines; but while our government carried it forward with sincere hope for its success, the Japanese were using it for their own ends. Manila had a glimpse of one of the moves in their game, when on November 6 newspapers announced that a special Japanese minister was traveling to Washington on the Hong Kong Clipper. The flying boat landed in Manila Bay and took off again November 8 with Saburo Kurusu aboard. He reached Washington on the 16th, and on the 18th he called on Secretary of State Hull and President Roosevelt to present his credentials and initiate the hypocritical negotiations under which Japan concealed her final moves toward war.

7. *Reinforcements: November 20*

ON NOVEMBER 20 a convoy consisting of the S.S. *Coolidge* and the USAT *Winfield S. Scott* entered Manila Bay escorted by the heavy cruiser *Louisville*. The ships had left Hawaii on the 6th, and it was only then that the rank and file aboard were officially informed that the code word "Plum" stenciled on their gear stood for the Philippines. At night the ships steamed under complete blackout; but except for one day when the *Louisville* rolled over on her side and, swinging her guns, took out after a dark blot on the horizon, the voyage was made without incident; and an hour later the *Louisville* was back in her place.[1] They stopped off Guam while the *Scott* went in for water but no one went ashore. They came into Manila Bay in the full heat of the day and the *Coolidge* lay for over three hours at Pier 7, which was the longest pier in the world, before her passengers were allowed to disembark [2]—even then officials had formalities to observe.

The *Scott,* among other items, carried a deckload of light tanks.[3] Aboard the *Coolidge* were four Air Corps units: the 5th Air Base Group, which almost immediately moved down to Mindanao; and the 21st and 34th Pursuit Squadrons and the 27th Bombardment Group (Light), all three of which remained on Luzon. These units were the last reinforcements received by the Air Corps in the Philippines.

The fighter squadrons, which belonged in the 35th Pursuit Group,* were at roughly half pilot strength—the 21st with 15 [4] and the 34th with 16; [5] but both had brought out their full ground echelons. The remaining pilots were expected on the next ship with the rest of the Group,[6] but they never reached the Philippines.† The squadrons had brought no planes with them as they expected to be equipped at Nichols Field on their arrival. But though they found preparations going forward furiously at Nichols Field, there were no P-40s waiting for them. Instead they were issued some of the well-worn P-35s that had formerly been used by the 3rd, 17th, and 20th Squadrons.

The 21st Squadron, which was under the command of Lieutenant William E. Dyess, was based at Nichols Field, from which the 17th also operated. They flew in their P-35s until December 4, when they began receiving brand-new P-40Es from the Air Depot as fast as the planes could be assembled. Their old P-35s were passed on to the 34th Squadron, which thus finally acquired a total of about 25 planes.[7]

After five days at Nichols Field, the 34th was taken by its commanding officer, Lieutenant Samuel W. Marrett, out to Del Carmen, one of the new airfields, where they set up operations as well as they could. They

---

* The 35th was also the parent group of the 20th Squadron.

† The Group went to Australia; but from there Headquarters Squadron and the 35th Interceptor Control Squadron were sent on to India in the convoy that left Melbourne on February 12, 1942.

were a very youthful outfit, and except for Marrett himself, the Operations Officer, and the Adjutant, the air echelon was composed entirely of second lieutenants.[8] Del Carmen must have been something of a shock to them. It was a raw dirt strip cut out of the countryside close to a small river. The town of Floridablanca was three miles away, but it had little to offer. The field itself had no facilities of any kind, and the Squadron were thrown entirely on their own resources. They had to build their gun emplacements and revetments. There was no running water and no latrine and the stream was used for all purposes. The dust on the strip presented an enormous problem, as it did, for that matter, on most of the new strips on Luzon; but at Del Carmen it was something special. It lay six inches deep over the whole strip and a quick squadron take-off was a sheer impossibility. It might be as long as three to five minutes after one plane had taken off before the pilot in the next could see at all. Moreover, due to the fact that their P–35s were long overdue for an engine change, this dust helped make maintenance even more difficult than it would normally have been under such primitive conditions.[9] The men worked hard to establish themselves, though, of course, they did not know that they had just thirteen days to prepare for war.

The 27th Bombardment Group had also arrived without planes, besides being minus one squadron. Its 52 A–24 dive bombers, which would measurably have corrected the lack of dive bombardment in our Philippine air strength, had been left behind on the San Francisco docks. While the Group was still at sea, the rumor went round that the planes were following them on the *Meigs;* [10] and just before December 8, the Group Commander, Major John H. Davies, received word that the transport carrying his planes had left Hawaii. But by then it was too late; the planes never came. Hope, though, died hard, and even after several days of war, the mere rumor that their planes were on the docks was enough to send the 16th Squadron rushing to the waterfront.[11] It is a cardinal principle of warfare never to send an organization into a combat zone without its tactical equipment; but when the 27th Group left San Francisco we were still at peace. Still more ironical, however, was the fact that when a small contingent of the Group's pilots finally found their planes waiting in Australia, the planes could not be used for several weeks because they lacked several essential parts.

In the meantime the 27th was sent out to Fort McKinley, which now served as a reception center, and set up their camp on the parade ground. The field they were to use when their planes arrived was San Marcelino,[12] near the head of Subic Bay above Bataan. When Major Davies went up to look at it, he found a natural field close up against the mountains with trees and brush surrounding most of it. The usable part was perhaps 300 by 1800 yards and natives were still picking rocks out of its sandy sod.

It was a desolate spot, in a dry river bed, and Clark Field was 30 miles away across the mountains. As at Del Carmen, there were no facilities of any sort and a detachment was sent in to start building quarters and help work on the strips while the rest of the Group stayed on at Fort McKinley, waiting for their planes and wondering what to do with their time. Finally they were set to filling sandbags and building revetments at Nielson Field, which was bare of natural camouflage or protection of any sort. In their frustration, the men seem to have gone in for filling sandbags in a large way. When they had used up 100,000, Captain Edward N. Backus was sent off to draw another 150,000. As less than 500 were available at the depot, Backus went to see the colonel in charge. The colonel laughed, and told him that though he had authority to draw sandbags locally and the manufacturers could turn out 100,000 a week, he did not think there was enough of an emergency to justify spending Government funds for such a purpose. This was the 6th of December.[13] The skeptical colonel had something on his side, however, for the half-built revetments were never used. Next day the filled sandbags were loaded on trucks, carted over to Air Head-quarters, and stacked around the walls.

Several days after the Group's arrival four of the more decrepit B-18s were turned over to the air crews and the process of getting in flying time was begun in a more or less hair-raising fashion. But these prewar jaunts to and from San Marcelino and Clark Field were about the only missions flown by the 27th Bombardment Group in the Philippines.

The 5th Air Base Group had been sent out to set up a base for the 7th Bombardment Group, which, with its B-17s, was expected early in December. The day after landing their commanding officer, Major Raymond T. Elsmore, reported to FEAF Headquarters, where it was decided that he and his group should take over the operation of Clark Field. He went up there the same day by air to look the situation over, but on his return to Manila he found a call waiting for him to report to Colonel George, who was still A-4 of FEAF. While he had been up at Clark it had been decided to open up Del Monte, on Mindanao, as an air base, but George said that whoever went down there would be starting from scratch. There was only one field big enough to accommodate all types of planes, and there were no facilities at all—no hangars, no barracks, no supplies, no nothing, as George put it. He had told Elsmore that the 5th Air Base Group could have Clark Field, but he hoped they would go to Mindanao.

Elsmore asked if he could talk it over with his officers, and George said to go ahead. It was not an easy decision to make, for Clark Field, besides being the best and largest airfield in the Philippines, with plenty of barracks and quarters to take care of the Air Base Group, was also the base for the only bombardment group. But when it came to a vote almost all the men voted to take on the pioneering job. In the discussions that followed, Colonel Brady had stated that it would take the Group two to three weeks to get ready; [14] but within three days after two small interisland steamers had been turned over to them, men and supplies were aboard and moving out of Manila Bay. Next day Elsmore and his staff flew down in two B-18s which, after considerable wrangling, had been assigned to them for base planes. Off the island of Masbate, they overtook the two ships with the Group on board, [15] proceeding one behind the other. They made small and apparently immovable tips to the arrowheads their wakes had traced on the Sibuyan Sea. But the planes bore west of the ships' heading, across Cebu with its pointed grass-green mountains, and Bohol, and the Mindanao Sea. Then as they came in above Macajalar Bay, the high Bukidnon Plateau opened before them like the revelation of a different world. Its rolling grass plains were seamed by deep and twisting ravines, and on either side the mountains stretched to the southward under canopies of broken clouds.

The shadows of the planes came up from the sea, swept inland, leaping the ravines and racing past the winding red dirt roads, and finally touched wheels again as the planes landed on a little golf course set among pineapple plantations. Here they were met by the manager of the Del Monte Corporation, J. W. Crawford, who also held the contract for erecting their barracks. There was not a stitch of cover for the airdrome, and the second day after his arrival, Elsmore started locating and laying out seven more fields within a 15-mile radius.

By then the two steamers had docked at Bugo, a little hamlet on the tip of Macajalar Bay, where the road from Del Monte came down off the hills and turned along the coast for Cagayan. The Del Monte Corporation had a cannery there and a pier at which the two little steamers, the *Legaspi* and *La Touche,* tied up. The men spent the next couple of days unloading them and getting their supplies up the 18 miles of climbing road to Del Monte. They pitched their tents alongside the field. Major Elsmore commanded the base but the men worked under Captain Herman A. Little. It was a neat camp; the tents were beautifully lined up. You could have laid a straightedge down the entire row. Then they started on the air strip.

It was the best natural meadow the men had ever seen. The sod was on hard ground and would hold anything in any weather. No grading was necessary. All they had to do was cut the grass. They got hold of a tractor mower and the few farmers in the outfit took over. They refused to let anyone else in on the job unless he was a qualified farmer.

On December 3 they were joined by two Ordnance Companies: the 701st (Air Base) and the 440th (Bombardment), which came in to Bugo on the *Mayon,* but their ranks were not full. A second contingent was to leave Manila on December 10 on two small ships, loaded with ammunition and 110,000 gallons of aviation gasoline, and arrive only after a harried voyage.* These outfits together built their camp at Tankulan, about a mile and a half from the airfield. This spot, which

* These two ships were the *Pisquataqua* and the *Samal.* The chief difficulty they had to surmount was the conviction of the *Samal's* skipper that they should go ashore and take to the hills. Several times they sighted planes, which added to the skipper's enthusiasm about the woods; and there was a good deal more trouble in Cebu, where they had to unload supplies and ammunition and most of the civilian passengers, and hold onto the skipper at the same time. They set out for Mindanao by night and just at dawn they sighted a Japanese destroyer which had made a run across the Mindanao Sea to intercept them; but by then they were in sight of Bugo dock and out of the destroyer's range. . . . The final contingent, of the 701st Ordnance Company, left Manila several days after this on the ill-fated *Corregidor,* which went astray in our own minefields at the mouth of the bay and was blown to splinters with a heavy loss of life. Lt. Macgowan, who commanded this contingent, was rescued and later fought on Corregidor.

became known as Camp 29, was where most Air Corps personnel were to put up during their stay at Del Monte. As soon as the airfield was finished, it was designated Del Monte No. 1—the golf course being Del Monte No. 3, though it had been in use as an airfield for some time before the 5th Air Base Group arrived.

Mainly in those early days, the men worked on their camps and the airfields. It was a busy life, but a peaceful one; and the bare grasslands with the sweep of cloud shadows upon them made a few men think of the prairies. In the short time since their arrival, though, Del Monte had changed; and now native Filipino help had come in to work on barracks and air strips. Trucks besides those brought by the three outfits were hired from local sources, and the roads continually flew plumes of dust. But many of the men could not shake their sense of remoteness. They had not yet had time to explore Cagayan, the little seacoast town west of Bugo and 20 miles away by road. To them, at night, the hard and angular shapes of the mountains carried desolation.

Then on December 6, the dawn sky was filled by the roar of airplane engines, and before the night shadow was fully lifted from the airfield, B-17s began dropping down to it one by one, their silver shapes dimming as they sank out of the upper light. There were 16 of them—the 14th and 93rd Squadrons.* They had left Clark Field hurriedly the night before, and because they expected to stay only three days, they had brought very few supplies.

None of the barracks had yet been completed and, as there were not enough tents to house all the air crews, many of them slept in their planes. Del Monte's communications with the rest of the world were still very uncertain, and the men had little information of what was going on on Luzon. Time hung heavy on their hands. The only diversion was a visit to the P-X, a makeshift shack that had been run up almost on the day the base was opened. But all the P-X had to offer was a single brand of beer called "San Miguel Beer for Convalescent Mothers." It was weak, black, and mildly reminiscent of stout. The men bought it anyhow and took it back to the airfield. There, in the evening, Sergeant

---

* Two full squadrons were sent, barring Lt. John Carpenter of the 93rd, whose plane (which had been Lt. Connally's on the Pacific flight) both then and later had continual generator trouble. But Lt. Parsel replaced him to bring the 93rd up to strength.[16]

Wilbert A. McClellan of the 93rd Squadron began composing the song that ultimately grew into hundreds of stanzas of increasing ripeness. It was called "The Gypsy Ninety-third," and other men, some of them undoubtedly from other squadrons, aided in its composition. On the second night of their stay at Del Monte, which was the last night of peace, there were still only a few stanzas, but enough to sing, and they began mildly and factually:

> There's a pilot in the cabin,
> And a bomber in the nose,
> A tail full of gunners,
> And off she goes
> To some far-off place
> Of which we've never heard,
> But we don't give a damn
> In the Gypsy Ninety-third.

The men sang it to the tune of "Turkey in the Straw" as they sat in their tents or underneath their planes with starlight on the wings above them.

8. *Reconnaissance: American and Japanese*

THE SEQUENCE OF EVENTS that led up to the abrupt transfer of half the bomber force in the Philippines from Clark Field to Del Monte had begun in the small hours of the morning of November 28 with the receipt at Headquarters of the following radio:

#624
PRIORITY   NOVEMBER 27, 1941
COMMANDING GENERAL, U. S. ARMY FORCES IN THE FAR EAST
      MANILA, P. I.

Negotiations with Japan appear to be terminated to all practical purposes with only barest possibilities that Japanese government might come back and offer to continue. Japanese future action unpredictable but hostile action possible at any moment. If hostilities cannot, repeat cannot, be avoided the United States desires that Japan commit the first overt act. This policy should not, repeat not, be construed as restricting you to a course of action that might jeopardize the successful defense of the Philippines. Prior to hostile Japanese action you are directed to take such reconnaissance and other measures as you deem necessary. Report measures taken. Should hostilities occur you will carry out the tasks assigned in revised Rainbow Five which was delivered to you by General Brereton. Chief of Naval Operations concurs and requests you notify Hart.*

MARSHALL

General MacArthur acknowledged receipt of this radio at 4:53 that morning and reported that reconnaissance had been extended and intensified in conjunction with the Navy. "Ground security measures have been taken. Within the limitations imposed by the present state of development of this Theater of Operations everything is in readiness for the conduct of a successful defense."

FEAF Headquarters had been notified as well as Admiral Hart, and later in the day General Brereton received directions by radio from General Arnold to instruct all establishments and units under his command to take immediate measures to protect themselves against subversive propaganda, espionage, and sabotage. "This does not, repeat not, authorize any illegal measures. Avoiding unnecessary alarm and publicity protective measures should be confined to those essential for security."

General Brereton had returned from Australia with his party only two days before. After finishing their conferences in Melbourne, they had flown to New Guinea and taken off from Port Moresby because Eubank wanted to see if the flight from there to Clark Field could be made in one hop. It took the B–17 fourteen hours and there were about 200 gallons of gas left in its tanks when they landed. The narrowness of this margin demonstrated the need of an emergency landing field for planes coming up from Australia if Clark Field should happen to be closed in by weather and was the main reason for the quick decision to open Del Monte, for Del Monte and Clark Field were almost never closed in at the same time.

In accordance with his instructions from General Arnold, Brereton called all air commanders in to Headquarters at Nielson Field and ordered all air units on a full war alert. He summarized the international

---

* Admiral Thomas C. Hart, Commander of the United States Asiatic Fleet.

situation and emphasized its seriousness. All air troops were to be alerted and prepared for action at once—this applied to all command posts, communications and message centers, hospitals and transportation as well as to air crews. Blackout conditions were to be put into effect at once, shelter pits dug, gas masks issued, sandbags filled and defective bags replaced. Antiaircraft defense was to be ready and under guard and manned in dispersed positions near aircraft at all times.

Taking notes, Colonel Eubank jotted down instructions specifically applying to his command:

Practice bomb loading and fusing. . . . Protect all your facilities. . . . Check your alarm system and establish liaison with Ground Forces for local airdrome defense. . . . Planes ready for immediate action. No non-tactical missions. Complete combat crew and full load of ammunition to be carried at all times. Don't waste time. . . . Assemble officers and noncommissioned officers. Explain the situation to them. Tell them that work and hardship are a part of war. . . . Exercise close supervision and emphasize flight discipline. Conservation of equipment is all-important. . . . Absolute secrecy must prevail and no discussion of the situation outside of official assemblies.

Again emphasize war footing for all missions. . . .

On his return to Clark Field, Eubank called his men out on the line and talked to them there in the open sunlight in front of the Bachelor Officers' Quarters. Behind him the great cone of Mount Arayat dominated the plain, but its peak was insubstantial in the haze. Though Eubank's voice with its slight drawl was not raised, his words came to the men clearly as he told them of the imminence of war. He spoke briefly of the need and purpose of dispersal and explained why still more slit trenches needed to be dug.

Some of the men had the feeling that this actually was war itself, but others were sheepish about having to wear helmets and carry sidearms and gas masks, and they made cracks about "play soldiering." They were drilled from now on in a series of day and night practice alerts and, because bomb-handling equipment was one thing they had no lack of, they became proficient enough to load the entire group in thirty minutes. But there were no more leaves to Manila, and even when they went up to Fort Stotsenburg only half a mile by road, they had strict orders to keep their transportation with them at all times.

The next evening, November 29, was the night that the Army-Navy football game was to be rebroadcast in Manila. They make a great deal of the game on the Philippine station and both Services send cheer leaders to the shindig at the Army and Navy Club. This year Captain Colin Kelly was to be one of the cheer leaders and a good-looking mule had been lined up; but neither he nor any other member of the 19th or 24th Groups attended.* The only Air Corps Personnel there came from Headquarters or the 27th Bombardment Group, which had no planes. This alert was never relaxed in any particular; it was still in full force on December 8.

The need for long-range reconnaissance now became vital, especially as the air warning service was still in a thoroughly primitive state of development. It is true that the first radar set in the Philippines had just been installed at Iba; † but due to the vagaries of the Philippine telephone system it took from five to twenty-five minutes to get reports through to Air Headquarters at Nielson Field.³ As has been pointed out, moreover, radio communication between Iba and Nielson was at best uncertain. General Headquarters enjoyed no such services as the Japanese espionage network supplied to their commanders, and it was now evident that in air reconnaissance lay our sole hope of gaining advance warning of a hostile movement.

The zones to be watched were laid out on the map—the larger area being turned over to the PBYs of the Navy's Patrol Wing Ten under their Captain Frank D. Wagner. The bulk of their 30 planes, stationed at or near Manila, covered the China Sea west as far as the coast of Indo-China, northwest to Hainan, and north to Formosa. Besides these patrols,

---

* Nor did any Navy personnel attend. Radio reception was all fouled up anyway, so very little of the game came through.¹

† According to Col. A. H. Campbell, Chief of Aircraft Warning Service, a second radar set was in operation outside of Manila on December 8 (AAF IN WORLD WAR II, Vol. I, p. 186, note 96); but since no other source mentions it, the set at Iba was almost certainly the only set in full working order, as stated in the Brereton Diaries (p. 65), *24th Pursuit Group, History of the 5th Air Force,* Sheppard Statement, and elsewhere. Another set, similar to the one at Iba, was in process of being set up on the northwest tip of Luzon, 60 miles from Aparri; and still another (a mobile set) was on its way to the south of Manila when the Japs struck. It became mired in swampy going and its crew was forced to blow it up to keep it out of Jap hands. Some lighter units also arrived in the closing days of peace and a couple were supposedly in operation on Bataan after December 25.²

the entrances to the Celebes Sea were covered by planes attached to the seaplane tender *Preston* in the Gulf of Davao watching to the eastward, and four light planes on location with the *Heron* off the southeast tip of Palawan Island to watch the western passages. Farther south along the northern borders of the Indies, the Dutch were running their own patrols.[4] This left the area northward from Manila. It was divided into pie-shaped sections, one reaching to the tip of Formosa and the other covering northern Luzon, the small islands to the north, and then running up the east coast of Formosa.

These segments were assigned to the 19th Group. They began flying reconnaissance missions on the 29th of November, two planes taking off from Clark Field each day, though occasionally extra missions were run. Their orders were to look for enemy shipping but not to fight unless they met opposition, and not to cross the International Boundary.* For the first few days these missions were uneventful.

Then on December 2 the PBYs reported 20 Japanese ships in Camranh Bay, on the lower southeast coast of French Indo-China. Next day 50 ships were reported in Camranh Bay, including destroyers and cruisers. On December 4 there were none. Further reconnaissance had to be abandoned because of violent weather.[5] The disappearance of this fleet gave our people their first lesson in the adroitness of the Japanese in using the Pacific weather to veil their operations. For two days no one could tell which way the ships were moving. Then on December 6 the weather lifted over the Gulf of Siam and the fleet was discovered on a heading that would inevitably bring it to Thailand or the Malay States.

During those two anxious days, Admiral Phillips of the British Navy had been in Manila conferring with Admiral Hart. One of his prime objectives had been to get destroyers to screen his two great battleships, *Repulse* and *Prince of Wales,* for the British then had only six in Far East waters, all of which were needed for detached service. But on

---

* Among Air Force personnel a story has persisted that a few days before December 8 Maj. David R. Gibbs flew low across the southern end of Formosa in spotty weather and saw installations stacked with trucks, planes, tanks, and guns. Maj. Gibbs was lost on a flight from Clark Field to Del Monte shortly after hostilities began, so direct verification is impossible; but it seems improbable that Gibbs, then Squadron Commander of the 30th, would have exceeded very positive orders to that extent. Maj. Gen. Eubank, however, says that some fliers were supposed to have exceeded the letter of their orders, and in his opinion some undoubtedly did.

learning of the Japanese fleet's heading he took off at once by night for Singapore. Destroyers or no destroyers, he felt that he should be at sea.*

In the meantime our reconnaissance planes began to meet Japanese planes patrolling the sea northwest of Luzon. No incidents occurred, but, as the planes approached, each had its guns manned. Reporting on his PBYs, Captain Wagner said that they and the Japanese were "keeping a wary eye on each other and avoiding each other like stiff-legged dogs." [7]

The Japanese planes sighted by the PBYs were not the first, however, to come down the Luzon coast. On November 27, two pursuit pilots—Major William H. Maverick, attached to Headquarters of the 24th Pursuit Group, and Lieutenant Walter B. Putnam, commanding officer of the Headquarters Squadron—took their planes out to buzz the S.S. *Coolidge,* on which a friend was sailing for the States and which, with the USAT *Scott* and an escorting destroyer, had pulled away from Manila at noon.† The two fliers went well out and then, after they had brushed off the *Coolidge* satisfactorily, they came loafing back along the coast with most of the kinks flown out of their systems. In this relaxed mood, Putnam happened to look up. Straight above were nine planes, flying three three-ship leads, and heading up the coast as he was. He peeled back and tried to get up to them, but they were 10,000 feet higher and he could not come near them. He sent in a report to which the only reaction seemed to be that he must have been mistaken. But Putnam knew he had seen nine ships, and they were none of ours.

Putnam had a second experience, this time with one plane, that early raised his suspicions. Just after the beginning of December he was out on a routine night-survey mission led by Major Grover when a single plane with running lights flew hell for leather through their formation.

* Since there was no military alliance with Britain at the time, it was a difficult decision for Admiral Hart to make, but by coincidence four of our destroyers were refueling at Balikpapan (Borneo). Hart decided that there was nothing in international law that would prevent U. S. ships from making an indoctrinational cruise with ships of a friendly power. Before Phillips left he ordered the destroyers to Batavia for supplies and recreation. They should have reached Singapore in 48 hours. Unfortunately the Dutch port authorities refused to open the antisubmarine booms at Balikpapan before sunrise, and by the time the destroyers reached Singapore, the two battleships, unescorted, had long since left on their mission up the Malay coast.[6]

† Putnam was uncertain of the date and recollected it as being about three weeks before the war; but the *Coolidge* sailed on November 27.

For a second, P–40 planes were spilling all over the Luzon sky and it took them over an hour to get into formation again.[8] The lone plane kept right on going and they were never able to identify it.

Then, beginning with December 2, a single plane flew over Clark Field on four consecutive nights. It came about 5:30 in the morning, but no origin for its flight could be found at any Luzon airfield. After its second appearance, orders were given to force the plane to land and, if the pilot committed any overt act, to shoot him down.[9] A six-ship flight from the 17th Pursuit Squadron, led by Lieutenant Boyd D. Wagner, was therefore ordered to attempt interception on the night of December 4-5; * but their search mission was unsuccessful, largely due to the lack of air-ground communication. The radios in their P–40s were ineffective beyond a maximum range of 20 miles. The 20th Pursuit Squadron also made an unsuccessful attempt to intercept on the night of December 5-6. Then, on the night of December 6-7, all aircraft were grounded except the 3rd Pursuit Squadron; and the antiaircraft at Clark Field were alerted to shoot the plane down.[11] That night, however, the plane did not come.

That same night was also a quiet one at Iba, though the 3rd Pursuit Squadron were prepared to make a squadron interception. This was with the direct sanction of General Headquarters. When the newly installed radar had first picked up the tracks of unidentified planes off the Zambales coast on December 3 and Clark Field reported its lone plane for the second successive night, Colonel George, now Chief of Staff of the 5th Interceptor Command as well as A-4 on FEAF, had gone to higher headquarters immediately to report not only the presence of the planes but his belief that the two flights were co-operating with each other and were the immediate preliminary to Japanese attack. Yet he had great difficulty in persuading some higher officers that these tracks represented hostile aircraft and not merely some unidentified private or commercial planes—if indeed he persuaded them at all, for many of them were still talking and thinking in terms of war in 1942 and counting the equipment and supplies they were due to receive before the first of March.[12] But both MacArthur and Sutherland, his Chief

---

* The other members of this flight were Lts. W. J. Feallock, William A. Sheppard, John L. Brownwell, R. B. Church, and 2nd Lt. William J. Hennon.[10]

of Staff, agreed with George and ordered the interception that was attempted by the 17th Squadron.

At this time the decision was reached in General Headquarters to send all the B-17s to Mindanao to get them out of range of direct attack by Japanese land-based planes. If war came, the B-17s could themselves stage out of Clark Field, picking up their bombs and gasoline for the run to Formosa.* But at FEAF Headquarters the latest information was that the 7th Bombardment Group could be expected at any time with four full squadrons. Their plans called for basing the 7th at Del Monte as soon as it arrived, and, since the field there could accommodate at most six squadrons, only two of the 19th Group's squadrons were dispatched. All planes were to have cleared the field by midnight of the 5th. They began taking off singly at 10:00 o'clock, the airborne ships circling the field until the others joined them. But several of the planes were delayed on take-off and it was nearly three hours before they completed their formation and headed south, and the night sky above Clark Field was finally drained of the roar of circling engines.

At Iba, the men in the half-buried hut that housed the radar saw more tracks born on the screen. Outside on the blacked-out field the 3rd Squadron's new P-40s stood on the line. Beyond was the dark sea, above which only the radar's eye could trace incoming planes. They did not come in all the way; they stayed offshore in the farther darkness, beyond the sound of the sea, as though there were a point in time for them to meet before they turned back. Then at the end of the runway one of the P-40s came suddenly to life and the air strip lights bloomed faintly along the field as the plane took off. The pilot was the 3rd's commanding officer, Lieutenant Henry G. Thorne, and he took off alone. He made a long search for the strange planes, far out to sea, but he could not find them.[13]

The men were eager to try a Squadron interception and after Thorne's report had been turned in, they were told they could attempt it. All air-

---

* According to General Brereton the order was given on the 4th, but he maintains that the order originated with him and that "approval . . . was obtained . . . only with the understanding that they [the B-17s] would be returned to airfields to be constructed on Cebu and Luzon as soon as the necessary facilities could be prepared." (BRERETON, 35.) This matter of dispersing the B-17s will be discussed in Chapter 12.

craft on Luzon except their own were to remain grounded; [14] therefore any planes encountered would automatically be considered hostile. It was re-emphasized that they must act defensively; but if the Japanese came in close enough, the 3rd could go for them. [15]

In their weeks at Iba, the Squadron had been drawn much more closely into a unit. There was a great deal more work to be done than the 120 enlisted men could handle, and during the last days officers worked beside the men as crew chiefs or digging foxholes and slit trenches. They felt the nearness of war and were doing everything they could to prepare for it, but they were still slow-timing the engines of some of the last planes to reach them and getting in what gunnery training they could. Because of the shortage of .50-caliber ammunition, they still had to use P–35s which had .30-caliber guns mounted on the fuselage. Consequently there were almost no pursuit pilots who had fired the wing guns that P–40s were equipped with, and the 3rd Squadron offered no exceptions. The men and officers shared the same quarters, a single barracks building without partitions and a group of tents behind it. And as they went about their work together on the air strip beside the bare beach and the blue and empty sea, with their few small buildings in the open and the high and frowning mountains that stood between them and all the rest of Luzon, they had a deepening sense of their own isolation.

The day of December 6 must have worn slowly for them, but the night hours brought nothing. The men in the black-out radar hut discovered no tracks on the screen. It was a peaceful night at Iba, as it was everywhere in the Philippines, for as far as is known there was no plane that night in all the Luzon sky.

9. December 7: Final Inventory

WAR DID NOT COME to the Philippines on December 7, as it did to Pearl Harbor. The arbitrary date line, by means of which man seeks to count his days, requires that the sun that rises in Hawaii on December 7 rise over the Philippines on December 8. Actually the man in Manila has seen the same sunrise as his brother in Honolulu, though it has taken five and a half hours of the earth's slow turning to bring the sun above the Sierra Madres. So, ironically, it was only through a man-made contrivance that in the Philippines Sunday, December 7, remained a day of grace. Outing families could still rattle along Manila streets, six or eight or ten people crammed into one high-wheeled *calesa* drawn by a single pony-sized horse, and in the open country small groups in their Sunday best drifted as they always had along the dusty roads to the old, sweet-belled churches.

But the armed forces continued their preparations for war.

The Infantry was still mobilizing. Its strength in men amounted to perhaps 112,000, and was made up as follows: U. S. Army Ground Forces (including 12,000 Philippine Scouts), 22,400; Philippine Army (one regular and ten reserve divisions), 87,000; two Philippine Constabulary Regiments of reduced strength, 3000.[1] But their effectiveness by no means measured up to their listed strength, and General Wainwright's description of his North Luzon Force at this date gives a much truer picture.

Out of 28,000 men making up his command, 25,000 were untrained and led to a very large extent by inexperienced officers. The 31st Division, forming on the Zambales coast, was a case in point; it had had no combat practice, no combat training, little or no rifle and machine gun practice. It began mobilizing on September 1, but two of its infantry regiments were called up on November 1 and November 25 respectively. The majority of its artillery was not mobilized till after war started. For that matter, not one of the four other divisions in or attached to Wainwright's command had a full complement of artillery, and the guns they did have were ancient British 75s or 2.95-inch mountain howitzers for which, because they too were obsolete, no ammunition was being manufactured. They were short of all other types of ammunition and grenades. They had no antitank outfits, almost no transportation—"hardly a truck, hardly a car"—and their only means of communication was the public telephone system which the Japanese agents could tap or cut almost at will. Two of the five divisions were each lacking a regiment. The 26th Cavalry and Battery A of the 23rd Field Artillery were the only thoroughly trained troops in Wainwright's command, yet this green army was called on to cover an area of roughly 75 miles north and south by 100 east and west.[2]

The South Luzon Force under Brigadier General Albert M. Jones was in no better case—its main numerical strength then consisting of the 41st and 51st Philippine Army Divisions, which were mobilizing below Manila in the provinces of Cavite and Batangas. The 45th and 57th Infantry regiments of the Philippine Scouts, and the 31st Infantry, an all-American outfit, were being held in reserve. Besides these there were the four small regiments of harbor defense troops on Corregidor and its three satellite forts, Hughes, Drum, and Frank.

A good deal of commercial shipping had run into Manila Bay during the past few days, but on December 7 most of our Asiatic Fleet was widely dispersed. Admiral Hart had long realized that with one heavy and two light cruisers and 13 overage destroyers he had no chance at all of standing up to one of the great navies of the world. The heavy cruiser *Houston* was therefore ordered to Iloilo on the south coast of Panay. The light cruiser *Boise* which had brought in an Army convoy on December 4 was sent down immediately to Cebu. The light cruiser *Marblehead* with four destroyers was loitering off Tarakan, Borneo. Four more destroyers with the tender *Black Hawk* were presumably en route to Batavia and Singapore. This left three destroyers to patrol the Manila-Subic Bay area, and two which were in dry dock at Cavite as the result of a collision two months before, the *Peary* and the *Pillsbury*. All the 29 submarines of the fleet were also in the area as were the six motor torpedo boats of Lieutenant John D. Bulkeley's P-T Squadron Three, which had yet to prove their extraordinary ability and daring.[3] Finally, the Asiatic Fleet had Patrol Wing Ten, the disposal of whose PBYs has already been described. But these slow and lumbering planes, in spite of the extraordinary courage and pugnacity of their crews, were not adapted to offensive combat.

The weaknesses in the other services laid an added burden on the Air Force which it was ill equipped to carry. This fact apparently was realized in relatively few quarters. General Brereton was one of those who did recognize it, and Colonel George in his talks to the personnel of the 24th Pursuit Group tried to prepare the men for the odds they would presently face. He had explained to them that they were not expected to defeat the enemy in the air, but to fight a holding action until reinforcements could reach the Islands. Until then, the 24th Pursuit Group would be virtually a suicide outfit. On December 6, George brought the majority of the pursuit pilots together in the theater at Nichols Field and told them that the war was a matter of days, and possibly only hours, away. It was a grim talk, but there was no trace of defeatism in his attitude. He pointed out that they had about 70 first-line planes to throw against the huge Jap air fleet, but he believed they would turn in a good performance.[4]

He did not convince all of the younger pilots, but he made a deep impression that morning on a few of the older hands, and when Lieutenant Grashio offered to bet Dyess five pesos there would be no war with Japan, Dyess snapped it up and laid another bet that war would be declared before a week was up.

It was midmorning when the men came out of the theater. In spite of the heat, Nichols Field and the Air Depot were swarming with activity. Dyess's 21st Squadron was receiving and readying its new P-40s. When the planes were received they still had to have their guns installed and bore-sighted,* but in this last operation the men were handicapped by the acute shortage of .50-caliber ammunition, of which only a few rounds were available for test purposes.[6]

That was Saturday. Work did not stop with darkness, for the Air Corps was now working the clock around in its effort to be ready. Sunday made no difference, either, at Nichols Field, and men were still at work that evening when the sun went down. At that time the squadrons of the 24th Pursuit Group turned in a status report showing 90 planes in commission; but to understand their actual strength and consequently have some insight into the showing they made on December 8, it is necessary, even at the risk of being repetitious, to list the strength and location of the various Air Force units on the evening of December 7.

---

* "In bore-sighting the guns are fired and adjusted until they strike the spot where the sights are centered." [5]

Altogether there were 8100 U. S. Air Corps troops in the Philippines, besides some 1500 belonging to the Philippine Army Air Corps. The latter, stationed on Luzon at Cabanatuan, at Zablan Field, Manila, and at an auxiliary field in Batangas, also had a detachment at Lahug Field on the island of Cebu; but their equipment was pathetically antiquated. Of their 60 planes 42 were PT-13s, Primary Trainers. Their only combat aircraft were twelve of the P-26s discarded by our forces and three B-10s. The Filipino pilots heroically took these crates into combat, but their effective contribution was necessarily a small one.

Five hundred of the U. S. Air Corps troops were stationed outside of Luzon, principally at Del Monte on Mindanao. Here, on December 7, were the 16 B-17s of the 14th and 93rd Squadrons under Major O'Donnell and Captain Cecil E. Combs. In the course of the morning several officers of the Air Base Group took off in one of the two B-18s that had been assigned to them and made a reconnaissance of the entire island, flying low over Davao to have a close look at the airfield; but everything was serene.[7]

With two full squadrons at Del Monte, a total of 19 B-17s remained at Clark Field—eight each in the 30th and 28th Squadrons and three in the Headquarters Squadron.* Only 16 of these planes, however, were ready for immediate combat service on the night of December 7. Two were in the hangars getting a camouflage paint job, and the third was the plane that had lost its tail section while landing in a typhoon and was still out of commission.

Clark Field by now had acquired something of the aspect of an armed camp. Tent areas had been added on the far side of the road leading up to Fort Stotsenburg. There were first-aid stations round the field and the whole place was honeycombed with foxholes and slit trenches, most of them dug by a mechanical ditch digger. It was operated day and night by a relay of Filipinos and was now at work behind the Bachelor Officers' Quarters. Round the perimeter of the landing area, in their sandbag nests, were the antiaircraft guns of the 200th Coast Artillery (AA), a mobile unit consisting of one battalion of three-inch and one of 37-mm guns; and big revetments were being built for the

---

* Commanded respectively by Maj. David R. Gibbs, Maj. William P. Fisher, and Capt. William E. McDonald.

LOCATION OF
U.S. SQUADRONS
ON LUZON

DECEMBER 7

Aparri

Tuguegarao

Vigan

Lingayen Gulf

Baguio

▲ Rosales

Tarlac

▲ Cabanatuan

Iba
3rd Pursuit
Squadron

CLARK FIELD
Hq & Hq Squadron — 24th Pursuit Group
20th Pursuit Squadron
Hq & Hq Squadron — 19th Bomb. Group
30th & 28th Bomb. Squadrons

DEL CARMEN
34th Pursuit
Squadron

MANILA

NIELSON FIELD
HQ, FEAF

NICHOLS FIELD
17th & 21st Pursuit
Squadrons

NOTE —
14th & 93rd Bomb. Squadrons at Del Monte, Mindanao

B-17s, big enough, one pilot said, to have housed a battleship. Two of them had been finished, but even in them the big planes were open to strafing attack.

The air crews of the 19th Group, however, were less inclined to think of a raid against their own field than of the attack mission that had been planned for them against Formosa. It had been set up in some detail, and the reconnaissance missions had also served as dry-runs from which gas and bomb loads had been worked out.

Sunday at Clark Field, as elsewhere in the Philippines, was without incident. The planes returning from their reconnaissance towards Formosa had nothing to report except that the bad weather of the past two days continued to cover the northern Islands. The big bombers in their search for shipping were flying close over the water, hunting in the open lanes between the squalls. There was nothing to see; nor had there been on Saturday when Major Walsh in one of the Headquarters planes had gone up to within 15 miles of Formosa. Six weeks later they would have learned to be automatically suspicious of such a spell of weather, but on December 7 they merely had nothing to report.

The status report turned in by the 24th Pursuit Group gave the following location and combat strength of its squadrons:

1. 3rd Pursuit Squadron, *Iba,* commanded by Lt. H. G. Thorne, 18 P-40Es in tactical commission.

2. 17th Pursuit Squadron, *Nichols Field,* commanded by Lt. Boyd D. Wagner, 18 P-40Es in tactical commission.

3. 21st Pursuit Squadron, *Nichols Field,* commanded by Lt. W. E. Dyess, 18 P-40Es in tactical commission.

4. 20th Pursuit Squadron, *Clark Field,* commanded by Lt. J. H. Moore, 18 P-40Bs in tactical commission.

5. 34th Pursuit Squadron, *Del Carmen,* commanded by Lt. S. H. Marrett, 18 P-35s in tactical commission.[8]

It added up to 54 P-40Es, 18 P-40Bs, and 18 P-35s, an official total of 90 first-line combat-worthy planes.*

In actual fact, the Group's strength did not approach that figure. The P-35s had been used by all the different squadrons as work-horse planes

---

* It should be noted that the 3rd Squadron had 22 planes in commission, but had decided to use only 18 tactically.[9]

before being turned over to the 34th; they were lightly armored and armed; their .30-caliber guns were worn out from steady use in gunnery training; and all of them needed an engine change, a condition that was seriously aggravated by the heavy dust on the Del Carmen field.

The 21st Squadron at Nichols Field had received the last four planes to make up its total of 18 that same day,[10] the 18th being delivered after dark.[11] None of these last planes had been in the air before they were taken up into combat; and the squadron had not been able to finish slow-timing any of the other planes. In fact none of the 18 planes on the line had had more than three hours in the air.[12]

There were therefore but three pursuit squadrons in the Philippines on December 7 with first-line planes actually fit for combat. This force of 54 pursuit planes, coupled with the 34 B-17s in commission, made a total of 88 first-line aircraft in which our men were asked to face the Japanese Air Force. Not even at the start of the Revolution had American troops stood to heavier odds. They fought the brand-new P-40s of the 21st Squadron and the worn-out P-35s down to the last ship, but their performance was not first line. They were only better planes than the B-10s and P-26s the Filipinos went to war with. The pilots, moreover, still had to learn the limitations of the P-40s; and they had to learn them under actual battle conditions against odds that almost never were less than ten to one and usually were nearer twenty. Nor was their B-17 the Flying Fortress that ended the war over Germany with its power turrets, heavier armor, and tail guns. These B-17Cs and Ds could only protect themselves adequately in full squadron formation in level flight, but the way the men had to fight them during the first days—one, two, or three ships over the target—they might as well, as General O'Donnell says, have been flying spotted ponies.

The pursuit pilots still lacked oxygen; their ship to ground communications were inadequate; their air warning service was next to useless; and they were based on four fields all of which were known to the enemy through espionage and air reconnaissance. On these fields there were, of course, the other planes that added up the paper totals which made our air strength in the Philippines sound fairly impressive. There were the O-46s and O-52s of the 2nd Observation Squadron. There were 12 B-18s, two of them at Del Monte, which were used to run supplies and parts down to Mindanao with as great hazard to their crews from the weather as from the Japanese; there were eight A–27s, the dive bombers with their instrumentation in Siamese, only two of which could still fly; and there was a miscellaneous assortment of trainers, observation planes, and broken-down bombers scattered here and there on different fields.

And finally, of course, there was the 27th Bombardment Group—1200 officers and men whose planes had never come. On the evening of December 7, the officers gave a dinner for General Brereton at the Manila Hotel. It was quite an occasion and it is probable that none of the participating 27th noticed the General slipping out on them, first for a conference with Admiral Purnell and a little later with General Sutherland. From them he learned that in the opinion of the War and Navy Departments war might break at any time. Brereton called his staff together and had Colonel Brady warn all airfields to go on combat alert. At the same time plans for field exercises, which were to have brought the B–17s back temporarily from Mindanao to Clark Field, had to be canceled.[13]

Meanwhile, the 27th's party at the Manila Hotel continued on its course, breaking up finally at two o'clock on the morning of December 8.[14] It was a clear night then, with a soft southerly wind beginning to blow. Manila was quiet as the men found their way back to Fort McKinley through the blackout. Only the sound of their jeeps or, after they had gone, the quick clopping feet of a little Filipino horse taking home a *calesa* full of Sunday stragglers could be heard in the streets.

Less than an hour later the men watching the radar screen in the half-buried hut at Iba saw the tracks of the first big flight of Japanese bombers coming down from Formosa through the still darkness over the China Sea.*

---

* Sheppard puts the time at about 2:00 A.M.; but the 24th Group Narrative puts the time at about 4:00 A.M.[15] 2nd Lt. A. E. Krieger, the Assistant Operations Officer at Iba, says "the early dark hours" and adds that one of the pilots of the 3rd Squadron figured out that the Japanese flight came down within an hour of the attack on Pearl Harbor. Thorne, the Squadron CO, puts it at about 1:00 A.M.[16] I believe the time was between 2:00 and 3:00 A.M. At 2:30 A.M. the 21st Squadron at Nichols Field was ordered to stations,[17] which lends weight to Sheppard's statement, and it seems likely that the flight reported off Iba was the cause of the alert at Nichols. See Chapter 11, below.

III

Attack: December 8

10. *Iba: The First Phase*

THERE WAS NO QUESTION of the flight's identity. They had to be the Japanese, for all planes on Luzon, except the 3rd's, were grounded again that night. The men thought this was war at last, both the men in the cockpits of the planes, and the others standing by to see them off. No time was wasted, no words were needed. The interception had been carefully planned and every pilot knew his place in the formation they were to fly. The engines thundered as they were run up; then came a moment of comparative quiet before Thorne's plane moved out from the rest, roared briefly down the strip, and, almost in the instant of becoming airborne, turned away over the sea. One by one the others followed, the wash of their propellers driving clouds of dust back through the darkness. Then they were gone. The beat of their engines grew fainter than the soft wash of the sea along the beach. Only the men inside the sunken hut, their eyes intent upon the radar screen, could follow them.

The pilots knew their heading but they did not know at what altitude the Japanese were flying, for the radar set at Iba had no means of estimating altitude. So they themselves were at staggered altitudes to afford the greatest possible chance of interception. Their orders of the night before still held: if they found the Japanese within 20 miles of shore, they were to shoot on sight. But they saw nothing at all, though they searched far beyond their 20-mile limit in wide casts across the sea. It was only when they returned to the field that they learned that interception of a sort had been accomplished.

According to the radar presentation, contact had been made at 40 miles. The men watching the screen had seen what the pilots could not. The two lines representing the Japanese and the P–40 flights had faithfully converged; then, suddenly, at the very point of meeting, the Japanese flight had turned back. Without oxygen, the 3rd Squadron had been limited more or less to 15,000 feet, and undoubtedly the Japanese had been above them.[1]

The Japanese flight seemed pointless, and the returning pilots of the 3rd Squadron must have scratched their heads over it. It was both frustrating and mysterious. If the Japanese had had any serious intention of bombing, they would have sailed right on over the P–40s; for they knew already that our squadrons could not offer effective night interception. But instead they had turned back at the first indication that their presence off the coast was known.

The planes were regassed and the stand-by crews took over. The rest of the Squadron returned to the barracks which men and officers shared alike; and the report of the completed mission was sent on its way to Headquarters at Nielson Field. They did not have long to sleep. At about 6:30 one of the men on the first breakfast shift snapped on the mess-hall radio to pick up Don Bell's news broadcast. There seemed to be a great deal of radio interference that morning. But after a moment Bell's voice came through. He was talking about Pearl Harbor.

That was their first news of the war.

11. *Nichols Field: 8:30 A.M.*

At 2:30 A.M., the 21st and 17th Squadrons at Nichols Field were ordered to stations.[1] It was the sixth successive morning this had happened, but there was the same feeling of tenseness in the emergency operations tent as the men assembled in the dim glow of the blacked-out gas lantern. The night was hushed. The leaves on the trees round the Air Depot barely stirred in the breath of the new south wind. Beyond the open tent fly the men could see their planes on the line ghostly in the starlight.[2]

There was little talk among the 21st's pilots. They were an even younger bunch than the 34th Squadron; except for their commanding officer, Ed Dyess, all of them were second lieutenants and most were but a few months out of Flying School.[3] Colonel George's talk of two days before was fresh in their minds, and like the 3rd Squadron they were sure that this was it.

But after about ten minutes' waiting, they were told that the immediate emergency was over and those who had been routed out of sleep by the alert officer * now returned to their quarters. It began to seem as if this had been just another night of Japanese reconnaissance maneuvers.

About 4:30 the telephone in the tent rang and Dyess, answering, received the first fragmentary news of the attack on Pearl Harbor.† There had been an even earlier flash, caught about 3:30 by the commercial radio station at Clark Field, but as no verification had come through, no action was then taken beyond notifying the base commander.[5] The Navy, however, had had the news since 3:00 A.M.,[6] and most of their installations were alerted by 3:30.‡ A radio operator had picked up a message in the clear, in Morse. It was twice repeated, and he recognized the sending technique of the operator at Pearl Harbor.[7] This message was sent to Admiral Hart and to General MacArthur's Headquarters. Apparently it reached General MacArthur at about 4:00 and within a few minutes Air Headquarters also had been notified.[8] Official confirmation did not come through, at least to the 24th Pursuit Group, till about 4:45.[9] At 5:30 A.M. General Headquarters issued an official statement that Pearl Harbor had been heavily attacked by Japanese submarines and planes and that a state of war existed between the United States and the Empire of Japan.§

By this time the pilots at Nichols Field who had returned to their quarters after the first alert were all back at stations. The pilots of the 21st Squadron were ordered into their planes and told to start their engines. Shortly afterwards, however, Lieutenant Dyess told them to cut their

---

* 2nd Lt. Lloyd A. Coleman.

† Dyess does not give the time, but when Grashio returned from his quarters at 5 A.M., the news had come through.[4]

‡ Patwing Ten's PBYs in Davao Gulf loaded bombs at 3:15. Capt. Wagner's report, quoted in KARIG & KELLEY.

§ It is interesting to note that at 4:35 General Wainwright was informed over the phone by MacArthur's Assistant Chief of Staff for Operations that "Admiral Hart had just received a radio from Admiral Kimmel" of the attack on Pearl Harbor.[10]

engines. They climbed out of the planes but stayed with them, sitting on the ground in the shade of the wing. As they talked back and forth, they must have found the news confusing, for the idea had been thoroughly drilled into them that Japan was bound to strike first at the Philippines. Yet here the Japs were, attacking Pearl Harbor, 5000 miles to the east, and leaving them alone. It was hard to understand.

But, though no word came through to them, Japanese planes were at that moment bombing the Philippine radio station at Aparri. And just at dawn a force of Japanese dive bombers, heading in from the Pacific, caught two of the Navy's PBYs sitting on the water of Davao Gulf and sank them out of hand. Only by adroit maneuvering did the tender *William B. Preston* succeed in dodging the bombs and a little later evade four Japanese destroyers entering the gulf in obvious search of her.[11]

The day was clear and the south wind blew gently in a sun-filled sky. To the pilots of the 17th and 21st Squadrons restlessly waiting by their planes or at the telephones in the operations tents, it was incongruous. They were at war, but that was all they knew about it. It looked as if they were expected just to sit it out.

But at about 8:00, while one shift of the flight crews were eating breakfast, the 17th Squadron received orders to cover Clark Field.* A heavy fleet of Japanese bombers was reported north of Luzon heading down Lingayen Gulf towards the central plain.

The 17th took off and drilled straight north up the shore of Manila Bay. They took up their patrol line near Tarlac, east and west across the central plain. Still farther north on a line crossing Rosales the 20th Squadron was flying another patrol.[13] At Clark Field itself the B-17s were taking the air as a precautionary move in case the Japanese bombers broke through the two fighter patrol lines.†

---

* The 24th Pursuit Group Narrative puts the time at 9:30; but I have here accepted what seems the consensus of the pilots involved, all of whom put the time earlier, even though varying among themselves. Thus while Sheppard says "a little after 8:00," Brownwell thinks it was between 7:30 and 8:00, and Blanton says "approximately 7:00." At any rate the 17th Squadron pilots had just finished breakfast. Obert says it was shortly after sunup that they took off, but he later records that they flew two and a half hours' patrol, landed at Clark Field and regassed and ate lunch there, and had their last plane off the ground at 12:15, which indicates that they must have left Nichols about 8:00.[12]

† Here again there is divergence over the time, but again the consensus puts the alert for the 19th Group between 8:00 and 8:30, with only one bomber pilot supporting the 24th Group Narrative's time of 9:30.

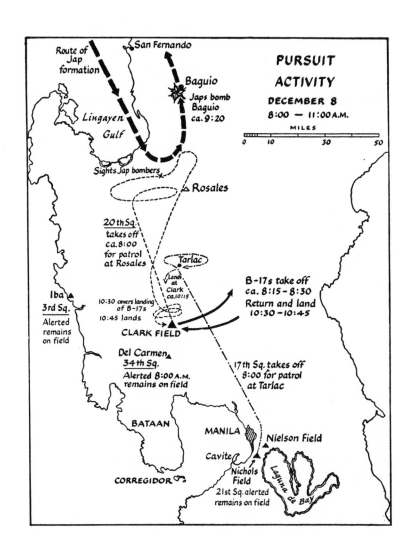

Route of Jap formation

San Fernando

Baguio

Japs bomb Baguio ca. 9:20

Lingayen Gulf

PURSUIT
ACTIVITY
DECEMBER 8
8:00 — 11:00 A.M.

MILES

0   10   30   50

Sights Jap bombers

△ Rosales

20th Sq.
takes off
ca. 8:00
for patrol
at Rosales

Tarlac

Lands
at
Clark
ca. 10:15

B-17s take off
ca. 8:15 - 8:30
Return and land
10:30 - 10:45

Iba ▲
3rd Sq.
Alerted
remains
on field

10:30 covers landing
of B-17s
10:45 lands

CLARK FIELD

Del Carmen ▲
34th Sq.
Alerted 8:00 A.M.
remains on field

17th Sq. takes off
8:00 for patrol
at Tarlac

BATAAN

MANILA

Nielson Field

Cavite

Nichols
Field

21st Sq. alerted
remains on field

CORREGIDOR

Laguna de Bay

The members of the 21st Squadron watched the 17th's planes take off, but there were no orders for them. They were tense with frustration, and as time passed the tension mounted. Olives and sandwiches were brought out to the operations tent and a tub full of Coca-Cola. They drank the Cokes, but they were too excited to do much eating. They went back to their planes to wait.

They weren't the only squadron wondering what it was all about. At Iba, the commanding officer of the 3rd had called Air Headquarters for instructions as soon as the commercial radio broadcast had come through. He was told to stand by. The 18 ranking pilots were assigned to the operational planes and went out on the line and climbed into the cockpits. They sat there all morning. Their breakfasts were brought to them, sandwiches and coffee. No instructions came through from Headquarters. They had no idea of what might be happening in the rest of Luzon. There was nothing for them to do but sit in their planes with the mountains at their backs and the sea in front of them, bright in the windy sunlight; and Herb Ellis yelled to Thorne that he ought to think up something historic to tell his command on such an occasion, like "Damn the torpedoes and take to the hills!"

The 34th Squadron at Del Carmen did not learn that there was a war on till 8:00 o'clock. Then Headquarters got through to them on the radio, which was their sole means of communication, ordering the Squadron on immediate alert, with pilots in their planes.[14]

At about 8:30, therefore, the interceptor situation showed the 20th and the 17th Squadrons flying two defensive patrols east and west across the plain at Rosales and Tarlac, while the 3rd was at Iba, the 34th at Del Carmen, and the 21st at Nichols with all operational planes manned and waiting further instructions.

At Clark Field, the 19th Group's B-17s were still getting into the air. Their orders were to stand by on control tower frequency, which meant that they could not get very far from the field.

12. *Clark and Nielson Fields: 4:00 A.M. to 12:30 P.M.*

SOME TIME AFTER 4:00 O'CLOCK that morning, while it was still dark, the telephone rang in Eubank's quarters and Major Kennard, one of the four men who shared them with him, answered it.* He was told that it was a special message for Colonel Eubank—Manila calling. Eubank came over and listened for a minute, spoke briefly himself, and then put the telephone down and said, "Well, boys, here it is. It's what we've been waiting for."

The message was from General Brereton, announcing the attack on Pearl Harbor. Eubank immediately called in his staff and gave them the news. Brereton's instructions were to be ready for a mission. There was no need to designate the target. Everyone knew it was Formosa. However, when Brereton prescribed the bomb load, Eubank suggested that it would be better to have the bombs stand by. Then if there were a change of loads at the last minute for a special target, they would not have to be taken off. And in case of a sudden attack on the field, it would be better not to have the planes standing loaded. The planes could be bombed up with no loss of time while the crews were being briefed. Brereton agreed and the bombs were ordered to stand by.

The guards on the planes were warned at once to be on the alert against sabotage; but the news of war was slow in filtering through to most of the lower echelons. About 5:30 Operations ordered all commanding officers to report to Headquarters. Day was just breaking as they came across the field. They were instructed to get their men together and tell them that hostilities had started and that Hickam Field had been attacked. Three pilots who had been scheduled to go out on patrol that morning reported to Operations a few minutes later in complete ignorance of the fact that there was a war on. Two of the patrols were canceled in order

* Maj. William J. Kennard, Senior Air Force Surgeon. The others were Col. Lester Maitland, CO of Clark Field; Maj. Lee Johnson, Adjutant; and Maj. David R. Gibbs, CO of the 30th Squadron.

to reserve as many planes as possible for any strike against the enemy. The third, Lieutenant Hewitt T. Wheless, was sent up alone.

A few pilots did not hear the news until they turned on their radios about 6:30 to pick up Don Bell's news broadcast. But within a few minutes after that, practically everyone at Clark Field knew of the attack on Pearl Harbor. The combat crews had collected at Headquarters for briefing, the bombs were ready near the planes. The Group only needed orders to load and take off.

The orders would have to come from Manila.

Shortly after Eubank had talked with his staff officers, a second call came through from General Brereton summoning Eubank and his Operations Officer, Major Birrell Walsh, to Air Headquarters at Nielson Field. It was about daylight when they took off in a B-18, leaving Major Gibbs in command of the Group.

At best Nielson Field is a bare place, lying clear of the city and well out in the open plain. There is no natural cover anywhere around it and on that morning, under an almost cloudless sky, its buildings must have seemed particularly exposed. The black and yellow squares of peacetime still marked the hangar roof.[1] Gangs of men were banking the walls of the new operations building that now housed Air Headquarters with sandbags; and trucks, hauling these from the half-finished revetments round the perimeter of the field,[2] still further emphasized the importance of the building by the network of tracks they left pointing to it.

The FEAF staff began gathering at 6:00 and when Eubank and Walsh arrived they were all there except for Brereton, who had gone into Manila to confer with MacArthur. He was still at USAFFE, but the rest met in his office—Colonel Brady, the Chief of Staff; Colonel Campbell, Air Warning; Lieutenant Colonel Caldwell, FEAF Operations; General Clagett and Colonel George; Captain Sprague, Operations Officer, 5th Interceptor Command; Major Lamb, Signal Officer; Captain Eads . . . with others, like Captain Ind, in and out.[3] There was a good deal of discussion and some argument, but it was the unanimous opinion of those present that the B-17s should be sent at once against Formosa. The bomber crews were ready; they had trained specifically for the mission; Takao Harbor had been designated as their target since December 6;[4] all they needed was the word to go.

Ind went to his office for the objective folders on Formosa and, returning, handed them over to Major Walsh.[5] Though considerable effort had been spent on these folders, the information they contained was pretty rudimentary. In Eubank's opinion it was definitely poor. This was not the fault of A-2. There had been neither time nor the means to secure data necessary in preparing calibrated bomb targets and approach routes; and, naturally, there were no air photographs.

It was a little before 8:00 when General Brereton returned to Air Headquarters. As he entered his office he asked what decision the staff had reached, but on being told said, "No. We can't attack till we're fired on," and explained that he had been directed to prepare the B-17s for action but was not to undertake offensive action till ordered.[6]

There is no question that this statement came as a shock to most of the men in the room. All were puzzled and incredulous. They could not understand why the attack on Pearl Harbor, which was certainly an overt act of war, did not automatically release them and United States forces everywhere from a purely defensive attitude. Moreover, not to strike now meant throwing away the best chance they were likely to have of hitting the enemy on his own ground.

The staff therefore found themselves back where they had been two hours before. The whole discussion on what to do with the B-17s was reopened and after a good deal of arguing back and forth it was decided that all they could do under the circumstances was to complete plans for the operation against Takao Harbor and in the meantime to send up two or three planes on photo-reconnaissance. Brereton then gave Eubank his orders, specifying that the first objective of the bombing attack would be Jap naval ships and transports and that three planes would undertake the photo mission, with emphasis on Japanese airfields.[7]

This discussion consumed the best part of an hour. Supposedly during it a call had been put in to USAFFE, but word had come from General Sutherland that the B-17s were not to carry bombs at this time.[8] Now, as Eubank went to the telephone to call Clark Field and set up the photo mission, Colonel George pointed out the danger in leaving the B-17s parked on the field. The path of the Japanese bombers that had been reported heading in from Lingayen Gulf was already being plotted in the Air Warning room. Ind's account quotes Eubank as replying that the B-17s couldn't be taken off for every alarm, they had to be serviced, and the crews had to eat.[9] Whether this was an accurate quotation or not, tension was plainly mounting as the period of inaction lengthened. But in any case, at Clark Field Major Gibbs, in response to a warning from the base commander, had ordered the B-17s into the air.*

Back at Nielson Field, Air Warning's staff and facilities were now being taxed to the limit of their capacity as warnings and messages began pouring in—enemy battleships off the north coast; Jap flying boats over the northern Islands; and then, just after 9:20, two reports close together that Baguio and Tuguegarao had been bombed.† On sighting the patrolling 20th Squadron, the Japanese had turned about, with the 20th in pursuit; but the Japs were over 22,000 feet, and with the 20th Squadron at 17,000 at the time they made visual contact, only two of the P-40s were able to draw up to the bombers in time to trade shots and get a few bullet holes for their pains. But the encounter settled all doubts, and the Japs by bombing Baguio had provided an overt act for the Philippines.

Brereton immediately put in a call to MacArthur's Headquarters and spoke personally to Sutherland, informing him of the two attacks and again requesting authority to undertake offensive action.[11] He then warned Sutherland, in Eubank's recollection of his exact words, that "if Clark Field is attacked, we won't be able to operate on it," and turning to Colonel Brady, who was listening in on another line, Brereton instructed him to make a note of the conversation. The request to take offensive action was, however, apparently still refused.[12]

Almost immediately after this, Eubank and Walsh, who had been at

* It has been stated that the planes were assigned patrol areas (for instance see BRERETON, 39-40); but if this was the case, it would appear that more than one pilot misapprehended his instructions and that from 8:30 to 10:30 a good many B-17s were milling about over Mount Arayat. Kreps, the 30th's officer of the day, says that they were sent up and ordered to stand by on control tower frequency, "which meant that we could not go more than a few miles from the field."

† Ind states that a report of Cabanatuan's being attacked also came in, with details of the destruction of the three B-10s of the PAAC stationed there.[10] But Lt. Col. (then Lt.) Joseph R. McMicking, who was on the airfield there that morning, does not mention an attack.

Air Headquarters for over an hour and a half, left for Clark Field with instructions to prepare for both the reconnaissance and the attack missions on Formosa. Whether authorization for the photo mission had come through from General Headquarters before their departure is a matter of some doubt. Both Brereton and the daily *Summary of Activities of the Headquarters, Far East Air Force* (hereafter referred to as *FEAF Diary*), the validity of whose December entries is, however, open to some question, state that a call from General Sutherland authorizing the reconnaissance came through just before Eubank's departure.[13] But as Eubank recalls, he did not receive orders to dispatch this mission till after his arrival at Clark Field—an insignificant point in the light of the next two hours, but indicative of the confusion that existed in all quarters that morning.

It was after 10:30 when Eubank and Walsh got back to Clark Field. By then Gibbs had recalled the B-17s, and the big planes were coming back in. There were a few broken clouds building up south of the field and a slight haze already touched the upper slopes of Mount Arayat; but to the north and northwest the sky was a clear blue with visibility unlimited. As the last B-17 rolled over the grass to its revetment, the P-40s of the 20th Squadron, which had been flying cover for the landing bombers, buzzed the field and came in to land, joining the 17th Squadron, which had landed earlier, so that by 11:00 both fighter squadrons were on the ground.[14] They had been flying patrol for nearly two and a half hours and needed to refuel. While the planes were being serviced, the men went after food; but as soon as they had eaten, they returned to their planes and went on the alert. The 17th Squadron, which had regassed first, was ready to go shortly after 11:00.

At that time, therefore, all the pursuit were on the ground and, except for the 17th, in their accustomed stations; and all were ready for action except the 20th, which was in process of refueling. All but two of the B-17s based at Clark were on the ground. These two ships were Lieutenant Wheless's, flying reconnaissance up somewhere near Formosa in heavy weather, and Lieutenant Carpenter's. This last plane, which had been consistently plagued by generator trouble, had not been able to take off with the others at the first alert; but at 10:30, just as the others had begun to return, it was ready to go. Carpenter was therefore designated for reconnaissance and sent off alone up the eastern sector of Luzon. The crew were in a good mood at finally getting into the air, and they loafed along up their beat, laughing at the reports spouting out of the radio about how Manila had been bombed and towns damaged all over Luzon. A little after noon, they received a message to return to base. They were pretty far north when they turned around and wouldn't be able to get back till about 12:30.

At the same time and about equally distant from Clark Field, but approaching it from the south, was a third B-17 coming up from Mindanao to have a leak in one of its wing tanks repaired. This ship, piloted by Lieutenant Earl R. Tash, had taken off shortly after 8:30 that morning. Word of the attack on Pearl Harbor had reached Del Monte by military radio about 6:30.[15] Orders were received from both Brereton and Eubank to send out reconnaissance, and the mission was performed by two planes flying round Mindanao in opposite directions,[16] though since they had no information on the positions of any U. S. Navy ships, the reconnaissance was not likely to prove of much value. These were the only instructions received at Del Monte during the day of December 8.* But though they were left almost completely in the dark as to what was happening, Major O'Donnell, who as Senior Air Officer commanded both squadrons, decided that Lieutenant Tash should take his plane up to Clark Field for immediate repairs. O'Donnell was impressed with the necessity of having every possible plane ready for combat.

A low overcast covered the field; but once through it the B-17 leveled off at 6500 feet in bright sunlight, with the south wind on its tail. A course was set for Laguna de Bay, the three-toed lake that lies south of Manila, and as soon as the pilots picked it up they began letting down to 2000 feet. They were proceeding cautiously for on the way up Del Monte had called in to quote a Don Bell news broadcast of Clark Field's being bombed at 9:00. It was then about 12:00 o'clock.

This was, of course, another of the countless rumors that cluttered the air over Luzon. But about 11:30 a message from Iba had reported a large

---

* Brereton, however, records in his Diaries that orders were issued to the two B-17 squadrons to move north to take offensive action at daybreak of December 9, and that he notified Sutherland of this order at 11:56 A.M., December 8.[17]

formation of planes heading in across the China Sea, presumably for Manila. The 17th Pursuit Squadron was immediately ordered into the air by Major Grover to patrol over Bataan and the entrance to Manila Bay and intercept whatever the Japanese tried to send through.[18] At the same time, the 3rd Squadron was ordered to intercept the hostile formation as it came in from the China Sea, and the 34th, still on the ground at Del Carmen, was told to fly cover over Clark Field;[19] but, as will be seen, the orders finally received by the 3rd were to fly standing patrol over Iba, and the 34th received no message at all. In the meantime, the 21st Squadron at Nichols Field finally got orders when the call of "Tally-ho, Clark Field!" came in over the Squadron radio.* Two flights instantly took off behind Dyess and headed straight for Clark Field, and as they gained altitude Dyess radioed Air Headquarters that they were on their way. The twelve planes had just reached the northern borders of the city when they were called back and told to fly standing patrol between Corregidor and Cavite. The third flight of the 21st Squadron had had trouble with their brand-new P-40s and did not get off the ground for a good five minutes after the others had left. They made the prescribed circle down over Laguna de Bay to check their guns over water but, in doing so, lost contact with the first two flights and set out for Clark Field by themselves, having presumably swung out of radio range when the orders to fly standing patrol had come through.†

This left the 20th Squadron to cover Clark Field. It was still refueling at 12:00; but at about 12:15 its planes were ready.[21] The 19th Group was then holding a staff meeting, for just before noon orders had finally come through from Air Headquarters to dispatch both squadrons on an attack mission against known airdromes in Formosa. The attack was to be delivered with 100- and 300-pound bombs at the last possible daylight hour.[22] Apparently orders for the photographic mission were yet in force, for the crews of at least two of the three scheduled planes were still preparing for it;‡ yet it seems curious that they had not taken off on their mission before noon. The only explanation given is that when the planes were scheduled it was found that there were not enough cameras to go round, and a B-18 had to be sent to Nichols Field for them. This plane, according to Captain William E. McDonald, returned to Clark Field shortly before 12:30.

There had been reports fifteen minutes before noon of an unidentified flight of planes out over Lingayen Gulf; but there had been no further word on it. Around the field, the B-17s were in process of bombing up. Some of the air crews were at mess, and others were just about to go after their food. The engines of the first flight of P-40s were being turned over.

Back at Nielson, in Air Headquarters, George had been "begging and begging" to have the Fortresses put in the air; but it would still be two or three hours before they took off, and meanwhile, through indecision, delays in transmitting orders, and broken-down and sabotaged communications, the sole fighter cover for Clark Field in the next twenty minutes amounted to as many of the 20th Squadron's planes as might get off the ground in that time; the six brand-new P-40s of the 21st Pursuit Squadron coming up from Nichols Field, of which, due to their condition, only three would be able to fly the distance; and a single flight of the 3rd Squadron which, as will be seen, quite fortuitously found themselves over Clark Field for a few short moments before the enemy appeared.

If this had been the goal of Japanese maneuvering, it could hardly have worked out more aptly for them; and their own pilots, sighting the glitter of the B-17s parked on the green field below, must have found it hard to accept the evidence of their own eyes.

The handling of our bomber force during those early morning hours has become the subject of a controversy which the passage of years has done little to dispel, for no record of the day's events exists that is wholly satisfactory to the historian. The key undoubtedly lies in Brereton's first conference with Sutherland, and of this conference there are two fundamentally opposed accounts. The first is Brereton's, on record, in his Diaries, published in the fall of 1946:

I reported to General MacArthur's Hqs. at Fort Santiago, Manila, at about 5 A.M. He was in conference with (I believe) Admiral Hart. After General

Sutherland had given me all available information I requested permission to carry out offensive action immediately after daylight. I told Sutherland I wished to mount all available B–17s at Clark Field for missions previously assigned and to prepare the B–17s at Del Monte for movement, refueling and bomb loading at Clark Field for operations against the enemy on Formosa. General Sutherland agreed with my plans and said to go ahead with preparations; in the meantime he would obtain General MacArthur's authority for the daylight attacks.

When I left General MacArthur's Hqs. I was under orders to prepare our heavy bombers for action but not to undertake any offensive action until ordered. . . .[23]

These orders, according to Brereton, did not come through till 11:00 A.M.,[24] though the *FEAF Diary* implies that permission was received in a telephone call from General MacArthur at 10:14, the pertinent entries being as follows:

10:14 General Brereton received a telephone call from General MacArthur. General Brereton stated that since the attack was not made on Clark Field that bombers will be held in readiness until receipt of report from reconnaissance missions. Lacking report of reconnaissance, Taiwan would be attacked in late afternoon. The decision for offensive action was left to General Brereton. All bombers were ordered to arm and be on alert for immediate orders.

10:20 Report of planes coming south proved erroneous. Planes reported coming south from Cagayan Valley turned around and are now proceeding north. The staff was called in and informed of General Brereton's telephone conversation with General MacArthur. General Brereton directed that a plan of employment of our Air Force against known airdromes in Southern Formosa be prepared.

10:45 Employment of Air Force directed by General Brereton as follows: Two (2) heavy bombardment squadrons to attack known airdromes in Southern Formosa at the latest daylight hour today that visibility will permit. Forces to be 2 squadrons of B–17s. Two (2) squadrons of pursuit to be on alert to cover operations of bombardment. Pursuit to be used to fullest extent to insure safety of bombardment. Two (2) squadrons of bombardment to San Mencelino [*sic*: San Marcelino was the name of the field] at dusk. To Clark Field after dark prepared for operations at daybreak.

This circumstantial, and curiously redundant, account appears, except in the matter of timing, to substantiate General Brereton's position. Opposing it is General Sutherland's account of the same conference with Brereton as given to me in Manila on June 4, 1945. As I have no knowledge of shorthand, my notes of the interview are mainly in the third person:

Gen. Sutherland began by saying that all the B–17s had been ordered to Del Monte some days before. On a check it was found that only half had been sent. GHQ wanted the planes in Del Monte because they would there have been safe from initial Jap attacks—they could themselves have staged out of Clark Field to bomb Formosa. This direct order had *not been obeyed*. And it must be remembered that GHQ gave out general orders and that AFHq were supposed to execute them. As Sutherland recalls there was some plan to bomb Formosa but Brereton said that he had to have photos first. That there was no sense in going up there to bomb without knowing what they were going after. There were some 25 fields on Formosa. On December 9th and 10th, photo missions were dispatched—Carpenter going on the first and returning with generator trouble; Connally going on the second but being turned back by fighters.* *Holding the bombers at Clark Field that first day was entirely due to Brereton.* [Italics mine—W. D. E.]

I then asked if there had been a definite order from GHQ to keep the planes off the ground all of December 8.

Gen. Sutherland does not recall such an order for the 8th. He is not sure such an order was issued. He does know that such an order went out of GHQ for the 9th, and it was emphatically given.

General Sutherland's statements were confirmed in September 1946 by General MacArthur, who stated that he knew nothing of a recommendation to bomb Formosa having been made:

My first knowledge of it is contained in yesterday's press release; that it must have been of the most nebulous and superficial character as no official record exists of it in headquarters; that such a proposal if intended seriously should certainly have been made to me in person by him [Brereton]; that he never had spoken of the matter to me either before or after the Clark Field attack; that an attack on Formosa with its heavy air concentrations by his small bomber force without fighter support which because of the great distance involved was impossible and would have had no chance of success.—TOKYO, Sept. 27 (UP).

There is no reason to suppose that MacArthur would necessarily have opposed an attack on Formosa in spite of the then prevalent belief among

---

* A correct recollection of small details, except for the fact that Connally turned back with engine trouble. A Jap fighter attack on Clark Field, however, kept him circling in the clouds for some time after his return.

air officers that he knew little about the proper employment of air power. It is possible also that his September statement may have been colored by his later experience in the use and development of air power while working with General Kenney; yet it is in the record that MacArthur's mind was open to the use of what air power he had for offensive operations. As early as November 7, in a message to Admiral Hart, he had defined his position as commander of USAFFE, under the strategic plan of Rainbow No. 5 in the following terms:

4. The mission of the Army is:
(a) Defend the Philippine Coastal Frontier in co-operation with the Navy.
(b) Conduct air raids against enemy forces and installations within tactical operating radius of available bases.
(c) Support the Navy in raiding enemy sea communications and destroying Axis forces.
(d) Co-operate with Associated Powers in accordance with approved policies and agreements.[25]

However, in the hectic early hours of December 8, it may have taken some time to gain contact with Washington, and it may well have been that MacArthur did not feel free to authorize offensive action till he had received official confirmation that the country was officially at war or till he himself had been attacked; and Sutherland's statement lends color to this. In discussing the attempted interception of Jap planes over the Philippines before the war, Sutherland said:

The last War Department directive received at GHQ before the war was to the effect that hostilities might start at any time. We here in the Philippines could not do anything to provoke hostilities but we could take any defensive action. This directive came out on December 1 or 2—perhaps five days before the outbreak of war. During those five days, Gen. George [George then still held colonel's rank] made reports on the radar station's (at Iba) having reported early Japanese flights. George wanted to intercept and came to ask permission. We told him he could effect it, but that he must act defensively; but if the Japs came in close enough he could go to it. . . . The boys had to operate purely defensively. There was no question of that; and, with the War Department directives, no choice on the part of GHQ.

One must surmise, therefore, that there was uncertainty in both headquarters until shortly after 10:00 (if we accept the record of the *FEAF Diary*) or till nearly 11:00 (if Brereton is accurate). But there seem to have been additional uncertainties in Air Headquarters. For one thing, the matter of making a prior reconnaissance undoubtedly weighed very much on Brereton's mind. As long before as December 1 he had asked permission to conduct high-altitude photo missions over Southern Formosa—a request that General MacArthur had refused, though agreeing a day or so later to extend the limits of reconnaissance from two thirds of the distance between Northern Luzon and Formosa to the International Boundary itself.[26] The need for reconnaissance was accentuated by a shortage of maps of Formosa—even after the outbreak of war, tactical personnel who had lost their planes were put to work at Clark Field to make copies of such maps as were available. In the absence of any record, the terms in which Brereton presented his recommendation for the attack on Takao Harbor must remain a matter of conjecture.

There was, however, one ramifying element underlying the conference between Brereton and Sutherland. Reading between the lines it becomes evident that contacts between Air Force and General Headquarters had at some points become difficult. Two evidences of this exist. First is the controversial matter of sending the B-17s down to Del Monte. General Brereton's Headquarters have consistently maintained that the proposal originated with them and that General Sutherland was reluctant in giving permission and only agreed, in the end, with the understanding that the Fortresses would be brought back to Cebu and Luzon as soon as dispersal facilities for them were ready, on the ground that no Infantry protection could be provided for bases on Mindanao.

Sutherland's categorical statement that MacArthur's Headquarters ordered all the Fortresses to be sent south is therefore made to seem inconsistent; but actually there is no reason why it should not be true, and General Headquarters in the last days before hostilities may well have ordered all the planes to Mindanao. However, since all such orders were transmitted orally, for the most part by telephone, this point also must remain conjectural. But in this particular instance, and again reading between the lines, one is aware of a reluctance on the part of Air Headquarters about basing the B-17s at Del Monte. The reason given for sending only half is not too convincing; for the expected arrival of four 7th Group squadrons would merely mean recalling enough of the 19th Group planes to make room for them when and as they arrived; and the 19th's ocean flight had already demonstrated that the arrival of the new group must be stretched over several days at least. A more convincing reason would have been the interruption to group training such dispersal would cause. Actually, the air crews of the 16 planes that were sent down expected only a three- or four-day stay, and Brereton himself points out that the planes were to be temporarily recalled to Clark Field for extensive field exercises,[27] this plan being canceled only in the late evening of December 7. Air personnel in FEAF and the Bomber Command had not yet conditioned their minds to the feasibility, or even the possibility, of operations apart from the kind of air base facilities to which their training accustomed them.

The second evidence, as it seems to me, of difficult relations between the two staffs is the fact that Colonel George went directly to General MacArthur's Headquarters to ask permission for the attempted interception of Japanese airplanes over Luzon before the outbreak of war. Whether George did this because he could gain no credence in Air Headquarters for his belief that the night-flying planes were Japanese, I do not know; nor do I know whether he went with General Brereton's approval, perhaps because it was felt that his word would carry more weight with General MacArthur. In any case it was an unusual procedure, so unusual that some air officers refuse to believe that he did go. But that he did is indisputable.

In the absence of contemporary records, the reader must draw his own conclusions about the actions and omissions of December 8. Shortly after his departure from the Philippines on Christmas Eve, General Brereton is known to have made a report to General Arnold. This report has never been made available even to the official Air Force Historian. General Arnold makes no mention of it in his GLOBAL MISSION: he only says that he has never been able to get "the real story of what happened in the Philippines." [28] He neither considered General Brereton's Diaries a complete and accurate account, nor did he feel that General Sutherland's statement furnished a complete explanation. Since General Brereton has refused to discuss any phase of his command in either the Philippines or Java, one must accept his Diaries, despite minor inaccuracies that suggest later editing, as the major source from the Air Corps point of view.

The official historian is inclined to lend more weight to the account given in the *FEAF Diary* and accepts it as the most nearly accurate source covering events on the morning of December 8. He, however, has some reservations which he has expressed in a footnote recounting the transmission of these summaries to the historical office and describing their appearance as follows:

The FEAF summaries, which are typed out on loose sheets of two different sizes and of varying weight and texture, all of them carbon copies except for the inserted notes of a staff conference held on 19 December, are bound together by an acco fastener within an ordinary manila cover. On the cover has been written in ink, possibly by historical personnel in the theater [India], "Early History 10th AAF"; but that has been struck out and in its place appears "General Brereton's Headquarters diary 8 Dec 41—24 Feb 42," and below that in pencil is written "Activity Report of FEAF." Other markings were apparently made by filing personnel of the historical office. The historian is given some pause by the fact that the daily summaries from 8 December through 13 December give the year as 1942 with corrections in ink for 8, 9, and 10 December. The year appears without change as 1941 for 14 December at which point the weight of the paper changes, but reverts thereafter to 1942 until the entries for 16 December. From that date forward the year is rendered corrctly in the original typing. Since one often writes by mistake the preceding year but rarely if ever puts down the new year ahead of time, the likelihood that entries for the earlier dates were compiled at some later time must be considered. Perhaps they represent a compilation taken from available records for assistance in the preparation of such a report as is understood to have been made by General Brereton in late January or early February . . . ; perhaps there is some other explanation. Whatever the case, the fullness and exactness of detail given, together with the fact that at so many points independent corroboration can be had, lead to the conclusion that the document represents a valuable record compiled closer to the events described than any other known source of comparable scope.[29]

I cannot bring myself to accept the *FEAF Diary* as a wholly reliable source for FEAF activities on the morning of December 8. In the timing of incidents I feel fairly sure that it has been re-edited—for instance pursuit activity conforms to that given in the 24th Pursuit Group history but does not conform as closely as does General Brereton's account to the experiences of the various personnel I interviewed. If the *FEAF Diary* was actually written in daily entries through the opening episodes of the war, it seems to me that the evidences of later editing (by whom, whether staff or historical personnel, is immaterial) seriously affect its value as a source for the opening days of the war.

In any case, the picture that emerges is one of confusion and indecision. The FEAF staff seem to me to have become so preoccupied with their planned attack on Takao Harbor that, when this was temporarily denied them, they were left at loose ends. A great deal has been made of the fact that the air crews were ready for this mission and that if they had been allowed to go the planes would not have been lost; yet when authorization for offensive action did come through, the raid on shipping in Takao Harbor was abandoned in favor of the one to be made at last daylight against enemy airfields. This decision was undoubtedly sound, especially if in the meantime the photo-reconnaissance bore fruit; for the Takao Harbor mission would at best have been one merely of opportunity. Yet the second mission would probably have kept the bombers on the ground, and vulnerable, for two hours more, and there is little evidence that great concern was felt for their situation except in Ead's account of George's begging that they be put in the air.

The whole discussion is, after all, one of purely academic interest. Like the long controversy over why Lee and his Confederates lost at Gettysburg there is but one sound explanation; and in the Philippines the personnel of our armed forces almost without exception failed to assess accurately the weight, speed, and efficiency of the Japanese Air Force.

General O'Donnell (a major then and waiting impatiently for orders at Del Monte) is probably nearest the truth in his comment that the opening of the war in the Philippines was just a disorganized business and that no one was really at fault for the way the Air Force got shot up. It was not a balanced air force. Everyone knew that something was coming but no one knew just what. They were not geared for war.

13. *Iba: The Second Phase*

ABOUT 11:00 the telephone and telegraph at Iba both suddenly went dead. From then on the only means of communicating with the rest of Luzon was the radio, and the unusual amount of interference made that increasingly uncertain. No instructions had come through from Headquarters since Lieutenant Thorne's original request for orders about 7:00 o'clock, and the 3rd Squadron's 18 planes were still on the ground.

The shadows of the mountains had receded as the day drew on, and the airfield with its little cluster of buildings and palm trees now shimmered in the full heat of the sun. Talk had worn thin. The men sitting in their planes smoked cigars from the P–X and worried about their guns that hadn't been proof-fired and listened to fragmentary reports that Baguio and Aparri had been bombed. They didn't know whether to believe them. Mostly their eyes kept watching the empty sky above the empty sea.

About 11:30 the radar picked up a large formation of bombers at extreme range, nearly 100 miles out. Thorne immediately had the men start their engines; but instead of coming straight in, the Japanese started milling back and forth, apparently to kill time, far out over the ocean. The 3rd Squadron remained on the ground with their engines running and using up gas. But shortly after, orders came through from Group Headquarters to take off and climb to 15,000 feet and fly standing patrol over Iba.[1]

They were in three flights of six planes each under Lieutenant Thorne, 2nd Lieutenant Woolery, and Lieutenant Ellis, but they never got together as a squadron. The pressure under which they had had to take off may have been partly accountable, but mainly it was due to poor communications. The air was in horrible shape by then, with contradictory orders coming in from every direction and everyone shouting, and at times it was almost impossible to talk even between planes flying wing to wing. In the confusion "B" flight lost the others—Krieger says that Woolery's radio had gone out of commission—so they headed at top speed for the Manila area, hoping to pick up orders from Headquarters once they were near enough.

They circled over Nichols and Nielson for a few minutes, but nothing happened. They couldn't get anything definite over the radio, but suddenly the "Tallyho!" call came through and someone started shouting what sounded like "Bandits over Clark!" and they flew wide-open up to Clark Field.

When they got up, seeing that everything looked normal, they decided it had been a false alarm. By then their gas had begun to run low, for they had made wide-open flights from Iba to Manila and from Manila to Clark, so they headed back to Iba to gas up and try to get some further orders.

In crossing the mountains they went up to 18,000 feet, which was just about their ceiling, flying without oxygen as they were. The mountains under the midday sun had almost no shadows; they looked smaller and far below. Then as the flight came out over the coast and began to draw near their home field, they saw a freighter and a P-T boat a little offshore. The P-T boat was zigzagging like mad, and they could see from her smoke and the long white feather of wake on the blue sea that the freighter was traveling at full speed. It looked queer. But they could get no orders. They couldn't get anything at all. Their radios had apparently been jammed. So Woolery decided to go on in. He started his approach with four of the planes following him down and the fifth, which was Krieger's, staying up to cover their landing.

Krieger, circling, saw Woolery's plane touch wheels and start to roll. The others were on their approach with their wheels down. And then the field went off in a single blinding flash that carried from the northwest corner clear through the length of the air strip. It was a terrible thing to see. The bombs fell in train across the field.

Krieger never saw what happened to the other planes of "B" flight. He gave his own ship everything it could take and started back up. Then he saw the bombers, directly over the field, proceeding serenely on their course at something above 28,000 feet. He could never have come up with them even if he had had oxygen.*

He was going up so fast that he had to level off around 10,000 feet to let his engine cool. He looked down and saw what appeared to be a squadron of P-35s circling the field, and for an instant he thought they must be trying to land and wondered how they could help seeing that the field had been bombed. Then it occurred to him that they might be Japanese and he started down for a closer look. They were. They were

---

* This Japanese formation was variously reported at 54 and 72 planes. The reason for these recurrent figures in all reports of Jap bomber formations is that 54 was the largest "box" they flew, but sometimes an extra unit of 18 was added. Krieger himself thought that there were 72 planes, which was a very heavy force for such a small field.[2] Actually, Japanese sources indicate a force of 54 bombers and 50 fighters.

flying a beautiful Lufberry circle around the field and strafing everything in sight. They were beautiful planes, all white, with big red spots on their wings. When they came out of the smoke and the sun glanced on their backs, he could see them clearly. It was his first sight of the Zero.[3]

He started to call "All pursuit to Iba," but just then the Clark tower came in with "All pursuit to Clark" and looking in that direction he saw a great column of smoke leaning in the sky. It towered above the mountains. He knew that pretty soon all available planes would be going there, so he called "All 3rd Pursuit to Iba," and laid his plane over and went down after the Japanese planes. He could not get his sights on them. They were flying so low it was impossible to get under them. He had never had any briefing on the Zero; he knew nothing of its potentialities; but if he had, it would probably have made no difference, for by then he had lost his head entirely. The only way he could think of to get at them was to join their Lufberry circle, which he did, shooting at the plane ahead. It dropped away and suddenly he realized that there was tracer coming past him. Looking back, he found three Zeros on his tail.

Somehow he managed to pull away from them, and about then he realized that he was down to his last 25 gallons of gas. He called for instructions and like a clear miracle Lieutenant Thorne's voice came in telling him to try for Rosales.* He headed for it and made it safely, but his gas ran out as he was taxiing back up the strip.[4] Thorne was waiting there with about four other members of the Squadron.† Before long they

---

* Rosales was about 50 miles north of Clark Field.

† Flights "A" and "C" stayed on patrol at 15,000 feet for almost an hour, till they heard and answered the call from Clark. Presumably they arrived between the bomber and strafing attacks for they saw no planes. Then they heard a call from Iba (perhaps it was Krieger). Climbing as they went, they raced back to Iba only to see the Japanese formation passing on out of reach and their own landing strip destroyed. Low on gas and groggy from lack of oxygen, Thorne ordered the Squadron to Rosales. But in the confusion of orders and the jamming of their tactical frequency, some of the pilots broke formation. One was Lt. F. C. Roberts, who ended up with his tanks dry over the field fighting Zeros. He crash-landed in the sea just off the strip and waded ashore.

"C" flight under Lt. Herbert S. Ellis picked up the second call from Clark Field and, returning, got into combat with the Japs attacking there. Ellis himself had to jump from his burning plane and was strafed in his chute but saved when 2nd Lt. John L. McGown of the 21st Squadron came along and drove off the Japs. 2nd Lt. George O. Ellstrom also lost his ship in combat over Clark.

It has been commonly stated that the 3rd Squadron lost most of its planes on the ground at Iba. That is obviously not the case. Woolery's was the only plane in tactical commission actually destroyed on the ground. Woolery himself was blasted from it into

were joined by Lieutenant Neri and 2nd Lieutenant Woolery. Then a lone B–18, shot full of holes, flew in from Clark Field with a pilot who had never handled a B–18 before and a radio sergeant for co-pilot. These men told them a little about the attack there. They had to wait till gas and ammunition could be trucked up to them, and that night they were ordered down to Nichols Field, where they found other members of the Squadron who had been scattered like leaves over Luzon.

Iba was completely destroyed. For a place of its size the Japanese had poured in an extraordinary weight of bombs, and they had accomplished what must have been one of their prime objectives, the complete destruction of the radar unit.

At the time of the attack the radar crew had been plotting the incoming flight and trying to get their plots through to Headquarters. They were killed at their posts, as were the two officers and two enlisted men in the control tower, who were trying to warn "B" flight of the bomber formation over their heads. All the other buildings were razed, and even the little grove of palm trees. No one survived who was not in a foxhole when the bombs struck. The single air strip was so pitted with craters that it was difficult to drive a truck down it. No exact figures on the casualties exist, but they were very heavy.* The men were completely dazed when they finally crawled out of the wreckage and began picking up the wounded. They had no way of communicating with the rest of Luzon now, not even radio. There was nothing left at all, except a few trucks. There were no drugs for the wounded. The dispensary had been completely wiped out.

Though the 3rd's Flight Surgeon, Lieutenant Frank L. Richardson, was a youngster, he had enough sense and enterprise not to call for help and just sit until it came, but to start moving with what motive power he

a shell hole, picked himself up, climbed into a plane standing on the field which was not in tactical commission, took off, and made Rosales shortly after Krieger. The other four coming in to land were destroyed. Three of the four remaining pilots out of the original 18 brought their planes through the day's combat, though Lt. Neri came into Rosales with a cannon shell hole in his wing. There is, however, some doubt as to whether 2nd Lt. Vernon Ireland crashed on the slope of Mount Arayat on December 8 or 10. 2nd Lt. Richard L. Root was killed on December 10; but Lt. Raymond M. Gehrig proved to be entirely indestructible.[5]

* Krieger in his narrative says there were about 50 per cent casualties.

could get hold of. He commandeered all the surviving trucks for his wounded and set out down the coast road towards San Marcelino. He couldn't do much for the men except give them a little whiskey he had salvaged. But whenever he could pick up ambulances, he transferred his worst cases to them and sent them on to Manila. It was days before he himself got in with the last of the train of wounded.

The unwounded survivors had to walk. They were organized into a sort of safari by Lieutenant Roberts and started out across the Zambales Mountains for Clark Field. There was supposed to be a cart track that would bring them out at O'Donnell; but many were lost in the mountains and did not find their way out for weeks. They straggled in, half starved, many of them shoeless, and most still showing the effects of the bombing.[6]

14. *Attack on Clark Field: 12:40 P.M.*

OF THE SIX BRAND-NEW P-40s that started out for Clark Field after checking their guns over Laguna de Bay, two almost immediately had to turn back when their engines, which had not been slow-timed, started throwing oil. The oil plastered the wind screens and the pilots, barely able to see, had no choice but to return to base. The four remaining pilots continued on to Clark: Grashio flying with Williams on his wing, and Cole with McGown.* Everything seemed peaceful as they came over the field. There wasn't a sign of hostile aircraft, but away off in the west above the mountains they could see a flight of planes heading towards the China Sea, and presuming that they must be the rest of their own squadron, the four instinctively took out after them.

This left the air above Clark Field entirely undefended, for the 34th Squadron at Del Carmen had not received the orders to fly cover and was still standing at alert on the field.† So, until the 20th Squadron,

---

* All were 2nd lieutenants.

† Major Stewart W. Robb states that "the organization was scrambled during the morning to fly a search mission but encountered nothing and was ordered to return to its field and stand by."[1] I have found no other reference for this mission.

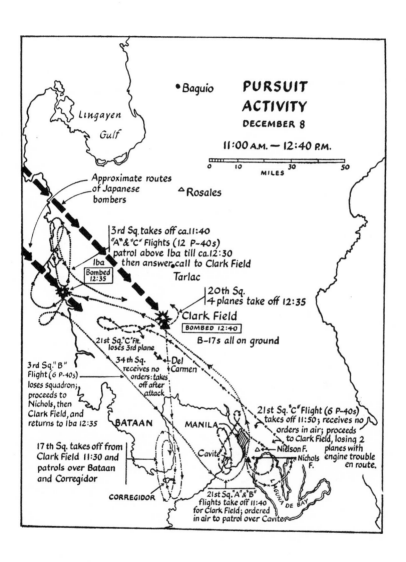

• Baguio

PURSUIT ACTIVITY
DECEMBER 8
11:00 A.M. — 12:40 P.M.

Lingayen
Gulf

0   10   30   50
MILES

Approximate routes
of Japanese
bombers

△ Rosales

3rd Sq. takes off ca.11:40
"A" & "C" Flights (12 P-40s)
patrol above Iba till ca.12:30
then answer call to Clark Field

Iba
Bombed
12:35

Tarlac

20th Sq.
4 planes take off 12:35

Clark Field
BOMBED 12:40
B-17s all on ground

21st Sq. "C" Flt.
loses 3rd plane

34th Sq.
receives no
orders: takes
off after
attack

Del
Carmen

3rd Sq. "B"
Flight (6 P-40s)
loses squadron;
proceeds to
Nichols, then
Clark Field, and
returns to Iba 12:35

BATAAN

MANILA

21st Sq. "C" Flight (6 P-40s)
takes off 11:50; receives no
orders in air; proceeds
to Clark Field, losing 2
planes with
engine trouble
en route.

17th Sq. takes off from
Clark Field 11:30 and
patrols over Bataan
and Corregidor

Cavite

Nielson F.

Nichols
F.

CORREGIDOR

21st Sq. "A" & "B"
flights take off 11:40
for Clark Field; ordered
in air to patrol over Cavite

LAGUNA DE BAY

which had just finished gassing up at 12:15, should get into the air, the fate of Clark Field depended entirely on the efficiency of the air warning system.

A test before the war had shown how uncertain this was likely to be. Native observers, but few of whom had been trained in plane identification, had to send their reports in over the lines of the Philippine telephone system to Air Headquarters at Nielson, where the reported flights were plotted [2] and the data relayed to Clark Field, from which in turn orders were issued to the various squadrons. In this cumbersome arrangement delays were frequent and inevitable. Direct communication between Clark, Nielson, and Nichols Fields was by a teletype circuit, which was supplemented by the telephone line and radio. Each of the three fields had an SCR 297 set which was used for both point-to-point and ground-to-air communication.[3] That morning there had been continual difficulty with the radio set, so when the wires went dead, Clark Field was virtually isolated.* No further reports, of course, had come in from Iba; and the hostile formation that had been reported over Lingayen Gulf at 11:45 had, apparently, vanished into thin air.

At 12:30 the staff meeting of the 19th Group, planning the raid on Formosa, was still in session. Near the end of the field the first flight of the 20th Squadron's P-40s were lined up to take off. The ordnance crews were busy with the B-17s and already had several of the big planes loaded. At 12:35, Lieutenant Fred T. Crimmins, Jr.'s ship was ready and he sent his crew off to get lunch. They had just time to make the third shift in the 30th Squadron mess. The radio was turned on there for the news, and to their astonishment, Don Bell was just coming in with "an unconfirmed report that they're bombing Clark Field." Crimmins himself walked across the field towards the hangars with one of the plane's waist guns, which needed a new buffer screw. Everything seemed routine. There was a B-17 in the hangar for a camouflage paint job, but at the moment no one was working on it, and Crimmins passed under its wing on his way to the shop at the rear. He had just handed the machine gun over to the sergeant there when the Base Fire Alarm started its grunt-

* Lt. W. E. Strathern, Operations Officer at Clark Field, to 2nd Lt. A. E. Krieger.[4] Japanese transmitting sets were found later both near Nichols Field and in the town of Angeles, about six miles from Clark Field.

ing, and both he and the sergeant ran back to the front of the hangar. A
P-40 was taking off and another was beginning its run across the field.
The insistent, hoarse bleating of the klaxon continued, and instinctively
both men looked downwind to the north.

High over the green points of the mountains they saw the planes. The
sky there was a clear and cloudless blue, and the bombers came on steadily out of the northwest in two perfect V of Vs, one behind the other,
their wings glistening in the sunlight. They were flying above 18,000 feet,
but the unfamiliar and unrhythmic droning of their engines was audible
through the uproar of the P-40s taking off. There were 54 of them,* 27 in
each V; and they held their formation with absolute precision, as though
they were on review.

There had been no warning of their immediate approach, and the first
wave was almost at the release line when they were sighted. Lieutenant
Strathern, the field's Operations Officer, sounded the alarm and ordered
the 20th Squadron off the ground; but there was time left for only four
of them to get into the air. The next five, which were in process of taking
off, and five others still on the line were caught in the bomb pattern and
were all destroyed.†

The bombs were dropped in train diagonally across the field. They began falling on the northwest corner, in the row of Officers' Quarters, and
proceeded through the parked P-40s, the Headquarters Building, and the
shop and hangar area. The bombs from the second wave followed almost
immediately. Like the formation that had attacked Iba, the Japanese
planes never deviated from their course but continued straight on into
the southeast until they disappeared in the haze and clouds.

Behind them they left the field blazing. Most of the buildings had
been hit, and many were afire. The men could do little to save them,
for there was no fire apparatus. Another casualty had been the communications center and as a result, after its initial call for pursuit, Clark Field

* Here again the figure is sometimes put at 72. However, the general impression was
of two exactly similar Vs, without any additional unit of 18, and this is confirmed by
Japanese sources which give the number of fighters that followed up the bombers as 34.

† No account is given of what was wrong with four of the 18 planes originally
in commission at the start of the day. Presumably they were in the revetments along with
the others.[5] Sheppard says that only three P-40s got into the air and names the pilots:
Lt. J. H. Moore, 2nd Lt. Randall D. Keator, and 2nd Lt. Edwin B. Gilmore.[6]

was unable to ask for help. With all wires cut, the base was entirely isolated.[7] It was difficult to see what had happened, for besides the pall of dust, mushrooming clouds of black oil smoke from a blazing oil dump behind the hangars came rolling across the field. The smoke grew so heavy that the sun was shut out; it was hard to see more than 50 or 60 feet.

As the crash of the bombing ceased and the uneven beat of the Japanese planes faded away, men began to lift themselves out of the slit trenches. The cries of wounded sounded through the smoke from all over the field. Almost all the casualties were people who had kept on running for cover after the bombs began to fall; most of those who dropped flat on the ground escaped injury. But many had been caught completely unaware. The Officers' Mess, which at the time was serving fifty or more, and the 20th Pursuit Squadron's mess tent, right beside the hangars, both received direct hits, as did the kitchens, in which many of the Filipino help were killed.*

In all the confusion, the job of handling the wounded was well done. Four emergency dressing stations had been set up around the field, and the men, instead of carting the wounded straight to the Field Infirmary, brought them to the first-aid stations where the surgeons were able to give emergency treatment, put tags on them, and carry out their evacuation in an orderly manner. The Field Infirmary had been wiped out but the men were treated on the lawn in front of it and more were handled at the 19th Group's Dispensary, and from there they were driven up to Fort Stotsenburg Hospital.†

The work had hardly begun, however, before the roar of airplane engines sounded over the field and Japanese pursuits broke through the smoke. The strafers made their runs from the open, east end of the field, coming in only a few feet above the ground and using their machine gun tracer to sight on the parked Fortresses and then letting go with

---

* An amusing incident at the start of the attack was provided by the operator of the mechanical ditch digger at work on the slit trenches behind the Officers' Quarters. When the first bomb went off, he leaped from the machine and pulled foot for the hills. Apparently he had no use for nor the least confidence in the ditches he had dug, for he wasn't seen at Clark Field again.

† The medical personnel had had a period of training before the war on evacuating wounded from the field.

their 20-mm cannon. Only a few B–17s were destroyed by the high-altitude bombing at 12:40; * and as Eubank made the round of his Group
immediately afterwards, he had felt pretty much encouraged by the
small amount of damage. But the strafers destroyed all but two or three
of the B–17s and damaged those.† They also attacked buildings, gun emplacements, and personnel at will. There was little to prevent them.

The only pursuit opposition at first was that offered by the four P–40s
Lieutenant Moore had led into the air. These had not yet gained combat
altitude when they tangled with the first incoming Zeros; but 2nd Lieutenant Keator shot down one of them almost at once and Lieutenant
Moore, a little later, brought down two others.‡ The P–40s, however,
were too heavily outnumbered to accomplish much.

A few minutes later, three planes of the 21st Squadron's lone flight returned to the field. Four of this flight, as will be remembered, had taken
off over the Zambales Mountains after "B" flight of the 3rd Squadron.
They had not gone far before they heard the call for "All pursuits to
Clark Field. All pursuits to Clark. Enemy bombers overhead," coming in
on their radios. They could hear the mounting excitement in the man's
voice; it became almost hysterical; and then they heard the bombs bursting in their headsets. As they turned back to Clark, they saw a tree of
black smoke standing on the plain; and it kept rising as they neared it;
and when they got close they could see the fires at its roots. Cole's engine
started shooting oil about then, and he had to turn back, so only the
three were left. Then McGown disappeared § and there were just
Grashio and Williams.

* Most accounts have put the time of the attack earlier. Lt. Tash, pilot of the B–17
flying up from Del Monte, had his ETA for 12:40 and was coming in to land with his
wheels actually down when the field blew up in his face. This time is supported by the
great majority of officers interviewed who were present on the field, all of whom place
the time as after 12:30. Dissidents are Lt. Wheless, who says that it was 12:15 when
he picked up a report of the bombing; the 24th Pursuit Group Narrative which puts the
time at 12:20; 8 and Col. Kreps, who says the first bombs hit at 12:22.

† Lt. Jack Adams flew his plane down, after repairs, on December 9. Lt. Lee B. Coats
took another down on December 12. One of the reconnaissance planes was destroyed
(Carpenter's) when run into by a P–40, and another plane that had been repaired met
the same fate. Wheless, of course, went out with his plane and fought it.

‡ This was the first confirmed American combat victory in the air in this war. Keator
was awarded the Silver Star.

§ McGown had probably spotted Ellis being strafed in his chute near Mount Arayat, as
described in Chapter 13.

Down below they could see the enemy planes darting in and out of the smoke close above the fires. The two P-40 pilots circled up on top, trying to nerve themselves to go down after the enemy. Then they saw one of the planes break into the clear only three or four thousand feet below them and they dove for it, and got it. Just then, as they saw the Jap start down, they discovered that there were two Zeros on their own tails, and they split, diving into the smoke cloud. One of the Zeros came in after Grashio and put a cannon shell through his wing; but he got away and returned to Nichols Field.*

Fourteen miles south, at Del Carmen, the pilots of the 34th Pursuit Squadron had been waiting in their well-worn P-35s when they saw great clouds of smoke and dust climbing in the northern sky.† Lieutenant Marrett immediately took the Squadron up to intercept without orders.[10] There was a 6000-foot ceiling at Del Carmen, and as the lead flight reached the base of the clouds they were jumped by two Zeros. These were driven off by the arrival of the other two flights; but Marrett's guns had failed to operate and he was compelled to return to base, leaving the Squadron under the command of Lieutenant Ben S. Brown.[11]

Heading towards Clark, the 34th got into their own private war with several Zeros. The Japanese were very cocky and came right into the American formation, and the ensuing fight spilled itself all across the sky. The American pilots soon discovered that the Japanese planes could outmaneuver theirs in every respect except maximum diving speed, and owing to their own inexperience and the worn-out condition of their guns, the fight went on for some time in a seesaw fashion, with no confirmed kills being registered, though planes on both sides were hit.‡ By the time the fight was broken off, the Japanese strafers and dive bombers

---

* Grashio recalls that Dyess was waiting to see his pilots in, that there were more Cokes in the Operations Tent, and that this time the boys were hungry enough to eat the sandwiches.

† Robb puts the time at 11:00, which is manifestly impossible.[9]

‡ Brown states that he got one Zero, and Robb claims a total of three were shot down during the action. In this entire early phase of the war, there was seldom opportunity to confirm combat victories unless they were witnessed by troops on the ground. The 24th Pursuit Group Roster lists a total of 103 enemy planes shot down in the Philippines campaign, but there can be little doubt that the actual number of Japs shot down considerably exceeded that figure. . . . Robb had his engine shot out and barely got back to Del Carmen to make a dead-stick landing with both tires flat.[12]

had finished their work on Clark Field, and the 34th returned to Del Carmen.

The only other American pursuit to get into the fight that day were the six planes of "C" flight of the 3rd Squadron. Apparently they came over Clark at the beginning of the strafing attack and became tangled up with a bunch of Zeros almost at once. They were very low on gas by then; at least one of the planes ran dry in combat and its pilot, 2nd Lieutenant Ellstrom, was strafed in his chute.* Two more P-40s were lost in this action. The first crashed with its pilot, 2nd Lieutenant Ireland, into the side of Mount Arayat.† 2nd Lieutenant Ellis had to bail out of his. He was cutting round a cloud, looking for a Zero he had just chased into it, when he discovered that his own ship was not only on fire but its tail surfaces were practically burned off. It was impossible to pull up to kill his speed, so he jumped anyhow and made it safely to the ground, except for a crack on the head from his own plane that kept him from flying from then on. "C" flight was not able to prevent the Japanese from strafing the field, but they had at least drawn blood, and Ellis alone was officially credited with three Zeros.[14]

In the meantime Lieutenant Tash's B-17 had arrived over Clark Field at the exact moment of the Japanese high-altitude attack. Because of the report relayed to them from Del Monte that the field had been under attack, they had approached cautiously, keeping within the cloudbank over Arayat and searching with field glasses through the holes in the overcast. But at 12:35 Clark Field lay peacefully on the plain, the unpainted B-17s and P-40s shining in the open sunlight. They let down through the overcast, broke clear of it, and then, crossing the field at 500 feet, let down their wheels. At that instant the first bombs struck the row of quarters and the incredulous men at the windows of the big plane watched the string of explosions run out across the field. Tash reacted instantly,

* The 24th Pursuit Group Roster lists Ellstrom as killed in action on December 10. There is some obvious confusion in the Roster between the 8th and 10th, in respect to the 3rd Squadron, for several men are entered as killed in action at Iba on December 10, by which time the gunnery training field had been completely abandoned. Therefore it seems likely that Krieger's account, even at second hand, in this particular case is probably nearer the facts.[13]

† 2nd Lt. Vernon R. Ireland's death is also listed on the 10th in the Roster, though there seems to have been no pursuit action at Clark Field that day.

ordered wheels up, and headed back and up under full throttle towards the overcast. As the ship banked, the navigator had a glimpse of the bombers, gleaming in the sunlight and still in perfect formation, entering the same clouds far above them.*

They went up to 4000 feet and then, on the far side of Mount Arayat, they circled among the clouds and tried to figure out what they ought to do. Hasty calculations showed that they had enough gas to get back to Del Monte, with 35 minutes' extra flying time. They decided therefore to stay where they were until they had used up this margin and then to take another look at Clark. If the field looked all right, they would go in; otherwise they would return to Mindanao.

Once in their circling they saw another B-17 in the distance. They flew towards it, hoping to get into formation with it; but the other pilot took off for cloud cover. This was the plane that had been up the east coast of Luzon on reconnaissance and had been recalled at noon. The pilot, Lieutenant Carpenter, had seen Tash's plane but had not been able to identify it as friendly.

At the end of their allotted time, Tash started back for Clark. The air was clear of planes as they neared Arayat, but as they came closer to the field with its towering pillar of smoke, they could see planes flashing in and out of the smoke above the shattered buildings and the burning aircraft. At first Tash and his crew mistook these for friendly pursuit flying the regular traffic pattern before going in to land, and they themselves went jubilantly ahead, letting down their wheels once more, and firing two red flares, the signal of the day. About four miles out, however, just as they were turning into the base leg, a pursuit plane hurtled out of the clouds in front of them in a long vertical dive that carried it straight into the ground. At the same instant the co-pilot reported anti-aircraft fire and Tash decided that Clark Field was no place for them. As he banked away, Sergeant Sowa in the top dome reported three planes diving on them from 2000 feet above.

Tash took the B-17 down under full power to the treetops, and as they

* The crew of this ship were: Lt. Earl R. Tash, 2nd Lt. Douglas H. Kellar, 2nd Lt. Arthur E. Hoffman, S/Sgt. M. Bibin, S/Sgt. J. U. Sowa, Pfc. A. E. Norgaard, Pfc. J. S. Penney, Pvt. R. C. Krowd. Also aboard the plane was Cpl. Johnson of the 14th Squadron who had come up to have a tumor removed from his eye.

leveled off the fighter planes closed in. They peeled off their original formation and came in singly from the rear and banked away to the left as they finished their run. Sergeant Bibin, the bombardier, who had volunteered to handle one of the waist guns, was struck in the chest by the opening burst from the leading Japanese plane. He was knocked to the floor but did not lose consciousness. The Jap pilot came in so close on the B-17's tail that the tracer from his wing guns was converging out in front of Tash and Kellar. The aileron cables were half cut through; so were the flap cables; and one of the propellers was hit. After that Tash had to fly the ship dead level for fear of spinning in.

As the first Zero finished its run, the second took its place on the B-17's tail, where the side and top gunners couldn't get at it; but as the third Jap peeled off, Pfc. Norgaard, manning the top radio guns, caught the Zero in his sights and his tracer chewed right down the length of its belly from the prop spinner to the tail wheel. The Japanese did not go down, but he was flopping pretty badly the last time they saw him. The other two Zeros left them alone after that and they went on through the deepening overcast, still at low altitude, so that they had to feel their way between the Southern Luzon mountains. They had one more bad moment when they picked up the high Del Monte tableland in the clear ahead of them and saw smoke rising from the area in which the airfields lay. They hadn't enough gas left to do anything but go on in. But the smoke proved to be merely a brush fire, and they made a safe landing at a little after five o'clock.*

The pursuit action, and the diversion, if it could be called that, created by the passage of Lieutenant Tash's plane, had no material effect on the strafing of Clark Field. The Japanese worked over the burning Fortresses, the hangars, and the shops with no more direct opposition than the antiaircraft could produce. That was little enough. The planes broke so sharply out of the smoke, they came in so low, and the 37-mm guns were so slow at traversing, that the gunners could not follow the planes across the field, though one crew did get the plane attacking them when it was observed that the Japanese pilot kept repeating the exact line of

* Sgt. Bibin recovered after a long convalescence.

his run. They pointed their gun to pick up his exit, waited till he came again, and took him going away.*

The attack had broken so suddenly and unexpectedly after the departure of the high-altitude bombers that many of the air crews who had run out on the field as soon as the last bombs fell were caught in or beside their planes, and the strafing was carried out with such savage persistence that most of the men on the base were pinned down in their slit trenches until it was over. The heat of the fires, the choking clouds of smoke, the roar of airplane engines and the gunfire made any organized resistance impossible; but both Eubank and Gibbs continued to move among the dispersed planes encouraging the men and directing their efforts in defending the aircraft and fighting fires.[15] Some of the enlisted men had gone to the B–17s without orders and were firing the machine guns in the grounded planes against the enemy.† Others filled in among the antiaircraft gun crews as casualties occurred. The two B–17s that had been laid up for paint jobs were taxied out of the burning hangars, but both were destroyed almost immediately after coming under enemy fire.‡ In spite of the strafing and through all the confusion, the task of evacuating the wounded went on without interruption. There were more to pick up than the ambulances and stretcher crews could handle, and both officers and enlisted men took reconnaissance cars and trucks out on the field to aid them.§ Standing out among the others were the 19th Group's Flight Surgeon, Major Heidger, and Lieutenant Joseph V. LaFleur, of the Chaplain's Corps, each of whom performed his appropriate duties with a calmness and deliberate courage that not only gave heart to the wounded and dying but helped restore confidence to all those who saw them at their work.‖

* As previously stated, the A/A consisted of one battalion each of 3-inch and 37-mm guns of the 200th Coast Artillery.

† Among these the following received D.S.C.s: T/Sgt. Anthony Holub, who had just completed an engine change on his plane; Pvt. Joseph G. McElroy; and, posthumously, Pvt. Greeley B. Williams, who was killed still working his machine gun. There were others whose work deserved equal recognition.

‡ Lt. Fred T. Crimmins, Jr., brought one out unassisted; the other was brought out by Lt. Ray L. Cox and 2nd Lt. Austin W. Stitt.[16]

§ Pvt. Robert J. Endres performed conspicuous service in this way.

‖ Colonel Kreps speaks movingly of Father LaFleur. "He was out there . . . going around in the open as a matter of course, tending to the wounded and the dying. He

When after 45 minutes * the Japanese at last withdrew, they had done a thorough job. Clark Field as a tactical base was virtually destroyed. The casualties were very high, about 250 wounded, besides civilians, and 100 dead. There was not a single flyable plane on the base. Two or three of the B–17s were pieced out with parts of completely ruined planes sufficiently to be flown down to Mindanao within the next few days, but they were never in good tactical commission. The plane taken to Del Monte by Lieutenant Adams next morning lost two engines during take-off for its first assigned combat mission on December 12, had its hydraulic system go out, and crashed into Lieutenant Tash's plane. All other planes on Clark Field were wiped out. Though most of these were observation types or outdated or obsolete bombers like the B–18s, B–10s, and A–27s, they also included the P–40s of the 20th Pursuit Squadron. The field was pockmarked with bomb craters. The hangars and shops were gutted, and though the first fury of the fires had begun to die down, smoke still rose high and black above the base, like mourning for the dead, and the trucks and ambulances still crawled ceaselessly across the field and funneled into the road to Fort Stotsenburg.

Numerically the striking force of B–17s had been cut in half. But in efficiency their loss was infinitely greater, for from now on all B–17s would have to be based on Mindanao and use Clark Field merely as a staging area. The wear and tear on engines and air crews alike would be far more than doubled, and so would be the time spent in arriving over targets.

But those facts did not immediately concern the people at Clark Field. Their first instinct was to take stock of what they had. All communications were out for some time; but finally Eubank was able to get through

---

was a short slight man in his early thirties, a young fellow, but older than most of the boys, a Louisianan who spoke with a marked Cajun twist to his speech. He wore glasses, was very quiet. He used to conduct Catholic services in the early morning and later Protestant services. In the days following, on Bataan, he always seemed to find candy and cigarettes for the boys from some place. He went to Del Monte, elected to stay with the boys instead of evacuating, waved good-by, cheerful and casual." (Father LaFleur was lost among the men in the sinking of a hospital ship.) Eubank says of Heidger, "The Flight Surgeon, Heidger, had a station near the field and the smoke was pouring over it from an oil fire and Heidger was remarking how lucky he was to have a smoke screen provided, courtesy of the Japanese."

* In Eubank's recollection the strafing lasted only about 30 minutes; most other sources indicate a slightly longer attack.

to Brereton with his grim news. By then the engineers, who had moved out on the field with their equipment almost as soon as the last strafer turned away, had packed in enough craters to mark out a little narrow strip diagonally across the field, and Lieutenant Carpenter, who had been ordered to fly down to Mindanao but was too low on gas to obey, came in to land. At five o'clock Lieutenant Wheless returned from his Formosa patrol. Until the 21st Pursuit Squadron came in late in the afternoon, those two B–17s were the only planes fit for combat on Clark Field.

I V

The Effort to Reorganize: Two Days
of War

15. *December 9*

THE SUCCESS of their attack must have surprised the Japanese command nearly as much as it did our own people in both Air and General Headquarters. They had planned to make their strike at dawn; but the same heavy weather encountered by Lieutenant Wheless in the Bashi Channel had held their planes on the ground for several hours. By the time they were finally able to take off, it was unlikely that they would find any planes left on Clark Field. For, after the warning of Pearl Harbor, it seemed almost certain to them that the B-17s would either be sent south for dispersal or else would be headed north to attack Formosa while their own groups were on the way down to Luzon; and on some of the Japanese airfields that morning the men actually were wearing gas masks because of a false report of approaching hostile planes. The Japanese pilots therefore must have stiffened with incredulous elation as they cleared the Zambales Mountains at 12:30 and saw the big bombers still grounded on the open field below them.*

---

* This glimpse of the Japanese side of December 8 is drawn from several interviews contained in *Interrogations of Japanese Officials* in *U. S. Strategic Bombing Survey (Pacific)*, *Naval Analysis Division*. The opening attacks were carried out mostly by naval planes. Their first purpose was the annihilation of the U. S. Air Force in the Philippines. Attacks on our Naval Forces were a secondary objective which became less important with the retirement of almost all U. S. ships at or before the onset of hostilities. The naval planes making these initial strikes belonged to the 11th Air Fleet, which was attached to the 2nd Fleet, Southern Force. It comprised three Air Flotillas, one of which, based at Saigon, was used solely in the Malayan Campaign. Its strength is therefore not listed

That was the last attack delivered by the Japanese on December 8; but it was many hours before even a semblance of organization began to emerge from the confusion that apparently enveloped the Air Force command as well as many of the lower echelons. The effort to bring Clark Field back into use hinged entirely on the initiative of scattered individuals. A surgeon * superintended the digging of a sort of super foxhole in which to set up his infirmary and kept his detachment on duty beside the field through the ensuing days of bombing. An old-line mess sergeant, though ordered to have his equipment ready to evacuate, decided that someone ought to get out a lunch for the men who had stayed on the base and set up his shop at the hangar end of the field.† Lieutenant Colonel Eubank himself worked with the men who had stuck to their jobs, guiding in planes with flashlights and helping regas them with his own hands.‡ The first hours were chaotic. In fact it was almost

here. The other two flotillas, with their Headquarters and listed strength, according to the interrogated officers, were:

21ST AIR FLOTILLA (HQ, Tainan)		23RD AIR FLOTILLA (HQ, Takao)	
1st Group (Takao)		*Takao Group* (Takao)	
72 VF (Zeke)		54 VB (2) (Betty)	
24 VF (Reserve)		18 VB (2) (Reserve)	
6-9 VS (Recon.)		*3rd Group* (Takao)	
Kanoya Group (Taighn)		72 VF (2) (Zeke)	
54 VB (2) (Betty)		18 VF (2) (Reserve)	
18 VB (2) (Reserve)		6-9 VS (Recon.)	
Toko Group (Palau)			
12 VP (4) (Mavis)			
4 VP (4) (Reserve)			

This makes a total of 330 combat naval planes available on Formosa for the first day's attacks. In addition there were apparently about 150 army planes. There seems to have been some confusion in the minds of the Japanese officials, for they speak of attacks on Clark and *Nichols* Fields, and do not mention Iba. The listing above is from Interrogation #15, USSBS #74, Capt. Takahasi, who was on the Staff of the 11th Air Fleet.

* Maj. Emmett C. Lentz, who in the opinion of Kennard, the Air Force Surgeon, did as much as any one man to restore morale at Clark Field.

† This was M/Sgt. (now Lt.) George R. Robinet of the 30th Squadron. He became famous here, on Bataan, and later yet in Mindanao for the quality of his mess, and even in Japanese prison camps the people who ate with Robinet ate better than the rest.[1]

‡ There seems to be no question that a substantial proportion of the personnel on the base took off after the attack. Eubank, who is universally known for his loyalty to men in his command, maintains that the men behaved well. But he is speaking of the engineers, who did a fine job, and of his own combat crews, most of whom stood by him. The service troops were, for the most part, completely green and, though they later developed into some of the best infantry on Bataan, their morale in the first days of the war had badly disintegrated. The causes seem to have been the weight of the attack, the

four days before things were under control at Clark Field, and the work accomplished was done in piecemeal fashion with what manpower came to hand. Navigators, their planes destroyed, were put to work making copies of the very few maps they possessed of the southern tip of Formosa; * and both combat and service crews immediately embarked on the task of putting the least damaged B–17s back into commission and salvaging all usable parts from the ones that had been hopelessly destroyed. They could afford to let nothing go to waste. Major Gibbs made it the duty of the 30th Squadron to see that no plane came in for service or repairs without receiving them at once.² But Clark Field remained a broken air base. For almost a week the dead were left lying with the burned-out skeletons of their aircraft. In the confusion a dispute had arisen as to whether the Medical Department or the Quartermaster's was responsible for their identification and burial; and during the bright moonlight nights that followed, as well as in the glare of the sun, their bodies remained with the living, pathetic but grim reminders of the way in which the power of the enemy had been misjudged.

That evening there were two B–17s on Clark Field in tactical commission. Three of the damaged planes were found to be capable of repair; but only two were evacuated to Del Monte, and of the two one never flew a combat mission.† In addition there were the 16 Fortresses at Del Monte, one of which was damaged.‡ This meant that the Air Force had 17 planes left with which it could carry the war to the Japanese.

Now at last the need of dispersed airfields, servicing facilities, and supply depots became desperately apparent even to those who had blindly obstructed their development before the war. The destruction of Clark Field had left Nichols the only air base adequately equipped to service pursuit, and it was almost certain to be the next primary target for the Japanese. Therefore, when the 21st and 17th Squadrons landed after

inexperience of young officers in handling and caring for their men, and the fact that both officers and men had had poor psychological preparation for any such onslaught.

* One of these amateur cartographers said that the maps were "made free hand by untrained people and the work was constantly being interrupted by alerts and air raids." It was probably as well that no opportunity for using them developed.

† The first was the plane taken out by Lt. Adams on the morning of December 9. The second was taken out by Lt. Coats on either the night of December 9-10 or 11-12. The third B–17 was run into by a P–40 out of control.

‡ Tash's plane.

nearly three hours of fruitless patrolling over Cavite and Bataan, it was decided to send all planes of both squadrons that were fit for combat up to Clark and keep at Nichols only those requiring maintenance, together with such strays of the 3rd Squadron as had or might yet come in.

The pilots of the 17th and 21st had seen the smoke of the bombing, but not knowing the cause, and in the absence of any instructions, they had kept to their assigned patrols.* In the late afternoon, the 21st took off again, to be followed in about an hour by the 17th.† At 4000 feet they saw again and headed for the smoke above Clark Field. It towered out of the plain, a black, motionless column, for now there was not a breath of wind. It was sweet flying weather. The haze had cleared and hardly a cloud remained in the sky. To their left as they flew north Manila Bay was a deep, unruffled blue, and beyond it the Bataan Mountains stood clearly defined by the low afternoon sunlight.[4]

When they came over Clark Field, the hangars and oil dumps were still burning. It took a long time for the Squadron to get down, for each successive landing on the little patched-up air strip raised blinding clouds of dust, and the next pilot had to wait for several minutes before he could see to go in. The twilight was fading into darkness as the last one landed, his plane faintly outlined by the deep red glow from the burning hangars.

When they climbed from their cockpits the whole field seemed deserted, but after a little while an old master sergeant appeared and rounded up enough men to service the planes. The pilots then located the 24th Group Headquarters, which had been moved into a patch of woods just south of the field,[5] and reported to Major Grover. They were instructed to be ready next morning to fly cover for B-17s that were coming up from Del Monte. They had 11 P-40s of their own; but shortly after their last plane landed, a P-40 belonging to the 17th Squadron came in with its radio out of commission and the pilot ‡ attached himself to their squadron.

---

* The 24th Pursuit Group Narrative indicates that the 17th Squadron, after seeing the smoke, proceeded to Clark, arriving too late to be of use. Kizer more or less supports this; but the other pilots interviewed say that the Squadron remained patrolling over Manila Bay till they went into Nichols Field.[3]

† The 21st took off about 4:30 and the 17th at 5:30.

‡ 2nd Lt. John H. Posten, Jr.

The 17th had come over Clark while the 21st were still trying to get down and, observing the condition of the field and the near approach of darkness, had turned off for Del Carmen with the exception of Posten, who, having no radio, had gone on in according to his original orders. The dust at Del Carmen was even worse than at Clark. It lay six inches deep on the strip and the landing planes raised plumes nearly as long as the field itself. But there were no bomb craters to dodge and the Squadron got down safely before black dark, saw their planes serviced, and dispersed them for a quick take-off in the morning.[6] Rations were on the scant side, for the 34th's resources were limited. As the night closed in on the raw strip with its crude control tower and huddle of tents, the men became aware of a new and hostile element surrounding them on the darkening plain. Fires sprang up mysteriously in empty fields and lights appeared where no one had seen lights before, framing the little air base. When parties were sent out to investigate, they found nothing but the fires. Whoever lighted them had melted into the darkness and the woods.

It was the same all over Luzon. In the first dark hours before the bombers came, fifth columnists, known as Sakdalistas, had started placing their rockets and signal flares around Manila, at the corners of Nielson and Nichols Fields, near Army camps—even on the parade ground of Fort McKinley.[7] No sentries saw them at their work, but when the beat of Japanese engines sounded in the moonlit sky, the birth of lights preceded them across the plain, leading the pilots on direct lines to their targets. So a gasoline truck,* burning in the open 200 yards away, made a sighting point on the Pan American Airways radio station,[9] and two bombs dropping within 30 feet completely wiped it out.[10]

The attack came at 3:00 o'clock in the morning;† it was not very extensive. Bombs fell on Fort McKinley, but, except for the loss of the Pan American beam station, the greatest damage was suffered at Nichols Field, where a stick of bombs hit Hangar No. 4 and took out the north

---

* Col. Vance, however, saw no evidence of this burning truck and believes reports of flares exaggerated.[8]

† Though the time given for this raid varies, the consensus puts it at 3:00 A.M. The 24th Pursuit Group Narrative puts it at 3:15; and *The 27th Reports* contains a separate account placing it at 4:30. Colonel Fellows, however, says that it came at 1:00 and Colonel Thorne remembers it as around midnight.[11]

end of the Bachelor Officers' Quarters. There were several casualties, and two of the B–18s were destroyed.[12] These ships, in spite of their ramshackle condition, were beginning to assume real importance to the Air Force. The whole countryside from Fort McKinley to Nichols Field was laced by arcing tracer fire as the Filipino troops cut loose at the attacking planes. Since they had nothing heavier than .30-caliber machine guns, they did no damage to the Japanese bombers which circled at will and at low altitude over their targets.

There was no air opposition; but interception had been attempted on the preceding alert, which had occurred shortly after 2:00 o'clock. Clark Field was still only in telephonic communication with Headquarters at Nielson so when plots showed an approaching hostile formation, Major Grover ordered one flight of the 17th Squadron at Del Carmen into the air. The extraordinary dust conditions and the fact that the take-off had to be made in almost complete blackout made it an almost impossible assignment. Three planes, led by Lieutenant William J. Feallock, got into the air successfully; but the pilot of the fourth * took off too soon in the blinding dust cloud, crashed into another plane, destroying both, and was himself burned in the wreckage. The other three planes circled Manila, and, as might have been expected from earlier failures at night interception, found nothing. On their return to Del Carmen they were lucky to get in safely, for the lights along the landing strip had been narrowed to slits so fine that the pilots had to come right down on the treetops before they could see them at all.†

No further incidents occurred at Del Carmen that night; but at Clark Field the 21st Squadron lost a pilot and two P–40s during take-off for a dawn patrol, and one B–17 was destroyed in the resulting crashes. The men had been waked early by Grover after a night spent on the open ground, and Dyess briefed them, laying particular emphasis on the need of care on take-off. Every pilot was to watch him closely and follow his

---

* 2nd Lt. Lawrence K. Lodin.

† Lt. Col. John Brownwell puts the time at 2:00 A.M. and says three planes got off safely. The 24th Pursuit Group Narrative says four planes, which is confirmed by implication in Sheppard's account. Sheppard says the flight went off at 4:30 A.M. as relief for a mixed flight from Clark, but there is no confirmation of such a flight by any other source. Obert says three P–40s were burned in Lodin's crash, but he was not present on the field.[13]

exact route. His take-off was good, but they had to wait at least five minutes for the dust to settle, and because of this one pilot taxied himself into a bomb hole, and then 2nd Lieutenant Clark * lost the direction entirely and crashed into the B–17 and was burned. The others knew it was going to happen as soon as Clark got rolling. All the time he was taxiing they could hear Dyess in their headsets calling down from where he was circling in the new light up above the field that Clark was sure to crash; but either Clark did not understand or his radio had gone out. Then McGown also lost himself in the dust and went straight on off the field into the trees beyond. He destroyed his plane but came through it himself. Grashio's engine cut out at 7000 feet and he had to come in again. With no power it was impossible for him to follow the prescribed approach and he was consequently fired on by the antiaircraft.[14] Clark Field was still a jittery place.

This left the rest of the 21st to perform the patrol with a total of eight planes, the eighth being Posten's. There was of course no oxygen at Clark, so the 21st learned that day what it was like to fly for hours without oxygen at altitudes of 15,000 feet or above. Night, according to Dyess, "found me so done in I doubt if I could have seen a Jap even if he had been in the cockpit with me." [15] He brought his Squadron into Rosales that evening. There were only three ground men available on the strip, so the pilots, tired as they were, had to check their own planes and gas them from 55-gallon drums.

The 34th and 17th Squadrons flew individual patrols that day: the 34th ending up for the night at San Marcelino where there was neither food, bedding, nor drinking water for them.[16] The 17th was sent to Clark Field and went to the camp that had been established by the 20th Squadron in the hills a few miles north of the field. It was known as "20th Camp" and had a mess going, a few cots, blankets, some nicely dug foxholes, and living quarters constructed out of bamboo poles laced with vines and covered with banana leaves. Best of all there was a stream of fresh water in the woods for washing and bathing.[17] Almost all the pilots who stayed there in the remaining days of Clark Field were to remember 20th Camp with longing in the days to come.

---

* 2nd Lt. Robert D. Clark. The B–17 was Eubank's.

None of the three squadrons, nor the pooled fighters of the 3rd Squadron and members of the 17th and 21st left behind at Nichols who flew patrols over Manila Bay, had encountered any enemy planes. It had been a long and fruitless day of flying. The pilots were left exhausted and, in the case of the two squadrons at San Marcelino and Rosales, with practically nothing to eat. As they lay out on the open ground or on the bare floor of a half-finished shack and looked across the moonlit strip at the dark and watching wall of jungle growth, the men must have speculated about Pearl Harbor, though of course they had no conception then of the extent of the disaster. They still thought of themselves as engaged in the holding action Colonel George had talked about. Help would come in time, in a couple of months, perhaps; but now their most immediate concern was to get back to base, and food, and decent drinking water. There was little refreshment in water still warm from boiling.

They were baffled, too, by the apparent inertia of the Japanese. They had expected new waves of attacking planes; but, except for their own, the skies had been empty of pursuit all day, and the only bombardment they saw was a lone B–17 dispatched from Clark Field at 8:00 that morning on a photographic mission to Formosa.[18] It had had to turn back with a burned-out generator before it had made half the distance, but when it came over Clark Field, the pilot was told to keep in the air till dark, and for the rest of the day the plane could be seen from time to time circling through the clouds above Pamapanga Province.*

Then, in the afternoon and evening, the two squadrons of B–17s from Del Monte came in to land at Clark Field and San Marcelino. There were 14 of them, altogether, and they had been ordered up with the intention of sending them against enemy airdromes in Southern Formosa.[19] During the night, however, reports of large Japanese convoys approaching Vigan and Aparri came into Headquarters. The Formosa mission was abandoned and, instead, it was decided to hit the convoys with all available air power in the morning.[20]

There was no subsequent opportunity of attacking Formosa. Headquarters had now begun to understand the full implications of the situa-

* This was Carpenter's plane, which had constantly been plagued by generator trouble. However, this plane was destroyed only a few days later when a P–40, piloted by 2nd Lt. Robert Newman, crashed into it on take-off.

tion of the Philippines. They knew that Guam and Wake Island were under attack.[21] This fact, coupled with the damage suffered at Pearl Harbor, meant that all hope of quick reinforcement from the United States must be foregone. The Army in the Philippines would have to get along with what it had.

All during the day messages had trickled in of troops in Japanese uniforms materializing in the northern barrios, or merchants, even town officials, turning suddenly into Japanese officers, and hostile bands moving down on radio stations, observation posts, and telephone switchboards.[22] As more and more communication lines were cut, the situation in the north became increasingly conjectural. But now, at last, the convoys offered a definite target for the Air Force to attack with all it had.

Except for the 21st Squadron at Rosales and the mixed collection of strays at Nichols Field, every plane fit for combat would attack in the morning: the 15 B–17s;* the 17th and 34th Pursuit Squadrons, to act as fighter cover and then attack on their own account after the bombardment had finished its work; even three B–18s that had been turned over to the plane-hungry pilots of the 27th Group were to try their luck.[23]

16. *December 10: Vigan*

As THINGS TURNED OUT, only five B–17s of the 93rd Squadron formed the bombardment on the mission attacking the Japanese convoy off Vigan. It would seem an almost laughably small force today, but it looked all right to the air crews on Clark in the cool pre-dawn of December 10; and it proved to be the heaviest bombing mission flown by the United States Air Force until December 22, when nine B–17s were to take off from Batchelor Field in Australia, more than 2000 miles to the south, to attack another convoy in Lingayen Gulf.†

Some of the men felt pretty eager. They hadn't yet had their taste of combat. Clark Field was a grim place, but it did not look as grim to them

---

* Wheless's plane at Clark Field, still in combat commission, was to join the 14 brought up from Del Monte.

† But of these nine planes, only four managed to get over Lingayen.

as it did to the men who had been subjected to the bombing. They felt that December 8 had been a wasted day. Except for the early morning orders directing reconnaissance of Mindanao, no word had reached Del Monte from Headquarters and they had sat out the whole day by their planes. But on the morning of December 9, the 93rd Squadron was ordered to hunt a Japanese raider reported 125 miles off Legaspi. Six ships * under Major Combs took off at 7:30, loaded with twenty 100-pound demolition bombs.[1] They spent most of the day flying back and forth over the Catanduanes Islands but saw no sign of the raider. Then, according to his orders, Combs brought the Squadron up to Clark Field. They arrived late in the afternoon with the gas fairly low in their tanks.

It took them a long time to get down, and it was past sunset when the fifth plane landed. By then, the 14th Squadron's eight planes under Major O'Donnell were flying in through the twilight. But the Clark Field radio ordered them over to San Marcelino; and Combs, who was still circling over Clark, flew over with them to watch them land. No B–17 had ever set down there. The valley the field lay in was a narrow well, rapidly filling with darkness, and Combs watched O'Donnell's planes circle, space out, and drop down into it, their landing lights shrinking fast as they came in to the rough grass and then running out suddenly across the field at the point of a plume of dust. As the first ships went in, the edges of the field sprayed machine gun tracer, but all the planes got down safely.[2]

The fire came from native Filipino soldiers stationed on the field as a ground force. They had been issued uniforms only a week before; they had had almost no training in plane identification; Luzon was full of fifth columnists; and nobody knew what was going on anyway. The big planes coming in at dusk were natural things to shoot at. One plane received a bullet through the wing before the troops quieted down,† but fortunately there were no casualties.

Having seen the 14th Squadron safely landed, Combs flew back across the mountains to Clark. It was now nearly pitch dark and it was lucky

---

* Lt. Tash's plane was out of commission after being shot up over Clark Field and the eighth plane (Parsel's), as will be seen, was on reconnaissance.

† Piloted by Capt. Elmer L. Parsel. Parsel had flown an individual reconnaissance mission over Davao, which had been bombed by the Japanese on December 8, and coming in behind the 93rd Squadron he was ordered over to Marcelino with the 14th.[3]

that he was thoroughly familiar with the field, for they refused to turn on any lights for him. He made his sight on Mount Arayat and went in safely with his own landing lights. Eubank and McIntyre came out to meet him and guided him to his parking place, a process that took over half an hour. The B-17s were widely dispersed around the field and men with hooded flashlights were already at work, gassing and servicing them. The small moving lights, the occasional vague illumination of the big silver bodies of the planes, the silence, and the smell of death had turned Clark Field into a strange and ghostly place. Only the great cone of Arayat towering in the night sky remained an unchanging reminder of the world as it had been.

Before daylight detailed information on the Japanese convoy off Vigan was brought in by a fighter pilot. Lieutenant Grant M. Mahony of the 3rd Squadron, flying alone in his P-40 on a night reconnaissance mission, had counted and described the ships and determined their location.[4] This was the first recorded individual mission of a pilot who was to fight the war as if it were his personal crusade against Japan.* It was flying of a high order, carried through in thick weather, over a complete ground

* Few men have fought this war, or any war, harder than Mahony fought it, for he had the high emotional qualities that came with his Irish blood. Though he was often gay, there were also times, when he thought of his dead friends or the innocent people he had seen fall victim to Japan, that a black spell lay on him. He did not especially like the Army. He was not a superlative flier, in the sense that Wagner was, but he fought in his plane with a deadly purpose that made him nearly as effective. It became his mission to kill Japanese. He flew in combat against them in Java, in Burma, and then in China. In the end it brought him to his death on the very scene of his first mission, in Lingayen Gulf, in January 1945. The circumstances are worth recounting.

Previously he had been given a desk job in the United States; but he had to get back into the war against Japan, and finally he was sent back to the Philippines as Deputy Commander of the 8th Fighter Group, flying P-38s.

On his final mission his group had been assigned to escort A-20 bombers that were to attack the landing beaches in Lingayen Gulf. As they came in from the sea, Mahony saw a Japanese seaplane sitting on the water off to his left. He told his men to go on with their mission; he himself would take care of this plane and then rejoin them. The Japanese had set up a seaplane base at Puerta Princessa off which the seaplane was anchored, and as Mahony came in on his strafing run, all the antiaircraft around the base concentrated on his P-38. He finished off the Jap plane, but just as he was pulling out, his left wing was hit by the ackack and his plane caught fire. It was seen to cross the beaches and then, an instant later, it crashed in the jungle.

Col. John R. Alison, then Chief of Staff of the 308th Bombardment Wing, witnessed

blackout, and against enemy fire.[5] His information was vital for working out the timing of this co-ordinated mission, as the slowness of the P–35s presented difficulties. They had a listed top speed of 290 miles; actually, badly in need of an engine change, they would be lucky to reach that. In addition, they had no protective armor for the pilots, no leak-proof tanks,[6] and were lightly armed, with their two .30-caliber guns of uncertain performance. But they had to be used.

Take-off from Clark Field was set for 6:00 A.M. At 5:30, however, one of Combs's planes was taken away from him for a photographic reconnaissance of Formosa.* He was left, therefore, with only five planes,† still loaded with their twenty 100-pound demolition bombs. With this light load they were supposed to attack Japanese transports.

Combs took the Squadron up the middle of Luzon, and then turned due west to come over the target from the land at 12,000 feet. The ships lay under them in a line off the beach. A few were pulling out to sea, which made it look as if the Japanese had already got ashore. Farther out were two or three cruisers, and to the pilots' inexperienced eyes the decks looked livid with fire. But most of the ackack was well off them, nor was it actually very heavy. They saw some of the transports sprout white wakes and start to squirm from under them, and they went on in in sudden high excitement, shouting, "Christ Almighty. There they are," as if they had just seen them, and roaring over, and dropping their bombs.‡ They wheeled out over the sea and made a second run from

the incident from the deck of a cruiser which was covering the landings. As soon as possible he instituted a search for the crashed plane. It was found, but Mahony's body had disappeared. It should be added that at the time of his death, Mahony had flown more combat hours than any other fighter pilot in our Air Force. Few men have served this country to better purpose or with more sincerity.

* Like the previous attempt, this mission failed, the pilot, Lt. Connally, turning back with engine trouble. As he returned, he sighted a large formation of enemy pursuit and, on reaching Clark Field, found them attacking the base. He had to stay in the clouds all day, landing after dark.[7]

† Pilots: Maj. Combs, Lts. Vandevanter, Ford, Shedd, and Young, the last replacing Lt. Bohnaker, who had arrived at Clark Field with a bad case of malaria.[8]

‡ All dropped their bombs but Vandevanter, whose racks refused to work at 12,000, so he dropped to 7000 feet where they worked perfectly. The ackack looked heavier to him and he had a wing holed by shrapnel. He reached Clark after the others, was told not to land, and circled in the clouds till 2:00 P.M., when he was ordered to Del Monte. Not having gas enough to make it, he went in to Tacloban on Leyte, a 2600-foot strip,

west to east. As they headed inland again, Young, in the weaver position on the tail of the flight, saw some P–40s coming in.

The B–17s kept well on inland over the mountains before turning south for Clark. They had made some hits, and they thought they had left one transport sinking. Only three hours after take-off they were back at Clark, with Combs screaming for more bombs. But the people at Clark were jumpy about another raid. They were still loading a ship of O'Donnell's 14th Squadron, and they told Combs to get himself and his Squadron off the field and head for Del Monte. Just before he took off, Eubank came over to ask him whether they had had any fighter opposition. When he learned that they hadn't, Eubank said, "Thank God. I've been sending off O'Donnell's ships one at a time."

When Combs got up, only one of the other pilots, Lieutenant Ford, managed to form on him. The others returned to Del Monte individually. That was the first United States Air Force bombing attack in this war.

In the meantime, the pursuit at Vigan were attacking on their own account. They were headed by the 17th Squadron, which had been flying top cover for the B–17s,[9] with a few casual flights from Clark Field and Del Carmen that had come up to join them.[10] Both fragmentation bombs and machine gun fire were used against landing barges and the ground installations already established on the beaches.[11] Two planes were lost from engine failure, but both pilots bailed out safely, found each other, and within a week had made their way home on foot across the mountains.*

The 34th Squadron, however, were late in coming up. They not only missed the B–17s entirely; through no fault of their own they arrived barely in time to see the finish of the P–40 attack. Before dawn the pilots had flown from San Marcelino, where they had spent a foodless and nearly sleepless night, back to Del Carmen. There they found orders waiting to take off immediately for Vigan. The planes were hurriedly serviced and, though the dust again delayed them, they got into the air with 16 planes in two flights, led respectively by Lieutenants Marrett and

landing with brakes. He spent the night there, confiscated gas from Pan American, and badly damaged his horizontal stabilizer taking off.

* Lt. Sheppard was one. The other pilot was 2nd Lt. Edward E. Houseman of the 20th Squadron, who had flown up in an odd P–35 from Clark Field.[12]

Brown. This was stiffer treatment than the worn engines could stand up under and, as the Squadron flew north, they started to give out. One by one the pilots had to turn back, so that when the Squadron finally flew out over Vigan, there were five planes left in Marrett's flight and only two in Brown's.[13] The P-40s had done quite a job on the beaches, completely disrupting the landing;[14] quite a few barges were sitting down in the water; and Brown, who was supposed to be furnishing top cover, couldn't see any enemy planes. So he took his flight of two down after Marrett and what was left of the Squadron went in together against the transports and the barges around them. Their two .30-caliber and two .50-caliber guns were pretty light armament for such work, but they sank a good many of the small barges and set three of the big transports afire.

One of these ships was a 10,000-ton vessel that Marrett had been concentrating on, and he wouldn't leave it alone. He made his final pass at barely masthead height through close and heavy fire, including that of nearly 20 destroyers and cruisers, and this time he got home. He must have hit the ship's magazine. It might have been carrying mines to judge from the violence of the explosion. Just as Marrett started to pull up from his dive, it blew up under him. The other members of the Squadron saw the wing torn off his P-35. The plane whipped over in one clean flash and dived into the sea. It was gone before the fragments of the transport started returning to the water.[15]

It was an outstanding piece of flying. In spite of the subsequent publicity given Captain Colin Kelly's attack on a Japanese warship, Marrett in his obsolescent plane had turned in a performance that for skill, determination, and courage was unsurpassed. It was hard for the returning members of his squadron, in making their reports, to find words that did justice to his flying.

When they reached Del Carmen, the eight planes * that had been compelled to turn back from the mission were waiting on the line. They had a short interlude of quiet. Then, entirely without warning, twelve Zeros swept in, strafing the field. The gas and oil trucks were blown up, twelve of the P-35s were destroyed, and six more were damaged.[17] Lieutenant Brown, who at Marrett's death had inherited the Squadron command, now found himself and his pilots in virtually the position of the

---

* One plane lost its engine over Vigan, and the pilot had to bail out.[16]

27th Bombardment Group, a flying organization without planes. And, except for a few missions, they were to remain inactive at Del Carmen until December 25.

It was the greater loss because within an hour every pursuit ship was to be desperately needed in the air.

17. *December 10: The 14th Squadron*

THE 14TH BOMBARDMENT SQUADRON, like the 34th Pursuit, spent the night at San Marcelino. Most of the pilots had never even seen the field before and bringing the big ships down was quite an experience. As Teats wrote, "Right then the safety margins of peace in heavy bomber operation disappeared. We found out a lot about those big Fortresses we hadn't known. We discovered that we could take off from any field we could land in. We took off and landed, no matter what the wind direction was. We operated at maximum most of the time. We threw the book away. . . ." [1] There were no quarters for them, so they slept in their planes or on the ground under the wings, with the dew dripping on them like cold rain. But at least they were better off than the 34th, for they had a little good water left in their canteens and a foraging crew sent in to San Marcelino came back with eight loaves of bread they had discovered in an empty store. These were divided up one to a plane, providing the 64 men with supper and breakfast.

O'Donnell took off in the morning before daylight for Clark Field. He needed orders, and he was temperamentally unqualified to merely sit and wait. He also wanted to have some idea of what was going on. Figuratively as well as literally the 14th Squadron was still completely in the dark. All they knew about this war was what they had seen of Clark Field in the evening, before being turned away to this barren and deserted valley.

Taking off in the darkness at San Marcelino was a feat in itself. There were no obstruction markers, and the mountains were invisible. With moonlight or starlight, they could be picked up against the shine of Subic Bay; but there was not even starlight on December 10, and as soon as the big ship was airborne, it had to be put into a 45-degree turn.

O'Donnell made it. After the roar of his engines had lifted beyond the mountains, the men went over to Communications to wait for orders. Communications was an old B–18 shoved off the field into some thick brush with its radio tuned in on the Clark frequency. Here they received O'Donnell's instructions to follow him at dawn.[2]

It was pouring rain then, and the overcast was stuck on the mountaintops and they had to work down under it coming in to Clark. But only three of their ships were allowed to land. On the field they were expecting an air raid. The air warning system was practically extinct; there were a couple of spotters on nearby hills and on the control tower itself, but that was all. Even the klaxon was gone. When a raid was expected, a red flag was hung out of the control tower.[3]

The three ships that had been turned away * went back to San Marcelino and circled the valley close under the overcast until their gas had nearly run out. They were not brought into action at all that day. On landing they found that bombs and gas had been trucked in and they loaded with 500-pounders with the idea of staging their own mission against a reported Japanese carrier. But before they could take off, orders arrived sending them back to Mindanao.†

The three ships that went in to Clark Field to load up were piloted by Captain Kelly, and Lieutenants Schaetzel and Montgomery. Captain Parsel's B–17 was on the field being repaired; but O'Donnell had already taken off with eight 600-pound bombs aboard for Vigan. There he had picked out a cruiser and a destroyer escort to go for; but, like Vandevanter, he had trouble with the operation of his bomb racks. He wouldn't give up, in spite of heavy antiaircraft fire, and made five runs on the two ships, using up three quarters of an hour over the target.[5] No hits were observed, but there were no bombs left in the bays when he turned back for Clark, where he regassed and took off for Del Monte.

Before Kelly's, Schaetzel's, and Montgomery's ships had finished

* The pilots were Godman, Teats, and Keiser.

† Actually, Godman's plane was grounded with engine trouble. Capt. Parsel was to join the other two, but he had already flown a mission to Vigan, attacking a cruiser and firing a transport. Godman came out with Schaetzel later in the night.[4]

loading, they were sent away because of a red alert. Schaetzel and Kelly had orders for Aparri, but they flew north individually, Schaetzel with eight 600-pound bombs and Kelly with three. There had been time to put only one of the 600-pound bombs into Montgomery's ship; but as long as he had to stay in the air anyway, he decided not to waste his time and set out for Vigan.

This individual mission with an individual bomb was the beginning of an arduous day. The bomb was dropped with no discernible effect on the Japanese shipping and Montgomery turned back to Clark for another load. He was allowed to land and this time twenty 100-pound bombs were put into his racks and he was sent off to bomb transports at Aparri. It was now 2:00 o'clock, and neither he nor his crew had eaten anything except the loaf of bread at San Marcelino for the past twenty-four hours. But they saw no enemy pursuit and they came out over the long straight beaches off Aparri and let go on the transports. When they were through, one ship was burning well and appeared to be sinking. The whole crew felt better as, for the second time, they headed their ship towards Clark Field. But now as they came over it, they were ordered to keep straight on for Mindanao. Darkness overtook them; they ran into violent weather and for two hours they flew on instruments. When they should have hit Del Monte, they couldn't find it and worked on westward hoping to get in somewhere down along the coast. Finally, with the gas run dry in his tanks, Montgomery set the ship down in the sea off Zamboanga. It sank, but all the crew managed to make shore.[6]

Kelly and Schaetzel had orders to find and attack a carrier reported north of Aparri. As we have seen, they followed separate routes. When Schaetzel came out over Aparri, he and his crew saw the transports lined up beyond the beach and bombed them through broken clouds from 25,000 feet. The clouds prevented their seeing whether they had registered any hits; but they had no time for a second look as four Zeros came bursting up to intercept them. The Japanese pilots were aggressive and tenacious, refusing to be shaken off until Schaetzel put the B-17 into a 45-degree dive for the lower cloud level. He held the dive for 18,000 feet and he told Teats afterwards that the last time he looked at the air speed indicator it read 350 and was still going up.

Though he knew there were mountains inside those lower clouds, he did not give them a second thought for, just as the ship found cover, the ammunition ran out, leaving it as helpless as a plucked turkey. But he survived, to land finally at San Marcelino. The ship was streaming oil, it had one engine out, and its tail section was as full of holes as a cheese. It was a mess, but it could still fly, and none of the crew had been wounded.[7]

Colin Kelly had taken his own route northward. He crossed Vigan at 20,000 feet in clear weather and looked down with his crew mates on the Japanese landing operation. There were no enemy pursuit in sight and the Fortress proceeded uneventfully, cutting over the northwest coastline and swinging down through the Babuyan Channel towards Aparri. As they approached, they saw below them six cruisers and, as they thought, one battleship bombarding the shore. The cruisers were working in close to land, while the big ship, four or five miles offshore, blasted away with its big guns in solitary dignity. The men in the Fortress stared down on it for several minutes, but they did nothing to disturb it, or the other ships. Instead, they turned north once more over the Babuyan Islands towards the Luzon Strait.

Though they saw Japanese shipping scattered everywhere through the island waters, there was no sign of the carrier. As they searched, scattered and thickening clouds forced them to let down until, by the time they were approaching Formosa, they were at barely 4000 feet. It was nearly noon then; and Formosa itself was hidden in a rainstorm, so Kelly took the plane back up to 20,000 and swung it round. There seems to have been very little discussion about their next move. Every man aboard the B–17 could see in his mind's eye that big ship standing off Aparri all by itself.

They were still at 20,000 feet as they came up to the target; but this time they were instantly spotted by the cruisers, which began to take violent evasive action, throwing up antiaircraft fire as they did so. The flak was light, however, and inaccurate. For some reason the battleship not only did not use its antiaircraft guns, it made no evasive maneuvers whatever, but continued its undeviating course along the coast. The bombardier, Corporal Meyer Levin, was able to begin his run ten minutes out and the B–17, now utterly in his hands, became tense with a quiet of its own, independent of the droning engines and the sound of antiaircraft, while Levin worked over the dials of his bombsight.

The three bombs were dropped in train. At Levin's shouted "Bombs away!" Kelly once more resumed control of the plane and turned it sharply towards the coast. The rest of the crew stared from the windows, trying to follow the downward course of the bombs. The first struck about fifty yards short, but the second was close alongside, and the third hit fair on the ship's after turret. They could see the flash of the explosion; then smoke blossomed suddenly from the stern, and an instant later an oil slick showed on the water. The smoke increased and slowly covered the ship, so, though they circled twice, the crew could not see whether any heavy damage had been done.

Several Japanese fighters now appeared in the air under the B–17, but the passes they made were fainthearted and a burst or two from the waist guns sufficed to cool their interest. As the B–17 crossed over the shore line near Aparri, however, the navigator, 2nd Lieutenant Bean, saw two three-plane flights take off from the coastal strip. They were climbing very fast, as if they meant business, and he noticed them especially because, unlike most Japanese fighters, which were finished silver or white, these were painted a soft, pale green. However, when the Fortress passed over the edge of the undercast of cloud, he lost sight of them. This undercast thickened steadily, and as they crossed the mountain ranges, Kelly gradually let down until the big plane was flying only about 300 feet above the clouds. Bean forgot about the six Japanese fighters he had seen take off at Aparri. He had been on the lookout for fighters through the overhead glass dome, but now, realizing they were close to home, he leaned forward to glance at the altimeter. As he did so, the dome, in which his head had been framed a moment before, was smashed to atoms and in the same instant an explosive bullet hit the instrument panel, breaking it loose and leaving it hanging from the wires that led to the dials. In the same burst the radio operator, Sergeant Delehanty, at the left waist gun, was beheaded and Pfc. Altman was wounded.

A second burst cut through the left wing tanks, setting the wing afire,* and the flames spread rapidly on the flowing gasoline. A third

* The ship was a B–17C. Its tanks were not self-sealing.

attack cut the elevator cables, and the ship plunged in a steep dive under full power. By this time the fire had broken through into the body of the plane and was obviously beyond control. After a quick consultation, Kelly ordered the crew to bail out. Bean and Levin tried to open the bottom emergency hatch but found the pins corroded and only after great difficulty were able to remove one and pry the hatch part way open. Levin went first and just as Bean left, he saw Robins, the co-pilot, moving towards the top escape hatch. The ship blew up a moment after Bean's chute had opened. He counted four other chutes as he started floating down, and then he saw the Japanese fighters that had attacked the plane sweep round and come in to strafe him and the other crewmen in their chutes. The planes were painted the same pale green as the fighters Bean had seen taking off at Aparri, and he realized that the Japanese must have been stalking them all through the homeward flight, using the undercast for cover, except for an occasional peep out.

The Japanese pilots made three passes at the men hanging helpless in their chutes and then made off when a P-40 from Clark Field headed over to investigate. Bean was the only man hit in these attacks, his ankle being chipped by a bullet as the last Japanese pilot bored in to within 30 or 40 feet of him. He was nearly three hours rounding up the other members of the crew after they got down, but he could find no sign of Kelly or Robins.

Robins, however, had been blown clear of the plane in the explosion and had automatically pulled his ripcord. He was picked up by an ambulance from Clark Field, badly burned, his face, hands, and clothes completely black.

The wreckage of the plane was found scattered along a little country road about two miles west of Mount Arayat. Kelly's body lay close by, his chute unopened.*

* This account is based closely on Lt. Bean's, with occasional reference to the report of the flight made to the Commanding General, FEAF, February 19, 1942, and Kelly's posthumous citation for the D.S.C. (GO 48, USAFFE, December 21, 1941). Also to those of other officers present at Clark Field when the crew were brought in. In view of the extraordinary publicity given Kelly for this mission, it might not be inappropriate to list the others in the crew. They were: co-pilot, 2nd Lt. Donald D. Robins; navigator, 2nd Lt. Joe M. Bean; bombardier, Cpl. Meyer Levin; gunners, S/Sgt. William J. Delehanty; Sgt. James E. Halkyard; Pfc. Robert E. Altman; Pfc. Willard L. Money.

Two more individual missions to Aparri, by Lieutenants Wheless and Pease,[3] neither productive of confirmed results, completed the bombing record of the 19th Group on December 10.* The total of accomplishment had not been great, and it was offset still further by the loss of two B-17s. But some lessons were being learned. The fact that the Japanese were well aware of the blind spot of the B-17Cs and Ds, their most determined attacks being made from the rear, emphasized the necessity of holding formation over hostile territory. The loss of Kelly's plane in sight of Clark Field was a pointed demonstration. Then, also, they found out that bombing a moving vessel, from altitude, in turbulent air, even with the Norden bombsight, was a vastly different proposition from hitting a stationary circle on the training grounds at Muroc, California. They were beginning to learn about the weather, which

The report to the Commanding General, FEAF, is very circumstantial and credits Kelly with opening the seams of the battleship ("more on the starboard than the port side," though how that was observed from nearly four miles is not detailed) and causing its beaching. The basis of these claims is debatable. According to Bean, the explosion was a large one but not so loud as to make one believe the magazine had been fired. Robins at the time reportedly did not think they had sunk the *Haruna* (actually it was neither the *Haruna* nor any other battleship, for the Japs used none in these landings). There were strange auspices over the mission, beginning with the incredible good luck of finding a big ship virtually alone, which sent up no flak and took no evasive action. Flak from the distant ships was too inaccurate to be a disturbing factor. Levin, one of the best bombardiers in the Group, enjoyed the unique opportunity of a ten-minute run. It was good bombing, and he deserved equal credit with Kelly but received relatively little notice in comparison. Then after the initial good fortune there is the triumphant return from the mission, with death all the while stalking under the clouds. But compared to other sorties of that day, Montgomery's, for instance, or O'Donnell's, or Schaetzel's, its chief distinction was the fact that the pilot lost his plane and his life. Actual results were inferior to those achieved by fellow pilots without fanfare by the engine chorus of the press and press relations. This is no discredit to Kelly, who was a superior officer and pilot; but it was senseless procedure, adversely affecting the morale of fine units and justifiable only in that it produced heroes for public distraction from the fact that our armed forces had precious little else but courage left to fight with.

* At about 11:30 A.M., five PBYs of Patwing Ten, under Lt. Comdr. J. V. Peterson, attacked a Japanese battleship, believed to be the *Kongo,* in the China Sea about 300 miles west of Manila. It was one of a task force consisting of two battleships, two heavy cruisers, and four big destroyers. They got three or four direct hits on the stern, stopped her dead, while the other ships ran off, abandoning her. (Peterson's Report, as directly quoted in KARIG & KELLEY, 151 ff.) Patrols sent out later failed to find her. Two PBYs were shot down in these patrols. On December 12, the Japanese surprised seven PBYs on the water at Olongapo and destroyed all. On December 15 the eleven PBYs remaining in Luzon were sent out southward into the N. E. I., where they operated chiefly thereafter, though they were still to fly a few dramatic and extremely hazardous missions back to the Philippines and even, in the very last days, to Corregidor itself.

Dec. 10

Dec. 10

Aparri
Gonzaga

Dec. 10

Vigan

Tuguegarao

SEQUENCE OF
JAPANESE
LANDINGS ON
THE ISLAND OF
LUZON
DECEMBER 1941

Dec. 22

Dec. 22
Lingayen
Gulf

San Fernando

Baguio

Rosales

Tarlac

Iba
Ft. Stotsenburg

Clark Field

LUZON

San Fernando

BATAAN

Manila
Ft.
McKinley

Dec. 24
Dec. 23

CORREGIDOR

Dec. 24

Nasugbu—Mauban
Lucena
Batangas

Atimonan

Dec. 27

MINDORO

Legaspi

Dec. 11

MASBATE

could close in within half an hour, blanketing the target that had been reported open when a mission took off. They were also revising their conceptions of the Japanese Air Force.

The small accomplishment was less a discredit to the air crews than an example of the disorganization of the Air Force command. Combs, it is true, had been dispatched with five planes; but the handling of the 14th Squadron is hard to understand. They were originally supposed to stage from Clark; but at the last moment, when O'Donnell was coming in to land, actually with his flaps down, they were waved away to San Marcelino, which had neither food nor quarters for the men nor facilities for the planes and on which a landing had to be made in the dark, on an undeveloped strip, without lights, and under fire of friendly but unwarned troops. It is difficult to see what greater risks could have been run by continuing on in to Clark, where during the dark hours the entire Squadron could have been loaded, or, if necessary, the crews could have loaded their own planes, to fly a full squadron mission to Aparri in the morning. Instead, next day, three planes were kept roaming the air, bombless, for hours and finally returned to Del Monte unused, and the planes that were permitted to land at Clark were compelled, because of the fear of daylight raids, to make individual attacks, two of them, as related, without full bomb loads. It was incomprehensible procedure. Many of the pilots were articulate about it at the time; some of those surviving still are.

However, it was water over the dam. Another fact was made bitterly apparent that morning. Five B-17s, a squadron of P-40s, and seven obsolescent P-35s had badly disrupted the Japanese landing at Vigan. The men who had been there realized how little additional air strength would have been required to roll the Japanese off the beaches and out to sea. The missing dive bombers of the 27th Bombardment Group, for instance, could have had a field day with the Japanese transports that morning. But as it was, the Japanese were only checked. By the time ground troops could be brought up, they were well established. At Aparri they had made good their landing with virtually no resistance *

* It is interesting to note that in his book Wainwright places the landing at Aparri on December 12. He also says, "They were combated by one B-17." He made no effort to strike the Japanese there as he knew that they could be better contained at the Belete Pass, which

and, having acquired an airfield there, were in a position to use land-based aircraft on Luzon.

The 19th Group was now forced back on Del Monte. The missions of December 10 were the last pulled by American bombers out of Clark or any other field on Luzon for over three years. But Del Monte itself obviously could not long be used as a base, for it had no depot or servicing facilities. And as events proved, only two missions were to be flown from it directly before the 19th Group was once more forced back, this time to Australia. Thereafter Del Monte had to be used as a staging base for missions originating from Batchelor Field or Java.

For December 10 also marked the end of interception by the 24th Pursuit Group. In the hours immediately succeeding noon, the Japanese launched their heaviest air drive against our installations, and when the sun went down, American fighter strength had been reduced to a bare 30 planes.

18. *The End of Interception*

THE STRAFING ATTACK on Del Carmen in which the 34th Squadron had suffered such a heavy blow was a mere preliminary diversion to the main Japanese attacks. But it paid them twice over: both in the destruction of the P–35s and also by flushing the pursuit at Clark a good half hour before the big attacks were due, during which time they were using up their gas. Clark Field was alerted at 12:28 * and all planes

was their only egress south from the Cagayan Valley, and where he had one of his battalions well dug in.[9]

* There is again some discrepancy in accounts of the time of the main raids. Obert and Posten both fix it at 1:00 P.M., which seems to fit in with Dyess's time of 12:28 for the alert at Clark. Rowe, however, remembers it as being nearly 2:00. *The 27th Reports* says "shortly after noon." But Gerrity says 11:30; Ind puts it at 11:00; and the 24th Pursuit Group Narrative says the alert came at 11:15. According to Dyess, the pilots at Clark were told they had two minutes before the Japs were due. In the rush to take off, the field became a single solid cloud of dust. Dyess himself found that he had forgotten his goggles and chute and flew into combat without them. As he broke clear of the dust into the brilliant sunlight, he found his plane almost touching wings with another P–40. It was Wagner. "He laughed like a hyena. I laughed too—rather shakily, I think—then we pulled apart."[1]

were immediately ordered into the air, the 21st and 17th Squadrons taking off together in mixed flights.[2] Only a few pilots managed to reach Del Carmen in time to intercept the Japanese force there, but they did well, shooting down four of the enemy and scattering the rest.[*] It was short-lived triumph.

When the Japanese came, they were in very heavy force. The first wave of bombers alone had cover from some 40 fighters; and the total fighter strength thrown by the Japanese over central Luzon that afternoon exceeded what our own Air Force could put in the air by at least 100 planes.[†] The American pursuit did not number more than 46 P-40s.[‡] But in spite of Naval reports that there was no fighter opposition to the Japanese attacks of December 10, every plane that could fly was in the air above Manila or Manila Bay.[6] Only two flights, however, were able to break through the Japanese fighter screen [7] to attack the bombers.

The Japanese had chosen their time well. The second shift of the standing patrol from Nichols was just ending its three-hour trick and was due to land in the next few minutes for relief and refueling. Their gas was nearly used up: some planes had enough left for fifteen minutes' combat, but others had barely enough for ten. Several of the pilots were finishing their sixth consecutive hour on patrol without relief,[8] and they were glad to return to base. They were on their way in when, hearing the Nichols Field control tower come in on their headsets to warn them of the approach of enemy formations, they looked back.

The bombers, in three formations of 27 each, were following the inner shore of Manila Bay down from the north. They were high up, almost 20,000 feet, and far above the level of the returning P-40 patrol. The

---

[*] 2nd Lt. Carl P. Gies shot down two. Lt. Allison W. Strauss and 2nd Lt. Edwin B. Gilmore each counted one.[3]

[†] Estimates of the size of the bombing formations vary, but Naval observation and Rowe put it at over 50 bombers. Obert says more than 60 were in each of the two formations, and Vance is inclined to confirm his figure.[4]

[‡] The 17th Squadron started the day with 18 planes, lost two; 2nd Lt. Morgan S. McCowan crashed his plane into a tree at Clark to avoid hitting men on the ground; 2nd Lt. Gies's plane was too badly shot up in the brush at Del Carmen for further use. The 21st still had, presumably, twelve. The Nichols patrol had about 18, according to Krieger, but Rowe says it had only ten. The last figure would lower the total to 38 P-40s.[5]

sky was now almost cloudless over city and bay; and every detail of streets and rivers, docks, airfields, and Naval Base was clearly etched in the still afternoon air. The approach of the enemy bombers, at their great height, must have seemed slow, almost leisurely, to men standing in the streets; they looked bird-sized; but no birds could have matched the precise formation of their silver wings, which the Japanese pilots maintained with characteristic and inexorable perfection.

Cutting in from a more westerly angle and at much lower altitude was another and slightly smaller force of pursuit planes and light bombers. They were heading towards Cavite. In the instant of seeing them, the patrol pilots saw also the puffs of antiaircraft fire from the Naval Base, black and white against the sky, and suddenly the unruffled, deep blue water of the bay was laced by the wakes of boats escaping from the docks.

Their eyes accumulated these details during a few brief seconds of nightmarish suspension of the other senses. Then Lieutenant Feallock, who was leading one flight of the patrol, called the Nichols tower to report their low reserve of gas and ask instructions. The tower told him to use his own judgment, so he called in the other pilots, asking whether in their opinion the interception ought to be attempted, in the hope of doing some damage before their tanks ran dry, or whether they should try to save their planes by running for an outlying air strip. They all decided to attack, and the patrol began the long climb back towards the formation of bombers, which was now deliberately wheeling on Cavite.

They never got upstairs, for suddenly the sky around them filled with Zeros, and their small formation was broken into a dozen dogfights—each P-40 with its individual swarm of enemy pursuit. The fight tumbled back and forth across the Manila sky at furious speed for nearly fifteen minutes, before the P-40s began coughing dry of gas. By then they had come down well below 5000 feet and the citizens of the outer Manila suburbs were able to watch aerial combat at housetop level. The patrol did well in its few minutes of action, but no flier made any claims for ships shot down. The action was so fast that a pilot could not see what became of the ship he had last shot at: he went straight for the next one in his sights, or else he found some Zeros clamped on his own tail.*

All of the patrol were shot up, but most of them crashed from lack of gas. A few succeeded in reaching Clark Field; the rest came down anywhere they could, in small fields, roads, or the shallow waters of Manila Bay. Members of the 17th and 21st Squadrons, joining in the fight from Clark Field, found themselves carried as much as 100 miles across the Luzon sky.† Three pilots were killed, at least eight more crashed or bailed out.‡ They downed more Zeros than they lost P-40s, but against such odds that was not enough. The Japanese bomber pilots were able to complete their runs entirely without interference.

They did not even have to worry about antiaircraft fire. There were only 15 antiaircraft guns for the whole Manila area. Four of these were Army, in the triangle formed by Nichols and Nielson Fields and Fort McKinley, all of which they were supposed to cover.[9] The Navy had nine 3-inch guns at Cavite.[10] But none of them, because of their antique, powder-fused ammunition, had range enough to reach the altitude at which the heavy bombers were approaching; and civilians in the streets, as well as Army and Navy men at their posts, watched the harmless

* The speed at which this action was fought is illustrated by the experience of one pilot. The fight had come down to 5000 feet when he got in his first good shot and saw the Zero stagger and fall off. Just then his own plane was hit from astern. He half-rolled and during the maneuver looked at the tail of his plane. It had a large shell hole through it, and he wondered why it stayed on. An Immelmann turn threw the Jap off and when the American rolled out he found two Japs dead in his sights. Just as he was going to pull the trigger, his engine quit. He dove quickly with the two Zeros fast on his tail. They hit him again as he banked and his ship rolled on its back and started to spin. He had no idea how he got out of the spin at that low level; he was sure his time was up; but when the ship came out of it, it was practically dragging its belly in the water of a little creek. The engine coughed back to life for a few brief instants and he lit out up the creek between some houses and trees, with the Zeros peppering away behind and hanging on all the time. The metal of his fuselage was peeling forward with the volume of their fire and it wasn't long till the plane wasn't any more good. When the engine quit entirely, he remembered the chute, pulled up in a stall, and bailed out at about 500 feet, with the Japs chasing him all the way to the ground. Filipino farmers armed with pitchforks, bolos, and antique muskets picked him up and took him to a house where they forced two half pints of their liquor on him. The liquor was more lethal than their guns but it never caught up with him.

† 2nd Lt. John Posten did not break off his fight till he had gone clear over Subic Bay and then barely made it back to Clark Field.

‡ Killed were Lt. Glen M. Alder, 2nd Lts. F. M. Holbrecht and R. M. Root. Among those shot down or crashing with dry tanks were Lts. W. J. Feallock, R. M. Gehrig, and 2nd Lts. A. E. Krieger, G. S. Benson, and J. A. Phillips.

bursting of the shells a thousand feet and more under the oncoming formation and realized the terrible extent of their helplessness. The guns were kept working, but it was only when the dive bombers or strafing pursuit came in low that they were able to draw blood.

The big bombers stayed up out of reach. They wheeled over the Manila docks and dropped one stick across the shipping now frantically trying to clear the breakwater into the open bay. Only one ship was hit, but the planes weren't really concerned with shipping. They kept on towards Nichols and Cavite. They took their time. Their bombing was deliberate. Now and then they held their bombs to make a second or even a third run on the target, as if the lead bombardier wasn't satisfied with his aim. There was nothing, after all, to prevent their making as many runs as they chose.

Within fifteen minutes, the first wave of heavy bombers was followed by a second, equally large, equally deliberate, and equally effective in their bombing. Nichols Field was fairly well smashed up; and this attack, combined with one two days later, practically destroyed its effectiveness as an air base. The bombs were dropped in train. They started at the outer edge of the field, near the sluice by the engineer barracks, and came on across, blowing everything in a solid pattern as they reached the installations. The main hangar and the Philippine Air Depot were gutted. Several planes were burned on the ground.* The big fuel tanks were hit, sending out great rolls of black smoke that spread heavily over the whole area. Working under this pall, the men on the base could hear and feel the bombs falling on Cavite.

Cavite was completely wiped out. Shipyard facilities, barracks, hospitals, warehouses, all went down under the weight of bombs. The loss of life was heavy; it would have been calamitous but for the fact that the shipyard workers had been excused that day to move their families to safer areas. As it was, the fires spread so rapidly that many people were

---

* Among these planes was one of the three B–18s originally scheduled to attack the Japanese landing at Vigan. The other two had been ordered off the field at an earlier alarm, but the third, with a dead right engine, was caught by the first strafers and blown up by the explosion of its own bombs. Ind implies that many planes were destroyed on the field and gives a detailed description of his visit there two days later, with broken planes everywhere about. Obert and Krieger both say that there was negligible damage to planes, but it is likely that their minds were mainly concerned with pursuit.[11]

trapped in the burning buildings. A submarine and mine sweeper were lost; another submarine, docked for repairs, was towed to safety, as was the destroyer *Peary,* which thus took another step along the unhappy course that ended finally in Darwin. Only the Ammunition Depot remained. Fires had raged on three sides of it, but it was saved, almost miraculously, through the efforts of the base personnel directed by Admiral Rockwell.

This demonstration of Japanese superiority in the air was enough to convince Naval officials that surface ships could no longer hope to operate in or near Manila Bay. Their decision to withdraw to the south was fortified by the loss on the same day of the British battleships *Repulse* and *Prince of Wales,* off Kuantan, Malaya, also as the result of Japanese air attack. Without their heavy guns the odds against the little Asiatic Fleet became even greater, and the following night Admiral Hart ordered two destroyers and two submarine tenders and five auxiliary vessels to safer waters. They slipped away in the darkness and with them went nearly 200,000 tons of merchant shipping. The submarines were to stay on till the end of December, as were the destroyers *Peary* and *Pillsbury*. The PBYs continued to operate out of Manila and Olongapo until December 14, when the remaining serviceable ships, amounting to less than a squadron, were also ordered to the East Indies.

Four damaged PBYs were repaired, and these continued to be based near Manila till Christmas Eve. But the P-T boats stayed on through the Bataan fighting, and so did the old submarine tender *Canopus,* four mine sweepers, and three little gunboats. They operated mainly from Corregidor and the little port of Mariveles on the tip of Bataan. It was a tiny force, relatively as small as Colonel George's Air Force was to be; but it also played a stirring part in the defense of Bataan and Corregidor.

The Air Force, of course, had not yet come under Colonel George's command, nor would it for two weeks more. It was still under FEAF when they reckoned up their balance after three days of war.

On the night of December 10, they had a total first-line strength of 18 B-17s, which were scattered on five different fields and of which twelve at most could be presumed fit for combat,* and 30 pursuit. But

---

* At CLARK FIELD were: *Bohnaker* (whose ship had been flown by both Young and Pease), *Connally, Carpenter* (whose ship would soon be hit by a crashing P-40), and

only 22 of the pursuit planes were P–40s; the remaining eight were the nearly worn-out P–35s.

Then there was the Philippine Air Corps's 6th Squadron, which had been led into combat that afternoon by Captain Villamor against Japanese bombers over Zablan Field; * but it was obvious that their antiquated little P–26s could not hope to compete in the same league with even the poorest Japanese fighter planes. A few B–18s survived, some odd transport ships, and a miscellany of primary trainers and observation types too obsolete to have been used in any capacity, though some of them were soon to perform heroic service. The 2nd Observation Squadron's more modern O–52s and O–46s had either been destroyed by enemy action or so seriously damaged as to be useless. With the Japanese steadily moving in at Vigan and Aparri, the need of aerial reconnaissance was becoming hourly more vital; and, as it was evident the continued use of the few remaining pursuit planes to intercept vastly superior forces would result in their quick extermination, General Headquarters decided that they must be reserved for observation, and the order came down through FEAF that evening that no more combat missions would be flown.

There was a good deal of resentment among the pilots, who felt that they were just beginning to get the measure of the enemy.† How-

Coats (whose plane had survived the attack on Clark Field). At DEL MONTE were: *Tash* (still under repair), *Adams* (who had brought a repaired plane from Clark Field and who was to crash into Tash's plane, seriously damaging both ships), *Chiles* (replacing Shedd), *Parsel, Teats, Keiser, O'Donnell, Smith,* and *Wheless.* At SAN MARCELINO were *Godman* and *Schaetzel,* who left for Del Monte at 11.00 P.M., but Schaetzel went into Cebu on a false report that the Japs had Del Monte and had to wait there two days for a new aileron cable. At TACLOBAN (Leyte) was *Vandevanter.* At SAN JOSE (Mindoro) were *Combs* and *Ford,* who had picked up a similar report. Combs knew the Islands well from an earlier tour of duty and remembered the little field beside a sugar Central run by a man named Obregat. The Obregats opened their house to the fliers, who enjoyed their first and last hot baths and good meals for many days.

* Capt. Jesus A. Villamor. On December 10, Capt. Villamor led three P–26s into action against Japanese bombers and broke up their formation. Villamor received the D.S.C. and general credit for shooting down one bomber.[12]

† One of the chief hazards faced by pilots of P–40E airplanes during these first days of war had been the continual gun failure and the fact that the guns could not be charged in flight by means of the wing gun-charging system installed in every P–40E. This was due to orders received from the Matériel Division a few weeks before the war by the Philippine National Air Depot, then assembling the planes, and by squadrons that accepted delivery, to disconnect the wing charging systems. No explanation was given. This meant that time and again a pilot took off on a combat mission and found after clearing his guns

ever, since observation planes were permitted to defend themselves, a good deal of latitude developed in the interpretation of the word "attack" and several noteworthy, if minor, actions were to develop out of routine reconnaissance.

Yet, by and large, the pattern of the air war on Luzon had been established. The Japanese superiority was acknowledged, and even the most hidebound military reactionaries in Manila must at last have been able to read the handwriting on the wall.

that only three, two, or even none would fire and could take no corrective measures unless he returned to an airfield where the guns could be recharged by hand. After three or four days, pilots began reconnecting the systems and used them with no ill effect to the gun mechanism; but how many had died as a result of this unaccountable order, or how many planes were needlessly lost, cannot be accurately estimated. That the effect on pilots' morale was dreadful only a fool could deny.[13]

V

Interlude: The Philippine Scene

19. *Air Taxi*

ONLY PEOPLE UNDER ATTACK can ever understand the full disorder of war. It is indiscriminate; it finds the cracks in civilization; and like disease it seems to feed upon itself. Sometimes also it does odd things. In Manila, after the third day, it affected even the dead.

These weren't the new dead only, like those whose charred and swollen bodies lay beneath creeping blankets of flies in the ruins of Cavite or the burned-out rubble of native barrios set afire by the incendiary bullets of a casually strafing Japanese pilot. *They* were soon accustomed sights to people in the central provinces. Even the little boys who stood on the backs of carabao submerged in the gray mud wallows and looked up to see the sudden silver glitter of bombs squirted like water from the belly slits of the high bombers could understand how such dead came to be. But there were also the older, dignified, and buried dead in Grace Park Cemetery who now had to share the elaborate sanctuary of their tombs and monuments with the transport planes of the Philippine Air Lines.

A little over a year before war broke out there had been two air lines in the Islands. The Philippine Air Taxi Company, the older line, called "Patco," had for General Manager and Senior Pilot a man named William R. Bradford. Bradford had long foreseen and been articulate about the threat to the Philippines. By 1940, recognizing its imminence, he advised his company against expanding, and instead, in September of that year, Patco suspended operations and Bradford himself went into the Air Force, first as Base Engineer at Nichols Field and later, on the organization of FEAF, as Technical Inspector for the Air Service Command under Colonel Churchill. At that time he was undoubtedly the most experienced pilot in the Philippines. In his ten years of service with Patco he had flown about 5000 hours—the equivalent of seven solid months of flying time—and his knowledge of the Islands was both wide and intimate. Towards the end of the Bataan campaign, he not only staked his life many times on this knowledge, but many other men besides were to depend on it and his flying skill. However, that lay with the future. In the meantime, Patco's franchise was bought in by the Philippine Air Lines.

Paul I. Gunn, the operations manager of this younger company, was another flier of unusual skill and experience, and practically unlimited resourcefulness. He had put in twenty-one years' service with the Navy and Marines; but he was a domestic man in his instincts, and when he came out to Manila in 1939, he brought his wife and four children, two daughters and two sons, with him. In 1941 he was not very widely known, outside of air line circles. He was then forty-one years old, a tall, thin man, with steady blue eyes in a deeply tanned face, deliberate in his speech and slow in movement. When he joined the Air Force the day after war started, it was natural for the younger pilots to think of him as an old-timer. They called him "Pappy" Gunn, and it was by that name that men all over the Southwest Pacific theater of operations came to know him. Few men out there had as wide celebrity. Certainly no man fought more indefatigably to beat the Japanese, and probably no man under General rank contributed more through his individual efforts to beating them. Like Grant Mahony, Pappy Gunn governed himself as though there were two wars against Japan: the one the United States had on its hands, and his own. He fought them both.

The first thing Gunn had to find was a safe field for his six transport planes to operate from. They were two-engined Beechcraft, small, light, fairly fast, but completely unarmed. There wasn't enough antiaircraft to go round among the military installations, so it was obvious that the planes of the Philippine Air Lines weren't likely to get any protection. What Gunn needed was a place where the Japanese wouldn't think of looking for an airfield; and that gave him the line that led him ultimately to Grace Park Cemetery.

It lies in the northern districts of the city. Its western slope is entirely a Chinese section; and here stand the tombs of the wealthy dead, elaborate, templelike structures, large enough to mark the whole area as a burial place even from high altitude. The airfield of the Philippine Air Taxi Company used to be on the higher ground behind this Chinese section, but little by little the cemetery had grown round and finally absorbed the field entirely, incorporating the old cinder runways in the pattern of its driveways. All Gunn had to do was knock down a few of the tombs and monuments that might have clipped the wings of his planes. He figured that the Japanese, being a superstitious race who stand in awe of death, would not molest a graveyard. He was right. He never lost a plane on this airdrome.

Here, at first, he set up operations without any fanfare, carrying passengers out to Zamboanga, Davao, or Del Monte, all in Mindanao. Sometimes instead of passengers his planes flew food down to the 5th Air Base Unit at Del Monte—Gunn himself took turkeys down to the men there to provide them with their Christmas dinner, but that was to be the next to the last trip he made to Mindanao from Luzon. Most of the time he was carrying passengers when he went south. He never knew who they all were. It seemed as though there were an awful lot of colonels that "wanted south" after December 10. He did not know what became of them beyond the fact that most got aboard ship at Zamboanga or Davao, at least before Davao was closed by the Japanese landing on December 20. He didn't care, for that matter. He wanted to stay on the ground as little as possible and, once he had unloaded, he would set right out on the return trip.

He had only two American pilots: Captains Harold G. Slingsby and Louis J. Connelly.* Two of his men had returned to the States before the war, and just before it broke the fifth had gone over to Hongkong with CNAC. His Filipino pilots were good; but Gunn kept the toughest assignments for himself and Connelly and Slingsby. It put a heavy load on the three men; and when the real push to get out of Luzon

* Gunn and Slingsby almost miraculously came through the war and are now back in the States. Connelly was killed on his first mission over Lae.

developed, Gunn was making two round trips a day to southern ports, sometimes flying over 2000 miles without relief. The Army called on the Philippine Air Lines for other jobs also, one of which was flying the payroll over all the Islands: to Cebu, Del Monte, Tacloban, Iloilo, Legaspi, Masbate, Cotobato, Davao, Zamboanga, Dipolo (Mindanao), and Dansalan, where the Navy had some PBYs.

All these flights were under constant threat of enemy attack. It made no difference. They took to flying as close to the ground or sea as was humanly possible. In many of these flights, Gunn never took his plane above 500 feet. Usually he flew around 100 feet, especially in enemy territory and over the sea, the object being to fly low enough to keep the enemy from picking up his shadow. And a plane that close was hard to see and hard to hit. People who knew what they were doing began to look for their planes every evening, homing to Manila. They would come in, skimming the treetops and the roofs, suddenly bank, and go down on the runways. Their flying skill was enormous. They got to know the land and the valleys and the Southern Luzon mountains as a woodsman knows his woods. Gunn's mechanics claimed that he would come in with leaves and seaweed on the belly of his ship.

Under the Army they organized regular missions for flying in drugs and medical supplies—probably these were the first courier missions in the Southwest Pacific. They took serum and vaccine up to the front lines near Lingayen. "They would go any place. They were utterly intrepid."

Bradford flew some of these missions. He and Connelly and especially Gunn were the most active in this transport service. They lost only one plane in the air.* The Japs sprang it in the narrow valley that cuts across the eastern end of Cebu. Gunn was alone in the plane, on his way back from Del Monte. It was December 13, the day the Japanese first bombed Cebu City. Maybe he was just a little careless. The Zeros jumped him off the flank of the mountains and the Beechcraft was all shot up. He got away by getting it down almost to grass level and he nursed it all the way back to Luzon, threading the valleys and heading straight for Grace Park. His course brought him across Zablan Field,

* A second was shot up on the ground on Bataan Field. The other four were all used in evacuating FEAF and key personnel to Australia.

which was the home field of the Philippine Army Air Corps, and the Filipinos let loose at him with all their .30- and .50-caliber machine guns. The plane was barely limping before they hit him, and he knew that he couldn't make it in to Grace Park, so he tried to come in over Nichols Field and crash-landed there in the blackout, about 11:00 o'clock.

These missions seem haphazard, almost inconsequential, now, against the larger pattern of the developing war. But out of his ground flying, Gunn brought the seeds of an idea that germinated later in the conversion of A–20 bombers to strafing purposes by installing four .50-caliber machine guns in the nose.* The A–20s, shooting up the Kokoda Trail, helped save Port Moresby; and out of them came the idea of converting B–25s in the same way. One can almost say that in these early unarmed flights at wave level was the beginning of the battle of the Bismarck Sea.

In Australia, also, Gunn and his tiny organization formed the start of what became the Air Transport Command; but as that branch of the Air Corps slowly grew down under, Bill Bradford developed a strange scarecrow version of the same thing for Bataan in its last days, the organization known as the Bamboo Fleet.

Both men must be remembered.

20. *Bush League Air Force*

THE FILIPINOS on Zablan Field who had cut loose when Pappy Gunn came limping home through the dark felt entitled to shoot at anything that flew in range. The Japanese had combed them pretty thoroughly that day: first with a low-level strafing attack that came so suddenly they had no chance to get into the air; then the Japs had dive-bombed them, using antipersonnel bombs that exploded 50 feet above the ground and umbrellaed down, so for the second time the base personnel had had their noses in the dirt; and finally the heavy bombers had come over at 30,000

---

* Attack bombers were not Gunn's invention. As Col. Vance has pointed out, the 3rd Attack Group, which became the 3rd Bomber Group, was flying low attack missions in the Louisiana Maneuvers in August 1941. But as we shall see, Gunn was at work adapting the A–20 in the early summer of 1942, though it was only when General Kenney arrived that real development of the A–20 as a strafing plane took place.[1]

feet and let go a stick of big ones obviously intended to yank Zablan Field and everything on it up by the roots. The fact that the Japanese misjudged the strength of the ground wind and that the bombs reached just beyond the field seemed only mildly palliative. The concussion had tossed men around like chips, and when they picked themselves up for the third time that day they were annoyed, frustrated, and pretty well disgusted, for by then practically every man on the base had heard about the magazine article one of the pilots had brought in. It was called "Japan's Bush League Air Force" [1] and it belonged to the school of American self-advertisement that gained part of its effects through belittling the achievement of other nations, especially unfriendly ones.

If this was the bush league, then no one at Zablan Field wanted to get a look at the big time. They had seen what the bush leaguers could do to other fields as well as Zablan. The great rolls of smoke towering above Nichols and Cavite in the southwest had been visible by day; at night there was the red glow under the clouds. And at night also Manila was regularly alight with the flares and rockets of the Japanese sympathizers.

The men at Zablan could do nothing about that. Their business was to fly; but they labored under a continual sense of frustration, which is one of the most difficult handicaps any soldier has to contend with. Their pilots had been trained to defend their country in the air; but they did not have the weapons to do it with and must, instead, watch a few American pilots carry the burden they felt was properly their own. At maximum performance, the old P–26s they had inherited were little better than training planes. The worn engines could hardly be expected to produce even the 230 miles per hour they were supposed to, and they had only two .30-caliber guns to shoot with. Against the Japanese air attack they were blown aside like bees in a hurricane.

But they still managed to sting, and what their machines lacked in power, the pilots made up by their own fire. On the December 10 raid against Zablan, when Captain Jesus A. Villamor led three P–26s against an attacking Japanese formation, Lieutenant Jose Gozar picked himself out a bomber. But on his first pass his guns jammed. Instead of breaking off, however, Gozar tried to ram the bomber. Two or three of his rushes proved all the Japanese pilot could stand. He pulled foot and, seeing him go, the other Japs characteristically took after him.[2]

Then on December 12, over Batangas Field, 56 miles to the south of Manila, Villamor took six of his P-26s up against 54 Japanese bombers. When he saw the first Japanese flight coming over, Villamor said, "I felt afraid, but I went upstairs anyway. Then I saw the second flight of 27 planes, and I thought they were Americans, and I said to myself, 'This is going to be a heck of a good fight.'" But they were Japs. That made him so mad he went right for them and the rest of the boys went with him.

The Jap bombers had a covering force of Zeros but, before the latter could drive off the P-26s, Villamor had shot down one bomber and scattered the rest. Then the Zeros were on them. One of the Filipinos was wounded and took to his chute, and Lieutenant C. M. Basa was killed when seven Japanese planes ganged on his slower ship and just rode him into the ground.[8]

That encounter more or less finished the career of the Philippine Army Air Corps in the air. Thereafter, like the 24th Pursuit Group, they were given reconnaissance work. Half their planes were detailed for Northern Luzon at Clark Field under General Wainwright's orders, and the rest worked out of their own field of Zablan under General Parker. They did not fly the extended patrols the P-40s did, but worked in close to the Infantry, hedgehopping, and using every stitch of natural cover they could find. When orders for the withdrawal to Bataan came through on December 24, they still had six P-26s and twelve Basic Trainers in serviceable shape, but to their chagrin they were ordered to destroy them together with all installations. This unfortunate order was only a part of the wild confusion of the Air Force High Command; but to the Philippine Army Air Corps, it was sheer tragedy.

21. *Moonlight Parlor*

THE AIR BASE PERSONNEL at Del Monte were glad to get the turkey Pappy Gunn flew down to them before Christmas, for they had precious little else. Food had begun to run short long before then, and bread had been scarce almost from the start. Practically all they had was corn willy and pineapple which appeared three times a day. The mess sergeants tried fixing pineapple to taste different. They served it broiled, fried, baked, and stewed but they found that the flavor of pineapple is a rugged thing; it can be fooled with but it can't be licked. Some of the men began having dreams. When they weren't eating it, they were looking at it—acres and acres of planted pineapples.

In their isolation the war, during those first two days, had a queer sense of unreality for some of them. It was only when the B–17s came back from the raids of December 10 that the men around the field understood a little of what had happened at Clark and began to realize what it might add up to for themselves. But others of them were even more out of touch, working on the construction of four subsidiary fields at Dalirig, Impasugong, Palais, and Tigitip.[1] For these men, the sound of engines and the sight of one of the big Fortresses breaking down out of the over-cast and heading for Del Monte was the nearest thing they had to home. But they weren't left much time to brood.

There is a lot of work to pioneering an air base in as remote a spot as Del Monte—people who haven't turned their hands to it are not apt to understand how much; and the 5th Air Base Group hadn't been given much equipment for the job. Most of the time, in fact, they were operating on a shoestring. They had one ordnance machine shop truck and one welding truck; but with these they managed to turn out an immense amount of work, both in making parts for aircraft repair, in improvising mounts for twenty .50-caliber and various .30-caliber machine guns taken out of aircraft supplies, and also in rebuilding their rolling stock. They had come down with little transportation. A few trucks were secured through civilian sources, but the problem of maintaining them soon became acute. Some of the men developed extraordinary ingenuity in adapting parts of one make to fit another, and towards the end of Del Monte's existence some strange and hybrid vehicles began to raise the dust along its roads. The most notorious of these was a cargo truck consisting of a Diamond-T motor and steering gear, a Dodge front end, a Ford rear end, a Chevrolet cab, and an Ordnance bed. It was known as the "six and seven eights."

During the early weeks the only ground troops near Del Monte were a scant battalion of Filipinos commanded by Captain Magee. Since a Japanese landing at Bugo seemed very likely, the base personnel were organized into an emergency rifle brigade, and on top of their other work held several maneuvers along the surrounding gullies and ravines. Even so, they felt very insecure, for it was some time before they could assemble the .50-caliber machine guns and install them round the field. In the beginning they were set up in individual, shallow, sandbagged pits; but later, when time permitted, deep emplacements were dug and the guns mounted almost flush with the ground. Gunners had to be trained and Sergeant Sullivan was put in charge of this department. He gained superior results from completely green hands, most of whom got the larger share of their training in actual defense of the field against strafers. They sent several Zeros away with smoking engines; and though they could not do much to damage bombers, they did shoot the float off a navy dive bomber. Sullivan himself was outstanding and completely fearless. Once, leaving his post for more ammunition in the midst of an attack, he took shrapnel in his leg so badly that he could hardly walk, but he returned to man his gun until the bombers left. They couldn't keep him in the little hospital that had been set up on the clubhouse grounds beside the golf course. He insisted on going back to his guns, feeling responsible for their performance. His name was put in for a Purple Heart when that award still stood for more than it means today. He made a strong impression on the men who served under him. "Remember old Sullivan?" one of the youngest men in the outfit said. "He was a first-class drunkard, but he was sure a pretty good shot."

This was a rhetorical statement. Opportunities for heavy drinking were scant. At first there was some Scotch to be had, for those who could afford it; later there was some bourbon and then the supply whittled down to Canadian Club. Finally there was a liquor labeled "Very Special Brandy." The men had no idea where it came from; but it was the roughest stuff anyone in the outfit had ever had. One drink would have curled the hair on a sea cow.

They found out about it when they finally got a few hours of leave to spend down on the coast. Bugo was a way station, with just the Del Monte cannery, the steamship pier, and a few houses. The men went on down the road to Cagayan, where they could get fried chicken and pop at the "Moonlight Parlor."

This was nothing but a two-by-four shack in the middle of the town, but it became more or less of a hangout for all the enlisted men. It was run by Filipinos. The Filipinos were always wonderful to the boys. They wanted to make money out of them, of course, but they were awfully nice doing it. If a man had enough time off, he would try to work in two meals at the Moonlight Parlor. In between he would go up to the Cagayan Hotel for a bath. At Del Monte's Camp 29 there was just a little creek to bathe in, so they always tried to work in a bath in Cagayan. But it wasn't always possible, for the hotel had one bathtub and sometimes there would be a line waiting for a shot at it, and then, of course, a man never knew if the hot water was going to hold out for him. After that, if he had time, he might or might not get a haircut, but he always ended up by going over to the brewery to check up on whether any beer had come in from Cebu. No mail reached Del Monte, and somehow having beer come in from Cebu made a sort of substitute for getting mail. Then the only thing he had to make sure of was meeting his truck for the trip back. The twenty-odd mile walk uphill in the dark, with perhaps some fidgety Filipino patrols to pass on the road, was a long, tiresome, and uneasy business. But it was so hard to break away from the pleasures of Cagayan that a good few men had to walk the distance in the course of our defense of the Philippines.

Not many men, however, got leave to see Cagayan during the first weeks at Del Monte. On top of all the construction work, they had to carry on the routine air base duties, and every plane was met, its service performed, and the personal needs of the crew looked after as far as the air base's limitations permitted. Whatever their own shortages, no crew went off on a mission without a meal of hot coffee and sandwiches.*

The greatest difficulty they had to meet was camouflaging the B-17s. The air crews returning from Luzon had become rabid on the need of camouflage. There wasn't a stitch of cover at Del Monte No. 1, but there happened to be some paint and a single spray gun. Almost at the last minute before leaving Manila, Major Elsmore had discovered that the bomb trucks assigned to him were painted a poisonous and highly visible yellow. He applied for some GI paint, but he could get hold of only the

---

* Lt. Edward Bewley met every plane whatever the hour of its arrival and men still speak of the welcome sight of his spectacles and skinny frame materializing in the darkness to learn their bomb and ammunition needs and then lead the crew off to chow.

one spray gun. It was now worked twenty-four hours a day. The paint, unfortunately, was glossy and all the same shade of green. The men tried to tone it down and mix new colors to break the outlines of the planes; but the finished camouflage, according to Teats,[2] was a sorry job. Some of the planes looked vaguely green; the others were a liverish sort of brown, or just plain drab; but they still reflected sunlight, and, parked on the bare grass uplands, they could still be seen in bright weather from a long way out.

It was obvious that further means of camouflage would have to be found. They went down to Cagayan and bought up fishnets. But the fishnets did not work out very well, for it took too long to set them over the ships and tie in foliage. So a crew of Filipinos were organized to go down to Bugo and cut coconut palm fronds along the beaches with a crew of air base people supervising and trucking the fronds in. Ten truckloads were needed to cover one B–17; the 18-mile haul was up steep and winding roads; and the fronds had to be supplied fresh every third day. It became an almost unending job just to keep the planes covered while they were on base. The finished job looked odd from the ground, but it turned out to be effective from the air during the short remaining days of the 19th Group's stay.

They were to fly only two more attack missions while based at Del Monte No. 1.

22. *Mission to Legaspi*

ON THE MORNING of December 12, 16 B–17s, in their new and peculiar war paint, were parked around the bare Del Monte field,* but only six of them were ready to go. The combat crews had put in a full day and a good part of a rainy night trying to get them in shape. Officers and men worked together under the direction of the crew engineers, who now

---

* Lt. Schaetzel was still on Cebu; but the others had returned during the morning of December 11. Lt. Montgomery and his crew had been fetched back from Zamboanga by Majs. C. B. Whitney and W. Rotherham of the 5th Air Base Group in one of their un-armed B–18s.

were doubling as line chiefs; but they lacked the proper tools and parts. "It never occurred to them to wonder whether a job could be done. They did it, tools or no tools, in the flickering light of lanterns or the narrow spot of a flashlight." [1] The trouble was that the work took so long. They were learning the hard lesson that mechanized war, whether on the ground, at sea, or in the air, without the proper backlog of material and trained technicians, is wasteful not only of machines and men, but of time, which can never be replaced. It was not their fault. They tried to run a mission to Vigan anyway.

They were to attack Japanese shipping again and O'Donnell was to lead the flight. It produced no important or definite results and is mentioned only for the fortuitous part taken in it by Captain Combs as a step leading to the final and celebrated mission to Legaspi. There can be no better illustration of the way the men had to operate or the handicaps they worked under.

Communications with Luzon were poor. The SCR-297 radio set on which they depended for contact with Headquarters was operating beyond its maximum zone of effectiveness, and often the orders that did come through conflicted with one another.* They had only the haziest picture of what was happening north of them; and they did not yet know of the Japanese landing at Legaspi, already solidly established, a move intended to draw General MacArthur off balance and lead to the ultimate division of his forces. To add to their own problems, Filipino reports had come in that the Japanese at Davao were armed and organizing an attempt to drive north across Mindanao against Del Monte. With no proper infantry support, it looked as if the planes would have to be pulled out to Australia or Java, and the suggestion had already been radioed up to FEAF.

The take-off for Vigan was set for about 7:30 that morning; but one of the planes—the one that Lieutenant Adams had brought down—was the survivor of the Clark Field attack. It was halfway across the airfield when two engines cut out. At the end of the field is a very deep ravine, almost a canyon. The ship's hydraulic system was out, and with no brakes all Adams could hope to do was ground loop. In doing so he

* GHQ (MacArthur); FEAF, HQ (Brereton); Bomber HQ (Eubank). Col. Connally mentioned three orders coming in, all in conflict, from these three sources.

clipped the nose of another plane that had been parked close to the end of the field and broke his own in two.* So, to bring O'Donnell's flight up to something like strength, Combs took off in the sixth serviceable ship. But he never caught up with O'Donnell, who went on to Vigan, dropped his bombs, and returned to Del Monte without landing on Luzon.

Combs himself went in over the target alone at 25,000 feet. He found some Japanese destroyers, but just as he started his run a whole mess of things went wrong in the plane. First, the radio operator passed out from lack of oxygen; he had clipped his tube in closing his box. Then, when they decided to go on with their run, radio operator or not, half the bombs hung up and suddenly the bomb bay motor caught fire. But they finally got the bombs away and the fire out, and Combs immediately turned and went into a steep dive to bring the radioman to, which he fortunately did at 15,000 feet.

After all this kicking around they decided to go in to Clark Field to regas and when they landed they found they were the only B–17 on the field and base operations wanted to discourage their staying any length of time. But Combs was told to see Eubank for special instructions and then learned for the first time about the Japanese landing at Legaspi. A Japanese carrier was reported lying off the town. Eubank said that it must be hit with everything they could send, and the sooner the better. He also wanted Combs to take Major Gibbs down in his B–17. Gibbs was to take over the command at Del Monte from O'Donnell, who was to be recalled to Clark Field.† But as it turned out, Gibbs had some unfinished business he wanted to clear up; he told Combs to go along and

---

* The other plane was Tash's.

† The recall of O'Donnell, undoubtedly, came from misunderstanding on FEAF's part of the reasons behind the request to move the B–17s to Australia. The lack of facilities, the real need of maintenance work that could not be performed, were the major reasons. The threat from the Japanese at Davao was merely a final incident. But O'Donnell's recall was practically banishment since he had to assume command of what was now a ground echelon at Clark; it was unjust, as General Brereton admitted later, since if O'Donnell had a fault, it was his extreme combativeness. Moreover, when, after Gibbs's loss was manifest, Maj. Walsh was sent down, the B–17s were started out to Australia within two days. Later, in Java, O'Donnell was made G–3 of FEAF, an admission on Brereton's part that he had made a mistake and still later confirmed by O'Donnell's (now Maj. Gen.) superior performance with the B–29s of the 20th Air Force in the Marianas. But in the meantime, the air crews of the 19th Group, beset with their problems, lost a man with the kind of leadership they sorely needed.

said he would fly down later in the day in one of the B–18s. So Combs loaded a second Fortress crew aboard his plane and took off for the return flight.

They had 18 men in the ship and not enough chutes to go round, and on the way they ran into a very heavy thunderstorm. It was a storm that a B–17 could take, but not a B–18. The rain was like a wall through which the ship kept boring; the roar of it against the skin almost drowned the engines out; and the big ship was tossed all over the lot. But they got through it, and spent 45 minutes feeling their way in to Del Monte. The only lights were two flare pots, one at each end of the field, for the pilot to line up on, and in the dark and rain Combs had to take his ship down again and again before he could pick them up. In later times he would have had the crew bail out and let the ship go; but even if he had had enough chutes, it would have made no difference then, for the men realized that not only the war but literally their own lives depended on their planes, and they would go to any lengths to save them.

As soon as he had landed, Combs got hold of O'Donnell and they discussed the Legaspi mission. There was some disagreement. Combs thought they ought to hit the place at dawn with what they had; but O'Donnell wanted to put it off another day to let the crews get in more maintenance on the planes. The pouring rain had still further slowed the work for men who had to handle heavy parts with their bare hands. It was obvious to him that piecemeal attacks such as they had been making were not producing real results. But it was decided that they would send up two ships next morning on reconnaissance, and Lieutenants Bohnaker and Smith were assigned to the mission.[2] In the meantime they awaited the arrival of Major Gibbs.

But he never came. Back at Clark Field Operations had had a report of the storm encountered by Combs. It was too big to go around, for the gas load of the B–18 just permitted the run into Del Monte and back with very little leeway at either end, and they were already trying to eat into the gas reserve at Del Monte as little as possible. By this time they had worked out a regular nightly run from Clark Field to Del Monte for the B–18s to take down parts and engines salvaged from the burned-out planes; and pilots who made the run remember these flights as the roughest work they put in during the war. The lumbering old bombers had a maximum speed of only about 160 to 170 miles an hour; they were un-armed; and they weren't built to take tropical storms. The pilots sweated the trip out all the way, both down and back. They could have their choice of starting late in the day to get down to Del Monte in the dark, deliver their load, and come back to Luzon before daylight; or they could start after dark and land after sunrise. Either way they were exposed to Japanese pursuit. It was a rough choice.

When they learned that Gibbs was going to make the flight in a special plane, other pilots tried to persuade him not to take off till midnight; but, having received his orders, he was insistent on getting down as soon as possible and set departure for six that evening. The plane took off into a sunset sky. Men on the base watched it reach into the clouds. It was never seen again.

When word of Gibbs's failure to reach Del Monte came through, Major Birrell Walsh was assigned in his place and went down the fol-lowing night; and it was in this uncertainty of command that the mis-sion to Legaspi was undertaken. The carrier was known to be there, for Lieutenant Bohnaker saw it on December 13. The weather remained spotty, and Bohnaker, flying at 2000 feet, suddenly broke from a cloud to find himself directly over the ship, its fighters neatly stacked along its flight deck. The Japanese must have had a bad minute; but Bohnaker had specific orders not to attack, and he left the ship alone. It was too bad, for next day no one had a chance at her.

In spite of their best efforts, they again were able to get no more than six ships in commission, and from the very start a hoodoo seemed to hang over these. Lieutenant Connally, who was to lead the mission, blew a tire and never got off the ground. Lieutenant Coats took over the lead, but he had to turn back with engine trouble and was soon followed by Lieutenant Ford, who turned back for the same reason. That left just three ships to go in over Legaspi.

They were piloted by Lieutenants Wheless, Vandevanter, and Adams, who, with his regular crew, had taken over Bohnaker's plane. They had covered about half their distance when they ran into a thick overcast and Lieutenant Wheless became separated from the other two. He had lost his No. 2 engine and was compelled to drop to 10,000 feet before he could get it started. By then he was approaching Legaspi, so he continued at that level, hoping to slip in on the target ahead of Adams and Vandevanter and take the Japanese by surprise.

Actually the other two were far ahead of him; but they in turn had lost track of each other so they were 90 seconds apart when they came over Legaspi and started their runs on the Japanese shipping. The bay was crammed with transports and warships, the former lined up along the shore and disgorging troops and supplies. Adams went in first. Both he and Vandevanter were at 21,000 feet. They bombed in train, Adams dropping all his on a single run and Vandevanter making three. As the bombs fell the crew of Adams's plane sighted a flight of six Zeros coming up at them, so swiftly that they gained on the Fortress even as they climbed.

Adams dived for a cloud bank 10,000 feet below, but the Zeros came in on the big ship and attacked it as it was still going down. In one devastating minute they had crippled her. Both the navigator and the radio operator were wounded in the first pass, the former in one arm, the latter seriously in the leg. The air crew had hit three or four of the Japanese fighters—they thought three were shot down; but the others followed them into a second cloud bank at 3000 feet.

All this time they were heading home; and now, as they came out of the second cloud bank with two engines dead on one side, they found themselves over Masbate Island, with a stretch of beach below, and Adams called over the interphone to get ready for a crash landing.

The ship was falling rapidly. The beach turned out to be almost nonexistent, impossible even for a crash landing, but just beyond was a little flooded rice field, separated from them by a line of tall trees. Though there seemed to be no conceivable chance of missing them, Adams, by switching his two remaining engines on and off, managed to jump the trees and brought his lurching ship down on the other side in a beautiful belly landing. The crew were tumbling out almost before the plane came to a halt and one of the Japs, who had overshot them, circled and came in to strafe the grounded ship. His bullets passed the length of her fuselage but did not set her afire. After the Jap fighters had gone, the crew decided not to burn her, hoping to come back to strip her of parts. Instead, they started across the island, carrying the wounded radio operator

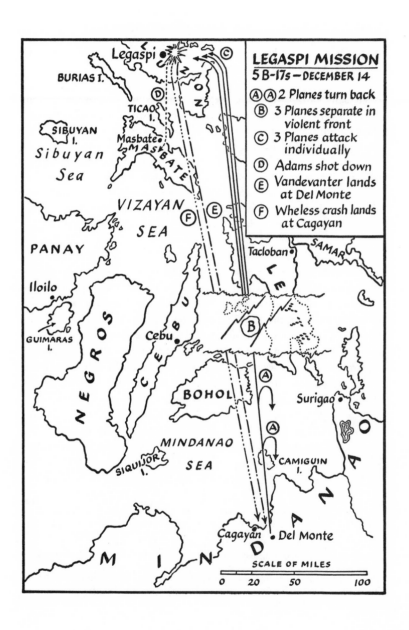

LEGASPI MISSION
5 B-17s – DECEMBER 14

Ⓐ Ⓐ 2 Planes turn back
Ⓑ 3 Planes separate in violent front
Ⓒ 3 Planes attack individually
Ⓓ Adams shot down
Ⓔ Vandevanter lands at Del Monte
Ⓕ Wheless crash lands at Cagayan

on a makeshift stretcher and assisted and escorted by an armed band of Filipinos, mounted on their tiny horses.*

Vandevanter, miraculously, made his second and third bombing runs after Adams had left, dropped all his bombs, and got away himself without a casualty of any kind. He was safe, hidden in the weather front on his way back to Del Monte, when at last Wheless broke from the cloud cover above the bay to find the whole hornets' nest of Japanese stirred up for him. There were six transports lined up at the docks and he had started his run on them when 18 Japanese fighters jumped him from above. Wheless was now flying at something under 10,000 feet; but being already committed, he went on in, dropping his bombs in train.

The ship had eight 600-pound bombs in the bays; and all eight were dropped. But the air crew had too much work on their hands to make definite observations of the results. Four Zeros piled on them during the run, one each from right and left, and two in tandem on the tail. The two on the sides were shot down at once, though the first burst of fire from the second Japanese plane blew the top off the head of the radio operator, Pfc. W. G. Killin. In the meantime, the B–17, held in the iron groove of her bombing run, was at the mercy of the two fighters attacking from the rear. They riddled her. But as soon as the bombs were out, Wheless swung the big ship on the rudder to let the side guns bear on the Zeros behind her, and one was instantly shot down.

Now, with three of the enemy to her credit, the B–17 was turned for home. She had been badly mauled, and the other Japanese fighters, 15 of them, were swarming at her. They confined their attacks entirely to the rear and for 30 minutes they emptied their guns into the big bomber. But they couldn't pull her down.

---

* Adams's crew were weeks in getting back to Del Monte. After crossing the island they spent their first week at a gold mine which had a private hospital where the wounded radioman, Pfc. Anthony E. Jumia, Jr., was cared for and in which they left him when they decided to try to reach their base. Before going, they recrossed the island and destroyed their plane. They finally reached Panay in a flimsy outrigger canoe. There they served in a field artillery unit under command of Col. B. G. Chynoweth and then moved with his tiny forces to Negros, from which with the field artillery they were finally withdrawn to Cagayan on Mindanao. After ten days' further service with the artillery on beach defense they were permitted to go to Del Monte and rejoin the 19th Group, which was then serving as infantry.[3]

Two of the waist gunners were wounded and out of action after the first few seconds of this running fight: Sergeant Russell Brown and Corporal W. W. Williams. That left one man, Sergeant John M. Gootee, to man the side guns, but he had a bullet through his right wrist and had to handle them entirely with his left hand. With the ship on course, the navigator, 2nd Lieutenant W. F. Meenaugh, and the bombardier, Sergeant R. W. Schlotte, came back to lend a hand, the former taking the dead radio operator's place at the belly gun. But it had been put out of action by the same burst that killed the radio operator; and within ten minutes from the time the Japanese first attacked both the side guns jammed. They had shot down three or four more Japanese by then; but after that there was nothing more they could do but fly the plane, until the Japanese fighters had run out of ammunition.

The No. 1 engine was dead, its throttle cable shot in two. The No. 4 gas tank had been hit by a cannon shell which had opened a six-inch hole, allowing all the gas to run out. The radio had been destroyed by another explosive shell. The oxygen system was shot out. Out of eleven control cables, only four—right rudder, two aileron controls, and one elevator control—were intact, which made it very difficult to maneuver the ship and almost impossible to turn it. The tail wheel had been shot completely out of its mount and both front wheels were flat. When they made a count of the bullet holes in her, they found over 1200. But somehow the ship still flew, and the Japanese, Wheless said, pulled close alongside and peered through the windows at the remaining members of her crew. Then they left her.

The ship had come down to 3000 feet after her 75 miles of punishment, and they kept her at that level for the rest of the way home. It was just dark and a weeping rain had begun to fall as they came in sight of the mountains of Mindanao. In such weather and with his plane in distress, Wheless saw no chance of bringing her in to Del Monte, so he turned aside to the small airfield near the beach at Cagayan. As the bomber sagged heavily to earth, they saw that the field was barricaded; but it was then too late to try anywhere else. With a heavy crash the B-17 burst through the barricades and rolled forward 200 yards on her flat tires. Then the brakes locked and the plane stood straight up on her nose. But in an instant she settled back on the tail and her crew slowly climbed out of her.[4]

That was the Legaspi mission. Six planes had been scheduled for it; three reached the target to make individual attacks; one returned to base, and two were lost, though the crews of both were saved, except for the two men killed in action. In results they had nothing definite to show but the near-misses on transports claimed for both Vandevanter's and Adams's ships * and some nine, possibly ten, Zeros shot down. However, in that crowded bay it was probable that they did more damage than they claimed.

There were now 14 B–17s left. Within a day of his arrival at Del Monte, Major Walsh requested permission to take these ships out to Darwin for maintenance, and to rest the crews. Permission was granted, and the first six took off on the long hop at 2:00 A.M. on December 17. They worked under pressure to get the ships away, for both Walsh and FEAF Headquarters were now alert to the possibility of a Japanese attack on the field. Four more planes went out on the 18th, one on the 19th, and the last three on the 20th. It was high time. The day before at dusk, Japanese planes had found and strafed Del Monte, and destroyed three B–18s in process of being camouflaged, but apparently they missed the Fortresses. Next day, however, they attacked in force.

23. *Episode at Vigan*

AT VIGAN, on December 16, an American pursuit pilot, Lieutenant Russell M. Church, Jr., his P–40 in flames from antiaircraft fire, continued his bombing run on a line of parked Zeros and crashed beyond the air strip. This was nothing like the Kamikaze attacks that the Japanese developed later in the war and tried to popularize with their own peculiar and

---

* Wheless made no claims. The citation of Adams for the D.S.C. says he destroyed a large transport. The citation of Vandevanter for the D.F.C. says that he sank one and damaged two transports, though the 19th Bomb Group Diary does not substantiate these claims.

thoroughly logistic sense of what constitutes honorable conduct. Church had his chute. He could have jumped, and no one would have spoken or thought critically of him if he had; but, like others, he knew that a plane by then meant more to the Army than a pilot. There were plenty of pilots left, some of them more skillful than he. But with only 20 P-40s, not even a burning ship should be wasted. A competent and conscientious man, Church made his own decision and took his plane down.

The pursuit were no longer flying under squadron organization; but two pools of fliers and planes had been set up at Clark and Nichols Fields respectively. The ground crews serviced the planes as they came in and the pilots took the missions in rotation. They were, for the most part, the older, more experienced men, and the missions were mainly reconnaissance. The whole of Luzon was covered each day: the planes from Clark Field taking care of the northern section and those from Nichols flying the southern beats, to Legaspi, out over the Island passages, and Mindoro.

The P-40s generally went in pairs; but many missions had to be undertaken by a single plane; and these long and solitary flights through skies dominated by the enemy put a heavy strain on the pilot. Even when he was well clear of areas of Japanese activity, the mountains with their sudden storms, the strangeness of the green jungle, and the little nipa-roofed shacks suddenly encountered in their tiny clearings, served to emphasize the pilot's own loneliness. But for many of them it was the over-water flying that was hardest to get used to. If a pilot went down then, it was for keeps; for, even if he managed to get free of his plane, there were the sharks. Some pilots never got over this uneasiness; but all of them had more than a taste of it before they were done. Then, at times, the sight of men working in a rice field on a steep mountain terrace, the motionless shapes of carabao standing beside their square and blocky shadows, like children's toys, in the hazy sunlight, or a native cart, raising its delicate feather of dust along an open country road, as though no word of war had reached to these untouched and forgotten corners, lent unreality to the plane's flight, and the pilot, unless he was on guard, would relax his watchfulness. Most of them learned quickly that unending vigilance was the price of their survival, and that sixth sense of awareness that belongs to both the hunted and the hunting and is only latent in civilized and peaceful men became the instinct by which they lived.

But a few men at each field developed the ability to capitalize on the very lack of support that made these flights hazardous, striking when the Japanese least expected aggressive action from a lone plane. Grant Mahony, on reconnaissance out of Nichols Field to Legaspi, suddenly went in to strafe the Japanese-held radio station and some of their parked planes. When nine pursuit came diving down on him, he led them off on a chase round the 8000-foot peak of Mount Mayon. Mahony had learned, as Wagner also had, that the P-40 at low altitudes could pull away from the Zero; but this was one thing that as yet the Japanese did not know and they went after Mahony like yelping hounds. The whole pack of them were still in hot pursuit as he brought them round full-circle back across their own airfield at tree height for a second strafing attack. Only then, with the radio station demolished, several planes burning on the field, and the fuel dump ejaculating rolls of black smoke, did he set out for home. He lost the Japanese in the creases of the mountain valleys and returned to Nichols Field to make a difficult landing on the patched-up air strip with some of his bombs still dangling from their faulty releases underneath his wings.[1]

On the same morning * Boyd D. Wagner, flying out of Clark Field on a similar, solitary reconnaissance, was jumped north of Aparri by five Zeros. Like Mahony, instead of high-tailing it for cloud cover, he took his ship right down to wave level and headed inland. Two of the Japanese pilots had evidently been detailed to take care of the lone American pursuit plane, for when Wagner looked back, he saw them sticking hot on his tail. He found that they weren't to be shaken off, so he tried a maneuver that no Japanese pilot had ever had worked on him before.

Men often spoke of Wagner as a "born" flier, because there was nothing that he couldn't do with a plane; but he was more than that. Like many skillful people, he was not satisfied with the skill he had but worked indefatigably to improve it. His nickname of "Buzz" came from his habit of buzzing other planes in the air. Long before the war

---

* Though the 24th Pursuit Group Narrative gives the date of Wagner's mission as December 13, it was evidently on the 11th. An AP story, Manila, December 12, gives an account of this Aparri encounter of his, as does the War Department Communiqué No. 6, also dated the 12th.

he had begun to use unsuspecting and frequently outraged commercial jobs as his figurative clay pigeons, working out on them the best angles of attack and the handling of his own ship and an endless and often spectacular variety of evasive tactics. As he was also a trained aeronautical engineer, he undoubtedly knew as much about the performance characteristics of the P–40, when war came, as any other man.

Now, with the two Zeros still chasing him, Wagner suddenly throttled back and let the astonished enemy flash past over his head while he poured his own machine guns into their tails. Before either of the Japanese pilots could think up any evasive tactics for his own benefit, both Zeros were flaming and on their way into the ground. Wagner then turned back and, still hedgehopping, came in across the airfield at Aparri, catching the Japanese there completely by surprise. They had twelve planes on the line. Wagner strafed them as he roared down the field and when he zoomed up at the far end, five of them were burning. Then, to quote his own laconic report: "My gas was running low, so I returned home." *

Results like these were heartening to the whole Army, yet to the pursuit pilots they did not mean the same thing as an actual attack mission staged as such. They chafed under their confinement to reconnaissance, for, with each passing day, as the Japanese established more and more airdromes, first principally round Aparri, then at Legaspi, and finally at Vigan, the American pilots could see for themselves the gradual constrictive process that would ultimately mean the extinction of their own air effort. The hit-and-run tactics, developed in sporadic attacks like Mahony's and Wagner's and in other unreported brushes, became the basis of the combat tactics by which the P–40 was finally turned into an effective airplane. But it was increasingly evident on Luzon in December that our dwindling number of pursuit planes could less and less afford to be risked in an offensive strike.

However, when the report came in on the evening of December 15 that there were 25 new Japanese planes on the air strip at Vigan, it was decided to stage a dawn attack on them, and three of the most experienced fliers at Clark Field were assigned to the mission. They were

* The 24th Pursuit Group Narrative states that Wagner shot down four Zeros.[2]

Lieutenants Wagner, Church, and Allison W. Strauss, all members of the 17th Squadron.

The Japanese had established their beachhead at Vigan on December 10. On the 13th they began moving in more men a little to the south of the town; but their chief purpose seemed plainly to be the securing of air bases outside the areas controlled by our troops, and most ground action was of a sporadic and local nature. General Wainwright's orders from General MacArthur were simple: "In the event of a landing, attack and destroy the enemy." [3] But even if he had had trained troops, Wainwright could not have attacked, for there was no room between the crowding mountains and the beach to deploy forces large enough to handle the situation. He contented himself with intensified patrols, knowing that in due time the Japanese must come south to him along the shore. It was a situation in which air power and air power alone would have been effective. "That was the day I realized, for all time, the futility of trying to fight a war without an Air Force." [4] But the only plane over the transports and beaches during those intervening days was a P-40 reconnaissance ship. And the Navy's handful of motor torpedo boats were far south. . . .

"The shooting war opened on the sixteenth of December." [5] It opened with an action that Wainwright thinks of as "touchingly symbolic of all other combats in the futile fight for the Philippines. Two busloads of Jap troops moving south from Vigan were ambushed by a platoon of Filipino infantrymen under command of a Lieutenant Williams. The ambush took place at a little point named Tagudin. . . ." [6]

But there was symbolism also in the death of Church, whom Wainwright does not mention.

The airfield was a single, north-south strip, close to the beach, about four and a half miles southwest of Vigan, and the three P-40s came to it from the sea as dawn was breaking. Strauss stayed up in the paling sky to furnish top cover, while Wagner went in with Church on his wing. Each of the P-40s carried six 30-pound fragmentation bombs, three under each wing. As they neared the field they saw the 25 Japanese airplanes lined up beneath them on the turf. It was darker down there, where the gray, predawn shadows were creeping towards the mountains. The air was perfectly still as Wagner put his plane over and started down.

Wagner went through without a scratch; but by the time Church started, the Japanese antiaircraft guns were going full blast, and they now had only the one plane to concentrate on. At the very beginning of the dive, the nose of the P-40 burst into flame. It was then that Church had to make his split-second choice, for he could still have let the plane go. But the P-40 did not waver in its dive. Even with the fire pouring back over the cockpit, Church controlled his ship through its full run, dropped his bombs on the target, and went strafing down the line like a comet. From where they circled above and beyond the field, Wagner and Strauss followed the flaming course of his ship. It never rose, but carried as straight as though the controls were locked until it crashed, about a mile away, in the flat land towards Vigan.

Church's death touched off a spark in Wagner. In spite of the heavy antiaircraft fire, he made five more strafing runs across the field. Only one Japanese plane succeeded in getting off the ground. The pilot tried to take it up just as Wagner was coming in. The Zero was half hidden from Wagner by his own wing, so to get a clear view of the whole strip he rolled his plane over on its back. No other pilot in the Philippines could have done it with a P-40 at strafing altitude. When he saw the Japanese plane, Wagner righted his ship and throttled back to let the other gain headway, and then shot it down.

Ten planes were destroyed and seven more left burning when Wagner and Strauss finally gave over and turned home. Even the Japanese had been impressed. They buried Church [7] with full military honors.*

* Church was, supposedly, put in for the Congressional Medal, for which he would seem a fitting candidate. There is some conflict about Strauss's presence on this mission. Brownwell says that Wagner and Church were alone. The Obert Report does not mention Strauss nor do the citations for the mission. But both the 24th Pursuit Group Diary and the Sheppard Statement place him over Vigan as top cover for the other two, and Sheppard says Strauss joined in the strafing. Strauss was subsequently shot down over Darwin while engaged with a superior number of enemy pursuit and himself posthumously decorated with the Silver Star.

V I

Withdrawal of FEAF: December 24

24. *The Airfield at Lubao*

To MOST of the Air Force troops, without planes either to service or to fly, the battle for the Philippines seemed fought in a sort of vacuum that was to end only on December 25, after the complete chaos of the retreat to Bataan. Once there, they came under the command of Colonel George and drew from him purpose, discipline, and the sense that they were fighting for a cause. But the 16-day period that intervened between December 8 and Christmas Eve was one of continual shifts and changes. Units were moved round Luzon until it seemed to the men as if they were, actually, pins on a Headquarters map. In a few instances the administrative officers developed hysterical tendencies and became less than useless—the ground echelon of one fighter squadron went through the first week of war under four sergeants. Other units were broken up by their assignments.

There was the case of the volunteer outfit called up from the Matériel Squadrons at Nichols Field. Two hundred men were asked for and on the 13th of December they set out from Manila in four open boats to establish an air base at San José on the island of Mindoro. One boat, containing men from the 48th Matériel Squadron, reached its destination; and these 50 men operated the field for stray P-40s and such members of the Bamboo Fleet as came drifting in until the Japanese drove them into the hills on March 8, 1942. They did not have much to resist with. There were only 30 rifles in the outfit. Some of the men surrendered two months later; some died; the rest became guerillas, and of them only one got out of the Philippines before the war's end.

Most of the grounded air squadrons, of both the 24th Pursuit and the 27th Bombardment Groups, were turned into airdrome troops. Since the start of the war, the airfield program had really come to life. Undertaking it as a full-time job, Colonel George was all over Luzon during this period, with Captain Eads as his engineer, and in the first week of the war they put in five 5000-foot dirt strips, south of Manila, entirely with native labor and handwork. This was indeed a far cry from the old, lush, drowsy days of peace and the Philippine Department, when six months would be spent merely to secure the lease of a worthless piece of land * and the construction of the airfield dragged out for over a year. Now, without graders or bulldozers, but using only primitive means, stone boats, and carabao carts that must be unyoked to dump them, and baskets carried by men and women, George and Eads were building air strips literally in a matter of days.

As soon as they had one finished, one of the grounded squadrons would be moved in to man it. The 3rd, for instance, which had been so beaten up in the bombing of Iba, went down to Tanauan south of Laguna de Bay.[1] There were three strips there, and the men took over the job of camouflaging them with imagination and thoroughness. They would wear denims and get themselves Filipino straw hats and act like native labor. They made portable nipa shacks that could be put out on the fields and had straw shocks on hurdles set out in other sections. When Bill Bradford or another American pilot buzzed the field for a landing, the transformation was amusing and grotesque.

None of these five southern strips was ever used by the B-17s it was designed for, and the work of building them now seems an utter waste. But then men still believed that help would come. Even with the loss at Pearl Harbor it was hard for them to understand how their country, the most powerful in the world, might fail to get help through to them. But a few of the fields completed north of Manila were used for varying brief terms by the pursuit, and because the one at Lubao was notable for its camouflage—not only the Japanese, but the American pilots as well failed to find it until they had been led into it on the ground—and

* Zamboanga was a case in point—the field laid out in a rice paddy which needed thousands of tons of coral fill was dickered over for half a year.

also because the service performed there by the 21st Squadron as airdrome troops was fairly typical, it seems worth describing in some detail.

The end of interception on December 10 found the Squadron divided: the ground echelon had remained behind at Nichols Field, while Lieutenant Dyess and the pilots who had survived the first three days of war were at Clark Field. Their youth and comparative lack of experience meant that they were unlikely to have a chance at flying, so, when they were ordered back to Manila, Dyess was relieved at the prospect of getting his whole Squadron together again. From the first he appears to have felt the importance of maintaining the Squadron's morale as a unit, and, whether he disapproved or not of the practice of manning the remaining planes with a pool of fliers and crew chiefs, there can be little doubt that he began here to build his Squadron up into as effective a unit as he could, with the idea of eventually getting them back into the air war. A lanky, long-legged, blond Texan, with a cool and logical mind, Dyess had the gift of handling men under stress. Because of it he eventually achieved his goal.

In Manila the Squadron were put up at LaSalle College and, when the ground echelon moved over from Nichols, it was like a reunion. They stayed there together for three or four days before receiving their new assignment. This once more meant a division of the Squadron, a few of the men being taken into the Signal Corps, for which their chief duty was to go round Manila picking up radios and receiving sets and any other kind of radio equipment they could lay their hands on. At almost the same time the rest of the Squadron were ordered to a new field then being finished in the area just north of Manila Bay, near the little town of Lubao.

It was supposed to be completed, but when Ed Dyess arrived ahead of the Squadron, he found the runway still under construction. There were no ground installations of any kind, nor revetments for the planes, and Dyess stayed to take charge of the 300 Filipino laborers until his own men could come up from Manila. All of them, Americans and Filipinos together, worked in shifts twenty-four hours a day to complete the field, and when they had it done, it was a wonder.[2]

The runway was cut out of a plantation of sugar cane. They divided it in two halves, covering the first with windrows of dead canes to look from the air as though it were being harvested. When in taking off and landing, the planes scattered these windrows, the Filipinos would rush out to sweep them back in place. The other half was left bare, like a new planting.[3] Parking strips ran at right angles from the main runway, with revetments dug into the ground and sandbagged five feet high, wide and deep enough to cover the planes. At each corner was a bamboo pole with chicken wire stretched over the top. Short upper sections of cane were notched and put through the wire with elaborate care to make them match the surface of the living growth. They had to be changed every two or three days to keep the false cane looking fresh. Then in front of each revetment bamboo cups were placed in the soil two feet apart to hold full-length canes, so that the parked planes were invisible to even a low-flying enemy pilot, yet it took only a moment to pull out the wall of cane and run the ship out on the field.

Every day Japanese bombers on their milk run down to bomb Manila and Corregidor flew directly over the field in flights of up to 50 planes without suspecting its construction or, later, its operation. They always came from the same direction and at the same altitude, and this positive target finally became too much for an antiaircraft battery that had been set up about two kilometers away beside the San Fernando road. They let loose one day at a flight of the bombers and knocked one down.

The men on the Lubao field saw the fire start in the Japanese ship where the wing joined the fuselage; and it grew bigger as the plane started down. The pilot kept advancing the throttle as if he were trying to pull the ship out of its dive, but all he did was to increase the velocity of its downward rush. It came roaring into the sugar cane behind the parking strips and almost buried itself in the ground before it exploded. Flaming gasoline set the cane on fire and the whole airdrome force turned out to fight it. When they reached the spot of the crash all that was left was the tail of the plane sticking up out of the ground and a couple of arms and legs. All the other Japanese planes had kept circling while the ship came down, but they never spotted the airfield.*

* Dyess writes that the explosion had scattered maps, charts, and papers over a wide area, and "I set the Filipinos to gathering these up. I told them to bring me everything they might find. They obeyed me to the letter, one of them handing me the jawbone and big teeth of a Japanese flier." [4]

The men had been quartered in a deserted nunnery about a mile away; but when the remaining P-40s at last flew in sometime after dusk on Christmas Eve, the crew chiefs refused to leave them. They moved over to the field for good and slept in the revetments with their planes. It seemed a long time since they had had their own kind of work to do and they were hungry for news of what their planes had accomplished in the intervening days.

A lot of catching up on maintenance as well as news was needed, for the planes were pretty well roughed up when they reached Lubao. In the past two days they had staged two attacks against Japanese landings in addition to their reconnaissance missions. In the first of these on December 22 against the Japanese beachheads in Lingayen Gulf they had had to take off in an overcast that ran from 500 to 2000 feet and was so heavy that their formation could not assemble but proceeded singly northward through the clouds. They had lost no planes, but two or three had been shot up and one barely made its way back to Clark Field to land with a frozen engine. More serious, however, was the wounding of Lieutenant Wagner. As he was turning for home a 20-mm explosive shell had hit his wind screen, filling his chest and face with glass splinters, one piece entering his eye. It was to halt his flying for many days to come.*

No one could doubt that this was the main Japanese invasion thrust against Luzon. The attack mission and later reconnaissance flights brought in a count of nearly 100 vessels of all sorts in Lingayen Gulf. The 80 transports among them were estimated to hold 80,000 to 100,000 men. Opposing them General Wainwright had two divisions of his raw little Northern Force of 28,000. In the course of the day's fighting, the Japanese drove between them near the heel of the Gulf. The 71st Division, cut off to the north, had to withdraw inland. To save the exposed

* Some doubt exists over the date of this mission and even whether it should be classed as an attack mission at all. The date here given is based on the 24th Pursuit Group Roster, which puts the wounding of Wagner at Lingayen on December 22, which seems logical. Some corroboration exists in Sheppard's circumstantial account of the mission, in which he took part, though he dates it on December 23. However, Wagner's citation for the Purple Heart states that he received the wound over Vigan on December 18, and Ind says he was wounded over Vigan, without mentioning when. The 24th Pursuit Group Narrative does not mention the mission at all.[5]

flank of the 11th Division, deployed round the south shore of the Gulf, Wainwright brought up the 26th Cavalry, which, at a little town called Damortis, hit the advancing enemy so hard that with only a little more force—a few more tanks, a few more planes—to back them they might well have rolled the Japanase right off the beaches. Support was not forthcoming, and grudgingly the lone regiment began to give ground in a retreat that did not end until they reached Bataan nine days later. But in those nine days they set up a record for themselves that no unit in the Philippines, if indeed any in our history, has exceeded in effective valor.

The possibility of reinforcements from the Southern Force or from reserve troops near Manila was abruptly killed when, twenty-four hours later, the Japanese landed at Atimonan on the east shore of Luzon about 75 miles from Manila. This was not only a direct threat to the city but also to all Army forces in the south. It set the stage immediately for the withdrawal on Bataan, but, to hold the Japanese on the beaches as long as possible and let the troops still further south, near Legaspi, come through, all available pursuit planes were ordered to attack the landing on December 24.*

Eighteen planes—twelve P-40s and six P-35s—were the most that could be put in the air for this mission. Six of them came from Nichols Field,[7] all that survived there; the rest were from Clark. They attacked the 40 transports in Lopez Bay with fragmentation bombs and strafing, driving home through unusually heavy ackack. Most of the planes took punishment and two of the P-35s were so badly damaged that they crashed on their way home. One dove into Laguna de Bay, from which the pilot was fished uninjured by a native and highly excited fisherman.†

By noon of that day the acceleration of the Japanese drive in the north

---

* In the 24th Pursuit Group Narrative the landing is stated to have been made in San Miguel Bay and attacked by our planes on December 23. I find no other mention of San Miguel Bay in any primary source, though Ind, here as throughout, accepts the *24th Pursuit Group.* WD Communiqué No. 26 substantiates the December 24 date (which is also given by Obert), claiming that the air attack on the landing was delivered at Atimonan. Further though not final confirmation is given in the *Japanese Field Diary* and *Map* in ATIS Bulletin No. 761.[6]

† Presumably 2nd Lt. James McD. Rowland, though Sheppard says the incident occurred after a reconnaissance mission. Obert writes, "From all reports, Lt. Rowland was almost a one-man air force that day. Although encountering heavy enemy fire, he remained in the area and made attack after attack against enemy warships and transports." [8] Rowland was later killed in action over Java as described below, Part Two, Chapter 6.

—which was then reaching for the Agno River, already well south of Lingayen Gulf—had become a direct threat to Clark Field and Fort Stotsenburg, and the pursuit planes were ordered to Lubao that afternoon. They left just before the order for the evacuation to Bataan came through, and for the rest of the late afternoon hunted their way to the field here and there across Luzon above the wildly confused traffic of the retreat. Altogether, on Christmas Eve and Christmas Day, some 25 or 26 planes reached the field. It was not wholly finished, and work was now slowed by maintenance demands of the planes, which continued to operate from the little strip while the rest of the Army on its retreat into Bataan—Air Force, Artillery, Tanks, and Infantry, except for General Wainwright and his rearguard, the 11th and 21st Divisions and the inevitable 26th Cavalry—poured down the San Fernando road a few yards beyond the green walls of cane.

Then, in Lieutenant Dyess's words, "On New Year's Day, 1942, in mid-morning, we finished our airfield. By mid-afternoon the onrushing Japanese advance had made Lubao field front line territory. By evening we had received orders to abandon it." [9]

It was the last of the fields north of Manila to be abandoned. From now on men worked to build air strips on Bataan itself, for they still had hope of airplanes coming in. On December 17 word had been received that the convoy carrying the dive bombers of the 27th Bombardment Group was heading for Australia. Presumably it would bring pursuit planes also.

25. The A–24s Arrive at Last—in Australia

FROM THE MOMENT of their landing in the Philippines, the career of the 27th Bombardment Group had been one of sheer frustration. Without their planes they had turned their hands to any sort of job that came along, from filling sandbags to supplying detachments to serve as airdrome or antiaircraft troops at San Marcelino, Nielson, and Nichols Fields; and then twelve of their most experienced pilots, who had been sent on loan to Clark Field to fill in as pursuit pilots, found themselves relegated to ground duties after all.[1] The news that their planes were on the way from the States at last, even though their destination was probably a port 3000 or 4000 miles to the south, would have heartened the entire group; but the efficiency of the Japanese espionage made it imperative that the departure of a handful of their pilots to ferry the planes back to the Philippines should be handled with the utmost secrecy. With only three planes allotted him from the pool at Nichols, Major Davies picked 20 of his pilots for their "dependableness and ability," to use his own words,[2] and early on the afternoon of December 17 called them to Head-quarters.

Air Headquarters had by this time been removed from Nielson Field to Fort McKinley, for Nielson, in the opinion of some, lay precariously open to parachute attack[3] and also lacked sufficient housing and office facilities. At Fort McKinley, the former Officers' Club had been taken over. Far beneath it sappers were still hard at work driving the tunnels that were to provide bomb shelter for the staff. South and east of the ridge on which the building stood one could look across the lower fields to the untouched town of Pateros with its tranquil yellow church, whose bells still rang, and beyond its little tower to the mountains, aloof among their clouds.

The 27th Headquarters, however, was a house in one of the Officers' Quarters, which, though overlooking the same peaceful scene, was merely a light, gray-painted frame building. Here round a table spread with maps that showed the landing fields of the proposed fighter ferry route up through the Netherlands East Indies, Major Davies briefed them for the trip south. Presumably their planes would be in Australia; but where in Australia he was not sure. Davies, big-boned, black-haired, taller than almost all his men, said that they would go south until they found them. They could take not more than 30 pounds of personal belongings and they were to tell no one where they were going. At 6:00 that afternoon they would meet to start for Nichols Field.

But it was 8:15 when they finally set out in four sedans—a slow trip along the blacked-out highway, halted constantly for identification in the thin, dim rays of sentries' flashlights. To reach the field, also, they had to pass through Baclaran, which had recently been bombed while the Japanese were trying to hit Nichols Field. The big fleet of bombers on two runs had twice miscalculated and overshot their mark, and the little barrio of flimsy houses, close packed on either side of the road, had been wiped out. In the heavy darkness the stench was appalling, especially to the pilots who had not been down before. They could see now and then the broken remnants of a house faintly silhouetted by the glow of the fires still burning in Cavite. In the utter silence there was only the sound of their own cars and once or twice a single pistol shot, isolated, unexplained, and strangely foreboding.[4]

They left the cars and moved in the darkness on foot across the narrow bridge to quarters that had been assigned for them. The building had been hit in one of the raids and the entire rear had been blown out so that most of the rooms were open to the sky. Rubble covered the floors. The only room left relatively intact was what had been the living room, and here, round a single candle, the men were told that they would take off at 3:00 A.M. Three planes had been allotted them from the Nichols pool—a C–39 and two B–18s, one of which was a survivor of the decrepit four that had been first assigned to the Group.[5] Air raids and a brush with Zeros had not improved its sinews. They found also that a pilot from the 24th Pursuit Group had orders to make the trip with them. This was Grant Mahony.

There was time to kill and some of the men went to the various rooms and tried to get some sleep; but few slept. Most of the others sat out in front of the house. The warped skeletons of the hangars were weirdly lighted by the fires still burning on their floors. The smell of gas from a broken main hung in the night air; but it could not cover the smell of the dead in Baclaran.

At 3:00 o'clock those inside the house were roused and the whole band moved out onto the field. The C–39 was the first plane to go, with six aboard her, Lieutenant Frederic G. Hoffman of the Philippine Air Depot piloting. The co-pilot, 2nd Lieutenant A. R. Salvatore, had never seen the inside of a C–39, but he was co-pilot anyhow. The men got in with their bags and Mahony with his flashlight walked out ahead of the plane, guiding it among the bomb craters and piles of rubble to the end of the 2500 feet of usable strip. There he climbed in and the engines were run up. At the far end of the blacked-out runway a mechanic blinked a flashlight. The engines roared and the trees beyond the field came back fast, but the overloaded ship lifted finally and turned its nose for Mindanao.

It was a cold, rough trip. The ship had some thirty shrapnel holes and the wind roared through her like a gale. They hit a tropical storm that took everything the pilots had to bring the ship through. But at dawn it cleared a little, and they picked up the shore of Mindanao and found their way in to Del Monte.

They had to spend the day there, for daylight flying wasn't a good bet for the unarmed ship over the concentration of warships the Japanese were reported to have round Mindanao. So they waited till 2:00 A.M. of the 19th to take off for Tarakan in Dutch Borneo. Even at that as they skirted a line of islands a little after dawn they sighted a Japanese carrier. The minutes dragged and the C-39 seemed to hang in the sky as they waited for the Zeros to take off, but none did, and then they ran into weather once more and were glad of it. But it became terrible as they approached Tarakan and they could not find their way in, so they flew on south with dwindling gasoline, hoping to run out of the front and figuring there was just gas enough in the ship to make Balikpapan if they didn't have to hunt for the place. They met a high mountain range but they did not dare use the extra gas to climb above it, so the plane threaded its way down canyons and between the peaks. They got through and hit Balikpapan on the nose and set down with 28 gallons of gas in the tanks.

"That night everyone ate boloney and cheese and drank Dutch beer. The Dutch were quite good to the 27th and made the boys feel at home. One thing had the whole crowd puzzled and that was the large round hard pillow in each bed. It turned out to be a 'Dutch Wife' that one slept with in the absence of the true McCoy!" [6]

The next night they reached Makassar in the Celebes, and the night after Koepang, in Dutch Timor, where they were guests of the RAAF. The Australians treated them well, though some of the Southern boys felt uneasy at being called "Yank." From there they flew to Darwin, where they joined the two B-18s, which had made a faster trip down, flying to Tarakan from Nichols in one hop. All three planes were in rickety shape; but Davies immediately began to arrange their return trip with loads of desperately needed .50-caliber ammunition.

While in Darwin they learned that General Clagett had flown out of

the Philippines in one of the 19th Group's B-17s, which had been transferred to Batchelor Field a few miles below Darwin and were now operating from there. General Clagett's mission was to organize the Air Corps
units expected, now, to arrive at Brisbane. General MacArthur believed
that the convoy might still get up to the Philippines if enough Naval
escort were provided; but he planned to have the Air Corps units left
at Brisbane for assembling aircraft while the remaining troops and supplies were moved into the Philippines if that were still possible.[7]

The 27th pilots, however, were interested only in getting to their planes.
They had hoped to find them completely assembled. Now, waiting for
permission to leave Darwin, some of the men began to feel skeptical. Not
till December 23 did permission to move south finally come through and
they boarded a QUANTAS * Airways flying boat for Townsville.

It was Christmas Eve when the flying boat landed in the Brisbane
River alongside the armed ships of an American convoy. The sight was
heartening, but the tired, ragged-looking little group of pilots that got
out of taxis in front of Lennon's Hotel felt like curiosities. They were.
The people of Brisbane, eyeing their tin helmets, gas masks, and pistols,
and seeing the fatigue lined in their faces, realized suddenly that somewhere, not too far away, a war was really going. It gave them something
of a shock.† But the men got over it quickly. They were in civilization
again, in Australia's best hotel, with good food, clean sheets, with drink
to be bought, and it was Christmas Eve. It seemed almost like the Promised Land, and in a way it was to be, for no troops in the world's history
ever received a warmer welcome than the Australians offered ours.

But the A-24s, that were so desperately needed in the Philippines, had
come with 24 trigger motors for the guns where 80 were needed and
apparently no solenoids at all. The gun mounts broke when the guns
were fired and the planes had no self-sealing tanks. The instruments were
bad, the tires were defective, so that ultimately several of the planes were
flown with truck tires on their wheels. Adapters and gunsights were

---

* Queensland and Northern Territories Air Services.

† "Shocked also was one such GI Colonel, who, being CO of the Brisbane area, happened along. His expression, at seeing our US insignias, our rough-looking appearance, and
our recently acquired Australian shorts, was indescribable. He immediately demanded of
Major Davies an explanation of our 'non-regulation' attire and was promptly set right by
the diplomatic but forthright explanation." [8]

missing, and the planes were old, worn-out, and had already served through one maneuvers in the States. They were Navy planes so that all bombs had to be modified to fit the Navy racks. To the pilots who had come down from Luzon, the chance of flying them back in time seemed hopeless.

26. *December 22: The Long Lingayen Mission*

IN THEIR OWN WORDS, the pilots of the 27th Bombardment Group had been "a little awed by the huge expanse of nothing in Australia." [1] Darwin was a place of "mosquitoes, heat, and not much beer. A frontier town of few women and fewer comforts." [2] The Australians had some planes and ground crews there; but the planes were Wirraways with long glass canopies like greenhouses, essentially trainers and entirely inadequate for combat. And there was a Hudson bomber or two.

The field looked good to the 27th pilots, perhaps because they had received their training in light bombardment. It had proved too light to hold up the Fortresses, so the B-17s that had come down from Del Monte were based at a newly completed field named Batchelor about 45 miles to the south. If Darwin seemed desolate to the 27th pilots, Batchelor Field, to the Fortress crews, must have looked like the outpost of a lost world.

The raw new strip lay out by itself in the red dust. The highway was routed more than five miles to the east, and though the single-track, narrow-gauge railroad ran nearby, it carried very little traffic. The southern railhead was the town of Daly Waters, 250 miles beyond. From there the highway offered the only link to the south, crossing the desert for 600 miles before it came to Alice Springs. The stops along the line had sad, lost echoes in their names—Adelaide River, Brock's Creek, Burrundie, Pine Creek, Katherine, Mataranka, Birdum—as all names have in that tortured and irrational land where water and women become the focus of man's existence and his dreams. The threadlike track passed over empty watercourses that in the monsoon season became flooding torrents, covering the lowland ranges that for eight long months had parched in the relentless sun. Now and then the track passed within sight of low, broken tablelands; but elsewhere the earth lay monotonously flat beneath its cover of sparse trees casting a sparser shade; and often the white man's homestead, beside its inevitable water hole and yard, was less noticeable than the weird clusters of monolithic anthills. It took some fliers weeks to train their eyes to spot a human habitation from the air.

The first B–17s to reach Batchelor Field came in on the morning of December 17. There were six planes in the flight, with Captain Combs commanding. In addition to its regular combat crew of eight, each ship brought two maintenance men. Major Walsh arrived on the following morning, leading in four more ships, and took over the command, and on December 19 a single plane arrived with one maintenance man, an extra officer, and two passengers. The last were General Clagett and his aide, Major Erickson S. Nichols, on their way to Brisbane. The final flight of three B–17s came in on the 20th with seven maintenance men aboard and two extra officers.[3] They reported that Del Monte had finally been spotted by the Japanese.

These 14 Fortresses were all that ever came out of the Philippines; and they, with the 143 men they brought with them, constituted the only real, striking air power the Allied Nations had in the Southwest Pacific. None of the planes was in good condition. The crews were tired out; but the first thing they did on reaching Batchelor Field was to dig foxholes for themselves. That somehow gave the place a more familiar look.

There was not much else to see round the field except their own planes parked along the taxi strip and in a small natural meadow southeast of the runway. There was no control tower. The only building then was a frame shack set up by the Australians out of sight among the gum trees near the northeast corner of the landing strip. The Americans had a tenting area facing this shack, also under the trees.

Some way beyond the tents, on the narrow dirt road that led out to the highway, was the only civilian home in the area. The two daughters in the family used to sit out on the porch in the evenings, and every night some of the men would walk up the road past the house just to look at them. The great thing about Batchelor, though, as the Aussies liked to point out to the Americans, was the running water. It came from an old volcanic crater miles back in the bush, but as the pipe was laid above ground, the water became so hot during the day that no one could drink it. It was too hot even for bathing.

The thermometer often registered 118 degrees in the shade, and with the constant rains the air became as enervating as a Turkish bath. Maintenance work was very difficult. Sometimes it seemed to take as much strength as a man had merely to walk from the tents to where his plane was parked. There were, of course, no better facilities for maintenance than had existed at Del Monte, and when orders came through to attack Japanese shipping in Davao Gulf, they had only nine planes in shape to fly the mission. Even that number represented a major effort.

The plan was to hit the Davao area just at sunset and then go on to Del Monte for service and gas. They had to install bomb bay tanks for the extra gas needed to cover the 1500 miles so they were to come in over Davao with only one bomb bay loaded—each plane carrying four 500-pound bombs. In a way it would be a blind mission, for they were not too sure that Del Monte still remained in American hands. Radio communication between the Philippines and Batchelor Field was primitive, slow, and a little like something out of musical comedy. As Combs described it, an order originating from Headquarters, in Manila, or later in Corregidor, would be sent over to the Naval Station at Cavite, which radioed it to a ship out in the harbor at Darwin, which handed it over to a commander in the Navy at his room in a Darwin hotel, and he, observing the international courtesies, gave it to the RAAF who saw that it got to the American Air Officer; and usually it was handed in to the little tent in which Walsh and Combs had their quarters sometime towards the middle of the night. Almost never was a message received within twenty-four hours of its origin. In that interval anything could have happened at Del Monte.

The time lag in the case of this first mission out of Australia was more than forty-eight hours between the Japanese landing and the arrival of the B–17s over the target. The landing had been known and reported in Manila on the 20th.[4] It was not till December 22 that the B–17s hit Davao.

They took off at 10:43 in the morning, in good weather, Captain Combs leading the flight, and the other eight ships with Parsel, Keiser, Connally, Ford, Godman, Tash, Teats, and Coats as first pilots.[5] Their passage northward above the Ceram Sea and the green chain of the Moluccas was without incident. They raised Mindanao exactly on schedule, closed up their formation, and pointed at 20,000 feet for Davao itself.

Ahead of them the great peak of Apo * was buried under its pile of clouds. The clouds were bright-edged in the sunset, but behind them over the island, to the north and east, the sky had darkened with storms and the gathering night, and against this towering curtain of the weather, the formation of nine bombers in their shoddy camouflage suddenly dwindled into insignificance.

An overcast covered the gulf, but they found breaks in it as they came over the port. Perhaps the forty-eight-hour delay had helped them after all, for the Japanese were evidently taken completely by surprise. No antiaircraft fire broke up through the filmy gray carpet under the planes, though the Japanese had a battleship or heavy cruiser, and light cruisers, destroyers, and transports jammed into the harbor. The overcast made definite observation impossible, but the bombers hit the dock area heavily and sank one 10,000-ton tanker.† No time was wasted over the target, however, for they were already observing the axiom that had become almost a motto for the Group—to hit high, fast, and *once*. With all their planes emptied but one, which had three hung bombs, the formation swung inland and before the Japanese could get organized enough to send up one shell, the nine Fortresses were lost in the gathering darkness and the storm whose black heart they had seen as they approached Mindanao. The planes became separated in the violent weather, but one by one they found their way into Del Monte Field and landed safely. There was a long moment of suspense when Combs's plane stopped rolling, but the men who came out of the night were Americans.

Del Monte had now had its own baptism of fire. Twelve Zeros had stolen in to strafe the base on the 19th, and on the morning of the 21st the Japanese had come over with 54 bombers, eight four-engined flying boats leading the procession.[6] The field had been badly plowed up; there

* Standing just west of the gulf, Mount Apo rises 9690 feet.
† Combs recalls that the Japanese later credited them with this ship.

had been casualties; two men had been killed.* It was obviously no longer sound practice to keep B–17s on Del Monte No. 1 in daylight hours.

The men on the base were almost pathetically glad to have the planes come in. There had been no advance word of their arrival, and now as fast as the B–17s landed, the troops rushed out to take charge of them. No more than six, however, could be serviced and reloaded at the same time.[7] There was only one gas truck that was a prime mover, and it had to be refilled from trucks carrying gas in drums and pumping with electric pumps salvaged out of airplanes. The work was performed in the rain by the light of lanterns and flashlights, and at 3:00 o'clock next morning only six ships were ready for take-off.

The time had been set at an operations meeting called by Combs as soon as the air crews had had their meal of corned beef and coffee.[8] Orders had been waiting for them at Del Monte to attack the 80 Japanese transports in Lingayen Gulf and then go in to land at San Marcelino. These orders were already nearly thirty-six hours old, and in Combs's opinion, to carry out the second phase of them would probably mean throwing his planes away. Neither he nor his pilots could understand any possible purpose in it. For it would mean landing at a field that had no proper facilities and not an atom of antiaircraft defense, when presumably they would be pursued by enemy fighters. The nine planes were the only combat-worthy bombers in the Southwest Pacific and Combs considered it absolutely essential to save them if he could; but he hardly knew what to do. Finally he decided to take off with as many of his planes as were ready by 3:00 o'clock, in order to bring them over

---

* The dead were Maj. Chauncey B. Whitney, Base Operations Officer, and Pfc. Allan Thibido. It might be remarked here that criticism attributed to 2nd Lt. Frank Kurtz (now Col.), in the book QUEENS DIE PROUDLY, about the management of Del Monte by the 5th Air Base Unit, held true only for the first days of the war: "Here on this beautiful field we saw people who did not seem to know there was a war on. The only military were some kind of transportation outfit. The first day we were there I got hold of a couple of privates and gave them orders to dim headlights of every car, no matter whose, that approached the field, but when the boys, carrying out my orders, stopped a staff car, the Transportation Officer decided he'd stop all that nonsense." This officer was undoubtedly Maj. Whitney. To men fresh from the bombing on Luzon, procedure undoubtedly seemed criminally lax. Yet the units on Mindanao maintained their base till after Corregidor surrendered, built fields all over the island, and performed every task asked of them, including the rescue of crashed tactical personnel of Lt. Kurtz's 19th Group.

Lingayen at dawn. They would attack the shipping as ordered and then fly back over San Marcelino. If there was then no pursuit and it looked feasible to land, they would do so; but if not, they would keep on to Australia. So the men were sent back to their planes to get what sleep they could.

The six planes ready for take-off at 3:00 A.M. were piloted by Combs, Tash, Parsel, Coats, Teats, and Keiser. The rain had not let up all night; it was driving across the field in sheets when the men climbed into their planes. Combs's engines balked; he could not get them started, and Parsel had to take over the lead of the first three-ship flight. His ship roared down the field towards the inky gulf of the canyon at the far end and lifted into the darkness. Only the top position light of his plane showed his course, and the rain soon drowned it out. Tash followed him.

The second flight then took off with Coats leading and Keiser and Teats on his wings. Very soon after take-off, however, one of Coats's engines started missing and he was compelled to turn back; but instead of going in to Del Monte again, he decided to take the plane all the way out to Batchelor Field. That left only four B-17s to go up to Lingayen.

As soon as Coats dropped out, Keiser and Teats turned to join the first flight, which was waiting for them out beyond Cagayan, over Macajalar Bay, and perhaps 20 miles from Del Monte. They were above the rain, but at their altitude it was very hazy and a still higher overcast shut out the moon and what starlight there might have been. As the last two planes swung over to intercept the course Parsel and Tash were flying, a new, bright light appeared on their right following a line about 20 degrees off their own. From its course they felt sure that it could not be one of the old B-18s on a ferry flight with parts and supplies from Clark Field; and Teats took his plane over to investigate. At 1000 yards the crew identified the stranger positively as Japanese.

Teats tried to maneuver his ship to bring some of its guns to bear; but it was so sluggish with its overload of bombs and gas that the Japanese pilot merely hung his plane on the Fortress's tail. "It was maddening. He could fly much slower, and every time we turned or maneuvered, he . . . followed us. It was like trying to evade our own shadow. When

I realized that we couldn't shake him and get in suitable firing position, I started to climb." [9]

Teats's one idea was to keep the Japanese from following the other three ships, which were now almost out of sight in the mist. For a while the Japanese pilot tried to climb with the Fortress; but on finding that he could not match the pace, he leveled off a few thousand feet below. Even at a lower altitude he began to fall behind, and Teats, heading west, led him on until he lost interest and turned back. Then at last the Fortress was swung to the north once more.

In spite of the maneuvering with the silent Jap, the navigator's heading [*] was so accurate that when dawn broke, after two hours of flying on instruments, the Fortress was within five miles of its calculated position. But its course to the target had been separate from that of the other three planes, and it had to go in alone. Curiously enough it had arrived first, and the Japs were very little aroused by the lone ship in the clouds. A few cruisers were throwing up some flak but it was light, short, and far behind, and the B–17 cruised over the invasion fleet for fifteen minutes while the bombardier [†] looked for the biggest target. He picked out two 25,000-ton transports lying close together near the shore, and as Teats took over the plane after the bombing run and circled sharp to the south, the air crew saw two of the bombs score waterline hits, one near the bow of each ship. They were only 100-pounders, but they must have done some damage.

By then the Zeros were coming up through the thin overcast. They broke into the clear about 2000 feet under the B–17, in a formation front of 14 planes, and all fired one long and simultaneous burst. To the bottom gunner in the Fortress it looked like "a fiery burst of blossoms in the lightening sky";[10] but the bomber was not even touched.

As soon as they had fired, all the Japanese pursuit turned back. Probably an order for their recall had come in over their radios, for by this time Parsel and Tash, with Keiser some little way behind, were making their own runs on the fleet.[‡]

[*] He was 2nd Lt. F. K. McAllister.

[†] Sgt. C. R. Payne.

[‡] There is some uncertainty about the position of Keiser's plane. Vandevanter, who was his co-pilot, says they went in on the leader's wing (Parsel's). But Hoffman, who was Tash's navigator and kept an accurate log of his missions, says Parsel and Tash went in

They had come north along the east coast of Luzon and then cut west-ward, crossing the mountains near Baguio, though the town was hidden under a dense blanket of cloud, and approached the Lingayen shore at 21,000 feet with their three planes in the eye of the rising sun.

The sunrise, one of the most beautiful the fliers had ever seen, flooded the entire sky. The clouds and mountain edges underneath the three planes were dipped in crimson; and as they neared the coastline, they saw the color reaching infinitely beyond them across the China Sea. But the gulf lay in the shadow of the land.

When they looked down into this belt of darkness, it seemed as though the whole Japanese Navy lay under them. Eight rows of transports paralleled the land and, close in, a long line of cruisers and destroyers were bombarding the shore. It was hazy near the water, but everywhere they looked they could see landing barges, lacing white wakes in and out among the bigger ships in restless service of the beaches. For the first time the men in the three B–17s began to comprehend the full power that the Japanese could bring against them.

Then, far back where deeper shadows clung in the folds of the land, they saw the answering flashes from the American guns. The gunfire looked thin and scattered and hopelessly small against the invasion fleet, but the men in the Fortresses could not forget it. It was their last glimpse of the American battle for Luzon.

They wasted no time above the target. They made all their runs in the line of approach, straight west across the invasion fleet. They were scared. Inside their planes the air was bitter cold, and they were shivering, for they had only the same thin clothes they had first taken down to Del Monte on December 6. There was almost no antiaircraft fire to inter-fere with their runs; but as the light below spread into the Gulf, they could count more and more shipping stretched out along the coast as far as they could see, and the small answering fire seemed to fade out.

Two of the planes were loaded with 300-pound bombs.[11] The other, like Teats's, had only 100-pounders. But once the bombs were dropped, their one idea was to get out of there. Some of Tash's crew had seen

together and that Keiser never did catch up. As they left the target, however, another bomber was coming off the mountains. They thought at the time it was Teats, but it was almost certainly Keiser.

orange-painted Japanese fighters take off along a little strip beside the beach; and in nine minutes two of these planes had climbed to 18,000 feet without losing ground to the B-17s, which in their own right were making a ground speed of 300 miles an hour. This performance offered a new lesson in the capabilities of the Japanese Zero. But neither the orange-painted pair nor the planes of the standing patrol that had turned back from their pursuit of Teats and now made a pass at Keiser were able to close the gap enough for an effective attack.

It would have been suicide, however, to attempt to land at San Marcelino while they were still within view of the Japanese pursuit, so the four B-17s continued on into the south till they reached Ambon, in the southern Moluccas, where the Dutch had set up a small air base.* Here they spent the night, for they had been flying for 25 out of the past 32 hours, with little or no sleep at Del Monte, and the Dutch pressed hospitality upon them. It was past noon on December 24 when they finally returned to Batchelor Field,[12] completing the 4600 miles they had flown to drop a little better than a ton of bombs apiece on each of their two targets.

Of the four planes † that had been left behind at Del Monte, only one did any further bombing. When Combs finally got his engines started, it was too late to overtake the others, so he took off alone to attack Cotabato in western Mindanao, where Japanese activity had been reported; but finding nothing, he returned to Batchelor. The remaining three planes took off from Del Monte at 30-minute intervals beginning at 4:30. They had planned a joint attack on Lingayen, but their rendezvous failed, and as they had orders not to go up singly, they started back for Australia. Two of them flew straight back, but the third, piloted by Lieutenant Godman, went down to bomb Davao in the dawn before returning to Batchelor Field.

While these ships were homing, Operations at Batchelor was trying to stage further attacks. Two planes were sent up to Del Monte on the

* Teats, after his maneuvers to shake the Jap plane, hadn't gas enough to reach Ambon and had to go in to San José, Mindoro, but overtook the rest at Ambon.

† Coats, as will be recalled, had returned direct to Batchelor Field after losing an engine at the start of the flight.

23rd; but both were turned back—one with supercharger trouble and the second when it heard that the field had been under heavy attack that day. Its engines were behaving badly when it reached home, and the 19th Group's Status Report at Batchelor for December 24 showed: "Three B-17s on mission. Four here in commission. Seven here out of commission." [13] Long flights, overtime at maximum performance, and lack of adequate servicing were bearing inevitable fruit. Seven planes in commission formed the entire American bomber force in the Southwest Pacific. But on Christmas Day it was to fall still lower.

The three planes listed "on mission" had gone up to Del Monte on the 24th. They expected to find orders waiting for them, but as none had come through they decided to bomb Davao at sunrise Christmas morning. While taxiing out, one of them blew a tire and had to be left behind.* The other two took off, each plane loaded with seven 300-pound bombs and the 2100 gallons of gas needed to take it back to Australia; and, climbing to 15,000 feet, they leveled off and headed together for Davao.

Lieutenant George E. Schaetzel was leading the flight of two, with Lieutenant Alvin J. H. Mueller in the wing position. Perhaps the fact that it was Christmas morning helped keep the planes in close formation; but close as they were, there was not yet light enough for the crew of one plane to see men's faces in the windows of the other.† The air stream and the drone of engines sealed them in and their ship acquired a living identity of its own wholly apart from the memories, hopes, or fears of any member of the crew, while the other ship, in the dark sky above the tumbled clouds and the wild and empty mountains, became for the time being as aloof in flight and seemingly inhuman as any

---

* Piloted by Lt. Weldon H. Smith. There were no facilities or wing-jack at Del Monte to lift a ship while a main tire was changed, but that did not bother the crew. They blocked up a wing and dug a pit under the punctured tire, repaired the damage, re-mounted the wheel, filled the hole, knocked out the wing blocks, and took off during a strafing attack by Jap planes, proceeded to Davao, and bombed shipping in broad daylight.[14]

† The members of the two crews were: in Schaetzel's plane, 2nd Lt. E. C. Wade; 2nd Lt. Stanley Cottage; 2nd Lt. A. E. Oliver; T/Sgt. F. D. Secrest; S/Sgt. J. L. Cannon; Sgt. V. Spaziano; Pfc. J. A. Resl. In Mueller's, 2nd Lt. R. G. Teborek; 2nd Lt. G. M. Markovich; S/Sgt. W. J. Weiss; T/Sgt. C. R. Shellito; S/Sgt. C. W. Anderson; Pfc. E. R. Olsen; Cpl. F. A. Harvey.

bird. But, as they made their approach on the airdrome at Davao, with the dawn breaking, the side gunners could see the men inside the other plane and raise a hand in greeting. It was a comforting thing in an alien sky above an enemy base. Then, a few minutes later, antiaircraft bursts came up between them.

The Japanese were developing the place as a staging area for their next move into the Netherlands East Indies, and they had obviously brought in a lot of antiaircraft, for the fire was heavy and accurate. While still in their bombing run, Schaetzel's plane was hit once and Mueller's, which like Colin Kelly's was one of the old "C" models, was hit twice; but both completed their runs and dropped their bombs across the airport. Almost immediately afterwards they were attacked by ten Japanese fighters, including both Zeros and Messerschmitts; and at the very first pass, one of the engines in Schaetzel's plane was shot out and one of the gunners, Sergeant Cannon, fatally wounded.

The loss of the engine slowed Schaetzel's plane enough to make it dangerously vulnerable to attack, but Mueller stayed with it, and for the next twenty minutes interposed his own ship between Schaetzel's and the Japanese pursuit. The gunners in both ships fought off every attack, though two * in Mueller's were seriously wounded, and Cannon had fought his gun until he could no longer hold himself up.

Both B–17s were badly holed, but where Schaetzel's had perhaps a dozen hits, Mueller's had taken almost as heavy a beating as had Wheless's on the Legaspi mission.† Though they had climbed during the running fight to 28,000 feet, the Zeros, because of Schaetzel's dead engine, were able to swarm all over them even at that altitude. When the Japanese finally gave up and turned back to their own base, the B–17s had over 1100 miles to cover; but they were able to keep together all the way and limped into Batchelor Field in the afternoon. Mueller's plane was so badly disabled that only the pilot's skill averted a serious crash as it landed. If they had not met good weather almost the whole way home, they could never have returned at all.

* Cpl. Harvey; Pfc. Olsen.

† Citations for Mueller and his crew state conservatively that the plane had "more than 100 holes." Most pilots describe it as being nearly as badly sieved as Wheless's. One Zero was shot down.[15]

It made a grim ending to Christmas. The wounded men were taken to the hospital in Darwin, while Captain Combs spent all the rest of the day unraveling red tape to arrange for Cannon's burial beside the field * and Major Walsh made out his status report for December 25:

Three B–17s in commission here. One at Del Monte, status unknown. Seven here out of commission.†

Of those seven, three now needed a depot overhaul, which meant sending them all the way to Melbourne, some 2000 miles to the south.

The eleven remaining planes were the ones that General Brereton found at Batchelor Field four days later on his arrival from the Philippines. These eleven went up to Java to begin the defense of the Netherlands Indies.

27. *Departure of FEAF*

GENERAL BRERETON with a few key members of his staff had pulled out of Manila on the evening of December 24 in fairly dramatic circumstances. He had maintained for some time that it was no longer possible for FEAF Headquarters to function in the Philippines and had advocated its removal to a base in which it might operate to some purpose. Radio communications were so tenuous that Brereton at this time had no real idea even of how many B–17s the 19th Group had left; and after the Lingayen mission of the 23rd, General MacArthur himself reported that his bombing potentialities were exhausted.[1] On December 24, with his own Headquarters beginning its removal to Corregidor, he finally gave Brereton permission to leave.

It was now obvious that Manila's fate was sealed by the Japanese landings in Lamon Bay. After their first landing at Atimonan, a second was made at Mauban, about 17 miles up the coast. These two forces, once they worked into the clear, would have direct access to Manila over Highways 1 and 21. But in the course of the same day the Japanese

* In June 1945 Cannon's body had been removed to Sydney.
† The plane at Del Monte was Weldon Smith's. It came in to Batchelor Field near sunset.[16]

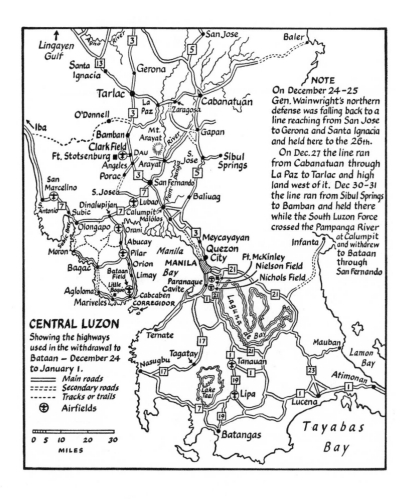

NOTE

On December 24-25 Gen. Wainwright's northern defense was falling back to a line reaching from San Jose to Gerona and Santa Ignacia and held here to the 26th.

On Dec. 27 the line ran from Cabanatuan through La Paz to Tarlac and high land west of it. Dec 30-31 the line ran from Sibul Springs to Bamban and held there while the South Luzon Force crossed the Pampanga River at Calumpit and withdrew to Bataan through San Fernando

CENTRAL LUZON

Showing the highways
used in the withdrawal to
Bataan — December 24
to January 1.

═══ Main roads
:::::: Secondary roads
----- Tracks or trails
⊕ Airfields

0 5 10   20   30
MILES

made yet a third landing, this time on the west coast a bare 60 miles southwest of the city.*

Though the last landing was on a much smaller scale, its effect was to create a pincers within a pincers. The main pressure on General MacArthur's army, of course, was developing between the five Japanese divisions driving down from Lingayen Gulf and the combined landings in the south; but the latter in turn exerted a lateral pressure between their east and west elements that not only put the newly completed airfields at Tanauan and Lipa automatically at the disposal of the Japanese but also directly threatened to cut Highway No. 1. This road was the sole escape route of the Philippine-American troops in the Legaspi area and it was necessary for them to fall back in full haste before they could attack the beachheads in Lamon Bay.

In fact the retreat of the South Luzon Force to Bataan, which began here, had to be carried through what amounted to a gantlet for nearly its entire length: first between these southern Japanese forces and then, above Manila, across the front of the Japanese Lingayen army which was being held in check by Wainwright's thinned and tired regiments on a line between Baliuag and Bamban. It was an ordeal that might well have demoralized more experienced troops. Two divisions of the underarmed and partially trained Philippine Army did break: the 91st in the north and the 51st in the south. But in the closing hours of December remnants of the 91st still held in the line at Baliuag in company with a regiment of the 71st and one battalion of field artillery, while the last elements of the South Luzon Force under Brigadier General Albert M. Jones were crossing the Calumpit Bridge behind them. In this South Luzon Force was the 51st Division, which, once it had been rallied, had held together all through its retreat.

The rear-guard actions fought by these green Filipino troops will probably never be recorded in detail, and against the panorama of the Pacific war they may seem small, disorderly affairs, for many of the men who took part in them had had less than a month under military discipline, some as little as three days. They were underarmed, lacked adequate tank support, and had no air cover at all. Some, as will be noted, did

---

* At Nasugbu, Batangas Province, from which Highway 17 offered a first-class separate route into Manila.[2]

not even know how to set up the heavy guns that had been assigned to them. Yet they brought off their retreat according to schedule. The Japanese Lingayen army did not reach the Calumpit Bridge until General Wainwright personally gave the order to blow it up on New Year's morning after all but a platoon of Engineers had crossed. And it was not till much later the same day that the Japanese forces in the south finally entered Manila.

The time that had been gained was the key to the whole stand on Bataan. It made possible the removal of Air Corps and service troops, hospitals, heavy machinery, and Quartermaster stocks that would otherwise not have reached Bataan at all. But it was a hair-raising business from beginning to end, for it had to be carried out over a single road.

Besides Highway No. 3, which was the main route to the north, there were one or two secondary roads leading out of Manila. But they all came together in the village of Calumpit, whose bridge provided the only road crossing of the Pampanga River. More than half of the men and a good proportion of the supplies that eventually reached Bataan were to cross over this single span. Eleven miles further on, Highway No. 3 came into San Fernando,* a town of twisting narrow streets through which the retreating troops must filter as they turned southwest on the homestretch for Bataan. But here again there was only one road, dirt surfaced for the most part, and running through the open country round the head of Manila Bay.

To gain the time necessary for the evacuation of Manila and then to join their two forces at Calumpit and make good their retreat through San Fernando was the task General MacArthur's Headquarters imposed on Generals Wainwright and Jones. It called for cool heads, courage, and sound organizational ability. Fortunately, both men had these qualities in full measure, and the calm atmosphere near the front firing lines provided a heartening contrast to the confusion in Air Headquarters at Fort McKinley.†

---

* This was San Fernando, Pampanga, not to be confused with the other San Fernando, La Union Province, on the shore of Lingayen Gulf.

† 2nd Lt. Gerrity of the 27th Bombardment Group, who had been assigned to Wainwright as Air Liaison Officer, wrote in his diary: "I had been depressed talking to people behind the lines down south, but the calm atmosphere near the front firing lines gave me a boost." [3]

No one seemed to know what was going on. Fort McKinley appeared to exist in a vacuum. For the past few days the military situation had seemed easier, so the first intimation of the removal of General Headquarters to Corregidor came as a shock. This was particularly true in the case of the Air Surgeon, Major Kennard, who had returned from Fort Stotsenburg only the day before. Up there the feeling had been that the fighting was going better, and to Kennard the Air Force personnel had seemed more unified and in a better mental attitude than at any time since the start of the war.* When he returned to Fort McKinley, things seemed to be going more smoothly at Air Headquarters too. Then on the morning of the 24th he had to go in to the Philippine Department Surgeon's office in Fort Santiago to confer with Colonel Wibb E. Cooper and his assistant, Lieutenant Colonel Manning. There he found that Cooper had moved to Corregidor with part of General MacArthur's staff.

At the time, a red alert was sounding over Manila and all the people went down into the tunnels. The Japanese came over in one of the heaviest attacks they staged during the war. For the past few days they had been working without much success on the shipping that still remained in Manila Bay, including the two destroyers *Peary* and *Pillsbury;* but on this Christmas Eve morning they shifted their attention to the port area and the people sheltering under the old fort beside the Pasig River could feel the rolling shock waves that came from heavy bombs. The entire waterfront became a shambles. Streetcars were thrown against buildings, the rails ripped out of the pavement and left crumpled like straws. Windows through all the lower city were blown out and whole sections of walls torn away; and bomb craters left many of the streets impassable except to foot traffic. The Engineer Island area at the mouth of the river was almost obliterated. When Kennard was let up out of the tunnels with the others, the air even inside the fort was choking with the dust of pulverized cement and stone, and a pall of dense smoke already overhung the city so that the Pasig River flowed with the same dull ominous green sheen it shows at the breaking of a heavy storm.

---

* In his capacity as Surgeon for the Air Force, Kennard was on General Brereton's staff, which with his continual visits to outlying squadrons kept him in touch with all the varying degrees of command inside the Air Force. He was also Surgeon for the Air Service Command.

When Kennard got back to the Surgeon's office he found Lieutenant Colonel Manning burning papers in a corner. The old fort, being built entirely of stone, was fireproof, and all through the offices men were piling papers on the floor and setting fire to them, including, among others, the famous Orange Plan. In a way, this action proved to be symbolic as far as the Air Corps was concerned, for its withdrawal to Bataan was almost completely unorganized. No one seemed to know what anyone else was doing and getting there was something that more or less just happened. In the end it was nearer a rout than a withdrawal.

By the time he was ready to return to Fort McKinley, Kennard had learned that Manila was to be evacuated by all military and government establishments so that MacArthur could declare it an open city; but no orders affecting the removal of the Air Corps had reached his own office. The first indication he had was when Lieutenant Roland J. Barnick called in for the necessary medical equipment and personnel to set up an advanced Air Headquarters on Bataan.* A detachment of cooks and service troops had already been assigned to him and he was nearly ready to go.

Kennard assigned various medical men and saw them started. About 3:00 P.M. a telephone call came from the Flight Surgeon at Nichols Field, Lieutenant Colonel Charles H. Morhouse, who said that all units at Nichols had been ordered to move into Manila and take a boat over to Bataan. Morhouse needed ambulances and trucks for his own people.

Kennard got Morhouse's ambulances over to him and saw them off towards Manila. The rim of the bay was still covered by its heavy cloud of smoke and from Nichols Field one could see that more fires were going at Cavite. It was fairly late in the afternoon when Kennard returned to Fort McKinley.

He found Headquarters in a state of utter disorganization. Instructions were being given in a hectic manner and no one seemed to know what anyone else had done or where he could be found. Lieutenant Colonel Charles H. Caldwell, FEAF Personnel Officer,† was no longer

---

* This appears to have been a little before noon.

† In a reorganization of FEAF on December 17, Caldwell had been shifted from A-3 (Operations) to A-1 (Personnel); Eubank had been made A-3; Maj. R. F. C. Vance was A-2 (Intelligence), a post he had been assigned to verbally on December 8; and George remained A-4 (Supply).[4]

there. Kennard could not find anyone who knew where General Brereton was. Colonel George also was absent. Actually he had gone to Bataan the day before with Captain Eads to locate sites for new air strips, but no one to whom Kennard talked had any idea of where he had gone or when he would return. No one, in fact, seemed to know who was in command.

Frequent alerts added to the confusion. Everyone would go down into the unfinished tunnel underneath the Officers' Club; but as no raids hit Fort McKinley that afternoon, they would all presently troop back up and return to their respective sections. It was about 6:00 P.M. when Kennard finally went over to the Air Service Command to see if Colonel Churchill knew what was going on.

The Air Service Command was the one orderly spot in Headquarters. Colonel Churchill had his people busily at work packing up the files; but he himself had little information to offer beyond the fact that all Air Force units had been ordered to Bataan. There was a report that the armies were deteriorating and another that the Japs had made a new landing near Pollilo Bight, due east of Manila. Tanks had been rushed north in the afternoon, but the movements of the tanks did not provide much of a clue to the situation. They were always going or coming in a hurry. It seemed plain that the Colonel was about as much in the dark as anyone else, but because he was the senior officer then at Headquarters, Kennard felt that there was little he could do but sit around and wait till Churchill made a move. A unit of the Signal Corps under Captain L. A. Mason was standing by also. The incongruous thing about the situation to the younger officers was that here was a senior staff officer with obviously little knowledge of what was going on.

Though he did not mention it to Kennard, Colonel Churchill had spoken to General Brereton only a little over two hours before. He had been inspecting air strips south of the city and on his return one of his staff met him with news of the impending move to Bataan; but the officer could not tell him any more than that, so Churchill, like Kennard, had set out to make the rounds in search of information. FEAF Operations was empty, nor was there a sign of life in either the Chief of Staff's office or the AGO; but when Churchill opened the door of Brereton's office, he found the General sitting there alone at his desk.

Brereton immediately asked where his airplane was. This was a Beechcraft that had been sent down to Del Monte with rations the day before. The pilot, who was Pappy Gunn, was presumably on his way back, but Churchill could not tell Brereton when to expect him, and in his turn he asked about the move to Bataan. The General told him merely that the Air Force was to move and that there were no written orders. Nothing was said about the impending departure of the FEAF staff nor of any change in the Air Force command.[5] It was only later, when his Executive Officer, Lieutenant Colonel Maitland, came in with the announcement that he himself had been selected by Brereton as one of the FEAF party to evacuate Luzon, that Churchill learned of the change and that the air command was probably to go to George.

One of the very few people in Fort McKinley to realize that the FEAF staff were pulling out was Captain Ind, who had returned as Intelligence Officer of the 5th Interceptor Command * after a brief period with Public Relations in General MacArthur's Headquarters. The reports on the Japanese raid against the Manila waterfront had just come in when Ind was requested by FEAF Operations to supply additional flight maps to the south. Soerabaja, Bandoeng, and Batavia were specified as well as Darwin. It was Lieutenant Colonel Caldwell speaking.

Ind, who was full of curiosity, decided to take the completed maps round to FEAF Headquarters in person and there found Caldwell in conference with General Brereton, Colonel Brady, and Lieutenant Colonel Eubank. From words let fall as the maps changed hands, Ind had no doubt that FEAF Headquarters was about to be transferred, and somewhat later he had a brief session with Brereton in which neither man referred to the General's near departure or the people who were to be left behind.[6]

Brereton's position during these trying hours is not difficult to understand. He had come to the Philippines with the knowledge that he was expected to pit a small, unbalanced air force against overwhelming nu-

* The reader will recall that the three integral parts of FEAF were the Air Service Command (Col. Churchill), the 5th Bomber Command (Lt. Col. Eubank), and the 5th Interceptor Command (now under Col. George, who had succeeded General Clagett on the latter's departure for Australia, December 19).

merical odds and had accepted its command with a profound conviction of the unwisdom of attempting to do so. On his arrival he had been bitterly disappointed by how little had been accomplished by his predecessors. Now he had lost most of his air force. He had only a handful of bombers—he was not at all sure how many—in Darwin. There were no longer enough pursuit for effective interception. The air war in the Philippines, as far as he was concerned, was over. Future reinforcements would come in to Australia or the Netherlands East Indies, where the re-forming of units would have to take place. It was plain that a strategic headquarters would have far greater scope there than on Bataan.*

Early in the afternoon of the 24th he had been summoned to General Headquarters where, after a brief conference with MacArthur, he received his orders.

> 1. You will proceed to the south with your Headquarters, Far East Air Force. Your mission is to organize advanced operating bases from which, with the Far East Air Force, you can protect the lines of communications, secure bases in Mindanao, and support the defense of the Philippines by the U. S. Army Forces in the Far East. You will co-operate with the U. S. Navy and the air and naval forces of Australia and the Netherlands Indies. . . .[8]

On his return to Air Headquarters, Brereton called a staff meeting which Brady, Eubank, Colonel Richards,† and a very few other officers attended. The smallness of the meeting was in part due to the necessity for secrecy, which did not need to be stressed, for Radio Tokyo had kept the Pacific world informed of Brereton's movements during his November trip to Australia. At the meeting Brereton announced that George was to take over the Air Force command in the Philippines and then named the men who were to go out to Australia. The party would not be a large one; ‡ but the problem of transportation presented diffi-

---

* In his Diaries Brereton says he was ordered south by MacArthur, apparently against his will, for he asked to remain.[7] Eubank, however, says that before December 24, Brereton had suggested that FEAF Headquarters should go where it could operate and that finally General MacArthur gave permission for him and a few of his staff to go. Desire on the part of a professional soldier to be where he has tools to fight with would seem neither unnatural nor discreditable.

† Col. H. H. C. Richards was, next to Brereton, the senior AAF officer in the Philippines. However, he was not a member of the FEAF Staff, but Senior Air Staff Officer on General MacArthur's staff.

‡ The members of FEAF selected to go out with Brereton were: Col. Brady (Chief of Staff); Lt. Col. Eubank (A-3); Lt. Col. Caldwell (A-1); Capt. Norman J. Llewellyn and

culties. All B–17s had by now left the Philippines and the only means of getting off Luzon by air was in the unarmed transport planes of the Philippine Air Lines, or in one of the Navy's PBYs. Captain Gunn had not yet reported in from Del Monte and Brereton was informed that his planes would need up to 48 hours' maintenance to prepare them for such a flight. The Navy, however, had a PBY scheduled to leave that night for Java with four places available in it for Army personnel. Brereton decided to go out in this plane, taking Brady, Eubank, and Llewellyn, his senior aide, with him and leaving the rest to follow as quickly as transport could be provided. At 4:00 P.M. December 24 he officially closed his Headquarters at Fort McKinley and radioed the commanding officer at Darwin that Headquarters, FEAF, were transferred as of that hour and date.[9]

There now occurred what was in effect a complete hiatus in the Air Force command. With only two hours to pack in, Brereton and the three men who were to accompany him left Fort McKinley at once for their own quarters. So apparently did most, if not all, of the other officers slated to go out with FEAF Headquarters. George, who was to take the command, was not on hand till later in the evening.

George's movements during the afternoon are obscure. According to Ind, he did not return from his Bataan trip till late in the afternoon; then, on being informed of the withdrawal to Bataan and Brereton's departure, he went almost immediately to Manila to confer with Mac-Arthur and Sutherland and there learned that he was to have the command.[10] Ind conveys the impression that this was George's first intimation that the command would be his; but George must have known earlier than this that he would succeed Brereton, who from the first had intended to have George as his fighter commander, and who had taken George into his confidence.[11] In any case, he was not available through the afternoon to anyone in Headquarters, and, when he finally returned in the evening, the Air Force units were already streaming into Manila from the south, heading either for the waterfront or out along

Lt. E. W. Hampton, his aides; Maj. Samuel S. Lamb (Signal Corps); Capts. W. G. Hipps and L. E. Hobbs (formerly with the 27th Bombardment Group and now attached to FEAF); and two enlisted men—T/Sgt. J. E. Felton and S/Sgt. Frank Dean.

the roads leading to the north, most of them ignorant of the military situation, all of them confused as to the meaning of MacArthur's proclamation of Manila as an open city (they thought this meant that they had to get out at once, destroying everything they could not immediately take with them), and few with definite orders beyond the bare fact that they were to go to Bataan either by boat or by truck convoy. Manila itself was hideous with explosions and great bursting fires set off by the demolition squads at Cavite, Nichols Field, and all round the city proper; and, walled off by the confusion at the docks, most of the troops had to find their way through by hit or miss, commandeering their own transportation.

No plan was followed.* It was left to the individual units to make their own way. That they all came through as well as they did spoke well for the initiative and enterprise of the unit commanders, though some, naturally, made a better showing than others. But it was a confused and chaotic movement, carried through in the utter absence of an over-all Air Force command.

In the meantime the evacuating staff were having their own difficulties. During the two hours they were in Manila, the Japanese elected to bomb the city once more and, as Brereton records, the house in which he had his quarters was hit twice. "For the first time . . . no one seemed to mind particularly, except the servants, who promptly cleared out." [13] These hours, however, must have been hard on Eubank, who had been smashed up about eight days before in an auto accident in the Manila blackout † and was now getting around with two sprained ankles and a broken wrist.

* Warning of the move had been fairly short. "During the night of December 21-22 I was called on the phone by one of my staff officers who said that he had been called by G-4, Hq., USAFFE and told to prepare a plan for the movement of all Air Force units to Bataan. He transmitted the message to someone on the FEAF staff and was told that we should prepare the plan. I joined him in my office and together we tried to prepare a plan. We struggled with it for a couple of hours but ran into so many difficulties because command decisions from FEAF were necessary that we had to give it up. The next day I explained to General Brereton what we had attempted to do and why we couldn't complete the plan. . . . Of course the evacuation order, which was transmitted verbally, contained the first information we had as to what water transportation would be available for the move." [12]

† Kennard said that during this period more men were being injured in blackout driving than from enemy bombs.

It had happened shortly after O'Donnell's recall from Del Monte, and Eubank had been on his way down from Clark Field to see General Brereton, in part about that episode. It was necessary to take him to Sternberg Hospital. The accident, to General Brereton, who was naturally upset both by the recall of O'Donnell and by the subsequent loss of Major Gibbs, must have seemed the last straw. Operations at Clark Field had not been going too well anyhow, but now with Eubank out of the picture, nothing seemed to go right. Brereton sent for Major Kennard and insisted that Eubank must be patched up enough to return to Headquarters. It was rigorous treatment, and when Kennard protested, Brereton exclaimed, "I don't want his arms and legs—what I want is his brains." Eubank was released from the hospital and returned to Fort McKinley, using crutches and with a cast on his arm.

Brereton and his party reported at Cavite about dusk. From there they had to take a boat across the bay to Mariveles, the tiny port on the southern tip of Bataan, where the PBY was waiting.* Night had fallen before the passengers were aboard. Mariveles was blacked out and its little harbor, shadowed still deeper by the lower slopes of Mariveles Mountain, was like an inkpot as the PBY moved out, turned, and began its run across the water. The heavy plane was already up on the step and nearly airborne when a fishing boat loomed in the darkness directly ahead. The pilot made a violent and almost miraculous water loop, but the port wing of the plane struck the vessel's mast and the wing-float was broken off.[14] Without it the plane could not fly and there was nothing for the passengers to do but take their boat back across the bay to Cavite.

After some delay, they were told there that another PBY was available at the far end of Laguna de Bay. Like the first, this plane was one of four that had been put back in flying condition after being knocked out at the beginning of the war and held in the Manila area for reconnaissance work and to provide transport for high officials. During daylight hours they were kept hidden in the deep rush banks that fringe Laguna de Bay, and this second ship was at its daytime anchorage near Los Baños.

* Brereton says that the PBY was waiting at Cavite; but Eubank and also Kennard, who talked afterwards to the pilot (Lt. Harmon Utter, U.S.N.), both say that the ship was waiting at Mariveles.

It meant a 50-mile drive through the blackout and bucking the tide of troops evacuating from the south. Once Brereton's car was side-swiped by a truck and had to stop while the crumpled fender was torn off.[15] When they came out from under the pall of smoke that covered all Manila, they had faint light from a quarter moon; but it was already low in the west, which gave them added concern, for they needed its light in taking off from Laguna de Bay.[16]

At Los Baños they were put in the care of a Filipino guide who was supposed to lead them to the hidden plane. He started off in the darkness and they followed, single file, each man carrying his baggage, down a narrow, winding, carabao path that stretched on interminably, while all the time the moon sank lower. The uneven going in the dark was sheer torture for Eubank, hobbling along on his sprained ankles; but when they finally reached the shore, there was no plane. The guide had brought them to the anchorage of the first PBY—the one over which mechanics were now desperately working back at Mariveles.

Once more the party had to retrace their way up the dark path until after a while they found a rowboat, and setting forth in that they at last discovered their second plane.[17] The take-off was without incident and, though they were behind schedule, so that daylight found them still in fighter reach of Mindanao, there was a solid overcast to cover them.

V I I

The Retreat to Bataan

28. Fort McKinley: "Where the hell is all the Staff?"

THE AIR CORPS TROOPS that found their way onto Bataan on Christmas
Eve and Christmas Day numbered about 7000 men, but they were a
demoralized and disorganized command. As we have seen, the movement was already under way when Colonel George took over, after the
departure of General Brereton, and there was little he could do with
communications what they were except make sure that all unwarned
units, including his own 5th Interceptor Command Headquarters [1] and
the remnants of FEAF, were started also.

It must have been past 6:00 o'clock before George, after returning
from his twenty-four hours of scouting for airfield sites on Bataan, left
his own Headquarters for his conference at General Headquarters in
Manila. Confirmation of the fact that he was to take over the Air Force
command * can hardly have surprised him, yet one wonders what
ironic thoughts must have passed through his mind on the dark drive
back to Fort McKinley.

He had foreseen what a first-class air power would do to our Philippine defenses, but for a while his had been one of the very few voices
crying for more planes, more antiaircraft, more dispersal. It was only
after General MacArthur's assignment to over-all command and the

* Brereton makes no reference in his Diaries to George's taking over command of the
AF in the Philippines and, while technically the Air Corps was now directly under Mac-
Arthur with George as his Executive Officer, it seems a curious omission.

coincidental decision in Washington that the Philippines could be defended that George's views began to find effective backing. But by then it was too late. The planes, the men, and the new command rushed over were not enough. George himself, no longer Chief of Staff, spent most of the first two weeks of war in building the airfields which he had tried so hard to get before. And now at last, when the B-17s had been withdrawn entirely from the Philippines and only 16 battle-worn P-40s and four P-35s were left on Luzon,* he had the Air Force command.

Yet there is evidence to show that George was thinking less of himself and his pitiful remnant of planes at this time than of the men for whom he had suddenly become responsible. Most of them were technicians of one sort or another whose training had done little to prepare them for the kind of fighting they would have to do. They had little real discipline. They did not know how to take care of themselves in the field. And now they were all streaming towards Bataan, many without orders as to how they were to get there or where they were to go once they arrived. The prospect might have daunted any man.

It was past eight when at last he entered Air Headquarters in the Officers' Club and found what was left of FEAF still at dinner. They had been having a silent and gloomy meal. The darkness of the night outside seemed to have invaded the building; there was a lost feeling, as if no one knew where these men were or cared what became of them. And then George's solid, stocky figure appeared in the door and he came in asking if they had all eaten, if they had saved anything for him.

Colonel Churchill from the end of the table asked the question that had been in all their minds.

"Hal, where the hell is all the Staff?"

George told him, and there was a short but pregnant silence as the two men looked at each other. Churchill was senior officer of FEAF, and by the ordinary process the air command would have been his.

George said quietly, "Well, Colonel, this is the situation. General Mac-

---

* The 24th Pursuit Group Narrative says that there were six P-35s, but two had been lost that morning, as mentioned in Chapter 24 above. By January 1 there were only two P-35s in commission on Bataan in any case. There was also one P-40 which had been flown down to Del Monte by Lt. Brownwell on a courier mission and retained there for reconnaissance, and another, piloted by Lt. Feallock, went down on December 30.[2]

Arthur has taken over command of the Air Force, and I am his Deputy Chief of Staff. I don't know whether you like this, but that is the way it is today."

Neither then nor later was there any question of Colonel Churchill's full and unwavering support, and George went on to say that most of the units were on their way to Bataan, or would be by next morning. "We are all going over to Bataan."

There was another silence, which Major Kennard broke by asking, "What are we going to eat there?"

George said, "Hell, there's rice. There's fruit. The natives live there. The Igorots live there."

But George was entirely wrong about this, though it was to take time to convince him. In the first place the Igorots did not live there. They were farther north. No one can live in the mountains of Bataan unless he packs his own food in with him. Once in a while you can find a Negrito hunter roaming there, but that is all. Kennard, who had served longer in the Philippines, explained this. "We'll need a hell of a big food supply," he said.

George turned on him. "Can't you think of something besides adding to my troubles?" he demanded harshly.

But it would have to be faced. There had been talk of making Bataan into a great storehouse, but due to meager appropriations and MacArthur's decision to fight his battle on the beaches, little had been accomplished before the war. Some work had been done on Bataan Field; and in the spring of 1941 the Engineers had begun work on their depot above Mariveles. The site they chose was in deep woods, and, because of its height above the sea and the coolness of its shadowed air, the place was known as Little Baguio.*

But that was all that had been done on Bataan up to December 8. Most of the Army's essential food reserves were still stored in Manila, though rations for 10,000 troops for six months had been placed on Corregidor.[3] It should be remembered that the original plans covering a retreat to Bataan called for a defense by small units, and the Japanese attack had caught our Philippine forces in a phase of their expansion

* Baguio, the summer capital of the Commonwealth, high in the Mountain Province, was a cool haven often visited by Army men and their families.

in which their numerical strength had outgrown their matériel resources. One of the most serious shortages, actually a desperate one, was transportation.[4] For the past two weeks the Army had been throwing ordnance and Quartermaster's stores into Bataan by boat, lighter, and every conceivable type and size of truck that it could commandeer. A lot had been taken in; but now instead of a small force, some 90,000 men were retreating to Bataan.*

In the Officers' Club at Fort McKinley the discussion about living off the land was ended, and Colonel George told the men around him that they could go over to Bataan how and when they wished. He had no definite idea of where they were to locate their outfits but areas were supposed to be marked out for them when they got there. He himself then left the club to return to his own 5th Interceptor Command Headquarters and get some sleep.

When he had gone the others gathered outside the club.† All of them decided to put off the trip to Bataan till next morning, and after a few more minutes they separated to return individually to their own quarters.

But sleep was impossible. Demolitions at Nichols Field, Cavite, and all round Manila were making the night hideous. The uneasy underside of the great pall of smoke that covered all the sky was flickeringly lit by flashes from the countless smaller fires, but every now and then it would be torn asunder by heavier explosions that shook the ground even in Fort McKinley. And in the intervals of comparative silence, as the night grew, a new sound was gaining force and authenticity—the uneven, ceaseless mutter of truck trains rolling up from the south. Occasionally a line of trucks pulling out of the fort area itself would drown out this sound, but, little by little as they drew away, the diminishing roar of their engines would be absorbed by the softer but deeper sound of the general retreat. Within this mutter of retreat were the

---

* From the start of the defense of Bataan, according to General Sutherland, both General MacArthur and himself believed that June 15 "was the absolute maximum we could hold out."

† Besides Kennard there were Col. Churchill; Capt. J. E. Caldwell, who headed the service section of FEASC; and Maj. Lee Johnson, who had been Adjutant General of Clark Field and was slated to become Personnel Officer in the revised 5th Interceptor Command set up by Col. George on Bataan.

voices, the sharp and distant calls for directions, the answers, the abrupt challenges of sentries, heard and lost again, like the far, persisting cries of migratory birds.

After two hours Kennard gave up all thought of sleep and drove into Manila to round up three small panel trucks that he had secured earlier in the day as substitutes for ambulances. He loaded these with cartons of soap and the kind of supplies it seemed to him that other people might not think of, and also 350,000 quinine tablets and boxes of bandages from the Medical Supply Depot.* There he also picked up some Squadron first-aid kits that had been made up to his orders and packed in foot lockers. Then he took the trucks out to Fort McKinley and told the men to report at daylight.

Some time before an Army nurse, Lieutenant Willa Hook, had asked Kennard to bring her car down from Fort Stotsenburg on one of his trips and he had driven down in it on December 22. He now undertook to deliver the car to her at Sternberg General Hospital but was unable to find her. He did, however, run into Lieutenant Colonel Maitland, who, as we know, was one of the officers selected to go south and was still waiting for an airplane to take him. Maitland told Kennard about his mission and offered to take letters out for him. Kennard gave him a brief note for his wife and then for the second time drove back to Fort McKinley. The demolitions were still going on and the truck trains were still rolling through the city. From time to time Japanese planes would fly over, but there was no way of telling whether they dropped bombs or not; and now civilian Filipino refugees had begun to appear in the slowly moving traffic. No rest was possible for any man. Kennard sat out the hours before dawn, and about 8:00 he started forth with his small caravan, stopping only at Sternberg Hospital to talk for a few minutes with Major Craig and other doctors who planned to stay with their wounded patients and go into prison with them when the Japs took over.

Then with his trucks he found a place in the long lines moving out of the city towards the north, where, through the demolition blasts, they soon began to hear the rumble of artillery.

* The Air Corps had no Medical Supply Depot of its own but drew on the Philippine Medical Supply Depot, which furnished them with every medical supply at their disposal and often gave the Air Corps priority.

29. *Nielson Field: "Amounting to nearly a rout"*

CONSIDERING THE MANNER in which orders were sent out by Air Head-quarters and the vacuum that developed there almost immediately after-wards, it is remarkable that the Air Corps units in retreat held together as well as they did. Many were commanded by young officers who had little knowledge of how to look out for their men. Suddenly they were called over the telephone and told to get moving. Not a word of ex-planation was given except that Manila was to be an open city. ". . . The greatest haste (amounting to nearly a rout) and speed were urged. You couldn't take any more luggage and equipment than you could carry and no specific things were designated to be taken." [1] When they called Fort McKinley back again for more definite instructions, they got no answer. "Air Force Headquarters just quit work and disappeared all at once." [2]

Squadrons, scattered to begin with, were ordered to unite on the Manila docks, in the blackout and chaos resulting from the Japanese bombing. No policing of the district seemed to exist, at least for directing traffic, and the confusion was indescribable. Men were getting aboard any boat they could find room on. Most of those for whom there was no space turned back into the blacked-out city to forage for their own transportation. Some of these discovered that the Army warehouses were spilling out great mountains of their stocks while Quartermaster officers begged all who came by to help themselves before the demolitions started. The word got around (as word of free food inevitably does in any army, even one under full retreat), so almost every truck, bus, and commandeered auto that pulled out of Manila that night with Air Corps personnel was loaded down on its axles with food.

As with most outfits, their orders to start rolling reached the 27th Bombardment Group between 1:00 and 1:30 P.M. on December 24, and their withdrawal to Bataan on that "wildest and most fantastic day" [3] in the Group's annals was typical of the experience of other units.

Their commanding officer, Major Davies, it will be recalled, had gone south on December 27 with 20 of their most experienced and dependable pilots to look for the Group's missing dive bombers and if possible to fly them back.* Two more of their senior officers had gone into FEAF Headquarters. On Bataan the Group was to come under the command of Major J. W. Sewell, its Executive Officer, who was to do a superb job at turning them into infantry and who died in action towards the end of the Bataan episode; but when orders for the retreat came through the three outlying combat squadrons were all commanded by lieutenants, one of whom nominally commanded the Group.

Only two days before, the three squadrons had been assigned from Fort McKinley to three widely separated stations at which they were to serve as airdrome troops. The 16th Squadron, under Lieutenant Glenwood Stephenson, was at Lipa, where a field was being opened about 40 miles south of Manila, and they, like the 3rd Pursuit Squadron at Tanauan, were now directly threatened with being cut off by the Japanese force landing at Nasugbu. The other two squadrons had both gone north of Manila: the 17th, under 2nd Lieutenant W. G. Stirling, to a small new strip near San Fernando, the town in which the route from Manila turns sharp west for Bataan; and the 91st, under Lieutenant W. E. Eubanks, Jr., who was also nominal commander of the Group, to San Marcelino, the field above Subic Bay that had originally been assigned to them as their own base. Left in the Manila area, besides a few Headquarters Squadron men and officers, were the 120 men under Lieutenant J. B. McAfee at Nielson Field.

This detachment at Nielson Field had taken over running the airport on December 13, the day FEAF Headquarters moved to Fort Mc-Kinley; and they had been having a fairly rough time of it,* for the field was peculiarly open to air attack † with no nearby natural cover for camouflage. They must have done a pretty good job, for they suffered

---

* See above, Chapter 25.

† It is interesting to note that the Japanese faced the same difficulty of camouflage at Nielson at the time of the American return to the Philippines. They tried to solve it by taxiing their planes out down the highways, sometimes for as much as a mile, and turning off into the fields. They were, of course, trapped, for all the American planes had to do was fly a standing patrol over the field and highway approaches. Filipino countrymen and Manila civilians have told me how enjoyable it was to walk out along the roads and see a Japanese pilot just sitting in the cockpit of his plane and weeping with frustration. In time the American pilots got most of these planes in their parking corners; the fragments of many must still lie where they burned.

less from bombing than from strafing attacks. No planes were burned on the field by enemy action. But the Japanese had early discovered the lack of antiaircraft; the Zeros worked the field over every day; and by the third week of December some of the men were becoming a little bomb-happy. As one of them wrote in his diary, "I get awful upset by the bombing—the strafing is the worst though. It's deadly. The bombing just scares you and the strafing kills you." There was one bright moment, however, when a Filipino soldier aimed his old Springfield at a strafing Zero and brought it down with a bullet through the pilot's head. The men in their slit trenches saw it crash in a graveyard.[5]

During their first nights on the field, they had watched occasional flares and rockets of the fifth columnists tracing the outlines of the city and the surrounding military installations, including their own air strip, and they had experienced the same feeling of surveillance from the darkness that the men at Del Carmen felt on the first night of the war. But the Filipino troops around Manila caught and killed some of the Sakdalistas at their work, leaving them wherever they were killed as a warning, and by December 23 the flare-shooting had become much more discreet.

In the morning of the 24th they began to notice that more and more trucks were heading north on the main road into Manila and the usual crop of rumors swept the field. As the day wore on and the parade of Japanese bombers came in across Manila Bay, they watched the bombing of the waterfront and saw on their horizon the blue sky blacked out and the white buildings of the city shadowed by the rising smoke clouds. But the movement of trucks up from the south kept on without interruption past the airfield and into the shadow of the city.

Then, abruptly, at 1:30, Lieutenant McAfee received telephone orders from Air Headquarters to send his men to the docks and load them on a boat. He was to be there by 7:00 o'clock and join up with both the Headquarters Squadron from Fort McKinley and the 16th Squadron, which was on its way up from Lipa. As was the case with Lieutenant Stephenson at Lipa, the only explanation of this sudden move was that Manila was to be an open city, and to both men this seemed to mean either that the Japanese had broken through in the north or that the outfit was to sail somewhere,[6] presumably to the south. Stephenson was too far away to get further information; but, after commandeering enough trucks and seeing the men start loading, McAfee went over to Headquarters. There he found everyone "running for their life," as he writes in his diary, and he got the impression that the Japs were only a few miles away. He took time only to pick up a handful of underwear and socks and rushed back to Nielson Field.[7]

Preparations for leaving were carried on with the utmost speed, and the confusion increased as the afternoon lengthened. There were three observation planes—O-49s—that were to be flown to Corregidor, together with an A-27, one of the two that had been in commission at the start of the war. McAfee was a good deal troubled over their delivery, for he had no experienced pilots in the detachment, and the three men he had assigned to the O-49s—2nd Lieutenants Dillard, Stafford, and Owen—were fresh from flying school. The planes were hidden off the field down a side road, and because of the close watch kept by the Japanese it would be impossible to taxi them back to the field. The pilots would therefore have to take off from the road itself, between low trees, hedgehop over to Corregidor, and, if they were not shot down on the way, as seemed almost certain, set down on its tiny, 1500-foot Kindley Field. As 1500 feet was considered too short a distance to land the A-27 in, McAfee had assigned it to himself.[8]

At the moment, however, it was out on a reconnaissance flight, and he had to get his men started. He sent them off about 4:00 o'clock, keeping only the three assigned to the O-49s and himself on the field together with four enlisted men. Almost immediately after the others had gone, nine P-40s landed on the field, one of the pilots losing control of his plane and flying straight through the hangar wall, where the ship burst into flames. The planes were supposed to go to Lubao Field but had been unable to spot it from the air. They needed directions and gas, and McAfee with his three pilots and four enlisted men helped them gas up and saw them take off. As their planes lifted, the gas dumps at Nichols Field were set afire. The pillar of flaming smoke from the explosions towered far above all other clouds before it mushroomed and gradually merged with the general pall that was already gathering a false twilight over the entire bay area. This was the beginning of the heavy demolitions.

As if it had been his cue, Pappy Gunn suddenly flew in to land and taxi his small Beechcraft into a revetment. He was looking for General Brereton, who, as we know, had been asking for him. When he found that the General wasn't there, Gunn flew right out again.[9] He had come to arrange for the evacuation of the portion of FEAF that was unable to go out with General Brereton in the PBY. Two Beechcrafts of the Philippine Airlines were to make the flight, starting from Grace Park at 3:30 Christmas afternoon. Gunn himself and Captain Slingsby were to be the pilots, taking five passengers in Gunn's plane and six in the other.*

McAfee and the seven men with him naturally knew nothing about this as they watched Gunn take off and head his plane at treetop level round the eastern borders of the city towards Grace Park. They watched his course intently through the smoking skies until his plane had disappeared, for it was time to get their own observation planes away. All three managed to take off safely, and McAfee returned to the field to wait for the A–27 to come in and wonder how the three little observation planes were making out.†

The A–27 returned at last only to have the pilot crack it up past repairing against its revetment. That left McAfee no choice but to rejoin his detachment on the Manila docks, and he set out at once with the four enlisted men. He managed to find the Headquarters Squadron under 2nd Lieutenant Kane,‡ and with them was Major Sewell. According to their orders they still had to hook up with the 16th Squadron.

The 16th, with Lieutenant Stephenson at its head, rolled onto the docks around 8:00 P.M. They had spent all of the 23rd getting themselves settled at Lipa, and then at 1:00 P.M. of the 24th the orders to move reached Stephenson. He was eating lunch and, apparently, he took time to finish it. He didn't like the bit about leaving his equipment, and after a

---

* Capt. Gunn's passengers: Lt. Col. Caldwell, Lt. Col. Maitland, Capt. Hipps, Capt. Hobbs, Lt. Hampton, all of FEAF. With Capt. Slingsby were Maj. Lamb, Sgts. Felton and Dean of FEAF, and three unspecified passengers. Probably they were Lts. Strauss, Keenan, and McCallum (see below, Part Two, Chapter 4). Gunn is the authority for Slingsby's bringing six passengers. This specification of the FEAF evacuation is made as most sources have stated that they went south in two PBYs. Brereton does not say how any but his own party escaped. It took Gunn's two completely unarmed transports two days to reach Australia, but they made it safely.

† All three pilots reached Corregidor safely, though two nosed up on landing.[10]

‡ 2nd Lt. George W. Kane, Jr.

moment he decided just to ignore that whole angle. So the 16th arrived with all its rolling stock, food, field kitchens, clothes, and camp equipment.

Having brought the stuff that far, Stephenson had no intention of leaving any of it behind, for it was obvious there would be no room for any of it on any boat then at the docks. Indeed, there wasn't room for all the men trying to get aboard. He decided, therefore, to keep on for Bataan under his own power while McAfee went over in the boat.[11]

By ordinary standards the boat they found was barely big enough for the 120 men in McAfee's detachment. Three hundred crammed aboard. Dirty, tired, not knowing where they were to land, they did not have a life vest in the crowd; but, as McAfee himself was leaving the docks, "some witch" put a couple of packages of Cycle Cigarettes into his hand for a Christmas present. It was too dark for him to see if it was man or woman, bird or beast.[12]

Manila Bay was a wild place that night, with boats and submarines steaming in all directions, and the Filipino skipper got pardonably confused and finally decided just to sit down where he was and wait for light. A Navy patrol boat found them there in the dawn and told them they were right in the middle of a mine field. But it led them safely through and into Mariveles Harbor, where they disembarked under attack by Japanese bombers. They had no idea of where the 16th Squadron would be—no more in fact than the 16th itself had then—so, breakfastless, they started out along the road that follows the east coast of Bataan, each man with his laundry bag upon his back.[13]

The 16th Squadron was making a fairly smooth trip of it; but in the meantime the other two squadrons, the 17th and 91st, pulled out of their fields. Somehow word or orders, no one seemed to be quite sure which, reached the 17th at San Fernando that they were to take boat at Manila for Bataan. They hit the road without their equipment, though not before Lieutenant Stirling had called Lieutenant Eubanks at San Fernando to pass the word. When they reached Manila, they could find no boat to move them—no lighters, nothing. So they turned around and took the road back to San Fernando, turned west in the town without a stop, and went on down to Bataan. They arrived late on Christmas afternoon at the camp the 16th Squadron had set up near the village of

Cabcaben. They were half starved, but in spite of their hectic hegira they had not lost a truck or a man on the road—a remarkable performance since the whole Squadron had spent the better part of the night driving through the blackout.

Five miles away, Major Sewell had set up another camp for the Headquarters and 91st Squadrons along a beautiful, clear stream. The 91st had made nearly as hectic a departure as the 17th Squadron. San Marcelino's remoteness would have made communication with Headquarters difficult at the best of times; now it proved impossible, and all the 91st had to go by in the way of verification was Stirling's hurried telephone call. This had indicated a need for haste amounting almost to rout. According to reports, the Squadron did not take time even to finish their lunch, but set out at once for Bataan, leaving almost all their equipment behind them.[14]

Good fortune and individual enterprise combined to bring the 27th Group together on Bataan in condition at least to feed themselves. They still had no idea if they were in the right place; they had no idea of where to find Air Headquarters; they had no idea of who was in command. With varying efficiency they had followed their orders to go to Bataan. At least they had arrived.

30. Clark Field: "They closed the gate and threw the key away . . ."

IN ONE WAY OR ANOTHER the experience of the 27th Bombardment Group was typical of what happened all through the Air Corps on that unhappy Christmas Eve. At Zablan Field, Major Andrews of the Philippine Army Air Corps received orders to burn all installations, including the 18 remaining serviceable planes,* and to hit the road with his 780 officers and men in time to get through San Fernando before midnight.

---

*In an interview in the U. S. 9000 series in the A-2 Library Files, Col. Charles O. Backes, then commanding the Philippine Army Air Corps, says no planes were left save half a dozen basic trainers which were taken to Corregidor. Both Lt. Col. Andrews and Maj. José Francisco, then serving with him, are circumstantial in their account.

Twelve of the planes were basic trainers, but six were P–26s that were later badly needed for courier service. They were burned with the rest. The Filipino troops and cadets did a thorough job, and their technical equipment, photographic laboratory and supplies, their dump of aviation gas and all their hangars, except one that the Japanese had bombed to start the afternoon, were blazing when the last truck pulled off the field at 6:00 P.M. They did not know what they were supposed to do, once they reached Bataan, or where they were to camp. They just had orders to go and their line of 42 trucks found an opening in the unending stream rolling north on Highway No. 3. On the way they may have passed some bewildered-looking Air Corps units traveling in the opposite direction, for the 27th Bombardment Group's 17th Squadron was not the only outfit to start south from San Fernando with the idea of taking boats over to Bataan. At least one other came down all the way from Clark Field.

This was a detachment of the 30th Bombardment Squadron under Lieutenant Sig R. Young. Since the second day of the war the Japanese had been strafing or bombing Clark Field—usually both—several times a day; and, as the base lay on the milk route their bombers were running down to Manila, there were constant alerts from dawn to dark. The warning system had been reduced to lookouts in towers on top of the hangars who ran up a red flag when they spotted a plane and then did their best to make it to the ground before the bombs did.* The various Air Corps units were scattered in camps through the surrounding farming region or in the woods above Fort Stotsenburg. The 20th Camp, which was used mainly by pursuit personnel, has already been mentioned.† The 19th Bombardment Group had established themselves on a small hill in a cane patch about a mile and a half from the airfield, but after a week the 30th Squadron had set up housekeeping a little way off at a place called Santos's Farm. Besides the work of servicing such planes as still operated from Clark Field, the men were chiefly engaged in salvage operations; and a good deal had been accomplished. Besides the B–17 parts ferried down to Del Monte by the hazardous nightly

---

* Carpenter speaks of as many as ten or 15 raids on some days; and the detachment of the 27th Bombardment Group figured there were 35 during their five-day stay.[1]
† See Chapter 15 above.

trips of the old B–18s, a sizable additional reserve was being built up. Lieutenant Young's detachment of 40 men had been assigned to this work.

Morale at Clark Field had reached a deep low in the days immediately after December 8. It took the majority of the men some time to get over the shock of the initial Japanese attack. Nothing in their military training or their experience as American citizens had prepared them for its devastating violence. At one blow they found themselves reduced to the status of the have-nots of the world. Instead of the machine shops and depots they had been accustomed to, they were compelled to scrape through piles of burned-out rubble for the parts they needed to keep life in the few planes they had left. The frequency of the Japanese air raids made any effort to rebuild the base pointless without proper antiaircraft defense, and, actually, to many of the men their own continued service there must have seemed purposeless and wasteful. They suffered, too, from constant apprehension of a paratroop attack, yet except for the officers, to whom sidearms had been issued just before the war, most of the ground elements of the squadrons and the air-base troops were unarmed.

During these trying days the base commander was a big, black-bearded major, M. F. Daly, an ex-football player of the class of 1927 at West Point, who was to lead almost the last defensive effort on Bataan. The 24th Pursuit Group was still under Major Grover; and, dating from the day of his recall from Del Monte, the ground echelons and grounded air elements of the 19th Bombardment Group had been commanded by Major O'Donnell. It was about noon of the 24th that they were suddenly ordered to Bataan.

"This Headquarters is closing. Go to Bataan."

Those were the only orders O'Donnell ever received about leaving Clark Field. He could get nothing more. At the time, he did not have trucks enough to move his men; but more were expected in and he wanted to find out if he could wait until they came. They arrived while he was still trying to get through to Headquarters, so the men were started off, some by truck and some by train.

They had loaded bombs on the railroad cars, and the men rode on top of the bombs, and the slow little trains, puffing along through the open country on their single track, offered glaring targets for enemy pilots, but for some reason the Japanese left them alone during the trip down. At San Fernando the Carmen line branched off to serve the sugar fields around San Jose; but it ran in the direction of Bataan only as far as Lubao, and the cars were unloaded there, and a bomb dump was begun under the direction of an ordnance officer, Major James Neary.

In the meantime the demolition of Clark Field was proceeding in considerable confusion, due mainly to the general conviction that not a moment was to be lost. As O'Donnell said, "They blew up all the bombs and gas. They closed the gate and threw the key away." No one was quite sure of what anyone else was doing. Men acted as though they had lost their heads. They would leave one job to tear across the field and knock in the heads of gas drums, touch them off, and then rush back again. But, as the hours passed, the cumulative effect of these haphazard operations began to show in the rising column of smoke, the base of which soon covered all the field in grim reminder of December 8.

The hurry and confusion were, of course, entirely needless, and in succeeding days unit after unit that had reached Bataan in a state of near-destitution was to send back to Clark Field for tents, bedding, food, or tactical equipment. The Japanese did not reach it till after December 30. On that night, Lieutenant Edgar Whitcomb of the 93rd Bombardment Squadron, who had been assigned to communications, led a detachment of enlisted men back to Clark Field from Cabcaben to hunt for additional radio equipment. They arrived at dark. The base was utterly deserted; and, as they rummaged through the burned-out shops, they could hear the firing on the front lines about five miles off through the darkness. But they went on with their search, and, after they had done, they took extra time to visit what had been the P–X to see if there was any beer. As they might have expected, the place was bare as a hungry dog's bone; * but their stopping there illustrated the change in morale. On the evening of December 24 men acted as though the Japanese were at the very gates.

---

* The detachment were not surprised. But they did find a few cases in San Fernando on their return trip and bought them with funds forehandedly and hopefully collected from the Squadron for that purpose. With the beer they saw the New Year in on the beach at Cabcaben, looking across Manila Bay at the last demolition fires still burning in the city.

Lieutenant Young's detachment was one of the last to leave. How or why he had been ordered to proceed to Manila was something he never understood. The orders came to him that way, and he packed his men into trucks and started down. They did not attempt to rejoin the 30th Squadron, which had already left its camp at Santos's Farm, anyway, and was by then well on its way to Bataan.

The 30th was having an easy and orderly trip. One reason for this was that it was one of the first outfits to hit the road and consequently found relatively little traffic. Another reason may have been that it had put in the two previous days in traveling to and from Manila on one of those unexplained and incomprehensible moves that so bedeviled Air Corps personnel in the beginning days of the war. On the 22nd, the Squadron was ordered to leave all its belongings at Clark Field and proceed to Fort McKinley; but when it got there, no one seemed to know what was to be done with it. Finally a small detachment was armed and sent down to Tanauan, presumably as airdrome troops, while the rest of the Squadron was ordered back to their camp at Santos's Farm. This experience had opened their eyes to the necessity of looking after their own interests. When the order came on the 24th to proceed to Bataan, they made the move with full cooking equipment and full supplies, including turkey for their Christmas dinner.

But Lieutenant Young and his detachment arrived too late to eat it. When they came out on the Manila docks, they were told not to board the only boat with room to take them. After a moment's indecision, they decided that the proper procedure was to board the boat first and then continue the argument. They did so and they were still aboard when the boat finally pulled out into the bay.

31. *Nichols Field: "All units seemed pretty much on their own"*

THE LAST AIR CORPS TROOPS to leave Nichols Field were men from the 17th Pursuit Squadron. It was past 7:00 o'clock on December 24 when their trucks rolled cautiously out on what was left of the bridge over the Paranaque River and headed up the South Road for Manila. Behind them the runways were being blown; and, as the men looked back from the dark road, it seemed as if the whole base were ablaze: quarters, shops, hangars, even the already burned-out buildings of the Air Depot. Nichols Field was done for. The only people left there were the Engineers who were handling the demolitions.

The Squadron was making the move to Bataan under command of a 2nd lieutenant, David L. Obert, who was the third officer to take command of the Squadron's ground echelon within the past eight days. During the first week of war, the men had operated under the direction of four capable sergeants, who took over the job of servicing all pursuit planes at the field and found enough for the men to do to keep them from entire demoralization. The senior administrative officer had moved his command post so far back in the general area of Fort McKinley as to be practically cut off from the Squadron. The men under Sergeants King, Green, Day, and Edsall were doing a capable job, but it was not a good situation, and as soon as he heard of it, Lieutenant Wagner, who was up at Clark Field with his air echelon, sent down four pilots to take over. Lieutenant Brownwell was in charge, with 2nd Lieutenants Stone, Obert, and Crosby as his assistants.*

They reached Nichols Field on December 16; but on the 19th Brownwell was sent down to Mindanao to fly reconnaissance. He turned the Squadron over to Stone and almost on a moment's notice took off for Del Monte. Once the Japanese began operating from the Davao airfield, the sky over Mindanao had become too hot to use B-18s for daylight reconnaissance, and General Brereton had asked Brownwell to supply a P-40 pilot. Feeling that he was the most experienced flier of the four, Brownwell undertook the mission himself. The P-40 he drew was fresh from the Air Depot. Its guns had not been test-fired and it had only six hours' flying time; but it proved a stanch plane, and Brownwell was still flying it when his mission ended. He had expected it to be a short one, four or five days over all; but as events turned out, he continued to fly reconnaissance over Mindanao and the surrounding sea until almost the end of American resistance in the Philippines.

---

* Lt. John L. Brownwell; 2nd Lts. Earl R. Stone, Jr., Stephen H. Crosby, Jr.[1]

Two days after Brownwell left, Stone was injured in landing his P-40 on a barricaded runway on Nielson Field, and Obert inherited the Squadron command.* He could hardly have had time to become accustomed to the idea before being ordered to move the Squadron to Bataan. But Obert enjoyed what, on that wild day, must have been the almost unique distinction of receiving a definite assignment. The Squadron was to collect necessary equipment to set up servicing and maintenance facilities at a fighter strip then being constructed near the village of Pilar and report on the Manila docks inside of six hours to load on a boat for Bataan.

The orders had arrived about noon. By 4:00 o'clock it was manifest that the men could not be outfitted and all the equipment gathered in time to make the 6:00 o'clock deadline, so Obert decided to send the men ahead separately to the boat with what stuff they already had, under one of the administrative officers, Lieutenant Hall, while he and Crosby with a few picked men rounded up and loaded the rest of their equipment on available trucks to make the trip by road next morning. But, being a little disturbed by this deviation from the letter of his orders, he left Crosby at Nichols to continue the loading and himself made a hurried trip out to Fort McKinley to get his plan approved. There, as McAfee had earlier, he found that Air Force Headquarters seemed to have evaporated, and "all units seemed pretty much on their own." [3] The remaining personnel were "highly excited and were scurrying round collecting personal equipment and burning papers." [4] No one had time to listen to the problems of a young second lieutenant; but he did learn that all supplies left at Nichols Field would be destroyed that evening.

By the time he had driven back, the Engineers were already setting the gasoline stores afire. Though he and Crosby rushed their remaining preparations, the ground under their truck tires was shuddering from the main explosions even before they had cleared the field. They had light from the burning dumps to help them pick their way through the bombed-out native village of Baclaran; but as they proceeded towards

---

* McAfee described two instances of P-40s crashing his barricades on December 20 and 21, without naming the pilots. Presumably one was Stone. McAfee was disgusted and wrote of the second: "He got out with the remarkable statement that 'The Japs can land on this runway.' There stood his ship all torn to Hell." [2]

the heart of the city, the going became more difficult, and their little caravan was caught and almost submerged in the tide of the general retreat. The roar of trucks echoing in the streets and the blasts of the demolitions formed a pattern of continuous rolling thunder round the shore of the bay and out beyond the city. Over everything the recurrent, clamoring rise and fall of air-raid sirens marked the presence of enemy planes above the smoke.

It took the 17th a long time to work their way in to the dock area. Close in to shore they could see ships upon the water; farther out the bay was dark, and if any ships moved there they were invisible. Still farther out, beyond the edge of the smoke cloud, as one neared Corregidor, there was starlight; but the men on the docks had no idea of that.

It had occurred to Obert that, in addition to maintenance equipment, it would be a good idea to take along enough food and clothing to take care of the Squadron's needs at least until the Quartermaster was located on Bataan. Near the docks, as he had half surmised they might, they found trucks abandoned by the troops who had taken ship. They rounded up enough of these to bring their caravan up to ten and loaded them at the Quartermaster warehouses in the area.[5] The two young officers may have felt appalled by the general situation; but as far as their own command was concerned they were learning fast.

32. Quezon City: "They chose to stay"

AT ABOUT THE TIME Lieutenant Obert was hurrying over to Fort McKinley to find out if it was all right for him to evacuate some of his squadron by road instead of by water, a young engineering officer in the northeast outskirts of Manila made a decision vitally affecting the future operations of the Air Force on Bataan. Captain Richard W. Fellows, in command of the Philippine Air Depot, elected to remain in Manila for as long as necessary to finish the work he had in hand and also to move his Depot supplies out of the city and over to Bataan, an undertaking manifestly impossible in the eight hours allowed him by his orders. All his staff stayed with him of their own free will until their jobs were done. It is not too much to say that their work made the stand of the little Bataan air force possible; for without the planes, engines, parts, and tools that were brought out of Manila, the P-40s must have died on the ground of sheer intestinal attrition, and it is hard to see how Dyess's strike in Subic Bay could ever have occurred. But to understand the reasons that lay behind their making this decision, it is necessary to know something of the first move the Depot made from Nichols Field to Quezon City.

It began on the second day of the war. Till then, except for a sub-depot established at Del Carmen near the end of November to handle P-35 equipment,* all air engineering facilities and supplies continued to be concentrated in the single crowded group of buildings round the north and west sides of Nichols Field. This had long been a matter of concern to responsible officers. Plans for moving the Depot to a less conspicuous location and dispersing its various units had been drawn up and submitted and resubmitted in the two years before the war; but they had come to nothing,† and as new buildings were needed they were merely placed beside the old.[1] The Depot personnel prepared for hostilities as well as they could: blackout measures were provided for engineering hangars and shops, slit trenches dug, and walkways built to give access to the roofs of the eleven main buildings. But it was obvious that once Nichols Field came under attack, it would no longer be possible to operate the Depot.

When Fellows received the command shortly before the war, the staff consisted of 14 men, but within a few days he lost the two senior officers. Captain Harold V. Munton, Supply, went to Del Carmen to command the sub-depot; and Lieutenant Frederic G. Hoffman, the senior Engineering Officer, was ordered to Australia to organize the erection of planes there.‡ Their places at Nichols were taken by their respective juniors, Lieutenants J. F. Batchelor and H. E. Warden. Most of the staff were very young. The only older man was a Russian-American officer in charge

* Almost all the P-35s, it will be recalled, were with the 34th Pursuit Squadron at Del Carmen, which was the Squadron base from November 25 onward.
† Mention has been made of Col. George's ineffectual attempt to provide a safe storage area for Depot supplies. See Chapter 4, above.
‡ Chapter 25, above.

of Depot Shops, Lieutenant Michael M. Ushakoff. He had the reputation of being something of a character, but he also had a gift for improvisation that made him a useful man to have around in hard times,[2]
and he seems to have fitted in with the rest of them. They were pretty
independent in their outlook, but they quickly proved themselves to be
an adaptable, resourceful, and completely self-reliant unit.

The Depot finished assembling the last P-40E of the last shipment to
reach Manila and delivered the plane to the 21st Pursuit Squadron just
before the Japanese attacked. It then immediately turned itself to the
business of war. This began in earnest with the arrival of the first damaged pursuit planes at 10:30 on the morning of the 8th; and from then
till 11:30 that night, when the last plane on which immediate repairs could
be made was again in flyable condition, the men worked without inter-
mission, at high tension, and for the last five and a half hours under
blackout regulations. Two P-40s and four P-35s could not be repaired
because of a shortage of parts. These were taken out of the engineering
hangars and dispersed, and the men were then sent home.[3] Only 80 enlisted men were attached to the Depot; all the rest were civilians—60 of
them American, the remaining 350 Filipinos, Chinese, or Mestizos. Their
morale, especially among the civilians, was high; from the arrival of the
first injured plane they had realized they were beginning a struggle in
which their backs are already to the wall.

Not long after they had gone, Nichols Field received its first raid. It
was not a very heavy attack, but there had been absolutely no warning
signal; and Fellows made up his mind then and there that he was going
to move his command out of Nichols Field.[4] It was vitally important, if
the Air Force was to survive at all, to get the P-40 and B-17 spares and
shop equipment into safe storage.

A year before the war a survey had been made of Quezon City on the
northeast borders of Manila with the idea of transferring the Depot there
in an emergency. Early in the morning of the 9th, therefore, Fellows
called the Air Service Command asking for suggestions and to have
buildings assigned to him. He also requested transportation. He was told
he could get neither. There were no available buildings or trucks. But if
he wanted them, he could have 20 enlisted men from the 48th Matériel
Squadron assigned to the Depot for temporary duty. He took the en-

listed men and got the staff together for a council of war. They decided to move anyway and started making their plans.

The first move was to send off an officer and 15 armed men to Quezon City to take over a cabaret known as the Santa Anna. It had a huge dance floor that would serve as a temporary storage till they could get the buildings they wanted.

The next problem was transportation. They managed to adopt five trucks from Base Transportation. Two large shop trucks, empty, but battered from the previous night's bombing, were taken over, repaired, and put into use. Some small Air Corps tugs belonging to the Depot and assorted barges were used to move heavy stuff as close as they could get by river. As soon as they could gather enough men, they organized foraging parties to scour Manila, especially the dock area, for any government or civilian trucks they could get hold of. But finding enough men was perhaps the greatest difficulty of all.

Only three of the 80 enlisted men reported for duty that morning. The rest, with the majority of all personnel at Nichols Field, had scattered over as much as ten miles of the surrounding countryside after the night's bombing. A search had to be organized with these three men as a nucleus before anything else could be accomplished. In the end 27 more were rounded up and these, with the detachment of 20 from the Matériel Squadron, made a total of 50 enlisted men.

Fellows had decided that it would not be advisable to expose his civilian workers to the chance of being bombed without warning, so he directed them to assemble at the Santa Anna Cabaret. There were very few absentees, but 150 of the native civilians were discharged at this time, a few because their loyalty was open to question, but most because they were relatively new men and too little was known about them. With 40 more enlisted men assigned to him from various units during the next few days, and including his staff, Fellows therefore had a working crew of 352 men with which to move the Depot to Quezon City. They accomplished it, working twenty-four hours a day, in ten days.

Headquarters were set up in San Carlos Seminary, a former girls' school, which also furnished quarters and mess for the officers and enlisted men and storage for the P–40 airplane spare parts, which were kept in the seminary chapel. The engineering section took over a bicycle factory on Sunset Boulevard. A cement plant half a mile away was used for the storage of 18 spare P-40 engines that had been brought out of Nichols Field. An unfinished house became their sheet-metal shop and Depot Engineering Headquarters took over a Japanese-owned compound, consisting of four two-story buildings surrounded by a high wall. All blueprints and technical orders were stored in this place and the buildings served as barracks for the American civilians and the enlisted men of the engineering section.

To protect these buildings the Depot organized its own guard of 60 men. Though they were armed at first only with rifles or revolvers, they ultimately acquired six Lewis machine guns and four Thompson sub-machine guns and began to feel like quite an outfit. The whole organization was scattered over an area of seven square miles, but communications and co-ordination had been worked out to give Headquarters in the San Carlos Seminary constant and full control of all activities. By December 19 they were ready to resume full Depot operations, including assembly of airplanes.

They had set up five assembly units near various streets or boulevards wide enough to serve as runways for P-40s. Each unit was placed under natural cover, for there were still groves of trees here and there throughout this new city development, and the sites were further camouflaged to conceal them from all but the closest ground observation. Here they began to rebuild four P-40s out of twice that number of wrecks.

Considering what they had to work with it seems an extraordinary achievement. Besides this work, moreover, they were being called on to perform tasks usually handled by base, tactical, or headquarters organizations. They were asked to move large quantities of gas and oil from one storage site to another, or to deliver 10,000 gallons of gasoline to the field at San Marcelino, 100 miles away by road, and service a flight of B-17s as soon as they returned from a bombing mission on which they had already been dispatched at the time the Depot received the order! [5] Sometimes urgent requests for equipment involved its delivery by air. On the morning of December 10, at 9:30, Lieutenant Warden with one enlisted man as co-pilot and crew took off in the Depot's C-39 to deliver hand gasoline pumps and parts to Clark Field, to Rosales, still farther north, and to Del Monte in Mindanao. There were probably more Japanese planes over Luzon on the 10th than on any other single day of the war. The C-39's armament consisted of one Thompson sub-machine gun; its chances of getting through were less than one in ten; but it made delivery at all three fields that day as requested, came down to spend the night in Cebu, and returned to Manila in the morning of the 11th.[6] This same plane was the one later flown to Australia by Lieutenant Hoffman with a load of 27th Bombardment Group pilots.

During this period the Depot, like all other Air Corps organizations, seems to have gone ahead with its work in entire ignorance of the development of the land campaign in the north. The staff, like the men, not only lived on rumors, they had to base their plans on them. The one most consistently prevalent was that Manila could not be held much longer, and plans were drawn up to transfer the Depot to Del Carmen in case the city was directly threatened. But at the same time they were steadily expanding their facilities in Manila and were getting ready to shift their engine overhaul unit from the bicycle factory to a larger, more modern building, when at 4:00 in the afternoon of December 24, the order to evacuate the Depot to Bataan hit them like a thunderstroke. There had been no warning. They were assigned to the Cabcaben area; and they were given only eight hours to get their men aboard ship.

This meant that everything they had accomplished since the start of the war would be wiped out. It was hard to take it in; but there was no mistake about it. Colonel Churchill of the Air Service Command had personally called Fellows. His orders were based on the orders that had come to him from higher authority. By midnight Manila was to be an "open city."

Fellows pointed out that he could not begin to move his essential equipment in the allotted eight hours and asked for an extension of time. He was told that midnight was the deadline; and there would be no extension. He then requested additional transportation and asked what he should do with his civilian personnel. Colonel Churchill said that only water transportation was available. As for the civilians, they were not covered in the instructions he had received.

All this time Fellows was thinking of the four P-40s in the hidden assembly pens on the boulevards. One of them was nearly ready and work on the other three would be completed in from two to six more days.[7] He told Churchill; but the orders were specific: all equipment that could not be carried along would be destroyed. There was a pause. Then Churchill, who knew as well as Fellows how desperately those planes were needed, said into the telephone, "They aren't my orders." It seemed to be all there was to say.

But Fellows had already made his decision. He called a meeting of all Depot officers and laid the evacuation orders before them. A detail from the sub-depot at Del Carmen would be sent down on Bataan to establish a camp near Cabcaben. All officers were to report there unless they chose of their own free will to stay on in Manila. He made sure that everyone understood the consequences involved in that choice. Besides risking capture by the enemy—there were rumors that both North and South Luzon Forces had broken and that the Japanese were moving on Manila from both directions—any officer who failed to obey these orders exposed himself to any punishment that higher authority might wish to inflict in wartime.

There was no hesitation. All of them decided to stay on. To abandon or destroy their equipment and supplies at this point, particularly the four nearly completed P-40s, was unthinkable; and they began at once to work out their own program of evacuation.

In some ways it was simpler than the move from Nichols had been. They no longer had to plan on doing maintenance for a large air force. Their job now would be piecing out and patching for a few P-40s in the field and carrying enough parts for their upkeep. Moreover their transportation section, instead of being the weakest, was now the strongest element in the Depot organization. By various means they had raised their total rolling stock to 15 heavy trucks, four civilian pickups, a big truck with a ten-ton hoist, three motorcycles complete with sidecars, and a civilian bus that seemed to have strayed into their compound more or less as a stray horse sometimes turns up in anybody's paddock. Three of the heavy trucks had been equipped as field repair machine shops. They also had twelve Air Corps tugs and a variety of trailers, wagons, and dollies. Compared to the rolling stock they had begun the war with this looked pretty impressive. But suddenly, as had happened on December 9, they found themselves acutely short of man power.

As the movement to Bataan gained headway, the enlisted men who had been assigned to the Depot were recalled by their original units. The staff tried every means from cajolery to outright threats to keep the men on, but on Christmas morning they had only 20 of them left. This group was made up mainly of their truck drivers, who had been averaging 15 to 18 hours a days since the start of the war. They were a tough, loyal bunch of men, and they went on working now without a break till the evacuation was completed. They did much of their driving under blackout; they came under fire of strafing Japanese planes; and they often had to travel alone. Fellows had decided to leave his civilians behind, but they were held in their assigned stations and helped with the loading in Manila; on Bataan after two days some 300 enlisted men were assigned to him and helped with the unloading. But it was the group of 20-odd drivers who bore the brunt of the actual transportation of the Depot, with one exception.

The exception was the Filipino captain of the *Dos Hermanos,* a little, 200-ton, coastwise ship which the Depot finally got hold of to transport their heaviest equipment. This boat was loaded way over capacity with their 18 Allison engines and seven Wright engines for B–17s, bench equipment, and some 70 tons of hand tools, parts, and supplies, including tons of sheet metal and 150 bottles of oxygen. The *Dos Hermanos* stole across the bay on the night of the 27th and appeared early next morning off the village of Lamao, where a rickety apology for a pier stuck a little way out into the water. It had no facilities and the unloading had to be done by hand. With their shortage of men and the constant bombing by the Japanese, it took them two full days to empty the little vessel. But the Filipino skipper stayed with them. On the approach of the Japanese bombers, he would cast off from the pier and anchor offshore with every possible appearance of innocence. Then, as soon as the raid was over, the men coming out of their slit trenches would see the *Dos Hermanos* edging in to the pier again, and the work would be resumed. What became of the captain, the crew, or the *Dos Hermanos* afterwards is not known.

In the meantime, on December 26, the first P–40 to be completed was flown off one of the Quezon City boulevards by Lieutenant Warden and delivered to the Air Corps on Bataan. That night two more were finished, and they were flown over to Bataan on the 27th. They had to pick their take-off time carefully, for that day the Japanese bombed Manila solidly for two hours. It was apparently a terror raid, and the first of a series, directed against civilians and especially aimed at churches and colleges and convents. The great Cathedral of the Immaculate Conception was sought out and attacked three separate times. Altogether 14 churches and colleges were damaged or destroyed in these raids, huge fires burned, and there was a heavy loss of civilian life.

On the night of the 27th, with their heaviest equipment already in transit, all the staff and military personnel of the Depot left for Bataan with the exception of Lieutenant Warden, who was to deliver the last plane as soon as it was ready, Lieutenant Batchelor, the Assistant Supply Officer, and the truck drivers, who were to continue making their trips between Bataan and Manila until the city actually fell. When that happened, any Air Corps items that were still left would be destroyed by a nucleus of key civilians, and these men were to remain organized in case a shift of fortune brought about the Army's return.

Though these assignments were carried through, the timing was very close. Lieutenant Warden took off in the last P-40 on the morning of January 1 while the Japanese were entering Manila from the south. But four of the trucks were trapped in the city. It took twenty-four hours to make the round trip to Bataan, and the road had grown tougher in the past two days, especially as one approached Manila. One of the four drivers, Staff Sergeant James Tribby, had had a five-mile race with a Japanese Zero along Quezon Boulevard only the day before. He could have jumped, but his five-ton truck had a capacity load of food, and he refused to abandon it.* By zigzagging down the boulevard at top speed, he finally escaped, himself and his motor uninjured, but with the truck body peppered with bullet holes. He went on to Bataan, unloaded, and that night he returned, only a few hours, as it happened, before engineers along the San Fernando Road began to blow the bridges.

The four trucks caught in the city were driven into the Pasig River. Smoke overhung them and they were burning as they sank, for that day the Pasig itself was on fire. The great storage tanks along the shores were being emptied into the stream; the oil had caught fire and flowed

---

* All drivers did not stick so faithfully to their trucks; for several men pressed into service by the Depot on Christmas Eve dumped their loads along the side of the Bataan road, and later 15 of these were picked up by crews coming up from Cabcaben.[8]

down under the bridges, a slow and terrible river of flame.[9] A sense of doom was on the city. There was a new silence in the streets. The roar of trucks, the crash of hurrying tanks, the weary mutter of feet going north in the night had all passed on. Now black-clad priests were kneeling in prayer before the crumpled walls that once had formed the old and lovely Church of Santo Domingo, and Filipino men and women groping in the rubble of their homes found the ashes cold.

But over near the Japanese Club a strange group gathered with Japanese flags in their hands. They were the native-born Japanese, the appeasers, the traitors, and the craven, all rejoicing in their snow-white gowns. Armed men appeared at the crossings along Taft Avenue with the Rising Sun upon their sleeves. And from far off, at the outskirts of the city, came the faint sounds of a brass band practicing welcoming airs.[10]

Two of the four truck drivers managed to escape to Bataan. They got across the bay in native *bancas*, the small, outrigger sailing boats that Filipinos use mainly for fishing, and made their way to the Depot camp above Cabcaben.[11]

The camp was situated just south of Bataan Field, down over the bank and off the main Bataan road, where it turns to cross the creek. It was a shallow, wooded valley, with a small piece of open grass close by the road; and sometimes at night, when the bombing had stopped and the big guns up the road at Orion were quiet, the men had an almost peaceful awareness of the running water. They built bins, catalogued their stuff, organized their mobile units, and set up their own mess. In the hard days that followed, it did mechanics good to visit there. They no longer had planes of their own to work on, for they had been converted into infantry, and, instead of the tools they had been trained with, they were lugging Springfield rifles around through the Bataan jungles; but a glimpse of the Depot along the brook reminded them of the kind of work they used to do.

In their last runs out of Manila, besides their own supplies, the Depot trucks packed in quantities of clothing that eventually filtered down to nearly every unit. Part of it, for instance, was used to outfit the nurses on Bataan. But at the end the trucks carried nothing but food, and very soon the Depot Staff began to have misgivings over the first priority they had given their own supplies. For an enormous quantity of stores, food as well as ammunition, that ought to have reached Bataan never got there. It remained stalled on the railroad line between Lubao and San Fernando.

Somehow, whichever department it was that handled transportation, whether Engineers or Quartermasters, had the impression that the village of Lubao was the railhead. But actually the main line tracks led from there into 289 miles of private railroad line belonging to the Sugar Centrale that operated all the surrounding region. The tracks made a lacework through the cane, which at that time was twelve to sixteen feet high and would have concealed any amount of rolling stock until it could have been unloaded; and part of the trackage reached nearly ten miles towards Bataan.[12]

On December 30, Fellows, with Captains Munton and McFarland,* went up to Lubao to investigate a report that cars of Air Corps gasoline were blocking the tracks. When they arrived, the railroad siding was undergoing an attack by Japanese dive bombers. There were eight cars on the siding, and a train of forty cars stood idle on the main line. The Japanese got several hits on the eight cars, one of which caught fire. It was loaded with ammunition, which soon began to explode. The three officers examined all the cars and found them to be loaded with 75 anti-aircraft and .50-caliber machine gun ammunition, and Quartermaster gas and food supplies. None of the cars carried aviation gasoline.

They then went on up the line seven and a half miles to Guagua, where they found a block of some sixty cars. These had the same type of load as those at Lubao. And again there was no aviation gasoline. It was not till they reached San Fernando that they found their consignment: two tank cars and several more loaded with gas in 50-gallon drums. These cars stood with nearly two hundred others full of all kinds of supplies in the San Fernando yards. There was no way of getting the two tank cars out of San Fernando with the tracks blocked at Guagua and Lubao. They could not locate any Army railroad personnel and the Filipino dispatchers knew nothing. They then went to Del Carmen, found a plantation-owned engine, and sent it to Lubao, hoping to salvage some of the cars there by hauling them into the sugar cane.

By the time the plantation engine pulled in, Lubao was undergoing its

* Capt. Cecil S. McFarland, Gasoline and Oil Officer for FEAF.[13]

third attack by Japanese dive bombers. Ammunition was exploding briskly among the eight cars on the siding, and the eighteenth car of the long train was burning hard, completely blocking off the twenty-two behind it. In addition, a bridge down the line linking the main tracks to the plantation system had caught fire. The Filipino engineer had to be forced at gun's point to risk his engine and himself across it, but he coupled onto the first seventeen cars and snaked them safely back into the concealment of the tall cane. In the meantime, Fellows, Munton, and McFarland helped two Air Corps Ordnance officers push one of the eight cars on the siding a safe distance from the others. It was loaded with .50-caliber ammunition, of which there had been a serious shortage even before the war.[14]

These eighteen cars, as far as they ever learned, were the only ones to be salvaged out of all the rolling stock they had seen that day at Lubao, Guagua, and San Fernando; and the loads of few, if any, of the rest can have been saved, for by January 1 General Wainwright was already pulling out of San Fernando and by the 2nd the Japanese were attacking his front lines at Guagua. Who was responsible and how the misconception about Lubao's being the end of trackage arose in the first place has not been told; but it seems extraordinary when one considers the venerable standing of the Orange Plan that no extensive use was made of the Sugar Centrale's rail net.* The course of events would not have been materially changed however, if the food and ammunition had reached Bataan. Only for the soldiers in the front lines, who became so weak that food had to be carried to them in their foxholes, the starvation date would have been pushed back awhile. The three officers returning to their Depot below Bataan Field, of course, had no way of knowing how soon that date would come.

---

* Part of the stalling of rolling stock was undoubtedly due to the almost unanimous desertion of the railroads by native employees. But still stranger was the omission in War Plan Orange of Army operation of the railroads.[15] Lubao was considered the end of the line by the Quartermaster Department.[16]

33. *The Bataan Road: "Trucks were really high-tailing it"*

WHATEVER MAY HAVE BEEN WRITTEN or yet may be written about the retreat to Bataan, it was really the Japanese themselves who ensured its success.

There was only one road leading into Bataan. For nearly 100 miles this road stretched round the bay from Manila to the southern end of the peninsula, every mile of it open to air observation and attack. Yet, except for the small and inconsequential raids near Lubao on December 30,[1] the Japanese air force made no sustained or systematic effort to interfere with the retreat until the removal to Bataan was nearly completed. No man or woman who traveled over the Bataan road on Christmas Eve or Christmas Day will ever understand why they did not, nor, indeed, will anyone else.

They had control of the air. The 16 remaining serviceable American pursuit planes that found their way to the hidden airfield at Lubao could hardly have furnished cover for even one key point, had the Japanese chosen to attack it in force, and to have attempted it would probably have meant the loss of all our pursuit. The Japanese needed only to blast the two main bridges on the San Fernando road—one above Meycauayan, and the one at Calumpit that provided the sole road crossing of the wide and unfordable Pampanga River—to have utterly disrupted the American effort to defend Bataan. General Jones's South Luzon Force would have been cut off on the open plain, and General MacArthur would have had the bitter choice of bringing General Wainwright's army down to join in a hopeless stand or of writing off the South Luzon Force entirely. The latter course might have simplified some of the immediate problems of Wainwright's retreat and relieved the pressure on his right wing; but the defense of Bataan would then have begun without the stores of food, medical supplies, ammunition, and heavy equipment that poured in over the Bataan road, not only on the 24th and 25th, but during the six succeeding days as well.* Without these supplies and General Jones's divisions, green though most of them were, neither of the two Bataan defense lines could have been manned and the defense itself would have been over before it had properly begun.

To point this out does not detract from the performance of anyone involved in covering the retreat, least of all Generals Wainwright and Jones, who carried through their successive withdrawals and effected the juncture of their two forces at Calumpit under very heavy pressure. For the Japanese Lingayen army, driving down from the north, made for and barely failed to take the bridge on December 31, and next day threw fresh reserves into an attempt to break through Wainwright's lines at San Fernando.⁵ But this evident anxiety on the part of the Japanese infantry command to cut the road made its neglect by their air force all the more incomprehensible.†

They cannot have been unaware of the retreat. Japanese planes were over the road all Christmas Eve. Even at altitude the air crews of the big formations on their way to bomb the Manila waterfront could hardly have failed to observe the increasing flow of military traffic north from the city along the San Fernando road. Traffic blocks at Meycauayan and particularly at Calumpit, where the importance of the highway bridge was still further emphasized by the railroad bridge right alongside, must have cried their significance to high heaven. Above Calumpit the road ran for miles through naked, open fields, where there was not even a tree or a shred of cover of any kind, where even a kitten on a rainy day would have been visible from the air. But the afternoon before Christmas Eve was clear and the road was filled by a close-packed line of busses, trucks,

* The road was still open when Lt. Obert went into Manila on the 27th-28th for more blankets and mosquito netting for the 17th Squadron. But on the 31st, as he returned from another trip, the Jap dive bombers were out in numbers attacking traffic and villages all along the road.² Between the 24th and 31st a huge store of medical equipment and supplies was moved over to Bataan—80,000 tons in all—by lighter and truck convoy, even beds. From the 25th on, a 20-truck convoy under Lt. Bert Golden made two round trips every 24 hours, operating night and day, with the remarkable record of not losing a truck.³ But the greater part of the equipment and supplies for Hospital No. 1 at Limay had been stored there some months before in accordance with the War Plan.⁴

† Commenting on the stupidity with which the Japanese used their air force during the American retreat, General Sutherland said that, though their show on the opening days was beautiful, they never showed smart again, not when they had to find their own targets, and added feelingly, "Thank God for it."

great tank trailers, ambulances, and heavy guns—155s on their own carriages and dismounted Naval guns from the Cavite Navy Yard on trucks. They made good time through the beginning of this stretch; but the pace slowed as they approached San Fernando.

Here in the narrow streets of the town the line of retreat from the south met and converged with another from the north. This second stream, besides the Air Force units from Clark Field and detachments from Fort Stotsenburg, included Filipino infantry, elements of Wainwright's little army falling back to reserve areas closer to Bataan, though the battle line on Christmas Eve was still 50 miles to the north along the Agno River.[6] The Air Corps units from the Manila area must have eyed with astonishment the small, brown-skinned men marching in their bare feet, with their GI shoes slung by the laces from their rifle barrels * and many of them wearing blue denims instead of uniforms and paper hats instead of helmets.[8]

The only road that led southwest out of the town towards the base of the Bataan Peninsula was too narrow to carry the combined streams of retreating troops, which consequently were dammed up in the town itself. Trucks, cars, guns, ambulances were parked everywhere through the bystreets, even on the sidewalks and over the surrounding fields, and by noon of Christmas Day, when Colonel George worked his way through San Fernando in the new Packard car he had inherited from General Brereton along with the disorganized command, this packed mass of vehicles and troops still jammed the town.[9] A single dive-bomber attack would have turned the place into a shambles, yet the Japanese ignored it on both days.†

For ten and a half miles beyond San Fernando, until it came to Lubao, the highway wound from one small village to another. Maps gave it a first-class rating, but like all Philippine roads it was narrow. In many

---

* General Wainwright's Filipino troops began the campaign in their conventional sneakers, but these had quickly been worn out by the continual marching. They were replaced with GI shoes. But the American last was not adapted to the Filipino's foot and the troops could not wear them. Yet neither did they feel it proper to throw away such valuable articles, so they carried them as described.[7]

† In fact no Japanese air attack was made on the town till January 1 when the South Luzon Force was filing through the streets with Wainwright's battered right wing close behind. Even then the Japanese planes concentrated more on Wainwright's lines outside of San Fernando and the damage in the town itself was relatively slight.[10]

places it was built up like a dike across the sweep of marshland and when a breakdown occurred it was necessary to organize one-way traffic or else tip the vehicle entirely off the right of way. Usually the men took the latter course, for there was almost no policing on the road and the constantly increasing number of trucks coming back out of Bataan after more supplies added to the congestion.

Lubao lay in the sugar district, and here the route was hemmed in by high green walls of cane. Instead of being able to look far out across country the men could not see a plane until it was very near, which gave them the feeling of being coffined. All Christmas Day formations of Japanese bombers roared across on their way down to Corregidor, to which they had now transferred their attention. The retreating troops beneath them were in constant fear that their own antiaircraft crews manning the few guns emplaced along the road would stir up the crossing planes; but fortunately the gunners held their fire and the retreat continued unmolested, past Lubao and on through two tiny barrios named Santa Cruz and San Roque, until it turned into the homestretch down the east side of Bataan.

The memory of this Bataan road still haunts the men who traveled it. For about two thirds of the way, as far down the peninsula as Orion, it had been tarred at one time or another, but so lightly that the crust broke under the weight of traffic that hit it the first day. South of Orion the only paving was a strip of rough stone blocks, twelve feet wide, set into the red dirt, and it soon petered out. The passage of a single jeep was enough to set the dust flying. With the full tide of the retreat pouring over it the road was marked from end to end by a dust cloud that seemed at times to rise 1000 feet. An east breeze rolled it higher still and in the bright sunlight, against the shadowed mountains, it must have been visible from 50 miles away.

Beneath this cloud the retreat pounded south at a rate amounting to nearly a rout. When Major Kennard reached it early in the afternoon at the head of his little caravan, trucks were really high-tailing it down the road. A few officers tried to slow things down, but they got nowhere. There were no military police, and the whole area was a mass of confusion, with people asking where they were supposed to go, where the Quartermaster was, what had become of Headquarters. All the Air

Corps seemed to be funneled in on that road; but besides them there were the Medical and Quartermaster outfits, Engineers, Artillery, and Infantry; and the whole mass of trucks, guns, ambulances, busses, jeeps, gun carriers, tanks, and plain ordinary mule-drawn wagons were jammed together in dust so thick that some of the men were wearing gas masks and often it was impossible for drivers to see the tailgate of the truck just in front. Everything that moved absorbed the color of the road itself. Even the trees and the thatch-roofed little houses of the Filipinos beside the road were coated with the same heavy and indistinguishable rusty gray.

Here, again, there were breakdowns all along the ditches, and in one spot a line of eight or ten big guns—155s—so new that the grease had not yet been cleaned off them. When Major Kennard first saw these guns they were entirely deserted; but he later learned a little of their history. They had been handed over to the Filipinos, who, without being trained to handle them, had taken the guns south. When the general retreat started, they had brought the guns north, first to Manila and then faithfully all the way round to the base of Bataan; but there at last they had deserted them. In a day or so, however, the crews became ashamed about leaving their guns and went back for them and finally brought them south as far as Limay. Finally some Coast Guard personnel were sent up from Corregidor to teach the crews how to handle their guns, clean them, and get them properly emplaced; and their deep voices became something one listened for even in Little Baguio.

The Filipinos in the little villages looked wonderingly at the endless line that pounded past their doors. No effort had been made to evacuate civilians from Bataan. Instead many more came in both with and behind the troops, their high-wheeled carts making teetery, wild escapes through the dust from under the very snouts of the heavy trucks. Nothing was done about these people, either, though they were to be an added drain on the meager food supply and undoubtedly furnished cover for the fifth column that functioned actively throughout the defense of Bataan.

The civilians turned aside at one village or another; but the troops, without specific orders, had no idea of where to bivouac. The areas supposed to be marked out for them were nonexistent. It finally boiled down to each outfit's leaving the road as far south as its commanding officer thought he ought to go or wherever he happened to find what looked to him like a good camp site. Most of them were concentrated round Limay, a small village that boasted a pier jutting out into Manila Bay, a handful of native houses, and some dingy barracks in which a Medical Detachment was setting up the hospital that became known as Hospital No. 1. It was close to the road, and it may well have been that this one spot of orderly activity, or perhaps even a glimpse of the nurses in their white uniforms, had a magnetic influence.

From its start, Hospital No. 1 was under the command of Lieutenant Colonel James W. Duckworth, and to the end of its career, long after all other American commands had dissolved in the terrible Death March, it continued to operate under his direction at Little Baguio with its efficiency and discipline unchanged from that which marked its original organization.

The doctors, nurses, and corpsmen that made up the pioneer detachment had left Manila in twelve busses at 5:30 on the morning of December 24, each bus carrying a mixed group so that if some did not get through the rest would still be able to organize the hospital. It was an example of "tactical loading," the importance of which had not yet been fully realized back in the United States, or if it was realized was certainly not yet in practice. The nurses wore their white duty shoes and the uniforms that so soon became mere memories for them and the wounded men under their care. But that morning it was sunny and the busses made good time, for they were ahead of the general retreat, and the brown-skinned children along the road called high-pitched greetings and lifted their fingers in the V-for-Victory sign. The busses pulled up in one village for the nurses to buy bananas, and one of the corpsmen broke the food taboos by eating native-cooked wild rice. When a nurse chided him for eating contaminated and probably worm-infested food, he grimly prophesied that they would be eating worse than that before they were through. But they didn't take him seriously. How could they? "We laughed at him," wrote Juanita Redmond. "We felt very lighthearted. After the long strain of the past weeks, this trip was like going on a picnic. Even the planes that came over and sent us ducking into the ditches couldn't keep our spirits down very long. And soon after sundown, we thought, we would reach the hospital and find comfortable beds to roll into and sleep off the weariness of the hours of jolting stiff-backed travel." [11] But the "hospital was a shock, and the Nurses' Quarters consisted of a one-story wooden structure with six beds in it. There were fifty nurses, and someone said in a small tired voice, 'Do we sleep on the floor?' "

But at least it was silent there on Bataan, until the grind of the retreat began along the road outside. There were no planes and no bombs fell. "You could look up and see stars shining in the sky and smell the warm rich tropical earth untainted by explosives." [12] They went to work to organize their hospital on Christmas morning. By the 26th, when the rest of the Medical Corps began arriving from Sternberg and the other hospitals scattered through Manila, they were ready to receive the wounded. That night 300 patients came in to them by boat; [13] and next morning the first of the stream from the front lines began, a stream that never stopped its flow until the end of shooting.

34. *Christmas at Little Baguio*

WHEN THE SUN SET on Christmas, nearly all the Air Corps had reached Bataan. They were scattered the length of the peninsula, and as a command they were disorganized and fairly well demoralized, with no idea of where Headquarters was or what their duties on Bataan would be. Some units, fortunate enough to have old-line, self-reliant mess sergeants who refused to move without their field kitchens and plenty of rations, had had food; but many went to bed supperless, some without having eaten since lunch the day before. The men slept on the ground. Tents or shelter of any kind were rarities, and, because of the haste and near-panic with which they had pulled foot out of their old bases, it often turned out that there were not blankets enough to go round. Luckily the night was warm and clear, and the men on the beach at Cabcaben could look across the bay to the fires still burning in Manila. They speculated about whether the Japs had taken the city yet. There was some talk about what wives, sweethearts, and families would be doing back home; but most of the men kept off the subject of Christmas. Now and then some forehanded pioneer turned up with a bottle of grog * and a few toasts would be drunk, though most of these were in a man's own thoughts. They were still ignorant of the general situation; most of them believed that a rescuing convoy was bound to reach them; but to some that night the thought came for the first time that they were likely to leave Bataan only as prisoners of war—if they left Bataan at all.

There were no available communications. The only way for a commanding officer to get information was to climb into his jeep and start off down the road asking people questions. On Christmas Day it seemed as if no one knew any of the answers. About all he could expect to find out was where other units were located.

The greatest concentration, as already stated, was round Limay. In the village were the Air Base outfits, including the 19th and 20th Air Base Squadrons and the 27th, 28th, and 47th Matériel Squadrons. Two units of the 27th Bombardment Group—Headquarters and the 91st Squadrons —went up a valley about a mile away from the village, where they were joined three days later by the 17th Squadron. It was a wonderful site with its stream and huge trees all about to make good cover and the men thought they were going to stay in this hideaway till the absent pilots returned from Australia with their dive bombers.[2] Nearby in Rodriguez Park the Philippine Army Air Corps had staked out their camp. They had spent the first night of their trip from Manila sleeping in their trucks along the roadside; but, as they started off in the morning, Major Andrews recalled how he used to come over to Bataan in his Boy Scout days and camp in Rodriguez Park on land then worked by the Cadwallader Gibson Lumber Company; and pushing on ahead, he found the old site as he remembered it and had their camp area staked out by the time the men had come up.

The 19th Bombardment Group and the two remaining squadrons of the 27th Bombardment Group, the 16th and 17th, were at Cabcaben, about nine miles south of Limay. Between the two villages there was only the tiny barrio of Lamao. For the rest of the way the road wound through a thick growth of trees and jungle underbrush, following the

* A tantalizing sidelight on the liquor situation is recorded by Lt. McAfee in his Diary. Much concern was felt that the liquor in the Army-Navy Club might fall into the hands of the Japanese, who notoriously reacted badly to alcohol, so it was all loaded on a boat "and damn if the Japs didn't bomb and sink the boat." [1]

rise and fall of the land with relatively little grading. But just above Cabcaben it broke suddenly into a clearing.

This was Bataan Field, still a raw slash that ran 5000 feet on a slight down grade from the base of the wooded hills to the shore of Manila Bay. The road crossed the lower end of it, and as the Bombardment Squadrons rolled across it on their way to Cabcaben, a company of the 803rd Aviation Engineers were working on the strip. It had been roughed out by civilian contractors and, though it was large enough to take P-40s, there was still grading to be done on it. Work on two more strips, at Cabcaben and Mariveles, had barely started, but the airfields in the north of Bataan, at Pilar and Orani, were also nearly finished. They were, however, mere dust strips built over what a few days previously had been rice paddies. The problem of handling the dust became acute even before the fields were ready to receive the planes,[3] and the four pursuit squadrons that went in to take them over on the 25th and 26th tried various expedients, including that of sprinkling the runways with a mixture of molasses and water.

The 17th Squadron, as we know, had moved in to Pilar and was joined there by the 20th, which came down from Clark Field. The 3rd Squadron, coming over from Manila by boat, made its way to Orani, the most northern of the five Bataan fields, though its operation was officially assigned to the 34th Squadron. The 34th, which was only a few miles away at Del Carmen, did not arrive till the 26th. It had gone through a curious, brief period of demoralization, and except for the initiative of an officer not connected with the Squadron might never have reached Bataan as an organized unit.

It will be recalled that the 34th, like the 21st Squadron, had arrived from the States with half its officer strength, and of these men only three were first lieutenants. On the second day of the war they had lost their commanding officer and suffered a raid on their field at Del Carmen in which twelve of their 18 worn-out P-35s were destroyed and the other six heavily damaged. In consequence the Squadron, which had come under the command of Lieutenant Ben S. Brown, remained inactive till Christmas. They moved their camp well back from the field, but they left the battered planes lined up on the strip so realistically that in the next two weeks the Japanese staged 19 bombing attacks on the base.[4]

During this period the morale of the Squadron began to disintegrate. The men did not have work enough to keep them fully occupied, and Del Carmen, even in the general ignorance of the military situation in which Air Corps troops then existed, seems to have been specially isolated. The pilots were young and for the most part fresh out of Flying School. They had no experience and apparently little aptitude in handling men. The result was that the Squadron nearly fell to pieces, and the men were actually on the point of taking to the hills when Captain Munton, who had come to set up the new Air Depot at Del Carmen, stepped in to reorganize the unit and try to give the men some morale. It was a very temporary responsibility that Munton assumed, but it came at the vital moment. The Squadron got hold of itself again as a unit, moved down to Orani on the morning of the 26th,* after receiving a big Christmas feed the night before from the operators of the neighboring sugar mill, and, within a week, with Lieutenant Robert S. Wray as its new commanding officer, it was flying reconnaissance missions with the P-40s assigned to the field.

The only Air Corps unit that had not reached Bataan by the morning of the 26th was the 21st Pursuit Squadron. The 21st remained at Lubao as air-base troops until the night of January 1, when the Japanese advance threatened to bring the hidden field under artillery fire.[6] Colonel George stopped on his way in to Bataan to visit them there early Christmas afternoon [7] and inspected the 25 planes—P-40s, P-35s, and one lone surviving and useless A-27, still with its Siamese instrumentation—that comprised American air power on Luzon.† The men had had a night and morning to put in on the ships and altogether 16 P-40s and four P-35s were rated fit for combat. But the rating was purely relative, for by peacetime standards every ship needed a depot overhaul. It must have been hard to remember that it was only 18 days since peacetime standards had been in force.

---

* After this, Capt. Munton transported all the Depot supplies he had assembled to the Depot at Bataan Field and later was himself in charge of Supply there.[5]

† This figure does not include the new P-40s assembled in the Air Depot and flown from the Quezon City boulevards to Lubao by Lt. Warden in the next few days. Presumably at this time George did not know of them or could not have counted on them if he had. Altogether 18 P-40s and two P-35s were taken into Bataan on January 2. On December 30, another P-40 was flown down to Cebu and Mindanao by Lt. Feallock.

If he felt any bitterness as he looked over the planes, hidden under their revetments of green cane like mice in meadow grass, George did not show it to the men. He knew that within a few days the planes must be moved down on Bataan, where they would have to operate from fields that the Japs had watched building. As soon as they left Lubao every move they made would be marked down.

Once George had told a group of pursuit pilots that they would never win the war thinking how strong the other fellow was.[8] This was not merely an aphorism to him but a principle of his own life, and it became almost the guiding principle of the whole army on Bataan. But now as he observed the ingenuity with which the field had been camouflaged and the obviously high morale of the Squadron, George himself must have drawn encouragement from what he saw. The night before he had seemed almost overburdened by the responsibility he had accepted with his disorganized command. He summed it up for Ind. "I have twenty airplanes. I have got a lot of trucks, and I have got five thousand kids without a leader." * But here at Lubao was evidence that one squadron at least had learned how to look out for themselves, that they had discipline and high morale. It must have been then that George first realized Dyess's capacity for command and marked him as a possible successor to himself.

Three miles west of Lubao, George made another stop to look over a new strip being roughed out by two or three engineers with next to no equipment and only Filipino labor.† The day had become unbearably hot and time was running short, but George went over every foot of the work with the men, listening to their problems and making suggestions. He stopped twice more for similar inspections at Orani and Pilar. Then at last, with most of the day gone, he got into his car for the last time and set out to find his own Headquarters.[11]

The sheer amount of work confronting him would have appalled a

---

* Like some of Ind's quotations of George this should be taken with some reservation. Actually between 6000 and 7000 Air Corps troops moved onto Bataan. Five thousand were involved in the surrender on April 9, and that figure does not take into account the men lost and missing in battle, the relatively small number that escaped to Corregidor, or the 650 members of the 19th Group that left for Mindanao on December 29.[9]

† This strip was never completed. The Japs, while never finding Lubao, spotted this one and repeatedly bombed it.[10]

man of less determination. They were all starting from scratch. Even his own Headquarters Staff remained to be organized. All his units would have to be located and a communications network of some sort established. He was determined to get as many of the tactical units out of Bataan as he could; but until he could get them out, or until planes could be flown in from Australia, useful work would have to be found for them.

Shadows were lengthening as the new Packard car, now so dust-beaten that all its color and finish had disappeared, turned west at Cabcaben and started to climb the steepening grade towards Little Baguio. The road became narrower as it climbed, and the trees grew taller. The air was cool, and there was a sense of stillness, almost of peace, in the jungle on either side. The high canopy of leaves shut out the sunset; in the earlier dusk beneath them the immense, soaring trunks of the eucalyptus trees shone luminously white. Now and then the Packard had to make room for a truckload of troops; now and then a little group of tired and bewildered men afoot stepped down into the ditch to watch the car go by—casuals hunting for their outfits.

Some of them had been bombed as they came ashore in Mariveles. All had climbed the long steep winding road out of the little port to the Engineers' camp at Little Baguio and had been told to keep on going. Most of them had seen no food since noon the day before; but one or two had had better luck.

Lieutenant Young and his detachment that had come round from Clark Field by way of Manila, landed earlier than most and therefore foraged Mariveles with greater success. They bought up a day's baking from a native bakery, they found a five-gallon crock of strawberry jam, and two hardier souls turned up at the rendezvous with a gallon of gin and three gallons of rum. With this plunder they went on halfway up the zigzag road to Little Baguio and sat themselves down and had their Christmas dinner.

There was also a large group of casuals that, during the evacuation of Manila, were turned over to a young pursuit pilot, a second lieutenant, who was told to escort them over to Bataan and see that they got back to their original units. Like all others who came ashore at Mariveles that morning, they had spent nearly eight hours crossing the bay and creeping through the mine fields and they were hungry when they left the boat. But they didn't find anything to eat in Mariveles. And the road running out of town disappeared up a steep and jungle-covered hillside that looked awfully unpromising. But finally there was nothing left for them to do but set out along it, on foot and unfed, to try to find their units. It was a little past noon when at last they straggled up to the Engineers' camp at Little Baguio to witness a wonderful scene. The Engineers were sitting down to Christmas dinner.

The Engineers, having fixed themselves up pretty well, were beginning to feel like the ants in the fable about this inpouring of unprovisioned troops along the road; and they were not too cordial to a bunch of strays officered by a mere second lieutenant. But the men hung around just the same, with the instinctive tenacity that keeps hungry men as well as hungry dogs hovering in the neighborhood of food even when they have been told they can't have any. They weren't exactly hopeful; but the camp seemed like a good place to be in, with its low, clapboarded buildings, its orderly lines of trucks, its sense of establishment, its shadowy coolness, and above all the smell of food. And then, as if the Lord had taken notice, the air raid siren blew.

The Engineers, who had embroidered their installation with a fine system of foxholes well back from the buildings, fairly evaporated into the jungle. But the second lieutenant had learned a lot in his 18 days of war, and he could now recognize a dispensation of Providence as well as any man. So he sat his casuals down in the places of the Engineers and they all started wolfing the Christmas dinner while the Japanese planes came on. The roar of the engines gained power and suddenly echoed off the mountain wall. The shadows in formation rushed across the high green canopy of leaves directly overhead. But no bombs were dropped, and in a moment the engines faded out in the direction of Corregidor. Through the new silence the siren's voice sounded the All Clear and the Engineers began to return. There seems to be no record of what, if anything, was said by either party before the casuals went on their way.

That had happened at noon. It was near dark when George's car drove up to Little Baguio and found a parking space among all the trucks and cars that were now massed in the area. Lieutenant Barnick had set up

Air Headquarters camp across from the Engineers, on the bay side of the road. The Air Service Command and Signal Corps had moved in with him. They had not found the Quartermaster yet. The only food was C-rations in cans; and some of the men could not stomach it and turned away, though later a can of C-rations would seem like a feast.

George saw immediately that the camp could serve them only temporarily. It lacked running water, for one thing; it was too close to the ordnance dumps clustered through the trees; and it encroached on the Engineers, who had enough on their minds without having the Air Corps underfoot. But for the time being they must make this place do; and, as the men came round him in the gathering darkness, he made them a little speech on digging foxholes and latrines. Though there was hard sense in what he told them, the way he said it sent a ripple of laughter round the group.[12] It was a healthy sign. But he understood the lost look he had seen on many, especially of the younger, faces; and when at last he returned to the Engineers' camp, where a room had been turned over to him, he must have carried thoughts of his own wife and children. Inside the door the Engineers had set up a Christmas tree. It was a small tree, and not particularly healthy, but they had hung two or three ornaments from its dusty branches.[13]

It took the men twenty-four hours to get over Christmas; after that their morale improved and kept on improving. They were officially informed that General Brereton and his Headquarters had gone south; but they also learned to know their new commanding officer. For the next three days, till December 28, George spent most of his time scouting out better camp sites for the various units and keeping contact with the squadrons still in the north. Men began to realize that the feeling of helplessness that had pervaded everyone came from lack of leadership. Now for the first time they began to understand George's qualities. He would not give an inch in the performance he demanded of a man; but somehow the interest and warmth of heart that marked his personal relations with people he knew well and loved were communicated to his command, and, while they had begun to realize something of the grimness of their future, they knew that at last they had a leader.

PART TWO
Java

1. The Opening Situation

WHILE THE BATTLE for Luzon closed in on Bataan, where the opposing armies were to become locked in a three months' stalemate, the Japanese were preparing to launch their campaign beyond the Philippines for the conquest of the Netherlands East Indies. Their advance through the islands was to be marked both by its fluidity and by its momentum. In two months, almost to the day, it had reached its objective: Batavia was in Japanese hands and Java had fallen.

The Japanese method of advance was built round their air power,[1] as every phase of their Pacific campaign thus far had been.* It was extremely simple, but entirely effective. After establishing themselves at a given base, the Japanese would send their planes against the next immediate objective until Allied air resistance there, if any, had been overcome and the coast defenses softened up. Their warships then moved down to open the beachheads for the troops, who followed closely in the small and shabby transports that looked so inadequate but were ideal for

---

* Air power had been the dominant factor at every stage of the Japanese campaign, as it was also to prove in our own return to the Philippines and in the reduction of the home islands of Japan. That is not to say that air power *by itself* could have won the Pacific war. But in reaching the enemy across the vast distances of the Pacific theaters, ships and ground troops became subordinate to the airplane. Once, however, the objective was reached, and the main battle was joined on land, the infantryman was once more restored to his traditional place as the dominant factor in war, and the plane's mission was to support him and therefore subordinate to his. (The Navy's use of air power perforce involved a much more inseparable welding of the functions of ship and plane.) It was in their extraordinarily imaginative and flexible employment of ground force and air power that Generals MacArthur and Kenney were so successful. The Japanese never exhibited the same degree of imagination; yet it is interesting here to note that their air power had (1) by the strike at Pearl Harbor cut off all possibility of a relief expedition from the east, (2) eliminated American air power in the Philippines and driven what Naval strength we had clean out of the area, (3) sunk the *Prince of Wales* and the *Repulse,* opening the coast of Malaya to landings anywhere, and (4), as will be seen, it was with their air power that they pinched off the staging fields through which fighter planes could be brought to Java, sank one shipload of them, and virtually eliminated air cover for the bombers we had based there.

the purpose. Mostly shallow-draft and coastal types, they could hug the shores, and loss of one or even half a dozen meant a relatively insignificant loss in men and matériel. In their landings, too, they never had to count on more than local opposition, for outside of Java and Sumatra there were few roads and barely 50 miles of railroad in all the Indies. This made necessary the capture of only occasional coastal points in order to dominate large areas; and usually the distance the Japanese had to cover to reach their next point of attack was so short that it gave the Allied Naval forces no opportunity to attack them in transit. It was one of the bitter ironies of this bitter, brief campaign that in their progress down through the islands, the Japanese, who were at once the attacking and the numerically superior force, should also have the advantage of shorter and interior lines.

The reason for this is explained by the map. The peninsula and islands that make up Malaysia are spread over the Southwest Pacific in the shape of an open fan. The handle lies in the Philippines; Borneo, Celebes, and the Moluccas, together with the intervening ocean alleys of the South China Sea, Makassar Strait, and the Molucca Passage, are the ribs; and the outer edge of the fan is formed by the Malay Barrier, the slender chain of land that begins with the tail of Thailand, the Malay States and Singapore, and continues through Sumatra, Java, Bali, Lombok, Soemba, Timor, and the small islands that reach across the Arafura Sea to Dutch New Guinea. The fan covers an enormous area. Following the curve of the Barrier it is 4150 miles from the northwest tip of Sumatra to the eastern end of New Guinea. Airline it is just over 3000 miles from Singapore to Port Moresby. But the radius, or the rib, of the fan from Davao to the Java coast is just about 1400 miles.

It was down the ribs that the Japanese attacked. All the major Allied bases, on the other hand, were strung out in a thin line along the outer Barrier. The line was anchored on the west by Singapore and on the east by the North Australian port of Darwin, itself 1000 miles from the next deepwater Australian port; and Singapore and Darwin are 2080 airline miles apart. Most of the bases, however, were in Java itself. The Dutch had built airfields on the islands to the north: three on Borneo, at Tarakan, Samarinda, and Balikpapan; another in Celebes, at Kendari; and one on Ambon. Though these fields had no facilities, they could

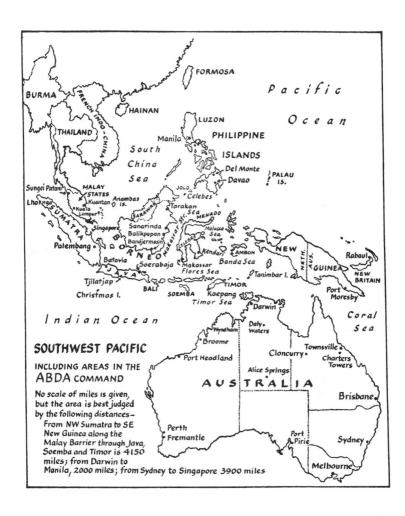

FORMOSA

BURMA

Pacific

Ocean

HAINAN

THAILAND

LUZON

Manila

PHILIPPINE

South
China
Sea

ISLANDS

Del Monte

Davao

PALAU
IS.

Sungei Patani

MALAY
STATES

JOLO

Celebes

Lhoknga

Kuantan

Anambas
Is.

Tarakan

MENADO

Kuala
Lumpur

SARAWAK

Sanarinda

Molucca
Sea

Singapore

Balikpapan

B O R N E O

Bandjermasin

CELEBES

Kendari

AMBON

NEW

Palembang

Banda Sea

Batavia

Soerabaja

Makassar

Tanimbar I.

GUINEA

Rabaul

NEW
BRITAIN

Tjilatjap

Makassar
Flores Sea

TIMOR

Christmas I.

BALI

SOEMBA

Koepang

Port
Moresby

Timor Sea

Darwin

Coral
Sea

Indian Ocean

Wyndham

Daly
Waters

SOUTHWEST PACIFIC

Broome

INCLUDING AREAS IN THE
ABDA COMMAND

Port Headland

Cloncurry

Townsville

Charters
Towers

Alice Springs

No scale of miles is given,
but the area is best judged
by the following distances –
From NW Sumatra to SE
New Guinea along the
Malay Barrier through Java,
Soemba and Timor is 4150
miles; from Darwin to
Manila, 2000 miles; from Sydney to Singapore 3900 miles

A U S T R A L I A

Brisbane

Perth
Fremantle

Port
Pirie

Sydney

Melbourne

be used as staging fields for long missions to the north. But they were without antiaircraft protection and were inadequately garrisoned with native, poorly armed, and unenthusiastic troops, and the Japanese were able to absorb them quickly. Once they were lost, the air situation in Java became hopeless. To have any chance of successful operation against a numerically stronger enemy, an air force must have its own bases organized in depth. This was impossible in Java, or anywhere else along the Malay Barrier, for the entire weight of the Japanese assault was from the north and perpendicular to the thin Allied defense line. The Japanese pushed their three invading armadas down through the South China Sea, Makassar Strait, and the Molucca Passage. Only in their conquest of Malaya did they make use of the outer edge of the Malaysian fan; but this land campaign, while strategically a vital part of the attack on Java, was in itself tactically directed only against Singapore.

Moreover, the geography of the islands aided the Japanese in providing air cover for their three amphibious assaults. Members of the Allied command had originally expressed a good deal of confidence that the Japanese would overextend themselves as they came south and that, as a result, their air power would become diffused. But this did not prove so. By making use of the airfields they captured and by building others themselves, the Japanese were able to form a network of air bases with only 300-mile hops between fields and thus could concentrate their air power quickly in any part of the Indies. Since they also held the initiative, it was possible for them to build up local superiority at any point they wished without relaxing their over-all pressure throughout the theater of operations.* To our own people, with barely enough resources in men and matériel to meet a single one of these threats as it rose, it must have seemed like fighting forest fire. Checked in one spot the flames invariably broke out somewhere else. General Brereton wrote in his diary that "the Japs fairly leaped from airfield to airfield in their southward advance." [3] That was undoubtedly an exact description. With their flanks covered on the west by the Malayan campaign and secured in the east by the effects of their raid on Pearl Harbor, the invading Japanese convoys had nothing to distract them from the sole task of getting south.

---

* Japanese air cover was so dominant that our Naval forces were never able to make a successful daylight attack. [2]

The small Dutch defense forces were never adequate for the protection of the Indies. Their army numbered about 100,000 men, mostly Indonesians, incompletely equipped with a strange and impractical assortment of left-over arms. The urgent necessities of the Allies on critical fronts were greater than either Britain or the United States could hope to fill; and much of the matériel that came to Java in the final months before war started had been captured from Axis armies on the battlefield. When Captain Ind was there in July 1941,[4] he reported that the Dutch had seven different calibers of cannon and that in the last shipment to reach them were a pair of Italian Caproni types for which, of course, there was no way of getting shells. By the end of August their situation had become so critical and their requests had been so often, of necessity, disapproved in Washington, that the Netherlands Indies Government sent representatives to appeal to General Marshall personally. He has recorded how they asked for, among other items, an initial allotment of 25,000,000 rounds of small arms .30-caliber ammunition, and how the most that could be made quickly available were 4,000,000 rounds that would have to be shipped from Manila. To make them up to the Army in the Philippines, replacement shipments were to be started immediately from San Francisco; but these in turn meant that the reserves for United States troops then in movement to Iceland would be dangerously depleted.* It was a little like a man playing the shell game against himself; but it did not materially help the Dutch, whose shortages extended far beyond the item of small arms ammunition. Chief among them was the scarcity of antiaircraft guns and the utter absence of any form of radar.

The Netherlands air force was composed of about 200 planes of all types;[6] but they also were left-overs, outmoded, and obsolete. The bombers were an export version of the B–10 our own Air Force had discarded long ago. They were slow and dreadfully vulnerable, without armor plate, and armed only with a .30-caliber gun in the rear station,

---

* It now seems hardly credible that finding a mere 4,000,000 rounds of .30-caliber ammunition could ever have been such a problem for the Chief of Staff of the United States Army. "Money in large appropriations had been made available, but not available was the time in which to convert this money into munitions ready for issue." Time is the greatest single factor in war—a fact this nation is forever forgetting.[5]

with no turret, but with an ordinary old C-4 mount.* Their fighters, of which they had roughly the equivalent of four squadrons, were mostly Brewster Buffaloes, solid, heavy, thick-barreled ships that had originally been designed as carrier planes for the United States Navy. They could buck themselves off a field nearly straight up into the air and they could dive like sacks of lead; but while the Dutch model was considerably faster than the one the British had been using in Malaya, which had a top speed of about 190 miles an hour,† they still could not fly in the same league with the Zero, which had 100 miles an hour advantage and a rate of climb that was three to five times faster. Besides these types, the Dutch went into combat with a few P-36s, bought in 1940, and also a plane called a Curtiss CW-21B. This was a training plane that had been rejected by our Army as requiring a genius to land it; but in some ways it was the best fighter the Dutch had and was armed with four .303 Browning machine guns. There were 13 of these planes stationed at Soerabaja when the Japanese first came over. Six of the 13 were knocked down in that first raid. The remaining seven went up against the next one, and two of them returned.[8] The Dutch defending Java would fly anything, but not from choice. General Van Oyen, who commanded their air force, told General Brereton that the Dutch had tried to purchase the latest model U. S. planes, "but every effort was met with the statement that Japan, the only possible enemy, did not have modern aircraft." [9] That may have been so, but the actual fact was that the United States did not have planes enough for its own needs.

The Dutch naval force in the Indies was efficient and had good morale; but it also was small. At the start of the war it consisted of four light cruisers, six destroyers, and 18 small submarines. There were, besides, a few sloops and several torpedo boats whose usefulness was confined chiefly to the close, home waters round Java and its neighboring small islands. The Dutch themselves never suffered any illusions about their navy's being able to turn back a full-scale assault by Japan, but neither did they have any illusions about their own expendability. By the time Java fell, they had fought their tiny fleet down to its last surface ship.

* Technically, the plane was a Glenn L. Martin model 139W.
† George Weller, in his account of Malaya's fall, "Singapore Is Silent," gave a graphic account of these Brewsters.[7]

Even while General Brereton was flying southward from Manila on December 25, the pattern of forthcoming events was beginning to take shape. The immediate weight of Japanese pressure still lay in the west, where Hong Kong had surrendered that same grim Christmas Day, where Thailand had come to terms two weeks before, and where the Japanese army under Yamashita was driving the British fiercely down the Malay Peninsula. But now also, at the end of December, the Japanese were busily preparing their base at Davao and were about to move in on Jolo.* They had made good their landings at Miri and Kuching, near the north and south borders of Sarawak on Borneo's west coast, and were pouring in their troops there; and already their air reconnaissance was being reported over the east coast south as far as the great Dutch oil center of Tarakan.[11] The need for naval and aerial striking power to defend the northeast approaches to the Indies, long urgent, was now becoming desperate; but the Allies had little left to draw on.

When General Brereton landed at Soerabaja on the 25th, he learned that the total Allied naval strength in the Southwest Pacific (not counting Dutch sloops and torpedo boats) amounted to one heavy cruiser, eight light cruisers, 23 destroyers, and 36 submarines;[12] but at that time all Dutch and British surface units were engaged in escorting convoys, mainly into Singapore. They were to remain on this duty until early February.[13] This left only our own small Asiatic Fleet, under Admiral Hart's command, to meet the Japanese convoys coming down through the Molucca and Makassar Straits. They had some Dutch submarines with them, and they also had the invaluable services of Patrol Wing Ten, whose PBYs, now operating out of Soerabaja, were flying reconnaissance over the entire theater and on occasion were even staging bombing missions of their own, like the costly attack on Jolo on December 27 when four out of six PBYs were shot down.† The Dutch could provide no aerial striking power from Borneo, for during the second week of fighting all the bombers in their air force had been sent to bases in Sumatra. From there they were flying missions to support the British on Malaya,

* Jolo, in the Sulu Archipelago, lies southwest of Zamboanga, in the chain of islands between Mindanao and the northeast shoulder of Borneo.[10]

† The PBYs had gone up to attack a concentration of Jap shipping and were intercepted by fighter planes. Many of the crews were saved; but within seven days the Japs were ashore and setting up a fighter assembly line.[14]

and by the end of the year their total air strength had been cut to 158 planes of all types.[15]

The British were much too preoccupied by their own situation, which was deteriorating with dismaying rapidity, to feel able to send help anywhere else. Firm statements that Singapore would be held were issued at intervals in official quarters; but the retreat of the army had gained such momentum that the Australian, Lieutenant General Henry Gordon Bennett, as early as mid-December had warned his superiors in Australia that Singapore must fall if the retreat were allowed to continue at its present rate.[16] Far from being able to help their allies, the British could not even provide air cover for their own troops. They had put an Air Chief Marshal, Sir Robert Brooke-Popham, in command of Singapore, but they had given him no modern planes with which to defend the base; and his ceaseless requests for effective fighter planes remained fruitless until the situation had gone past all saving.* As a result the bomber force with which the British and Australian pilots on Malaya began the war consisted of a handful of Hudsons, a few obsolete Blenheims, and some strange archaic ships called "Wildebeestes," already sold to the Indian Government for £60 apiece but held in Singapore because there were no substitutes. These Wildebeestes had an attacking speed of roughly 85 miles an hour, and though they were classed as torpedo bombers, they had never been fitted to carry torpedoes; but they were sent out to bomb the Japanese landings just the same.[18] The fighter pilots continued to take their lumbering Brewsters into combat, but their numbers were thinning fast. Reconnaissance over the jungle and the shore of the China Sea was handled by a group of civilians known as the Malayan Volunteer Air Force. Without previous combat experience or training of any sort, these men went out on their missions in little Puss Moth monoplanes and Tiger Moth biplanes, unarmored and unarmed, with a top speed of between 90 and 100 miles an hour,[19] defenseless as sparrows beneath the hunting Zeros. When mention is made of the whiskey-drinking complacence of the British planter class in Malaya and Burma, a word ought also to be said about these volunteers. They did not last long.

---

* Brooke-Popham, while in Java for staff talks during September, had told McClure Smith of the *Sydney Herald:* "Every week I ask London for three things, torpedo planes, dive bombers, and tanks." [17]

The only piece of real air striking power available for the defense of Borneo and the northern ocean passages leading down into the Indies was our own force of B–17s of the 19th Group, still based at Darwin after their withdrawal from the Philippines. After a series of conferences in Soerabaja with Rear Admiral William P. Purnell, Admiral Hart's * Chief of Staff, and Admiral William A. Glassford, Jr., U. S. Navy Task Force Commander, General Brereton agreed that the B–17s should be used in support of the Naval forces to delay the southward advance of the Japanese; and it was his intention then to establish his own headquarters with Admiral Glassford.[21] In the meantime, while he himself flew to Bandoeng to confer with the Netherlands East Indies Army Commander, General Hein Ter Poorten, and with General L. J. Van Oyen, Chief of their air forces, he ordered Lieutenant Colonel Eubank † to find an airfield suitable for Fortress operations and to make a survey by air.

A young Dutch pilot took Eubank round in a training plane. There was no time to make a complete inspection of all the fields that sounded possible from the descriptions given him; but he found one near Malang, about 60 miles south of Soerabaja, that could be used; and on Brereton's return from Bandoeng it was decided that the B–17s should move up from Darwin at once.

Original plans had called for establishing FEAF Headquarters at Darwin and developing the town into a major base; but it had almost no facilities and it was too far away for effective operations north and west of Java. These factors, together with difficulties of supply, had already induced the Navy to set up their operational command in Soerabaja.[22] For the B–17s there were the additional inducements that they would be a great deal nearer Palembang in Sumatra, the source of all their high-test gasoline; the Dutch bombs, though marked in kilos, were all American made and would therefore fit the Fortress bomb racks; and the Dutch also had facilities for making oxygen.

On December 29, Brereton took off with Colonel Brady and Captain

* Admiral Hart, en route by submarine from Manila, had not yet arrived.[20]
† It will be recalled that Brereton had been accompanied aboard the PBY by his Chief of Staff, Col. Brady, his aide, Capt. Llewellyn, and Lt. Col. Eubank on the flight from Manila.

Llewellyn for Darwin to get things moving while Eubank was left behind to set up bomber operations at the field near Malang, which the Dutch called Singosari.[23]

2. *The 19th Group Moves Up*

ONLY ELEVEN of the 14 B–17s that General Brereton found on Batchelor Field went up to Java.* Seven of them were ready to move at once, when he arrived, and they took off on December 30. Three more followed on the 31st. The eleventh plane was having electrical trouble on its No. 2 engine; it finally got away on January 2; but it was not assigned for a combat mission till the 14th, and then it aborted, again with engine trouble.† This meant that until January 11, when the first reinforcements began to arrive in Java after flights from halfway round the world, the Far East Air Force had exactly ten heavy bombers with which to operate against the invading Japanese convoys.

The air crews were tickled pink over the prospect of moving up to Java,[3] though they were pretty well aware of the odds against them. All

---

* General Brereton says in his Diaries that twelve B–17s went up to Java—"Nine of the bombers could move at once and three more within three days." [1] And under date of December 31, a radio from Darwin, signed Brereton, was sent stating that nine B–17s under command of Col. Eubank "proceeded by daylight today to Malang, Java, for immediate operations in accordance with assigned mission." But the movement of the planes occurred as stated in the text, eleven planes in all going up.[2] It does not seem likely that a twelfth plane could have gone to Java. The remaining three, *Nos. 40-2072, 40-3062,* and *40-3091,* all needed depot overhaul. One was turned over to the Army Transport Command for noncombat service when ATC was born under the command of Capt. (Pappy) Gunn. The other two appear to have been left at Batchelor, where they were stripped of parts under the direction of Lt. Mueller. (Lt. Col. Hoffman to the author at Batchelor Field, June 26, 1945.) None of the three numbers appears on the 19th Group's combat records after this date.

† This time the trouble was not electrical. The supercharger regulators had gone out on the two right side engines. The plane was old *3072* that had been over Clark Field when the Japs struck, with Tash as pilot, and now on the trip to Java it had the same crew except for Sgt. Bibin, who was wounded over Clark, and Krowd, replaced by Cpl. A. E. Karlinger. On January 4 it was sent from Malang to Australia, returning for good on the 12th to Java. Its first combat mission out of Malang was as one of seven planes against Sungei Patani on Malaya, staging from Palembang, Sumatra, with Vandevanter pilot, when as stated it aborted and returned to Palembang.

the officers had been called into one of the base tents where, standing in front of a map of the Southwest Pacific, General Brereton did some plain talking. Using the map, he showed them how and where the Japanese threat was forming against the northern Indies—Borneo and Celebes—and indicated the lines along which it was likely to develop as it came south. Java was the key to the whole Malay Barrier, and he explained that they were being sent up to do what they could to hold it because they were the only air power the Allied Nations had in the entire South Pacific area. He told them with some bitterness how he had tried to keep their highly trained bomb group from being sent out to the Philippines in the first place before there was adequate fighter cover for them. It was a bad situation, but there was no choice.* Instead of a group they now amounted to just about a squadron. Still, they were glad to be going.

Partly this was because any move that took them away from the heat, the flies, the dust and desolation of Northern Australia would have seemed good. But also they expected to make a better showing once the new B-17Es they had been told were on the way caught up with them in Java.† Their old B-17Cs and Ds had neither top turrets nor tail guns; but according to reports the new ships would have both. And then they knew for a fact that the facilities in Java were beyond comparison better than any Darwin had to offer. The air crew that had gone up to Soerabaja on the 27th to get General Brereton had had nearly two full days there to look the situation over.‡ They returned with glowing accounts of streetcars, blonde women, and cold beer.[6]

In addition to its regular crew of eight, each of the ten bombers that made the flight to Malang on December 30 or 31 carried three passengers. Five were extra officers; one was a Headquarters sergeant; the other 24 enlisted men were for maintenance.[7] This meant that they would have roughly two mechanics for each of their badly worn planes and that until the new ones did catch up with them and new personnel arrived, the

---

* As far as I know there is no record of this talk beyond the recollections of those who heard it, on whom at the time it made a deep impression.

† On December 28, 1941, General Arnold had cabled Generals Brereton and Brett that 80 heavy bombers were being ferried to the Far East "at the rate of three per day."[4]

‡ The plane, *No. 3070*, was piloted by Parsel and went up with only a six-man crew.[5] But they were enough to cover the ground.

19th Group would be operating on a shoestring. But the men weren't troubling their heads over such things on the way to Java. The weather on both days was fine and the flights were peaceful. The men peered down at the chain of islands in the blue sea with all the eagerness of tourists. The islands were pretty to look at and seemed incredibly green after the wastelands of Australia. When interest in them began to wane, the identification of Bali by the navigators was enough to bring the men back to the windows. Everyone wanted a look, but the altitude was too great for any practical observation and the subsequent discussion had to be based on hearsay or recollections of photographs in the *National Geographic.*

Then they were over Java, a velvet land with green mountains and greener valleys, every inch of which seemed under cultivation. A railroad line that ran east and west, paralleling but a good way inland from the southern coast, was their guide. After a hundred miles, it turned north and the bombers followed it into an upland valley narrowing between four mountains, and one by one in the late afternoon dropped down through lengthening shadows to the long sod runways of the airfield.

This was Singosari, six miles out of Malang. It had two enormous hangars side by side. There were brick barracks for the men, old but clean and lacking only beds enough to go round, so many of the men had to sleep on straw-filled pallets thrown on the stone floor. Like all the fields the Dutch built, it was well camouflaged, the long runways being almost indistinguishable from the surrounding fields; but because the revetments had been designed for nothing larger than medium bombers, the Fortresses once more had to be parked out in the open.

During the first days at Singosari it made no difference. The Japanese were not yet in striking distance of Java and the men had time to look around and make themselves feel almost at home. The Dutch in Malang, who were enormously excited by their first sight of four-engined bombers and took them as emblems of salvation, practically turned over their city to the 19th Group and on New Year's Day gave a dinner in their honor which the men still talk about. In it they encountered for the first time the celebrated *rijstaffel,* a course that begins with a platter of

rice to which various meats (ham, mutton, chopped bacon), grated coconut, shrimp, fish, sauces, and spices are added, each from its individual
dish, until the services of a dozen or more waiters have been employed.
According to Teats, there were something like 16 courses.[8] After the
lean rations they had lived on since December 8, it seemed a wonder
that the entire 19th Group was not permanently foundered.

Out at the airfield the food was not as good and, as far as the enlisted
men were concerned, there never seemed to be enough. After a while
they caught on to the fact that the Dutch personnel at the field answered mess call about eight times a day, which meant scant pickings
at the three conventional American meal hours. But when they had time
off they could always go into Malang for a good feed: to the Toko Oen
restaurant for a real steak, or to the Ket Van Kie for fried shrimp, or to
the Palace Hotel. There were night clubs to visit, and store windows to
look at, and the movies in which, oddly, the talking was plain American
and the subtitles incomprehensible Dutch. The men were apt to be
silent and a little subdued after the movies, especially if the picture
happened to be one they had seen a year or so before back in the States;
and they would return to Singosari with their thoughts on their own
people at home. It was a dark ride back to base, for both Malang and of
course Singosari were blacked out from the time they arrived. And then
word got round that you could telephone the United States direct from
Malang. Man after man put in his call, but it cost $13 and often took
days, sometimes weeks, to get through, and in the last hours of Java
the greatest preoccupation of some men was not whether they would
get out in time but whether their call home would be put through before
the island fell.

Singosari was a good base, and the 4000-foot sod runway held up
well and was all right to land on until the heavy rains began in mid-
January. The big hangars allowed the men to have full light for maintenance work at night. The nights were cool, too, for the field was a
thousand feet above sea level. At midday it would get very hot, but a
thin rain always came in the afternoon, falling gently for about an hour,
veiling the green hills, and bringing the coolness with it.

It was a very brief interlude.

On January 2 they sent off their first mission to the north, Captain Combs leading eight planes, this time as commanding officer of the Group. Lieutenant Colonel Eubank had been setting up his 5th Bomber Command when the B–17s came into Singosari and he gave the Group command to Combs. The ten planes were in bad shape: they had just one combat crew and about two mechanics for each, and they were terribly short of parts; but Combs was as proud of the outfit as any group commander probably ever was. They were to stage out of Samarinda, in Borneo, and from there strike a concentration of Japanese shipping reported at Davao. They knew that bombs and high-octane gas would be waiting for them at Samarinda, for one of the Fortresses * had gone up on December 31 with three Dutch liaison officers and returned on New Year's by way of Kendari, in Celebes. The crew reported both fields possible for B–17 operation, the one at Kendari very good.

Two hours out over the Java Sea, however, the formation ran into weather so rough that Combs was finally compelled to turn back to Malang. But next morning they took off again, this time with nine planes. During the extra twenty-four hours the maintenance men had been able to get one more ship back in shape.† Seventeen extra men were taken for maintenance since there were no facilities at Samarinda, and Major Walsh and Captain Broadhurst accompanied them to serve as Operations and Engineer Officers respectively. It came close to being the whole 19th Group.

The strip was cut out of the heart of the jungle, and it was really secret. The Dutch insisted that the American planes never set a direct course for it, so they flew off the coast of Borneo till they picked up a designated river and then followed the stream's course back into the hills. High broken clouds rested on the lower mountains; their shadows, huge and dark upon the jungle, barely moved. Only the shadows of the nine planes, in flights of three, raced on the treetops. The green strip, when they found it, looked small and lost. There was nothing to indicate that it was an airfield, though the planes were at low altitude; but after a minute some natives straggled into view and began drag-

---

* Broadhurst's plane. One of the Dutch officers, Lt. Bergvelt, was left at Samarinda II.[9]
† The tenth plane was out because of a lack of hydraulic fluid; but the shortage of fluid was relieved on January 4.[10]

ging log barricades off the strip; and the planes were able to land a little past noon.[11]

The job of servicing and loading them took all the rest of the day, and the men worked on after dark by the light of torches. The Dutch had a dozen Brewster Buffaloes on the field, but they had precious little else. There were neither mechanical fuel pumps nor bomb trolleys.[12] Everything had to be done by hand and the men were driven nearly frantic by the slowness of the natives who rolled the 50-gallon drums out of the jungle to the waiting planes.[13] The drums had to be hoisted up on the wings and poured into the tanks one by one—an interminable and bone-racking process. Through a translator's error the Dutch had brought out 1100-pound bombs instead of the 600-pounders asked for. The substitution took further time,[14] and then there was difficulty in getting the Dutch fuses lined up right.[15] One ship, too, had broken an oil line on the way up from Java,* but by 8:00 o'clock, all were finally ready, gassed, and loaded with four 600-pound bombs apiece, and at last the men could knock off for their scant meal of bread and a nearly inedible stew that was the best the Dutch had to offer.

They took off next morning before dawn. At 5:00 o'clock the jungle was shaken by the roar of engines running up. Propeller blasts drove gusts of dew from the trees. A fading moon made the sky mistily luminous, but the strip remained a black trough in which only the moving spots of flashlights or the orange flames of the exhausts showed where the bombers stood.

At five minutes past the hour Combs's ship taxied out to the head of the strip. It loomed enormous in the darkness, turning itself with slow and awkward movements, like the walking steps of a bird whose true strength lies along its wings. It paused a moment, facing the opening of the sky, as the slow beat of the engines lifted to a screaming pitch and the deep orange of the exhausts faded to thin collars of pale blue. The blast of the propellers swept back upon the men standing by as the ship began to roll. They lost it momentarily in the shadows far down the strip; then they saw it rising into view once more and for an instant its wings seemed to span all the sky. Then it swung away far out of sight beyond the jungle edge.

* Schaetzel's plane.

One by one seven others followed, taking off at four-minute intervals.[16] The oil line on the ninth, Schaetzel's, had failed again, and the crew were forced to remain behind with the maintenance men, the Dutch, and the natives, listening to the sound of engines fading away until once more stillness returned to the little strip and the jungle sounds were restored to life.

The eight airborne planes had 840 miles to cover to Davao. They flew in formation, climbing steadily, Combs leading the first flight and Parsel the second, while Connally and Kurtz made up the third.* By the time they raised Mindanao, they were at 25,000 feet and the high cold had entered the planes. They swung on inland in order to make their approach on Davao from the northwest. They were looking for Malalag Bay in which they had been told there was a lot of the Japanese fleet. There was, though they did not spot it right away.

The pattern of land and sea lay small and distant underneath them. The sea was deep blue, and the mountains, flattened by altitude, had stiff and narrow shadows. Where the planes flew it was all clear sunlight, but the gulf below was partly obscured by low and broken clouds, and it was only as they came full out above the water that they saw Davao Bay itself was crammed with shipping. Six freighters in line followed each other's wakes slowly up to port. Twelve big transports filled up the dock area and there was small stuff lying round everywhere they looked.

Then Stone,† Combs's bombardier, picked up Malalag Bay, and the formation swung through a 120-degree right turn and headed down the west shore of Davao Gulf, with the great peak of Apo reaching up towards them on the right, and beyond it by the waterside the town of Digos that other members of the 19th Group would come to know later in their prison years; and beyond Digos was a little cove caught in a fishhook of the land.

Within its narrow space the Japanese had crowded a mass of warships. The bomber crews counted one as a battleship,‡ five as cruisers,

---

* Bohnaker and Keiser were on Combs's wings, Smith and Teats on Parsel's.
† 2nd Lt. M. D. Stone.
‡ Actually a cruiser, later acknowledged by the Japs to be severely damaged.

and six as destroyers. Off to one side lay twelve submarines. And here, as in the upper bay, were quantities of smaller craft, and all packed in so close that from the B–17s it seemed as if they had been tied up deck to deck.[17] It looked, too, as if the Japanese had been caught completely off base, for there wasn't a sign of smoke or steam in any of the ships. None took evasive action, and the antiaircraft fire was late in coming up. When it did, though some reached to 25,000 feet, it was not heavy enough to interfere with the bombing run and it looked bad only to the last two planes.

The three flights went in at one-minute intervals. Their bombs exploded among the cruisers and destroyers. They counted three direct hits on the battleship. They claimed one destroyer sunk out of hand. Some of the bombs dropped among the submarines. As they pulled away they saw five Zeros around 10,000 feet and heading for them; but the Fortresses, which had made their approach, penetration, and withdrawal at rated power, were doing better than 300 miles an hour; and the Japanese fighters were unable to pull up to them. At 2:30 that afternoon all eight B–17s were back at Samarinda, with no casualties and hardly a scratch on any of the planes.*

It was, perhaps, the most successful bomber mission that the Far East Air Force, in its first incarnation, staged; and a proper elation gleams through the abbreviated report sent off from Samarinda for Malang by Major Walsh that afternoon.† There was the feeling that an installment on the December 8 account had been paid back. But compared to the 54 heavy bombers that the Japanese had put over Clark Field alone, it seemed a pretty small installment. The combat crews, especially, who had looked down on the stacked nest of warships in Malalag Bay, had moments of frustration when they thought of what might have been accomplished if they had had 30 planes—or even 18—in their formation, instead of eight.

It was not possible to stage another attack out of Samarinda as only

* Japanese records do not acknowledge loss of the destroyer.[18]
† The radio message was sent through Dutch Headquarters at Bandoeng for forwarding to Malang. It was received at Bandoeng at 5:30 P.M., January 4, but there, apparently, it died, and consequently neither Eubank and the 5th Bomber Command at Malang nor FEAF Headquarters at Darwin knew the results of the mission nor the status of the planes till they reached Malang the following day.

enough 100-octane gas remained to service each plane with 1700 gallons. This meant returning to Malang, which was done on the following morning, though not until the Dutch officials had held them up for nearly two hours while a methodical search was made (not without justification) for a missing Angora blanket. All hands who had flown up from Java on the 3rd returned with the planes. They attempted no more squadron missions from Samarinda, for it was obvious that the new sod on the strips would not stand up under heavy aircraft once the rains began.*

Instead, the next mission was staged through Kendari, on the southeast corner of Celebes, the best camouflaged and one of the best of all the Dutch bomber fields. Nine of the B-17s went up on January 8—the tenth was still out for lack of parts.† This total strength of nine represented two days' unremitting effort by the combat crews, including officers, who worked with and under directions from the maintenance men. Again their objective was the Japanese shipping in Davao Gulf; but this time they planned to strike the place at dawn.

They took off half an hour after midnight in black dark, with a 2000-foot and practically solid overcast to bore up through, so it seemed a miracle when all eight following planes found Combs and made formation with him. They flew formation all the way to Mindanao, and how any of them managed to follow Combs through the enormous front they met is something he will never understand. Of course they had their night lights, but the pale blue blurs on the wings were barely visible through the streaming windshields even in moments when the planes passed through broken areas in the clouds. Much of the time the weather was so heavy that the lights were smothered and the big bombers, tossed with a violence none of the fliers had experienced till then, were flying blind. Yet when they came out south of Mindanao and started firing their guns to clean them there were still six planes with Combs. The missing two had had to turn back with engine trouble.‡

---

* Only two more B-17s ever landed on this field: the first (Connally) on January 11; the second (Hillhouse) on January 19.

† On the 5th, Eubank radioed Darwin for "all available spark plugs, three generators, one broken expander tube, one set aileron bearings, one tachometer drive shaft, six oxygen check valves, six fuel pressure transmitters, one propeller assembly complete." [19]

‡ Teats and Smith.

They had made their landfall too early, so Combs went inland over Mindanao to kill time. There in the darkness and another front he lost four of the planes. Two of these turned back to Kendari carrying their bombs.* The other two came in separately in the early dawn and bombed a good-sized transport and missed it.† Combs, with his flight, went on to bomb the ships in the gulf as they had planned.‡ Though the weather over the gulf was too thick for accurate observation, it was plain that a good part of the Japanese concentration had moved out. There were still some warships in Malalag Bay, however, including the big one they had bombed before. It was surrounded by a busy circle of tugs and small boats as though the Japanese were trying to move or raise it. They attacked it again, getting one waterline hit and one direct hit that started a fire, while one over bomb to their great satisfaction lit square on an anti-aircraft battery on shore.[20]

Long before noon all the planes were back at Kendari, and next day they returned to Malang. Since the 2nd of January the planes had been out on mission for a total of seven days, including their first abortive attempt. In that time they had flown between 6000 and 7000 miles, some of the way through very heavy weather, to drop a total of forty-four 600-pound bombs in the target area. The combat crews, doing most of their own maintenance, had had almost no rest. A few of the men were beginning to show signs of accumulated overfatigue.[21] They were looking forward to a short respite when they flew into the upland valley and came down on Singosari; but they found that they were scheduled for another mission next day. The Japanese shipping they had missed from Davao Gulf was off Tarakan.

3. ABDACOM: The High Command

THE MISSION was flown on January 11 solely at the insistence of the Dutch. Colonel Eubank § wanted to wait one more day because of the heavy

---

* Broadhurst and Kurtz.   † Parsel and Connally.
‡Combs, Bohnaker, and Keiser.
§ Eubank received his promotion to full Colonel (temporary) on January 5.

front below Tarakan; but the Dutch, who had been rushing all their bombers back from Sumatra, concentrating them at Samarinda, were determined to strike the Japanese at once. General Van Oyen, their air commander, notified Eubank that the Dutch planes would attack no matter what the weather was. Under such circumstances, Eubank did not feel that he could keep his planes back, so he said all right, he would send in the Fortresses.

The men, who had only returned from Kendari at noon on the 10th, worked all that day to get their planes in shape for a high-altitude mission. By night they had seven ready and these took off at 5:55 in the morning of the 11th. One hour out of Malang they hit the front. It stretched east and west from horizon to horizon and was absolutely solid from sea level up to and above 25,000 feet. The planes spread out before boring into it, and from that moment they were blind. At times the fog and cloud became so thick that the men inside the planes could not see the ends of their own wings, and the pilots, in continual fear of collision, flew on instruments for the four remaining hours it took to reach their assembly point. This had been agreed on in case of their becoming separated; but only three—Combs, Connally, and Kurtz—got through to it. The other four lost radio contact, turned back inside the front, and came into Malang during the hour after noon.[1]

When Combs broke out of the front just before reaching the assembly point, he found no other planes. He circled there awhile, waiting for the others to come up and wondering what he ought to do. But none of the others joined him. Towards Tarakan, which now lay only 50 miles to the north, enormous cloud masses, broken from the front, drifted in utter stillness, and as the air crew looked down the shadowy, incredible crevasses between them, their Fortress seemed dreadfully alone.

Combs decided to attack. It didn't make much sense for one plane to go in by itself, but he thought that if the Dutch were going over in their old B–10s, the least he could do was to make a gesture for the U. S. A.

He was already above 20,000 feet and he climbed to 23,000 as he approached the target. Though the sea was veiled by a thin overcast below the base of the great clouds, there were spots in which the water showed clear and dark, and suddenly in one such space they saw the Japanese convoy. There seemed to be hundreds of ships, and Stone, the bombardier, took the Fortress over on a ten-minute run. Every time he got lined up on a ship he saw a bigger one just beyond and had to go for it. Then three Zeros cut round the shoulder of a cloud onto their tail, and Combs told Stone to pick the nearest, not the biggest, ship and let his bombs go.

The Zeros were very aggressive and hung to the Fortress for 35 minutes. In his efforts to shake them off Combs started looking for a cloud. There were some huge thunderheads and black piles of smoke from the oil-fields the Dutch themselves were burning, and Combs picked the biggest and blackest one he could find. He was just getting into the heart of it and feeling pleased with himself when the radio operator yelled, "For Christ's sake get into a cloud. Here come the little bastards again." The Zeros had bored right in with the Fortress and they didn't give up till the crew had shot down two of them.

Fifteen minutes later Kurtz and Connally came over without meeting any opposition at all. They dropped their bombs, but they wasted no time trying to see what damage, if any, they had done, for they were low on gas after hunting for each other and Combs in the front. Kurtz barely made it back to the coast of Java, landing at Soerabaja. Connally found his way into Samarinda where the clouds came down nearly to the treetops. The Dutch bombers were all at the field. That was the ironical part of the whole mission. They had found the front too heavy for their old B-10s to take and had turned back. Next day, though, nine of them attacked the Japanese convoy at very low altitude, and only one came back.[2]

This mission was the beginning of Eubank's difficulties with the Dutch—at the end he ran into really bitter feeling when he was trying to get his planes and people out in the last days before Java fell. It was not unnatural, indeed it was almost inevitable, for such incidents to occur. Four nations were taking part in the defense of the Malay Barrier, each with interests of its own to serve. The British were preoccupied by their appalling reverses in Malaya and Burma. The Dutch were wholly devoted to saving their island empire. The two American Army commands—FEAF and USAFIA,* the last a supply and training command

---

* United States Army Forces in Australia. In strict accuracy it was known first as USFIA (U. S. Forces in Australia) but the title was changed to the more pronounceable USAFIA when, on January 5, Headquarters moved to Melbourne.

set up at Brisbane after the arrival of the first American convoy on December 22—were, at least in this early phase, still looking towards the relief of the Philippines.* The Australians, following the British line, at first wanted American air power used in defense of Malaya and Singapore as well as the Australian continent; but by mid-January the drive of the Japanese down through the Indies had so alarmed them that they were exerting pressure even in Washington to have American air units, that had already been scheduled for operation in Java, withheld for the protection of New Guinea and their own northeastern cities.[8]

The need for unity of command and co-ordination of military effort began to overshadow all other problems in the Southwest Pacific theater; it became one of the major concerns of the British and American Chiefs of Staff, then meeting for the first time in Washington;[9] and on January 2 the formation was announced of a Supreme Command for all American, British, Dutch, and Australian forces in the Far East. This

---

*It is not easy to determine at what point the Philippines were written off in the minds of the various commands in the Far East area. Evidence exists that the U. S. Navy had done so as early as December 16, though General Marshall still counted on "energetic support of the Philippines."[3] By February 9, when Col. John A. Robenson was raising heaven and earth to procure ships and supplies in Java to run the Jap blockade up to the Philippines, the only hopeful response he won from any quarter of the Supreme Command came from Admiral Helfrich, the Dutch Naval Commander.[4] Originally, the primary mission of both FEAF and USAFIA was the support of the Philippines. (For FEAF see Chapter 27, Part One; for USAFIA, General Marshall's cable to General Brett, December 25, which made clear that the long-range air equipment was to be used to support the Philippine garrison.) As late as January 8 Brereton was reminding Australian officials of this fact.[5] But after the formation of ABDACOM early in January, the general strategic policy was changed, with operations in the theater designed, first, to hold the Malay Barrier; second, to hold Burma and Australia as essential to the support of India and China; and third, to establish communications through the Dutch East Indies with Luzon and to support the Philippine garrison. All air resources were funneled into the defense of the Malay Barrier, and both Brereton and Brett seem to have become converted to the theory that withdrawal to India and attacking through Burma and China offered the best chance of beating Japan. Brereton noted in his diary for February 24, on the eve of his evacuation of Java, that "my desire for some time has been to give the Japs territory and get back where we could reorganize the striking force, and I didn't care whether it was India or Australia. Brett gave me my choice and I picked India, maybe because I was sick of islands, even one as big as Australia."[6] And on February 21 Brett radioed the War Department, "Through Burma into China is my belief real theater for American forces exists."[7] In any case FEAF flew no more attack missions to support MacArthur's forces in the Philippines after the one of January 8-10 through Kendari, which has been described above.

command was to be headed by the British General Sir Archibald P. Wavell, with Major General George H. Brett, U. S. Army,* as his deputy; and almost inevitably it was to be called ABDACOM.

It would be at once tedious and impractical to give here a complete account of the ramifications of ABDACOM; but some outline of its structure and development is necessary if one is to understand the pattern of air operations in Java, particularly as it affected the American bombardment units and a little outfit of American fighter pilots and mechanics who brought up a total of 37 P-40s from Australia and fought in them till only six shot-up planes were left. To the men in these combat and ground crews, running missions and working on their planes as much as eighteen and twenty hours a day, an aura of almost fantastic unreality overhung the High Command.

The belief that Headquarters has lost touch with the situation exists in any combat outfit in any war and the closer the men are to the enemy the more profound their conviction is. Generally some discount should be made, but in Java there was undoubtedly basis for their belief. Organization of the air command in ABDACOM, for instance, was not completed till February 16, eight days before evacuation of American and British troops began. In a way, General Brett spoke for the lower echelons as well as himself when, after informing Washington on February 20 that evacuation plans had been prepared, he added bitterly that "tenacious adherence to age-old custom of procedure is of primary importance here. Aggressive initiative is of secondary consideration and committees are the rule. Staff procedure is obstructive, complicating, and cumbersome. If the war is to be won it is most evident that a different

* In the directive Brett received two days later for the formation of ABDACOM, he was promoted to Lt. Gen. to give him rank consonant with his high staff position. He had been acting as observer and consultant in Europe and the Middle East when, on December 21, he was given command of USAFIA. At that time he was under General MacArthur and his mission was to set up a service of supply for USAFFE and get supplies to the Philippines. General Clagett, who had reached Australia from Manila on December 19 (Part One, Chapter 26 above), was named as his assistant, and the commander of the troops on the convoy that reached Brisbane on December 22 (Brig. Gen. Julian F. Barnes) was ordered to report to one or other of these officers. Brett had been expected in Darwin on December 22. Actually, he arrived January 1, having spent some time in conferences on the way out, in India, China, and Java, to familiarize himself with the needs of the various commands.[10]

attitude of aggressive action must be taken." Perhaps here, too, a certain discount should be made. More was asked of Wavell than any man could have performed. He was contending not only with Japan's long-planned attack but with London's reluctance to believe that Singapore was not impregnable. A few more Spitfires and tanks arriving in time would have made a vast difference in Malaya. Moreover, when Wavell assumed his duties in Java, he was already a tired man.

He arrived with some of his staff on January 10, to be met by Generals Brett and Brereton at Batavia, where the work of building the new command was begun. The four Army, four Navy, and six Air organizations involved were all brought under three top operational commands: Army, (called ABDARM) under the Dutch General Hein ter Poorten; Navy (ABDAFLOAT) under the American Admiral Hart; and Air (ABDAIR) under the British Air Chief Marshal Sir Richard E. C. Peirse. This line-up bowed to the interests of the three nations chiefly engaged in the defense of the Malay Barrier. Chiefs of Staff for ABDACOM itself, ABDAFLOAT, and ABDARM were all British, while the post of Deputy Commander of ABDAIR was reserved for an American. It was first offered to Brereton.

He accepted it conditionally, but a shift in American commands made his retention of the post impossible for the time being, and it was given to General Brett, who thus filled a double function in ABDACOM. General Marshall felt that it was important to keep line command of American forces in Australia and Java separate from staff command inside of ABDACOM. While subscribing wholeheartedly to the principle of combined command, General Marshall wanted the line commander to feel sufficiently independent to appeal directly to the War Department if he felt that an order from ABDACOM jeopardized American interests, though he warned that this authority of appeal must be used sparingly. Therefore, Brett's appointment as Wavell's deputy meant that he could no longer command American troops in Java or Australia, so Brereton was appointed to replace him in command of USAFIA. Brereton returned to Australia on January 18. But he was to exercise the USAFIA command for only nine days. On January 27, the War Department agreed to Wavell's request for Brereton as Deputy Commander of

ABDAIR. Brereton turned the USAFIA command over to General Barnes and flew back to Java on the 28th to take up his new staff duties and resume active command of the Far East Air Force, which in the meantime had also moved its Headquarters up to Java and was operating under Colonel Brady's direction.*

Such continual shuffling of the top command, hard as it must have been on the men personally involved, left the lower echelons floundering in constant bewilderment. To make matters more difficult, Headquarters of ABDACOM were moved out of Batavia after three days to Lembang, a resort high in the mountains about ten miles north of Bandoeng. The site had been chosen for its coolness and in the hope that it would prove secure from Japanese bombing—as indeed it did.† But it was remote from the centers of both air and naval operations at Malang and Soerabaja, and this remoteness was accentuated by poor communications. Time was lost in the effort to improve them, and work on them was still going forward when the top command pulled out of Java.¹² It was in this atmosphere of almost Olympian detachment that ABDACOM completed its cumbersome machinery of joint command,‡ while the Japanese convoys piled down through the Indies.

* The movement of Hq FEAF was another example of the confusion prevailing at this time. Col. Brady with three officers and two enlisted men left Darwin to set up a new Headquarters at Soerabaja on January 10. They were joined on the 14th by four more officers and one enlisted man from Darwin, at which time both contingents moved to Batavia where, on the 16th, the final detachment from Darwin joined them. Next day they received orders to move on to Bandoeng and they accomplished this move on January 18. Five days later, on the 23rd, they shifted their quarters in Bandoeng to a new location in a downtown hotel, which made the fourth move in ten days. Then, on February 6, the Headquarters was moved, for the last time, to a military academy in Bandoeng and on that day the diarist wrote, hopefully, "Order is beginning to emerge in the administrative functions with the following setup: Maj. Gen. Brereton, CG FEAF; Lt. Col. (C. H.) Caldwell, Chief of Staff, acting; Lt. Col. (H. E.) Strickland, G-1; Maj. (R. F. C.) Vance, G-2; Lt. Col. (Emmett) O'Donnell, G-3; Lt. Col. (Birrell) Walsh, G-4." On February 4, Caldwell replaced Col. Brady, who had been sent to Burma to look over the situation in that area.¹¹

† The Japs apparently never attacked the Headquarters at Lembang but confined themselves strictly to tactical targets.

‡ It must be remembered that in ABDACOM, however ineffectual it was in stemming the Japanese tide, the basis for future combined operations under a united command was laid down.¹³ But as worked out at Lembang, the organization was unwieldy and top-heavy. As one officer expressed it, "The staff was way too large. We spend our time supporting ourselves instead of the combat squadrons. There were too many pilots behind

The basic strategy of ABDACOM—the combining of all forces to hold the Malay Barrier—rested on the assumption that Singapore itself would hold. It also depended on keeping open the chain of island airfields on Bali, Soemba, and Timor through which alone fighter planes could stage from Australia into Java; and since original plans called for opening communications with the Philippines as well, P-40 detachments were to be established at Samarinda, Kendari, and Ambon. The last was the little island at the tail of the Moluccas, almost exactly halfway on the air line from Darwin to Mindanao. As late as January 15,

desks and shuffling papers and some of the work could have been consolidated." The way this comment applied to the air command is made clear by a study of the table below:

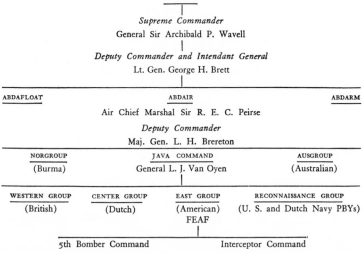

ABDACOM

|

Supreme Commander
General Sir Archibald P. Wavell

|

Deputy Commander and Intendant General
Lt. Gen. George H. Brett

|

ABDAFLOAT	ABDAIR	ABDARM
	Air Chief Marshal Sir R. E. C. Peirse	
	Deputy Commander	
	Maj. Gen. L. H. Brereton	

NORGROUP	JAVA COMMAND	AUSGROUP
(Burma)	General L. J. Van Oyen	(Australian)

WESTERN GROUP	CENTER GROUP	EAST GROUP	RECONNAISSANCE GROUP
(British)	(Dutch)	(American) FEAF	(U. S. and Dutch Navy PBYs)

5th Bomber Command   Interceptor Command

Under the 5th Bomber and the Interceptor Commands were the little operational commands of the actual flying units. For most of the time these units were all the real striking air power the Allies had in the theater, since the Dutch Air Force was quickly wiped out and the British lost most of their Hurricanes (that arrived too late to do any good) in Singapore and Palembang. About half a dozen finally came down to share in the last two days' defense of Java. Thus the two little American outfits were, in the end, all the air that the staffs outlined above, on the stepladder that culminated in the cool, remote resort of Lembang, had to command. In their days of greatest strength the grand, combined total of all personnel, combat and ground together, in these two outfits rose to a paper strength of 310 officers and 943 enlisted men. That was on February 21. It would seem that seldom in the history of war have so few been commanded by so many.

ABDACOM announced that these fighter planes would be sent in "as soon as special non-aromatic 100 octane fuel can be produced and camouflage pens are available." *

Such long-range plans banked heavily on the arrival in time of air reinforcements from the United States. General Brett had been informed on January 10 that besides one light and two heavy bombardment groups, his command would include four pursuit groups. Eighty of the heavy bombers were known to be on the way, but pursuit planes, like light bombers, would have to come out by ship to Australia for assembly there; and as will be seen this process was to involve unexpected delays and hazards from lack of parts and trained pilots. Only 39 assembled P-40s ever reached Java, the first 13 arriving on January 24 and 25.† By that time the Japanese had taken or were within striking reach of the three airdromes to which ABDACOM intended to send fighter planes.

On January 10 and 11 the Japanese had seized Tarakan in Northern Borneo and Menado at the top of Celebes. Within two weeks they were driving south again. One force moved down the Borneo coast to land at Balikpapan on the 23rd. Next day a second force, coming down from Menado through the Molucca Passage, took Kendari, while at the same time a force of four carriers, with appropriately heavy support, began air operations against Ambon. The Dutch air force on Ambon consisted of two Brewster Buffaloes, which were wiped out in the first raid.[15] Besides them there had been some Australian-manned Lockheed Hudson bombers on the island ‡ and a few PBYs of Patrol Wing Ten, operating from a base the tender *Heron* had set up.§ Now, without even the

---

* All gasoline produced in the Netherlands Indies was of the aromatic type, under which the linings of the American self-sealing tanks rapidly deteriorated.

† But, as will be seen, not all of these 39 planes were in combat condition—probably not more than 34.[14]

‡ At twilight on December 28, three of these same RAAF Hudsons had attacked the ill-fated destroyer *Peary* in the Molucca Passage under the impression that she was a Japanese light cruiser. She had dashed out of Manila Bay on the night of December 26, hidden out in little bays next day along the shore of Negros under a camouflage of green boughs; and on the afternoon of December 28 she had successfully come through a series of attacks by Jap bombers and torpedo planes. Then came the Aussies, getting a near-miss that killed two of her crew and cut her main steering lines. When she finally reached Ambon the RAAF pilots were still celebrating the probable sinking of the "cruiser," but the *Peary's* people vociferously straightened out the record.[16]

§ The *Heron*, an 840-ton converted minesweeper, was sent to the *Peary's* assistance and was attacked for over seven hours by Japanese planes without being sunk.[17]

semblance of fighter protection, they were forced to pull out and when enemy transports appeared offshore, the island could offer no air opposition of any kind. Ambon was in Japanese hands on February 1.

Samarinda, the last of the staging fields by which fighter reinforcements could have been flown to the Philippines, was pinched off on February 7; but by then its loss had become relatively unimportant. With Japanese bombers based at Ambon, Kendari, and Balikpapan, not only was the air ferry route between Java and Australia directly threatened, but the air fields on Java itself were no longer safe from attack.

To meet the exigencies of the new situation, ABDACOM now made plans, besides stationing a full American fighter squadron at the Koepang airdrome on Timor, to build up a composite wing at Darwin.[18] Darwin, in spite of the obvious drawbacks of its remoteness, exposed position, poor facilities, and totally inadequate communications, was slated for development as a major base for future offensive operations.* But neither project could be realized. Here as in all previous instances the people in ABDACOM found that time, their own lack of means, and the Japanese were arrayed overwhelmingly against them.† So quickly did the situation deteriorate that as fast as a scant squadron of P-40s could be assembled in Brisbane it had to be flown all the way in to Java. There were no planes to spare for Koepang or even Darwin; and yet the greatest combat strength achieved at any one time in Java never amounted to over 26 planes.‡

---

* Darwin had been specified as a base by General Marshall on December 22, 1941. When Brett arrived January 1, 1942, he approved plans for its development and intended that it should be the largest advance base in Australia to support operations developing in the N. E. I. After Java fell, Brett and Brig. Gen. Ralph Royce, who became his Chief of Staff, both seem to have retained the idea of using Darwin as a springboard for attacking the Japs up through the N. E. I. But shortly after he reached Australia in March, MacArthur scrapped the plan in favor of the campaign up through the South Pacific, though he kept up appearances in Darwin to protect his own flank and as threat to that of the Japs.[19]

† General Brett was urgently aware of the need of holding Koepang but he had run into Australia's increasing reluctance to use any military strength of any sort except in her own defense. On January 31, in a message to Washington, he said, "Defense [of Koepang] should be provided by Australia and NEI. NEI cannot assist due to present employment of forces. Australia considers defense of Koepang of less importance than defense of Darwin. Australia is endeavoring to divert American squadrons to Port Moresby for defense of east coast. . . . If war is to be carried to the north it is absolutely imperative that the line of communication from Darwin to Java be kept open."

‡ This top strength was attained on February 14.[20]

General Marshall had from the first feared just such dissipation of American strength and in his message of January 10 he specifically directed that there should be "only a minimum of piecemeal employment of the air force." Units were not to be considered ready until they had been organized into combat teams in Australia, nor must units be employed short of their destination as they came past areas of action. But in its desperation ABDACOM could pay scant heed to these restrictions, and its operations in the final defense of Java rested entirely on improvisation. It meant that the men in the tactical commands had to operate pretty much on their own.

4. Arrival of the 17th Pursuit Squadron (Provisional)

THE FIGHTER OUTFIT that moved up at the end of January to undertake the defense of Eastern Java was known as the 17th Pursuit Squadron (Provisional). It was almost inevitable that the Squadron should be given this number. When orders for its formation came down on January 10, there were just 17 flyable P-40s in Australia. This meant that the little expeditionary air force consisted of 17 pilots, 17 crew chiefs, and 17 armorers, with one line chief, one first sergeant, and three radiomen. But there was also a sentimental reason for the number. Thirteen of the pilots had seen service in the Philippines, and of them eight had belonged to the 17th Pursuit Squadron. When they took off from Brisbane under the command of Major Charles A. Sprague,* they still believed that they were headed back to Bataan to rejoin their old squadron.[1]

That was why they had been sent south by Colonel George. Fourteen of them made the trip out in two of the Philippine Air Lines' Beechcraft planes, one flight leaving at 4:00 in the morning of December 31,

---

* Sprague, who still had a captain's rank, became a major by virtue of the Squadron command but was not commissioned till after he reached Java. He had been Operations Officer of the 5th Interceptor Command, first under General Clagett, then under Col. George. He had been, apparently, very close to George, sharing his quarters, and was one of the Colonel's disciples.

the second two days later. It was a hazardous trip, with danger of interception for more than half the route. Enemy planes were thick over Bataan and the whole Manila Bay area; they were reported to be active in the islands south of Luzon; and at this time, also, they had begun attacks on Tarakan, at which both flights would have to land.* The little, unarmed transport planes were in poor condition for the long over-water hops, but the first, piloted by Captain Connelly,† went the route successfully and landed its passengers at Darwin on January 2. From there the pilots were taken on to Brisbane next day in General Brereton's personal LB-30.‡

The second Beechcraft, however, was in far worse shape than Connelly's. It had previously been both strafed and bombed at Nielson Airport, and when the men gathered round it in the early afternoon of January 2, they eyed it with profound misgiving. They were a little shaken, anyway, because twelve Japanese bombers had just given the village of Orani a going over as they came through, and now beyond the edge of the airfield smoke clouds were rolling towards the mountains. The sight did nothing to improve the appearance of the plane.

The left wing, broken off in the bombing at Nielson Field, had been fastened on again with bailing wire and the whole leading edge of it replaced by a piece of tin roofing. With a suddenly roused statistical sense, the men counted 130 bullet holes in the fuselage and realized that, while the plane was designed for only seven passengers, they were going to load eight into it, besides 50 gallons of extra gas in five-gallon cans. A length of pipe with a funnel in the end had been rigged to lead through the wall of the cabin into the wing tanks, so they could refuel in flight.[2] With all of them inside, it didn't leave jump room for a flea, and when Captain McFarland § lifted the plane off the dusty strip it seemed a miracle.

---

* The Dutch fighter unit of six planes at Tarakan had been wiped out before the southbound pilots landed there. All that remained were a few burned-out Brewsters round the field.

† Connelly was one of Pappy Gunn's former pilots in the Philippine Air Lines. (See above, Part One, Chapter 19).

‡ The LB-30 was the export version for British use of the B-24. For my account of this flight I am largely indebted to Sheppard's Statement.

§ McFarland had been Gasoline and Oil Officer of FEAF. (See above, Part One, Chapter 33.)

They flew the length of Bataan above a broken overcast, expecting at any moment to see Jap planes break out of the clouds behind them; but they never saw a Jap. The only sign of them, after the Beechcraft had left Luzon, were piles of smoke above Iloilo on the south shore of Panay. From the appearance of the smoke they thought that the city must have been attacked very recently. Their major difficulties did not involve the enemy as much as the condition of their own plane. When they came down at Del Monte just before dark, they found that their right brake was hardly holding at all and the left brake was gone entirely. The tail wheel wouldn't lock, either. It must have been an erratic landing. They spent two nights and the intervening day working on the ship with the help of some 19th Group mechanics and the 5th Air Base people. They did not accomplish much on the brakes and the tail wheel was hopeless so they took off on the morning of the 4th with a 300-foot ceiling which at least would hide them from the Japanese. A magazine-sized map of the Pacific was all they had to navigate with and when they finally made a landfall in the lowering weather they could not tell whether they were north or south of Tarakan. They tried south, which of course proved to be the wrong direction, so they went back to the north. The last five-gallon can had been emptied down the funnel long before they spotted the airfield and the engines were coughing for gas when the wheels touched ground.

Here they discovered that the right engine was running on only one magneto, but as there was no possibility of having it repaired at Tarakan, they took off anyway. The weather was growing worse, with the ceiling so low that they flew at less than 100 feet, following the dark coast of Borneo southward till they came to Balikpapan late in the afternoon.

Next day they decided to abandon the ferry route through Celebes and Timor in favor of Bandjermasin, in the south of Borneo, and Java, a course that involved shorter over-water flying. But at Bandjermasin the right engine quit for good and, after twenty-four hours of fruitless work on it, they sent a message to the Navy at Soerabaja, begging transportation. A PBY stopped for them on the afternoon of the 6th and carried them to Java.

At Soerabaja the party split up. One of the pursuit pilots, Lieutenant Sheppard, who had been suffering from a very bad throat, was found to have diphtheria and had to be left in a hospital. McFarland waited for new parts for the Beechcraft, which he later repaired and flew in to Java. The rest moved on to Australia to join the seven pilots who had come out ahead of them. In Brisbane they found four more members of the 24th Pursuit Group and these 17 men * formed the nucleus round which the American pursuit forces in Java and Australia developed.

The 17th was the first of five provisional pursuit squadrons hastily thrown together in Brisbane during the hectic weeks of January and February when the Japanese tide was at its peak. Elements of two of these squadrons—the 20th and the 3rd—managed to get up to Java and were absorbed by the 17th Squadron, in which they did their fighting. But the last two squadrons—the 33rd and 13th—were both wiped out, as will be told, with only five of their planes ever getting into combat. When, therefore, the 17th was disbanded on March 1, just fifty days after it had been formed, not one of these units remained and a large proportion of the men were dead. But, though their part in the war had been tragically brief, they had helped win time for the units coming after them. No other fighter squadrons were to enter battle with as little training as the majority of their own men had had. Except for the Philippine veterans, most of the pilots who came out from the States in the first convoys were fresh from Flying School; very few had flown a fighter plane, much less fired its guns.[3]

The 17 P-40s of the 17th Squadron came from a shipment of 18 that arrived on the convoy of December 22. The eighteenth plane had been crated without its rudder [4] and stood uselessly on Amberley Field while the Squadron prepared for the long trip north. Major Sprague had twelve of the veteran pilots with him.† From the 48 casual pilots and

---

* Pilots coming out in the Beechcraft on December 31 were: Lts. Coss, Blanton, Kruzel, Dale, Neri, Gilmore, and 2nd Lt. Gies; in the plane that left Bataan on January 2 were, besides Sheppard, Capt. Sprague, Lts. Wagner and Kizer, and 2nd Lts. Hennon, Rowland, and Irvin. The four who had come out earlier were Lts. Mahony, Strauss, Keenan, and McCallum. Mahony came out on the 18th of December with the 27th Bombardment Group; the last three on December 25 in Capt. Slingsby's plane, which carried three unspecified passengers. (See above, Part One, Chapters 25 and 29.)

† In the directive creating the 17th Squadron, Sprague was authorized to draw on any of the pursuit pilots then training at Amberley Field except Mahony, Wagner, Strauss, and Keenan, who were reserved for the command of future squadrons.

flying cadets who had accompanied the planes, four of the most promising were chosen to fill out the Squadron.*

The work of assembling the planes was done by ground crews of the 7th Bombardment Group. They had some help from the 8th Matériel Squadron, but it was the 7th Group who provided the real driving force.[6] They had been bound for the Philippines to meet their planes, which the air echelon were to fly out to them, when their convoy was diverted to Australia by the outbreak of war. A heavy bomber outfit, all their work for the past year had been in B–17s. Now with no planes of their own they were suddenly called on to put together not only fighter aircraft but 52 A–24 dive bombers that had been consigned to the 27th Bombardment Group. Both types were new to them; but the 7th Group, which like the 19th was one of long standing, had among its line chiefs some of the most experienced and resourceful men in the Air Corps. These old hands took over the whole show,† organized assembly and inspection at Amberley and Archer Fields, and quickly mastered both types of plane. The men worked two shifts, twenty-four hours a day. In a week 27 dive bombers and two fighters were ready to fly.‡ By January 9 all the P–40s had been assembled.[8]

It was some days before all 17 could be operated as a squadron, however. For, while the P–40s were mechanically complete, except for the missing rudder, and had none of the armament difficulties that beset the dive bombers,§ they had been sent out without any Prestone. None could be found in the convoy, though every ship was searched; ‖ but enough turned up in Brisbane for two engines, and the men transferred this from one plane to another as each one was test-flown.[9] All the Prestone in Australia was requisitioned, and when it had been rounded up, the whole supply was just enough for 18 P–40s.[10] But that meant that the 17th Squadron might start north as soon as it was ready.

---

* The four were: 2nd Lts. R. S. Thompson, W. C. Stauter, C. E. Trout, K. D. Brown.[5]

† Capt. James E. Tull (Chaplain) said, "The real heroes of this project, as in many others, were not officers, but enlisted men. The job of assembling and inspecting all these planes required a technical skill which was possessed by none of our officers."

‡ January 1 Report of Maj. Davies, in command, to General Brereton.[7]

§ As described in the final paragraph of Chapter 25 (Part One) above.

‖ It will be recalled that this same failure to provide coolant had bedeviled the P–40 squadrons in the Philippines during the preceding July.

There had been little time for squadron training. The four new pilots had had at most fifteen hours in P-40s. As for the Philippine veterans, they grabbed planes whenever they could get hold of them and went off on wild flights over the city. They made a deep impression on the men in the 7th Group, who listened to the grim tales of war on Luzon and were disillusioned about the relative strength of the Japanese and American forces fighting there. These veteran pilots were still a ragged-looking crew, according to Chaplain Tull, "careless about personal appearance and such niceties of military etiquette as saluting and saying 'Sir.' One afternoon a flight of them buzzed the main street in Brisbane, flying down below the tops of some of the buildings. It was an unpardonable sin, but they didn't care. They were going back to the Philippines to fight and probably to die."

The Squadron left Brisbane on the morning of the 16th in two flights, Sprague himself leading the first nine planes away at 8:30. The second flight, under Lieutenant Walter L. Coss, followed half an hour later. Few people saw them start on the first leg of their 2000-mile pull to Darwin. Circling to complete formation, they then turned into the northwest, and their little wedge was soon lost against the wide Australian sky.

Brisbane with its hills and its smooth and shining river must have looked especially good that day, both to the veterans, who knew what they were up against, and to the four new pilots, who were facing an unknown. Not all of them were to see combat; but of those who did, one would be seriously injured in his crashing plane and three were to be killed in action. One of the three was Sprague.*

There was new shipping in the Brisbane River. The big hull of the *President Polk,* fresh from its maiden voyage, lay beside the docks. Among the men and equipment she had brought were 55 casual pilots and 55 P-40s. From them reinforcing squadrons would be formed as soon as

---

* There is a story that when the 17th was to be formed Sprague and Boyd Wagner tossed a coin to see which one should have the command. Wagner lost the toss and Sprague went north and, as we shall see, failed to return. Later, in New Guinea, a newspaper correspondent jokingly congratulated Wagner on the fact that though he might have lost the toss, he actually had won in the end. "No," said Wagner. "I still lost. Bud was a good friend of mine." [11] But even had Wagner won the toss, it is unlikely that he could have gone with the 17th. His eyes were still full of glass particles of the splintered windscreen that had nearly blinded him in the Philippines.

men and planes could be got ready. More ships loaded with 322 P-40s were reported already on the sea.*

The original convoy that had brought out the 17th's own planes had all, except for one ship,† long since gone north, reloaded with ammunition, supplies, and three National Guard units of Field Artillery for the Philippines. The 17th Squadron pilots, who thought that they were bound for the same destination, had no way of knowing that the convoy had been diverted to Darwin and that they themselves, like one of the artillery units, would wind up, not in the Philippines, but in Java.‡

Both flights were accompanied by escort planes over the first leg of their trip, which lay 700 miles up along the Australian coast to Townsville, with a stop halfway for gas and servicing at Rockhampton. Two RAAF Fairey Battles waited on Amberley Field for Coss's take-off; but when Sprague's flight turned into the northwest, it was joined by an aged, weather-stained, twin-engined Beechcraft that would have looked familiar to the veteran pilots even if they had not already known that the man who had hold of the controls was Pappy Gunn. The way Gunn took a plane off the ground was as distinctive as any trade-mark. He, too, supposed that they were headed for the Philippines, and with his wife and children still in Manila had a far greater personal incentive for returning than any of the younger men.

At Rockhampton they lost their first P-40. The electrical system on Gies's plane failed, forcing him to land on what proved a very short runway without brakes or flaps and with his propeller out of control. He tried to ground loop but overshot the field and crashed into a fence.

* The *Mormacasun,* with 67, and a ship unknown with 255.[12]

† The ships in the Philippine-bound convoy were the USNT *Chaumont,* the USN Yacht *Niagara,* the USAT *Meigs,* the USAT *Holbrook,* the freighters *Admiral Halstead* and *Coast Farmer,* and a fast Dutch ship, the *Bloemfontein,* which took the 131st Field Artillery to Soerabaja, landing them there on January 13.[13] The ship that did not go north with the rest, according to Robenson, was the USNT *Republic.*[14]

‡ On December 21, while the convoy was still at sea, General Barnes, in command, received instructions from General MacArthur to disembark Air Corps personnel in Australia to erect aircraft and to send the rest of the troops and equipment on to the Philippines if Barnes felt this was possible and could secure naval escort. As the ships had been loaded without any tactical purpose and all manifests were hopelessly confused, every hold had to be entirely emptied, but Barnes had them reloaded and started them off on December 28. With General Brett's arrival, however, all U. S. troops in Australia came under his command and one of his first acts was to turn the convoy into Darwin and notify General MacArthur on January 1 that the tactical situation made this necessary.[15]

It meant leaving him behind with orders to get himself back to Brisbane while the remaining 16 pilots went on to Townsville. There Brown, one of the new men, washed out his ship by collapsing the landing gear,[16] so only 15 were left to take off next morning for Cloncurry and the long grind beyond it over the Australian wastelands.

The hop to Cloncurry over the low coastal mountains was accomplished safely with Pappy Gunn's Beechcraft now providing their sole escort. Here Coss's flight spent the night * while Sprague's pushed on 550 miles to Daly Waters and then 310 more to Darwin.[18] Steady traveling of this sort wears hard both on the engine of a fighter plane and on the pilot. It wore doubly hard over the desert lands where the air was always turbulent and the little P-40s bounced about like bees. The pilots had to fight the controls all the way. When they looked down, there was only the thin cover of gum trees to see, stretching endless miles on the pale sandy soil. Sometimes the sand was marbled with orange or purplish veins; but generally there was nothing but the gray dust under the gray trees. Finally even the gum trees disappeared and the little flight of planes was over the unbroken desert, that in the whole 550-mile stretch between Cloncurry and Daly Waters, offered only two check points. Both of these were mere sheep stations,[19] marks so small in the vast wastes that only a trained eye might hope to find them. Yet the flight came through safely to Daly Waters, gassed, and took off once more to the north. From then on they had a thread of road to follow and it guided them to Darwin in the late evening, when the bay was still scalloped from the sunset glow, though the land already lay under the shadows of approaching night.

Next afternoon Coss's flight caught up. They too had suffered no mishaps along the route; but ironically, while waiting for orders, the Squadron was to lose another plane. Trout came down with dengue fever and had to be hospitalized. That left them 14 P-40s.

They were three days more in Darwin. The RAAF treated them cordially, but it was a restless time. They had little to do beyond maintenance on their planes, and, shortly after the second flight's arrival, the enlisted men flew in in two C-39s to take over the work. Most of these

* Gilmore, however, says that Coss's flight took off an hour after Sprague's with Gunn escorting it, while Sprague did navigation for his own flight.[17]

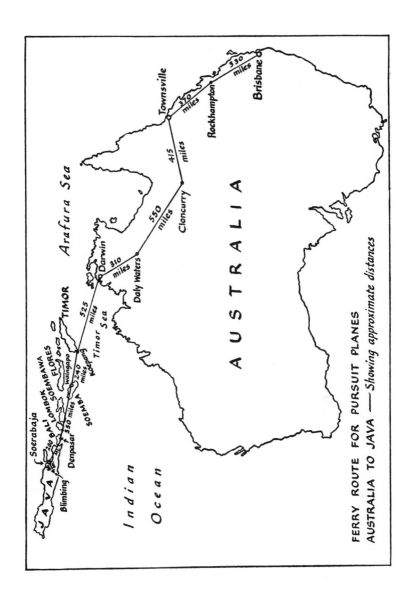

FERRY ROUTE FOR PURSUIT PLANES
AUSTRALIA TO JAVA — Showing approximate distances

enlisted men had come to Australia only a few days before aboard the *President Polk*. Their first job had been erecting the P-40s shipped out with them; but when a call for armorers and crew chiefs came through, they volunteered without the slightest conception of where they were headed for. They "took their tool kits, an extra aileron or two, a couple of spare tires, and nuts and bolts of assorted sizes," wrote one of the pilots.[20]

That was the extent of their maintenance equipment. They never did get any more except what they were able to salvage themselves from crashed planes. Instead they developed a high degree of resourcefulness and an almost unlimited capacity for work under pressure; and they had the conviction that theirs was the best Air Corps outfit doing business in this war. Many of them had never flown before the morning they took off from Brisbane. They had a rough time crossing the desert. A few were violently seasick and "went hand over hand to the tail of the ship on the cables that stretched down each side of the plane. The cables were for the static lines of parachute troops, but they served a good purpose." * It was 120 degrees in the shade at Daly Waters that day and after gassing there the planes stayed hot even when they had risen to 10,000 feet. Yet when the men climbed out of the two transports at Darwin and walked over the airfield for a first look at their P-40s, they had the air of seasoned operators, and already it was plain that they identified themselves with the 17th Squadron.

They started in immediately, attaching 45-gallon belly tanks to the planes and tuning the engines for the more than 500 miles of over-water flying to Koepang. They needed no one to tell them how much depended on their work. There were no Mae Wests for the pilots, and no flying boats or rescue craft to follow up the flight. If a plane went down at sea, it would be for keeps.† In the steaming monsoon heat, precision work of any kind came hard enough, but they also had to fight the incredible flies of Darwin that blackened a man's hands and face, crept into his mouth and ears and nostrils, and drank from the inside of his eyelids.

* Cpl. Kenneth H. Perry's Diary, quoted by Weller.[21]
† One of the later flights to start for Java would have been compelled to take off without even parachutes if enlisted men on a transport also bound for Java had not handed over their own chutes to the fighter pilots.[22]

At night, while mist and wild rains drove in over the bare port town, the work of unloading American ships proceeded very slowly. Only two ships at a time could be tied up to the available pier, and there had been trouble at first with the Australian wharvies, who had their own ideas of the hours, pace, and weather conditions, war or no war, under which a man should work and who refused to work at all if American troops were put on the job with them.[23] In four days they barely dented the holds of the first ship at the pier. Twenty-five more crowding the bay to wait their turn offered a ripe target to the Japanese. The American base commander, a tough old cavalry colonel named John A. Robenson, decided to disregard the pleas of the Civil Administrator and the Brigadier commanding Australian troops in the area, both of whom feared political repercussions, and, borrowing bayonets from the Navy, since the American troops had arrived without any, and posting guards and machine guns along the pier, he put the troops to work at the ship and in a few days had ironed out most of the difficulties with the labor union involved.

Besides the waiting cargo ships, there were other vessels moving in and out of the port. The hospital ship *Mactan* stopped for a day with wounded from Luzon on its way to Sydney; * the *Bloemfontein,* carrying the 131st Field Artillery,† set sail for Java, escorted by the cruiser *Houston;* and a submarine, loaded with .50-caliber ammunition, stole out of the bay one night, bound for Corregidor. At about the same time, Colonel Robenson received lengthy orders to proceed at once to Java, taking six assistant officers, on a mission to procure supplies and ships for running the Japanese blockade to the Philippines.‡ He was to have a fund of $10,000,000 to draw against. Next day, with some awe, he signed his name to a letter of credit for 5,000,000 gulden.[24]

But the pilots of the 17th Squadron knew little or nothing of these activities and probably cared less. Time is the devil for men who wait,

---

* The *Mactan,* a ship purchased and converted by the Red Cross in the Philippines, left Manila December 31 and reached Sydney after a slow voyage, unmolested by the Japanese, on January 27 with 224 wounded.

† This was the 1st Battalion of the 131st Field Artillery Regiment. The 2nd was sent to North Africa, and the 1st, after reaching Australia, became known simply as the 131st Field Artillery. So also in the case of 2nd Bn, 147th FA, which became known as the 147th Field Artillery, and the 1st Bn, 148th FA, which came out at the same time—the last two remaining in Darwin.

‡ An account of his mission is contained in Chapter 9, below.

and for them Darwin had no diversions, except an evening in the blacked-out Darwin Hotel, drinking a bottle of Australian champagne, which is not the best in the world, for an exorbitant price. The town had long since been drunk dry of everything else, and cigarettes also were at a premium, an American brand being worth pure gold. Most of their time the pilots spent out at the RAAF field, fussing round their planes and wondering when their Philippine orders would come through.

It was not till January 21 that they learned they were to go to Java. On that day General Brereton flew in from Brisbane and talked to them much as he had talked earlier to the 19th Group. He said their job was to do what they could to slow up the Japanese offensive movement. They might get some support from British Hurricanes, if any came out of Singapore; but probably it would not be much for things looked black in Malaya. It would be better to count only on themselves, do the best they could, and when the time came, he told them, "we'll see that you get out." [25]

The Squadron started on the morning of the 22nd, all 14 P-40s * following Gunn's ancient Beechcraft out across the Timor Sea to Koepang. There, at Penfoei airdrome, American gas was waiting for them. It had been brought in only a short time before by the destroyer *Peary*, which had lost both her boats in transferring the heavy drums from her creaking decks to a beach close by the airfield.[27] She had been forced to pull out in such haste that one of her boat crews was left behind; but, though she eluded the Japanese bombers and got safe away to Darwin, her time was running out.

At Penfoei the Squadron split once more into two flights. Sprague's went on that afternoon to Waingapoe on Soemba Island, with Pappy Gunn's Beechcraft leading them over the 240 miles of water like a winged old bellwether. Coss's flight waited at Koepang for the indefatigable Gunn to double back for them.

The moon was brilliant that night. On the Penfoei airstrip, out beyond the hangar, the light had an almost flowing quality, and the black palms swayed against a milky sky. There was nothing to interrupt the croaking of the lizards in the bush outside the pilots' quarters, nor the strange

---

* It is not quite clear how the flight to Koepang was made. Apparently, though, it was made with both flights in separate formation following Gunn's plane.[26]

night-crying of the jungle birds. It was peaceful as a thousand other moonlight nights that had covered Timor with silver; yet the pilots and the little garrison of Australian infantry had an indefinable sense of the nearness of the Japanese and they were anxious to be gone. And that night, Irvin, as Trout had in Darwin, came down with dengue fever, reducing the Squadron strength to 13 planes.*

These 13 P-40s reached Soerabaja on January 24 and 25. Sprague's flight came in the first day unescorted, for Pappy Gunn had taken his unarmed transport back alone to Koepang to wire Darwin to send up a P-40 tire—one in Sprague's flight having blown out during take-off.† Captain Connelly, of Gunn's former Philippine Air Lines, who was flying two members of Colonel Robenson's mission to Makassar that day, brought the tire with him as far as Penfoei airdrome, where Gunn picked it up, and the war in the Southwest Pacific began to look almost as if it were a family concern. Returning to Waingapoe through scattered storms, Gunn saw a six-engined flying boat high in the clouds over Soemba, so it was obvious that even if the Japanese did not know that an American fighter squadron was staging through the islands, they were keeping close watch on them. And the same day some Zeros, coming in to strafe Penfoei airdrome, spotted Irvin's plane and destroyed it.

But Coss's flight got away from Soemba without interference. They covered the 550 miles to Soerabaja in one hop, for there was nothing but a field on Bali, at Den Pasar, with no supplies of any kind. Later flights coming up from Darwin made use of Den Pasar; but they found it dangerously open to attack.

On the 26th the enlisted men arrived and the first thing they wanted to know as they piled out of their transports was how the engines had stood up. On the whole, they were pleased, for twelve of the Squadron's 13 planes were in commission. But they lost another that afternoon at the end of their first mission. Sprague took six planes out over the Java Sea to furnish protection for a crippled Dutch submarine limping home from Makassar Strait. The weather was extremely bad and

* When Irvin recovered, he returned to Darwin and begged himself another P-40 and came to Java with the second flight of the 3rd Pursuit Squadron (Provisional) on February 11.[28]

† This was Gilmore's plane. Gilmore picked up dengue fever on Soemba but managed to fly to Java with the second flight of his own squadron.[29]

steadily grew worse, and after an hour the flight had to be recalled. Landing through heavy squalls, Lieutenant Neri's plane spun in and crashed.[30] Neri was terribly cut about the head and face and one ear was sliced clean off.* He did not fly again in Java. So, out of the 17 planes with which the Squadron had left Brisbane, they had twelve left when they moved down on February 1 to their permanent station at Blimbing, twelve miles from the town of Djombang and 60 miles southwest of Soerabaja.

The field had been built in record time under the direction of a Dutch liaison officer, Lieutenant Gertz, and Captain Willard Reed of the U. S. Marine corps.† The Dutch had an uncanny knack at camouflage but they never excelled their work on the field at Blimbing. When the Squadron moved down, they had to have a Dutch plane lead them in. The Japanese, who hunted for it often and once had four Zeros circling directly over it, never found the field till the last day before Java fell.

It lay in an amphitheater of low hills, among terraced rice fields, and was itself constructed from rice fields drained and sodded. The only way to find it was by using check points. "After flight up a river until a bridge was sighted, a 45-degree turn was made to the left, flying was continued for one minute, and by that time the plane would be over the field." [33] Fitting into the checkerboard pattern of the ricefields, its shape was like a cross, but the long east-west strip barely overreached the cross runway, so that Gilmore described the field as being like a "T." [34] For fast take-off, they stationed eight planes at the bottom of the long arm and the remaining four at the south end of the crossarm, and later they became so proficient at synchronizing their cross runs that, in the heyday of the Squadron's strength, 16 planes were able to take off in three

* Weller wrote that "after Neri had gone a couple of his friends went out to the scene of the crash and saw something white in the grass. It was the ear. They put it in a small blue box and carried it around for a while, intending to return it formally to its owner. But the ear became impossible to live with and finally, like a lot of other things, got lost." [31]

† Capt. Reed was one of a group of officers who came to Java to give instruction in piloting PBYs. Of the three who remained in Java after war started, Reed, and Lts. John A. Robertson and Thomas Hardy, only Hardy came back to the States. Reed died in the crash of a P–40 near Blimbing. Robertson was killed flying a PBY for Patwing Ten over Makassar Strait.[32]

minutes. But only the best pilots were able to use the cross runway, which was so short that on muddy days they had to give the ship full throttle in 65 or 70 inches of mercury to get it off the ground.[35]

It was a simple place. The operations building was a square bamboo hut, and there were smaller alert shacks at each end of the field. They had some bamboo and dirt revetments to house planes under repair, but the serviceable planes were parked in the open under the trees that edged the field. Men and officers were quartered in the buildings of an abandoned sugar refinery at Blimbing, five miles from the field. The officers lived on one side of the company street and the enlisted men on the other in little four-room houses, which had tile floors and were very clean but had no furniture except the cots provided for the Squadron.[36] The Dutch provided their food at no cost. Though it was not very good, the men accepted it cheerfully as the best that could be procured.

The pilots' working day began at 4:00 or 5:00 o'clock, though the early shift of enlisted men had gone out to the field two hours before that, if indeed some of them had not been working straight through the night. Before starting they were served coffee in the old sugar mill by the Dutch ladies of the village; then at the field, after inspection, their breakfast was brought out to them from the mill and they ate it in the alert shacks or standing beside their planes. It usually consisted of bread, two slices of meat, and two cold fried eggs made into sandwiches. Lunch was also served at the field—of a paste or putty, as Blanton described it, of chopped vegetables and meat and rice, usually cold by the time it reached them. Their time to leave the field varied a good deal according to the weather. If the thunderstorms that generally followed sunset happened to come earlier, they could go back to Blimbing secure in the knowledge that the Japanese would not attack in the late afternoon or evening.[37] For the Jap did not like rough weather or night flying and never attacked without leaving himself time to get back to base by sunset.

They had two days to settle down in before the Japanese bombers began hitting Java, and in that time they learned to know a good deal about their commanding officer. Sprague, a slender, red-haired Irishman from California, was a West Pointer, but he had his own ideas of discipline. He wanted it to come from below, and when he got to Blimbing, he made this clear to every man in the Squadron. He told the enlisted men that keeping the planes in commission was their job. After the planes were ready to fight, the men's time was their own. No leave passes would be issued on the station, for every man was free to go anywhere and do anything as long as there was nothing more to be done for his ship. He was to be the judge of that, and no enlisted man ever abused Sprague's trust.

He told the officers that there would be no saluting for a while. They were a scratch outfit, with almost nothing to back them and no time or strength for nonessentials. All of them were in it together. As one of the enlisted men wrote, "The officers behaved that way to us, and we behaved that way to them"; [38] and a pilot, in turn, said of the men, "The 17th Pursuit Squadron was the hardest-working outfit we have ever seen." [39] It continued to work out that way even when new arrivals swelled their ranks on February 12 to 47 officers and 81 enlisted men.[40]

The driving force in Sprague's nature made it work. There was never any question of where he stood in the war. His experience in fighter planes was somewhat limited, because he had held staff jobs almost from the time of his graduation from Flying School. But he would listen to his pilots.[41] He has been best described by young Corporal Perry, who, on the day Sprague was reported missing in the wild fighting over Bali, wrote in his diary: "He flew for the love of flying and fought for the love of fighting and to avenge the deaths of his partners in the Philippines. He instilled his courage and fighting spirit into all the pilots and men and there was no one who did not admire him. He was a square shooter and hell on wheels for the Japs. . . . He was usually first to take off on an alert and never asked his pilots to do something he could not do himself. The 17th will long remember him." [42]

This was the fighter force that took over the defense of Eastern Java. Only at the very beginning, when the Dutch squadron of 13 CW–21Bs flew with them over Soerabaja, and in the last few days of their brief career, did they receive any outside fighter support. For the rest of the time they were fighting on their own.

The Dutch air warning system was not much help to them. Without radar and relying on native observers who reported any activity they saw to a central control room in Soerabaja, it seldom gave them more than twenty minutes' warning of approaching enemy planes, when it took

forty minutes for the slow-climbing P-40s to get into position at their
ceiling of 26,000 to 28,000 feet; and as the observers reported friend and
foe alike, they were often sent chasing after American bombers, and once
even spent two hours hunting for themselves.[43]

But most of the time they fought the Japanese at odds of anywhere
from three to fifteen and more to one. The record they wrote was one of
the great ones of the war. To the end the Japanese radio kept reporting
"swarms of fighters rising from fields all around Soerabaja," while, actually, it was the six to 26 shopworn P-40s rising from the single field at
Blimbing. Sprague's work was so well done that his death, though it sad-
dened them, did nothing to diminish the Squadron's ability to fight.

5. *The Bombers*

WHILE THE 17TH SQUADRON was island-hopping its way up from Darwin,
the first phase of the battle for Java reached its climax. On the night of
January 23-24, which the P-40s had spent together on Soemba, four of
the old, four-stacker American destroyers attacked a Japanese invasion
fleet off the Borneo coast, just above Balikpapan. Dutch planes and the
PBYs of Patrol Wing Ten had been shadowing the fleet as it moved
down Makassar Strait. The Dutch had attacked on the afternoon of the
23rd; but messages from Patwing Ten still indicated the presence of 13
destroyers, four cruisers, and five or more armed transports. It made
quite an order for four overage destroyers, badly overworked since the
first day of war and all in need of overhaul.*

They were to have had the support of two cruisers; but on the way up
from Koepang, the *Boise* hit an uncharted pinnacle rock that laid her
bottom open, forcing her to limp back to the south coast of Java, and
ultimately on to India; and the *Marblehead* lost a turbine, which cut her
speed to 15 knots, so the four destroyers were compelled to go in alone.
But, as things turned out, they had a field day.

---

* The *John D. Ford*, for instance, had gone two years without an overhaul. The other
three destroyers were the *Parrott*, *Pope*, and *Paul Jones*. All four were under the command of Comdr. Paul H. Talbot.[1]

The Japanese ships were silhouetted for them against a curtain of towering, bubbling fires from the oil refineries of Balikpapan, which the Dutch themselves had blasted, and the American destroyers got right into the midst of the enemy fleet with their torpedoes before the Japanese discovered what was happening to them. Completely surprised, they apparently thought that they were under submarine attack, for their destroyers went chasing round among the transports with the American destroyers and dropping depth charges right and left. When they realized that they were being hit by surface craft, their confusion increased; and at the end of the engagement, as the withdrawing American crews looked back, the Japanese were still valiantly gunning for each other in the smoke and darkness.

Altogether our Navy claimed six enemy ships, including one destroyer. But the commander of an adventurous Dutch submarine, which had popped up inadvertently in the middle of the action and remained to watch the whole show, reported that the four antique American destroyers had made away with 13 Japanese ships.*

Effective though this stroke was, the Navy had nothing with which to follow up the blow. The *Marblehead* with her turbine trouble, and the four destroyers all showing the effects of continual overwork, had to turn in for repairs. Most of them now lacked torpedoes, which were becoming increasingly hard to replace. Except for our submarines, which from the beginning had never ceased their long patrols, all other American warships were either under repair or engaged in convoy duty. The Dutch fleet, though in much better condition, had gone to the northwest up the strait between Sumatra and Borneo, acting on reports, later found to be inaccurate, of a new Japanese threat in that direction; and the British were wholly occupied at Singapore. Wavell himself had left his headquarters at Lembang to visit the base, where, at the end of January, the decision was taken to abandon Malaya and withdraw all troops to Singapore Island.†

* Dutch claims here, as throughout the brief campaign, were wildly out of line with actuality. Our Navy people came much closer to the truth, though the "destroyer" claimed was actually a minesweeper.[2]

† Wavell left his Headquarters a second time in February to visit the Burma front, taking with him Col. Brady, who remained in Burma.

Meanwhile the Japanese advance in other quarters met only the weakest sort of local resistance. Reports reached ABDACOM of raids and landings at Rabaul and Kavieng, in New Britain and New Ireland,* with the consequent threat to Papuan New Guinea and the lifeline between Australia and America. The Japanese force at Kendari, on the southeast shore of Celebes, was known to be gaining strength. Within the week convoys would move against Ceram and Ambon, the preliminary step to cutting communications between Darwin and Java. But the greatest and, as it then seemed, the most imminent threat to Java was the main Japanese force in Makassar Strait.

Though work on the *Marblehead* and the destroyers was pushed as rapidly as possible, the ships were not ready for sea till February 1. Then, on their way north towards Makassar Strait, they were spotted by enemy aircraft, and with the memory of *Repulse* and *Prince of Wales* still fresh, they prudently retired. On February 4, a second attempt was made with a combined Dutch and American force of destroyers and cruisers, including the *Marblehead* and *Houston;* but it also was turned back short of its objective.† In fact, after the initial strike by the four old destroyers, the Navy never succeeded in making a surface attack on the main Japanese concentration in Makassar Strait again; and, as had happened before, the B-17s found themselves carrying the fight to the enemy alone. They flew the first of a long series of missions over Balikpapan on January 24.

There were eight planes in the formation, but only two were the old, familiar B-17Ds of the 19th Group. The other six had dorsal fins, turrets, and tail guns, marking them as the new and long-awaited B-17Es. They had come halfway round the world to get to Java: five of this particular flight had crossed the Atlantic, Africa, India, and the Indian Ocean,

---

* Rabaul on January 23; Kavieng on the 25th.

† For nearly forty minutes on the morning of February 4, Japanese bombers attacked the little fleet of four cruisers and seven destroyers in Madoera Strait. The *Houston* lost her after turret to a direct bomb hit; and the *Marblehead* was so desperately hurt by two direct hits and a near-miss that laid her bottom open that she barely won back to the little, south-coast, Java port of Tjilatjap. After sketchy repairs, she set out for the States on a 48-day voyage that is a history in itself. But the *Houston* stayed on to fight through the last bitter hours of the Java campaign, and even without her turret she was still the strongest ship in the Allied fleet when the Japs sank her.[8]

while the sixth was one of three planes that had pioneered a new route over the Pacific. All belonged in the 7th Bombardment Group, and it was the 7th's commander, Major S. K. Robinson, who led the mission.*

Of the 50 bombers that eventually reached Java,† all but nine went out by what was known as the African Route. It had been pioneered as far as Cairo months before by planes being ferried to the Middle East, and to the experienced Pan American pilots who had flown it time after time, the trip was routine. But many of the Army navigators were mere cadets, so new to the business that they had not yet received their commissions, and to them it seemed a strange and hazardous route, beset by weather worse than they had ever dreamed of.

MacDill Field at Tampa, Florida, was the base from which all flights originated. From there they flew south to Trinidad, then Belem, and Natal on the easternmost tip of Brazil. The airdromes were not equipped to service the four-engined bombers. Spare parts were nonexistent. A pilot who lost a tire might be lucky enough to find a stratoliner tire that would do, as Rouse had at Waller Field in Trinidad; but he was forced to wait thirteen days at Natal for a new propeller, after bending his own in an unfortunate landing.[5] Belem was a spot where you could generally find one or more ships in difficulties. Here Captain C. V. McCauley lost his No. 1 engine with a bent piston rod and cracked cylinder skirt. He knew that it would take forever to get a new engine sent out, but there was a crashed B-17 up the river from Belem and his bombardier was Lieutenant Hugh McTague, the Assistant Engineer of the 9th Squadron. So McCauley sent McTague upstream to get a replacement engine out of the wreck.

McTague started off with a barge and a bunch of natives and found

---

* The first of the 7th Group's planes had reached Java on January 10, when three LB-30s landed at Bandoeng, spent the night there, and moved on next day to Malang. The Group, which had been flying in B-17s, was scheduled for new equipment, and their old planes had been sent to other units. But there were not enough of the new Es to go round, and a portion of the 11th Squadron had to be equipped with the LB-30s at the last minute. The pilots were allowed a few hours' transitional instruction and sent off. One pilot said that he "received 20 minutes' transition instruction and the plane was his."[4] "In those days they gave you a thousand dollars for the crew and said your next duty was to report to FEAF and you'd better be on your way. So you put the thousand dollars in your pocket and started out."

† The *Summary of Air Action* lists the arrival of 38 B-17s and 12 B-24s (or LB-30s).

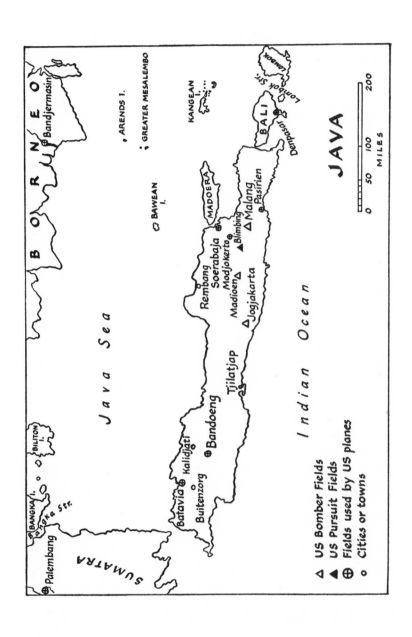

BORNEO

Bandjermasin

ARENDS I.

GREATER MESALEMBO

KANGEAN I.

LOMBOK

Lombok Str.

BALI

Denpasar

BAWEAN I.

MADOERA

Rembang

Soerabaja

Modjokerta

Madioen

Blimbing

Malang

Pasirien

Jogjakarta

Java Sea

Tjilatjap

Bandoeng

Kalidjati

Batavia

Buitenzorg

BILITON I.

BANGKA I.

Banka Str.

Palembang

SUMATRA

Indian Ocean

JAVA

MILES

0   50   100   200

△ US Bomber Fields
▲ US Pursuit Fields
⊕ Fields used by US planes
∘ Cities or towns

the plane near the edge of the river with one wing completely buried in the mud. It was of course the wing with the No. 1 engine that was down; but, as McTague looked the plane over, he realized that if he did not use the No. 1 engine he would have to change the wiring and the whole rig to set it in place. So he hauled the plane out of the mud—a difficult process with only native help and no tackle—and after a time they managed to get the engine out of the wing. They cleaned it carefully before taking it back to Belem, making it quite presentable, and McTague never said anything to McCauley about the engine's having been underneath the river ooze. He just put it in their own plane and started it, and it ran all the way to Java for them. It went through the Java campaign and was still running when they got out to Australia. The number of that plane was *452;* it kept on running with the same four engines till it finally crashed on a reef outside of Milne Bay; and it was an example of the endurance, almost the fortitude, of B–17 engines and B–17s themselves.

It was by shifts like these that some of the crews got out to Java. Some of them had to learn as they went along. A good many of the crews had never been in a B–17 or LB–30 before setting out from MacDill Field. The sudden expansion of the Air Corps had spread experience dangerously thin. Take Hardison's ship, the *Suzy-Q:* Captain Hardison himself was the only man aboard who had had any service in a B–17.[6] Lieutenant Smelser's co-pilot "had never seen a four-engined bomber before," according to Smelser, who might be forgiven possible exaggeration since he had to do most of the flying over the 21,000 miles to Malang; and on the Atlantic hop, his navigator, fresh from navigator's school, got them 230 miles off course so that when the plane finally touched down at Hastings it had 20 gallons of fuel inboard and only slightly more outboard. Except for the fact that Smelser happened to be a celestial navigator on his own account, the bomber might have joined the list of five planes lost along the route.*

Hastings was the British airdrome at Freetown. The planes that reached it had nearly all had a taste of the tropical weather they were to take

---

* Considering the limited four-engine experience of many of the crews, the rudimentary briefing they received, and the lack of facilities along the route, this loss of five planes out of 58 dispatched was a remarkably good record.

in larger doses when they reached the Southwest Pacific. The *Suzy-Q* had nearly 1500 miles of heavy front to bore through when it went across. The navigator never had a glimpse of the stars, but to the crew it seemed that they saw everything else when they were in shape to see at all out of the windows of the tossing plane. Over the equator, at only a thousand feet, the wings started icing and Hardison had to take the ship way down before it melted off. St. Elmo's fire visited the ship a little later, wreathing the propellers with its wild cold light and throwing into dark relief the writhing clouds beyond the wing tips. The men, seeing it for the first time, had a moment's heart-stopping fear that their plane was on fire; but later they learned to take the phenomenon for granted, and on many missions the strange light rode with them through heavier fronts than any they encountered over the Atlantic.

From Hastings the route led to Accra, though the planes had to swing wide out to sea to avoid Vichy French territory. Then they headed inland and north to Kano, which is the largest walled city in the world. The builders, long ago, had left an open strip of ground inside the walls, a hundred yards wide, for growing food in case of siege. Now, suddenly, with wall and gates, it was made obsolete by the passage of the great planes' shadows.

Kano to Khartoum across the African desert was one of the longest stages of the trip. Most of the planes made it at night with nothing to see in the vast empty land below except occasional desolate mountains or the pin-point lights of campfires. As they stared down the crews were more aware of their remoteness from home than at any other point in the long flight. They were happy to land at the RAF airdrome outside Khartoum in the morning, and some of them breakfasted on goat liver, buzzard eggs, and camel milk.[7]

From Khartoum, where all the crews were automatically given cholera inoculations, the planes flew either up to Cairo before turning eastward, or else they were sent straight east to Aden and then northeast to Karachi. Either at Cairo or Karachi they first learned that Java was their destination. It was the first indication they had had that the Air Force had been driven out of the Philippines, or at least that was how it seemed to them then, for no word had yet come out about the performance of Colonel George's tiny force of P-40s on Bataan. They began to wonder what sort of place Java would be to operate in and, a little grimly, what they would have to work with when they got there. All at once they realized that they were coming close to the war, and at Karachi more than one crew began putting in extra time on their guns.

They had a good deal still to learn about the guns. The top turret seemed all right, though it proved to be too slow to follow a Zero making a frontal attack.* But the bottom turret in the first B–17Es was a baffling thing and already, long before they entered combat, had become the prime frustration of all crews.

It was of the ball type but operated by a remote control device that looked as if the inventor might have been Rube Goldberg himself. The gunner lay on his belly in the bottom of the plane and sighted in a mirror, with the guns in back of him. Theoretically all he had to do was manipulate the mirror till he had picked up the enemy pursuit and then bring the image of the attacking plane inside the crosslines etched on the glass. At that point the gunner pressed the trigger and the guns did the rest. It was a fine idea, but as far as is known no gunner was ever able to pick up the image of an enemy plane in time. Probably not a hundred rounds were fired out of the belly guns of the 37 B–17Es of this type to reach Java, and then mostly for testing purposes. Soon they had to give up all thought of using the contraption as it was intended. Some crews loaded the guns with tracers, tied a cord to the trigger, and kicked it now and then in battle to give the Japs, who had a profound distaste for tracers, the impression that the guns were manned. But usually the guns were taken out of the ship and set up on homemade mounts around the airdromes for use as antiaircraft while, for the sake of appearances, the crew replaced them in the turret with black broomsticks. Finally they began removing the turret bodily and sealing up the belly of the plane, giving it more speed and range.†

The last stop was at Colombo, on Ceylon, and appropriately enough in beautiful and luxurious surroundings. Here, as the men dined on the veranda of a vast hotel above the Indian Ocean, some of them first en-

---

* Capt. Bostwick said, "The raticles had a tendency to lag, but the men later corrected that up to a point." That was in Australia; they had no time for such work in Java.

† Some of these made-over B–17Es were later employed as flare ships in the first experiments in night bombing out of the Australian airfields.

countered refugees—people from Malaya and Singapore and even, for the crews arriving towards the middle of February, a first scattering of evacuees from Java.

There were drawbacks, however. The British, who said there was no room to spare in Colombo, pointedly urged them to move on; and the weather forecasts for this last and longest stage of their long journey proved vague and inaccurate. All the way from South America information had been sketchy at best and little could be learned even of conditions at the next airdrome. Maps, particularly of Africa, were unreliable; but as far as India general weather conditions were so well known that forecasts were not too far off actuality. It was a different story beyond Colombo, and almost all the planes met fronts and storms much heavier and covering greater areas than they had been led to expect: thunderheads that pilots could not see the tops of even at 17,000 feet, so that they had to be flown through; and rainstorms hard enough, in the words of one pilot, to take the paint off the rivets on the wings.[8]

Generally the flight was timed to bring a plane off the western shore of Sumatra about daybreak, and as they picked up the land the pilots would turn southeast along the coast line, often dropping down to 1200 or 1400 feet to keep below the level of the low green mountains. The crews, tense and anxious at the guns, watched the sky for enemy pursuit; but, though once in a while a Fortress reported meeting a Dutch flying boat on patrol, more often they saw no planes at all. Land and sea unrolled peacefully beneath them, and there would be only the cloud shadows drifting on the jungle slopes, or perhaps a solitary freighter, stitching its wake upon the lonely sea. At times it was difficult to realize that war was being fought so little to the north of them.

But then a plane like Lieutenant K. D. Casper's, low on gas and calling the field at Palembang for permission to land, would be warned off because Japanese planes were at that moment attacking it. And when the All Clear came, the bomber would have to slip furtively in, regas, and get away again as quickly as it could.

Most of the Fortresses, however, went straight through to Java and landed at Bandoeng,* where they received orders to go on to Malang

---

* Batavia was the first stop for a few planes, but they had to fly over to Bandoeng for their orders, anyway.

and report to the 5th Bomber Command. As soon as they landed, they found themselves swept into the current of the war.

Their first impression was of the enormous tiredness they saw in the faces of the 19th Group men, and listening to these veterans they began to realize how little there was to work with. An eight-plane mission was discussed as if it were not only a major effort but something of a miracle. The field at Malang was being operated on a scratch basis, without anti-aircraft defense worth the name, and with nowhere near enough Air Corps personnel to go round. Most of the air-base functions were performed by the 1st Battalion of the 131st Field Artillery. These men had arrived at Soerabaja from Darwin on January 13, aboard the *Bloemfontein,* without their guns and with no real idea of what they were supposed to do.[9] They began by taking a few old French 75s, with wooden carriages, and, by sinking the trails in the ground, elevated the muzzles to make them seem like antiaircraft guns. The only ammunition they had was shrapnel, and while they never got close to a Japanese plane, the old guns made a fine noise and helped discourage strafing and dive bombing when the Japs started coming over Malang. However, there weren't enough even of these old guns to occupy a whole battalion, so the artillerymen turned their hands to anything there was to do from policing the quarters to gassing planes and volunteering as aerial gunners aboard B-17s. Only a few of the many who volunteered could be accepted and these went off on missions, some flying for the first time in their lives, and all of them using Zeros as their first aerial targets.

But the men of the 131st Field Artillery had not been trained to service aircraft, and it was there that the greatest shortage in man power existed. So air crews fresh from their world-girdling flights would find themselves at work on the battered 19th Group planes before their first day was over, as well as making one necessary modification on their own. Like the earlier B-17Ds, the 7th Group's new bombers had been sent out with only 25- or 50-round cans for the guns. The change to 100-round cans came none too soon, for more than one of the new ships, with its crew, was scheduled for a combat mission within forty-eight hours of the time its wheels touched down on Java.

The 7th Group never operated as a unit. Indeed, its four tactical squadrons, scattered to the four winds in the opening days of war, were never to join forces again. The air echelon of the first squadron to leave the States—the 88th Reconnaissance—had flown to Hawaii on the night of December 6 and arrived over Hickam next morning in the very middle of the Japanese attack with their tanks running dry and no ammunition for their guns. By a miracle all six planes in this flight, under Major Carmichael, managed to land safely and survive subsequent bombing and strafing,* but none of them got to Java. Instead, they were held in Hawaii for two months to fly antisubmarine patrols. Then, on February 9, they combined with five planes of the 7th Group's 22nd Squadron, that had reached Oahu ten days after the attack on Pearl Harbor, and one plane of the 38th Reconnaissance Squadron, to form a force of twelve which was attached to a Naval task force.† They headed towards the South Pacific along the newly opened southern ferry route and spent two weeks covering out of the Fijis. From there they moved on to Australia to base at Townsville, where they operated as both a bomber and a reconnaissance outfit, known successively as the 14th Bombardment, 14th Reconnaissance, 40th Reconnaissance, and finally, after March 14, as the 435th Bombardment Squadron, the designation under which they became famous.‡ By then, however, they were no longer in the 7th Group but had been absorbed by the reorganizing 19th.

In the meantime, the 7th Group's 11th and 9th Squadrons and the remaining planes of the 22nd were working their way out to Java over one or other of the two world-circling ferry routes. Arriving in flights of one, two, or occasionally three planes, they were at first based at Malang; but as their numbers increased they set up for themselves at Jogjakarta, 160 miles west of Malang, and later, as still more planes came in, they opened another base at Madioen, roughly halfway between and a little north of the other two fields. Group Headquarters were located at Jogjakarta, which became the home field for the 11th Squadron, while

---

* Eight planes made up the flight, but one failed to take off (engine trouble) and one had to turn back (ignition trouble), leaving six to complete the flight.[10] See also Chapter 1, Part One, above.

† This was Admiral Wilson Brown's *Lexington* force.[11]

‡ It became popularly known as "The Kangaroo Squadron" from its insignia of a kangaroo floating on a cloud with a spyglass at its eyes and a bomb wrapped in its tail.

the 9th and 22nd operated out of Madioen, though some planes of both squadrons were stationed with the 19th Group at Malang.[12]

Major Robinson, who was among the first of his pilots to arrive,* was concerned from the beginning about preserving his Group's identity. Like the 19th, it operated under the 5th Bomber Command, whose staff was made up almost entirely of 19th Group men, and the rapidity with which the Japanese drive developed and the constant shortage of planes in both line units made overlapping of 7th and 19th Group planes and crews necessary on all larger missions. Though flight command alternated more or less between the two units, considerable friction arose because of the divergent combat philosophies of the two groups.

As already pointed out, the tactical maxims of the 19th Group had all boiled down to hitting the target "high, fast, and *once*." Colonel Eubank insisted that his planes must never climb when attacked but must close up tight, fly level, and go on through to the target. The plan laid out beforehand for the mission was to be carried through, come hell or high water, though the officer commanding the formation might alter details as to altitude and such, depending on local conditions. But Major Robinson held to the old philosophy that the leader of the mission should command all phases of the attack and make all tactical decisions during flight.

Robinson was a fine officer, with the offensive spirit in a very high degree, and under his command the 7th were an aggressive and self-confident group. When the Bomber Command directed that they should take some experienced personnel along on one of their early missions, the 19th Group navigators and bombardiers assigned for the flight found themselves relegated to the waist of the ship where they had nothing to do but ride along as dead weight and suck oxygen—though one or two were permitted to act as gunners.† This treatment brought forth complaints so exceedingly articulate that Major Robinson was forced to call in all personnel, listen to both sides, and issue a verbal order

---

* He arrived on January 19, by the African route.

† The attitude of the 7th Group crews was not unnatural since, as one participant somewhat plaintively recorded, "The only catch to this master strategy move was that HQ, in order to safeguard itself against any remarks which might be made in the future about planes being sent into combat without experienced crews, sent only the lowliest 2nd lieutenants they could muster."

that griping would cease as of that date. After that, when 7th Group planes went out on combat missions, they seem, with few exceptions, to have carried purely 7th Group crews. They had to learn, as the 19th had learned, through hard experience.

Their very first mission had given them a violent introduction to the kind of fighting they might expect from the Japanese. On January 16 two B–17Es and three LB–30s took off together from Malang to attack Japanese air and naval concentrations at Menado in Northern Celebes. Three ships—one B–17 and two LB–30s—were lost, and the two that returned had been roughly handled. It was some comfort to know that on their part they had given the Zero pilots a problem of their own to chew on; but such losses were heavier than our forces could afford, and the LB–30s had proved a disappointment.

When the first three LB–30s rolled to a stop on the sod runway at Singosari,* which the rains had turned into a swamp in which planes landing or taking off threw up sprays high enough to completely hide the fuselage, the 19th Group veterans greeted them enthusiastically, for they had long wanted a ship with guns in the tail, and the LB–30s had two .50s there. They were nice easy ships to fly, developing high speed at low altitude, and because of their light weight, a pilot could do anything with them; but they were not rugged enough for the kind of fighting bombers had to face then in the Southwest Pacific. They had only one turret, no armor plate, and being without superchargers their ceiling was limited to a bare 20,000 feet—the altitude at which the Zero appeared to attain maximum efficiency.†

---

* These first three 7th Group planes to reach Java were piloted by Maj. A. A. Straubel, CO of the 11th Squadron, and Lts. J. E. Dougherty and Horace Wade. They had stayed together all the way out on their twelve-day flight from the States and they brought full loads of badly needed supplies, including quantities of sulfanilamide that was to help save the lives of the terribly burned crewmen of the *Marblehead* and *Houston*.[13] However, they had actually been preceded over the African route by two Ferry Command B–24s, refitted for transport service and unarmed except for tail guns. These two ships were piloted by Capts. Ben I. Funk and A. C. Davis and flew endless missions between Australia, Java, Burma, and the Philippines. Funk's plane, which became the more famous of the two, was affectionately known as "The Flying Red Cap" or "The Gravy Train" and carried men of all ranks from the Highest Brass to plain GIs all over the Southwest Pacific theater.

† Later, the newer B–24 models were to invade the theater and prove so effective that, with their longer range, they gradually replaced the B–17s. By then the caliber

None of the crews had had more than five days at Malang and the 5th Bomber Command was reluctant to send them out; but when orders for the strike against Menado came through, theirs were the only planes available except for still more recent arrivals from the States. The seven B-17s of the 19th Group in combat condition at that time had all been dispatched to Palembang, from which they were to bomb the Japanese-held airport at Sungei Patani in Northwestern Malaya at a distance which, by the prescribed course to the target, was far beyond the normal radius of the Fortress, so that on their return the planes were just able to reach an emergency Dutch airfield on the northern tip of Sumatra. This was the first of two similar missions undertaken solely at the insistence of ABDACOM. Both Bomber Command and the participating crews considered them perfectly futile,* for they knew that their intelligence was at least two weeks old when they received it so that the main Japanese drive must have passed well south of Sungei Patani, and, in any case, high-altitude bombers could not seriously damage an air strip. All the Japanese had to do was fill in the holes.† Still worse from the men's point of view was the fact that each of the missions consumed three full days when they felt that they might be putting in their time on shorter runs against the Japanese fleet with far less wear and tear on their already badly worn engines.‡ But General Wavell was set on pulling the raids: he wanted to "put heart in Singapore"; and the new 7th Group crews were sent up to Menado.

They staged through Kendari, spending the night of January 16 there and taking off in the early hours next morning. Two targets had been assigned: the B-17s were to attack shipping in Menado Bay, while the LB-30s bombed an airport in the vicinity. Unfortunately their orders

of Japanese interception had declined considerably; but even in December 1942 the B-24s had many "bugs" that had to be worked out by men in the combat zone, as shown in a letter from General Kenney to General Arnold, December 10.

* It must be said, however, that both the officers and, especially, the enlisted men enjoyed the overnight stops at Palembang, for they were made guests of the Shell Oil Company, whose Dutch managers put them up at the Shell Club, high above the heat and smells of the native town.

† Actually, when observation planes of the Malay Volunteer Air Force reconnoitered the following day, they saw no evidence of the bombing.

‡ The second raid, against Kuantan and Kuala Lumpur, was on January 28-29-30, when the five planes engaged could have been used for daily strikes against Japanese shipping at Balikpapan.

were so unclear that the LB-30 crews could not be sure where the airport lay and they had to spend fifteen or twenty minutes searching before they finally found the field at Langoan, beside a lake, about 20 miles south of Menado. Almost in the instant that the last ship reported its bombs away, they were hit by five Zeros,[14] and for six minutes the three bombers with their naked bellies were under fire. They managed to shoot down one of their tormentors before themselves escaping into the weather; but two of the ships—piloted by Lieutenants Dougherty and W. E. Bayse—had been fatally hurt. There were two wounded men in Bayse's plane * and four, less seriously injured, in Dougherty's. Only Major Straubel's got back to Singosari.

In the meantime the two B-17Es, flown by Major C. F. Necrason of the 9th Squadron and Lieutenant J. L. Dufrane of the 11th, had arrived over Menado to find four transports out in the bay and two more at the docks. On their first run, because of inexperience, they got themselves so blinded by the sun that they could drop no bombs, and on the second one plane had six bombs hang in the racks; yet as they withdrew the crews saw one of the transports capsize like a child's toy in the blue bowl of the bay. Their returning course took them over the airport where the plane with the hung bombs managed to kick out two more on the runways, but the last four remained in the racks. Five minutes after this they were attacked by 15 enemy fighters.

Two were Messerschmitts, the rest Zeros, and the Japanese pilots, according to their established procedure, made their passes from the rear or by diving under the bombers and pulling up behind to deliver their fire. The Fortress tail gunners let them come up close. Then, for some minutes before the Japanese discovered what had been added, it beat any skeet shoot ever seen. Five Zeros and one Messerschmitt went down. Four were accounted for by Necrason's tail gunners,† one by his

---

* Sgt. W. L. Oldfield and Pfc. R. D. Chopping. The latter, with a bullet lodged within an inch of his heart, continued to man his guns till, in his weakened condition, fragments of an explosive bullet knocked him down. The bullet was later removed, and he wore it round his neck on a string as an amulet. It served him well till, on his final mission before returning home, his plane was shot down over Rabaul on November 2, 1942.[15]

† The tail gunner in Necrason's plane, Pfc. Arvid B. Hegdahl, had shot down two Zeros before an explosive bullet shattered his right leg above the knee. He collapsed from loss of blood and was removed from the tail of the plane by M/Sgt. Louis T. Silva,

bombardier,* and one by the gunners in Dufrane's ship.† But the action was not wholly one-sided. Dufrane's ship had lost an engine while making its second bombing run; by the time the nine surviving Japanese fighters broke off the fight, forty minutes after their first attack, Dufrane had had a second engine shot out of commission. There were wounded in both Fortresses, and they were forced to land at Kendari for medical aid, gas, and repairs. An hour later, while they were still at work on Dufrane's engines, five Zeros swept in to strafe the field. Necrason took off in the face of the attacking planes and successfully fought off the three that went after him. The other two Zeros shot up the airport and further damaged Dufrane's plane on the ground. Dufrane spent two more days endeavoring to repair his engines. Then, with Japanese ground troops approaching the field, he blew up the B-17 and with his crew was taken back to Malang by one of the 11th Squadron's LB-30s.‡

While the two B-17s were being attacked at Kendari, the flight of three LB-30s continued on course towards Malang, with Bayse's and Dougherty's planes having more and more trouble in keeping up. Bayse was the first to drop out of the flight, turning off to land at Makassar, where his plane was found to be damaged beyond repair.§ Dougherty

line chief of the 9th Squadron, who took his place. At this time Silva seems to have been nearing sixty (on various enlistment papers he had given his age variously as forty-seven, fifty, and fifty-two)—which was compulsory retirement age, but had insisted on accompanying his squadron commander on the mission because of the lack of experienced gunners. He was officially credited with two Jap planes,[16] though his citation for the D.S.C. allowed him three. Major McTague said of Silva that "he was one of the best gunners in the Army, and he shot down Zeros demonstrating to green gunners. Officers tried to ground him two or three times, for he was much too valuable to lose, but you could not ground Silva. He wouldn't stay down. He was finally killed with McPherson at Horn Island [Australia, on July 20, 1942—W. D. E.]. He left something like twelve kids and no insurance. He was of Portuguese stock and looked Portuguese and spoke broken English, but he could do anything around an airfield—maintenance, armoring, anything. Without him the base at Madioen would have fallen flat on its face. It was old Army men like Silva that really kept the Group going. They could not have operated without the old Master Sergeants."

* 2nd Lt. E. J. Magee.

† Dufrane's citation for the D.S.C. gives his plane credit not only for the transport but also for destruction of seven Jap fighters. However, neither the 19th Bomb Group Diary nor the 7th Group's allows his crew credit for more than one plane.

‡ Piloted by Wade, who landed and took off at night.[17]

§ The crew were brought back to Java in one of Patwing Ten's PBYs, together with a load of parts taken from the ruined bomber.

hung on a while longer, but his gas was running low and it became increasingly difficult to hold his plane in level flight. Halfway across the Java Sea it was obvious that they could not hope to reach Malang and Dougherty turned aside to crash-land on a streak of sandy beach on Greater Mesalembo Island. It was a difficult landing, but he managed to set the crippled bomber down without further injury to the crew, and for nine days they waited there, with little but coconuts to live on and no proper shelter or medical care for their wounded, hoping that the wrecked plane would be spotted by a friendly aircraft. Luck went against them; the weather thickened; and when on the second day they heard heavy bombers flying north, the formation was high above the overcast.* As the days passed, they heard the engines of other planes, but they saw none and no planes sighted them. Finally the co-pilot † went off after help and, discovering a native village at some distance, set out for Java in a fishing boat. The morning after his departure, the rest of the crew again heard a formation flying north; but by now the weather had become so bad, with a dense overcast above a running sea, that they had no hope at all of being seen.

Three and a half hours later, however, they heard the engines of a heavy bomber flying low and very fast. Then they saw it, a B–17E, with its high back fin, sweeping suddenly in under the base of the dark clouds and only a little above the waves. They had hardly time to wave before it was swallowed in the flying scud and the sound of its engines died upon the wind. But the pilot had seen them on the beach, and next day they were picked up by one of Patwing Ten's PBYs.‡

The pilot of the low-flying Fortress was their group commander, Major Robinson, on his way back from the January 24 mission against Balikpapan. Eight B–17s, bombing in formation, had sunk one transport and left another listing and afire. Attacked as they withdrew, they had shot

---

* These planes were in a combined 19th and 7th Group mission against Japanese shipping off Jolo. Six planes reached the target, bombed a 10,000-ton tanker and blew it to bits, and then flew on to Del Monte and evacuated 23 officers, mainly pilots, of the 19th Group.

† 2nd Lt. C. A. Gibson.

‡ S/Sgt. W. B. Kolbus, who was one of the more seriously wounded members of the crew, played a major part in keeping up the morale of the rest. After this mission the LB–30s were relegated almost wholly to night attacks and reconnaissance.[18]

down five Zeros with light damage to only three of their own planes and had then scattered to return individually through the heavy weather to Malang.[19] There had been no casualties, and as things went it was one of the most successful missions they flew against the Japanese in Makassar Strait.

They had embarked at this time on a program, ambitious for them, of sinking a ship a day there; but such attacks were on too small a scale to do more than delay the Japanese, to whom one or two transports were but minor losses. The effort to fulfill this program was out of all proportion to the final result; and, as the Japanese developed their outer thrusts, first down the eastern coast of Celebes into the Flores Sea, and then, soon afterwards, south from the Anambas Islands to Sumatra, the air effort over Makassar Strait was diffused, and the two small undermanned bomber groups had more and more difficulty in supplying air crews and planes for the missions called for by Headquarters. The pressure on the 5th Bomber Command, even in this early stage, is illustrated by the fact that the January 24 mission was the second for Major Robinson and his third day of combat flight since his arrival in Java only five days before.

Robinson was the type of leader incapable of asking more from his men than he expected from himself. Intensely proud of his command and determined that they should make as good a showing as the 19th Group, but aware of their comparative inexperience, he was led into flying on missions that involved green and newly arrived crews as well as on those he would normally have scheduled for himself. Thus, on January 26, two days after spotting Dougherty's crashed LB-30, he and Lieutenant D. R. Strother took off on a two-plane mission to Balikpapan. Four hours out of Java the weather forced them to turn back; yet in spite of these eight hours of strenuous flying, the two took off again next morning, accompanied by another 7th Group plane and three from the 19th. This time they reached the target, where, besides claiming the sinking of one transport, they reported waterline hits on a second and on a cruiser, and two Zeros shot down.[20]

That was Robinson's fourth combat mission in nine days and Colonel Eubank ordered him temporarily grounded. The order did not stick. On the 28th, a five-plane mission against Balikpapan was set up for the

29th, with four planes coming from the 7th Group and one from the 19th.* But of the four 7th Group planes, two had reached Malang from the States only two days before and one had arrived that very afternoon. To Robinson it was unthinkable that these men should be sent into combat without experienced leadership and he pleaded so earnestly for permission to go with them himself that Eubank finally gave in. Robinson took off next morning in Captain Sparks's plane. He never returned.

Four of the Fortresses got up to Balikpapan † and went over the target in formation; but after they had completed their bombing run, the other crews saw Sparks's plane turn back for a second pass—whether because its bombs had hung on the first run ‡ or because Robinson was determined to observe the results of his attack was not known. While they delayed, the formation was jumped by 30 Zeros.

By the time they managed to pull clear of this attack, all four B–17s had been pretty well worked over. Sparks's plane was then at the rear of the flight and the other crews noticed at once that it was losing altitude. It kept up with them for a while but continued to sink lower every minute. At about 2000 feet it started to wobble, as if the pilot were fighting the controls. Suddenly it peeled off to the left and dove straight into the sea. No one was seen to jump and after the sea had closed again, there was no sign of either the plane or the crew upon the water.[21]

This was the first of a series of dark days for the 7th Group. Major Straubel, who had taken over command, went on with the work of establishing the Group at Jogjakarta. The pressure on the air crews had been eased somewhat by the arrival of the ground echelons of the 22nd and 11th Squadrons. These men had reached Soerabaja aboard the *President Polk* on January 28 after a jittery voyage from Brisbane; § and at almost

---

* Both *19th Bomb Group* and *Summary of Air Action* credit two planes on this mission as from the 19th Group and three from the 7th. However, four of the planes were flown by 7th Group pilots: *No. 2476,* by Capt. W. W. Sparks, Jr. (who had reached Malang on January 26); *No. 2455,* by Lt. P. L. Mathewson (who had arrived on January 26); *No. 2454,* by Lt. D. H. Skiles (who had arrived January 19); and *No. 2427,* by Lt. E. C. Habberstad (who had landed at Malang only that same afternoon of January 28). Lt. Ray L. Cox in *No. 2478* was the 19th Group pilot on the mission.

† Habberstad lost an engine an hour and a half out of Java and had to turn back.

‡ As Chaplain Taggart heard.

§ The *President Polk,* which carried a full cargo of ammunition,[22] together with the *Pecos* and *Hawaiian Planter,* was escorted by the cruiser *Houston* and two destroyers.

the same time 29 enlisted men of the 19th Group, who had been flown down from Mindanao, via Darwin, by Lieutenant Funk in his lightly armed B–24 transport and Lieutenant Wade in one of the LB–30s,* arrived at Malang. The two pilots had had some difficulty finding their way in to the Del Monte field, for, though Davao was brilliantly lit up when they crossed the Mindanao shore and they could see the pin-point lights of native fires everywhere below them in the dark and mountainous land, Del Monte itself was blacked out and the field lights had been painted over except for slits so small that when they finally were flashed on, their lights seemed less than candles from the air. As soon as the planes had been serviced and loaded, they took off again for Australia, reaching Darwin towards noon of the next day after eighteen hours of almost continuous flight.†

Yet, even with these additions, the combat units were still so short-handed that one of the 7th Group squadrons—the 22nd—had to be as-signed to the 19th Group. They took over the airdrome at Malang, while the 11th moved on to Jogjakarta. When Madioen was opened up, the latter had to supply personnel for that base as well. These shifts and the accumulating maintenance needs of the overworked and battle-damaged planes meant that from the start the ground crews were putting in an eighteen- and often a twenty-hour day.‡

Meanwhile the air crews, though relieved of some of the maintenance work, were finding the going rougher on their missions. On the 25th of January, four days before Robinson's loss, out of eight B–17s attack-ing at Balikpapan, only three returned safely that afternoon to Malang.

There were three submarine scares during the voyage, and one submarine was sighted though not sunk.[23]

* Two officers reached Malang with this consignment of enlisted men, but Wade and Funk had evacuated a total of 51 men from Del Monte on this mission, leaving the rest in Darwin.[24]

† They had picked up Shorty Wheless, then Operations Officer at Darwin, who was familiar with the layout at Del Monte, and carried in full loads of medicines and cigarettes.[25]

‡ The top-heavy staff structure, already alluded to in Chapter 3 (Part Two) above, de-veloped till out of 1132 personnel actually in Java, 87 were in the two strategic commands, either FEAF or the 5th Bomber Command—a ratio of one to thirteen, and the latter figure includes the staffs of the combat groups themselves.[26] However, in January our people were still planning on an ambitious scale and General Johns has reported how, when he reached Java on the 14th of that month, his first instructions were to provide airfields for 2000 air-planes by June. [27]

The other five were scattered widely: one, in fair condition, managed to reach Soerabaja; a second, so badly shot up that it was lucky to get down at all, went in at Bandjermasin in Southern Borneo; the other three made forced landings in various parts of Madoera Island, two of them with their wheels up.* After that it was eight days before the two groups between them could muster more than six B–17s for a combat mission, and in that time three of the formations dispatched from Malang were turned back by weather.†

It would have been costly bombing even if they could have been assured of sinking their ship a day; but they were not sure of it. The weather continued to cover the advancing Japanese convoys and the big bombers were hunting their targets through the cracks and fissures of the clouds. Again and again they dropped their bombs without knowing whether they had made any hits. This uncertainty about achieved results, the unreliable Intelligence they had to work with, the length of their missions, the lack of relief for combat crews, and the necessity of flying through the blind and violent heart of the vast equatorial front both on their way to the target and again before they could return to base, wore heavily on nerves already stretched fine. In some instances members of returning air crews were beginning to exhibit symptoms of hysteria. The situation called for leadership of a high order and the 7th Group were fortunate in having a man of Major Straubel's caliber to replace the missing Robinson. But in five days Straubel too was dead.

He had been summoned to a conference at Bandoeng on February 2 and had flown up from Jogjakarta in one of the old, unarmed, uncamouflaged B–18s that had brought the 27th Group pilots out of the Philippines and were now used solely for transport or courier service. His only crew on the trip were 2nd Lieutenant Russell M. Smith as co-pilot and Staff Sergeant George W. Pickett, crew chief. On their return on Febru-

---

* The third of these planes landed safely on a desolate strip of beach near Arosbaja. The pilot, Crimmins, who had been evacuated from Del Monte five days before, enlisted native aid to lay a wood and bamboo mat along the beach and three days later successfully took off and returned to Malang.

† Weather and lack of good Intelligence worked against the crews to such an extent that in the whole campaign for Java out of 304 sorties only 172 heavy bombers reached their assigned targets. In February the figures were 97 planes on the target out of 206 dispatched.[28]

ary 3 they had orders to fly round by Soerabaja to drop four passengers from FEAF. One of these was Colonel William H. Murphy, a communications expert from Hawaii to whom General Brereton had assigned the job of overhauling Java's creaky air warning system.* It was an ironical assignment. Apparently unwarned, Straubel's plane was caught in the first Japanese air attack on Soerabaja and shot down by Zeros about 30 miles west of the city. Straubel and Smith were miraculously thrown clear in the crash, but in their efforts to extricate the others from the flaming wreckage—Straubel went back into the fire three times—both men were fatally burned and died next morning in a Dutch hospital.[30]

It was but one incident in a black day for Java. The Japanese, with the airfields at Balikpapan, Kendari, and Ambon in their possession, could now send their bombers over all of Eastern Java and attack the P-40 ferry route from Australia in both Bali and Timor. Moreover, the long range of the Zero when equipped with an auxiliary belly tank enabled them to give their bombers fighter cover over the target—an advantage our own bombers never enjoyed.

In the first raids of February 3, the Japanese put in all 68 bombers and as many fighters over Soerabaja, Madioen, and Malang.† At Soerabaja, where 50 Zeros practically obliterated the valiant little Dutch force of Brewsters and Curtis CW-21Bs in the first few passes, the bombers concentrated on the naval base which in a very few days more they were to make untenable. The airdrome at Madioen, hit in a second raid, was severely damaged; but the heaviest loss to Allied air strength occurred at Malang, where a dive-bombing and strafing attack caught the Fortresses on the field.

There had been no warning and there was no defense except for that provided by the uptilted old French 75s of the 131st Field Artillery. The men worked these antique pieces for all they were worth; they battered

---

* The other passengers were the radar staff, 1st Lt. Glenn H. Boes and 2nd Lt. Irvin R. Kriel, and also a Maj. Joseph A. Burch for whom no particular connection with ABDACOM, FEAF, or any other unit in Java seems to have existed.[29]

† General Brereton gives the following figures: over Soerabaja 26 bombers and 50 fighters; over Madioen, 28 bombers and nine fighters; over Malang ten bombers and 15 fighters; in all 69 planes in each category.[31] However, the 19th Group reported nine dive bombers and 20 heavies at Malang [32] and McDonald's Diary says there were nine "strafers" and twelve bombers. It may be that the figures as submitted to Brereton confused Madioen and Malang; but in any case the totals given by Brereton most nearly reconcile other sources.

the air with noise and smoke; but they were so manifestly harmless that the Japanese pilots kept coming in at treetop level. Two B–17s, loaded with bombs, exploded within five minutes of each other. A third burned to the ground. A fourth, which was partly burned, caught fire again next morning and became a total loss.* A fifth Fortress, one of the old B–17Cs that did not have self-sealing fuel tanks, was making a test hop over the field. It was caught at low altitude by the attack, chased south by Japanese pursuit, and shot down with all its crew in the mountains about ten miles from Singosari.†

That was not yet the end of the day's black news. The 7th Group, running its first mission out of Jogjakarta that morning, had sent nine B–17s up to Balikpapan. Eight came back. The ninth made a forced landing on Arendis Island off the southeast coast of Borneo, hitting the beach wheels up and with one engine afire. The crew survived, but the eight returning planes carried two wounded with them and a third man dead from "oxygen want." ‡ That made a total of six B–17s for the day. The seriousness of the loss is shown by the status report handed up to FEAF next morning: eight B–17s and one LB–30 available for missions.[34]

It marked a turning point in the air phase of the battle for Java. From then on new bombers coming in from the States were barely able to keep pace with the losses. The airdromes were never safe from attack and being without adequate antiaircraft, planes that could not get off on a combat mission early enough to evade the expected raids were sent away from the airfields at the first alarm to spend the day cruising aimlessly up and down off the south coast of Java 100 miles west of Malang, putting hour after hour on the engines and increasing the frustration of the crews. This sense of frustration was aggravated by the removal of 5th

---

* This plane, just in from the States, became celebrated from its serial number as "old 27." After its demise, whenever an unexplained pair of binoculars, sunglasses, or similar article turned up in the hands of a new owner, the accused invariably said that he had "got it out of old 27"; and in time the plane's capacity became as extended as the cabin capacity of the *Mayflower*.[33]

† Piloted by Lt. Ray L. Cox, who had been more fortunate in the attack on Clark Field when he taxied a B–17 from a burning hangar into the teeth of the strafing. Two of the plane's crew were members of the 131st Field Artillery, volunteering as gunners.

‡ There were two or three cases of men dying from this cause—apparently a lack of tolerance for oxygen. Artificial respiration did no good unless the plane could be at once brought down to a low altitude. But with a formation under attack that was impossible. Lt. T. B. Swanson piloted the plane landing on Arendis.

Bomber Command Headquarters from Singosari to Malang on the day after the raid. The move was made for security reasons and to effect better communications with FEAF at Bandoeng; but all the combat crews could think of was their erstwhile companions sitting behind desks on good per diem in the luxury of the town. It was the old, old resentment of the tactical outfit against the Headquarters staff that has never been blunted by repetition.

6. *Reinforcements for the 17th Pursuit*

ON FEBRUARY 3 the 17th Pursuit Squadron fought without their commanding officer. Sprague had flown up to Air Headquarters on administrative matters and was half the length of Java away when the Japanese made their first attack on Soerabaja.

The Squadron was given about twenty minutes' warning that day, so by the time the first flight got up to Soerabaja, the Japanese bombers had already struck and were out over the Java Sea on their way back to Borneo. There were 17 of them—twin-engined, heavy bombers—and when they saw the P-40s they went into an on-line defensive maneuver, stacked down on the side of expected attack, that was new to the Philippines veterans. The P-40s were still 4000 feet below, and before they could pull up into range the chase had carried them over Bawean Island, 85 miles from Java.

Two had to turn back at that point from lack of gas. The other two pilots, Dale and Hennon, both of whom had seen action over Luzon, hung on. Dale made one pass from the rear at extreme range; but Hennon succeeded in working in close enough to shoot one of the bombers down. This was the first kill in the impressive score the 17th was to roll up during its very brief career.

In the meantime, south of Blimbing, Coss and Rowland in a two-ship flight * encountered six of the Japanese fighter force that attacked at

---

* There is some question about the exact details. Gilmore said that this was a three-ship flight, himself flying weaver for the other two, and that he broke away in a shallow left turn when the Japs jumped them, while Coss and Rowland went into a straightaway dive.[1]

Malang. The Japs, at 8000 feet and below the P-40s, were crossing the green hills as heedless as a bunch of sheep-killing dogs, and the chance looked too good to be passed up. As the P-40s dived, however, they were attacked in their turn by another Japanese formation that had been riding the high clouds above and behind the first. In the melee that followed, Rowland, who had survived the wild fighting over the Atimonan beaches of Luzon on Christmas Eve, was killed; but Coss came through and later, as he was returning to Blimbing, sneaked in on the rear of another Jap formation and shot down a Seversky type fighter to pay for Rowland.*

The pattern of this day, with its inadequate warning, and with the Japanese in overwhelming force and rendezvousing their bombers and fighter cover over the targets in absolute precision, was to be repeated on succeeding days with monotonous regularity. Out of the 138 planes the Japanese sent over Java, only two had been shot down. Against them, besides the B-17 destroyed, our people had to set the loss of Rowland, which brought the 17th's strength down to eleven P-40s, while the Dutch, who had made a hopeless fight in their CW-21Bs and Brewsters, lost 13 planes without downing a single Jap. It was obvious that the whole defense of Java depended on bringing in enough P-40s to protect the bomber fields and the absolutely vital naval base at Soerabaja.

The effort was made; but the odds were hopelessly against success. Koepang and the intermediate island airfields, already under Japanese surveillance when the 17th flew up from Australia, were now open to fighter attack. Moreover, the heart of the hurricane season was at hand and, as will be seen, the weather offered hazards as deadly as enemy interception.

It will be recalled that the 17th Squadron brought 13 of the 17 planes with which it had started out from Brisbane through to Java, and of these twelve finally reached the base at Blimbing. No other unit was able to make as good a showing. After the 17th's departure, 124 P-40s were dispatched to Java. Of these 65 were supposed to fly the route as the 17th had; the remaining 59 were loaded aboard ship at Fremantle—32 on the

---

* Coss himself had turned in a remarkable performance on Luzon. Shot down over Aparri in one of the first missions of the war, he had parachuted into the Cagayan River and though continuously strafed had made shore and then walked back 150 miles through the mountains and jungles to report to his unit.[2]

short flight deck of the seaplane tender *Langley;* and 27 in crates aboard the British steamship *Seawitch.* Out of this total of 124 planes, 26 managed to put wheels down on Java soil and only 25 ever got to Blimbing. The rest were lost along the way, from engine trouble, enemy interception, weather, or pilot inefficiency. The 32 aboard the *Langley* went down with the ship when Japanese bombers sank her 74 miles south of the little Java port of Tjilatjap on February 27. Only the *Seawitch* succeeded in landing all her consignment of crated P–40s. But she reached Tjilatjap on the 28th; and by then American Air Force troops were in full retreat from Java. There was no time left for assembling planes, nor man power to do the work if there had been; and the Dutch, who had so long and vainly pleaded for modern fighter planes for their own pilots, had to sink all 27 in their crates to keep them out of the enemy's hands.*

The 26 P–40s that did reach Java in time to take a part in its last defense were survivors of two provisional pursuit squadrons which, with a lone dive-bomber outfit, attempted the difficult flight up from Australia in the sixteen remaining days between the first air attacks on Soerabaja and the 19th of February, when the ferry route was closed for good by Japanese landings on Bali and Timor. Taking off from Brisbane, these three units had totaled 15 A–24s and 50 P–40s and represented a maximum reinforcement effort. They were, in fact, the only air units that the American command in Australia had been able to bring to any kind of combat shape since the departure of the 17th Squadron. But by any ordinary standards, they were not ready for combat at all. They were sent to Java simply because there was no one else to send.

Few of the pilots had had more than twenty hours in a P–40 before taking off on the flight to the north. The 17th Provisional Squadron had drawn on all but four of the veteran fighter pilots who had seen service on Luzon to fill its ranks. Succeeding squadrons had to be built round the replacement pilots who had reached Australia in the early convoys. With only three or four exceptions, these men were straight out of train-

---

* In some accounts the planes were supposed to have been burned. Col. William Hipps's version, here given, is the more likely because the *Seawitch* had, according to Sgt. Nicholson, who had made the voyage on her as a member of her armed guard, unloaded the planes onto lighters, and the congestion in the little harbor makes it quite likely that they were still on their lighters when time to destroy them ran out.[3]

ing school; and a War Department message of January 8, warning that "of pursuit pilots being sent to you, high percentage should have additional gunnery practice before combat," [4] proved to be an appalling understatement. Not only had these inexperienced pilots not fired front guns,[5] many of them had never even been in a combat plane.*

Out of such material, with their very limited equipment, the training center organized in Brisbane under Major Davies's operational control † had to produce combat units against vanishing time. Only three days after the departure of the 17th Squadron, the Japanese began their attack on Rabaul ‡ and pressure by the Australians for pursuit protection for Port Moresby and their own eastern coast was added to the constant demands of ABDACOM. Pupils and instructors alike felt this pressure; both knew what it meant in terms of wasted planes and lives when they started with barely trained squadrons on the long flight north. They knew it even before then on the two training fields at Brisbane—Amberley, where the P–40s were, and Archerfield, where Davies and his 20 veteran pilots were rebuilding the 27th Bombardment Group as fast as they could get their A–24s into action.

The condition in which these planes had been shipped from the States has already been described—without solenoids,§ or gunsights, with only 24 trigger motors for the front .50-caliber guns where 104 were needed, with defective rear gun mounts, worn-out tires, and mud picked up during the Louisiana maneuvers the year before still clinging to the undercarriage. It is small wonder that Major Davies in an official report

* The situation in respect to pilot training did not immediately improve, and as late as March 5, General Brett reported to Washington: "These pilots arrived in this country without having flown for over two months and over 75% of them had either no time at all or had flown only few hours in P–40s. Some specific examples: Following are cases of pilots having never been in a pursuit plane: 27 of 29 pilots of the 35th Pursuit Group; 95 of the 102 pilots of the 49th Pursuit Group."

† CO of the 27th Bombardment Group. Group Captain Lachal of the RAAF was responsible for organizing the center, but actual training was under Davies's direction.

‡ January 19. But a Japanese fleet had been spotted and reported off New Ireland on the 18th.[6] The newspapers had begun screaming over Australia's desperate situation.[7]

§ Chapter 25, Part One, above. General Arnold, in "Global Mission," has discussed the matter of the missing solenoids. According to him, they were with the planes all the time, in small boxes tacked to the inside wall of the crates, and were burned along with the crates by the men who unpacked the planes.[8] Eubank believes this to have been standard crating procedure, as Arnold states. Though this is certainly a possible explanation of the absence of the solenoids, I find it hard to accept in the light of the other missing items.

on January 3 should have written that in his opinion the parties responsible for the shipment should be prosecuted for criminal negligence.[9]

A request for shipment by air of the necessary gun sights, trigger motors, and solenoids was radioed to Washington that same day; * and the parts were sent out on bombers flying the African ferry route. But long before they had found their way to Australia, the collapsing situation had made the demand for every combat plane so desperate that the 27th Group started fitting out the dive bombers with what makeshifts they and the Australians could devise.

It involved unforeseen difficulties. The Australians were not used to working with close tolerances and were hesitant about undertaking the complicated and delicate machine work required for the trigger motors. Moreover, their machine shops were all equipped with British gauges and threads (the reverse of American) and it was not till February 1 that enough trigger motors were completed to equip one of the reorganized Group's three squadrons—the 91st. The other shortages were more easily taken care of. The Australians manufactured rear gun mounts; ordinary truck tires replaced airplane tires; and the guns that had no solenoids were outfitted with hand triggers that "worked well enough." [11] That was how the A–24s set out for the north, hauled through the air by their oil-hungry engines. They were no longer fully maneuverable under a full bomb load; they still had no armor plate or self-sealing gas tanks; without fighter cover they would be duck soup for a Zero. The pilots were well aware of this; they called them the "Blue Rock Clay Pigeons."

But in the meantime training of the casual pilots to fill out the ranks of their three squadrons had proceeded smoothly enough. The men received a total of fifteen hours' flying time divided between dive bombing, navigation, formation flying, and night flying. They were allowed six practice bombs apiece and 100 rounds of ammunition for gunnery training. But they were an enthusiastic lot; they worked hard; they had

---

* An earlier radio, General Clagett to General Marshall on December 31, 1941, had informed Washington of the defective shipment; but, according to General Brereton, the oversight was known in the States even earlier than that, and the parts had originally been shipped on B–17s coming via the Pacific. But these planes had been halted and held in Hawaii by the outbreak of war and had to wait the opening of a new and more southerly Pacific ferry route via Canton Island and the Fijis.[10]

few crashes; and most of them proved able pilots. Their gunners were any men they were able to pick up who were willing to go along and who could qualify as gunners. Qualifying meant chiefly that the candidate did not get airsick. This was the basis on which the squadrons were rated ready for combat. They did all right; but the 91st was the only squadron ready in time to make the flight to Java. The others were held up at Darwin when the Japs severed the ferry route. Their record was to be written mainly in New Guinea, except for one last mission to the Philippines.

While the pursuit phase of the training program had no such armament difficulties to contend with—even Prestone was now coming through in adequate quantities—the greenness of the replacement pilots proved an even greater handicap. As has already been pointed out, many had had no experience at all in combat aircraft; the rest with rare exceptions had had only a few hours. After the long layoff of their slow sea voyage, none of them were ready to handle P-40s. The result was inevitable, and on January 31 a message from the pursuit center reported that "the first three inexperienced pilots to fly P-40s cracked up on 29 January. It is absolutely imperative that initial transition for P-40s pilots be in slower type aircraft. . . ." [12] Lieutenant Gerald Keenan, who was in charge of the pursuit center, asked that some A-24s be turned over to him for this purpose. The request was refused on the ground that all A-24s were needed for combat.

This reason was hard to accept, as most of the A-24s were useless for combat until their guns were made workable. It seems to have enraged Wagner, Mahony, and Strauss, who were handling the actual flight training. Like Keenan they had come out of the Philippines with the sole purpose of bringing help back to George and the units left behind on Bataan; but the time for that had passed. Now it looked as if they would not get to Java in time to support the lone 17th Squadron with which the rest of their buddies had gone. On February 1, risking their commissions, they sent off a radio directly to Washington:

Seventy so-called pursuit pilots assigned to us for training, average total pursuit time approximately fifteen hours.

Have had eight accidents and one death all due to pilot inexperience. Estimate three months and fifteen wrecked planes to fully train these pilots for combat operations.

Request we be allowed two transport airplanes type C-53 for purpose bringing Colonel George and two squadrons of experienced pilots from Bataan, P. I. Consider ourselves very qualified for this mission. Excellent of success.

If request cannot be granted request we be allowed to proceed north with squadron of fully qualified pilots taken partially from light bombardment group.[13]

Though the pilots of the 27th Group endorsed this suggestion enthusiastically, the top command very thoroughly disapproved of it; * and the training command went forward as originally organized. But as the situation in Java deteriorated, the training period had to be continually shortened; and by February 12 the outlook was so desperate that General Brett ordered "operational training to be put aside." [15] The result was that most of the pilots of the last two squadrons to start for Java had had less than twenty hours' total flying time in P-40s. These were the 13th that set off aboard the *Langley* and the 33rd that met the Jap onslaught at Darwin. Their stories do not belong in this chapter, for neither survived to join the 17th. It is the 20th and 3rd Squadrons whose histories concern us here.

The 20th had originally been designated for the defense of Port Moresby; and on January 24, as a direct Allied reaction to the loss of Rabaul and the resultant threat to the sea lanes connecting Australia and the United States, the Squadron received orders to proceed to New Guinea. Before they could move, however, the Japanese capture of Kendari had so darkened the prospect in the Indies that these orders were countermanded by General Brett, and the 20th found themselves committed instead to Java, with instructions to take off as soon as possible.[16]

---

* At the end of January General Barnes sent a message to General Brett in Bandoeng reporting the delay in completing armament on the A-24s and suggesting, in view of their obsolescence and the need of transition planes in the pursuit training program, that they be turned over for that purpose while at the same time the 27th Group be equipped with P-40s and converted into a pursuit group. This request was also immediately disapproved by General Brett, who replied that "it is not understood how these planes which have been in Australia for over a month are now being reported as obsolescent. This office is fully conversant with the characteristics of this airplane. It is not desired that there be any change in the organizational equipment of any of the organizations now in Australia." [14]

Five days later, commanded by Captain William Lane, Jr., they were on their way with 25 P-40s.*

They arrived in Darwin on the 31st with 24 planes. One had cracked a wing in landing at Charleville; but its loss was made good when Lieutenant Strauss overtook them with a replacement from Brisbane. The other ship had crashed and burned † at Cloncurry.[17]

It was the heart of the storm season. As they came farther north, they had to fight heavy winds, and the desert under them was lost in the black rains. Even with a B–17 to escort them on the leg from Cloncurry, they had an anxious time finding their way into Daly Waters. There the pilots gassed their own ships with a few aborigines occasionally lending a hand, but a new storm pinned them to the field for still another hour before they could take off for Darwin. They felt more urgently the sense of time running out. Their own unreadable future, which till then had seemed geographically limited by the North Australian shore, was suddenly imminent. They slept that night with wind and rain driving in upon their thin-walled quarters from the Timor Sea.

At six next morning they started preparing for the long over-water flight to Koepang; but it was five o'clock in the afternoon before they had the planes ready, and then, an hour out, a tropical front too heavy for small planes to penetrate forced them to turn back. They came into the RAAF field ahead of it in the cloudy dusk like blown bees.

By dawn the storm had increased to hurricane pitch, with rain driving in visible waves across the field, and they had to tie the planes down. It did not break till noon of the following day, and then they were alerted by rumor of a Japanese carrier 500 miles out and flew patrol over Darwin. Finally, late in the afternoon of February 4, fourteen of them were able to take off for Koepang.‡

There was still a front over the Timor Sea; but this time they could get under it, and for the first half of their flight they were only 50 feet

---

* Most of the pilots were drawn from units of the 35th Pursuit Group, which had reached Australia during January. The 35th, as noted in Part One, Chapter 7, above, was also the parent group of the 20th, 34th, and 21st Squadrons, serving on Bataan in the 24th Pursuit Group.

† The pilot, Lt. George A. Parker, survived.

‡ Gambonini, who gives a very circumstantial account, says that only 13 planes took off. Most other sources, however, list 14, and *Summary of Air Action* names the 14 participating pilots.

above the water. Beyond the front a big B-24 picked them up and led them into Koepang, which they reached with something like eight gallons of gas left in their tanks.[18]

One of the planes, Lieutenant Robert McWherter's, could not take off next morning because of engine trouble. McWherter was left to make repairs and join the second flight when it came through; the other 13 were in the air at dawn and heading west towards Bali behind their B-24 guide. A little way out they sighted two planes that were too far away to be identified. These disappeared after a few minutes; but some time later Lieutenant Dwight S. Muckley, Jr., discovered that four more planes were shadowing them. This remote, aerial stalking went on until the P-40s were near Bali, when the strange planes vanished. As the fighter flight went down to land on the south coast air strip at Den Pasar, the sky held nothing but the clouds.

The pilots still, however, had an uneasy sense of being watched, and Captain Lane, who was particularly anxious to be away, ordered every plane to take off as soon as it was serviced. But only seven were able to regas and begin their patrol above the field before 16 Zeros broke out of the clouds over them. One other P-40, Lieutenant Gambonini's, managed to take off with partly filled fuel tanks; but the odds were too uneven and the ensuing combat lasted less than twenty minutes.* Two to four Zeros were claimed shot down as against three of the P-40s.† One of these plunged into the sea, taking its pilot, Lieutenant Larry D. Landry, with it. The other pilots parachuted, and two more with their planes more or less shot up managed to land on the Den Pasar strip. Captain Lane, Lieutenant Jesse R. Hague, and Lieutenant Muckley broke clear of the fight and headed for Soerabaja. All three got through, though Muckley's plane had been so badly punished that it was barely able to make the distance.

Japanese bombers were working over the city again that day; they were in the act of bombing Perak Field when Muckley landed. Some

---

* Estimates of the Jap strength in this small action vary from 15 (Gambonini) to 24 in Landry's posthumous citation for the D.S.C. The account given here is drawn from *17th Pursuit Squadron (Provisional)*; Citations for Muckley, Turner, Gambonini, and Landry; Gambonini Diary; FEAF Diary; WELLER (Fighters); and Sheppard Statement.

† By Lts. William L. Turner and Landry, according to their citations. Lane and Lt. Gene L. Bound are credited with a Zero apiece in AAF IN WORLD WAR II, Vol. I.

American mechanics, sheltering along the edge of it, saw him come in. "We noticed it was a bad landing. The ship hit, nosed over for half the length of the runway, then flopped back on the tail wheel and came to a stop. The engine ran for several seconds, then slowly spluttered and died. The pilot climbed out of the cockpit very slowly, and we noticed him examining his plane's tail." [19]

They could understand why when they looked the ship over. The right wing had been chewed up by machine gun bullets; the left wing had been hit by an explosive cannon shot; the aileron cables were severed and hanging loose; the rudder and elevators were locked and useless; there was a hole a foot square in the fuselage; the radio was shot to bits; the prop was full of holes; and the mechanics later noticed that a rear view mirror had been clipped off inches from the pilot's head. Besides that, Muckley had landed his plane on two flat tires—"no mean feat," as Corporal Perry wrote, "for a P-40." [20] The ship could never be fought again; but they patched it together enough to fly it to Blimbing where it was cannibalized for such parts as the Japanese had left usable.

Back at Den Pasar the two P-40s that landed after the brief dog fight, and the five that had never got off the ground at all, were attacked for a second time as 31 Japanese bombers slipped out of the clouds to make four separate and deliberate passes over the field. Two P-40s were destroyed outright by direct hits; two more were so badly riddled by shrapnel that it took three days to get them into shape to fly; * the other three managed to get across to Soerabaja next day accompanied by Mc-Wherter, who had come into Den Pasar with the Squadron's second flight, but they were a limping and badly battered trio.

The second flight, leaving Darwin with ten planes, lost two in crash landings on Waingapoe when they ran out of gas after a successful brush with a Japanese reconnaissance bomber.† Thus, out of 25 planes, the 20th Squadron delivered 17 to Java, eleven of them in condition for combat.‡

---

* Flown to Soerabaja by Lts. Thomas L. Hayes, Jr., and Cornelius F. K. Reagan.[21]

† Credit for shooting down this plane, which was positively identified as a Messerschmitt 110, was divided among Lts. McWherter, Bernard J. Egeness, and Andrew J. Reynolds.[22]

‡ Various sources, including the official Air Force history, put the total at twelve.[23] But there seems no doubt that 17 actually reached Java: three on February 5, two flights of eight and four on February 6, and the final two on February 8.[24] Gambonini lists 15 planes but phrases his entry for February 6 somewhat ambiguously.[25]

At that, they had far better luck than the 3rd Squadron, which came after them.

The 3rd, commanded by Captain Grant Mahony, had had less time for training, and they began their trip north by losing seven planes, all through pilot inexperience, before they even reached Darwin. There the remaining 18 were divided into two equal flights, Mahony himself taking one and giving the other to Lieutenant Allison Strauss.

Strauss's flight was first to take off on the long hop to Koepang, starting on February 9 with an LB–30, as usual, to provide navigation, and with three A–24s of the 91st Bombardment Squadron, which had come into Darwin just the evening before. One of the P–40 pilots, however, did not belong on the Squadron roster; he was Major William P. Fisher, who had flown into Darwin on the night of the 5th in one of two LB–30s that were evacuating Air Corps troops from Mindanao.* Fisher was about to embark on a new phase of his varied career in the Southwest Pacific. He was first encountered in this narrative as a member of the 14th Bombardment Squadron in broad daylight over the Japanese-held island of Ponape during the initial transpacific ferry flight before the outbreak of war; † he had then served on Luzon and Mindanao as commanding officer of the 28th Bombardment Squadron after its incorporation in the 19th Group; ‡ now, since his arrival in Darwin, he had received orders to report to FEAF Headquarters in Bandoeng for possible reassignment, which in fact was to appoint him Interceptor Control Officer for Eastern Java. A fighter pilot long before he had turned to bombardment,[26] he was undoubtedly, even after a long layoff, more competent to fly a P–40 in to Java than the majority of the 3rd Squadron's pilots. But an hour out, the engine of his plane lost a magneto and he had to turn back to Darwin. His was the only P–40 in the flight to make a safe landing.

The rest went on behind the LB–30 through broken weather. The

---

* The pilots of these LB–30s were Lts. Horace Wade and Murray W. Crowder. (Wade had already flown a similar mission to Del Monte on January 24-27 with Capt. Funk. Part Two, Chapter 5, above.) They took 19th Group personnel to Java on February 7, arriving at the same time as the submarine *Seawolf*, from Corregidor, was landing twelve Army Air Corps officers at Soerabaja. (*Seawolf* had also brought out twelve Navy Air Corps personnel, a heavy passenger list for a small submarine.)

† Part One, Chapter 1.

‡ *Ibid.*, Chapter 6.

three A-24s, whose worn old engines had small hope of matching even the throttled-down cruising speed of the P-40s,* lagged farther and farther in the rear until they finally faded out of sight. The weather grew steadily rougher. The little pursuits moved up closer to the big bomber as it sliced in and out of the drifting bellies of the clouds. By the time they were approaching Timor, the ceiling was down under 600 feet, and they saw that the land ahead was completely closed in by the dark heart of the storm. There was no chance for them to turn back. Their fuel margin was only just enough to carry them to Koepang and they followed the bomber on into the storm.

But in only a little while they realized that the navigator was lost. The bomber kept circling in apparently aimless search for the airfield. One by one, as their gas ran out, the pursuit pilots took their planes down to attempt crash landings or parachuted blind through the clouds. The LB-30, with gas enough to make the return trip, broke clear of the storm and headed back to Darwin. All eight P-40s were lost. One pilot, Lieutenant Phillip T. Metsker, was killed.[27]

Later in the same evening, the three A-24s found their way into the airfield. Their flight leader, Captain Edward N. Backus, who also commanded the 91st Squadron, had had seven years' experience in commercial airlines and refused to be baffled by the weather. But ironically the Australian airdrome troops had not been warned of the arrival of the A-24s and their antiaircraft gunners, mistaking the dive bombers for Japanese, cut loose at them with everything they had. Though all three pilots succeeded in landing, two of the planes were so badly damaged that they had to return to Darwin for further repairs. The third, however, was patched up sufficiently to allow Captain Backus to go on alone to Java next morning.†

* The A-24s had a listed top speed of only 247 miles an hour, when new. Memorandum to the Chief of Staff, December 1, 1941.

† According to the Group history, Lts. Abel and Criswell returned safely to Darwin, repaired their planes, and took off for Java with the rest of their squadron. The 91st had left Brisbane with 15 planes. One was left behind en route at Charleville, with engine trouble. Two more barely made the distance to Darwin and were left there for the same reason. The flight that took off on February 11 under Lt. Harry L. Galusha consisted of eleven planes. One of these overturned in landing at Waingapoe; ten reached Pasirian where they were met by Capt. Backus and led by him to Modjokerto, a brand-new field that had been fashioned for them out of ricefields by laying a woven bamboo mat, 3000 by 100 feet, and

The storm that had proved so fatal to Strauss's flight was to provide cover for Mahony's. Japanese pilots consistently exhibited an antipathy towards violent weather, and neither Mahony's P–40 pilots, nor the dive bomber crews that came through the islands a day behind them, reported hostile aircraft. The 3rd Pursuit Squadron's second nine planes took off for Koepang on February 10 and all nine arrived intact over Pasirian, a small airfield in the southeast of Java, on the 11th. But one ship nosed up in landing and another came in on its belly. Neither could be flown immediately to Blimbing; before they were repaired one had been caught on the strip and destroyed by Japanese strafers.* So, out of its initial quota of 25, the 3rd Squadron brought nine planes through to Java, of which eight finally reached Blimbing.[30] The pilots, together with those of the 20th who had preceded them, were absorbed into the 17th Squadron that, as a result, had now attained its greatest strength. The record for February 12 shows a roll of 47 officers, 81 enlisted men, and 30 planes, not counting the two at Pasirian. Of these planes 25 were in commission, and two days later that figure, through the unceasing efforts and ingenuity of the enlisted men, had swelled to 26.[31]

It was their high mark. From then on their strength steadily declined. There were no more reinforcements. On February 15, as the white flag went out from Singapore, the Squadron, detaching eight planes to fly the length of Java for a bombing attack on Japanese landing barges at Palembang, Sumatra, lost a plane in a crack-up at Batavia. That was the beginning of inevitable attrition that accelerated as the Japanese pincers closed on Java. They fought with what they had, but even the enlisted men knew that they would get no more support. Their nearest supply base, from which all of them had flown, was 3200

covering it with earth—all in three days' time and entirely by native hand labor, starting "from bamboo still growing in the tree." [28] Several of the planes bogged down. All needed repairs and there were only two mechanics in the outfit to oversee the work, which was done by officers and gunners working together. They lost two planes in accidents and cannibalized two more for parts. They were then ordered to a new station at Batavia and almost immediately thereafter to Malang, where they set up shop with seven planes in their squadron.[29]

* Pilots were Lts. Frank E. Adkins and Quanah P. Fields. The latter was a full-blooded Cherokee Indian and was later shot to death in his chute, thus becoming the first American Indian killed in this war.

miles away. No fighter unit in all history ever flew its planes so far to reach its battle station and was given so little to fight with when it had arrived.

7. A Decline in Morale

THE CAPTURE of Singapore was tangential to the general pattern of the Japanese assault on the Netherlands East Indies. The island could have been enveloped and by-passed far more easily than, a year later, our own forces were to by-pass and neutralize the Japanese stronghold at Rabaul, for in the narrow waters of its strait shipping was hopelessly vulnerable to air attack, and over Malaya Japanese air supremacy was absolute. But Singapore was the symbol of white domination in the Far East, and it was natural for the dominant British element in ABDACOM to regard it as the indispensable western anchor of their Malay Barrier defense line: they persisted to the end in using all British and Australian, and for a time most of the Dutch, surface naval strength in escort duties for its relief instead of building a real striking force to meet the gathering Japanese convoys. By the time they finally decided to consolidate these ships with the little American flotilla, it was too late. One Japanese assault was already penetrating the Malay Barrier to take Palembang on Sumatra; a second was forming off Celebes for strikes to the east of Java, at Bali and Koepang; and the central force that for so long had hung in Makassar Strait like a dark and gathering cloud was once more getting ready to move, this time to the capture of Bandjermasin on the southeast coast of Borneo, thus completing Japanese domination of that island. These forces in turn were to be supplanted in the climactic assault on Java itself by two vastly heavier convoys: the first of 41 transports originating at Jolo and heading straight down Makassar Strait and, after a single stop at Balikpapan, out across the Java Sea; the second, even larger, coming down out of the China Sea around the western curve of Borneo against Batavia and Western Java.

Against the cumulative pressure of these armadas and their over-powering naval escorts, the small combined Allied fleet would have neither chance nor hope of victory, for all the desperate courage of its ultimate sorties. And meanwhile, on Malaya, the Japanese army under Yamashita had proceeded almost unimpeded to the capture of Singapore, most of whose huge coastal defense guns, that in the past had overawed the Asiatic world and Britain equally, still pointed unhappily and futilely to sea.*

The men on the bomber fields in Java received the news of Singapore's surrender as forewarning of their own defeat. Like most of the rest of the world they had expected it to hold out longer. They were shocked; but they were not altogether surprised. Even the ground crews could see how things were going, and three days before Singapore fell an abrupt change in the pattern of their bombing missions had indicated a shift in the direction and the pace of the Japanese campaign.

For eighteen days the two groups had been pounding the convoy in Makassar Strait, 15 of the 22 missions scheduled between January 26 and February 12 going up to bomb either the shipping or Balikpapan port. Bad weather over the target and the altitude from which the planes bombed, usually 25,000 feet or over, minimized the effectiveness of these attacks. But the men believed that they were getting results † and the

---

* And the few whose traverse had been adapted to landward fire did not have enough elevation to offer effective counter-battery fire. It is interesting that as far back as the 1860's, one unawed Britisher, John Cameron, had written: "I would mention that there is not a single heavy gun mounted on any of the forts capable of being turned to deliver its fire inland." [1]

† Here, as elsewhere in the early months of the war, Air Force claims were consistently overoptimistic and were seldom substantiated in the final accounting at the war's end. (The same tendency applied, though in slightly less degree, to our Naval forces, except for the consistently realistic submariners. Cf. MORISON, III.) Results claimed by the two groups on the series of Makassar missions were one transport sunk, three transports damaged, and a hit on a carrier. But the "carrier" was actually an aircraft tender.

In a message dated February 21, General Brett officially claimed the following score since January 1 for all his air forces:

	Damaged	Sunk
Carriers	1	0
Tankers	0	2
Cruisers	12	0
Battleships	1	0
Transports	8	6
Destroyers	2	1

But the Joint Army-Navy Assessment Commission credits Army airplanes of *all* Allied Air forces in the theater with no more than three minesweepers, four passenger or cargo vessels, and one converted salvage vessel sunk, and a part in the sinking of two other cargo vessels

earlier missions, at least, were carried through with considerable determination, 60 of the 72 bombers dispatched getting over the target. Considering the conditions under which the men were operating—the lack of adequate shop facilities,* the state of the runways, turned by the rains into quagmires in which more than one plane just arriving from the States was hopelessly cracked up, and the stiffening of Japanese fighter opposition—this was not a bad record; certainly it was not approximated afterwards in Java.

The Zero pilots had discovered that the vulnerable point in the B–17E was the nose, which as a rule carried only a single .30-caliber gun.† The first evidence of this came on February 5 when a formation of six Fortresses on their way up to Balikpapan was jumped 35 miles east of Soerabaja by a flight of eight Zeros. Contrary to their usual procedure these Zeros, after pacing the bombers out of range for a few minutes, swept ahead and then turned head-on into them. The B–17s, still making their laden climb out of Malang, had reached barely 4000 feet and were therefore at a heavy disadvantage. As soon as they sighted the Japs, they closed their formation very tight, swung back on their tracks, and went into a shallow dive. The Japs made no attempt to co-ordinate their frontal attacks, but came in individually. Except for one lucky shot that blew out the oxygen system in the last Fortress, they did no damage and inside of twenty minutes they broke away, leaving the B–17s to proceed towards the south shore of Java, up and down which they beat for the next four or five hours till it was considered safe for them to return

for the entire period from December 1941 through March 5 in *both* Philippines and N. E. I. I find it hard to accept the JA-NAC figures as completely accurate also. Interrogations of captured Japanese officers do not *per se* constitute absolute authority in my opinion. In the invasion of the Indies the Japs used all sorts and descriptions of transports that they had swept the China shores to gather and that they treated as wholly expendable. Probably the truth lies somewhere between the JA-NAC assessment and the AF claims.

* The Dutch shops proved disappointing and a bomber needing depot overhaul still had to be sent south over 3000 miles to Melbourne. The Dutch could handle small repairs. Their shops were beautiful but they used almost entirely native labor, each man being taught to make one thing—a gear, a spring, etc. "They kept him at it till he could make that particular thing as beautiful as something out of a watch. The problem was to find people (instead of parts) to make what you wanted." There was no time for such research in Java.

† According to Lt. M. C. Rowan, Jr., his squadron, the 93rd, had a few planes with two .30-calibers in the nose. Another pilot says they tried out as many as six .30-calibers in the nose, though I have not seen this corroborated elsewhere.

to Malang.* But the next frontal attack by Zeros, which came only three days later, was an entirely different affair.

On the morning of February 8 nine B–17s of the 7th Group took off on a mission against the airdrome at Kendari from which the Japanese were now launching most of their raids on Java. An hour and ten minutes out of Malang one of the planes had to turn back when an engine failed, but the other eight went on, holding a loose javelin formation. It was a day of high winds and broken clouds in a bright sky. Beneath them the deep blue of the Java Sea was stippled by the running waves and the small islands were frothing white along their windward shores. It was the first really clear weather the air crews had seen in days and it seemed ironical that they should find the Japanese pursuits lying in wait for them among the clouds over the open sea beyond Kangean Island.†

The B–17s had reached only 14,000 feet in their long climb out of Malang; but Captain Dufrane,‡ who was leading the formation, took no evasive action, but held the bombers on their course. Mention has already been made of the fundamentally opposed combat philosophies of the 7th and 19th Groups.§ The resulting controversy had lately shown signs of coming to a head. There had been some stiff censure by the Bomber Command of flight leaders who deviated from the strict line of their orders, even in the case of enemy attack. The intention of Dufrane, a spirited and determined man, to leave no loophole for criticism and to carry his formation through to the target therefore seems plain; and indeed for several minutes it looked as if his show of determi-

---

* The 19th Bomb Group Diary ascribes the abandonment of the mission to the fact that in addition to the damaged plane the top turrets of two others failed to function during the attack. The B–17s claimed one Zero shot down, one damaged.[2]

† The Japanese fighters may have been on their way to Java to furnish cover for bombers over Soerabaja or to strafe on their own. But in the first case their first duty would have been fulfillment of their rendezvous, and at this time few strafing raids had occurred except in close conjunction with a bombing attack. The feeling at Malang was that the interception had been planned and was the result of espionage. Certainly there were watchers round the airdrome and crews of bombers taking off in the mornings on combat missions often saw smoke signals rising from the mountains, the number of fires equaling the number of planes in their formation.[3]

‡ Capt. J. L. Dufrane (then Lt.), who had participated in the 7th Group's first combat mission against Menado. (Part Two, Chapter 5, above.)

§ See above, Part Two, Chapter 5.

nation might pay dividends. For, though the Zeros still enjoyed a wide margin of performance at 14,000 feet, they made no immediate offer to close but, keeping well beyond range, paced the bombers through the fringes of the clouds till both sets of planes had climbed to nearly 17,000 feet.* Then, with the abruptness of a whiplash, they struck.

There were only nine of them,† but it was evident in the very first pass that these Japs meant business. The Zero that came head on against Preston's plane, which was flying wing on Dufrane's, bored in till Preston and his co-pilot, Knudsen, were sure they would crash. But the Zero pulled up in the last instant, clearing their wing by only 20 feet; the B–17 was filled by the flash of sunlight reflected from the fighter's white underside; the Jap pilot was plainly visible as he passed them; and the plane's Rising Sun insignia shone bloody red. After that the action was too fast for any man to register consecutive details. The Japs, as they always did, attacked individually, but this time with a split-second co-ordination that brought in three planes almost as one, from the front, the front quarter, and up underneath, where the Jap pilot would hang on his prop and pour his fire into the belly as the B–17 came over him.

The bomber formation had tightened before the attack and Dufrane continued to hold rigidly to his course. The next attack was concentrated entirely on his ship. Suddenly, while the Zeros were still at him, a mass of flame burst from the plane's belly. Men in the other Fortresses saw the auxiliary bomb bay tank drop out. It was burning as it fell, but the ship itself also continued to burn. Six men bailed out; and the plane started down. It exploded as the Zeros turned to strafe the men in their chutes.‡

With Dufrane's loss, Strother, who had just received notice of his promotion to captain, took over command of the formation, which had be-

* At 20,000 feet the margin began to dissipate; and above 25,000 it turned in favor of the B–17. The Zero then had difficulty in keeping up with the Fortress and had to attack from the flank or rear, which gave the gunners their best chance to shoot him down.

† The 19th Bomb Group Diary says there were nine to twelve Japs, as do other sources, including Lawrence; but five Zeros were shot down and when the fight broke off the retiring bomber crews counted four Zeros still in the air. Nine seems the logical number.⁴

‡ No one, of course, could tell whether Dufrane was one of the six who succeeded in bailing out, and over the open sea it made no difference. But probably he was still in the plane. He had set out on this mission with a premonition of his death and had told the Chaplain what he wanted done with his things in case he failed to return. Never before any other mission had he shown the least concern about such matters. (Maj. William C. Taggart to the writer.)

come fairly disorganized. While it was reassembling the Zeros left off strafing the men in the chutes to attack the B–17s from side and flank. During these attacks, one Zero was shot down; the men in Preston's plane saw it go into a spin and crash into the sea. Meanwhile Strother had headed straight for the nearest cloud cover; and, though the Zeros broke off for the moment, the Fortress crews realized that they had not done with them yet.

The new attacks came again from the front, front quarter, and below; but while the gunners now knew what to expect, they found themselves more or less helpless. The bottom turrets, already described, with their mirror sights and the gunner lying prone and back to his guns, were no use at all. The top turrets traversed too slowly to match the speed of planes coming at them from the front. This left only the .30-caliber nose guns, one to each ship, and they were too light and too few to keep the Zeros out.

On the first pass Prichard's plane, in No. 3 position on Strother's wing, blew up in mid-air. Pieces of it hung in the sky about the formation like sheets of blown paper before they started down; and the other air crews saw only a single chute open below the wreckage.* Five of the six remaining planes now jettisoned their bombs and bomb bay tanks, and barely in time, for the one in Preston's plane was hit as the bomb bay doors opened and was flaming as it left the ship.

Strother's plane had been hit in the same attack; an exploding oxygen bottle had blown out the bomb release mechanism so that the ship had to carry its bombs and the far more dangerous bomb bay tank through the rest of the action. Fortunately it did not last much longer. By the

---

* Though the crew had all been in Java ten days or longer, Prichard himself had reached Malang (via the African route) only at midday of February 5. This was his first combat mission. Crews of the lost ships were:

Capt. J. L. Dufrane	1st Lt. W. J. Prichard
1st Lt. R. V. W. Negley, Jr.	2nd Lt. W. T. Morgan
2nd Lt. S. S. Patillo	2nd Lt. Isadore Alfred
2nd Lt. W. W. Burney	2nd Lt. F. O. Luscombe
S/Sgt. J. W. Coleman	S/Sgt. R. P. Legault
Pfc. H. L. Ellis	Pvt. Joseph Hines
Sgt. L. H. Keightley	Pfc. Ignatius Barron
	Pvt. Horace Salmon

The 19th Bomb Group Diary gives no explanation of Dufrane's ship being undermanned.

time the six surviving B–17s finally reached cloud cover, a man in one ship had been killed and another, in a second, seriously wounded.* The tail of this last plane, Lieutenant Paul M. Lindsey's, had been so badly shot up that it took the combined strength of pilot and co-pilot to handle the controls.

There was a great deal of turbulence in the clouds—so much that keeping formation was impossible and the planes turned individually for home. When Lindsey's ship hit the turbulent air, the two men were no longer able to keep the nose down and she went into a flat spin. The co-pilot, navigator, and tail gunner all bailed out; but Lindsey, with one of his crew wounded, stuck to the ship and with the help of the bombardier, who had crawled up into the cockpit, finally got her nose down and brought her out at 7000 feet. By then the plane had dropped nearly 10,000. The two men put their feet against the wheel and shoved with their backs braced against the armor plate; but they could not keep the plane flying level till they had tied the steering column forward with a piece of rope to the brace above the rudder. Lindsey's compass had been shot out; none of the navigator's maps could be found; he had to find his way into Malang over what was still strange country for him and through steadily thickening weather and land his ship with her controls half gone; but he brought her in.†

This was the costliest mission in the history of the 5th Bomber Command. Only one of the nine planes dispatched that morning from Malang, the one that had returned early with engine trouble, came back undamaged. Nineteen men had been killed. The survivors realized that they had not made a good showing. They had learned too the necessity for some system of fire control. Till now this had been on an entirely informal basis, where it existed at all. While the 19th Group were using the B–17D they had generally had a man say when to start firing, but for some reason this procedure had been dropped with the acquisition of the Es and it was left to the judgment of the individual gunner when to start. Usually the gunner opened fire at about 1000 yards, and heretofore

* Pfc. H. D. Bilyeri in Habberstad's plane, killed; and Pfc. J. R. Mackely in Lindsey's plane, wounded.

† This was Lindsey's first combat mission, his only previous mission having come on the 6th, when with eight other Fortresses he had spent the day flying up and down the south coast of Java, as an air raid precaution.[5]

this had proved effective in keeping the Japs out, particularly after their first encounters with the Es' tail guns. But in a really determined frontal attack such as they had just experienced, the need of controlled fire was obvious. The men, however, were more impressed by the weak points in the plane's equipment, particularly the bomb bay tanks.

The non-self-sealing bomb bay tank had been a source of misgiving from the first, but it is unlikely that, before the double loss of Prichard and Dufrane, anyone had realized its disastrous potentialities. Coupled with the demonstrated inability of the top turrets and single .30-caliber nose guns to turn aside a frontal attack of this type, it made a profound impression on all bombardment personnel. There was a growing reluctance to undertake combat missions that involved carrying bomb bay tanks; and perhaps it was fortunate for the discipline in both groups that the new moves of the Japanese brought all bomber action so much closer to Java that there was little need of carrying auxiliary gas loads in the days to come; and if one pilot is to be believed, this reluctance in some cases reached the stage of outright refusal.

Unquestionably there was an abrupt decline in morale from which neither group, either before or after their subsequent merger in Australia,* ever wholly recovered. It is always difficult to assess the combination of factors that makes or breaks morale in a military organization; too many intangibles are involved. In the case of the 19th Group and the 7th, which it absorbed, there were plenty of work horses who carried the tough missions through to the bitter end of the Java fighting. These men continued to keep the groups going, but even when they finally came under a first-rate top command in Australia, the tone of the organization, to use the word in its medical sense, was never again completely sound.

The men, to begin with, were near exhaustion, mentally and physically. Oddly enough this applied in almost equal degree to the 7th Group, freshly arrived though they were. The bombardment personnel we sent to England did not have to fly a combat mission for weeks or months after they arrived, not till they had had time to become thoroughly oriented; but the 7th Group crews, after flying halfway round the

* On March 14, 1942, surviving personnel of both groups were to be brought together and reorganized as the 19th Group.

world to reach their base of operations, generally went out on their first combat mission within five days of reaching Java. While most of the pilots who reported to Malang were experienced fliers, there were some who had had no combat training, who had not even done formation flying, and these men had to practice flying on the wing on their way up to the target, which sometimes produced hair-raising sensations in the rest of the formation. And a great proportion of the crews were entirely new to heavy bombers and utterly green in their assigned positions. What this meant to men operating under extreme tension has been reticently and graphically described by one of the 7th's experienced bombardiers.

. . . We were on the line ready for take-off, and they called over to our plane. Number 53 was going to lead the flight, and they had just found on take-off that this was that bombardier's first mission. They called over to my plane and said for me to take the lead ship.

Just about then this bombardier came up: "Are you Sgt. Campbell? We are to change planes."

"Have you any bombing equipment over there in your plane?" I said.

"I don't know."

"Well, I'll take mine."

"What do I do?"

"If you see my bomb bay doors open up, open up yours."

"All right," he said. "How do I open my doors?"

"Use your bomb bay door handle."

"Then what?"

"Well, either kick them off or if you want to, use the manual release."

"Where is the manual release?"

I had to show him everything in a couple of minutes. I came to find out later that he had dropped a total of 20 bombs in his life and spent two hours of flying time in a B–17. And then they were going to send him out in a lead ship . . .*

And as Master Sergeant Campbell went on to say, somewhat dryly, "the pilot and the bombardier have to have experience together." It would have been all right if there had been a training program to take care of such replacements. But there was no time to set one up in

---

* M/Sgt. W. P. Campbell, in Carmichael. This series of Carmichael interviews (so named because Col. Richard M. Carmichael introduced the various men) was held December 5, 1942, in Washington, before and in very large part by General Arnold.

Java;* nor was there to be time for any kind of training for the 19th Group until the squadrons were finally brought together at one base in Australia on July 11, 1942. Till then their war had to be strictly cut-and-try, and they took off with any planes and personnel they had; and if they had to learn their jobs, they learned them under combat.

Lack of supplies, especially of airplane parts; the many futile, ill-advised, and wholly inadequate missions they were sent out on; the hours spent in beating up and down the south coast of Java: all these were elements in the decline of their morale; yet these things cannot wholly explain it. For the 17th Provisional Pursuit Squadron at Blimbing, with no replacements after February 12 and existing mechanically on nothing but the bones of their own wrecked planes, never lost their offensive spirit, any more than did the tiny Bataan Air Force, compared to whose resources even the 17th Provisional Squadron were well off. But these two outfits had natural combat leaders to command them; and while they had almost nothing to fight with, the pilots realized that, considering what they did have, their record was very high. But the bomber missions, as many of the 7th and 19th Groups were beginning to realize, were earning a minimum of military return.[6] Their conception of the strategic role of heavy bombardment was violated by the almost impromptu fashion in which the B-17s had been employed; and, as one sifts through their personal statements and diaries, their lack of confidence in the top command is inescapable. It even reached down to operational levels where, though men like Combs went into combat with his 19th Group and the Squadron leaders of the 7th took their turn with other pilots, there was already, as one pilot phrased it, "a good deal of this preserving the valuable men stuff."

No more insidious canker can attack the morale of a combat organization. It produced increasing tension between the tactical personnel and the Bomber Command, making itself evident in open recriminations. On the night of February 12, at Malang, a flight leader of the 7th Group

* Teats, in the Carmichael interview, said: "The training was what we learned day by day on combat missions. . . . In Java we got the first B-17Es. My [first] personal experience with the E was at 3 in the morning on a take-off. The runway was blocked off on one side. There were six inches of mud on the field. There was no transition flight training. The boys just stepped out of the Ds and into the Es, and took off with a full load of bombs. . . ."

killed himself. This man had a record of eight missions for the twenty-four days he had been in Java, only one of which had been abandoned. His act had a profoundly depressing effect not only among the men at Malang, but almost immediately among all personnel at Jogjakarta and Madioen.

It was at this point, with morale at all three bases striking an all-time low, that the Japanese move against Palembang shifted the focus of our bomber operations to Sumatra. The mission from which the dead man had returned on February 12 was the last one pulled in the Makassar series: * In the early morning hours ten B–17s in three separate flights bombed shipping through clouds and darkness with unknown results, except for the hopeful report of one flight that they "believed they hit a boat." [7] That same night of the 12th-13th three LB–30s took off from Jogjakarta to seek and bomb enemy ships reported off the Anambas Islands.

It was a long mission, 800 air miles to reach the target area in the South China Sea, longer still as the three planes flew, finding their way through the weather and searching for the convoy down the dark crevasses of nocturnal clouds. But they found nothing. The Japanese had already slipped away; transports loaded with troops no longer needed for the capture of Singapore had made their rendezvous with an escorting naval force, and now the combined fleets, mantled in the weather, were heading for the mouth of the Moesi River, whose shallow channel leads up to Palembang. This was the first step in the final pincer movement which was to cut off Java from all outside support. It developed with dismaying speed.

The last of the three LB–30s, returning from their fruitless quest, had landed at Jogjakarta at 8:30 in the morning of the 13th. Twenty-four hours later the Japanese attack on Palembang began. But it did not come from the sea: the convoy was still hidden under the reeking front that here, as in so many other instances, the Japanese seemed able to command at will. Instead, the first blow came from the air. On the morning of the 13th, 100 transport planes, many of them Lockheed Lodestars

---

* One other, and final mission, in the last days of Java, was pulled on shipping in Makassar Strait on February 24, by six B–17s of the 7th Group; but it does not belong in this continuous series of late January and early February.

with British markings, appeared over the city and the main airfield lying north of it and spilled between 700 and 900 parachute troops. There was no air resistance worth the name.* A few British Hurricanes based there, graduates of the fighting over Singapore, had been caught on the ground and thoroughly gone over by the Japanese six days before.[9] Though the survivors went up against the paratroop planes and claimed three bombers against a loss of one of their own number,[10] most of the fighting the RAF did that day was on foot, in company with some antiaircraft troops, and headed by a lone but tough battalion of Dutch infantry. The latter had the Japs cleaned up by nightfall, but no one expected that one battalion could hold out against the troops aboard the enemy convoy.

Strangely enough, ABDACOM Headquarters in high and remote Lembang had what amounted to a play-by-play account of this small action. Air Vice Marshal Hunter, commanding the RAF at Palembang, was in constant radio-telephone communication with them, and General Brereton has recorded the cool and even humorous manner in which he kept them informed of what was happening round his base.[11] The self-possessed British voice must have cut slices from what complacency Headquarters personnel may have previously felt. The fighting became suddenly more actual than the lines on their elaborate maps.

The one hope for Palembang lay in the newly formed, combined striking force of the Allied Navy which, under the erratic Dutch Admiral Doorman, had left the south coast of Java on the 13th to intercept and, if possible, turn back the Japanese convoy. Doorman was without the cruiser *Houston* which, as we shall see, had gone eastward on other work; but he came north through Sunda Strait between Java and Sumatra with five cruisers, including the British heavy cruiser *Exeter,* four Dutch, and six American destroyers. One of the Dutch destroyers was lost when it ran hard aground and Doorman had to leave a second behind to take off the crew. But he still hoped by coming round Banka Island from the east and north to surprise the Japanese unloading at the mouth of the Moesi River.

---

* An ABDACOM message of February 14 records an attack mission against the convoy by Dutch pilots in Blenheim bombers, though it is probable that the mission actually took place on the 13th. The pilots reported the convoy north of Banka Island and counted 20 warships and 22 transports.[8]

However, Japanese reconnaissance planes had been following his movements. They picked him up again at dawn of the 15th and by mid-morning the first wave of bombers was coming over the little fleet. For several hours the ships were subjected to an almost unbroken series of attacks. They came through with no fatal hits, though two of the American destroyers were badly shaken up. But with no chance of fighter protection and with his oil bunkers running low, Doorman decided that he could not take on the Japanese surface ships, and he withdrew to Java.

This outcome of the naval sortie was so in the pattern of what had gone before that it might have been foretold by the men in ABDACOM as they listened to Hunter's account of the paratroop attack on Palembang. Certainly their reactions, if not actually despondent, were gloomy enough to impel General Brereton to give a Saturday night party, and he has recorded that everybody came to it except Admiral Hart, who had received orders to relinquish his command and return to the United States.[12] This was partly due to insistent pressure by the Dutch to have one of their own people exercise the ABDAFLOAT command, and partly to a feeling in Washington that as long as the Dutch felt that way they might as well also assume responsibility for the inevitable defeat.* Vice Admiral Helfrich, commander of all N. E. I. naval forces, was named to succeed him. But no man worth his salt finds it easy to leave his command in a dark hour, and one can understand Hart's nonappearance at the General's party.

Admiral Doorman's withdrawal left Palembang wide open to the Japanese, except for what air opposition ABDAIR could provide. That did not amount to very much, though every mission scheduled by the Bomber Command in the five days from the 14th through the 18th was against the Japanese invasion force, either off the Sumatran coast, or in the Moesi River, or at Palembang itself. Their vanguard reached the outskirts on the 15th, and by the 16th they were in full control of the city

---

* In "Roosevelt and Hopkins," Sherwood states that Hart did not feel himself the man for the job and had asked to be relieved, and he implies that Hart was one of those commanders who had to be weeded from both services before a real fighting organization could be built.[13] Judgment is outside the province of this book; but if Hart asked for relief, it seems to me more likely to have stemmed from his inability to secure co-ordinated action when it might have paid off and reluctance to stage an all-out attack when he felt the time for it was past. Morison's account has been followed here.[14]

from the two airfields to the blazing native godowns of the lower town that had caught fire from the demolition of the American oil refineries. In those two days, using shallow-draught vessels and small boats, they moved a full division up the river against the light strafing of the few remaining Hurricanes, a lone attack by our B-17s, and a low-level bombing and strafing by a detachment of the 17th Provisional Pursuit Squadron, which had flown 800 miles from its home base at Blimbing to drop its bombs. Only one other B-17 mission reached the target—six of them bombing Japanese ships off the Sumatran coast on the 15th. Nine missions, involving 55 planes, were scheduled in the five-day period: seven missions, 43 planes, failed to reach the target; two missions, eleven planes,* dropped bombs on the enemy.

This appalling record was due principally to the weather. The tropical front that had shrouded the invasion fleet spread on ahead like weeping death till it covered not only Sumatra but all of Java with its storms. Two or three planes worked through individually, but finding themselves alone or unable to locate their objective, also turned back, while four times in as many days an entire flight abandoned its mission 75 or 100 miles short of the target. The second mission that did get through, on February 16, flew the whole distance to and from the target under ceilings that were never higher than 4000 feet and were generally 2000 feet or lower. It took them five hours to get up to Banka Strait; and they were still at 2000 feet when they came in over the mouth of the river—the trailing planes still lower; and then, miraculously, the sun broke through so that the bomber crews could see the men in the barges and small boats and on the decks of two big transports turning their faces upwards as the bombs dropped away. They were flying so low that some of the Fortresses were holed by fragments of their own bombs; but after the bombing run they dropped lower still to strafe the barges and drew answering machine gun fire through their wings, though the crews were too excited watching the Japs jump in the river to be much disturbed by that. No one was wounded; all planes returned.†

* Twelve planes were scheduled but one turned back with an engine out.
† There was no interception. Some Dutch pilots in Brewsters had been over a little before drawing off what Jap pursuits there were. The B-17s didn't often enjoy such luck. They made the most of it. One transport was left sinking. Capt. R. E. Northcut led the flight.[15]

But a single strike of this sort was small hindrance to the Japanese campaign. They already had Palembang. Within a few hours their fighters were landing on Palembang I, the field that for a few brief days had been home to the British Hurricanes. These Jap planes were not Zeros but the older Series 96 fighters that wore skirts over their unretractable wheels. Six of them took off next morning to meet the American attack.

The Jap pilots probably expected to meet Fortresses; but the B–17s did not get up to Palembang again, though at 7:50 that same morning a flight of five took off from Malang and spent nearly four hours fighting weather before abandoning their mission.[16] The planes that sliced out of the misty clouds below Palembang on February 17 were eight P–40s of the 17th Squadron, led by Major Sprague, and doubling as bombers with two 20-kilo bombs in the shackles under each wing.

Nine of them had left Blimbing on the 15th, Sprague taking off for Bandoeng alone for orders, and the other eight stopping at Madioen to pick up the bombs. They met at Batavia where, landing in the cloudy twilight on an unfamiliar field, Muckley, who had already had his share of bad luck,* cracked up his plane.[17] All the men were tired from their flight the length of Java. The weather that shook up Fortress crews could really manhandle P–40s; and at Batavia there was no one to service their planes, so they had that work to do before they were free to start looking up food and quarters in a strange city. George Weller, the correspondent for *Chicago News,* has described their arrival at the blacked-out Hôtel des Indes, where the manager finally consented to get them a supper while three newspapermen scouted the bedrooms for unoccupied beds which the manager swore did not exist.[18] Otherwise the pilots would have returned to the rainy field to get what sleep they might beneath their planes. The situation was an instance of the growing demoralization of command in Java. Men were assigned a hastily conceived objective and told to get there. Except for Muckley and Egenes, all the men with Sprague were old Philippine hands—Mahony, McCallum, Coss, Kizer, Kruzel, and Hennon—but they must have had the feeling that night of suspension in a vacuum. At best, for the sake of this one pass at a town already lost, they would be away from Blimbing for three days; and there were never

* Part Two, Chapter 6, above.

enough P-40s there to cover the eastern end of Java anyway. As it turned out they were nearly four days out on the mission, for the weather on the 16th closed in Batavia completely. But they took off on the 17th at 6:30, crossing the green flat lands to Batavia's port of Tanjong Priok, with its lacing of canals, and then swinging out over the Java sea. An hour later, halfway up Banka Strait, they turned in over the Sumatran shore, and lined up the Moesi River for their course to Palembang. That was when they met the Jap pursuits.

Five of the pilots dropped their bombs as they saw the Japs come in. Mahony had already started down at the barges in the river. Kizer and Hennon also hung onto their bombs though staying in the fight with the 96s. Sprague, Kruzel, and McCallum each shot down one, and Kizer, loaded as he was with his bombs, took care of another. That was plenty for the two surviving Japs. They pulled out and the P-40s all went down on the barges together, Hennon and Kizer bombing before joining in the general strafing.[19]

It was a fine day for the 17th, and the men felt a natural elation, though here again their attack came too late to have any real effect on the Japanese advance. Perhaps the two best features of the whole episode were the safe return of all eight planes to Batavia and the fact that during their absence from Blimbing there had been no enemy activity over Eastern Java. The P-40s refueled at Batavia and then flew south across the mountains to spend that night at Bandoeng. No more American planes attacked the Japanese in Sumatra for though two B-17 missions were scheduled for the 18th—one of four planes from Madioen and one of six from Malang —neither got through the weather. Yet even without that final failure, ABDACOM realized that Java would have to be abandoned.

On the 17th with Wavell's consent Brett notified Washington that a reinforcement convoy making up in Australia for Java with 3500 Air Force troops would be diverted to India.* Earlier, on February 8, General Brereton had said in Commander's meeting that he was prepared to recommend the withdrawal of the Far East Air Force to either Burma or Australia,[21] and both Wavell and Brett had criticized him as unduly pessimistic; and partly because of Wavell's criticism and partly because

* The actual figure on sailing was 2953 officers and enlisted men.[20]

of what he described as "some honest differences" with Air Marshal Peirse,* and finally because, as he wrote in his diary, "the morale of my own air force was low and my presence was required with it," [22] he asked to be relieved of his duties as Deputy Commander-in-Chief of the ABDACOM air staff. The fall of Singapore and the loss of Sumatra at least resolved the differences between the American and British elements within the Joint Command; there were no further demands for piecemeal employment of the bomber force in support of the British army on the Malay Peninsula; the only question now was the fate of Java itself; and from Brett's message it seems clear that in British and American minds Java was already written off.

In spite of his anxiety about morale, General Brereton did not succeed in making his visit to operational bases till February 17. He came into Malang late in the afternoon of that day through very heavy weather aboard an LB–30, with Air Marshal Peirse, Colonel Eubank, and Brigadier General Patrick J. Hurley in his party. General Hurley, who had reached Bandoeng two days earlier from Australia, had been sent out from Washington on thirteen hours' notice to co-ordinate and expedite the whole program of running supplies in to the Philippines [23] and was now on his way back to Australia. He had asked Colonel Robenson, the head of the supply mission in the Netherlands Indies, to report to him at Malang, and the latter's description of the Liberator's landing gives us some idea of the conditions under which the bombers were now operating.

The rain was pouring down with visibility zero and a ceiling of certainly not more than 75 feet. It had been raining for some time and the field was a quagmire with pools of water every place; there was no paved landing strip and to make it worse, the field had been bombed several times recently and the craters had not been filled in but were marked by large posts stuck in the ground on the four corners. It was the most discouraging looking landing field I ever saw and under the worst conditions. The young pilots round me were betting even money and some were giving odds that the landing, if attempted, would be a crash. Finally we heard the motors, first faintly and then as if closer; they would fade out, then come back. This lasted, it seemed, forever —probably ten or fifteen minutes. We could see nothing but rain and clouds,

---

* Apparently over operational procedure, for Peirse concurred in Brereton's air estimate of the general situation.

close-in black clouds. Finally this huge black plane came out of a heavy cloud, straightened out, and hit the ground. It did not seem to flatten, it didn't seem to land, it just hit—and was completely hidden with the splash of mud and water. It was a few seconds before any of us could determine just what had happened. When the picture cleared, the plane was still upright and apparently everything in good order.*

On Brereton's orders, the entire Bomber Command, both officers and men, had been assembled in one of the two hangars at Singosari. Lanterns dimly lighted the rows of tired faces. A couple of battle-shabby Fortresses, whose servicing had been interrupted, waited at one end. The heavy rain, which had been gaining force all evening, fell on the arched roof with a roar as uninterrupted and insistent as a cataract. Only by an effort were the men in the front rows able to hear what the General said as, for an hour and ten minutes, he read 74 citations and made the appropriate awards in what, as his diary is careful to point out, was the first Air Force decoration ceremony since the beginning of the war.[25]

Most of the citations covered the early missions in the Philippines, though a few were for the Java fighting; and of the names Brereton called some were of men left behind and some were of the dead. For those of the living who could hear his voice, it brought home in a strange way their own inadequacies for the job in hand. The others, half deafened by the downpour on the hangar roof, could only wait for the affair to end. But when General Brereton had finished, there were still speeches by some of the officers with him—the men in the rear ranks had no way of telling who they might be—and one of these strange gentlemen stepped forward and after a moment's hesitation suddenly threw up his arms and shouted in a voice that pierced the elements, "All I can say is, *Whoopee!*" He waited, perhaps for a response, but again there was only the roar of falling rain. The men were too astonished to react and waited grimly silent till all were done and the visiting officers had filed out. They still had the planes to service and the next day's mission to prepare for.

Brereton's party went in to Malang where they were introduced to the charms and virtues of the hotel at a dinner at which General Hurley

---

* The pilot was Lt. C. B. Kelsay. Difficult as landing was with a plane full of generals in such weather, a pilot might well prefer it to taking off with a full load of bombs.[24]

played the host so successfully that, according to Brereton, he kept the table in an uproar for two hours.[26] Afterwards Hurley received Robenson's report on activities of the Philippine supply mission and learned that two ships had already left Java ports on February 12 and 13 and were even then presumably heading towards the Timor Sea on their roundabout course.* Hurley left the matter of taking off for Australia entirely to the pilot's judgment, but by 6:15 next morning they were away. Meanwhile Brereton and Air Marshal Peirse sat up into the morning hours discussing the general situation, and Brereton then learned for the first time that Wavell had already been instructed to evacuate the Indies. Later, at breakfast, he was given an estimate of morale in both bomber groups by the Senior Flight Surgeon, Major William A. Morocco, who had only arrived in Java on February 8 by submarine from Corregidor. It was a depressing report as Brereton records it:

Combat replacement crews did not exist. Reinforcing aircraft contained only skeleton navigating crews. Fatigue and combat weariness had worn men to their last ounce of resistance. Pilots returned from attacks crying with rage and frustration when a crew member was killed or when weather or mechanical failure prevented successful completion of the mission. A flight commander, a fine leader, committed suicide. Boys were on the verge of mental and physical collapse.[27]

Whether this picture was unduly black or not, it served to make Brereton "thankful that I would not be called upon to ask much more of them." [28] He left Malang immediately to make a two-hour drive through the mountains to Blimbing, where the quiet confidence of Sprague's isolated little outfit of pilots and enlisted men deeply impressed him and Air Marshal Peirse. In fact Peirse wanted to take Sprague for his own staff; but Brereton, who planned to give Sprague command of the fighter group that was to be built up at Darwin, refused.†

* We shall encounter these two ships again below, in Chapter 8.
† The group Brereton refers to was apparently the collection of provisional squadrons of which three were now represented in the 17th. They were being loosely organized under Maj. Richard A. Legg, whose exact status through this period is difficult to define. There is some discrepancy here between Brereton's account and the Squadron Diary. Brereton says that after completing his inspection Sprague returned from Soerabaja "where he had been on daylight patrol." Actually Sprague and his seven pilots did not return from Bandoeng and the Palembang mission till nearly noon—of them all, according to the Squadron Diary,

February 18 proved to be another red letter day in the annals of the 17th Squadron. Sprague and the other eight pilots had not yet returned from the Palembang mission, so when at 11:15 they were alerted, Blanton led the rest of the Squadron into action. They had the incredible good luck to catch nine heavy bombers coming in on Java unescorted; as far as anyone knew, it was the first time the Japanese fighters had ever missed their assignment. By the time the fighters did arrive with the second wave of bombers, the sky over Soerabaja had been turned into a rat race of Jap bombers twisting frantically to escape or plunging earthward with characteristic streamers of black smoke.* As soon as they sighted the second formation with the Zeros over them, the twelve P-40s, now augmented by the newly arrived Mahony, whom only death ever successfully grounded in the face of action, turned on the new game. It was a fine fight till the Japs turned home. General Brereton, who had reached Soerabaja by then, watched it from the Interceptor Control Room, as did thousands of jubilant Dutch and Javanese in the streets. The 17th lost one plane.† Against the loss they put in a modest claim of four heavy bombers and one Zero; but the Dutch counted at least nine bombers surely killed.[30]

They never had such luck again, though next day six P-40s encountered six Zeros and in probably the sharpest dog fight of the Squadron's career shot down four Japs against the loss of three of their own planes and one pilot, Quanah P. Fields, the full-blooded Indian, machine-gunned as he hung in his chute.‡ That was February 19, the day on which the Japanese closed the eastern arm of their pincers, severed the ferry route for good, and sealed the fate of Java.

only Mahony reached Blimbing in time to get in on the scrap with the nine Japanese bombers, mentioned below, for which they took off at 11:15 A.M.[29]

* Unlike the Zero, which one incendiary bullet could turn into a ball of fire, the Jap bomber seldom burst immediately into flames but left a trail of oily smoke almost the whole way to the ground. WELLER (Fighters), and others.

† Lt. Morris C. Caldwell, who bailed out successfully, after shooting up two bombers, as his own plane dived to the ground.

‡ The Jap pilots had pursued their game with unusual savagery, and McAfee, who had to identify him, records the dreadful appearance of his body.[31]

8. *The 19th of February*

IN THEIR MOVES against the eastern flank, the Japanese had two primary objectives. They wanted Bali as an offensive air base for their final assault on Java, and they were determined to cut off all further fighter reinforcements from Australia. To insure the last they planned not only to get control of Timor, with its vital staging field at Koepang, but if possible to eliminate Darwin as a useful base. They used two occupation forces that sailed, one from Ambon on the 17th against Timor, and the other from Makassar on the 18th against Bali; and in addition they had the same striking force of four carriers supported by two battleships and three heavy cruisers that had earlier covered the attack on Ambon, and still earlier on January 23 had taken part in the reduction of Rabaul.* Though they were to achieve local surprise at both Bali and Darwin, the Japanese were not depending on it; and there was no surprise in the strategic pattern of their attack. Indeed for several days past ABDACOM had had a very clear idea of what was coming.† They simply did not have the force to meet it, and here again, as in so many previous instances, what force they did have was largely vitiated by the piecemeal manner in which it was employed.

As early as mid-January, messages from General Brett began to reflect ABDACOM's concern over the problem of reinforcing Timor; ‡ but finding the necessary troops, let alone the contemplated full squadron of P-40s, proved harassingly difficult. The Australians were more interested in building up strength at Darwin than in providing troops for outlying Dutch possessions;³ they had become increasingly preoccupied with the threat to New Guinea and their northeastern coastline; and in any case their stock of military man power was running dangerously thin. Not till February 4 could Brett complete arrangements to send a battalion of

---

* Morison points out that this was the most powerful striking force the Japanese had used on a single mission since the attack on Pearl Harbor, in which all nine ships had participated.¹

† FEAF Intelligence forecast to the day the first Japanese landing on Java.²

‡ See above, Part Two, Chapter 3.

Australian infantry from Darwin, together with a light antiaircraft battery and most of the American 147th and 148th Field Artillery.* These troops were embarked on two Australian ships, *Portmar* and *Tulagi,* and the American transports *Meigs* and *Mauna Loa,* with two Australian corvettes, the destroyer *Peary,* and the cruiser *Houston* as escort. It was this duty that had taken the latter eastward at the time that Admiral Doorman led the Allied fleet against the Japanese off Sumatra.

In spite of the urgent need of haste, the convoy was still further delayed while the various commands strove to supply fighter protection that, except for one lone plane, was never to materialize. On February 12, when the convoy was making up, there were two P-40s in commission at Darwin. They had been left behind with engine trouble when the 3rd Pursuit Squadron departed for Java, and with their pilots, 1st Lieutenant Robert J. Buel and 2nd Lieutenant Robert G. Oestreicher, these two planes provided all the fighter force there was in Northern Australia. The two last squadrons of the provisional group preparing at Brisbane, their training cut short, had been assigned to India on February 9, with orders to load aboard the tender *Langley* at Fremantle. They were already on their way when, on the 12th, General Barnes, of USAFIA, received a message from General Brett that it was "Essential you have squadron P-40s at Darwin for operation and convoy to Koepang by 13-14 February." [4] Then, only a little later in the day, the orders to load 32 P-40s aboard the *Langley* were repeated with the provision that two P-40 squadrons be assigned to cover the Koepang convoy.

In the confusion thus engendered, General Barnes first replied that 16 P-40s were already at Darwin, but later corrected himself to give the proper total of two P-40s. Considering the fact that the only two activated squadrons had been committed to the India convoy and were actually in transit, it is difficult to see how USAFIA could possibly have delivered two squadrons to Darwin in time to cover the convoy.† The best solution of the moment was to divert 15 P-40s of the 33rd Squadron which had just arrived at Port Pirie in their flight across the continent; and orders

---

* It will be recalled that the "147th Field Artillery" was actually only the 2nd Battalion of the 147th, and the "148th" was only its own 1st Battalion.

† The 49th Pursuit Group had reached Melbourne February 1 aboard the *Mariposa,* but they could not be called on since they were still in process of assembling their planes and organizing training at various scattered small Australian stations.

were therefore sent Major Pell, the Squadron commander, to start north immediately. But he still had the continent to cross, only now it was from south to north, and there was small likelihood of his reaching Darwin within the specified time. Pilot inexperience and lack of facilities on the long, forced flight took their inevitable toll; he had ten planes left when he came into the RAAF field at Darwin late on the 15th to find that he was too late and the convoy already gone.

The eight ships had slipped out of the harbor a few minutes past midnight that same day. Black darkness covered their going, for it was the night of the new moon, and hardly a soul in the bleak outpost community was aware of their departure. Yet before noon the Japanese were on their trail.

A heavy four-engined flying boat picked them up * and for nearly an hour shadowed them, lazily circling at high altitude and keeping beyond range of their guns. Everyone aboard the convoy felt that its presence heralded a bomber attack, and Captain Rooks of the *Houston,* believing that it might come at any time, radioed Darwin for fighter cover. His call was answered by a single plane.

When the message reached the RAAF field, Lieutenant Buel's P-40 was the only fighter on the strip. Pell had not yet come in with the 33rd Squadron, and Oestreicher was out on patrol. There was no chance of reaching the latter—whether because he was beyond the short reception range of the P-40 radio or whether as Wheless, the Operations Officer, stated, because his plane had no radio at all. Wheless at Legaspi had had his own experience of piloting a single plane against an overwhelming enemy force,† but he felt a grim obligation to send what air cover he had to the convoy's assistance; and Buel, without questioning his orders, took off alone.

When he reached the convoy, the Japanese flying boat had just begun a bombing run on the *Houston,* but either because the crew had sighted the lone P-40 or because they found the cruiser's antiaircraft fire too hot and close for comfort, they dropped their bombs well short and turned

---

* Accounts vary: one (*The Java Sea Campaign*) says there were two Jap seaplanes. I have here followed Morison's version, which does acknowledge the arrival of this fighter cover.[5]

† See above, Part One, Chapter 22.

for home. Buel's plane was seen leaving at the same time, but he never returned to Darwin. He was not heard of again.*

Though the expected air attack did not materialize that day and the convoy kept on its course throughout the following night without interference, no one nursed any illusions that the Japanese might have lost track of them. Next morning, as they approached Timor, they saw the paradelike formation high in the clouds to the north. There were 46 planes in all, 36 land bombers and ten seaplanes. The convoy scattered immediately, while the *Houston,* weaving in and out among the other ships, threw up such a curtain of fire that only the last wave of planes worked close enough to do any damage, and that was not serious.† But though the enemy had been beaten off, the situation of the convoy was still precarious, especially because the enemy's carrier force was believed to be operating somewhere in the vicinity of Ambon; [6] and after the ships had made a few more hours of cautious progress towards Timor, ABDA-COM decided that the reinforcement attempt would have to be abandoned and Captain Rooks was directed to bring his convoy back to Darwin.

They arrived on the 18th to find the harbor so crowded with shipping, some of which had come in since their own departure three days earlier, that there was dock room for only two of the transports at a time. The *Meigs* and the *Mauna Loa* therefore moved in to disembark their troops, leaving the *Portmar* and *Tulagi* anchored offshore to await their turn. Meanwhile the *Houston* and the *Peary* refueled with all speed and immediately headed westward for Tjilatjap under orders to join Admiral Doorman, who even then was preparing his move to meet the expected Japanese attack on Bali. But just outside the harbor the *Peary* spotted an enemy submarine and became involved in an action so prolonged that she had to return to the port to refresh her bunkers. This was the penultimate incident in the long series of misfortunes that had dogged the destroyer since her collision with the *Pillsbury* two months before the

---

* The assumption was that Buel pursued the enemy beyond his fuel radius and went down in the Timor Sea. Two years later, on October 17, he was awarded the Purple Heart, his only decoration for this only combat mission. It is interesting to compare this acknowledgment of heroism with another mission towards Timor, to be later described.

† Two men aboard *Mauna Loa* were wounded from a near-miss, and all four transports were slightly leaking. The *Houston* had recently added to her antiaircraft armament, and during all this early Southwest Pacific fighting she seems to have been the only ship with an effective record against attacking aircraft. In this action she supposedly got seven planes.

war * and she was still in Darwin next morning when the Japanese planes came over.[7]

When the 33rd Squadron landed at the RAAF field on the 15th, their P-40s needed so much maintenance after their long flight † that Pell reported it would take 72 hours to put eight of them back in combat commission.[9] Nevertheless, and tired as the men were, he and two other pilots took off that afternoon on a three-plane reconnaissance in search of the convoy. They sighted it about 4:00 o'clock.[10] By then, of course, both Buel and the Japanese flying boat had long since disappeared and the eight ships were steaming in formation steadily towards Timor.

The next three days were spent in maintenance on the planes, training, and patrol flights in which Oestreicher, who had been picked up by the Squadron, took part. Then at pilots' meeting on the 18th, Pell informed them that they had been ordered to Java [11] and scheduled their take-off for dawn of the 19th. It was in some ways a surprising decision, for, putting aside entirely the fact that the Squadron's departure would leave Darwin with no air cover of any sort, ABDACOM was already aware that the Japanese occupation force at Makassar had weighed anchor for Bali [12] and for three days past the island had been under such continual air bombardment [13] that, even if they beat the Japanese to the airfield, staging their P-40s through the islands successfully would call for Providential intercession. Nothing (unless it were Buel's lone sortie in support of the convoy, about which Bandoeng naturally knew nothing) could better illustrate the desperate expedients to which the top command was now reduced.

No Intelligence worth the name existed at Darwin,‡ and consequently no real information on the situation developing along the ferry route was

* In devotion, imaginativeness, and in actual services to the squadrons themselves, as well as in persistent misfortune, the *Peary's* brief war record bears a curious kinship to that of the pursuit squadrons. Readers wishing to refresh their recollection can find brief references to the ship's career above in Part One, Chapter 9 (just over note 3), Chapter 18 (following footnoted paragraph referring to note 11), and Part Two, Chapter 3 (footnote referring to note 16), and Chapter 4 (note 26).

† The maintenance crews did not reach Darwin till afternoon of the 16th.[8]

‡ Darwin was to remain more or less isolated from all the rest of the Southwest Pacific battlefronts, and, even when the higher command began furnishing Intelligence information somewhat later, it arrived too late to be of any tactical value and units operating there

available to the 33rd Squadron. To make matters even more obscure, radio contact with Koepang, always unreliable, failed completely that morning. Then, to add to the uncertainties of the flight, a coolant leak in Pell's plane delayed their dawn take-off for, knowing the critical need for every possible fighter, they spent several fruitless hours in efforts to repair it. Finally Pell took over another plane, telling the pilot to get himself to Brisbane as best he could and join another squadron; * and at 9:15 they at last took off behind a B-17E that had been assigned to lead them to Java.†

Less than twenty minutes after they had left, Operations picked up a message from Koepang reporting a 600-foot ceiling and the weather closing down. This was relayed to Major Pell through the bomber's radio, with advice from Captain Connelly,‡ of the Allied Combined Headquarters, that the Squadron return to Darwin.[16] Though the decision was still Pell's to make, he followed the suggestion, undoubtedly because of the inexperience of his pilots. As I have said, their training had been cut short, and except Oestreicher, none had more than 20 hours' flying time in pursuit planes—a few had even less. They dipped their wings and turned back, letting the B-17 go on its way alone; and it was just as well they did, for when the Fortress went in to land at Den Pasar Field on Bali, the enemy were already established there, and if the Jap gunners had not opened fire just as the ship approached the runway with flaps down and wheels lowered, the pilot would have taxied it right into their hands. By giving it full throttle he pulled the bomber out with only a few bullet holes and one man shot in the foot as souvenirs of the Intelligence briefing he had received; [17] but the P-40s, with gas running out, would have had no place to go.

As the 33rd Squadron cut back over Darwin, Pell took his own flight

---

even as late as 1943 had to depend on their own efforts for Intelligence, most of their information coming from units that had operated in the Philippines or Java.[14]

* The pilot was 2nd Lt. Robert H. Vaught.[15]

† It seems probable that this was Lt. Clarence E. McPherson's plane, the only B-17 flight from Darwin to Java, as far I know, that day, though it is hard to reconcile his arrival at Malang at 5:55 P.M. with the 9:15 A.M. take-off, unless he was kept out of the field for ARP.

‡ This was Louis J. Connelly of the Philippine Air Lines, already encountered in Part One, Chapter 19, and Part Two, Chapter 4, and who, besides many flights out over the islands, appears to have run operations at Darwin with Wheless.

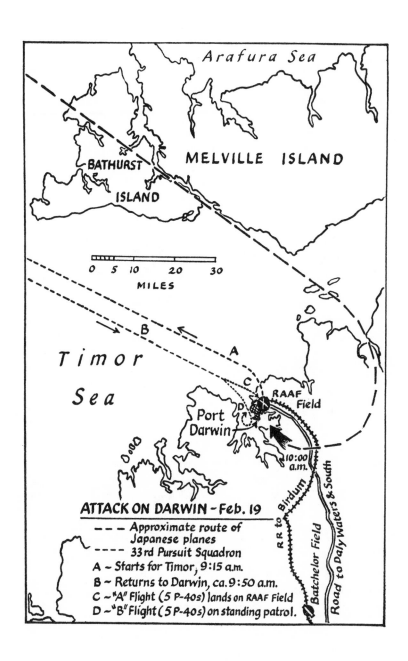

Arafura Sea

MELVILLE ISLAND

BATHURST
ISLAND

0   5 10   20   30
MILES

B

A

Timor

Sea

C

D

RAAF
Field

Port
Darwin

10:00
a.m.

ATTACK ON DARWIN – Feb. 19

— — Approximate route of
        Japanese planes
- - - - 33rd Pursuit Squadron
A ~ Starts for Timor, 9:15 a.m.
B ~ Returns to Darwin, ca. 9:50 a.m.
C ~ "A" Flight (5 P-40s) lands on RAAF Field
D ~ "B" Flight (5 P-40s) on standing patrol.

RR to Birdum

Batchelor Field

Road to Daly Waters & South

of five down to land, ordering the other five planes to patrol for two hours at 15,000 feet. It was a blue day with a fresh breeze blowing and some scattered clouds moving up in the southwest. Every detail of the port, the shipping, the streets of little flimsy houses, and the airfield stood out in the clear sunlight, and after the open sea it must have had a reassuring look to the returned pilots, as they started their slow climb to patrol altitude. They were flying two two-plane elements with Oestreicher as weaver above them; they were taking it easy, perhaps watching the first flight go in to the field, running out one after another on the runway, and taxiing to the hangar. When all were on the line, it was just a little before 10:00 o'clock,* and the patrol, swinging wide across the bay, had reached about 8000 feet. Something then made Oestreicher look upward over his left shoulder at the instant the first Jap plane peeled out 2000 feet above them. Recognizing the red Rising Sun emblems on the wings he shouted, "Zeros, Zeros, Zeros," into his radio and with the others dived away, dropping his belly tank as he went.[21]

The overwhelming surprise of the attack scattered the patrol so thoroughly that it never succeeded in forming again. 2nd Lieutenants Jack R. Peres and Elton S. Perry, who had been flying the lead element, were shot down out of hand and plunged into the bay. 2nd Lieutenant William R. Walker, with a bullet through his shoulder, managed to get back to the air strip and jump clear of his plane before it was shot up on the ground and burned to a cinder. 2nd Lieutenant Max R. Wiecks had to bail out. He landed ten miles out in the bay and did not make shore till after dark. Of the five, only Oestreicher fought his way clear and then, finding himself alone among the Japs, flew south into the clouds, from which a little later he ambushed two dive bombers, shooting one down.†

On the field there had been no warning, for Darwin had no radar units.‡ Major Pell was sitting with Wheless in the shade of a plane with

---

* As in the case of Clark Field time given for the first attack varies a good deal, from 9:30 [18] to 10:05, when Oestreicher reports seeing the first Zero.[19] 2nd Lt. Max R. Wiecks, who was shot down into the sea, had his watch stop at 9:55 and believes that that was when he hit the water. He had been in action about fifteen minutes; but damage to his plane may have stopped the watch. Ryan, who made a detailed study in Australia for the Air Evaluation Board, fixes it at 9:58.[20]

† Peres and Perry were killed. The others survived.[22]

‡ Col. Ryan says the first radar set was used "from about February 14, 1942";[23] but Wheless says definitely there was no radar then. A report that enemy planes were ap-

its radio turned on. But their moment of quiet was abruptly shattered by the crackle of Oestreicher's voice coming in on the receiver over their heads with his repeated shout of "Zeros!" Looking up, they saw the parade of Japanese planes approaching from the southeast.

There were more than 100 of them: * the heavy bombers on top, 18 in the first wave, bright and shining silver in the hot bright sky, with red suns and bursts of red and gold rays on their wings, were already turning with a kind of high disdain towards the dock area; farther down were 18 dive bombers, dull green planes with single engines; and heading straight for the field was a flight of 30 Zeros. After one glance, Pell started on the run for his plane, yelling to the mechanics to get the belly tanks off, but before the first P-40 could taxi out on the runway, the strafing planes were swarming all over them, and it was obvious that even if they did get into the air they wouldn't stand a chance. In spite of that, Pell

proaching Bathurst Island, 50 miles to the north, is supposed to have come in some time before, but immediately on receipt the frequency was jammed and no further information could be obtained. This story is apparently based mainly on a message from General Barnes, Melbourne, to TAG, February 22; [24] but I can find no indication that this message reached Operations, and certainly Wheless's account makes it seem very unlikely that even a rumor of hostile planes could have reached Maj. Pell. Nor does Oestreicher's report make any mention of this message.

* It is impossible to determine the exact number of planes sent over Darwin by the Japanese on February 19; and the figures given here are merely the author's best guess. No two sources agree. For instance, Morison mentions 18 heavy bombers in the first wave and then records a second wave of 18; [25] but *The Java Sea Campaign* says there were 72 bombers in all, plus 18 dive bombers, and these figures were accepted by Karig and Kelley. [26] According to the official Air Force history, there were "more than 50 bombers escorted by fighters," and this account then mentions a second attack two hours later by another equally large formation, [27] which Naval sources seem to consider part of the first raid. Col. Ryan believes there were 27 bombers in each of the two attacks, the second force being without fighter escort; [28] but his version does not agree with other sources such as Lt. Wiecks, floating in his Mae West out in the bay with plenty of leisure to count, who saw over 50 heavy bombers in a single formation. In other major attacks the Japs had shown a partiality for using 54 heavy bombers, and 54 seems the number they were most likely to have dispatched from Ambon (as indicated by Morison), though whether the second raid was by a second force of 54 or the first force returning after the dive bombers and fighters had cleaned up is uncertain. A few may have failed to reach the target. There is confirmatory evidence for 54 heavy bombers or more in the *Diary of Air Raids on Darwin* kept by Lt. J. R. Fabrie, F.A. He lists a total of 71 bombers on the first raid and 54 for the second. However, his count is 18 fighters in the first raid, where Wheless, the citations for Wiecks and others, and the *Statistical Summary of AAF in the Philippines and NEI* list 30-36 fighters. The only certain points are that the dive bombers numbered 18 and that the second raid was made by more than 50 high-level bombers without escort.

tried to make it, and one after another his four green pilots followed him.

Four of the five P-40s got off the ground. 2nd Lieutenant Charles W. Hughes, next behind Pell, was shot up as he made his run and crashed on the field, dead in his plane. With three Zeros on his tail, Pell himself worked only as high as 80 feet before his plane burst into flames. He bailed out, his chute barely opening before he hit the ground. For a minute he did not move, and it seemed that he must have been killed by the impact of his drop. Then he started slowly and painfully to crawl away. An Australian soldier leaped from a foxhole to help him, but the Jap pilots, who had seen him move, got to him first, strafing him as he crawled, and when they were finished with him Pell was past helping.

2nd Lieutenant Robert F. McMahon reached nearly 600 feet before a looping Zero clamped on his tail and shot him down. He was lucky enough to bail out and reach the ground with nothing more than an injured leg. 2nd Lieutenants Burt H. Rice and John G. Glover did better yet. The last to make their runs, they swung sharp to the left immediately after take-off and Rice, by alternately diving and zooming, shook off the Zeros and climbed to 5000 feet. Then as he made a sharp turn to get onto the leading Jap, he discovered that his controls were useless; his plane went into a spin, and he bailed out. In doing so he struck his forehead and was blinded.* As he hung in his chute, at first unconscious and then, after he had recovered consciousness, wholly unable to see, two of the Japanese pilots started gunning for him, circling his chute and coming in on him in turn. They would surely have killed him had it not been for Glover.

A moment after being airborne, Glover had the luck to catch one of the Zeros trailing Rice in his sights. He shot it down † and at the same time shook off his own pursuers. He was gaining altitude fast when he caught sight of the Japs circling Rice and without an instant's hesitation abandoned his own climb to cut in on their party by circling the chute in a tighter circle than theirs. In competition with the faster and more maneuverable Zeros, this was virtual suicide and almost all of the men on the airfield watched from their foxholes to see what would happen in spite

* Fortunately not permanently, though it was months before he regained his sight.

† As stated by Wiecks and also indicated in the second Wheless interview, but I do not know whether it was officially confirmed.

of the continual strafing kept up by the Zeros. At 3000 feet they saw Glover's plane suddenly drop off in a steep dive and then plummet for the earth. They thought he was done for, but at the last instant his ship leveled off, hit the edge of the field, toppled over and over in a cartwheel, and smashed into bits. Then, as the dust settled, Glover crawled out of the wreckage, got up, and walked off. After a few steps, he sat down on the runway and put his face in his hands. An Australian then ran out and pulled him to safety, just ahead of the strafers. He had to be taken to a hospital later, but he had saved Rice's life.* There was no further interception at Darwin. When Oestreicher came in at 11:45 to refuel and rearm his plane and change a damaged wheel, the first raid was over and he was just in time to be caught on the ground by the second.[29]

With no air opposition to trouble them, the Japanese bombardiers could be as deliberate as they chose, and their work showed the same precision that had marked the attacks on Clark Field and Pearl Harbor.† The surprise was equally complete, for the first bombs fell while the opening wails of the sirens still sounded. As the clerks and office workers who had been caught at their desks ran out into the streets, three vessels that were unloading at one of the two piers—an oil barge, a troopship carrying ammunition, and a British freighter with depth charges in her hold—all blew up together in a single, terrific, flashing explosion that rocked the whole Darwin area, starting the panic that was to empty the town.

Smaller explosions followed one after another as the pattern of the bombs moved across the docks and two more ships were hit. Then, while the high-level bombers circled lazily, waiting for their targets to clear again, the Jap dive bombers took over. Some concentrated their efforts entirely on the merchant shipping, but the rest went after the *Peary* and another of the old, flush-deck destroyers, *William B. Preston,* which had been converted into a tender for the PBYs.‡ Both ships had steam up and immediately got under way; but their maneuvers were hampered by the

* According to Wheless's account, Rice landed several miles away in a swamp. When he was found, hours later, he had managed to extricate himself from his chute and had plastered his whole face with mud to protect his wounds from the flies.

† As already pointed out, the carrier forces involved had taken part in the attack on Pearl Harbor.

‡ The *William B. Preston*, it may be recalled, was the tender stationed in Davao Gulf at the start of the war where she had undergone the first Jap bombing attack on a Navy ship in the Philippines.

close waters of the harbor, and the *Peary* also tried to throw a smoke screen round the Australian hospital ship, *Manunda*. The *Peary* took five direct hits; but though crippled and covered with flames she continued to fight back as long as the Japs came at her, her last gun being silenced only when the deck gave way beneath it. Shortly afterwards she sank, taking more than half her crew and all but one of her officers with her.[30]

The *Preston* also was hit, the blast killing several men and blowing the skipper overboard; * but her luck was better than the *Peary's* and she proved an unexpectedly tough customer for the dive bombers. Whenever one of her PBYs had become unserviceable, the crew had salvaged the .50-caliber guns and set them up on her afterdeck.[32] As a result, the Jap planes coming in low found themselves entering a hail of machine gun fire far heavier than any ship of *Preston's* class had any right to, and they soon began to treat her with a certain degree of caution. She was still afloat at the end of the raid, scarred, but able to make her own way down the long northwest coast to Broome.

Meanwhile the rest of the dive bombers, joined by some of the Zeros, had had their way with the merchant shipping and the harbor was a shambles of sunk, beached, and burning ships. Besides the *Peary* and the three vessels destroyed in the opening blast, five more ships were on the bottom and nine others damaged, three of them seriously.† But this was only part of the havoc raised by the Japanese squadrons. Three of the *Preston's* PBYs, caught on the water, were lost; one of the two piers was demolished; and when they had done with the harbor, the Jap planes turned their attention to the town and roared up and down the streets strafing everything they saw, houses, public buildings, people, dogs. In all, 243 people were killed and more than 300 injured.[34] But even the departure of the strafers did not mean the end of it, for at 11:55 fifty-four heavy bombers attacked the RAAF airdrome for twenty minutes, putting one runway out of commission and leaving nothing standing except the

---

* According to Karig and Kelley, the *Preston's* skipper, Lt. Comdr. Etheridge Grant, was crossing the harbor to his ship in a small boat which was capsized by the explosion of a nearby munitions ship, and after that he watched his own ship in action while himself clinging to a buoy.[31]

† Morison lists the U. S. freighter, *Admiral Halstead*, loaded with drums of aviation gas, as sunk, thus raising the total count to ten ships lost in the harbor; but, according to *The Java Sea Campaign*, she was later brought in to the pier and her cargo unloaded.[33]

little operations building, the Officers' Quarters and Mess, and the water tower. To Captain Funk, who arrived at twilight to fly General Hurley * down to Sydney, it was the most complete job of destruction he had ever seen, and a survivor of the *Mauna Loa* described it as "like the battlefields of France; hangars, planes, everything blown to bits; burnt holes all over the field." [36]

Darwin was no longer even the bare outpost it had been. It had become a ghost town where fires burning in the darkness showed the empty windows of riddled houses and stray dogs wandered in restless search of the people who had fled. Of all the government buildings, only the Police Station and Barracks, in ironic emptiness, remained; and the whole flat coastal area, now veiled in the smoke of burning fuel dumps and emptying its terrified inhabitants southwards along the single highway, lay in the gathering twilight like the corner of a lost and forgotten world. For what reports described as an "evacuation" was in reality a panic-stricken flight in which government officials and the larger part of the Australian garrison troops vied with the civilian population. So desperate was the demand for transportation that some people were compelled to make the first part of their frantic journey in the so-called "honey carts" that daily collected refuse from the outhouses of the town.† The handful of Air Force mechanics left at the field set up a lonely camp about five miles back in the bush and then drove their trucks in town to forage. At an open army warehouse the elderly and disgusted sergeant left in charge

---

* General Hurley had come in on the 18th from Java in Kelsay's plane and, after Pell's return, Kelsay was apparently assigned to lead the 33rd Pursuit Squadron in a second attempt to reach Java. Funk had recently arrived in Brisbane with orders to lead P–40s up to Darwin (though, of course, there were no P–40s there for him to lead) when new orders reached him to fly General Hurley from Darwin to Sydney. On his way up he caught a radio message that Darwin was under attack and changed his course to Daly Waters where he waited out the raid. Meanwhile, Hurley had been in the thick of the raid, had received Oestreicher's report at 11:45, and had been wounded in the head by a bomb fragment. Kelsay's LB–30 was among the planes destroyed on the field. So Hurley motored south all the way to Daly Waters in the midst of the frantic exodus and there Funk found him the next day. [35]

† "Confusion reigned after the raid. Despite well-laid plans of December 1941, both civilian and military personnel became panicky. Orders were issued for RAAF personnel to assemble one half mile out of town on the south road and one half mile into the bush to be fed. This order was passed verbally and after repetitions became so distorted that personnel were going three, seven, even eleven miles. Some went three hundred miles southeast to Daly Waters—one even hitch-hiked all the way to Melbourne, which took him thirteen days." [37]

told them to "Hell, go ahead and help yourselves." It was the one happy moment in that grim day, for the men took him at his word and stocked so liberally that their camp gained a local reputation for the quality of its mess. But, though there were other camps scattered back from the shore, that first night brought an indescribable sense of desolation, as though mankind had lost its right to live. Funk felt it too, when he brought his big B-24 in out of the night shadows to find only Wheless and Connelly at the field.

For all this destruction the Japanese had paid with the loss of only five planes definitely shot down. Five more were claimed as probably shot down, but even counting these the total was not enough to offset the Allied loss of 22.* Yet what was in many ways the most tragic loss of

* Nine of the 33rd Squadron's ten P-40s had been destroyed, plus two more P-40s out of commission on the ground; one LB-30 (Kelsay's); six Hudsons; one Wirraway; two PBYs of Patwing Ten in the harbor and a third outside.

It was indeed a sad showing and in his account of his own success, "Way of a Fighter," Maj. Gen. Chennault uses it to demonstrate the superiority of his own tactics. "In February 1942 the Japanese threw heavy raids against Rangoon and Port Darwin, Australia, in the same week. Over Rangoon five AVG pilots in P-40s shot down 17 out of 70 enemy raiders without loss. Over Darwin 11 out of 12 U. S. Army Air Forces P-40s were shot down by a similar Japanese force. . . . It was simply a matter of tactics." [38] The last sentence is undeniably true, but in emphasizing his own and his pilots' acknowledged excellence, Chennault does not present the full truth. AVG pilots had been training since October. Chennault very wisely would not commit pilots to combat till they were fully trained, and he was in a position to adhere to this practice. Moreover, the AVG had had complete data on specifications and performance of the Zero,[39] which U. S. Air Force pilots knew nothing about till they met it in combat on December 8, though Chennault states that he had provided Military Intelligence with dossiers not only on the first model Zero in 1940 but on its predecessor, the Nate 97, a year earlier.[40] Moreover, by February the AVG had been seasoned in combat where the training of the 33rd's pilots had been terminated so prematurely that most of them, as we have seen, went into combat with 20 hours or less of fighter flying time, and through circumstances beyond their control only five (not twelve) were in the air when the Japs came over. [Chennault himself refused to accept recruits with less than 300 hours' flying time only a little later.[41]] To use these two incidents as a comparison in tactics, therefore, is not to make a comparison at all. If the AVG pilots had been thrown into combat in the first few days after their arrival in China, it is unlikely that they would have done much better, whatever their tactics.

Chennault then goes on to say that "during the first year of the war AVG tactics were spread throughout the Army and Navy by Intelligence reports and returning AVG veterans. At least one Navy commander in the Pacific and an Army Air Forces colonel with the Fifth Air Force in Australia were later decorated for 'inventing' what were originally the AVG tactics." [42] No one disputes the "invention" of their tactics by the AVG and Chennault, but certainly after the first three days of the war the hit-and-run tactics were being developed on Luzon without benefit of Intelligence reports from China and the two-plane element was adopted by George's fliers before Christmas, for Wagner, Mahony, and

all on this day of unrelieved misfortune occurred not at Darwin but some hundred miles to the north and came as a wholly fortuitous dividend to the Japanese attack. As the bomber formations on their way to the target swept in towards the Australian coast near Bathurst Island, they spotted two small cargo vessels slowly steaming northeast on separate courses. Dedicated though they were to the obliteration of Darwin, the Japs could not forego such easy prey. Both ships were hit and set afire: one sinking where she was, the other barely making the beach where, however, she burned to a shell. They were the *Florence D* and *Don Isidro,* the two ships reported by Colonel Robenson, in his interview with General Hurley, as on their way with rations and ammunition for the beleaguered forces in the Philippines. At the time of the attack they had completed the long easterly run from Java and had just turned north to cross the Arafura Sea on a course that would have carried them west of New Guinea, up the east coast of Mindanao, and round the Surigao peninsula to Gingoog Bay in the province of Misamis Orientale. Three other vessels, originating in Australian ports, made this same run successfully between February 10 and mid-March. It was a dreadful irony that brought the two ships from Java to their turning point off Bathurst Island in the very hour when the Japanese were crossing. Careful and deliberate planning to that end could not have made the meeting more exact, and to the few men who knew their mission, it brought a foreboding of the inevitable doom that faced the army on Bataan.

Meanwhile the Japanese had taken Bali. The invasion force, consisting of two transports with a light cruiser and seven or eight destroyers for escort,* slipped down through Lombok Strait on the night of February

the rest were preaching it when they got to Australia. Actually the 5th Air Force learned more from the veterans of Philippine and Java fighting than from the AVG, as Maj. Gen. Wurtsmith pointed out (see above, footnote at the end of Chapter 5, Part One). To point out that George and his pilots developed similar tactics concurrently and independently is not done here to take any luster from the wings of Maj. Gen. Chennault and his AVG, but merely to show that there were other capable people in the Army.

* Reports by bomber pilots indicated the presence of three transports, two cruisers, four or five destroyers; [43] but their total corresponds nearly with Morison's, which is based on Japanese records.[44] More or less perfunctory Air Force training in naval identification accounts for the many claims on "cruisers" at this time.

18-19, and made a landing on the southeast coast within easy distance of Den Pasar, where the Jap troops quickly seized the airfield. There was no resistance, for, though there had been ample warning of the impending Japanese move, Admiral Doorman had permitted his combined striking force to scatter after its sortie into Sumatran waters, and when word reached him on the 17th that the Japanese were about to get under way, he was unable to collect his ships in time for a combined attack that would have found him in superior strength. He could not, in fact, bring any of his ships up to oppose the landing, and the only naval effort on that vital first day was made by a lone U. S. submarine whose torpedoes missed the anchored transports. The best Doorman could offer was an attack on the night of February 19-20 in three waves, a piecemeal effort dictated more or less by the time the ships were able to reach the scene of action. By then the damage had been done and the Japanese ships had already withdrawn or were on the point of leaving.* The only inter-ference encountered by the Japanese all during the 19th was furnished by the American bombers.

When news of the landing reached the airfields in the small hours of the morning, there were 13 heavy bombers in commission: three B–17s and three LB–30s at Madioen, and seven B–17s at Malang.† In addition, the 91st Squadron had arrived at Malang the day before with their seven remaining A–24 dive bombers.[46] The possibility of attacking the Japanese on the landing beach before daylight seems to have been brought up,

* The Dutch light cruiser *Tromp* was at Soerabaja; four U. S. destroyers were refuel-ing in a Sumatran bay; the British ships were off on convoy duty; Doorman himself with two Dutch cruisers and seven Dutch and two U. S. destroyers lay in the little south coast harbor of Tjilatjap. His plan for the attack sacrificed the full force of surprise and meant that the second wave of four U. S. destroyers and the *Tromp* ran into an alerted and aroused enemy. Orders were for a fast attack with all ships piling straight through Lombok Strait and round Bali for a rendezvous in Soerabaja, a risky proceeding in itself, as was borne out by the subsequent destruction of the destroyer *Stewart* there in dry dock. The net result was a tangled action in which Doorman gave up a destroyer sunk (*Piet Hein*) and a destroyer and a cruiser (*Stewart* and *Tromp*) so badly damaged that they never fought again, for one Jap destroyer disabled. The third wave of five Dutch torpedo boats came through the narrow passage without, according to reports, seeing a thing, which, as Morison dryly puts it, was "rather curious." [45]

† *FEAF Diary* states that 4 LB–30s were in commission, but only three are mentioned in *Summary of Air Action*, which is really a digest of all official sources. However, from now till reorganization in Australia all Operations records are very incomplete. People had reached the stage of merely laughing at Operations anyway, if they laughed at all.

but nothing was done about it; * the first planes took off at 5:00 o'clock.

Practically everything went wrong with this mission. The three planes made a long approach from the east of Bali that brought them over the target, less than 200 miles from base, more than two hours after take-off; they had become separated in heavy weather over Lombok Island and were therefore forced to attack individually; two of the planes had their bombs hang on the first run; clouds hid the target for both on their second runs, but even so the crew of one plane knew they had missed; the other plane held its bombs on this run and on a third and then on a fourth run jettisoned them when two Zeros came up to attack. Only the third plane claimed a hit on what the men mistook for a cruiser.[48]

The second mission of four planes, taking off an hour later, never dropped a bomb. Two Zeros and two "97s" attacked them before they reached the target and they turned back, after shooting down one Zero, and flew up and down off the south coast of Java till two in the afternoon. The next effort, by the three LB-30s from Madioen, was no more success-ful. Nine Zeros pounced on them while they were still at only 3000 feet; they managed to shoot down two of their harassers and shake off the rest, but they had absorbed so much punishment that they also abandoned the mission and landed two hours later at Jogjakarta. At 8:00 o'clock, two of the three B-17s at Madioen took off. These two bombed the Japanese ships, one claiming a hit on the "cruiser." Two Zeros then made a single head-on pass at them, which fortunately did no damage, and the bombers returned to South Java where they joined the other four B-17s already beating up and down the coast.

This was made necessary by the air sweeps the Japanese had now thrown over Eastern Java. Both bomber fields had already come under attack. There was nothing to stop the enemy, for the 17th Pursuit Squad-ron already had their hands full trying to clean the air over Soerabaja and lost three planes and a pilot in the process. On this day also the Japanese, operating from Sumatra, brought the western half of Java under attack, formations of 30 planes making separate strafing raids on the airdromes at Buitenzorg and Bandoeng, where, besides more than a dozen Dutch

---

* "General HQ had called at 2:00 A.M. saying they were landing that night on South Bali preparatory to taking the airport there. They wanted the 19th Group to bomb the landing lights. Why we didn't I'll never know." [47]

planes, they destroyed two out of three B–17Es that had just reached Bandoeng by the African ferry route.* But the very raids that kept the B–17s from returning to Malang and Madioen were responsible for the two most effective missions flown that day. Both were entirely impromptu, and in each case the planes involved had been ordered off their fields merely as an air raid precaution. Once in the air, however, the pilots took matters into their own hands.

The first was flown from Madioen by Lieutenant Kenneth D. Casper. His B–17 was one of three scheduled for the 8:00 o'clock mission, but it lost an engine during run-up, and it did not take off with the other two. It was still on the field when the first air raid alarm sounded at 12:30. There was no time to take the bombs out of it; the only thing to do was to get the plane in the air and clear of the field. Casper piled in with his crew and took off almost in the face of the incoming raiders † and headed south for the usual beat up and down off the Java coast. But the plane seemed to handle pretty well; it still had its bombs; and Casper began to think what a waste it was just to lug them around over the Indian Ocean; and after a minute he turned the plane's nose towards Bali and started climbing.

They were at nearly 28,000 feet when about two hours later they came over the target area. There was some turbulence; the sky around them was studded with big thunderheads; and the destroyer, when they spotted it, looked like a splinter on the sea. The bombing run was difficult, for the plane had to be maneuvered round the stormy clouds, but the bombardier, a big, taciturn 2nd lieutenant of Swedish extraction named Erling J. Nossum, refused to be ruffled and laid all eight of his 660-pound bombs alongside the ship. To the Fortress crew she seemed to lift almost clear of the sea with a welter of white water; and they thought they saw her turn over. They were convinced they had sunk her; but whether they had or not it was a remarkable piece of bombing; and even if the destroyer had survived,‡ the experience could have done her no good.[50]

---

* The Dutch lost two transport planes and four Hudsons on the ground at Buitenzorg; and one Hudson and several trainers on the ground at Bandoeng. The five Brewsters with which the Dutch tried to protect Bandoeng were all shot down.[49]

† McTague, the 9th Squadron's Assistant Engineer, says that Casper took off with three engines.

‡ Jap sources, however, list no ships sunk by enemy air action on the 19th.

At Malang it was the A-24s. Since dawn they had been waiting in front of their revetments while the two B-17 missions went out, and then the crews had watched the three Forts of the first mission return, bomb up, and take off again for another attack that proved even less effective than the first.* Backus was with Eubank, figuring out a mission they could pull against the ships at Bali. There wasn't any bomb-handling equipment for A-24s so, though the men later improvised a hydraulic hoist, that morning they had had to load the 500-pound bombs by hand. Five of the planes stood along the western border of the field, but the first two to be loaded, piloted by Captain Harry L. Galusha and Lieutenant Julius B. Summers,† were alone on the far side when at 12:45 the air raid warning sounded. Operations ordered the dive bombers back into their revetments; but in the confusion someone told Galusha and Summers to take off and fly around south of the field for the next hours. They took off at once and obediently turned south; and then back at the field the men in the control tower ‡ overhead the two pilots discussing their situation. "Shall we go over Bali way and see what we can see?" asked Galusha. Summers answered, "You're the man with the wife and kids—let's go." [52]

They went, and their luck rode with them. For they found two layers of stratus clouds at 10,000 and 11,000 feet, which concealed them all the way over to Bali. As they neared Den Pasar, the lower layer thinned away to show them, as if in a frame, a transport lying close inshore and a destroyer farther out on the narrow blue ribbon of the strait—though like the B-17 crews they also thought it was a cruiser. Galusha took the transport, Summers the destroyer, and they peeled off at 11,000 and went

---

* One dropped out and returned to Malang. The other two bombed from 27,000 feet, getting a near-miss on a destroyer.[51]

† Their gunners were T/Sgt. H. A. Hartmann and Pvt. D. S. Mackay.

‡ Lt. Stancill M. Nanney, who had come out of Del Monte in the Funk and Wade evacuation flight, was in charge of communications at Singosari and has graphically described their setup. When he reached Malang there was no control tower and Combs needed one, so Nanney and T/Sgt. R. W. Stephens took a panel truck and installed a communications command set with a CW transmitter. This made a mobile tower and in an alert it was their job to get out to the end of the runway and clear the planes and then clear off themselves for the woods. They had a permanent antenna rigged in the woods and when they had high-tailed it there, they would hook up to the antenna and could then monitor the planes, listen in on the pilots, and after the All Clear had sounded, they would go back to the field and call the planes in to land. They called it the "Mobile Control Tower." It worked so well that a similar outfit was used at Jogjakarta.

down together with their homemade bomb sights and released their bombs at 3000 feet. Each got a direct hit with one of his 110-pounders, a near-miss with his 660-pounder, and missed wide with the other small one. The Japs were evidently caught completely off guard, for the ackack was light and the only damage a small shrapnel hole in Galusha's plane. Before the Zeros found them they were back in the clouds and heading for Malang, somewhat troubled over what the authorities would have to say, yet very conscious of having staged the first dive bomber attack in U. S. Army History.[53] They needn't have troubled themselves; for when both Jap ships were reported sunk two hours later,* the authorities said nothing at all, and both pilots were subsequently decorated.

The record for the day was 18 sorties, with four direct hits claimed and twelve near-misses. That was not enough to stop the Japanese, or even seriously to hinder them. Admiral Doorman's sweep through the strait that night, as we have seen, accomplished little more; and next day the Japs were back again with reinforcements that more than offset what little pressure the Dutch were able to bring against them on the ground. The Japanese were not interested in immediate control of the whole island; all they needed then was the airfield; and once they had it, they brought in fighters and bombers and stepped up the pace of their attack till by the 24th they were sending 54 bombers and 36 fighters over Soerabaja in a single raid.[56] Moreover, while they were operating out of Celebes and Borneo, their planes could be expected only in the hours between 9:00 A.M. and 4:00 P.M.; but now they could hit any field at any moment of the day.

To the Allied air command the Bali landing spelled the end of the air defense of Java, and at Bandoeng the machinery of evacuation was put in motion that very day. As a matter of fact, Brereton had already decided to withdraw the American Air Forces, and two days earlier had called Eubank to Headquarters and instructed him to work out a plan. On the 19th Brereton finally received authority to commandeer

---

* This erroneous report came from Navy PBYs,[54] but neither ship appears to have been sunk. The transport, *Sagami Maru,* received a hit in her engine room, either from Galusha's bomb or from one of the B–17s, that disabled one engine completely.[55]

civilian planes, and the removal of civilian employees was begun. Then at a conference with Wavell, which was also attended by General Brett, Air Marshal Peirse, and Wavell's Chief of Staff, Lieutenant General Sir Henry Pownall, he announced his decision to pull out and said that he was wiring General Marshall for instructions. This was a bitter blow to Wavell, who felt that air resistance could be effectively maintained for two weeks more; but when he realized that Brett and Peirse agreed with Brereton, he asked the latter to delay forty-eight hours longer while he himself cabled the Combined Chiefs of Staff for additional instructions, not only respecting the evacuation, but for the dissolution of ABDACOM itself.[57]

Brereton acceded to this for the moment, but next day the rush of events had, in his opinion, become too headlong to justify any further delay in terminating American air operations on Java, and he informed Wavell that he was so advising the War Department. Wavell accepted this decision on condition that the American tactical air elements remain long enough to cover the departure of other units that were to leave the island.[58]

Implementation of plans for the evacuation were immediately speeded up. This was made possible through Colonel Eubank's foresight and his early determination to provide an evacuation ship for his ground echelons. It had not been easy to find one, but finally through the enterprise and persistence of Lieutenant Kurtz, who had been posted by Eubank as an Air Force liaison officer in Soerabaja, a 12,000-ton freighter of Dutch registry had been secured. The bulk of General Headquarters personnel were now assigned for evacuation on this ship also. She was ordered to wait in Tjilatjap, the only Java port not regularly open to Japanese air attack. At the same time, all Ferry Command deliveries of heavy bombers were halted,[59] and before the day was over Brett was able to report to Marshall:

Have laid all plans concerning evacuation and will make all effort to salvage everything possible. As Australia will be taken care of, the mass of all troops are being sent to India by me. . . .*

* The rest of this message was devoted to a recommendation that in the future U. S. officers be placed at the head of theater command, and Brett then went on to imply that

The "mass of all troops" referred to included the convoy, originally destined to reinforce Java, that had already been diverted to India and in two days would put out from Fremantle, bound for Bombay.* Besides the 59 P-40s aboard the *Langley* and *Seawitch,* there were ten others in the holds of the three transports. On the 21st Brett cabled that he was planning to divert enough more P-39s and P-40s from Australia, and from a convoy then on its way out, to bring the total fighter consignment for India to 160 planes; and though this would have bled Australian fighter strength perilously thin, he felt that it left "sufficient there to meet current needs. . . ." [60]

Actually both he and Brereton had become convinced that the only road to victory over Japan lay through Burma and China, and from their point of view in the midst of defeat—the second for Brereton in a matter of weeks—it is easy to see why they thought so. Brereton expressed it simply when he wrote in his diary that his "desire for some time had been to give the Japs territory and get back where we could reorganize the striking forces." [61] The instinct to find ample territory for maneuvering, instead of bases pin-pointed on islands where they could be easily outflanked, must have been overpowering. Brett, on the other hand, had approached the Southwest Pacific theater through India and China, and while he had had undoubted difficulties with British red tape, his sympathies were strongly British. Moreover, thinking as airmen, the two had seen most of their bomber reinforcements arrive through Africa and India. Finally there was the failure of the Navy in the Pacific which, combined with their own poverty in matériel and troops, must in their minds have ruled out the practicability of a campaign round the eastern perimeter of the Indies such as MacArthur and Kenney were to embark on only six months later, if indeed they considered it at all.† However, Brett recommended building up military strength in Australia and

---

"tenacious adherence to age-old custom . . ." (as quoted previously in Part Two, Chapter 3, above) was responsible for ABDACOM's weak showing, as indeed in part it was.

* See above, Part Two, Chapters 6 and 7. Besides the *Langley* and *Seawitch,* the convoy included the *Holbrook, Duntroon, Katoomba,* and the U. S. cruiser *Phoenix* as escort.

† Even today there are arguments on the wisdom of an approach through China (as *vide* Chennault), but it seems to me to show an almost flighty disregard of logistics as well as of the amazing U. S. Naval recovery—though the last of course would have been hard to foresee in Java on February 23, 1942.

planned to go there himself briefly after leaving Java, while Brereton proceeded directly to India.*

Brereton's instructions from General Marshall were to take out his own Headquarters "in such manner, at such a time, and to such a place within or without the ABDA area" as he should decide on; [63] but American troops with arms were to stand by the Dutch:

All men of fighting units for whom there are arms must continue to fight without thought of evacuation, but air forces which can more usefully operate in battle from bases outside Java and all air personnel for whom there are no aircraft and such troops particularly technicians as cannot contribute to defense of Java should be withdrawn.

With respect to personnel who cannot contribute to defense, general policy should be to withdraw U. S. and Australian personnel to Australia.[64]

Though this message, received on the 22nd of February, gave Brereton complete latitude as to his own movements, its sense would seem to indicate the War Department's purpose to transfer the major effort to Australia; and on the same day General Arnold wired Brett:

Believe it very important that on account of your shortage of experienced personnel Brereton remain with you and not repeat not go to Burma. The Burma situation will be handled from this end.[65]

The last sentence was clarified later in the day by another message which stated that the 10th Air Force would be established in India under the command of Colonel Caleb V. Haynes and would be under the direction of Major General Joseph W. Stilwell.[66] In still another message, Brett was informed that after his release by Wavell he himself should proceed to Australia where further orders would be waiting for him.[67]

It is difficult at this date to determine the order in which these messages were received at Bandoeng, or the interpretation laid on them at the time. Brereton apparently felt that his directive from Brett, coupled with the message he had received from General Marshall, already quoted, left him a free hand in choosing his next field of action.

Brett took off for Melbourne early in the morning of the 23rd. Late in the evening of the 24th, Brereton left for India in Crowder's LB–30.

* Brereton says that Brett offered him his choice of India or Australia.[62]

Wavell, for whom the prospect of withdrawal must have come especially hard, had not yet received his own orders to leave; but by the 25th he also was gone. His Headquarters were dissolved as of noon that day, and the ABDA command passed into the hands of the Dutch.

With Brereton went half of the ablest and most experienced operational officers—among them O'Donnell, Combs, who had commanded the 19th Group through nearly all the Java fighting, and such key members of both heavy groups as Parsel, Keiser, Tash, Schaetzel, Wade, Bayse, and Necrason. Brereton also took with him Grant Mahony who, as we shall see, had just succeeded Sprague in command of the 17th Pursuit Squadron, and Major Backus, who had commanded the dive bombers. In the confused and closing days of the Java battle these men were to be sorely missed, as they would be again in the difficult period of reorganization in Australia; yet at the time there was real concern in Headquarters that Brereton was not taking enough experienced men with him.

Before leaving, Brereton issued on the 24th a General Order relinquishing his command and commending all personnel who had served in it "for extraordinary effort and achievement under the most difficult conditions in the face of enemy action and overwhelmingly superior forces in a theater of operations comprising the Philippines and Southwest Pacific Command." [68] This marked the end of the Far East Air Force in its first, unhappy phase. It was also Brereton's farewell, and when Crowder's LB–30 lifted into the dark Java sky at 10:30 that night, it closed a chapter in history, for Brereton took no further part in the Southwest Pacific fighting; and as he wrote in his diary, quite understandably, he was glad to leave. [69]

There was still the job of getting out the troops and of fighting the remaining planes till they were no longer fit for combat. That was for Eubank and the steadily dwindling little group of pilots and air crews to work out as best they could.

9. *The Robenson Mission*

THE LOSS OF JAVA, which now all but the willfully blind knew to be imminent, was also to put an end to a determined, though curiously unsuccessful, attempt to supply the Philippine garrison from the Indies; and it is therefore necessary at this point to turn back in time and take up the story of our efforts to run the Japanese blockade, originating with the backing and personal interest of General Marshall himself, and particularly of the activities of the Robenson mission, which had set up operations in Soerabaja with a fund of $10,000,000 to draw on.

We have already had two brief glimpses of Colonel John A. Robenson, the leader of this mission—first as base commander at Darwin, where he had not hesitated to employ a show of force in straightening out his difficulties with Australian dock workers, and again as he stopped at Malang to report to General Hurley; and we have also seen how two of the ships dispatched by his mission were lost in the Timor Sea. During the five weeks he spent in Java, which covered nearly the whole life of his mission, Colonel Robenson succeeded in loading only one other vessel, and this did not get away from Soerabaja till after his own departure under orders for Australia, when the Japanese invasion fleets were already halfway out across the Java Sea. Yet, though in the end the mission was to prove an utter failure, the story of it is worth outlining for the glimpse it affords of the conflicting national and service interests, and also intrinsically for the flavor of adventure and gallantry, and the continual surprise of circumstance that marked not only the enterprises of Robenson's mission but those carried forward under still more adverse conditions by men at the other end of the line—a story that will find a place in a later chapter.

The first blockade-running message from the War Department reached Headquarters USAFIA, Melbourne, on January 18, and General Barnes *

* Barnes was placed in command of base facilities in Australia on January 17 when Brereton was named commanding general of all U. S. tactical forces in the ABDA theater,

replied the same day that he had initiated plans to ship supplies from the Netherlands East Indies on small craft and send ammunition in by submarine. Additional food and ammunition would be sent from Australia for similar transshipment as larger vessels became available. At the moment there was only one and it would be prepared for an attempted run. In the meantime others were being sought in both Australia and the N. E. I.* But this answer did not satisfy General Marshall and on the 19th he sent a message direct to Barnes, underscoring the necessity of immediate action and repeating the vital paragraphs of the first message:

Report on blockade indicates urgency my instructions not fully appreciated. . . . Time does not permit exclusive dependence upon dispatch of food supplies to NEI for transshipment. Imperative that local resources in every port be exploited to maximum through purchase and immediate dispatch. Vigorous execution necessary. Agents with cash must be placed on NEI and British Islands by plane. Actions and results are imperative.

MacArthur reports food situation PI becoming most serious. States blockade light, may easily be run by bold action. Imperative organize comprehensive efforts, run blockade and deliver supplies MacArthur. Use funds without stint. $10,000,000 now available. May be spent whatever manner deemed advisable. Arrange advance payments, partial payments for unsuccessful efforts, and large bonus for actual delivery. Determine method, procedure of payments, but must get results.

Organize groups of bold and resourceful men. Dispatch them with funds by air to NEI, there to buy food and charter vessels. Rewards for actual delivery Bataan or Corregidor must be fixed at level to insure utmost energy and daring on part of masters. At same time dispatch blockade runners from Australia with standard rations and small amounts of ammunition each. Make movement on broad front. Use many routes, great numbers of small or medium sized boats. Continue incessantly until satisfactory level supplies secured. Only indomitable determination will succeed. Success must be attained. Risk will be great. Reward will be proportionate.†

Brereton then assuming full command of USAFIA. But on the 18th Brereton was at Darwin, and he then went on to inspect Townsville on the 19th, Brisbane on the 20th, and only reached Headquarters in Melbourne on the 22nd.

* These and subsequent blockade-running messages are from Files, Historical Section, HQ USAFFE: radios and cables.[1]

† The last two paragraphs are repetition of the January 18 message. If evidence were ever necessary of the intense and personal response of General Marshall to the situation of troops under his command, this message alone should surely provide it.[2]

There seems to have been little hesitation as to the man best qualified to head the mission. Colonel Robenson had been both bold and resourceful in his handling of the recalcitrant wharvies at Darwin. Before sunset that evening he received a signal from HQ USAFIA (somewhat ambiguously addressed to "Commanding General, U. S. Troops, Darwin, N. T."):

You and six other officers will proceed by commercial or army plane on special mission to Java, NEI. Officers selected will be of junior grade, athletic, resourceful, and of sound judgement. Further detailed instructions follow by letter.[3]

Having found through an exchange of radio messages that he himself was the "General" referred to, Colonel Robenson lost no time in interviewing all junior officers in Darwin whose records indicated that they might have the required qualifications. By evening of the 20th he had chosen six—three from the Infantry: Captain S. J. Randall, Lieutenant F. H. Andrews, and Lieutenant J. C. Boudoin; and three from the two Field Artillery units: Lieutenant A. B. Cook and 2nd Lieutenants R. E. Stensland and P. M. Nestler. He also found an enlisted man, Private John E. Lundberg—a typist and stenographer—who in Robenson's own words "turned out to be the mainstay of our mission, the ideal man for the job."[4] Though the mission roster was now complete, they had to wait for two days for their instructions. These finally arrived by plane on the afternoon of the 22nd and contained both specific instructions for their mission and the over-all plan adopted in Melbourne to meet the War Department's directive.

There were three over-all objectives.

The first was to supply 60 days' rations for the army on Bataan, then estimated at 50,000 men, or 3,000,000 rations, which, figured at six pounds per ration, meant 8000 long tons. These were to be drawn from U. S. Army supplies already in the N. E. I. and shipped immediately to Bataan or Corregidor. At the same time two shiploads of supplies were to be forwarded from Australia to Makassar on the *Mauna Loa* and *Coast Farmer* for reloading there on small vessels.

The second objective was an additional 60 days of rations and ammunition which was to be delivered, as soon as other ships could be found, to Buton Island off the southeast corner of Celebes for transshipment on small boats.

The third objective called for still another 3,000,000 rations and ammunition to be sent on "ships later to be secured, either direct to the Philippines, or to intermediate points for transshipment, or by small boats to be obtained in the N. E. I." [5]

This was an ambitious program, though it showed no very clear comprehension of the speed and broad front of the Japanese advance; but even so it might have been partially realized had Robenson's mission met immediate and wholehearted co-operation from the various commands in Java. Certainly he was given wide powers.

His primary task was to implement the first objective of 3,000,000 rations, as well as ammunition "which should be dispersed widely in small amounts on various ships," and at the same time to detach two of his officers, sending one directly to Makassar and the other to Buton Island, to handle the transshipment of the cargoes expected from Australia. Letters of credit were arranged for: 600,000 gulden for the man on Buton, 800,000 for the man at Makassar, and as we have previously seen,* 5,000,000 gulden for Robenson himself; and if Robenson felt something like awe in signing his name to such a sum, the two younger officers, Lieutenants Andrews and Stensland, who were assigned respectively to the Buton and Makassar missions, must have been almost equally impressed.

Robenson was given authority to charter whatever ships were needed to forward these supplies and was further authorized to buy food in the islands to make up the ration cargoes if that were necessary. He was to urge U. S. Naval authorities to help by sending in what they could by submarines and destroyers, and local U. S. Army commanders to lend what planes could be spared for the same purpose. He was to use U. S. Army planes in moving his own people from place to place, and if U. S. planes were not available he was empowered to call on the RAAF. He had authority to seek personnel "for purposes of navigation or to superintend the accomplishment of the military mission" from civilian sources

---

* The value of the gulden was approximately 50 cents.

in Australia or the N. E. I., from U. S. Army and Navy units in both areas, and from the Dutch Army and Navy. He was given complete latitude in paying whatever sums he deemed necessary in chartering vessels to insure the utmost energy and daring on the part of the masters.

It may be said . . . that the cost of this venture should not be a deterrent to its accomplishment, nor should any means to attain the objective be eliminated from consideration. All imaginable types of deceit may be utilized by you or the masters of these vessels in getting their cargoes into the Philippines. For instance, camouflage or any other means of disguising a vessel or changing its characteristic appearance may be used. Neutral flags, such as the Vichy French flag, or Axis flags, German, Italian, or Japanese, may be painted on the vessel, displayed on occasion, or used in any method which will further the mission.

Many vessels should be employed on as wide a front as practicable. They should be started from various locations in Java and Sumatra. Routes to the east and west of Borneo and the Celebes, from the western point of New Guinea to the southern tip of Ambodia, should be utilized. It is possible that vessels with capacities of from 200 to 1000 tons will best assure getting these supplies to the Philippines.

The essence of the entire plan is speed. The situation regarding food in the Philippine Islands is desperate. Great secrecy should be observed. It is doubtful that any member of the crew of these vessels other than the master should know the purpose of the voyage or destination prior to sailing.[6]

There followed detailed instructions for handling their huge funds through Australian and Dutch banks. Everything seemed to have been provided for except the ships and how to get them to their destinations. The shortage of shipping in Australian waters was indeed the primary reason for sending Colonel Robenson to Java, for with the southward sweep of the Japanese a sizable amount of coastwise shipping from the Hong Kong-Singapore service had been driven into various ports in the Indies. Most of these ships were small—running from 200 to 5000 tons— and were of a nondescript type that would lend itself effectively to blockade running, and it was thought that they would provide a pool readily available for Robenson to draw on.

While the Robenson mission were preparing to take off for the Indies, Headquarters in Melbourne continued looking for ships in their own area, with constantly changing plans for their routing as new information and circumstances came to light. There were at the time six ships in Brisbane harbor—five of United States and one of Philippine registry—and of these General Brereton chose two largely because of their speed, the *Don Isidro* (19 knots) and the *Mormacasun* (22 knots), planning to send them with full loads of rations and ammunition round the northeast edge of New Guinea, and then directly into Mariveles at the tip of Bataan.[7] Originally it had been Brereton's intention to let the *Mormacasun* go only as far north as Makassar. Because of her speed and tonnage the freighter was indispensable on the Pacific run between the States and Australia, and, as he had pointed out on the 21st, there were greater prospects of success if her cargo were divided up among several smaller bottoms.[8] Actually, the scheme of having a ship of her size unload at either Corregidor or Bataan where there were no longer dock facilities was totally impractical, for she would have had to lie over two or three days at least, a ripe and open target for the Japanese bombers. But by January 23, Brereton had decided that any further delay in getting supplies in to MacArthur was "extremely hazardous" and he ordered both ships to make the run all the way through to Corregidor.[9]

However, he was reckoning without the extreme reluctance of the master of the *Mormacasun* to take his ship into any such troubled seas. This gentleman was able to find reasons and excuses for not complying with orders that no mere major general could cope with. First claiming that he was only under jurisdiction of the Maritime Commission, he then said he could not start for the Philippines without the concurrence of the union officials among his crew. Any consultation with crew members was out of the question because of the need for secrecy, and when this was pointed out to him he said that he had no charts, and if he did have them, his navigator was unfamiliar with Philippine waters. Upon hearing this, the Filipino skipper of the *Don Isidro*, Captain Rafael J. Sisneros, offered to contribute a full set of charts and then said that he would be willing to turn his own ship over to his First Officer and serve himself as the *Mormacasun's* navigator. At that point the unwilling master refused outright to undertake the mission.[10] Intending to replace him and his crew, General Brereton then ordered the loading of both ships to proceed; but before they were ready, the War Department directed him to release the *Mormacasun*. The *Don Isidro* therefore sailed alone, and the only requests made by her captain and crew were for eight .50-caliber machine guns with men to man them and compensation for the families of any crew members killed in performance of the mission.*

In the midst of these frustrating passages, Brereton learned that Admiral Hart had agreed to release one submarine to carry ammunition to Mindanao. Her capacity was 26 tons, and General Brett asked if Brereton could have that amount ready at Darwin within two days.[13] This submarine, the *Seawolf,* sailed with a load of .50-caliber and .75-mm ammunition, and she went all the way through to Corregidor, coming out of the dark channel water on the night of January 29-30 while eager men watched her from the shore.† She was the first vessel to run supplies through the blockade from Australia. Submarines were to prove the one certain means of getting in and out of Corregidor, but because of their small capacity, and the fact that they very soon became the only effective Naval striking force in the Southwest Pacific, the Navy was most reluctant to have them used on ferry service.[15] After the *Seawolf* no more than six submarines were to call at Corregidor before the surrender: two carried ammunition, but only two brought in food supplies, and of these one made delivery. We shall hear of them later.

Meanwhile USAFIA became concerned over the availability of cash for the Robenson mission, for all credits had been arranged in Dutch and Australian money. On the 22nd Brereton wired Washington:

. . . To further facilitate carrying out this difficult and important mission large sums of US currency may also be needed at short notice, since owners and masters in NEI will be reluctant to take risks for profits payable in local currency which may be worthless by the time their voyages are completed.

Therefore request eight million be deposited by telegraphic transfer and that remaining two million be forwarded in currency by plane. . . .[16]

---

* Brereton says that she sailed for Corregidor, but she seems to have followed a curiously roundabout route, for she was at Fremantle on February 4,[11] and then went to Batavia, where Robenson found her.[12]

† After delivering her cargo, the *Seawolf,* as noted in Part Two, Chapter 6, above, took on a full load of Army and Navy AC personnel for Soerabaja.[14]

This request was agreed to within twenty-four hours,[17] though Robenson was not informed of it till near the end of his stay in Java and then not through any Headquarters agency.

What he did learn was that his mission had been changed from one that was in large part a forwarding agency to one primarily of procurement. A message from Admiral Hart's Headquarters to USAFIA recommended sending supply ships to Mindanao since there was a large number of small boats available there to run the blockade through the islands to Corregidor. Intelligence reports indicated that Buton and Makassar were no longer safe transshipment points, and the Navy also considered that present hostile developments made any trip west of 130 degrees longitude "most difficult." [18] Since 130 degrees longitude lies only a few miles west of the western tip of New Guinea, this knocked into a cocked hat USAFIA's original plans of sending large vessels up into the Indies to transship their cargoes or, conceivably, to run all the way through to the Philippines. On the eve of his departure for Java, Robenson received new instructions:

> . . . Following changes in plan for your information and compliance. *Coast Farmer* will not be sent to Makassar. *Mormacasun* will proceed direct to final destination and will not stop at Makassar. Do not send *Mauna Loa* to Makassar. Unload *Mauna Loa* at Darwin. Further disposition of this vessel will be given later.*
> Officers directed to go to Makassar and Buton will proceed on their mission. There will be no supplies shipped to them. They will arrange to obtain subsistence by purchases and load direct on small vessels. You should maintain contact with these two officers and give them pertinent instructions depending on your instructions upon arrival in Java. There is no change in your own mission.[19]

The Robenson party took off from Darwin a little before dawn on January 24 in two army transport planes piloted by Captains Connelly and Slingsby, so that once again it seemed as if Pappy Gunn's old Philippine Air Lines was taking over our end of the war in the Southwest Pacific. The C–39 carrying Robenson, his four officers, and Private Lundberg, had an uneventful trip, except for meeting stormy weather, all the

---

* The reader has already been apprised in the preceding chapter of the disposition of this ship and the tragic outcome.

way to Soerabaja. The flight plan of the second C–39, piloted by Connelly, called for a first stop at Koepang to drop off a P–40 tire for one of the 17th Squadron's planes;* a second stop at Kendari, the nearest airfield to Buton Island, which had none, to leave Lieutenant Andrews and another tire, this time for a grounded B–17; † and then on to Makassar to deliver Lieutenant Stensland—the plane returning to Darwin on the following day.‡ Though the Japanese were reported to be bombing Kendari, their attacks had been light and supposedly came only between 2:00 and 3:00 P.M.; and Connelly expected to be in and out of the field before they came over. But for some reason, perhaps a sixth sense about what the Japs were likely to do next, which he and Gunn and Slingsby had all developed to a high degree, he changed his mind at Koepang and headed first for Makassar. There he and his passengers learned that the Japs had taken Kendari that very day.

As no useful purpose could be served by Lieutenant Andrews's trying to get to Buton Island, he remained in Makassar with Stensland. But before they were able to accomplish much, they were driven out by the approach of the Japanese, leaving just ahead of the enemy and rejoining Colonel Robenson in Java about February 8.

Headquarters for the mission had been established at Soerabaja, but Robenson himself had spent relatively little time there. Leaving Lieutenants Nestler and Cook in charge of operations—their instructions, reflecting a very short-lived optimism, were to round up four or five vessels of from 300 to 1000 tons displacement but capable of carrying at least 30 tons of cargo each, and load them with dry rations for immediate dispatch—Robenson went on to Bandoeng on the 25th with the remaining three members of his party to report to General Brett and establish contacts both with the various branches of ABDACOM and with any Dutch authorities who might help speed his mission. Speed, as he quickly

---

* This was Lt. Gilmore's plane, which, as we have seen in Part Two, Chapter 4, was waiting at Waingapoe while Pappy Gunn in his old Beechcraft flew back to Timor for it.

† The reader may recall that Lt. Dufrane's ship had landed at Kendari on the 17th with two of its engines shot out. The tire presumably was lost when Jap strafers attacked the plane on the field. But no one reported to Darwin that Dufrane had already destroyed his plane on the 19th and returned to Java. See above, Part Two, Chapter 5.

‡ This meant a round trip of over 2200 miles in an unarmed plane through skies in which Japanese pursuit were operating or might be expected to appear at any time— typical of the kind of service steadily performed by these three civilian pilots.

discovered, was not an ascendant attribute of this high headquarters; *
but Brett did make arrangements to have him meet Henry A. Quade,
the managing director of General Motors in the Southwest Pacific.

Quade's interests were instantly and deeply enlisted. He dropped all
other business, attached himself to the mission without pay, and devoted
himself heart and soul to the project of finding ships. Robenson could
not possibly have found a more useful recruit, for Quade knew everybody one should know in that part of the world and everybody knew
him. He saw to it that Robenson met everyone in Bandoeng who might
conceivably aid him, helped him open accounts with the Javasche Bank,
and introduced him to high officials in the Dutch Army Commissary
with a view to purchasing stores from them and also securing the services
of a Dutch captain, W. J. L. De Lange, as liaison officer for the mission.
With these two new additions to his staff, Robenson realized that he
would no longer need Captain Randall and Lieutenant Boudoin, so he
turned them over to General Brett, who assigned them to Headquarters
in Bandoeng. That night Robenson and Quade reviewed the whole situation in detail and decided that Soerabaja was obviously the place in
which to center their activities. But before returning, they thought it advisable to visit Batavia, where Robenson was introduced to the British
Consul General, the British Naval Commander, our own Naval Liaison
Officer, and several Dutch military and civilian officials who might later
be useful to him, including Admiral Helfrich. Of all these men, as it
turned out, only the Admiral was to exhibit any real interest in the success of the mission.

When he got back to Soerabaja with Quade and Private Lundberg,
Robenson found his headquarters functioning, though no business had
yet been done. However, during his absence, an expected convoy of
three ships—the *President Polk, Pecos,* and *Hawaiian Planter* †—had
docked and was discharging cargo, largely through the work of the 131st

---

* In the light of subsequent developments, one is irresistibly reminded of the experience
of another officer whose special mission took him to another supreme headquarters to
the East and who, after many days of waiting, chanced to glance through a window
and seeing someone moving there mistook this person for a tree.

† This convoy, which had come into port on January 28, had also carried the ground
echelons of the 11th and 22nd Bombardment Squadrons. Part Two, Chapter 5, above.

Field Artillery, who here, as in all other duties they were called on to perform in Java, turned to with a cheerful acceptance of the situation that more fortunate units serving with them still recall. This cargo, consisting mainly of ammunition, dry rations, and 100-octane gas, gave Robenson plenty of supplies on which to draw. For the moment the sole problem was to find ships and crews to run the blockade.

Word had reached Robenson that anchored out in the bay was a Filipino ship, the *Florence D,* which with her crew was now under control of our own Navy. One of his first calls, therefore, was at Admiral Glassford's Headquarters, but his reception as he recorded it was not encouraging. "My request for the use of this ship was not looked upon with much enthusiam, the Navy's argument being that the strategy of the war had gone beyond the Philippines and that ships' bottoms were too badly needed in other places then to run the risk of losing them on a more or less forlorn hope." [20] On this basis he was flatly turned down on his first visit, though he had shown them all his credentials and instructions. He told them that he would definitely be back; and he did return next day, and the next; and finally the ship and her crew were released to him.*

Practically all the ammunition aboard the *Polk* convoy and half the rations were turned over to Robenson, as well as most of the ships' stores. Part of the latter required refrigeration, but the only cold storage warehouse, which had a capacity of fifteen tons, had already been appropriated by the Navy. From this situation there developed a little passage

---

* This was, of course, a demonstration by Glassford's Headquarters of the pervading feeling of defeatism that had attacked Naval circles immediately after Pearl Harbor. In Washington, Stimson and Marshall had reacted strongly against it and, one gathers rather to Stimson's surprise, the President fully agreed with them "as against the Navy" that the Philippines must not be given up in any spirit of "scuttle." This attitude largely disappeared after the appointment of Admiral King as Naval Commander in Chief late in December [King was appointed December 20, took over the command December 25] as far as Washington was concerned.[21] But in Java, where perhaps U. S. Naval thinking was tinctured by British opinion, which had only its own unhappy experience in Hong Kong and Singapore to draw on, the prospects of a prolonged defense of Bataan did not appear very feasible. The fact that none of the three ships Robenson was finally able to dispatch reached its destination cannot be accepted here as evidence that the mission was impracticable or worthless, in spite of the fact that had all three arrived the Bataan defense would have been prolonged only a day or two longer. The purpose of the defense, however, was political and *moral,* as well as military, and to this the Naval authorities in Java were apparently blind.

between the services that might well have afforded the Colonel a mild satisfaction, though the fact is not emphasized in his account. Captain Gantz, Fleet Supply Officer on Admiral Hart's staff, had got wind of the Colonel's predicament and made a prompt personal call in which he blandly suggested that since the Army had no facilities to store its fresh rations, it might as well give them to the Navy, which had. Equally blandly, Robenson acknowledged the Navy's possession of the only cold storage, but pointed out that the *Army* had the supplies. He therefore suggested on his side that they make a deal—half the supplies for half the storage space. Thus in minuscule was a unification of the armed services accomplished. But it was merely temporary. In the end the shipment of fresh rations to the Philippines was found to be impracticable, and Robenson, well appreciating the Navy's power to help or hinder his mission a great deal, let Captain Gantz take all.

In the meantime, while the cargo of the *Polk* convoy was being unloaded and sorted for storage or reloading aboard the *Florence D,* the search for other ships continued.* The next one to be heard of was the *Don Isidro,* which, after circling the Australian continent from Brisbane to Fremantle, had now turned up at Batavia. Robenson and Quade immediately flew over to inspect her. Why she had come such a circuitous route or whether she still carried the cargo loaded in Brisbane is not made clear. Robenson says only that she was loaded in Batavia, mostly with flour, dry rations, and some ammunition, and that she sailed on the 12th of February.[23] We already know what became of her.

While in Batavia on this trip, Robenson and Quade planned to go on to Singapore to look for ships and crews. Fortunately this proved unnecessary, for at the Hôtel des Indes they met a Dutchman, a Mr. A. C. Bodeker, who according to Quade knew as much about the shipping business as any man in the Far East, and he consented to make a survey for them of just what ships between 200 and 5000 tons were available in the N. E. I. His report revealed the presence of 13 such ships under English or Norwegian registry—most of them with English or Norwegian

---

*Dock labor, native or otherwise, developed a critical shortage once the Japanese started bombing the port regularly. The only dependable man power (except for work performed by the 131st Field Artillery) came from a nearby penitentiary whose denizens worked under the chaperonage of armed guards.[22]

officers and Chinese crews, and some already loaded with stores of various sorts: sugar cane, medicines—especially quinine—timber, and so on. This was where Robenson's real troubles began.

His first move was to request that an order of restraint be put on these ships to prevent their leaving the port of Soerabaja, that they be unloaded and prepared for new cargoes to be decided by his mission. However, before the order could be delivered to Dutch authorities at the port, the British Vice-Consul cleared six of the 13 ships, and it was not practical to recall them. Seven, however, remained and Robenson went to work to get hold of them.

Their release, as he discovered in the course of a sort of Pilgrim's Progress up the mountains of Officialdom, involved the concurrence of the British Vice-Consul at Soerabaja; the British Consul General at Batavia; the Supreme Command, General Wavell; the Allied Naval Commander, Admiral Hart; the Dutch Naval Commander, Admiral Helfrich; the British Naval Commander, Commodore Collins (at Batavia); and the Chinese Consul at Soerabaja. The Dutch Government's offices of the Attorney General and of Commerce were also deeply involved. Of them all he wrote afterwards, "The Dutch authorities were the only ones who extended us enthusiastic co-operation, especially little Admiral Helfrich who, in spite of all his duties and worries, gave this matter his personal attention and allowed me several interviews and gave me his assurance that everything he could do to be of assistance to our mission would be done. He himself suggested and charted the best route that should be taken by our blockade-running vessels." [24]

The procedure by which these ships were to be turned over to Robenson was for Admiral Helfrich to requisition them from the British Government; but though all commercial vessels in the N. E. I. technically came under control of the Dutch as soon as they declared war on Japan, they were unwilling to requisition them without previous assurance that the British would consent. Once consent had been received, the Dutch promised to put the requisition through and then immediately release the ships to the Robenson mission. They proved as good as their word and as a matter of fact, after Admiral Helfrich succeeded to the ABDAFLOAT command on February 14, Robenson's problems were greatly simplified.

Before that occurred, however, the seven ships left out of the original 13 had dwindled again to four; and these four, while remaining in Soerabaja, became the subject of an interminable controversy with the whole matter finally coming under consideration of the High Command in Lembang. It would have required only a word from them to have the four small, old, coastal steamers released to Robenson; but apparently they simply could not make up their minds whether to take such a drastic step. Considering the type of vessel, small and slow as they were, useful only in coastal or island waters, such extreme hesitancy, or reluctance, is difficult to understand. According to Quade's long report on his negotiations, which he dispatched from Bandoeng on February 9, the proposal had come before some of the top people in ABDACOM at least twice, and at one point the British Naval Commander at Batavia even cabled the Admiralty in London. This message, however, and a follow-up message as well, elicited no reply.* Presumably, the Admiralty had weightier matters to decide.

In any case, the proposal was ultimately scuttled. Brigadier Lloyd, of the British Staff, informed Quade that at the final conference "Naval opinion was expressed to the effect that the plan was unfeasible and would be tantamount to sending ships out with the certainty of their being sunk." †[25] In the face of this statement, General Brett said that the High Command definitely would not ask Admiral Helfrich to requisition the ships. Notice of this decision was apparently communicated at once to the British Naval Commander and Consul General in Batavia, for the Chief of Shipping for the N. E. I. Government telegraphed Quade that he had been informed QUOTE THE FOUR SHIPS WERE TO PROCEED ON THEIR PEACEFUL AVOCATIONS UNQUOTE.[26]

It was a bitter disappointment, and Quade, allowing his feelings to show, wrote:

There is a very great deal I would like to say about this whole matter. During about eleven days of intensive scurrying around trying to locate ships and then to find who had authority to release them, we had almost no co-

* Quade's letter, which was in fact his resignation from the mission, is quoted in full in Robenson's Story, Chapter VI.

† Brett wired Barnes on February 8: "The Naval authorities have refused to allow the use of any of the 12 ships mentioned in your cable."

operation whatever—and apparently very little sympathy. When we finally pinned down the only quarter that presumably had power to act in this matter, our attempts to obtain the ships were completely squelched. Considering the scheme as unfeasible ended the matter of the four ships. . . .

I appreciate there is nothing to be gained by crying over this sort of treatment, but it is obvious this apathy makes your mission all the harder of fulfillment because you will apparently get no appreciable assistance from the authorities as far as obtaining ships is concerned. Yours is now the "simple" task of picking up a number of ships in an area and at a time when anything that floats is under the control of one Government or another.[27]

During the next few days Robenson spent most of his time in Soerabaja. He had still further cut his staff by releasing Lieutenant Stensland, F.A., to the 131st Field Artillery. Quade had resigned. He had left with him Lieutenants Cook, Nestler, and Andrews, and the invaluable man of all work, Private Lundberg. By this time, also, their Dutch Liaison Officer, Captain De Lange, had joined them.

De Lange, whose job in civilian life corresponded to what we call a "County Agent" in this country, knew where foodstuffs were being grown and had an intimate knowledge of all means of transportation in the islands. He suggested to Robenson that the mission buy live pigs, slaughter, dry, and salt them, a process that would take about ten days. Robenson told him to go ahead and very shortly afterwards De Lange reported that he had found the pigs they needed in Bali, and 3000 were purchased. These live pigs had to be shipped to Java, for the facilities for slaughtering them and curing the pork were far more sanitary in Soerabaja. Native cargo boats, of about 50 tons, were used to bring them over; but before half of them were delivered, the arrival of the Japs at Den Pasar halted all further shipments—though the whole 3000 had been paid for. Japanese planes, patrolling the narrow strait with vulpine constancy, soon made the passage a death trap for any craft larger than native canoes, and even those could not count on immunity. The last of the pig boats to leave Bali began its trip with 150 pigs aboard and a native crew of eight. Japanese pursuits spotted it before it was quite halfway across, but the crew did not put back. In one of those inexplicable freaks of war, the boat failed to sink or burn, though strafed again and again by the attacking planes. When it finally reached Java, however, only one of the crew and six pigs were still alive.

While that put an end to the pig project,* the search for ships still continued, but with the same disheartening lack of sucess. The *Don Isidro* had sailed from Batavia on the 12th. A day later, insignificant in the great blue crescent of Soerabaja's harbor, the *Florence D* weighed anchor and set her course through Bali Strait and towards the same rendezvous with the Japanese bombers north of Darwin. Like the *Don Isidro's,* her crew and skipper, Captain Camelo L. Manzano, were Filipinos and neither asked nor expected special favors or undue rewards. She had for cargo what Robenson described as "the best-balanced ration of essentials and luxuries that any ship ever carried to troops," † and his heart and hopes obviously went with her. Besides her main cargo there were 7000 rounds of three-inch antiaircraft ammunition,[28] badly needed medical supplies including a large quantity of quinine, and in the captain's cabin a special package addressed to General Wainwright. It contained a case of beer. Robenson, who was a classmate and had been on his way out to the Philippines to serve as Wainwright's Chief of Staff when the outbreak of war diverted him to other duties, had not forgotten how the General loved his beer.

The very day these two ships were sunk, the first of the only three blockade runners ever to reach the Philippines docked at Anakan in Gingoog Bay on the north coast of Mindanao.‡ This was the *Coast Farmer.* First scheduled for Makassar, she had left Brisbane on February 4 with 3000 tons of rations and a heavy load of ammunition.§ A month later she returned safely to Brisbane.||

* Money for the undelivered pigs was fully refunded before Robenson left Java.

† Robenson records that the luxuries included canned fruits, jams, jellies, candies, cigarettes, molasses—items men on Bataan no longer knew except in dreams.

‡ According to Brett's report.[29] Brigadier General Charles C. Drake in his "Report of Operations, Quartermaster Corps, U. S. Army, in the Philippines Campaign, 1941-1942," but compiled after the war, gives February 20 as the date.[30] However, a message from Wainwright, Fort Mills, March 26, confirms Brett's date.

§ She carried 2000 81-mm mortar shells, 30,210 rounds .50-caliber and 801,000 rounds .30-caliber ammunition. She reached Brisbane on March 19, after 43 days in waters controlled by the Japanese.

|| In his highly readable account of the New Guinea campaign, "The Toughest Fighting in the World," [31] George H. Johnston repeats an apocryphal account of a run to Corregidor in January by the *Coast Farmer,* which he described as one of the most astonishing blockade-running feats in modern history. Unfortunately it did not occur, nor could it have, as the reader of these pages can see for himself.

Four other blockade runners left Australian ports between the 17th and 22nd of February. Of these two reached Cebu, their port of destination. The *Dona Nati*, arriving March 6, brought in by far the heaviest cargo to win through the Japanese blockade: 5000 tons of rations, 1,500,000 rounds of .30-caliber ammunition, 4000 rounds of 81-mm mortar shell, 5000 rounds of antitank rifle grenades, and a large amount of medical, engineer, and signal supplies. The *Anhui* reached Cebu on March 14 * with a smaller load but on her deck she carried three crated P-40s. These planes were to play a part in the last flickering of resistance in the Philippines. But out of the 10,500 tons of rations brought in by the three ships, no more than 1100, as we shall see, got to Corregidor.

Like the *Coast Farmer*, the *Dona Nati* and *Anhui* started from Brisbane. The other two blockade runners to leave Australia that month were from Fremantle. The *Yochow* sailed on the 17th, developed engine trouble, and turned back to Darwin, which she did not reach till March 8. A suspicion that she had been sabotaged was more or less confirmed when, after repairs had been made, the crew refused to continue. The *Hanyang* left on the 28th; but her crew took even less time to decide that they wanted no more of such a voyage and eight days later she too put into Darwin. Both vessels were unloaded there and then ordered to Brisbane.[33]

One more ship set out for the Philippines in February; but her port of origin was Soerabaja, and for her story we must return to the Robenson mission.

Two surprising things had lately happened to the Colonel. The first occurred about 5:30 one morning when he was waked by someone knocking on the door of his bedroom in the Oranje Hotel. The rooms at the Oranje were large and cool; each opened on its own veranda, so that even in daytime they were shadowed. At night, when the most careful footsteps in the long corridors beyond the slatted doors fell heavily, such knocking on one's own door had an ominous sound. Outside it was a U. S. Army captain whom Robenson had never seen before. He car-

---

* Here again General Drake's report [32] has different dates—March 10 for *Dona Nati* and March 20 for *Anhui*. I have followed those in Wainwright's message of March 26, the first of which checks with Brett's report. Brett gives no specific date for *Anhui's* arrival.

ried a package wrapped in soiled white canvas and tied with cotton rope—
a "safe-hand" package, he explained, for Colonel Robenson, and he was
very anxious to get rid of it. When Robenson asked what it contained,
the captain told him to open it and see.

Untying the rope, the canvas fell apart and spilled out on the floor were
carton after carton of U. S. paper bills: fifty-dollar bills, twenty-dollar bills,
tens, fives, twos (lots of twos) and dollar-bills. The scene reminded me of my
vision of how the pirates of my childhood books must have felt when they
opened the money chests they had taken from their victims.

"What is all of this and what is it for?" I asked. The Captain replied that
he knew nothing about it, except that he had been told to deliver this package
said to contain $250,000 to Col. John A. Robenson in Soerabaja and obtain a
receipt therefor. It was no small task to count that amount, but it checked out
okay and I signed a printed QM receipt form that was filled in with nothing
except the words: TO COL. JOHN A. ROBENSON, SOERABAJA—nothing said as to type
of package, contents, from whom—everything blank. The Captain said that he
had heard someone say that there were two more such packages on their way
to me. They never arrived.* What this money was for I shall never know, or
why it was sent to me.[34]

Apparently no one in Headquarters had thought of informing the
Colonel of the million dollars in cash being flown halfway round the
world. At the time he did not need it. He had more money with him
than he could use, and his letter of credit called for more cash than
even the bank had. So he bought a good leather suitcase for the money
and deposited it in a bank vault where it rested till just before he left
Java.

Robenson's second surprise was the unexpected arrival on February
14 of "permittance for departure" for the *Taiyuan, Proteus, Tuuni,* and
Bordvik, the four small ships so long held up at Soerabaja by conflicting

---

* I do not know what became of all the other installments. One was picked up in
Ceylon by General Brereton after his evacuation from Java.[35] Though the Colonel claims
that he was mystified, it seems to have been widely known at the bomber fields that the
money was for running the blockade, and all sorts of stories about it were current. T/Sgt.
Hickman recalled that "a quarter million dollars of currency lay in the hangar [at
Jogjakarta] a full day, unattended, with a flying jacket flung over it." Another story
claimed that a 2nd Lt. Taylor was supposed to have brought in half a million or a quarter
million dollars. But he couldn't get anyone to take it. He finally, as Lt. Col. McTague
recalls, found some kind of finance officer to sign for it. The rumors grew. A B–17 (2nd Lt.
Robert C. Lewis, pilot), destroyed just after arrival from the States, was supposed to
have contained a million dollars.

interests and red tape in Lembang and Batavia. How instrumental Admiral Helfrich had been in securing their release was not known, but the 14th was the day he took over the ABDAFLOAT command. No one took time to speculate and now that he had his ships it seemed to Robenson that his troubles were over. All he had to do was gather supplies and load them with the ammunition and send the ships on their way. He soon learned his mistake.

I first had to get the consent of the Master to make the trip. He was never told his destination but it was intimated that the trip was to be a hazardous one and that he would have no military or naval protection. The only incentive I could offer them was my pot of gold.

The ordinary American opinion is that anything can be had if one has sufficient money to pay for it. In general, that theory may be true—but a matter of life or death is another thing—the offering of one's life is seldom bought, it is invariably given through love or patriotism.

The dealings with these old sea captains of the China coast were not hampered by patriotism—they were interested in nothing except themselves, their shore pleasures, and Scotch. Many conferences were had in my office, sometimes individually, sometimes collectively, but always with a bottle of Scotch and at the end of each conference the Captain invariably agreed to take the risk. On the next day would follow either a letter or a visit from the Captain, subject of which would be: that his officers were unwilling to make the trip; that he had to have a new crew as he could not trust the Chinese whom he had; or that he didn't feel that he had the authority to commit the ship without the owner's consent—the owner either being interned in Norway or living some place in England. After two or three such letters or visits the Captain would come out flatly and refuse. The next step was to relieve the Captain and find another one." [36]

His negotiations for the 3040-ton *Taiyuan* involved all these and further complications. Before she could even be brought in to the wharf, Robenson had to find some way of disposing of her Chinese crew who, to a man, were under British indictment for mutiny. Dutch military and naval authorities could not, or would not, help him here as it was a purely British affair; and the British Vice-Consul, a Mr. L. A. Scopes, informed him that the matter would have to be settled in London and that the prisoners could not be taken from the ship until it had been decided just which British court they should be tried before.

Finally Robenson decided that since he could get nothing done by high authority he had better try low, and went to the local Chief of Police, who very quickly agreed to take over the job of guarding the crew if Robenson could supply a place for their detention, and then himself suggested such a place. This arrangement was satisfactory to the Chinese Vice-Consul also as long as the crew received their full daily pay until they were tried or returned to their ship.

The *Taiyuan* was now brought to the wharf and the next step was to clean out what Robenson called "the vilest ship anyone ever saw." This was the skipper's duty; on being confronted with the job the captain went into a state of depression and stayed drunk in his cabin for three days. As soon as he became sober enough to talk he refused to go out on the mission, as did also the three engineers and both wireless operators. After consulting the British Vice-Consul, Robenson bought all six men tickets to Batavia and passage for India. All six were drunk when they started, though the master had had enough glimmerings of sobriety, if that was what it was, to take the ship's log with him.

This was to occasion new difficulties, for after the appointment of the first mate, Mr. J. W. E. Warrior, in the captain's place, the British Vice-Consul at first declined to recognize him as a "master," but then switched his ground and held that the ship could not sail without its log. It was not till February 21 that these matters were adjusted. A new log was by that time originated for the ship, and Mr. Warrior was finally confirmed as its captain.

Mr. Warrior proved something of a problem on his own account. A hard-bitten, seafaring Welshman, who had rubbed the rough edges off a good many other men in the course of knocking about the world, he was extraordinarily resolute where money matters were concerned; and this perilous voyage, on which he was about to embark, was a money matter to him, pure if not simple, for as Robenson phrased it, "he could think of more monetary imbursements and advancements than a Philadelphia lawyer, to all of which we had to acquiesce."

With the shadow of invasion steadily darkening over Java, it became more and more difficult to find a complete crew, though Lieutenant Andrews was offering four times the normal salary, plus a bonus for safe delivery, and personal insurance in case of death. Moreover, loading ships had become a complicated process as the Japanese were bombing with increasing frequency and weight, and it was not safe to store large amounts of supplies at any one time on the wharf. Small and frequent deliveries had to be worked out with the railroad; but the work went so slowly that Robenson finally decided to take a chance rather than risk any further delay, for, besides the *Taiyuan,* the other three ships were now being prepared for the mission. At this point, a call from Headquarters to report to General Brett in Lembang took Robenson away for two days. By the time he returned on the 23rd, however, he found that Andrews had at last succeeded in rounding up a full crew, both officers and men—except for a wireless operator.

Wireless operators had become very scarce in Soerabaja. Lieutenant Andrews had signed up one man, but he had backed out. Remembering that his instructions authorized him to seek men "for the purpose of navigation or to superintend the accomplishment of the military mission" from, among other sources, "U. S. Military personnel either in N. E. I. or Australia," Robenson got in touch with Air Corps Headquarters in Malang. His first request for a radio operator was turned down flat, but he had learned the value of persistence. He repeated the request with the understanding that the service was voluntary and that a $5000 bonus would be paid.

It was now the 25th of February. Orders to close his mission and return to Australia had already reached Robenson, with instructions to report with his staff to Naval Headquarters in Tjilatjap not later than 4:00 P.M. on the 26th. It was evident that the evacuation of Java was under way. A final request to Malang was answered by "a half promise that Sgt. W. Warrenfeltz of our Air Corps at Malang probably might be allowed to go." [37] There was no more Robenson could do. That problem, together with the dispatch of the *Taiyuan,* had to be turned over to the Dutch liaison officer, Captain De Lange. All night on the 25th Robenson and his staff worked to check, close, and balance their accounts, the bank staying open till morning to assist them. Their final act was to reclaim the leather suitcase from the vault and once more count the $250,000 in bills. At 3:30 they returned to the Oranje and an hour's sleep, all except Private Lundberg, who continued at his typewriter cleaning up the final records and accounts. But by 5:30 his work, too, was finished, and they set out for Tjilatjap in two cars with their very scant belongings which, however, included the leather suitcase with its $250,000.

So now all that was left of the ten-million-dollar effort to run ships through the Japanese blockade from the Indies was the rusty little tramp steamer still anchored in Soerabaja harbor. While Robenson waited that afternoon in Tjilatjap, before his night departure in a Quantas flying boat, Captain De Lange reached him by telephone with the news that Sergeant Warrenfeltz had reported and that the *Taiyuan* would go out with the tide about 5:30.

Captain De Lange wished Robenson good-by and good luck. He had served the mission well, and Robenson considered him a bold and fearless officer, well trained and well informed. Like many of the Dutch who stayed, he knew how little time was left before the Japanese would take their country; but he chose to stay, accepting death if necessary, and doing what he could up to the very last.

The *Taiyuan,* carrying 1250 tons of rations, 10,000 rounds of three-inch antiaircraft shells, quinine and other medicine, did go out with the tide that afternoon of February 26, bound for Cebu. She did not deliver her cargo. With the redoubtable Mr. Warrior, Sergeant Warrenfeltz, and her scratch crew she sailed into the temporary night of the Japanese conquest, but for her it was not temporary.

10. *Closing Missions*

AFTER Admiral Doorman's ineffectual dash through Lombok Strait,* the Naval command made no further attempts to interrupt Japanese operations against Bali, and once more the burden of resistance fell almost wholly on the air units. The wake of the last destroyer had barely cleared the strait on the morning of February 20 before preparations for a combined attack got under way at Blimbing, Malang, and Jogjakarta. The

---

* Paradoxically in this region of unlimited oil, movements of the Allied Fleet were now being seriously curtailed by a shortage of fuel, so seriously that three days earlier, Admiral Glassford had ordered a tanker to Ceylon for oil.[1] Furthermore, the Naval evacuation had already begun and two U. S. auxiliary ships with two battered destroyers were even then on their way to a new base preparing in Exmouth Gulf on the northwest coast of Australia.

first mission of this type to be attempted by our Air Force, it involved the use of pursuit planes, heavy bombers, and dive bombers; and while the total of 26 planes seems pathetically small today, it would be hard to exaggerate the effort it represented for the tired men on the Java airfields.

The principal object of the mission was a dive bomber attack on the Japanese ships and shore positions by the seven A–24s. Sixteen P–40s were to provide top cover, and their presence allowed the Bomber Command to send out their three available LB–30s on a daylight strike with reasonable prospects of their getting through to the target and coming back. It was 6:15 and still dark when the LB–30s lifted from the sod runway at Jogjakarta and turned east towards Malang. At the same minute the P–40s began to take off from the little Blimbing Field, then headed southeast in flights of four. They were waiting at altitude in the brightening sky beyond Malang when the three big bombers came grumbling across the mountains. By then, far down in the dark and steep-walled valley, the A–24s had started their laden climb from Singosari. As they emerged from the reluctant shadow, the dive bomber crews saw the 16 P–40s forming over them—"a pretty sight" to the eyes of at least one gunner—and the combined formation proceeded in unison towards Bali and the rising sun.

There was new shipping. Two lay close inshore; and as the formation of planes approached the crews saw four more naval vessels, one of which they took to be a cruiser, steaming towards them down the strait.* The A–24s attacked first. They were flying at 12,000 feet, with the P–40s above them at 14,000 and the LB–30s at 13,500 well off to one side. The lead flight of three went for the cruiser; the second flight crossed over and dived on the ships inshore; Lieutenant Summers, who was flying tail-end Charley, let the rest go down and then picked what looked like the biggest ship for himself. Meanwhile, over at Den Pasar, 30 Zeros had shot up off the airfield like a string of hornets, but as the A–24 gunners lay over on their backs at the start of the dive, they saw the P–40s tearing into the Jap pursuits, and from then on neither they nor the LB–30s,

* The 19th Bomb Group Diary says they were "cruisers and destroyers." [2] Cpl. Lnenicka, gunner in one of the A–24s, said that the ships inshore were transports, that there were one cruiser and three destroyers.

which made their runs a few minutes later, had anything to fear from the Zeros. There was still the antiaircraft fire, however; it was very hot; and they lost two of their planes to it.

2nd Lieutenant Douglas B. Tubb was hit in his dive and never pulled out, but with his gunner, Private D. S. Mackay, plunged straight on for the full 12,000 feet into the sea. In the other plane, 2nd Lieutenant Richard H. Launder dropped two of his bombs on the cruiser and pulled out of his dive in the direction of the beach. He had carried the dive so far home that, according to Corporal I. W. Lnenicka, his gunner, they were then only 15 or 20 feet above the water. Either the guns of the cruiser, which was already burning from Launder's hits and three more by Major Backus, or the Japanese shore batteries caught the plane as it whipped over the narrow strip of land that joins Bali to the big peninsula called Tafel Hoek. The first shell damaged an elevator, though not desperately, but the second cut an oil line and immediately both men were covered and half blinded by oil. Launder, who had pulled up a little, saw an airfield dead ahead which he took for a Dutch base; but as he started to let down on it, he saw the red suns on the white wings of a parked plane and went dizzily on across the land and ditched his plane in the sea about eight miles up the coast and 150 yards offshore, "not too hard a crash," though both men were bruised about the head. They got ashore all right and at once set out to find their way back to Malang. It took them three days and two nights.

They began the trip equipped with one revolver (Lnenicka's) and two bars of chocolate (Launder's). They didn't dare go into Den Pasar, for they had heard that the Japs were in the town, but went on around as quickly as possible. After that the Balinese took charge of them, the native chiefs passing them on from village to village, and in each case presenting the two fliers with a few small Dutch coins—just why Lnenicka never figured out, for they were not allowed to pay for anything. The first 58 miles they walked. Then they found two bicycles and pedaled on till they reached a little fishing village halfway up Bali Strait where they negotiated for a proa to carry them over to the Java side. The boatmen demanded fifty dollars; but when the village headman heard of it, he was incensed and ordered the fliers taken over for nothing. They made the passage in thirteen hours on the second night, with one of their two paddlers, a Mohammedan, wailing prayers for good weather all the way across.

Of the five A-24s that got back to Malang, one other was so badly holed by flak that it could not be flown again; yet the dive bombers had not done too badly. They had made ten hits on four ships, two of which were so severely damaged that the Japs had to tow them away.* And the LB-30s, which attacked just after them, claimed three direct hits and a waterline hit on a cruiser, though this may have been the same ship that Backus and Launder had gone after. Two hours later, the three big bombers returned safely to Jogjakarta with reports of heavy antiaircraft fire over the target, but no enemy interception. The P-40s had done their work well, though at high cost to themselves. Four failed to return; two of the pilots were killed; and a fifth plane, trying to land at Blimbing with its elevators nearly shot away, crashed on the field.† But this accounting does not tell the full loss to the Squadron, for one of the dead pilots was Sprague.

His lieutenant colonel's commission had come through that morning just before they took off for the mission[5]—too short a time for any of them to think of him afterwards as "Colonel." Even the Squadron diarist wrote in the day's entry that "Major Sprague and Lt. Galliene had not reported in, and no information could be gained as to their condition or whereabouts." [6] No one knew what had happened to either man. When they first went after the Zeros that had swarmed up from Den Pasar, some of the pilots heard one man say over his radio that he could see the Major going in. They thought it must have been Galliene,[7] for none of those who returned remembered saying anything like that. Then as superior numbers began to tell, the P-40 flights were broken up and the fight became a wild melee, and while they managed to keep the Japs off the bombers, shooting three down and strafing a fourth on the Den Pasar strip in the process, they never regained formation. If a man dropped out, there was small chance of another man's seeing him go.

* According to an afternoon reconnaissance which reported a cruiser being towed by a destroyer, and a destroyer being towed by a cruiser.[3] An interesting footnote by Brereton, added after the event, states that all four of these vessels were sunk later by submarines. If true, the submarines were not of the U. S. Navy.[4]

† The plane was a total loss, but the pilot, Lt. Thomas L. Hayes, Jr., was able to walk away from the wreck.

When word arrived that afternoon that both other missing pilots had survived forced landings on the rough South Java beaches after running out of gas,* hope for Sprague and Galliene revived.[9] But it was false hope, for neither was heard from again.†

They waited three more days, during which they lost two more men in action over Soerabaja: Lieutenants Wallace J. Hoskyn and George W. Hynes, both shot down and killed on February 21.‡ Finally, on the 23rd, Grant Mahony was given the command. He held it a bare forty-eight hours in which the Squadron was nearly halved by the withdrawal under orders of 20 officers and 36 enlisted men for an unspecified destination. Then Mahony was called away "on a trip of inspection with General Brereton" [11] that as we know meant leaving for India, and on the afternoon of the 24th the Squadron came under the command of Lieutenant Gerald McCallum, a quiet man, who had run the little engineering shack in which such wonders of tinkering repair work were accomplished.

The base seemed very deserted that evening. There was less calling back and forth among the parked planes where the mechanics and armorers worked through the fading twilight; and in the bamboo Opera-

* Lts. William C. Stauter and Robert S. Johnson. Stauter's plane was wrecked and he himself injured and taken to the hospital at Malang. Johnson, with his engine coughing dry, squashed down intact on a beach so small it was impossible for the plane to take off again. But offshore he saw a schooner that somehow looked familiar. It proved to be the U.S.S. *Lanakai,* which he had seen in the moving picture *Hurricane,* and which had been sold to the Navy for a patrol boat. The crew had seen the P–40 flying low in search of a landing spot and came ashore to help dismantle her of her guns and burn her, and then they took Johnson back on board.[8]

† Months later, sitting on the beach at Darwin, Lt. Comdr. Frederick B. Warder, of the submarine *Seawolf,* which had been running a patrol off the south entrance of the strait that day, told George Weller, the correspondent, that at about the hour of the action, he had seen a parachute's white canopy open above the little island of Nusa Besar and float slowly to the earth. Weller wondered at the time if this could not have been Sprague's.[10] It might well have been, for Sprague's body was recovered there after the war by Graves Registration. Apparently he had been alive when he came down, but had died soon afterwards, and the local chieftain had given him burial. But then, according to the restless treatment which we accord so many of our war dead, his body was dug up and taken to Java for burial; and then it was dug up again and sent to Calcutta; and someday, presumably, if indeed this has not already happened, it will be dug up a third time and sent home. (Information supplied the author by George Weller, at Cambridge, Mass., March 14, 1947.)

‡ Other pilots in the same action were convinced that Hoskyn got two Zeros before going down himself, but they were never officially confirmed. However, Lts. Jack D. Dale and Frank E. Adkins each shot down one, and in addition two heavy bombers were credited to the Squadron.

tions hut men studied the Squadron record, chalked up on the board, as if it marked a chapter ending. Forty-six Japanese planes had been confirmed shot down against a loss of eleven P-40s and six of their own pilots killed or missing; * but since 23 of the enemy planes were bombers, they knew that at least 138 Jap airmen were dead. It was a record they need not be ashamed of.

They required no briefing to understand what was expected of them. They were to stay and fight as long as they had planes to fight with, and they realized that from now on they were operating on borrowed time. They had 18 P-40s left of the 39 that had reached Java. Only ten were in commission that evening, but by morning there would be twelve. Almost all had been more or less shot up; some had flown over 400 hours without overhaul; there was hardly an engine on the base that had not done 150 combat hours with only first-line maintenance; and lately the number of planes forced back to the field by engine trouble had increased sharply. The lack of facilities and the necessity of keeping all rated planes on constant alert through the daylight hours added almost insurmountable difficulties to the problem of maintenance. Their operations only continued to be possible because the Japs hadn't yet discovered the field. But more of the enemy came in sight of it each day and the men watching them from the alert shacks, or from the trees under which the planes were parked, knew that it was only a matter of tomorrow, or the next day, or the next, before some Jap pilot's eyes would trace the blunt cross of their runways in the green checkerboard of rice fields. When that happened, there would be an end of the Squadron's operations at Blimbing. They all knew this; they understood the mounting odds against them. Next morning their twelve patched-up planes took off against 90 of the enemy, and they lost McCallum.

They never reached the bombers. The Japs had had their lesson about coming in unescorted beneath the ceiling of the P-40s;† that day they

---

* The 46 Jap planes included 18 Zeros, four Army 96 Fighters, one Messerschmitt 110, and twenty-three 96 and 97 Heavy Bombers: but the Dutch credited them with more than 60. These figures and the pilot losses do not include the action over Bali in which Landry was killed; nor, of course, Metsker's death, or the loss of eight planes over Koepang, or other casualties in ferrying.[12]

† Though the service ceiling of the P-40E was officially 30,000 feet,[13] the plane was actually designed to fight at 15,000 to 20,000 feet, and during these early months of

had their 54 bombers stacked in formations of nine from 27,000 to 30,000 feet with six Zeros behind each formation; and the worn engines of the P-40s simply could not get them up there. They were still 1000 feet below when the Jap fighters dropped on them. At that altitude a P-40 did not stand a chance against a Zero, so the first two flights, McCallum's and Dale's, dived away; and it was then, as he hung back to cover the others, that the Zeros caught McCallum and shot his engine out. Some of the pilots saw the trail of smoke and the white blossom of his opening chute; but the action swept them on and they lost sight of him. Not till next day did they learn that he had been killed, strafed in his chute with the same savagery as Quanah Fields.* After that it seemed to make little difference that Kizer's flight, entering the action last of all, had timed their arrival perfectly to catch the Zeros in headlong pursuit of their comrades and had shot down two,† or that still later in the day Lieutenant B. S. Irvin, flying with Dale, had bagged a third.[16] Their sense of isolation had a new poignancy.

Nor was this tempered by the arrival in the afternoon of February 26 of six Brewster Buffaloes and six Hurricanes, all with Dutch pilots, to fly with the P-40s. The Hurricanes, stray survivors of Singapore and Sumatra, were useless for interception as they lacked oxygen equipment; moreover, they had been handed over by the departing British so recently that their Dutch pilots had had only two or three hours' experience in them. As for the Brewsters, everyone knew that at altitude they were sitting ducks for Zeros. The men of the 17th realized that these planes had been sent to Blimbing as a last resource. They had no way of knowing that even then the *Langley,* with 32 P-40s on her short flight deck, was approaching Java, or that the *Seawitch* would actually land 27 crated planes at Tjilatjap on the 28th. Yet even had these deliveries been completed and the crated planes assembled, they would have come too late to help the 17th Squadron.

combat in the Southwest Pacific there are few recorded instances of the plane's being fought above 27,000 feet.

* There were thirty holes in his chute and he had been hit twice in the head and twice in the heart.[14] Fields had been more terribly shot up, and McAfee has recorded having to identify him in the Soerabaja morgue "through an American penny in his pocket, mostly." [15]

† Lts. W. J. Hennon and A. J. Reynolds. In these last days the Squadron was flying three or more missions a day.

For by then the Allied fleet had been disastrously defeated in the Java Sea; * Japanese transports were already steaming for the landing beaches; and on the afternoon of the 28th, the Zeros finally found the airfield at Blimbing. But for a violent thunderstorm that broke over the valley at the time, the field would have been immediately attacked. As it was, the 17th were spared for one more mission, and on the morning of March 1 they took off with their full remaining force of nine P-40s, followed by six Hurricanes and four Brewsters, to attack the Japanese landings west of Soerabaja.

We shall take up this mission in its place; but now, briefly, we must return to the bombers.

Three hours after the combined mission struck the Japanese ships off Den Pasar on February 20, ten B-17s bombed the same target. Three, from Madioen and led by Captain Hardison, claimed sinking a large transport.†[18] The other seven were from Malang. They made two runs at 26,200 feet but missed with all their bombs. Neither formation encountered serious opposition. A single Zero, out of five sighted, made a halfhearted attack on the last plane of the second formation, and to the Fortress crews it looked as if the P-40s must have given the Japs all the fighting they wanted for one day. Nothing could have been farther from the truth.

The ten B-17s returned safely to their respective bases, and at Malang the work of refueling and bombing up was immediately begun. Air and ground crews were still at it when, forty-five minutes later, nine enemy planes appeared over the field, flying from south to north through a broken scud of cloud at about 10,000 feet. Everybody saw them; but as there had been no alarm, it was assumed that they were friendly, possibly P-40s. Then, as their radial engines were descried, some of the men decided that they might be Naval planes, probably of a new type, just arriving from the States. They watched the formation keep steadily on

---

* There is no need to describe here this naval action; but in it, between 4:00 P.M. and midnight on February 27, the Allied fleet under Doorman, though not greatly outnumbered, had lost nearly half its ships (two cruisers, three destroyers sunk, one cruiser and one destroyer damaged) against a single enemy destroyer heavily damaged.[17] Three more Allied cruisers and three destroyers were sunk in scattered actions on March 1.

† Sinking of this transport was not confirmed by postwar findings.

to the north till it had vanished in heavier clouds and then unconcernedly returned to their tasks.

Wishful thinking, and the unquenchable hope of reinforcement, in part accounts for this ready acceptance of unidentified planes as friendly; * but there is no reasonable explanation for the fact that, instead of being dispersed to their revetments, the B–17s had been parked in line at one end of the field, out in the open, and utterly vulnerable to a surprise attack. It hit them with vicious suddenness. Once hidden in the distant clouds, the Japanese planes had circled back; they now came gliding in on the field with cut engines at treetop level. The first intimation of their approach was the hail of machine gun and cannon fire striking through the parked Fortresses. Five caught fire. Three exploded almost instantly, and the other two burned beyond hope of any salvage. The Japs then worked over the rest of the base, passed on to strafe the town of Malang briefly, and were gone.†

The loss of the bombers was the more devastating because all five were in relatively sound condition. From then on the proportion turning back from missions with mechanical failure ‡ increased to such a pitch that only twice in the nine days before Java was evacuated could the Bomber Command put more than three planes over a target: once on February 24 when six B–17s attacked a Japanese convoy forming in Makassar Strait for the final thrust across the Java Sea; § and again in the closing hours during the night of February 28–March 1, when six B–17s and one LB–30 bombed the same convoy as it moved towards the Java beaches. But as these planes attacked for the most part individually and at wide intervals,‖ it is stretching the truth to class their effort as a single mission. Their work was notable more as a gesture than for

* Teats recalls that some men did feel sufficiently suspicious to call the Dutch control officer, but were assured that the visitors were "American planes of an unidentified type." [19]

† It was remarkable that only nine of the 1100 men on the field, Americans and natives, should have been injured.[20]

‡ For example: February 21, four out of six aborted; February 24, four out of five; February 25, six out of eight; February 27, three out of four.

§ In this attack, from 30,000 feet, many hits were claimed and two ships sunk.[21]

‖ Records of these closing missions are so sketchy as to be almost nonexistent. By interior evidence and available interviews it is known that out of seven planes, four made individual sorties (Hughey in the LB–30, and Smelser, Vandevanter, and Hardison). The remaining three (Barr, Beck, and Bevan) took off from Madioen together, if we can accept the sometimes questionable Hardison account as authority.[22]

any worth-while results * and did nothing to halt or even delay the Japanese.

The size of this convoy, which numbered more than 40 transports with 34 fighting ships in support, had powerfully impressed the Fortress crews,† yet it represented less than half of the assault force thrown against Java. To the west a second convoy of 56 transports and 35 warships moved down out of the South China Sea; and in addition a striking force that included four battleships and four carriers ‡ was to pass through Lombok Strait into the Indian Ocean to cut the one remaining line of reinforcement or retreat.

Meanwhile most of the bomber missions continued to be aimed at Bali and the airfield at Den Pasar in the hope of knocking out the source of the damaging fighter raids that now covered all three of their bases. The effort proved futile. Between the 20th and 23rd Malang alone suffered twelve separate attacks, and in the four days following the disastrous 20th eight more planes were lost on the ground. One was an LB–30, caught outside the hangar at Jogjakarta, which the Zeros hit for the first time on February 22,§ and on the same day the Japs also destroyed four of the old B–17Ds at Pasirian,‖ planes which, though no longer fit for combat, would be sorely needed for evacuation.[27] Then on the 24th three B–17Es were strafed and burned at Bandoeng.[28] To the Bomber Command it became obvious that to continue operations on the present

* Smelser took credit for sinking four transports and believed he "got at least six." Hardison claimed sinking a 10,000-ton transport packed with troops.[23] Bevan claimed direct hits on two ships.[24] Hughey could not find the convoy; Vandevanter bombed through the clouds and made no claims. Absence of Japanese corroboration does not necessarily invalidate these claims, though Smelser's seems optimistic.

† In their own words, it was an "enormous convoy . . . stretching up the straits interminably . . . counted more than 87 ships . . ." "My plane," said one pilot, "was at 20,000 feet when I first saw the convoy. I could look ahead and see ships clear to the horizon. That's how big it was."

‡ This was the same striking force that, under Admiral Kondo, had participated in the attacks on Darwin and Ambon, and still earlier on Pearl Harbor. Besides the eight ships mentioned, there were a light cruiser and eight destroyers.[25]

§ Two B–17s inside the hangar suffered no damage. The Japs went first for the only fire engine on the base, then destroyed the LB–30 at their leisure, and afterwards flew up and down the field waving to the men in their foxholes.

‖ Weller says there were five B–17Ds at Pasirian. Also destroyed was the P–40 Quanah Fields cracked up in landing after flying from Australia (Part Two, Chapter 6). Three mechanics of the 17th Squadron worked over this plane under fire till it was hopelessly riddled. They were S/Sgt. J. L. Swanson, Cpl. S. E. Cockcroft, and Cpl. A. V. Prioreschi.[26]

basis, without fighter protection and with their only three practicable airdromes under constant enemy observation, would mean the certain loss of all their planes. It was time to pull out. Shortly after noon on the 24th, therefore, a detachment of five officers and five enlisted men left Malang in a B–17D to organize an evacuation base at Broome, a small and now nearly deserted pearl fishing port on the bare northwest coast of Australia.*

The decision was Eubank's, taken within the clear definition of instructions he had received from Brereton on February 21. By these he was directed:

(1) To operate the American air units in Java as long as an effective operational force existed. The decision for the termination of operations was to be made by Eubank and Dutch Headquarters notified.

(2) To evacuate personnel not needed for the tactical operations of equipment available to Australia.

(3) As aircraft became unsuitable for tactical operations, to remove personnel so released from the combat zone.

(4) To include in each evacuation a proportionate share of personnel with combat experience. These to be used for reconstituting units.†

The purpose of the War Department to support the defense of the Netherlands Indies had been firmly stated ‡ and was subsequently reaffirmed by General Marshall in a sharply worded message respecting the proposed diversion § of fighter planes, including the P–40s aboard the *Langley* and the *Seawitch,* to India.[30] With the dissolution of Wavell's Headquarters, which became official on his departure for Ceylon on the 25th, but which to all intents and purposes was already in effect by February 24,‖ control of the Indies defense passed, as we have seen, wholly into Dutch hands; and the remaining Allied commanders—Admirals Glassford and Palliser of the U. S. and British Navies, and Colonel Eubank of the U. S. Air Force—presently found themselves under the

---

* The B–17, piloted by Capt. Dean C. Hoevet, returned immediately to Java.[29]

† These instructions, except for transposition from the first person, are taken from Eubank's account of the evacuation as it was incorporated in General Brett's long report of March 7 to General Marshall.

‡ See above, Part Two, Chapter 8 (note 63).

§ The proposal had been made on February 21. *Ibid.* (note 60).

‖ His orders to abandon Java arrived on the 23rd.

command of Admiral Helfrich and Major General L. H. Van Oyen of the N. E. I. Air Force. Both these men contemplated a last-ditch stand on the high Bandoeng plateau in which they expected to be supported by the Allied units; but in the light of the orders they had received, Palliser and Eubank reserved the right to withdraw their commands when in their judgment no further useful purpose could be served by continued fighting. Only Glassford was prepared during the final hours to accept the decision of his Dutch superior.[31] This confused situation was still further obscured by the peculiar lack of liaison observed by the departing Supreme Headquarters towards subordinate Dutch commanders— one might almost, indeed, call it secrecy—and it was not unnatural, in the rapid disintegration that occurred after the first Japanese landings, that the various elements of this unorganized command should find themselves at cross purposes. From this situation rose Dutch criticism of the manner in which the U. S. Air Force's evacuation was carried out so bitter that it amounted practically to a charge of desertion.*

The evacuation of the ground troops was unquestionably a disorderly affair, as retreats generally are, and, in spite of Eubank's foresight in securing a ship, the men were lucky to get out. But the Dutch accusations were ill-founded. They sprang from a misconception of Eubank's orders and a lack of contact with the tactical commands that were reminiscent of ABDACOM. Eubank planned to keep as many men in Java as the planes still in combat could carry out † and actually, as this narrative will record, the air units remained in action till they had only three heavy bombers left in combat commission. It is hard to see how Eubank could have timed the withdrawal of his command more closely.‡

On the afternoon of the 25th, at a meeting in the Operations hangar at

* Such, at least, was General Marshall's immediate reaction, and he ordered a full and factual report on the evacuation and the orders under which it had been carried out. This report, which exonerated Eubank and closed the incident, provides a valuable outline of the evacuation which is substantiated in the interviews on which this narrative is based.[32]

† This meant a crew and a half for each plane, with about four mechanics for the lot. These men were to leave as soon as their plane went out of tactical commission.

‡ It is pleasant to record that General Van Oyen subsequently wrote General Marshall a letter expressing gratitude for the services performed by U. S. troops in Java during those early and dark days, with particular mention of three officers, one of whom was Eubank.

Singosari, he told the men that they were to be transferred: the air crews to fly, the ground crews to go by rail and boat.[33]

II.   *Evacuation: The Ground Echelons*

THE MEN were not greatly surprised. Rumors had been getting very hot for two days past; and, though Eubank did not tell them where they were to go, or when, they knew it would have to be Australia or India, and it would have to be soon. Even so they were scarcely prepared for the suddenness with which the orders came. At 2:00 the next morning they were routed out, told to pack only bare necessities and to be ready to move within an hour.[1]

The night was pregnant with a sense of Java falling to pieces round them. Fifteen minutes earlier two Fortresses had roared off the field carrying 24 more officers and men to Australia. Now, as the trucks picked them up in the heavy darkness for the drive to Malang, they could hear two more B–17s being run up in preparation for a dawn mission over Bali—and it occurred to them that it would be days, or maybe weeks, before they learned whether the crews had made it back safely. Leaving was not as easy as many had thought it would be.

They did not like the feeling of walking out on the Dutch and Javanese. They liked it still less when they thought of the 131st Field Artillery. The National Guardsmen, who had turned their hands with unfailing cheerfulness to whatever jobs were asked of them, were under orders to join the Dutch with their old French 75s for a last stand near Bandoeng. Everyone knew that they did not have a chance of getting out of Java. Then there were four of their own men, left behind in the little base hospital because their wounds were considered too serious to risk their being moved.* Three seemed stoically resigned, but the fourth, reminding those who came to say good-by of what the Japs had done to other enemy wounded, begged over and over for a gun to defend him-

---

* The four men, all with compound leg fractures from bullet wounds, were Lt. J. P. Ferry of the 19th Group, and Pvts. A. B. Hegdahl, Joseph De Mott, and Pfc. Edwin M. Shipley, all of the 7th Group.

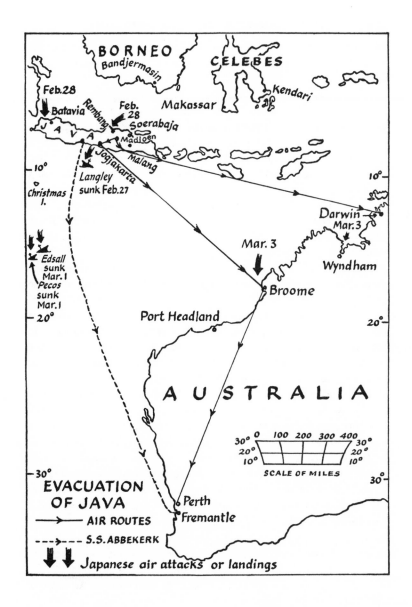

EVACUATION
OF JAVA
→——— AIR ROUTES
--→-- S.S. ABBEKERK

Japanese air attacks or landings

self with, and then broke down when it had to be denied him.[2] All these were in their minds as they rode the six miles through the heavy night to Malang.

A few of their number were already on the way to Jogjakarta in a truck convoy with what little equipment they hoped to take out with them.[*] By 3:30 the rest gathered in the blacked-out railroad station to board their train. The native cars had nothing but bare board benches, one along each wall and a third down the middle, and if the men had known how long they would have to ride on them, the complaints would have been even louder than they were.

The train went north all the way to Soerabaja before switching over to the line that would take them west through Madioen and Jogjakarta and ultimately bring them out at the south coast port of Tjilatjap, where their ship waited. In Soerabaja they were nearly caught in the most destructive air raid that had yet hit the city. Fifty heavy bombers came over while their train still stood in the station: they pulled out to the wailing of the sirens and barely ahead of the falling bombs.[3] But except for that experience, it was an uneventful journey. The train wound on across the green and sleeping hills all day, past towns with mosques and temples and villages half seen beyond the fringes of the rice fields. They watched the sun go down and shadows lengthen on the mountains. Night overtook them, the enclosing darkness bringing with it sharper awareness of the Allied failure and the sense of wasting time that soon afflicts all men in flight.

It was 9:30, eighteen hours after leaving Malang, when their train at last chuffed into Jogjakarta and they unloaded from the stifling cars and were taken through dark streets to billets in the classrooms of an empty school. Here they heard that the other ground units had already departed.[†] They themselves did not stay long. Joined by the few remaining members of the 11th Squadron, they were aboard their train at dawn and on the way to Tjilatjap.

---

[*] A few spare engines, a few parts, a single truckload of radio equipment were about all.

[†] The reader will recall that when the ground echelons of the 22nd and 11th Squadrons reached Java at the end of January, the 22nd was assigned to Malang and the 11th to Jogjakarta, but the latter also supplied the ground force for Madioen after that base was opened.

The movement to Tjilatjap was headed by a truck convoy which set out from Jogjakarta shortly after midnight on the 26th.* With it went most of the base personnel, together with the contingent from Madioen, a few men who had come from Malang by road, and the contingent of pilots and enlisted men of the 17th Pursuit Squadron who had left Blimbing on February 23 and 24. They were able to bring out a large part of their equipment, including, fortunately, the field stoves of the 11th Squadron. Preparations for departure were undertaken without any of the pressure that occurred less than twenty-four hours later at Malang; the men were given half a day to pack in; and the trip to Tjilatjap, even though made under blackout conditions, ought to have presented no special difficulties.

The convoy, however, had been placed in command of a bomber pilot who had no experience in handling transportation and who apparently gave no thought to providing markers at road intersections and detours but merely placed his car behind the lead car, which contained their native guide, and gave the order to roll. The lead car started off at a very fast pace. There was no moon that night. The route led through flat country. The roads were dirt and heavy with dust and ran a great deal of the way in dense woods. In trying to keep up with the lead car, the pilot-commander lost all touch with his convoy which, trying to find its own way without lights through strange country, soon fell into confusion, with trucks going astray at each new fork in the route and causing a halt while a car was sent in pursuit and the waiting trucks stood still in the dark with the dust choking over them. Finally a young medical officer and a still younger chaplain decided to assume command of the convoy.† They started posting men at each crossroads to direct traffic, these men being picked up by the last truck as it came by. Progress showed an immediate improvement and, as the night waned, they began to make good speed. Two trucks were lost, but no one was hurt; and at about 11:00 A.M., still without their two guide cars, they came in sight of Tjilatjap.

---

* Hickman says that they started out at 5:00 A.M., but he is the only source to name a later hour.[4]

† They were Lt. Donald D. Davis, M.C., and Lt. William C. Taggart, who in Australia later became Chaplain of the 19th Bombardment Group.

They had a long wait in the narrow streets of the town before they could work their way in to the port area. When they did reach the waterfront, they found it in indescribable confusion. Five or six commands were all trying to evacuate through this sole remaining open port at the same time, and no co-ordinating authority seemed to exist. Fifteen or twenty ships lay out in the harbor, boats and lighters plying between them and shore. There were two wooden wharves, one large enough for three ships, the other for only one. At the latter, two ships lay, one moored outside the other, their sides raised high above the dock planking by the tide. The men embarking on the outer ship had to cross the deck of the one next the dock, and instead of gangplanks there was a single stairway, not more than three feet wide, to serve them both. Colonel Robenson, who arrived about the same time with his staff, recorded his indelible impression of the scene:

> . . . On this stairway was a continuous line of soldiers which extended down to and across the wharf and out of sight, lost among the warehouses. Soldiers of all colors and many nationalities—white, black, copper, tan, yellow; American, English, Australian, Chinese, Dutch, Indian. Each soldier carrying all he could—barrack bags, suitcases, boxes, crates. There was no organization, each individual for himself. There was no fighting, each took and maintained his position, content to be in the line. To top off this picture, fifty per cent of the humans on the wharf were drunk or openly drinking. . . . There were none of the usual formalities of checking individuals, orders, authorization, equipment, etc.—all that one had to do to get passage on this ship was get in line, provided, of course, he was in some kind of uniform.[5]

The outer of the two ships was British, the *Kota Gedeh,* and loading troops for India, among them a small detachment of the RAF who had a battered 1937 truck on the dock that they were stubbornly determined to take with them, no matter what loading difficulties might be involved. The ship against the wharf was the 12,000-ton Dutch freighter *Abbekerk,* which had been reserved to take the U. S. Air Corps units out of Java. Her rusty sides gave point to a story current on the waterfront that she had been sunk at Singapore by Japanese bombers and later raised from the bottom of the harbor; * and, as their trucks crowded in through the port entrance, the ground men of the 7th Group eyed her with a good

---

* Weller says, however, that she had been sunk by the Germans in the Thames.[6]

deal of misgiving. Dismal as she looked, however, all they wanted then was to get themselves and their equipment aboard her as rapidly as possible.

But they soon found that except for personal belongings, some machine guns salvaged out of planes, and the field stoves of the 11th Squadron, they would not be able to take much. The *Abbekerk* had no side hatches, so all their vehicles would have to be abandoned. Besides ambulances, these included 72 trucks and jeeps, though what really upset the enlisted men were the brand-new Oldsmobile staff cars left behind for any native to drive off who wanted one. No system of loading existed. The lone American major, whose job it was to get supplies on board, had almost despaired of making any headway against the blind and compulsive preoccupation of the human line in feeding itself up the ship's side. He eagerly accepted the services volunteered by one or two Air Corps officers; a system of alternating traffic up and down the single stairway was organized; and as the men grasped what the officers were trying to accomplish they too lent a hand, and a semblance of order began to emerge. Yet, even so, the loading went forward with maddening slowness. The struggle to get the RAF truck over the *Abbekerk* and aboard the *Kota Gedeh* produced a long and at times acrimonious diversion. The sick and wounded, most of them sailors off the *Marblehead* and *Houston* who had been brought by train from the little Petronella Hospital at Jogjakarta,* had to endure a long and trying wait on the dock before an Air Corps surgeon managed to get them onto the ship.

Night fell, but the work continued under lights. Then at 8:30 an air raid warning put a halt to all activity. So many had by now boarded the two ships that a general disembarkation was obviously impossible. The men felt trapped and helpless. One by one the lights went out and the harbor darkened under the dark sky. Only the barest suggestion of moonlight came through the low and heavy clouds. Waiting and listening, the men could hear the drone of a circling plane. But no one saw it;

---

* These men, 47 in number, had been brought to Jogjakarta by Dutch doctors and nurses and had remained there under the care of Capt. Arthur Stafford, assisted by Lt. Davis and the Petronella staff, till their removal to Tjilatjap. Capt. Stafford's duty naturally kept him with the air echelon of the Squadron, and when he saw his charges off, he had only five more days to live.

and after a while it went away, the All Clear sounded, and loading was resumed.

They were still at it when dawn broke. At intervals all during the night, new groups of men appeared upon the dock to take their places in the boarding line; and long before the trainload from Malang was expected, the *Abbekerk* had become a crowded ship. She had cabin accommodations for twelve passengers. All above that number had to find space on her open deck. Besides our own troops * there were British and Australians out of Singapore, some American oil men, almost all of whom signed up with the armed forces later in Australia, and a few, perhaps 50, Dutch flying cadets, who were being sent out by their government in the hope that at some later time and in some other place they could get back into the fight against Japan.

Now in the brightening daylight the men, still edgy from the air raid alert they had had to wait out in helpless confinement on her deck, began to take new stock of the *Abbekerk*. They were not reassured. The ship's lifeboats could obviously carry few besides her crew. There were no life rafts, no extra life belts, nothing except some bundles of bamboo

---

* Among the late arrivals were Headquarters personnel from Bandoeng, mostly members of the Headquarters Battery of the 26th Field Artillery Brigade who, in the wild shuffling of units that occurred at the start of the war, had been sent to Java with the 131st Field Artillery aboard the *Bloemfontein*. Their commanding officer was Col. Albert C. Searle, an old Regular Army officer, a stickler in his manners, brusque and sharp. But in all the confusion of that evacuation through Tjilatjap, he, at least, was one man whose mind was clear as to his duty. After seeing his own command aboard the *Abbekerk*, he returned to Bandoeng to join the 131st Field Artillery. Lt. Stuart B. Avery, who served under him, described his leave-taking and the reason behind it.

At Bandoeng, when it became evident that Java was lost, the first reaction of Headquarters officers was to fight to the last man. Orders were issued: "Everybody will stay." But counter orders came quickly: "Everybody will go." Finally: "Only tactical troops will remain." That of course meant the 131st Field Artillery, our only ground troops in Java. When he heard of this decision just after receiving his own orders to evacuate, Col. Searle was unhappy. He went direct to General Brett and pointed out to him that all Regular Army men had been ordered out of Java, leaving only a National Guard outfit, all of whose officers were also National Guardsmen, to face the music. He therefore asked to be allowed to stay with them to represent the Regular Army in the inevitable surrender. Brett agreed to his request.

But Searle came down to Tjilatjap with his own men to see them safely aboard ship. He was strictly "Army" to the last, according to Avery, and brushed off any expression of sympathy. He gave a few last instructions, shook hands and crisply said good-by, and left. A few days later, he sent the last radio message out of Java.[7]

which had been brought aboard with the idea that they could be un-fastened and scattered overside for men to cling to. Her sole armament, a four-inch rifle mounted on the poop, was intended as a defense against submarines or surface craft. It would be useless against attacking bombers. And according to the grapevine, always gospel to the credulous, she car-ried a big load of bombs in her hold. They realized that once the *Abbekerk* put to sea, the lives of all aboard her would hang upon the cast of fate. As one pilot said, "If she was sunk, you drowned. There was no question of anything else."

An hour after sunrise the men were told that the ship would not be ready to sail till after 2:00 P.M., and that any who wished might go ashore till then. They poured from her deck like men escaping from the grave and spread out through the town, hunting for food and drink. But food was very hard to find. Refugees had been crowding into Tjilatjap all night long and the streets were jammed with streams of confused and hungry people. Most restaurant and hotel kitchens had long since been eaten bare; even the stores had been stripped of canned goods. But liquor was still plentiful, and a number of the men set out on a final celebration.

Wild rumors rode the crowds. The Japs had landed . . . they were sweeping across Java . . . they were already closing in on Tjilatjap. People wondered whether they would reach the port before the Ameri-can fighter planes arrived. Everyone seemed to know about these P-40s; it was an open secret that the *Langley* with a deckload of them was rac-ing for Tjilatjap. An air strip for the planes to take off from had been improvised outside the town and a roadway along which they must be towed up from the waterfront had been widened—trees, even houses, had been taken down to make room for their wings. Listening to all this talk, the Air Corps men thought grimly that the Japs must be equally informed and keeping particular watch upon the harbor waters.

There were several air raid alarms during the morning, and while nothing came of them, the men were under high tension as they filtered back to the wharf. By 2:00 P.M. the human line was once more climbing the stairway up the ship's side, augmented this time by the trainload that had arrived from Malang. But it took another hour for the harassed noncoms to round up all the celebrators, and it was past three before the last drunk had been shoved aboard.

Nearly 1500 men were now crammed on the deck of the *Abbekerk,* but the ship showed no sign of leaving. Word passed that the *Langley* had been sunk; they wondered how close in. At 4:00, the *Kota Gedeh* cast off and moved slowly down the harbor, the battered RAF truck on her deck a symbol of British doggedness. The men aboard the *Abbekerk* watched her with envy. Now that they were committed to their ship, they were anxious to be gone themselves. But the freighter still lingered, inviting immolation. At 5:00, the lifting wails of the air raid sirens turned all eyes to the sky, and for a second time the men had to wait out a half-hour alert penned like cattle on the ship.

Six o'clock came with no indication of departure. The field kitchen of the 11th Squadron, which had been set up on deck, started serving a dinner of corn willy for all comers. This was a slow and tedious process and in the midst of it the ship unexpectedly eased away from the wharf and began to move rapidly down the harbor. Three other ships were threading' the difficult passage ahead of her, and it now developed that the *Abbekerk* was under orders to join convoy with them. But the Dutch skipper had had his fill of convoys. For all her lamentable appearance his ship was capable of making 18 knots or better, and he had no intention of holding her down to the slow pace of the convoy. As twilight deepened, he turned off suddenly on a separate course, almost due south, for Australia.

The *Abbekerk* was now alone upon the sea. If she went down there would be none to see or lend aid, however dubious. But the fact that they were at last on their way roused the men to the need of working out some sort of organization for the voyage. This was haphazardly done, without an over-all scheme, with no attempt to assign space to individuals or groups—men were left to sleep wherever they could find space to lie down. But the need of ratic 'ng water was immediately obvious: each man was allowed half a cante⌐ ᐟ day for all purposes; and guards were stationed at the taps. Orders were 'ssued to throw no trash or garbage overboard, for fear of attracting submarines, and black-out regulations were laid down. But neither the ship's crew nor the evacuating troops were in a mood to accept these restrictions, which they persistently and openly violated. There was no discipline. The highest ranking officer aboard, a U. S. Air Corps major, seemed able to exert little authority over the troops or, for that matter, over some of the younger officers who, impelled to exercise their qualities of leadership, went about duplicating or countermanding existing orders to the confusion of everyone.

Next day, however, the ship appeared to be shaking down into routine of a sort, the principal complaint being about the food. Rations were very short, and nothing but hardtack and corned beef was available for the American mess, which meant that twice a day the men ate corned beef hash, with a single cup of coffee added at breakfast.* Yet, on that first morning, with a bright sun and a brisk running sea, the men were fairly cheerful.

This mood changed abruptly about noon with the sounding of the ship's alarm. In a tense silence, the major mounted the bridge and announced that all three of the ships they were to have joined in convoy had been sunk by Jap bombers, and that a pack of enemy submarines was reported lying in wait for them somewhere ahead. Every man was to be a lookout. It was as if a bleak wind blew through the ship. Games ceased. Men crowded the rails, straining their eyes for a periscope or the first horizon speck of an approaching plane. Even the heedless understood the uncertain balance on which their lives depended. The ship's crew manned the poop gun. Armorers among the troops mounted the machine guns on pieces of pipe which they tied to the rails with rope and wire.† Every rifle and sub-machine gun was loaded. There were even two or three shotguns in evidence. And thus armed, with all eyes scanning sea and sky, the *Abbekerk* continued on her course.

Nothing happened. As the afternoon wore on, some men began to

---

* The British and Australians preferred to organize their own mess, while the Dutch cadets ate with the ship's crew. The worst grievance of all on board was that of 24 crates of eggs on the ship, 23 were rotten.

† According to Sgt. Kezar and Cpl. Perry, only four of these were .50s.

think they might get through till nightfall without incident. But at 4:30 a cry of "Plane sighted" went up, and presently all saw it, just over the horizon, flying low, and obviously headed for them. They were sure it was Japanese long before they made out the red suns on its wings.

At the first alarm the skipper of the *Abbekerk* had changed his course to west; but, as the plane drew nearer, he suddenly turned north. Apparently puzzled by these maneuvers, the Jap pilot held off to reconnoiter, cutting leisurely circles at about 2000 feet above the ship. The plane was not a bomber as the troops had at first supposed; it looked like a lighter, reconnaissance job, and they thought it was probably off a cruiser or a carrier.

Crowded as her decks were, the *Abbekerk* must have looked relatively harmless to the Jap for, after several minutes of circling, he worked into the sun and then came down in a very shallow dive to strafe her. He had undoubtedly discounted the ship's stern gun, but the volume of small arms fire and the machine guns plainly disconcerted him, and he swerved sharply upwards out of range. He made three more passes. On the second some of the men saw two spouts rise off the ship's stern but whether these came from bombs or dropped belly tanks, they could not tell. The Jap did them no damage, and on his final pass they saw their own tracers entering the fuselage. Though the plane did not burn, it seemed to dip erratically once or twice before it disappeared; but, whether it crashed or not, they felt sure that it had reported their position—the ship's radio operator had heard the Jap's radio chattering as the plane went off; and now each man in his own way began to wait out the almost certain arrival of the bombers.

The remaining hours of daylight were the longest that most of those aboard the *Abbekerk* experienced in the war. The sun set a little past 7:00 that evening, but it did not become dark till after 7:30; and then a bright moon rose—"the biggest and brightest moon I have ever seen"—and they had the submarines to worry about also.

Men still speak of the miserable, sick fear that assailed them on that moonlight night. A blind hysteria pursued the ship. There was a feeling of utter disorganization. Two men tried to kill themselves. To add to their troubles, the weather turned rough and cold. Sleeping on the bare deck, with only a blanket, they were soaked and chilled to the bone. A radio rumor that MacArthur had reoccupied the land around Manila meant nothing to them. All they wanted was to get safe ashore.

But the rest of the voyage was uneventful. Four days later, the *Abbekerk* raised the Australian coast on the morning of the 5th and they landed that afternoon at Fremantle. They were taken by train to Perth and then on 60 miles inland to an Australian camp at Northam, where half of them were served a hot supper of lamb stew and tea, and the other half, probably as a treat, were given corned beef hash. The Australians had no cots for them, so they had to sleep, as they had for the past five nights, on the bare floor. But they were too tired to care: they were ashore; and for the moment Australia seemed safe from the Japs.

12. *The Loss of the* Langley

THE RUMOR that the *Langley* had been sunk, which reached the troops aboard the *Abbekerk* in Tjilatjap harbor, was well founded. It was fortunate for their morale that they did not know how few miles south of them she had gone down, for the Japs caught her on the 27th when she was in the last stretch of her race for Java. But her loss was only one act in a grim sequence which must be sketched briefly here if we are to complete the record of the five provisional pursuit squadrons that had begun their training back at Brisbane in January.

From the start, the mission of the *Langley* was clouded by confusion and uncertain purpose. The decision to use her for ferrying pursuit to Java had been reached as early as February 7; the only two squadrons then available in Australia, the 33rd and 13th, were assigned to her; and by February 12, the first contingent of planes from the 33rd Squadron, under Major Pell, was on its way across the continent to join the ship at Fremantle. But on that day, as the reader will recall, orders to cover the Koepang convoy intercepted Pell at Port Pirie, and he turned north for Darwin instead.* Actually ABDACOM had ordered two full squadrons sent to Darwin, though how they expected these to be provided and

* See above, Part Two, Chapter 8.

the commitment to the *Langley* to be filled before the ship sailed is hard
to understand.* The only other pursuit units in Australia were the newly
arrived squadrons of the 49th Group, which were still assembling their
planes and had yet to begin combat training.† Confronted by this Hob-
son's choice, General Barnes decided that Pell's planes would have to
suffice at Darwin till a reinforcing squadron could be sent up. In the
meantime, the remaining planes of the 33rd were placed under the command of Captain Gerald M. Keenan and ordered to Fremantle with the
13th Squadron. This seemed a reasonable enough solution of ABDA-
COM's conflicting desires; but it could hardly have worked out more
disastrously. For all but one of Pell's planes were wiped out at Darwin
on the 19th, and of the 33 pilots who boarded the *Langley* with their
32 P-40s and twelve enlisted men, two came back.

There had been a good deal of uncertainty, also, over the destination
of the convoy. Originally it had been consigned to Java. Three transports, carrying 2953 Air Corps troops,‡ with ten P-40s in their holds,
and the freighter *Seawitch* with 27 more P-40s, sailed from Melbourne
on February 12. The *Langley* and the escorting cruiser, *Phoenix,* were to
join them at Fremantle. But by February 17 it had become evident to the
American and British elements in ABDACOM that Java would have to
be abandoned and Brett, with mounting concern over developments in
Burma, on that day ordered the entire convoy to India. This roused immediate protests from the Dutch. They did not want the troops, but
they did feel that their only chance of holding off the Japs now depended on the prompt arrival of the P-40s, and their insistence on delivery was backed by General Marshall.§ Consequently, when the convoy
finally put out from Fremantle on February 22, the three transports were
still bound for India, but the *Langley* and *Seawitch* had orders to attempt
the run into Tjilatjap.

* ABDACOM must have known the situation, for the commitment schedule for
pursuit units had earlier been submitted by General Barnes and approved by General
Brett.[1]

† They had landed at Melbourne on February 1.[2]

‡ These troops included Headquarters personnel and part of the ground echelons of
the 7th Bombardment and 35th and 51st Pursuit Groups, the 51st and 45th Air Base
Groups, and various service units. As previously stated, the three transports were the
Holbrook, Duntroon, and *Katoomba.*

§ See above, Part Two, Chapter 10 (note 30).

They were to stay with the convoy till it neared the Cocos Islands, perhaps 800. miles southwest of Java; then, with the *Phoenix,* they were to cut back to Tjilatjap. This was obviously the safest course, but it meant extra days of steaming when the fate of Java was being measured in hours; and Admiral Helfrich ordered the two ships to leave the convoy at a point much closer Java, intending them to make an unescorted night approach that would bring them to port on the morning of the 28th. But once more time and the desperate need for fighter planes forced a change of plan. On the 23rd he ordered the *Langley* to proceed alone at top speed in an effort to reach Tjilatjap by the afternoon of the 27th.*

The risks were obvious and very great, yet if the planes were to do any good at all they must come at once, and the 32 P–40s aboard the ship were exactly twice as many as the 17th Squadron were able that morning to send up against the enemy. It would be impossible to exaggerate their importance to the plane-starved Java command. Admiral Glassford approved Helfrich's decision; [4] but at the same time, though no Japanese ships had yet been seen south of Java, he assigned the destroyers *Whipple* and *Edsall* † to meet the *Langley* and bring her in through her final morning's run.

The first three days of the *Langley's* voyage were deceptively quiet. Then, on the afternoon of the 26th, while still more than 100 miles out, she was picked up by two Dutch flying boats which reported that a Dutch minesweeper was coming up to escort her into Tjilatjap. This caused some confusion, for Commander R. P. McConnell of the *Langley* was expecting the two destroyers; and, after some delay, and finding that the minesweeper could not match even the ten knots of his own ship,‡ he decided to go on alone. During the night, however, he received a message confirming the Dutch PBYs and minesweeper as his escorts.

He turned back obediently to find them, but the planes were not sighted till well after daylight, and then they were circling the *Whipple*

---

* The *Seawitch* seems to have continued on the course laid out on the 22nd, to bring her to port on the 28th, for she left the convoy several hours after the *Langley.*[3]

† Both destroyers had been damaged by collision and in action; neither was in condition for combat.

‡ The *Langley's* speed was held down by the quality of the Indies oil, to which her engines were not adapted.[5]

and *Edsall* instead of the minesweeper. McConnell must have been a puzzled and frustrated man. He had his destroyer escort at last, but he was still 100 miles from port and the morning was well advanced by the time the three ships finally started their run for Tjilatjap. It was a sunny day, too, with a light wind and scattered clouds and visibility unlimited; ideal for air reconnaissance but deadly for ships upon the sea.

At 9:00 A.M. they sighted an unidentified plane. McConnell radioed for fighter cover; but none came, for there was none to send. By then the 17th Squadron was down to twelve P-40s in commission; even counting the surviving Brewsters and Hurricanes, there were hardly 30 fighter planes left in Java; and with the Japanese invasion fleets now closing in, these had to be saved for use against the beaches. The *Langley* and her two destroyers were left to take their chance alone.

At 11:40 the Japs came after them with nine twin-engined bombers, flying at about 15,000 feet. Just as they reached the bomb-release line, the ship was turned sharp right and the bombs dropped a hundred feet to port. The *Langley* was severely shaken and riddled with shrapnel, but she was all right; and as the Japs started their second run, she repeated her maneuver. But the bombardiers held their bombs for a third run; and this time as the ship turned, the planes turned with her.

Seldom has a ship been harder hit at a single salvo. She took five direct hits and three near-misses. The P-40s on her deck burst into flames; there were fires below; the water mains were burst; she was taking water and listing 10 degrees to port; and her steering mechanism was destroyed. The engines still ran, however, so Commander McConnell maneuvered her to kill as much wind as possible and the crew started fighting for her life. They shoved the burning planes overboard and tried to correct her list by counterflooding. But she was mortally hurt; her pumps could not keep pace with the leaks; and at 2:30 in the afternoon she was abandoned. All but 16 of her crew and the Air Corps personnel were taken aboard the two destroyers, and the *Whipple* then sank her, 74 miles south of Tjilatjap.

A little luck, a little less confusion, and she might easily have reached her goal; though, of course, it was already so late that her 32 P-40s could have accomplished nothing. From a tactical viewpoint Brett was right enough in not wanting them committed to Java in that final hour. Yet the *Langley* might just as well have started from Fremantle ten days or two weeks earlier and brought in her load of P-40s without opposition, when their presence would have really counted.

Hindsight, however, always comes cheap. In the Indian Ocean then the hunt was just beginning, for, though the planes that had found and sunk the *Langley* were land based and operating from either Borneo or Celebes,[6] the Japanese had also sent their carrier and battleship force through Lombok Strait, and these ships were now ranging south of Java in search of just such refugees and strays.

As the two destroyers headed west from the *Langley's* grave with more than 400 survivors divided between them, they received orders to proceed to Christmas Island, there to transfer their passengers to the Naval oiler *Pecos,* for they were needed elsewhere. The *Pecos* had left Tjilatjap that morning, bound for Ceylon and a load of oil, under escort of the destroyer *Parrott;* when these new orders came through, the destroyer turned off on another mission and the oiler changed course for the rendezvous alone. She reached it safely on the morning of February 28 to find the *Whipple* and *Edsall* waiting. But before the transfer could begin, Japanese bombers were seen approaching from the direction of Sumatra, and the three ships put out from the docks at full speed and headed for cover in a rain squall. The Jap bombers, however, were only interested in the docks and all three ships escaped.

Just before the ships plunged into the squall, a submarine periscope was sighted, so it was decided to keep south till they were out of range and then effect the transfer at sea. This was finally accomplished early on the morning of March 1, though for some reason all the P-40 pilots, except for two wounded officers—Lieutenants William P. Ackerman and Gerald J. Dix—were kept aboard the *Edsall.*[7] The destroyers then departed, leaving the *Pecos* to set her course for Fremantle alone.

It was the last ever seen of the *Edsall.* She, her crew, and the 31 pilots aboard her simply disappeared. Only after the war was it learned that two Japanese battleships had caught her that same afternoon and sunk her with all hands.[8]

But the *Whipple* was to renew acquaintance with the men aboard the *Pecos*.

For nearly six hours the oiler steamed southward through an empty sea but a sense of gathering doom rode with her, and the men were hardly surprised when an enemy plane came up to them from the northeast. It was a single-engined job, with retracted wheels—obviously off a carrier. As soon as the *Pecos* opened fire on it, the pilot turned away and finally disappeared; but now everyone aboard the ship knew what was coming. An hour and three quarters later the dive bombers were at them.

The Japs attacked in three waves, at roughly one-hour intervals, so the *Pecos's* fight lasted nearly three hours. The men fought with everything they had, the *Langley's* gun crews taking over as quickly as casualties developed; but they could not hold the planes off. There were six in the first wave, each of which made two attacks. The first three bombs missed; but the next wiped out a gun crew; then a near-miss amidships gave the ship an 8-degree list. She was already hurt: the second wave of planes really punished her. When they were through, the ship had a 20-foot hole in her side and was burning; her list had increased to 15 degrees; her foremast and radio antenna had been carried away; and a final hit forced the cutting of two boilers, reducing her speed.

Between attacks all hands turned to to fight the fires and correct the list. The fires proved not to be serious; but it was obvious that the ship had suffered basic damage and there were doubts about her ability to survive. A rumor started among the passengers that the order to abandon her had gone out. Several life rafts were dropped and men started going overside before the error was corrected, just in time for the ship to brace herself for the third wave of dive bombers.

This time there were nine. They scored no direct hits, but the third of three near-misses caused the ship to settle slowly forward, and finally she went down about 3:45 in the afternoon. The order to abandon ship was given a few minutes before she sank and the men went overboard with anything that would float. They were struggling in the water all about the ship when a fourth relay of planes came over and strafed them—though one man at the .50-caliber machine gun on her upended stern kept firing till her final minute.

Meanwhile, though the *Pecos's* radio had been jarred off frequency, the *Whipple* had picked up her distress call and immediately reversed course. She came up about two hours before midnight, trailing lines and cargo nets, and started picking men out of the water. Only 232 were taken aboard. Some of the rescued men reported having seen the conning tower of a submarine earlier in the evening. This was exactly the kind of bait a Jap would like to use. When the *Whipple* picked up the sound of propellers, she dropped depth charges and cleared out at once. The rest of the men were left to drown. How many had survived till then, no one knew. There had been 672 aboard the *Langley* and *Pecos* when the ships left port: 440 had been lost. In some ways it was as dark an hour for the rescued and their rescuers. But the *Whipple* reached Fremantle safely on March 5.

The *Seawitch* was luckier. Armed with only four old Vickers water-cooled .30-caliber machine guns, and with a gun crew of Air Corps mechanics who had never fired a machine gun in their lives, she made her approach to Tjilatjap on the night of February 27 after she had been looked over and obviously disdained by a Japanese reconnaissance plane. She arrived during the morning of the 28th and discharged her 27 crated planes on lighters. By then, of course, the *Abbekerk* had sailed. There were no men left to assemble the planes had there been time to do the work. They were destroyed in their crates by the Dutch; and after a day and a night in port the *Seawitch* set out for Fremantle with a few evacuees, among whom were some of the last British and Australian pilots to escape from Singapore. She made the return trip without incident.[9]

No further attempts were made to reinforce Java. There were neither planes nor men to send. And time had run out. It was the 1st of March. At Rembang, to the west of Soerabaja, the Japanese had already made good their landing.

13. *Evacuation: The Air Echelons*

REPORTS that Japanese invasion forces had been sighted in the Java Sea reached Bomber Headquarters on February 26. Late in the afternoon two B-17s * bombed and missed a convoy northeast of Bawean Island.[1] That night an LB-30 † flew a long search mission out of Jogjakarta. For six hours the bomber in solitary flight through broken moonlight and towering drifts of cloud covered the sea approaches. All it encountered was some weather south of Borneo, and it came home at dawn reporting nothing seen.[2] Yet the Japs were already well down, and the Bomber Command, mustering its resources, launched three missions against them during the day.

Five minutes after the LB-30 landed, four B-17s took off from Malang to attack a convoy 100 miles north of Java. Three of these planes turned back with engine failure. The one that went on found ships in the designated area and bombed from low altitude but, being alone, ducked immediately into clouds without observing results.‡ An hour later two B-17s from Madioen reached the target and, after counting 35 transports, bombed them through the clouds.[4] That was the extent of the heavy bomber effort on the 27th. The third mission was flown by the three remaining A-24s.§ Taking off from Malang at 4:15 that afternoon to attack the same convoy, they picked up their escort of ten P-40s ‖ and headed north to find themselves suddenly looking down on the naval battle that became known as the Battle of the Java Sea. Both fleets were heavily engaged. The Allied ships, nearest Java, were then moving on a southwesterly course. A little north and steaming roughly parallel were

---

* Pilots were Capt. Hardison and Lt. Bernice S. Barr.
† The pilot was Lt. Dougherty.
‡ Piloted by Lt. P. L. Mathewson.[3]
§ Four A-24s were scheduled, but the hydraulic system on one gave out. The pilots able to take off were Galusha, Summers, Ferguson. By this time Galusha had succeeded Backus in the Squadron command.[5]
‖ The P-40s were in two flights of four and six planes: Kizer, Morehead, Fuchs, and Lund in the first; and Dale, R. S. Johnson, Adkins, Dockstader, Kruzel, and Caldwell in the second.[6]

twelve Japanese ships. Still farther north, but heading almost due south, were what the pilots took to be six Japanese cruisers. Behind them, at considerable distance, was the convoy—43 transports by their count, with a naval escort of 15 ships.* The fliers had a real grandstand view, for the irrepressible Galusha, who was leading the mission, took them right across the whole show, displaying, as his companions said, "more nerve than brains,"[9] and only afterwards confessed that in spite of his orders to go after transports, he was looking for a carrier.† But no carriers were involved, and the A–24s with their escort of P–40s whirled away northward to attack the transports, one of which they definitely sank.‡

There was bitter irony in this passage of ten P–40s across the scene of battle. All of Admiral Doorman's requests for fighter cover had been denied, for the Air Command was determined to use everything it had left against the transports.§ His last appeal went out at 4:00 P.M., only a few minutes before the Japanese cruiser planes appeared and while the P–40s were still warming up at Blimbing. Doorman himself had no planes. He had put to sea late on the 26th expecting a night action and consequently the Allied cruisers had left their planes behind.[13] This meant that throughout the battle they could correct gunfire only while they maintained visual contact with the enemy, while the Japanese with three float planes could consistently spot their fire and at the same time keep

---

* It is interesting, and one more revelation of the lack of training in naval identification, to read that the fliers saw the Allied fleet as composed of six cruisers and five destroyers. Actually there were only five cruisers; but at this stage of the battle there should have been nine destroyers. The fliers may have missed the three British destroyers screening ahead of the column. Similarly, though their count of 18 Japanese ships was correct, they saw them as twelve cruisers, three destroyers, and three battleships, when there were really two heavy and two light cruisers and 14 destroyers. Their total of 43 transports may have been right (though there were presumably 41) but they described the escort as 15 destroyers when actually there were only four, with nine auxiliaries.[7] Yet in early U. S. Naval accounts identification was little better; they also saw a plethora of cruisers and battleships.[8]

† Galusha and Summers had flown the impromptu, unescorted mission over Bali on February 19. See above, Part Two, Chapter 8 (note 52).

‡ The dive bombers claimed three ships sunk,[10] but the accompanying P–40 pilots saw only one go down, which they described as 14,000 tons.[11]

§ Besides the P–40s and supporting Brewsters and Hurricanes at Blimbing (the last two types were not used on the 27th), the Air Command had a few Blenheim bombers, some of the antique British Wildebeestes, and two or three Hudsons. According to one account, some Dutch bombers attacked the Jap fleet at 4:45 P.M.[12]

every move of Doorman's under observation. Much of the action was blindman's buff with only one side blindfolded. One wonders how the outcome would have been affected had a few of the P-40s been assigned to knock down the Jap spotting planes.

When the three A-24 pilots returned to Malang, they found the base deserted except for their own people and two 19th Group officers * left behind with ten enlisted men to burn abandoned planes. Orders were for everyone to report to Jogjakarta, bringing all flyable planes. One of the three A-24s had been so badly shaken by the antiaircraft over the Jap convoy that it could not take off; so next morning the two surviving planes of their original 15 were flown across the mountains while the rest of the Squadron went by car. That night they were on their way to Australia.

The air evacuation was now running in high gear. Eubank held as many men on the base as he thought the combat planes could carry out, but at the same time he had at least two planes fly back from Broome each night to provide an extra margin in case of an emergency evacuation. It was lucky he did so. Even when the dive bomber crews went out, the planes were being overloaded. The first flights south had been made with twelve passengers in each B-17. This maximum load was now stepped up to 20. It was to go higher still.

The air crews in the evacuation flights were under heavy pressure, especially those who made a quick turnaround at Broome. They were once more doing their own maintenance, and the facilities for B-17s and LB-30s at Broome were nil. In any case there was hardly time to work over a rough engine. If it ran at all it was good enough. Details of the Naval disaster in the Java Sea had reached Madioen and Jogjakarta during the dawn hours of the 28th. The men knew that with the Navy beaten there was nothing left to hold the Japs off the beaches. Their own two groups had seven planes in combat commission—six B-17s at Madioen and one LB-30 at Jogjakarta. These and whatever the pursuit squadron could put up at Blimbing were all the effective air there was in Java.

A sketch of the flight record of Teats's plane will illustrate the pace

---

* Lts. Sig R. Young and Frederick W. Walker, Jr., who had volunteered to do the job.

at which the men were working. They took off at 2:00 A.M. on the 26th with twelve passengers. Nine hundred miles southeast, after just six hours, they were over Broome. The flight had been easy enough, though one engine developed an oil leak a little before they landed. They worked on it for four hours but could not repair it, so the return flight had to be made on three engines, using the fourth only in taking off and landing. It took them six hours and a half to get back.

Though more men were flown out of Malang that night, Teats's plane was one of four scheduled to attack the approaching Japanese convoy on the 27th. The crew put in extra hours getting it ready for the mission, but the oil leak again developed and on three engines, with full bomb load, they could not make altitude. Teats had to turn back, as did two other pilots, Captains Fred M. Key and Dean C. Hoevet, leaving the fourth, Mathewson, as we have already seen, to attack the convoy alone.

This was the day the 19th Group moved out of Malang, so the three ailing Fortresses headed for Jogjakarta, from which both Teats and Key were scheduled to make evacuation flights that night. As soon as they landed, they were told that a raid was due, and a few minutes later the yellow alert flag went up.* They took off once more to fly the usual beat up and down the south coast for the next two or three hours. While thus occupied they met a flight of nine twin-engined Jap bombers heading north and somewhat higher than themselves. Neither side made any hostile gestures, but the B-17 crews wondered what the Japs had been after. On their return to Jogjakarta they learned that the *Langley* had been sunk by nine bombers. Undoubtedly they were the same ones.

When they landed at Jogjakarta for the second time that afternoon, the crew had spent 20½ hours out of the last 36 in the air; they had put in more than eight hours on maintenance; and they now had to prepare their plane for the flight to Broome. It was 5:00 A.M. when, after about three hours' sleep, they finally got away with 19 officers and enlisted men aboard. The engine again developed its oil leak, but they were getting used to traveling on three engines and, while the flight took close to seven hours, they brought their passengers safely in to Broome.

---

* Besides the siren Jogjakarta used flags, run up on the control tower flagpole, for air raid warning. Yellow meant alert; red, planes sighted and attacking; green, All Clear. A black ball was to be used for a gas attack.

They now had almost 24 hours on the ground, a large part of which had to be spent working on the plane. However, by noon of March 1 they were in the air on their way back to Jogjakarta, this time accompanied by another B–17 piloted by Captain Edwin S. Green. It was another slow flight, with poor visibility all the way. Java was closed in when they reached it about sunset, and they had a difficult time finding their way in to the field.

Some planes had already gone out that afternoon; one carrying Colonel Eubank had left shortly before they landed.* But there were still 260 men waiting to be evacuated. These included the crews of six B–17s and one LB–30 which had flown ten sorties against the Japs since midnight,† and the remaining members of the 17th Pursuit Squadron who had arrived during the afternoon. The job looked hopeless but luckily another B–17 came in out of the twilight, and by crowding every plane to the limit, all the men were taken out. Teats's plane took off at 10:45 with 26 passengers. They hit Broome just at sunrise, refueled, and went straight on to Perth, another 1000 miles and 7½ hours farther south.

That completed their record in the evacuation. Altogether they had brought out 57 men. During the past four days they had spent more than 50 hours in the air, and except for the first trip south, this flying had all been done on three engines.[14] They had earned a respite.

Most of the men who came out on Teats's last flight were pilots of the 17th Pursuit Squadron. They had flown their final mission early that morning. It was the last effective mission to be flown by Allied air forces in Java, and the only one of any significance sent against the Japs' eastern invasion convoy.

This convoy had turned back at the start of the naval action on the 27th and waited 100 miles north of Bawean Island for the issue to be de-

---

* Eubank's plane took off about 6:00 P.M.

† There is no real record of all the missions flown March 1. Messages dated March 2, without origin, to TAG list three other unspecified missions by eleven U. S. planes. It is hard to credit these. Eubank himself reported ten missions flown between midnight and noon of March 1. Actually these included seven individual sorties against the landing convoy, as already noted. This figure tallies with the recorded missions flown during the day. The last, however, was in the afternoon, Mathewson taking off at 2:50 against ships off Bali. There may have been unofficial missions, but to me it seems unlikely.

cided. Thus Java had received an extra day of grace, as did the ten surviving Allied warships which lay in Batavia and Soerabaja desperately preparing their escape.* But for the 17th Squadron the 28th was just another routine day. They flew two missions over Soerabaja reinforced by four of the Dutch Brewsters.† As usual nowadays they were unable to get up to the level of the Jap bombers and came back to Blimbing empty-handed, while one of the Brewsters was lost when its engine failed.

The Squadron now had 13 P-40s, twelve of which they listed in commission. That proved an optimistic figure. Two were unable to take off with the afternoon flight and one of the ten that went was in such bad shape mechanically that it could not keep up with the rest.‡ This left them nine planes for their final mission.

Orders for it had already reached Major Fisher at Interceptor Control in Soerabaja. The Jap convoy was on its way in, headed for the coast west of Soerabaja, and the 17th was to attack the landing at daybreak on March 1 with all available planes. When Fisher reported to Headquarters that there were only nine shaky P-40s, Eubank instructed him to make a personal check of the condition of the Squadron. The mission was to be performed if it was humanly possible.

Fisher went out to Blimbing late that afternoon and found both pilots and enlisted men pretty well aware of the score. During the day the machine guns they had set up round the field for antiaircraft had been removed by Dutch troops for use against the Japanese landings. Then, a little before Fisher's arrival, a Zero had spotted the now defenseless airfield and, as we have seen, only a providential thunderstorm had saved it from immediate attack. The men did not need to be told that the mission coming up would be the Squadron's last.

It was set up for a 5:30 take-off. The nine P-40s were divided into flights of three. Kizer, who had succeeded to the Squadron command,

* Of these ten ships only four (U. S. destroyers *Edwards, Alden, Ford,* and *Paul Jones*) got away. The cruisers *Houston* and *Perth* and the Dutch destroyer *Evertsen* were sunk in an action in Sunda Strait in the early hours of March 1, while the British cruiser *Exeter* and destroyer *Encounter* with the U. S. destroyer *Pope* were caught north of Soerabaja shortly after noon the same day.

† The Squadron history lists two missions, but Gambonini records three in his diary—two in the morning at 8:00 and 11:00, and one at 2:30 in the afternoon.[15]

‡ At this time one flier sadly wrote: "My plane has two tires that have huge blisters on them. It has no brakes and no generator and hydraulic fluid is leaking into the cockpit."[16]

would lead the mission and the first flight with Adkins and R. S. Johnson on his wings; Dale would lead the second, with Caldwell and McWherter; Kruzel the third, with Reagan and Fuchs as wingmen. The six Hurricanes were to follow the P-40s in: since this was to be a low-altitude mission, their faulty oxygen equipment could be discounted. Last of all would come the four remaining Brewsters.

The Japanese made their landing in Rembang Bay, 100 miles west of Soerabaja, with moonlight and a quiet sea to aid them. Scattered attacks by U. S. heavy bombers and nine old British Wildebeestes * did little to damage and nothing to delay them.[17] Before dawn their main force of troops was ashore and the beachhead established with shore batteries and a heavy concentration of antiaircraft.

The P-40s approached the coast flying very low across the paddy fields and then swung in a wide arc to the east to get the rising sun behind them. As they came out over the water, they saw a line of 30 transports curving with the beach. Between these ships and the shore a multitude of small boats and barges were plying back and forth. Back a little from the bay were shadowy concentrations of landed troops, and farther inland, breaking out from the main bodies, were lesser groups, feeling their way towards the low green hills, like small, exploratory troops of ants. There was actually an antlike quality to the whole scene, busy, methodical, ruthlessly unconcerned with human factors. But this illusion was abruptly shattered as the antiaircraft on the ships and along the full length of the beach opened on the approaching fighters.

The P-40s were caught in a furious cross fire. Caldwell's † plane was hit instantly. It crashed in the sea. Almost in the same instant Reagan's plane burst into flames. A fellow pilot escorted him across the beachhead and saw his plane start for the ground but was driven off by antiaircraft

---

* For a description of these antique ships and their performance, see above, Part Two, Chapter 1 (note 17). These, at Madioen, were fugitives from Malaya and were flown by Australian and New Zealand pilots who swore they "had gotten them from the Singapore Museum." They loaded up with 50-kilo bombs and, according to a B-17 pilot then at Madioen, "flew across the convoy at 500 feet, returned, landed, looked at the hundreds of holes in their wings, laughed like hell, got another drink of whiskey, and went back."

† Lt. Morris C. Caldwell, who had already been shot down once over Soerabaja on February 18.

fire before Reagan crashed. He was not seen again.* R. S. Johnson's plane was also hit and started throwing oil, and he had to break off. He reached Blimbing in an oil-black ship, oil-black himself and half blinded, with two inches of oil in his cockpit.¹⁹ Then Frank Adkins carried his dive so far home that his plane hit the sea as he pulled out. He got control of it, but the Japs, firing level, caught him as he was going away, and the plane started burning. He managed to get a little altitude and bailed out just over the Jap lines. A heavy caliber shell hit Kruzel's engine but for some reason it did not quit and Kruzel stayed with the others strafing the antiaircraft batteries up and down the beach and on the transports, with occasional passes at the barges, till his ammunition had run out. Then he turned for home, as did the others, one after another, to arrive singly, only when their guns were empty.²⁰

They had sunk a few barges and they silenced enough antiaircraft batteries so that the Hurricanes and Brewsters came through successfully. But the cost went beyond the loss of Reagan and Caldwell and, as they then thought, Adkins. The six P-40s that came back had been so terribly shot up that it was doubtful whether even six flyable planes could be constructed out of the ten still left on the field. However, while the men were looking them over, counting bullet holes and assessing damage with a kind of awe, they learned that orders releasing them from further combat had come in from Air Headquarters. They were to turn their equipment over to the Dutch and then report at Jogjakarta. The problem of how to build combat planes out of their wrecks no longer concerned them.

An hour later it did not concern the Dutch either. At 9:00 A.M. two Zeros came in to strafe the field. With no opposition of any sort to hinder them, the two Jap pilots ranged back and forth till they had hunted out and destroyed every one of the parked planes. There was nothing left for the Squadron to do but pack their scant belongings and climb aboard their trucks and single staff car and pull out.

* Lt. Cornelius F. K. Reagan. "McWherter was flying on the Kentuckian's wing and signaled Reagan, whose motor was spitting flames, to fly with him to the beach and then bail out. Reagan understood and waved back. Possibly he was shot or his parachute was holed. Whatever the reason, he did something McWherter never forgot. He plucked himself a cigarette, rolled back the canopy, reached forward, and lighted the cigarette on the burning motor, and put it in his mouth to await the end." ¹⁸

They had a rough trip across the mountains. Twice they were lost and forced to backtrack. As their route lay diagonally across the line of Japanese advance, they were often close to the guns. They saw the smoke of the burning towns and in the villages they passed through the Dutch were blowing up their mills. It was past 4:00 when they finally rolled into Jogjakarta. The field had just been strafed. It was a nuisance raid. The real harm had been done two hours earlier when Jap bombers hit two parked LB–30s and damaged them beyond hope of repair.

It now seemed unlikely that all pursuit personnel could be taken out. The question hinged on whether any planes would get up from Australia, and no men were ever happier to see a plane touch wheels to earth than the men of the 17th were when Teats's three-engined Fortress followed Green's out of the twilight sky.

Then, while they were rolling drums of gas out to the newly arrived planes—for all native help had long since vanished from the field— Adkins appeared in their midst with a wild and wonderful account of his escape. After bouncing off the sea, being set afire by Jap tracers, and bailing out, he hit the ground barely 300 yards from the Jap lines. The Jap troops saw him come down and started after him. He himself immediately took out for the interior and at the crucial instant saw a native pedaling a bicycle frantically along a neighboring road. He cut the man off and commandeered a ride on the handlebars. The terrified native started off at a tremendous rate, but after a few minutes began to show signs of engine failure; and, seeing that the Japs were gaining ground, Adkins unceremoniously ditched him, took over the pedals himself, and in a few minutes distanced his pursuers. After that he pumped for miles along strange roads and finally picked up a carload of Dutch officers on their way to Jogjakarta. They took him aboard their car; and here he was, turning up like a good-luck piece in time to take off with the rest.

But there were still doubts about all of them being able to get out, for though five of the B–17s from Madioen * came in to Jogjakarta before

* At least one of the B–17s at Madioen took its own route direct to Australia. It had flown the last U. S. bombing mission in Java and was the last plane to leave Madioen. It "had a busted tail wheel. The crew jacked it up and fashioned a skid of 2 x 4s and one chunk of 4 x 4 and braced it with cable. They figured it would do just to take off with, which it did, and they flew on to Darwin, where they made a perfect landing. When

starting for Australia, all were already heavily loaded. As they took off one by one in the darkness, it looked more and more as if some of the 17th were not going to make it. And about 10:00 P.M. Captain Lane, who had charge of their evacuation, told the men that if safe loading was to be observed, 15 of them would have to stay. He called for volunteers.

Meanwhile there were increasing difficulties with the Dutch on the base. About 2:00 P.M. orders had been received from Bandoeng that both Madioen and Jogjakarta were to be destroyed and all planes moved to Malang. Colonel Eubank refused to comply. He again notified General Van Oyen that in his opinion operating out of Malang would result in inevitable and unjustifiable losses on the ground, and that he intended to carry out his plan of transferring all American Air Forces to Australia.[21]

He had no other choice if he was going to save his planes. His bomber force was now reduced to two B–17s in commission. One LB–30 and two more B–17s could be put in commission in twenty-four hours if facilities existed for doing the work, but both Madioen and Jogjakarta had been repeatedly hit in the past two days and there was no reason to believe that the fields could be protected. There were no more pursuit planes in Java.

After Eubank's departure at 6:00 P.M., the Dutch, while making no further effort to retain the B–17s, became increasingly insistent about blowing up all facilities and both the runways. Though none of the bomber pilots had been aware of the fact, all the strips on all three bomber fields had been mined for some time. They just needed to be touched off; and as the night closed down the instinct to finish the job and depart for their ultimate stations became almost overpowering for the few Dutch troops. All round the field the crash of explosions in

they looked over the skid, they found it was OK, so they took off again with it and made another good landing at Melbourne. M/Sgts. Walter Ashby and Louis Silva were the inventors and Lt. McPherson was the pilot. The Dutch had the field mined and all the time the men were building their skid under the plane the Dutch were threatening to blow the field up and it would be necessary to stop the work to persuade the Dutch to wait a little longer. Finally they finished the job and took off and the Dutch blew up the field practically under the plane's tail." McPherson was the pilot who had nearly set his plane down on the Jap-held field in Bali. See above, Part Two, Chapter 8 (note 17).

the darkness told of bridges and key roads being blown to halt the enemy. The runways and hangar faces were wildly lit by the rise and fall of fires still burning from the last strafing raid. No attempt had been made to put them out. It would have made no sense. Nothing was left, and the Dutch, waiting by the switches and staring at the silhouetted wings of the big American bombers that had failed to save their island, could hardly be persuaded to wait till they had gone.

But at last only two LB–30s were left on the field. All the B–17s had taken off, sluggish with their overloads of men. When Captain Lane called on the 17th Squadron for volunteers to stay behind, the enlisted men took it up with the bomber crews, and the crews went to their pilots. The pilots agreed to divide the surplus among their ships. Everyone was to go and everyone knew and accepted the risks. There would be no chance for passengers of a plane ditched at sea.

The first of the two LB–30s took off at a quarter to midnight. Forty-five minutes later, at 12:30 on the morning of March 2,* the second went down the runway and lifted with laboring engines into the dark sky. No more U. S. planes remained at Jogjakarta, and when the beat of the bomber's engines finally subsided, the American air effort in Java had been officially closed.†

At 7:15 the plane delivered its 35 passengers at Broome, completing

* Some accounts, including that in the official Air Force history,²² state that the evacuation here described took place on the night of March 2-3. But their accounts are based on Lt. Edward O. Yerington's "The Evacuation of Java" in the memorial history of the 435th Reconnaissance Squadron. A careful reading of Yerington, however, shows a discrepancy in his dates. He says that he took off at 11:45 P.M., March 2, in the next to last LB–30, arrived at Broome at 6:30 next morning, spent the whole of that day and the following night there, and was then caught in the Jap attack on Broome, March 4 by his reckoning; but the attack occurred on March 3, so it is obvious that he must have taken off on the night of March 1-2, which I have here assumed. However, both McTague and DeWold in their interviews claim to have left March 2-3. But the events described by McTague as immediately preceding his departure from Madioen fit exactly the known record of February 28 and March 1, rather than March 1-2 as he places them. And DeWold is not specific in his facts. It was not impossible, but to me it seems likely that no further official evacuation of troops took place after the morning of March 2.

† It was not the last U. S. plane to leave Java, however. At Bandoeng, T/Sgt. Harry Hayes, in charge of inspection and repair at the Andir Air Depot, realized by March 2 that no plane would be sent back to get him out, and, selecting the most hopeful of three shot-up and bomb-damaged B–17Es, put it in shape to fly, with the aid of native labor from the local railroad shops. It was ready by March 4. With a civilian pilot (Gerald L. Cherymisin) and a Dutch air officer as co-pilot (Lt. Sibolt J. Kok), Hayes was preparing to take off

the military evacuation.[23] No planes or men had been lost. But Dutch, British, and Australian civilian planes continued to arrive all through that day and the morning of March 3, when, as we shall see, the Japanese wrote a final bloody postscript to the Java episode.

14. *Broome: An End and a Beginning*

THERE WERE NO DEFENSES at Broome. It had neither radar, antiaircraft guns, nor fighter planes. It stood alone on the great northwestern curve of the Australian continent, on a wide bay, open to the sea. Behind it to the northeast was a line of low and arid hills. To the south, hundreds of miles farther than the eye could reach, lay the desert. A barely discernible road, leading inland, linked the small web of streets to the single highway that issued from the eastern hills to follow a tenuous course southwest along the coast. By this route the nearest city, Perth, was 1600 miles away and a truck in the rainy season might take a month to make the distance. There was no railroad except for a single narrow-gauge track that wound up from the waterside, through the town, to some gold mines in the hills: along it on occasion a small-sized locomotive, shaped like the ones in pictures of our Civil War, laboriously pulled a string of tiny flatcars.

The town looked pretty enough from the air when the detachment sent down from Malang to set up an evacuation center there flew in on the morning of February 24; but they found it a desolate place, very hot, loaded with mosquitoes, and with half the houses shuttered and empty. Most of the town's women and children had already left and the rest of the inhabitants were moving out as quickly as they could find transportation, for the fate of Darwin was fresh in all minds.

Organization of the center had been placed under the direction of

when the Zeros caught the plane again and it had to be wheeled back under the trees for further repairs. That night, however, it took off on three engines, with Kok lighting the instrument panel with his flashlight, and, though neither he nor Cherymisin had ever flown a B–17 before, reached Australia safely. The date, March 4, is according to *Summary of Air Action* and Hayes's citation. In his interview with me Hayes stated that they did not take off till noon of March 6.

Colonel E. S. Perrin, who had been on Brett's staff in Java and had himself just arrived at Broome. He seemed to be chiefly concerned with developing the airdrome and left the five young bomber officers more or less to their own devices.* They had neither training nor experience for the job; there was little for them to work with; but they were lucky enough to have twenty-four hours to prepare in, and they thought they had everything pretty well under control when the first evacuees began to arrive aboard Empire flying boats, DC–3s, and B–17s on the evening of the 25th. However, the local hotel ran out of food before the last plane landed that night and at the airfield they began digging into emergency rations.

After that they were never able to keep up with the incoming flood. Three cooks and kitchen equipment were flown up from Perth on the 26th with fresh supplies, but next day Rouse, the rationing officer, had to borrow four more stoves and set up operations in the open, which he did behind the schoolhouse.[2] By the 27th refugees were arriving faster than they could be moved on to the south. Every available transport plane in Australia was pressed into service and pilots were stretching the limits of endurance, but about all they could do that day and the next was to get out the women and children.

By March 1, however, things seemed to be going better. More food was being flown in from the south. The planes were making a faster shuttle of the 2000-mile round trip to Perth. It looked as if they were gaining a little on the pool of transient refugees. Then, towards evening, planes really began pouring in from Java, and next morning Rouse noted in his diary that the "place looks like La Guardia Field. Entire small drome now covered with ships. Men are sleeping on floors, porches, or any other shelter they can find." He added with satisfaction that his own department was functioning smoothly and serving good food; but the same entry included an ominous note. He had begun sending out truckloads of food to wells in the bush, in case the Japs attacked with troops and the town had to be evacuated.[3]

---

* The detachment set up their organization with Capt. R. V. Schwanbeck, servicing and maintenance; Lt. Harl Pease, transportation; Lt. John Bridges, evacuation; Lt. D. W. Fagan, housing; Lt. J. A. Rouse, rationing. They were later joined by Lts. Carey L. O'Bryan, Jr., and J. W. Norvell.[1]

It was certainly the kind of target that the Japs could be trusted not to overlook indefinitely. A growing tension became manifest on the base. The men worked hard to get incoming planes refueled and out, but it was not always easy to keep them moving. Most of the crews and passengers on evacuation planes, no matter how tightly keyed by the circumstances of their own escape, suffered a letdown as soon as they landed at Broome. Australia was sanctuary. It was hard to persuade them of the need of moving on immediately.

That night of March 2 was an uneasy one for the men running the base. They were sweating out a B–24 that had gone back to Jogjakarta to bring out any men who might have been left behind.* It returned at dawn; but long before it was due, about 2:00 A.M., an unidentified plane appeared over the town, flying very low. Men at the airfield saw it and also what looked like signal lights flashing to it from the bay. Lieutenant Colonel Richard A. Legg, who had arrived at Broome to take over the air defense of Northwest Australia, personally investigated the source of these lights. They proved to have come from the radio station: the operator, assuming the plane to be friendly, had flashed the tower lights to warn it. But it was unquestionably Japanese, and Legg had no illusions about what its presence meant.

Though all planes were warned to clear Broome before 10:00 that morning, there were still six planes loading at the airfield and 15 flying boats in the bay when, almost to the minute, the Japs struck. They used only nine Zeros; but 50 could hardly have been more effective, so defenseless was the town. There was no warning of their approach. Two flying boats had just come in from Java. Small boats with passengers for Fremantle were clustered round the other 13. A B–24 that had just taken off was swinging out over the bay.

This B–24 was one of the three Ferry Command planes of its type that had reached the Southwest Pacific. All three had been working

---

* According to O'Bryan, the Dutch had agreed to light a bonfire on the field if it was still clear. But though the plane circled for half an hour in the darkness, no light appeared, and it had to turn back empty.[4] The plane that brought Yerington out was originally scheduled for this mission—another indication, incidentally, that he must have reached Broome on the morning of the 2nd rather than the 3rd.

overtime in evacuating refugees from Java and then in flying them on to the south. Of the other two one, Captain Davis's, was at Broome, waiting to take off; the other, Captain Funk's, had reached Melbourne. The one in the air was the same plane that had flown up to Jogjakarta. It had been serviced immediately after landing, loaded with wounded men from Java and their surgeon, Captain Stafford, with enough other passengers to make a list of 30 men besides the crew, among them seven enlisted men of the 17th Pursuit Squadron; and now, piloted by Lieutenant Edson E. Kester, with Lieutenant William E. Ragsdale as co-pilot, it had barely climbed to 600 feet when three of the Zeros went after it.

None of the B–24s had self-sealing tanks. Almost at the first pass, the ship puffed into flame, dived sharply, and crashed in the bay. The impact broke it into two pieces, and two of the 17th Squadron men, Sergeants Melvin O. Donoho and William A. Beatty, were thrown clear. They had a momentary glimpse of Captain Stafford trying to get his wounded out of the front section; then plane and men together disappeared, and the two sergeants were alone in the water, struggling against the waves and what they soon realized was a very strong current. They could not see the shore, but a tower of smoke against the sky served as a landmark. They headed in its direction, not knowing what had caused it.

Meanwhile the six remaining Zeros were quickly rejoined by the three that had shot down the B–24, and all nine made one leisurely pass after another till every plane in Broome had been destroyed. Their only opposition came from the side arms of a few frustrated men on the airfield and a single .30-caliber machine gun which a Dutch pilot had taken from his burning ship and fired from a slit trench, holding the gun in his hands till his palms were nearly burned through. Some thought he had hit one of the Zeros, for it was trailing smoke when the formation was last seen, far out to sea.

There was little satisfaction in a trail of smoke from a departing plane. Fifteen flying boats were burning in the bay. The loss at the airfield included the second B–24, two Dutch Lockheeds, and two B–17Es which would be sorely needed in the next two weeks. As a final dividend, the Zeros shot down a Curtiss observation plane, bringing the total of planes destroyed to 22.*

There were no other raids on Broome.† It was just as well, for there was now the ugly work of cleaning up to do, especially in the harbor, where 45 Dutch refugees had been killed. As they were brought up out of the water, the bodies were laid out on the little flatcars, many women and children among them, and then hauled up into the town by the ancient locomotive. Many of the American troops remember this funeral train; but the sight of it seemed to produce a curious apathy among the Dutch (an apathy later remarked on by most troops that came in contact with them in the Southwest Pacific). A spark seemed to have been extinguished. Except for one man who dug the graves for his wife and three children, they refused to help bury the dead, and the work had to be turned over to the local Home Guard, who burned the rest of the bodies.[9] No men could be spared from the airfield, for more planes had come in and everyone was working at top speed to service them so that the remaining women and children, at least, could

---

* The exact number of planes lost at Broome is difficult to fix. AAF IN WORLD WAR II lists the land planes as I do, except that no mention is made of the Curtiss plane, probably because its loss was insignificant. But there is considerable divergence over the number of flying boats. AAF IN WORLD WAR II lists twelve,[5] perhaps relying on Yerington's account.[6] General Brett's Summary of Activities for AG, March 4, numbers them at nine. (Incidentally, he mentions a Dutch DC–3 as destroyed on the airfield, as does Col. Perrin on March 5, and, as we shall see, Col. Ryan thinks there were two.) Col. Perrin's report of March 5 lists 14 flying boats, a figure which agrees with O'Bryan's. However, Knudsen, who like O'Bryan was on the scene, says there were 15 flying boats, and this figure agrees with Col. Ryan's study.[7] Ryan was at great pains to identify the various craft destroyed. He listed them as:

4 Dutch PBYs,
2 American PBYs,
2 Australian PBYs,
5 3-engine Dutch Dorniers,
2 Quantas Airlines flying boats.

In his list of land planes, Ryan said six were lost, but named two Dutch (KNILM) Airliners, DC–3s, in place of the two B–17Es. Their presence on the field was hotly denied by a Dutch officer calling at the Air Evaluation Board office in Brisbane when I was there, and there is general confirmation of the loss of the two B–17Es in all sources before mentioned in this footnote as well as in the 19th Group and 30th Squadron histories and *Summary of Air Action*.[8]

† On the same day three Jap planes flew a reconnaissance mission over Wyndham, sometimes reported as a raid.

get out of Broome before nightfall. Meanwhile a launch that had been sent out into the bay to look for survivors of Kester's B-24 returned reporting nothing seen.[10]

The two sergeants were still alive, however. Keeping together, they swam steadily all through the afternoon. Towards evening they were close inshore; but then the tide, which falls 29 feet at Broome, caught them and carried them to sea. They swam all night, with Beatty, who had begun to weaken badly, between Donoho's legs. Beatty kept urging Donoho to strike out for himself, but the latter refused. By next morning they had once more painfully drawn in towards shore. Near noon they saw a lighthouse. They were then within 200 yards of land. And now, no longer able to make headway while towing the other, Donoho at last agreed to leave Beatty and go ahead for help. But the tide had again set against him. For a while he was ready to quit. It was more reflex than any purpose that kept him going, and finally, after the tide had swept him five miles down the coast, he made shore—33 hours after the breaking plane had dumped him in the sea. He could not see Beatty, so he rested awhile before setting out for the lighthouse. He found it deserted and stumbled on along the shore. Towards sunset, hours after he had crawled up on land, he made the airfield, stark naked, sunburned, and exhausted.

Next day they found Beatty, who had somehow managed to pull himself ashore. He was delirious and nearly gone. They rushed him to Perth on the next plane leaving; but, though he was still alive when he reached the hospital, he never regained consciousness.*

By the night of March 6 the last plane had moved on. The temporary installations had been torn down. Broome, like Darwin, had become a ghost town where cats and dogs, abandoned by their owners, asked pity in the streets. The parade of transports and bombers with their loads of frightened and exhausted refugees might never have been; but now and then a radioed plea for food to be flown in to some remote Abo mission or settler's homestead where an evacuation plane had been forced down and its stranded passengers had eaten out the scanty stores

---

* For details of Donoho's and Beatty's experience in the sea I am chiefly indebted to George Weller's graphic account.[11]

of food came as a reminder that in the silent and defenseless lengths of coast land there were still people facing the prospect of invasion.

Two messages came out of Java that day, also, both from Bandoeng, both asking that a transport plane be flown in if possible. One, from Colonel Searle * to General Brett, reported that it was no longer possible to get to Malang. But, in the utter disorganization that followed the retreat, so long a flight could not be quickly set up; and next day a third and final message from Bandoeng reached the Air Board at Melbourne:

SENDING AIRCRAFT FROM NOW ON UNSAFE †

There was probably a twenty-four-hour lag between transmittal and receipt of this final message, for the Japanese had reached the outskirts of Bandoeng on March 5, their advance unchecked by what opposition the Dutch ground forces could muster. Three days later they captured Tjilatjap, and on March 9 General Ter Poorten surrendered unconditionally.

The creeping silence that had shrouded island after island in the Southwest Pacific now closed over Java. In Australia, Army officials, stunned by this quick collapse, examined their own situation. They found the prospects bleak.

Very few people realized how utterly defenseless against invasion Australia was during the opening days of March. One division of her first-line troops—the AIF: Australian Imperial Forces—had been lost in Malaya, and the others were still overseas; ‡ no U. S. Infantry units had yet arrived; § the Australian militia were at this time poorly equipped, poorly trained, and for the most part poorly led. Without air cover, they would not have stood a chance.

---

* Col. Searle, it will be recalled, had refused to evacuate Java but had stayed on with the National Guard units as representative of the U. S. Regular Army.

† From Records Section, USAFIA. Further efforts to contact Bandoeng, either directly or through Sumatra, failed. The last word from Java is supposed to have been spoken by a dispatcher from the commercial radio station at Bandoeng, just before it was destroyed: *"We are shutting down now. Good-by till better times. Long live the Queen!"* They rang in Dutch hearts then, as they did in the hearts of many others, but the years have invested them with a harsh irony.

‡ Though one AIF Corps had been withdrawn from combat and was on its way home.

§ The 41st U. S. Division did not land till April 6, the 32nd till May 14.

Of that there was almost none. The RAAF's improvised fighter planes, the totally inadequate Wirraways, had been used up in defense of outlying islands like Ambon and New Britain, and their Hudson bombers had proved terribly vulnerable to the Zeros. The 136 fighter planes in commission in Australia belonged mainly to the 49th Pursuit Group, which was still in training and would not have a squadron ready for action—even by the standards then in force—till March 10. One heavy bombardment squadron, then known as the 40th Reconnaissance Squadron, was stationed at Townsville. It had reached Australia on February 18 with twelve B-17Es.* But it was operating on Naval orders and with one sixth of its combat crews out with dengue fever. The only U. S. Air Corps tactical units immediately available to the Air Command were the two squadrons of the 27th Bombardment Group that had been unable to take off for Java before the Japs cut the ferry route on February 19.† They had got as far as Batchelor Field from which, in their 16 rickety dive bombers, they flew "fighter patrols" over Darwin for nearly a month.‡ But neither they nor anyone else had the slightest idea that they could stand off fighter planes and at every alert they were ordered to take off to the south, for Daly Waters, to save their own planes. Darwin had ammunition and food reserves to last about two weeks, though the base commander radioed that in his opinion the area could not be held more than six days against a Japanese attack. He wanted fighter cover. If it could not be supplied, he felt that his entire force should be withdrawn.§

The consignment of planes and matériel to Java and India had left Australia dangerously weak. At one point in February there were only 200,000 rounds of .50-caliber ammunition, which, as Colonel Ross G.

* Under the command of Maj. Carmichael, the Squadron had flown reconnaissance missions out of the Fijis for two weeks before completing their Pacific flight.[12]

† They were the 16th and 17th Squadrons. The former had reached Batchelor Field by February 18, but at Darwin Group Capt. Scherger (RAAF) refused to let them push on immediately to Koepang, and next morning came the raid on Darwin. They always remembered him kindly for that. The 17th Squadron arrived February 22.[13]

‡ It was a tedious, hot, and dusty routine, with pilots and gunners doing their own maintenance. But there were moments of genuine excitement: a search mission for a carrier erroneously reported off the coast, and the discovery and acquisition of an icebox which made the beer at $2.50 a bottle seem almost worth the money.

§ The Darwin Force consisted of one infantry brigade and two units of light artillery.[14]

Hoyt* pointed out, was less than one loading for 140 planes or 40 bombers.† General Brett, who had reassumed command of the U. S. Army Forces in Australia (USAFIA) on February 24, must have recalled wrily his statement of the 21st to General Marshall that enough fighter strength had been left in Australia "to meet current needs." ‡ In the event, he was proved right; but only because the Japanese, against the expectation of nearly everyone in Australia, did not choose to invade. At the beginning of March, the salvation of the continent seemed to hang on the result of the Java evacuation.

Though Brett had earlier promised that "all effort" would be made to salvage equipment, the troops saved almost nothing from Java except the planes they flew out in. These, aside from the transports, amounted to 20 heavy bombers: 17 B–17Es and three LB–30s. Three B–17Ds had been flown out over a month before the evacuation, so out of the 61 heavy bombers that had reached Java, 38 had been lost: six through enemy interception, six by accidents, and 26 on the ground.§ Of the 26 lost on the ground, at least 20 had been destroyed by enemy action.

* Air Officer, USAFIA.

† This was after the February 12 departure from Melbourne for Java of the convoy later diverted by General Brett to India.[15]

‡ See above, Part Two, Chapter 8 (note 60).

§ I am aware that my figures do not completely agree with those in the official history.[16] I have based mine on Eubank's statement that 17 B–17Es got out of Java in the evacuation. Two of these B–17Es were destroyed at Broome, as we have seen, leaving 15. This checks with the status report of March 6, giving 27 B–17Es in Australia, of which twelve belonged in the 435th Squadron. There is no difference of opinion about the number of LB–30s. Again AAF IN WORLD WAR II states that "at least" 37 B–17Es arrived in Java, and *Summary of Air Action* totals 37 or 38 arrivals by the ferry route, depending on the number that reached Bandoeng on February 19. I believe the correct total to be 38, which checks against the losses as follows:

> *Bombers to Java:*
>
> | | |
> |---|---|
> | from the Philippines, via Darwin | 11 |
> | B–17Es by the ferry routes | 38 |
> | LB–30s and B–24s by the ferry routes | 12 |
>
> 61
>
> *Bombers lost in Java:*
>
> | | |
> |---|---|
> | by enemy interception | 6 |
> | by accident | 6 |
> | on the ground | 26 |
>
> 38

These were very heavy losses for just two months of combat, and out of all proportion to the results achieved.* The causes were obvious enough: on the ground they were due to the combined lack of effective air warning, of antiaircraft protection, and of fighter cover; in the air to the length of missions, violent tropical fronts, piecemeal employment of planes, light nose armament of the B–17s, non-self-sealing bomb bay tanks, and weariness and declining morale among the air crews, many of whom were suffering from what was beginning to be known as combat fatigue when they came out of Java. Yet there were good things in the record. They had fought the planes hard. In the 45 days between January 15 and March 1, they had flown missions on 44. They had used their big ships in every imaginable way from bombing at over 30,000 feet to strafing from 1500 or lower; and, though 40 per cent of all planes sent out during January and February failed to reach their targets, the fact remained that these ships had furnished the only consistently aggressive and offensive action on the Allied side and had at least made the Jap slow up and take stock once or twice as well as warn him that it was not all going to be easy.

The dive bomber and pursuit squadrons had been in more or less the same case. The morale of both was high and, considering the number of planes they had to work with in Java, they had made a better showing; but the movement of planes from Brisbane had been incredibly wasteful. While the 91st Bombardment Squadron had managed to bring eleven of the 15 A–24s with which it started through to Java, it was able to put no more than seven in combat; but the pursuit ferrying record was infinitely worse. In all, 142 P–40s were started for Java by air and sea, but only 39 ever reached an airfield there,† and of them not more than

Bombers evacuated from Java:

B–17Ds on January 23 and 27	3
B–17Es during evacuation	17
LB–30s during evacuation	3
	23
	61

* Claimed: one destroyer, eight transports, and two tankers, sunk; 23 planes shot down. For discussion of their naval claims see the second footnote of Chapter 7, above.

† In this case also my figures differ from those in AAF IN WORLD WAR II, which gives 120 as the number "forwarded from Australia," and 36 as the number delivered by air.

35, probably only 34, were fit for combat use. Here again the reasons were obvious. Weather, insufficient pilot training, and almost nonexistent Intelligence made each flight a hazard in itself. But there was also the overlying pressure of a command fighting a hit-or-miss war with whatever it could lay hands on from moment to moment, which made it necessary for green squadrons to attempt long and difficult flights and undertake combat with pitifully inadequate training and thus hasten the wastage of their few resources. It is hard to believe that the men themselves were not aware of this; and, in hindsight, it is even more difficult to understand why delivery of planes by ship was not attempted earlier than it was.

As the men and planes converged upon Melbourne, they found themselves in what was virtually a vacuum. No provision had been made for their reception. They merely turned themselves loose on the town, finding quarters in hotels or private homes, for every door seemed open to them. Probably nowhere in the world have troops received as warm a welcome as did ours from these hospitable Australians. Everything a soldier fresh from combat could want was theirs for the asking, and they did not even need to ask. For two weeks it lasted, and so intense had

But for a true picture one must include the losses before leaving Darwin as well as those along the island ferry route. I have here accepted the figures in the squadron histories and in *History of the 5th Air Force* on the allocation and ferrying of pursuit to Java.

Movement of P-40s to Java, by squadrons, showing the number of planes leaving Brisbane and the number delivered, was as follows:

By *Air:*

17th Squadron, took off with	17	delivered	13
20th Squadron, took off with	26 *	delivered	17
3rd Squadron, took off with	25	delivered	9
33rd Squadron (from Port Pirie)	15	delivered	0
	83		39

By *Sea:*

On the *Langley*	32
On the *Seawitch*	27
	59

142

* The 20th Squadron lost a plane, replaced before reaching Darwin.

been the round of parties, the proffered courtesies, the gay nights, that they always thought of it as "The Battle of Melbourne."

They had earned a respite, yet at the same time all military organization seemed to have vanished; and, as the time arrived when it was obvious that the squadrons must get back into action, it was hard to pick up the pieces. The dive bomber pilots had rejoined their Group, and the 17th Pursuit Squadron had been dissolved, the majority of its pilots joining squadrons of the 49th Pursuit Group. But the men of the 19th and 7th Bombardment Groups, with half of their key personnel now in India, had a harder time readjusting themselves. Discipline had collapsed. The situation was so bad that three quarters of the officers might fail to attend a squadron meeting,* and when, abruptly, an important mission came up, it was necessary to send out parties to drum up the hotels to find enough men to man the crews.

* As an instance take this entry from a pilot's diary during this period: "No one was at the 8 o'clock meeting, so it had to be 1:00. Out of 82 officers, 20 present." [17]

Postscript

Java was lost.

In the Philippines only a handful of pilots remained on flying status, and only a small number of men were reserved to service their few planes on the three Bataan airstrips or at Del Monte and the other air-fields being built on Mindanao. The rest were organized into provisional units of infantry. Except for the radio, an occasional submarine or PBY arriving at the Rock, or a Liberator bomber coming into Del Monte, provided their only contacts with the outside world, though a few of the interisland steamers ran the Japanese gantlet into Corregidor and the ramshackle little transports and training planes of the Bamboo Fleet still hedgehopped precariously in and out of Bataan and Cabcaben Fields, bringing drugs and an occasional bit of sugar or fresh fruit from the southern islands. But these were slender life threads and affected only a very few of the troops. Except for one bomber mission from Australia that came too late to help Bataan, they received no reinforcement. Their only help lay in what they themselves were able to do.

Their record, on Bataan and Corregidor and in Mindanao, is still to be told.

Appendix
Tactical Air Units

19th Bombardment Group (Heavy)

SQUADRONS:

Headquarters
14th Bombardment
28th Bombardment
30th Bombardment
93rd Bombardment

BASES:

Philippines—Clark Field, Luzon
Del Monte, Mindanao
Australia—Batchelor Field, Northern Territory
Java—Singosari, Malang

PLANES:

B–17C, B–17D, B–17E

27th Bombardment Group (Light)

SQUADRONS:

Headquarters
16th Bombardment
17th Bombardment
91st Bombardment

BASES:

Philippines—None. Planes never arrived and the group, except for a
small number of pilots evacuated to Australia, served
as infantry.
Australia—Amberley Field, Brisbane
Archerfield, Brisbane
Batchelor Field, Northern Territory
Java—Modjokerto
Singosari, Malang

PLANES:

A–24

24th Pursuit Group
SQUADRONS:
Headquarters
3rd Pursuit
17th Pursuit
20th Pursuit
21st Pursuit
34th Pursuit
BASES:
Luzon, P. I.—Clark Field
Nichols Field
Iba
Del Carmen
Lubao
PLANES:
P–40E, P–40B, P–35A
2nd Observation Squadron
BASE:
Clark Field, Luzon, P. I.
PLANES:
O–52, O–46
Philippine Army Air Corps
SQUADRONS:
6th Pursuit
10th Bombardment
BASES:
Luzon—Zablan Field, Manila
Maniquis Field, Cabanatuan
Batangas
Cebu—Lahug Field
PLANES:
P–26A, B–10
7th Bombardment Group (Heavy)
SQUADRONS:
9th Bombardment
11th Bombardment
22nd Bombardment
BASES:
Java—Singosari, Malang
Jogjakarta
Madioen

PLANES:

B–17E, LB–30

17th Pursuit Squadron (Provisional)
20th Pursuit Squadron (Provisional)
3rd Pursuit Squadron (Provisional)

BASES:

Australia—Amberley Field, Brisbane
Java—Blimbing Field

PLANES:

P–40E

33rd Pursuit Squadron (Provisional)

BASES:

Australia—Amberley Field, Brisbane
     Darwin, Northern Territory

PLANES:

P–40E

13th Pursuit Squadron (Provisional)

BASE:

Amberley Field, Brisbane

PLANES:

P–40E

435th Bombardment Squadron (Heavy)

(Previous designations, holding through the dates of this narrative—
 14th Bombardment Squadron
 14th Reconnaissance Squadron
 40th Reconnaissance Squadron)

BASE:

Townsville, Queensland, Australia

PLANES:

B–17E

49th Pursuit Group

SQUADRONS:

49th Interceptor Control
7th Pursuit
8th Pursuit
9th Pursuit

BASE:

Camp Darley, Victoria, Australia

PLANES:

P–40E

Notes

(In the short title references listed below, published sources are distinguished by having authors' names or titles printed in SMALL CAPITALS; official reports, digests, summaries, and unit histories by titles printed in *italics;* and personal sources—interviews, prepared statements, diaries, or records of personal experience—in straight type.)

Foreword

1. *Report of the Commanding General of the Army Air Forces to the Secretary of War, January 4, 1944,* Section 3.
2. Kizer Statement.
3. Lieutenant Colonel WILLIAM E. DYESS: "The Dyess Story," 29.
4. General JONATHAN M. WAINWRIGHT: "General Wainwright's Story."
5. Commander WALTER KARIG, USNR, and Lieutenant WELBOURN KELLEY, USNR: "Battle Report: Pearl Harbor to Coral Sea," 137.
6. Message, General Marshall to CG, USAFFE, November 27, 1941.
7. *19th Bomb Group; Summary of Air Action,* for dates listed.
   Interviews:

> Andrews
> Sutherland
> Dougherty (in Carmichael)

PART ONE: The Philippines

1. *Pacific Flight*

1. *93rd Bomb Squadron.*
2. Lieutenant General LEWIS H. BRERETON: "The Brereton Diaries," 15 ff.

3. Lieutenant Colonel ALLISON IND: "Bataan: The Judgement Seat," 60.

4. Major EDWARD C. TEATS: "The Turn of the Tide," Installment I.
Interviews:

Eubank	O'Bryan	Snyder
Hoffman	Schreiber	McDonald
Broadhurst	A. W. Smith	Robinet
Whitcomb	Coats	Norgaard

2. The Philippine Department

1. BRERETON, 8 ff.; Brereton, Message to AGWAR, March 1, 1942.

2. WAINWRIGHT, 16, 25, 26.

3. According to *AAF in the War against Japan*, 5, the Group was activated on September 16, 1941; but *24th Pursuit Group* gives the date as October 1.

4. Krieger Narrative; IND, 80; Obert Report.

5. TEATS, II.

6. *Survey of the Philippine Islands*, Vol. I, 123.

7. WAINWRIGHT, 36.

8. *Ibid.*, 48; *Quartermaster Operations*, 32; see also DYESS, 39.

9. IND, 32, 54, 62. Captain Ind served as General Clagett's aide.
Interviews:

Andrews	Eubank	Sutherland
O'Donnell	Crimmins	Grashio

3. Inventory: May and June

1. IND, 6.

2. *The 27th Reports.*

3. IND, 20.

4. *24th Pursuit Group.*

5. Sheppard Statement.

6. *Ibid.*

7. *Ibid.*

8. *24th Pursuit Group.*

9. Sheppard Statement.

10. IND, 22.

11. *Notes on the Defense Problem of Luzon, made as a result of visit to the Philippine Islands between 30 May 41 and 3 June 41*, by Group Captain C. Darval, RAF. Paragraph 3.

12. *Ibid.*, Paragraph 7, Section G.

13. *Ibid.,* Paragraph 3.
Interviews:

Dale   Kennard   Krieger

4. *Air Forces: USAFFE*

1. IND, 30.
2. *Ibid.,* 51.
3. *Ibid.,* 54.
4. *History of the 5th Air Force.*
5. AAF IN WORLD WAR II, Vol. I, 80.
6. *24th Pursuit Group.*
7. *Ibid.*
8. Note by Colonel L. S. Churchill, October 11, 1950.
9. Sheppard Statement.
10. Far East Combined Bureau (British) Intelligence Summary, May 15, 1940.
11. CIU, Enemy Activity, File No. 1, Australian, dated February 20, 1941.
12. WAINWRIGHT, 13.
13. BRERETON, 24.
Interviews:

Eads   Kennard   Brownwell

5. *FEAF: October and November*

1. *24th Pursuit Group.*
2. *AAF in the War against Japan; 24th Pursuit Group; History of the 5th Air Force.*
3. *24th Pursuit Group.*
4. DYESS, 24; *24th Pursuit Group;* Brown Statement.
5. Obert Report; Brown Statement.
6. DYESS, 23.
7. *History of the 5th Air Force.*
8. *19th Bombardment Group History* (Smith).
9. *History of the 5th Air Force.*
Interviews:

Krieger	Kennard	Wurtsmith
Grashio	Eads	
Huffsmith	Broadhurst	

6. Mid-November

1. TEATS, III.
2. IND, 69.
3. BRERETON, 25.
4. *24th Pursuit Group.*
5. WAINWRIGHT, 11 ff.; IND, 79.
6. *Survey of the Philippine Islands,* Vol. I, 127.
7. Air Evaluation Board, Notes.
8. Associated Press Story, Washington, March 21, 1945.
   Interviews:

Fisher	O'Bryan	Dougherty
Combs	Eubank	Krieger II
Hoffman	Vandevanter	

7. Reinforcements: November 20

1. *The 27th Reports.*
2. McAfee Diary.
3. *The 27th Reports.*
4. *24th Pursuit Group* (Roster); though Dyess says there were 13. DYESS, 23.
5. *24th Pursuit Group* (Roster); though here again individual sources differ, Brown giving 19 officers, 275 enlisted men (Brown Statement), and Robb giving 27 flying officers, 4 administrative officers, 250 enlisted men (Robb Statement).
6. DYESS, 23.
7. Robb Statement.
8. Brown Statement; *24th Pursuit Group* (Roster).
9. Brown Statement.
10. *The 27th Reports.*
11. *Ibid.*
12. *Ibid.*
13. *Ibid.*
14. Elsmore Statement.
15. *Ibid.*
16. TEATS, III.
    Interviews:

Brownwell	Huffsmith	Carpenter
Davis	Eubank	Norgaard
Elsmore	Tash	O'Bryan
Bolitho	McDonald	

8. *Reconnaissance: American and Japanese*

1. Note by Colonel R. F. C. Vance, February 7, 1950; also McAfee Diary.
2. *24th Pursuit Group;* Sheppard Statement.
3. *24th Pursuit Group.*
4. KARIG & KELLEY, 129.
5. *Ibid.,* quoting Captain Wagner's subsequent report.
6. *Ibid.,* 130.
7. *Ibid.*
8. Sheppard Statement.
9. *24th Pursuit Group.*
10. Sheppard Statement.
11. *24th Pursuit Group;* Thorne Narrative.
12. IND, 83.
13. Thorne Narrative.
14. *24th Pursuit Group.*
15. Thorne Narrative.
Interviews:

Eads	Wheless II	Krieger
Eubank	McDonald	Krieger II
Hoffman	Broadhurst	Brownwell
Combs	O'Bryan	Norgaard
Kennard	Young	Tash
Sutherland	Putnam	

9. *December 7: Final Inventory*

1. *Survey of the Philippine Islands,* Vol. I, 124.
2. WAINWRIGHT, 14 ff.
3. KARIG & KELLEY, 136.
4. DYESS, 27.
5. *Ibid.,* 29.
6. *Ibid.*
7. Elsmore Statement.
8. *24th Pursuit Group.*
9. Thorne Narrative.
10. DYESS, 29; Fellows Report.
11. *24th Pursuit Group.*
12. DYESS, 29.
13. BRERETON, 38.
14. *The 27th Reports.*

15. *24th Pursuit Group.*
16. Thorne Narrative.
17. DYESS, 29.
    Interviews:

Grashio	Elsmore	Broadhurst
Brownwell	Eubank	Whitcomb
Krieger	Kreps	Schreiber
Andrews	Carlisle	O'Donnell

10. *Iba: The First Phase*

1. *24th Pursuit Group.*
   Interviews:

Krieger
Krieger II

11. *Nichols Field: 8:30 A.M.*

1. DYESS, 29.
2. *Ibid.*
3. *24th Pursuit Group* (Roster); DYESS, 29.
4. DYESS, 29.
5. *24th Pursuit Group.*
6. *The Java Sea Campaign;* also Gerhard Diary, which reports receipt of warning ("Cincaf Urgent") at 3:00 A.M.
7. SAMUEL ELIOT MORISON: "History of United States Naval Operations in World War II," Vol. III: "The Rising Sun in the Pacific," 168.
8. BRERETON, 38; IND, 87. Some personnel, however, remember it as being earlier.
9. *24th Pursuit Group.*
10. WAINWRIGHT, 18; also IND, 88.
11. KARIG & KELLEY, 138.
12. Sheppard Statement; Blanton Statement; Obert Report; *24th Pursuit Group.*
13. *24th Pursuit Group;* Sheppard Statement; Obert Report; IND, 94.
14. Robb Statement.
    Interviews:

Grashio	Brownwell	Green
Bradford	Posten	Kreps
Sutherland	Carlisle	McDonald
Eads	Carpenter	Krieger
Andrews	Fisher	Putnam

12. Clark and Nielson Fields: 4:00 A.M. to 12:30 P.M.

1. McAfee Diary.
2. *The 27th Reports.*
3. From the Interrogation of Colonel Harold E. Eads, April 6, 1944, by Major John C. Ankeney, 5th Air Force Historian. *History of the 5th Air Force;* also IND, 91.
4. BRERETON, 37.
5. IND, 91 ff.
6. BRERETON, 39.
7. *Ibid.*
8. AAF IN WORLD WAR II, Vol. I, 207.
9. IND, 94.
10. *Ibid.*
11. BRERETON, 40.
12. AAF IN WORLD WAR II, Vol. I, 207.
13. BRERETON, 40; AAF IN WORLD WAR II, Vol. I, 208.
14. *24th Pursuit Group.*
15. TEATS, I; Lieutenant E. H. Heald, then communications officer at Del Monte, in an interview with Captain Edgar Holt, May 15, 1944.
16. *Summary of Air Action.*
17. BRERETON, 41.
18. Obert Report; *24th Pursuit Group.*
19. *24th Pursuit Group.*
20. DYESS, 30.
21. *24th Pursuit Group.*
22. BRERETON, 41.
23. *Ibid.,* 38.
24. *Ibid.,* 41.
25. General MacArthur to Admiral Hart, November 7, 1941—SUBJECT: Control of Air Operations over Water.
26. BRERETON, 34.
27. *Ibid.,* 38.
28. General of the Air Force H. H. ARNOLD: "Global Mission," 272.
29. AAF IN WORLD WAR II, Vol. I, 206.

Interviews:

Kennard	Eads	Combs
Eubank	Broadhurst	Brownwell
Carpenter	Kreps	Grashio
Wheless II	McMicking	Young
Crimmins	Heald	Whitcomb
Carlisle	Tash	O'Donnell
McDonald	Vandevanter	

13. Iba: The Second Phase

1. Thorne Narrative; *24th Pursuit Group.*
2. Krieger Narrative.
3. *Ibid.; 24th Pursuit Group.*
4. Krieger Narrative.
5. *24th Pursuit Group* (Roster); Thorne Narrative; Krieger Narrative.
6. Thorne Narrative; Krieger Narrative.
   Interviews:

Krieger	Krieger II
Grashio	Kennard

14. Attack on Clark Field: 12:40 P.M.

1. Robb Statement.
2. *History of the 5th Air Force.*
3. IND, 91.
4. Krieger Narrative.
5. *24th Pursuit Group.*
6. Sheppard Statement.
7. *24th Pursuit Group;* Sheppard Statement.
8. *24th Pursuit Group.*
9. Robb Statement.
10. Brown Statement.
11. *Ibid.;* Robb Statement.
12. *Ibid.*
13. Krieger Narrative.
14. *24th Pursuit Group* (Roster).
15. Citations of Lieutenant Colonel Eubank (S.S.) and Major Gibbs (D.S.C.).
16. Citations of Crimmins and Stitt (S.S.).
    Interviews:

Grashio	Crimmins	Wheless II
Krieger	Kreps	Schreiber
Whitcomb	McDonald	Hoffman
Eubank	Kennard	Carpenter
Robinet	Young	Norgaard
Fisher	Green	Broadhurst
Carlisle	Tash	

15. *December 9*

1. *30th Bomb Squadron.*
2. Anonymous Diary.
3. *24th Pursuit Group;* Kizer Statement; Obert Report; Blanton Statement.
4. DYESS, 30.
5. *The 27th Reports.*
6. Sheppard Statement.
7. AP Story by Clark Lee, Melbourne, Australia, April 1942; IND, 108 ff.; Lieutenant JUANITA REDMOND, "I Served on Bataan," 20.
8. Colonel R. F. C. Vance, Notes, February 7, 1950.
9. IND, 107 ff.
10. Diary of Lieutenant THOMAS P. GERRITY, in the *Evening Bulletin,* Philadelphia, June 15-20, 1942, entry for December 9, 1941.
11. *The 27th Reports; 24th Pursuit Group;* Fellows Report; Thorne Narrative; McAfee Diary.
12. GERRITY, December 9, 1941.
13. *24th Pursuit Group;* Sheppard Statement; Obert Report.
14. DYESS, 32.
15. *Ibid.*
16. Brown Statement.
17. Blanton Statement.
18. *Summary of Air Action.*
19. Radio Message No. 1133, from General MacArthur.
20. *History of the 5th Air Force;* IND, 115.
21. Radio Message No. 741, Brigadier General Gerow to General MacArthur.
22. IND, 111.
23. *The 27th Reports;* GERRITY, December 10, 1941.
   Interviews:

Kennard	Sutherland	Brownwell
Bolitho	Carpenter	Grashio
Young	Eubank	Posten
O'Bryan	Whitcomb	Feallock
Snyder	Seamon	Wheless II
Crimmins	Coats	

16. *December 10: Vigan*

1. *19th Bomb Group.*
2. TEATS, I.

3. *19th Bomb Group.*
4. Sheppard Statement.
5. Mahony's citation (D.S.C.).
6. Memorandum for the Chief of Staff, December 1, 1941.
7. *19th Bomb Group.*
8. *Ibid.*
9. *24th Pursuit Group.*
10. Sheppard Statement.
11. Kizer Statement.
12. Sheppard Statement.
13. Brown Statement.
14. Citation of 2nd Lieutenant Jack D. Dale (D.S.C.).
15. Brown Statement; Robb Statement; Sheppard Statement; *24th Pursuit Group.*
16. Brown Statement.
17. *Ibid.*
   Interviews:

| Combs | Young | Grashio |

17. *December 10: The 14th Squadron*

1. TEATS, I.
2. *Ibid.,* II.
3. Sheppard Statement.
4. *19th Bomb Group;* TEATS, II.
5. Citation of Captain Parsel (D.F.C.); *19th Bomb Group.*
6. *19th Bomb Group;* citation of Captain Guilford R. Montgomery (S.S.).
7. TEATS, II; *19th Bomb Group.*
8. *19th Bomb Group.*
9. WAINWRIGHT, 27.
   Interviews:

Combs	Kennard	Wheless II
Cottage	Grashio	O'Donnell
Bean	Carpenter	

18. *The End of Interception*

1. *The 27th Reports;* GERRITY, December 10, 1941; IND, 118; *24th Pursuit Group;* DYESS, 32; Obert Report; Rowe.
2. DYESS, 32.
3. Sheppard Statement; citation of 2nd Lieutenant Gies (D.S.C.).

4. *History of the 5th Air Force;* KARIG & KELLEY, 146; Rowe; Obert Report; Colonel R. F. C. Vance, Notes, February 7, 1950.

5. Rowe; Sheppard Statement; Statement by Warrant Officer Ballard B. Small, October 15, 1942.

6. *The Java Sea Campaign;* as also, KARIG & KELLEY, 146.

7. *24th Pursuit Group.*

8. Rowe; Krieger Narrative.

9. *The 27th Reports.*

10. KARIG & KELLEY, 146.

11. GERRITY, December 10, 1941; IND, 131; Obert Report; Krieger Narrative.

12. AP Dispatch, December 18, 1941; citation of Captain Villamor.

13. Certificates by Captain Jack D. Dale, March 1, 1943; by Lieutenant David L. Obert, March 3, 1943; by Lieutenant William J. Feallock, March 8, 1943. Also letter from Colonel R. W. Fellows to the author, dated December 12, 1946. See also DYESS, 33.

Interviews:

> Posten
> Donohoe (in Grashio)

19. *Air Taxi*

1. Colonel R. F. C. Vance, Notes, February 7, 1950.
Interviews:

| Bradford | Gunn | Kennard |

20. *Bush League Air Force*

1. AP Dispatch from Clark Lee, December 19, 1941; also IND, 141.

2. Citation of Lieutenant Gozar (D.S.C.).

3. Citation of Captain Villamor (D.S.C.); also AP Dispatch, December 18, 1941.

Interview:

> Andrews

21. *Moonlight Parlor*

1. Elsmore Statement.

2. TEATS, II.
Interviews:

| Norgaard | Huffsmith | Seamon |

22. *Mission to Legaspi*

1. TEATS, IV.
2. *19th Bomb Group.*
3. TEATS, IV; *19th Bomb Group.*
4. NANA Story, by Royal Arch Gunnison, December 14, 1941, for some details.
   Interviews:

Elsmore	Schreiber	Seamon
Combs	O'Bryan	Wheless
Connally	Carpenter	
Kennard	Vandevanter	

23. *Episode at Vigan*

1. Citation of Lieutenant Mahony (D.S.C.); *24th Pursuit Group;* Thorne Narrative.
2. *24th Pursuit Group.*
3. WAINWRIGHT, 28.
4. *Ibid.*
5. *Ibid.*
6. *Ibid.,* 29.
7. Sheppard Statement; Obert Report; *24th Pursuit Group;* AP story by Russell Brines, Manila, December 28, 1941; citations of Lieutenant Wagner and Lieutenant Church (posthumous) for D.S.C.
   Interviews:

Brownwell
Feallock

24. *The Airfield at Lubao*

1. Thorne Narrative; *24th Pursuit Group* erroneously states that the 3rd Squadron was sent to Ternate.
2. DYESS, 34.
3. *Ibid.,* 35.
4. *Ibid.,* 36.
5. *24th Pursuit Group* (Roster); Sheppard Statement; IND, 154.
6. *24th Pursuit Group;* IND, 162; Obert Report; WD Communiqué, No. 26.
7. Obert Report.
8. Obert Report; Sheppard Statement.
9. DYESS, 38.

Interviews:

| Brownwell | Luther | Grashio |
| Kennard | Eads | Donohoe (in Grashio) |

25. The A-24s Arrive at Last—in Australia

1. *The 27th Reports.*
2. *Ibid.*
3. IND, 140.
4. *The 27th Reports.*
5. *Ibid.*
6. *Ibid.*
7. *AAF in the War against Japan,* 38.
8. *The 27th Reports.*
   Interviews:

Davies
Walker

26. December 22: The Long Lingayen Mission

1. *The 27th Reports.*
2. *Ibid.*
3. *19th Bomb Group.*
4. *History of the 5th Air Force;* WD Communiqué No. 20.
5. *19th Bomb Group.*
6. Elsmore Statement.
7. TEATS, VI.
8. *Ibid.*
9. *Ibid.*
10. *Ibid.*
11. *19th Bomb Group.*
12. *Ibid.*
13. *Ibid.*
14. TEATS, VI.
15. *19th Bomb Group;* TEATS, VI; Citation of Lieutenant Alvin J. H. Mueller (D.S.C., S.S.).
16. *19th Bomb Group.*
    Interviews:

Seamon	Elsmore	Hoffman
Combs	O'Bryan	Vandevanter
Bohnaker	Bolitho	

27. *Departure of FEAF*

1. *Digest of the Air Phase in the Philippines.*
2. WD Communiqué No. 27.
3. GERRITY, December 25, 1941.
4. BRERETON, 57; Colonel R. F. C. Vance, Notes, February 7, 1950.
5. Letter of Colonel L. S. Churchill, October 11, 1950.
6. IND, 165-166.
7. BRERETON, 61 ff.
8. *History of the 5th Air Force;* BRERETON, 62.
9. BRERETON, 63.
10. IND, 167 ff.
11. Colonel R. F. C. Vance, Notes, February 7, 1950; Major General Eubank in an unrecorded interview with the author, February 2, 1950, at Cambridge, Massachusetts.
12. Colonel L. S. Churchill to the author, October 30, 1950.
13. BRERETON, 63.
14. KARIG & KELLEY, 155.
15. BRERETON, 63.
16. *Ibid.*
17. BRERETON, 64.
   Interviews:

Eubank	Sutherland	Kennard
Combs	Morhouse	

28. *Fort McKinley: "Where the hell is all the Staff?"*

1. IND, 167.
2. *24th Pursuit Group.*
3. *Quartermaster Operations, 32.*
4. WAINWRIGHT, 15-16.
   Interviews:

Kennard
Sutherland

29. *Nielson Field: "Amounting to nearly a rout"*

1. *The 27th Reports.*
2. *Ibid.*
3. *Ibid.*
4. McAfee Diary, December 13 through 24, 1941.
5. *Ibid.,* December 23.

6. *The 27th Reports.*
7. McAfee Diary, December 24.
8. *Ibid.,* December 26; *The 27th Reports.*
9. *The 27th Reports.*
10. McAfee Diary, December 26.
11. *The 27th Reports.*
12. McAfee Diary, December 24.
13. *Ibid.,* December 25; also *The 27th Reports.*
14. Sheppard Statement; *The 27th Reports.*
   Interviews:

> Gunn
> Kennard

30. *Clark Field: "They closed the gate and threw the key away . . ."*

1. *The 27th Reports.*
   Interviews:

Backes	Robinet	Whitcomb
Andrews	O'Donnell	
Carpenter	Young	

31. *Nichols Field: "All units seemed pretty much on their own"*

1. Obert Report.
2. *Ibid.;* McAfee Diary, December 21, 1941.
3. Obert Report.
4. *Ibid.*
5. *Ibid.*
   Interview:

> Brownwell

32. *Quezon City: "They chose to stay"*

1. Fellows Report, 2.
2. Letter of Colonel W. J. Kennard to the author, November 25, 1946.
3. Fellows Report, 4.
4. *Ibid.*
5. *Ibid.,* 14.
6. *Ibid.*
7. *Ibid.,* 15, 18, 20, and 22.
8. *Ibid.,* 34.
9. TRAVIS INGHAM, "Rendezvous by Submarine," 34.

10. INGHAM, 33.
11. Fellows Report, 22.
12. *Ibid.*, 25.
13. *Ibid.*, 35.
14. *Ibid.*, 24, 26.
15. *Quartermaster Operations*, 20, 32.
16. *Ibid.*, 21.
    Interview:

Kennard

33. *The Bataan Road: "Trucks were really high-tailing it"*

1. Sheppard Statement.
2. Obert Report.
3. *Report on Philippine and Australian Activities,* by William J. Kennard, Medical Corps, 12.
4. *Medical Department Activities,* 54.
5. WAINWRIGHT, 43, 44.
6. *Ibid.*, 41.
7. WAINWRIGHT, 46.
8. Captain GENE DALE, Captain JOHN MORRETT, Captain BERT SCHWARZ: "We Lived to Tell," in *Collier's,* March 3, 10, 17, 1945.
9. IND, 179.
10. WAINWRIGHT, 44.
11. Redmond, 29 ff.
12. *Ibid.*, 33.
13. *Ibid.*, 35.
    Interviews:

Kennard
Sutherland

34. *Christmas at Little Baguio*

1. McAfee Diary, December 27, 1941.
2. *The 27th Reports.*
3. Obert Report.
4. Robb Statement.
5. Robb Statement; Brown Statement; Colonel W. J. Kennard to the author, November 25, 1946.
6. DYESS, 38.
7. IND, 182.
8. *Ibid.*, 158.

9. *Ibid.*, 168.
10. Sheppard Statement.
11. IND, 182 ff.
12. *Ibid.*, 186.
13. *Ibid.*, 184.
    Interviews:

Kennard	Eads	Krieger
Andrews	Feallock	

PART TWO: Java

1. *The Opening Situation*

1. Admiral ERNEST J. KING: "Our Navy at War," Report Covering Combat Operations up to March 1944, page 25; also KARIG & KELLEY, 165 ff.
2. KARIG & KELLEY, 169.
3. BRERETON, 100.
4. IND, 48.
5. General GEORGE C. MARSHALL: "Victory is Certain," being the Biennial Report of the Chief of Staff of the U. S. Army—July 1, 1941, to June 30, 1944—to the Secretary of War, page 7.
6. *AAF in the War against Japan*, 42.
7. GEORGE WELLER: "Singapore is Silent."
8. GEORGE WELLER: "Luck to the Fighters," an account of the 17th Pursuit Squadron (Provisional) in Java, published in *Military Affairs* (VIII, Winter 1945).
9. BRERETON, 85.
10. KING, 28.
11. *AAF in the War against Japan*, 41, 43; BRERETON, 72.
12. BRERETON, 84.
13. KING, 28.
14. KARIG & KELLEY, 165.
15. *AAF in the War against Japan*, 42.
16. WELLER (Singapore), 239.
17. *Ibid.*, 115, 187.
18. *Ibid.*, 141 ff.
19. *Ibid.*

20. BRERETON, 72.

21. KARIG & KELLEY, 164.

22. *AAF in the War against Japan,* 44; KARIG & KELLEY, 166.

23. BRERETON, 72.

Interviews:

Kezar

Eubank

2. *The 19th Group Moves Up*

1. BRERETON, 72.

2. *19th Bomb Group;* also TEATS, VII; and according to Combs, who commanded the first flight of seven planes.

3. TEATS, VII.

4. *History of the 5th Air Force.*

5. *19th Bomb Group.*

6. Anonymous Diary.

7. *Summary of Air Action.*

8. TEATS, VII.

9. *Summary of Air Action.*

10. *19th Bomb Group.*

11. *Ibid.*

12. NANA story by Geoffrey Tebbutt, February 11, 1942—delayed. Tebbutt was at Samarinda on the 4th to watch the planes take off.

13. TEATS, VII.

14. *19th Bomb Group.*

15. TEATS, VII.

16. *19th Bomb Group.*

17. TEATS, VII.

18. *19th Bomb Group;* TEATS, VII.

19. *19th Bomb Group.*

20. *Ibid.*

21. TEATS, VIII.

Interviews:

Combs   Norgaard   Vandevanter
Eubank II   Cottage

3. *ABDACOM: The High Command*

1. *Summary of Air Action.*

2. *19th Bomb Group.*

3. Radio, Colonel Merle-Smith, U. S. Military Attaché to Australia, December 16, 1941; and Marshall to Merle-Smith, December 18, 1941. Also, HENRY L. STIMSON and MC GEORGE BUNDY: "On Active Service in Peace and War," 396.

4. Robenson's Story, Chapter VI.

5. BRERETON, 72.

6. *Ibid.*, 99.

7. Air Evaluation Board, Notes.

8. BRERETON, 72, 79.

9. MARSHALL, 10.

10. *History of the 5th Air Force.*

11. BRERETON, 77-83; *History of the 5th Air Force; FEAF Diary.*

12. *AAF in the War against Japan,* 47; KARIG & KELLEY, 167; *History of the 5th Air Force.*

13. MARSHALL, 11.

14. *17th Pursuit Squadron (Provisional).*

15. WELLER (Fighters).

16. KARIG & KELLEY, 159 ff.

17. *Ibid.*, 161.

18. Air Evaluation Board, Notes.

19. *History of the 5th Air Force;* Air Evaluation Board, Notes—Colonel J. P. Ryan.

20. *17th Pursuit Squadron (Provisional).*
   Interviews:

| Combs | Avery |
| Eubank | Fisher |

4. *Arrival of the 17th Pursuit Squadron (Provisional)*

1. Sheppard Statement.

2. Kizer Statement; Sheppard Statement.

3. *History of the 5th Air Force; The 27th Reports.*

4. Hickman Diary, January 1, 1942.

5. *The 17th Pursuit Squadron (Provisional); History of the 5th Air Force.*

6. *The 27th Reports.*

7. *Ibid.*

8. Hickman Diary.

9. *The 27th Reports.*

10. *History of the 5th Air Force.*

11. WELLER (Fighters).

12. *History of the 5th Air Force,* I, quoting General Clagett's letter file.

13. Historical Section USAFFE: Radios and Cables.

14. Robenson's Story, IV.

15. *History of the 5th Air Force.*
16. Gilmore, in Sheppard Statement.
17. Sheppard Statement.
18. *17th Pursuit Squadron (Provisional).*
19. Sheppard Statement.
20. Kizer Statement.
21. WELLER (Fighters).
22. *Ibid.*
23. Robenson's Story, IV.
24. *Ibid.,* V.
25. Sheppard Statement.
26. *Summary of Air Action;* Sheppard Statement.
27. WELLER (Fighters).
28. *17th Pursuit Squadron (Provisional).*
29. Sheppard Statement.
30. *17th Pursuit Squadron (Provisional).*
31. WELLER (Fighters).
32. *Ibid.*
33. Sheppard Statement.
34. *Ibid.*
35. Morehead, in Dockstader Statement.
36. Dockstader Statement.
37. Blanton Statement
38. WELLER (Fighters).
39. Gilmore, in Sheppard Statement.
40. *17th Pursuit Squadron (Provisional).*
41. Sheppard Statement.
42. WELLER (Fighters).
43. *17th Pursuit Squadron (Provisional).*
   Interviews:

Tull   Wagner   Avery

5. *The Bombers*

1. KARIG & KELLEY, 173 ff.
2. MORISON III, 290.
3. KARIG & KELLEY, 186 ff.
4. *19th Bombardment Group History* (Bruce).
5. Rouse Diary.
6. PRISCILLA HARDISON: "The Suzy-Q," 8.

7. Knudsen Diary.

8. Rouse Diary.

9. *History of USAFIA* (in *History of the 5th Air Force,* I, Appendix II).

10. MORISON III, 266.

11. *19th Bombardment Group History* (Smith).

12. *Nuetzel's Notes.*

13. *19th Bombardment Group History* (Bruce).

14. *19th Bomb Group.*

15. *Nuetzel's Notes.*

16. *19th Bomb Group.*

17. *Ibid.*

18. Citations of Lieutenant Dougherty (D.F.C.) and Staff Sergeant Kolbus (S.S.); *19th Bomb Group.*

19. *19th Bomb Group.*

20. *Ibid.*

21. TEATS, IX; *19th Bomb Group;* also Rouse Notes on 7th Group.

22. Message, General Barnes to General Brett, January 19.

23. Hickman Diary.

24. *19th Bomb Group.*

25. *The 27th Reports.*

26. Air Evaluation Board, Notes.

27. Brigadier General DWIGHT F. JOHNS: "We Are Doing What We Can with What We Have," in *Military Review,* April 1945.

28. *History of the 5th Air Force.*

29. *Summary of Air Action.*

30. WELLER (Fighters); *28th Bomb Squadron;* BRERETON, 86.

31. BRERETON, 86.

32. *19th Bomb Group.*

33. WELLER (Fighters).

34. *FEAF Diary.*

Interviews:

Funk	Hardison	Norgaard
McTague	(in Carmichael)	Eubank
Smelser	Shriever	Cheatham
Davis	Hayes	Fraley
Bostwick	Dougherty	(in DeWold)
Campbell	Carmichael	Taggart
(in Carmichael)	Bostrom	McDonald
Kezar	Trenkle	
Kezar II	Combs	

6. *Reinforcements for the 17th Pursuit*

1. Sheppard Statement.
2. *17th Pursuit Squadron (Provisional)*; WELLER (Fighters).
3. AAF IN WORLD WAR II, Vol. I, 398.
4. *History of the 5th Air Force.*
5. *The 27th Reports.*
6. OSMAR WHITE: "Green Armor," 32.
7. Gowen Diary, January 24.
8. ARNOLD, 290.
9. *The 27th Reports.*
10. BRERETON, 74.
11. *The 27th Reports.*
12. *History of the 5th Air Force.*
13. *Ibid.,* I, Document 65.
14. *History of the 5th Air Force.*
15. *Ibid.*
16. *Ibid.*
17. Gambonini Diary.
18. *Ibid.*
19. Perry, quoted in WELLER (Fighters).
20. *Ibid.*
21. *17th Pursuit Squadron (Provisional).*
22. *Ibid.*
23. AAF IN WORLD WAR II, Vol. I, 387.
24. *17th Pursuit Squadron (Provisional).*
25. Gambonini Diary.
26. Sheppard Statement.
27. Gambonini Diary; Sheppard Statement; *The 27th Reports;* WELLER (Fighters).
28. JOHNS.
29. *The 27th Reports.*
30. *17th Pursuit Squadron (Provisional).*
31. *Ibid.*

Interviews:

Nicholson	Tull
Wagner	Walker

7. *A Decline in Morale*

1. WELLER (Singapore), 253.
2. *19th Bomb Group;* Rouse Diary.
3. *28th Bomb Squadron.*
4. *19th Bomb Group.*
5. *Ibid.; 28th Bomb Squadron;* Rouse Diary.
6. *19th Bombardment Group History* (Smith).
7. *19th Bomb Group.*
8. *Summary of Air Action.*
9. WELLER (Singapore), 257.
10. *Summary of Air Action.*
11. BRERETON, 91.
12. *Ibid.*
13. ROBERT E. SHERWOOD: "Roosevelt and Hopkins," 492, 494.
14. MORISON III, 311 ff.
15. *19th Bomb Group.*
16. *Ibid.*
17. *17th Pursuit Squadron (Provisional).*
18. WELLER (Fighters).
19. *17th Pursuit Squadron (Provisional);* WELLER (Fighters); Major JOSEPH J. KRUZEL: "From Hawk to Thunderbolt," in *Mechanix Illustrated,* February-March, 1944.
20. *History of the 5th Air Force.*
21. BRERETON, 88.
22. *Ibid.*
23. General DWIGHT D. EISENHOWER: "Crusade in Europe," 25.
24. Robenson's Story, VI.
25. BRERETON, 93; also a UP story, datelined February 19, "somewhere in Java."
26. BRERETON, 93.
27. *Ibid.,* 94.
28. *Ibid.*
29. *17th Pursuit Squadron (Provisional); FEAF Diary; Summary of Air Action;* BRERETON, 94.
30. *17th Pursuit Squadron (Provisional);* KRUZEL; Blanton Statement; Gilmore, in Sheppard Statement; WELLER (Fighters); BRERETON, 94; *Summary of Air Action.*
31. *17th Pursuit Squadron (Provisional);* WELLER (Fighters); McAfee Diary, February 23, 1942.

Interviews:

Cheatham	Rowan	Trenkle
Smelser	Bohnaker	Dougherty
Preston	Lawrence	Shriever
Campbell	Taggart	Teats
(in Carmichael)	Kezar	(in Carmichael)
McTague	Cottage	Fisher

8. *The 19th of February*

1. MORISON III, 296, 315 ff., 320.
2. Colonel R. F. C. Vance, Notes, February 7, 1950.
3. Message from General Brett, January 31, in *History of the 5th Air Force.*
4. This and subsequent exchanges over supplying fighter protection for the convoy are from *History of the 5th Air Force.*
5. MORISON III, 314 ff.
6. *Ibid.,* 315.
7. *Ibid.,* 317.
8. *33rd Pursuit Squadron.*
9. *History of the 5th Air Force.*
10. *33rd Pursuit Squadron.*
11. *Ibid.*
12. MORISON III, 322.
13. KARIG & KELLEY, 209.
14. Air Evaluation Board, Notes—Colonel J. P. Ryan.
15. *33rd Pursuit Squadron.*
16. *Ibid.*
17. *Summary of Air Action.*
18. MORISON III, 318.
19. *33rd Pursuit Squadron.*
20. Air Evaluation Board, Notes—Colonel J. P. Ryan.
21. *33rd Pursuit Squadron.*
22. *Ibid.*
23. Air Evaluation Board, Notes—Colonel J. P. Ryan.
24. AAF IN WORLD WAR II, Vol. I, 393.
25. MORISON III, 318 ff.
26. KARIG & KELLEY, 206.
27. AAF IN WORLD WAR II, Vol. I, 393.
28. Air Evaluation Board, Notes—Colonel J. P. Ryan.

29. *33rd Pursuit Squadron.*
30. MORISON III, 319; *The Java Sea Campaign;* Air Evaluation Board, Notes—Colonel J. P. Ryan.
31. KARIG & KELLEY, 208.
32. MORISON III, 318; KARIG & KELLEY, 208.
33. MORISON III, 319.
34. Air Evaluation Board, Notes—Colonel J. P. Ryan.
35. Robenson's Story, V; *33rd Pursuit Squadron.*
36. *The Java Sea Campaign.*
37. Air Evaluation Board, Notes—Colonel J. P. Ryan.
38. Major General CLAIRE LEE CHENNAULT: "Way of a Fighter," 114.
39. *Ibid.,* 113.
40. *Ibid.,* 93-94.
41. *Ibid.,* 180.
42. *Ibid.,* 114.
43. Message from GHQ, Java, unsigned, February 19.
44. MORISON III, 320.
45. *Ibid.,* 321-330.
46. *The 27th Reports;* though *19th Bomb Group* says it was the 19th.
47. Knudsen Diary, February 19.
48. *19th Bomb Group.*
49. Message from GHQ, Java, unsigned, February 19.
50. *19th Bomb Group; Summary of Air Action.*
51. *19th Bomb Group.*
52. *The 27th Reports.*
53. *19th Bomb Group; The 27th Reports.*
54. BRERETON, 97.
55. MORISON III, 321.
56. WELLER (Fighters).
57. BRERETON, 95.
58. *Ibid.,* 96.
59. *History of the 5th Air Force.*
60. Brett (Java, ABDACOM) to AGWAR, February 21.
61. BRERETON, 99.
62. *Ibid.*
63. *Ibid.,* 97.
64. *Ibid.,* 98.
65. *History of the 5th Air Force.*
66. *Ibid.*
67. *Ibid.*
68. *Ibid.*
69. BRERETON, 99.

Interviews:

Wheless II	Wurtsmith	Eubank
Wiecks	McTague	Vandevanter
Kezar	Nanney	Eubank II
Funk		

9. The Robenson Mission

1. Barnes to War Department, January 19, 1942.
2. Marshall to Barnes, January 19.
3. Robenson's Story, V.
4. *Ibid.*
5. *Ibid.*
6. *Ibid.*
7. BRERETON, 83; Message, Brereton, USAFIA, to ABDACOM, January 23.
8. Brereton to Marshall, January 21.
9. Brereton, USAFIA, to ABDACOM, January 23; Brereton to Commanding Officer, Base 1, Darwin, January 23.
10. BRERETON, 82.
11. Brett to War Department, March 25.
12. Robenson's Story, VI.
13. Brett to Brereton, Melbourne, January 20.
14. McAfee Diary, January 30 and 31.
15. MORISON III, 205-206.
16. Brereton to Chief of Staff, Washington, January 22.
17. Marshall to Barnes and Brett, January 23.
18. Commander in Chief, Asiatic Fleet, to Brereton, USAFIA, Melbourne, January 23.
19. Brereton to Commanding Officer, Base 1, Darwin, January 23.
20. Robenson's Story, VI.
21. STIMSON, 395-396.
22. Robenson's Story, VI.
23. *Ibid.*
24. *Ibid.*
25. *Ibid.*
26. *Ibid.*
27. *Ibid.*
28. Brett to War Department, March 25.
29. *Ibid.*
30. *Quartermaster Operations,* 39.
31. GEORGE H. JOHNSTON: "The Toughest Fighting in the World," 97.

32. *Quartermaster Operations,* 39.
33. Brett to War Department, March 25.
34. Robenson's Story, VI.
35. BRERETON, 105.
36. Robenson's Story, VI.
37. *Ibid.*
   Interviews:

| Carpenter | McTague |
| Hickman | Kezar II |

10. *Closing Missions*

1. MORISON III, 330.
2. *19th Bomb Group.*
3. *The 27th Reports;* BRERETON, 97.
4. MORISON III, 304.
5. KRUZEL.
6. *17th Pursuit Squadron (Provisional).*
7. WELLER (Fighters).
8. *Ibid.*
9. This account of the combined mission of February 20 is taken from *19th Bomb Group; The 27th Reports; 17th Pursuit Squadron (Provisional);* Gambonini Diary; *History of the 5th Air Force;* WELLER (Fighters); BRERETON, 97; *Summary of Air Action;* AAF IN WORLD WAR II, Vol. I, 394; KRUZEL; and *Notes on American Fighter Activities in East Java,* by Major William P. Fisher.
10. WELLER (Fighters).
11. *17th Pursuit Squadron (Provisional).*
12. *Ibid.*
13. Memorandum to the Chief of Staff, December 1, 1941; also AAF IN WORLD WAR II, Appendix.
14. WELLER (Fighters).
15. McAfee Diary, February 21.
16. *17th Pursuit Squadron (Provisional).*
17. MORISON III, 343-358.
18. *19th Bomb Group.*
19. TEATS, IX.
20. *19th Bomb Group; 28th Bomb Squadron;* TEATS, IX; Rouse Diary, February 20; WELLER (Fighters).
21. *28th Bomb Squaaron; Summary of Air Action.*
22. HARDISON, 53.

23. *Ibid.*
24. *Summary of Air Action.*
25. MORISON III, 333.
26. WELLER (Fighters).
27. *19th Bomb Group.*
28. Message from Thorpe, Bandoeng, February 24.
29. *19th Bomb Group; Summary of Air Action;* Rouse Diary, February 24.
30. Marshall to Brett, February 26.
31. MORISON III, 376.
32. Marshall to Brett, March 3; Brett to Marshall, March 7.
33. *30th Bomb Squadron.*
    Interviews:

Lnenicka	Dale	Kezar
Wagner	Davis	Smelser
Fisher	Hoffman	Eubank II

11. *Evacuation: The Ground Echelon*

1. *30th Bomb Squadron.*
2. Hickman Diary.
3. *30th Bomb Squadron.*
4. Hickman Diary.
5. Robenson's Story, VII.
6. WELLER (Fighters).
7. Robenson's Story, VII (quoting Major R. C. Bower).
   Interviews:

Kezar II	Nanney	Avery
Hickman	Davis	DeWold
Cosgrove	Taggart	Sargent (in Young)

12. *The Loss of the* Langley

1. *History of the 5th Air Force.*
2. *49th Fighter Group.*
3. *The Java Sea Campaign;* MORISON III, 360 ff.
4. MORISON III, 360.
5. *Ibid.*
6. *Ibid.,* 362.
7. *History of the 5th Air Force.*
8. MORISON III, 378.

9. Details of this episode are drawn from *History of the 5th Air Force;* MORISON III, 359 ff.; KARIG & KELLEY, 220 ff.; *The Java Sea Campaign.* Interview:

Nicholson

13. *Evacuation: The Air Echelons*

1. *Summary of Air Action.*
2. *Ibid.*
3. *Ibid.;* TEATS, IX.
4. *Summary of Air Action.*
5. *The 27th Reports.*
6. *17th Pursuit Squadron (Provisional)*; *Summary of Air Action.*
7. MORISON III, 334.
8. KARIG & KELLEY, 237.
9. *The 27th Reports.*
10. *Ibid.*
11. *17th Pursuit Squadron (Provisional).*
12. KARIG & KELLEY, 232.
13. MORISON III, 343.
14. TEATS, X.
15. *17th Pursuit Squadron (Provisional)*; Gambonini Diary.
16. WELLER (Fighters).
17. *Summary of Air Action.*
18. WELLER (Fighters).
19. *Ibid.*
20. KRUZEL.
21. Eubank's report, quoted in Brett to Marshall, March 7.
22. AAF IN WORLD WAR II, Vol. I, 399.
23. *435th Overseas,* 53.

Interviews:

Lawrence	McTague	O'Bryan
Connally	Epperson (in Kezar)	Seamon
Davis	DeWold	Carpenter
Vandevanter	Hayes	Bostwick
Hoffman	Eubank	Kezar
Smelser	Eubank II	Norgaard

14. *Broome: An End and a Beginning*

1. *History of the 5th Air Force;* Rouse Diary, February 24 ff.
2. Rouse Diary, February 26.
3. *Ibid.,* March 2.
4. WELLER (Fighters).
5. AAF IN WORLD WAR II, Vol. I, 399.
6. *435th Overseas,* 56.
7. Air Evaluation Board, Notes—Colonel J. P. Ryan; Knudsen Diary.
8. *19th Bomb Group; 30th Bomb Squadron; Summary of Air Action.*
9. Rowan Diary, March 3.
10. Knudsen Diary, March 3.
11. WELLER (Fighters).
12. *435th Overseas.*
13. *The 27th Reports.*
14. *History of the 5th Air Force.*
15. Gowen Diary, February 18.
16. AAF IN WORLD WAR II, Vol. I, 400-401.
17. Knudsen Diary, March 18.
    Interviews:

    O'Bryan   Godman
    Eubank   Royce

List of Sources

1. Publications

Short Title

AAF IN WORLD
WAR II
THE ARMY AIR FORCES IN WORLD WAR II
(Volume I: "Plans and Operations, January 1939 to August 1942." Chicago, 1948.)
(Volume IV: "The Pacific—Guadalcanal to Saipan, August 1942 to July 1944." Chicago, 1950.)

ARNOLD
General of the Air Force H. H. ARNOLD: "Global Mission." New York, 1949.

BRERETON
Lieutenant General LEWIS H. BRERETON: "The Brereton Diaries." New York, 1946.

CHENNAULT
Major General CLAIRE LEE CHENNAULT: "Way of a Fighter." New York, 1949.

DYESS
Lieutenant Colonel WILLIAM E. DYESS: "The Dyess Story," edited with an introduction by Charles Leavelle. New York, 1944.

EISENHOWER
DWIGHT D. EISENHOWER: "Crusade in Europe." New York, 1948.

HARDISON
PRISCILLA HARDISON: "The Suzy-Q," with Anne Wormser. Boston, 1943.

HOUGH
Captain DONALD HOUGH and Captain ELLIOTT ARNOLD: "Big Distance." New York, 1945.

IND
Lieutenant Colonel ALLISON IND: "Bataan: The Judgement Seat." New York, 1944.

INGHAM
TRAVIS INGHAM: "Rendezvous by Submarine." New York, 1945.

JOHNSTON
GEORGE H. JOHNSTON: "The Toughest Fighting in the World." New York, 1943.

KARIG & KELLEY
Commander WALTER KARIG, USNR, and Lieutenant WELBOURN KELLEY, USNR: "Battle Report: Pearl Harbor to Coral Sea." New York, 1944.

KENNEY
GEORGE C. KENNEY: "General Kenney Reports." New York, 1949.

Short Title

KING   Admiral ERNEST J. KING: "Our Navy at War," Report
                     Covering Combat Operations up to March 1944.
                     Washington, 1944.

MARAUDER   THE MARAUDER: A BOOK OF THE 22ND BOMB GROUP. Sydney,
                     Australia, 1944.

MARSHALL   General GEORGE C. MARSHALL: "Victory is Certain," Being
                     the Biennial Report of the Chief of Staff of the U. S.
                     Army—July 1, 1941, to June 30, 1944—to the Secre-
                     tary of War. New York, 1944.

MORISON III   SAMUEL ELIOT MORISON: "History of United States Naval
                     Operations in World War II."
                     (Volume III: "The Rising Sun in the Pacific, 1931 to
                     April 1942." Boston, 1948.)

MORISON IV   The same.
                     (Volume IV: "Coral Sea, Midway and Submarine
                     Actions, May 1942—August 1942." Boston, 1949.)

REDMOND   Lieutenant JUANITA REDMOND, A.N.C.: "I Served on
                     Bataan." Philadelphia and New York, 1943.

SHERWOOD   ROBERT E. SHERWOOD: "Roosevelt and Hopkins, An Inti-
                     mate History." New York, 1948.

STIMSON   HENRY L. STIMSON and MC GEORGE BUNDY: "On Active
                     Service in Peace and War." New York, 1948.

WAINWRIGHT   General JONATHAN M. WAINWRIGHT: "General Wain-
                     wright's Story," edited by Robert Considine. Garden
                     City, N. Y., 1946.

WEINSTEIN   ALFRED M. WEINSTEIN, M.D.: "Barbed Wire Surgeon."
                     New York, 1948.

WELLER   GEORGE WELLER: "Luck to the Fighters," an account of
  (Fighters)   the 17th Pursuit Squadron (Provisional) in Java.
                     Published in *Military Affairs* (VIII—Winter, 1945).

WELLER   GEORGE WELLER: "Singapore is Silent." New York, 1943.

  (Singapore)   OSMAR WHITE: "Green Armor." New York, 1945.
                     W. L. WHITE: "Queens Die Proudly." New York, 1943.
                     W. L. WHITE: "They Were Expendable." New York, 1942.

                              2. Articles

DALE   Captain GENE DALE, Captain JOHN MORRETT, Captain BERT
                     SCHWARZ: "We Lived to Tell," as recounted by Corey
                     Ford and Alistair MacBain. *Collier's,* March 3, 10,
                     17, 1945.

Short Title

GERRITY Diary of Lieutenant THOMAS P. GERRITY, edited by Carleton Kent. *Evening Bulletin*, Philadelphia, June 15-20, 1942.

JOHNS Brigadier General DWIGHT F. JOHNS: "We are Doing What We Can with What We Have." *Military Review*, April 1945.

KRUZEL Major JOSEPH J. KRUZEL: "From Hawk to Thunderbolt." *Mechanix Illustrated*, February-March, 1944.

TEATS Major EDWARD C. TEATS: "The Turn of the Tide," as told to John M. McCullough. *Philadelphia Inquirer*, December 31, 1942—January 18, 1943.

3. Reports and Summaries

Air Service Command in the SWPA, by Captain E. A. Holt.

Air Transport in the Southwest Pacific Area (Statement to War Correspondents, April 27, 1945) by Colonel Ray T. Elsmore.

AAF in the War against Japan *Army Air Forces in the War against Japan*, 1941-1942. Washington, 1945.

Diary of Air Raids on Darwin, by Lieutenant G. R. Fabrie.

Digest of the Air Phase in the Philippine Islands. A-2 Library Files, 9910.

5th Air Force Combat Reports. A-2 Library Files—U. S. Possessions—Philippine Islands, 9910.

Japanese Land Operations. A-2 Library Files—U. S. 9000.

Java Sea Campaign Office of Naval Intelligence Combat Narratives: *The Java Sea Campaign*.

Medical Department Activities *Medical Department Activities in the Philippines from 1941 to 6 May 1942, and Including Medical Activities in Japanese Prisoner of War Camps*, by Colonel Wibb E. Cooper, Medical Corps.

Narrative of Events in Malaya and the Philippines. A-2 Library Files—U. S. Possessions—Philippine Islands 9910.

Notes on American Fighter Activities in East Java, by Major William P. Fisher. A-2 Library Files—NEI Possessions—Java, 9910.

Short Title

> *Notes on the Defense Problem of Luzon, made as a result of visit to the Philippine Islands between 30 May 41 and 3 June 41,* by Group Captain C. Darval, RAF. A-2 Library Files—U. S. Possessions—Philippine Islands, 9800.

Nuetzel's Notes

> *Notes on the 7th Bombardment Group* (with list of deaths occurring in Java), by Captain Henry B. Nuetzel.

Quartermaster Operations

> *Report of the Commanding General of the Army Air Forces to the Secretary of War,* January 4, 1944.

> *Report on Interviews Held with Wounded Americans Evacuated from the Philippines on the American Red Cross Ship "Mactan."* January 27, 1942. A-2 Library Files—U. S. Possessions—Philippine Islands, 9910.

> *Report of Operations, Quartermaster Corps United States Army in the Philippines Campaign, 1941-1942.*

> *Report on Philippine and Australian Activities,* by William J. Kennard—Medical Corps.

Summary of Air Action

> Army Air Forces Historical Studies: No. 29—*Summary of Air Action in the Philippines and Netherlands East Indies. 7 December 1941 to 26 March 1942.* Prepared by Assistant Chief of Air Staff, Intelligence, Historical Division. January 1945.

Survey of the Philippine Islands

> *Survey of the Philippine Islands.* Prepared under the direction of the Chief of Staff by the Military Intelligence Service, War Department General Staff. February 15, 1943. (3 Volumes.)

USSBS

> *United States Strategic Bombing Survey* (Pacific). Naval Analysis Division—Interrogations of Japanese Officials. (2 Volumes.)

4. Unit Histories

FEAF Diary

> *Summary of Activities of the Headquarters, Far East Air Force,* 8 December 41—24 February 42.

History of the 5th Air Force

> *History of the Fifth Air Force and its Predecessors.*

17th Pursuit Squadron (Provisional)

> *Report of the Seventeenth Pursuit Squadron (Provisional)—Activity in Java.*

19th Bomb Group

> *Diary of Operations of the 19th Bomb Group in Java, 8 December 1941—24 February 1942.*

Short Title

19th Bombardment Group History, by Major J. H. M. Smith.

19th Bombardment Group History, prepared under the direction of Major William H. Bruce, Intelligence Officer, Pyote, Texas, AAB.

Notes on Early History of the 19th Bombardment Group, by Colonel Edwin B. Broadhurst.

24th Pursuit Group   *Narrative of Activities of the 24th Pursuit Group in the Philippine Islands.*

The 27th Reports   *The 27th Reports.* History of the 27th Bombardment Group (L) in the Philippines, Java, Australia, and New Guinea.

28th Bomb Squadron   *28th Bombardment Squadron (H) History* from December 8, 1941, to October 29, 1942. [Also Notes on *28th Bombardment Squadron History,* by Captain Richard H. Beck.]

30th Bomb Squadron   *30th Bombardment Squadron History* (by 1st Lt. Harold C. McAuliffe and 1st Lt. Alexander D. DeShago.)

33rd Pursuit Squadron   *Activities of the 33rd Pursuit Squadron (Provisional)— February 15, 1942, to February 19, 1942.* Letter dated 21 July 1942, 2nd Lt. Robert G. Oestreicher to Colonel Paul B. Wurtsmith, Commanding Officer 49th Fighter Group.

49th Fighter Group   *History of the Forty-ninth Fighter Group.*

93rd Bomb Squadron   *93rd Bombardment Squadron History,* by Captain Arthur E. Hoffman.

435th Overseas   *435th Overseas* [435th Reconnaissance Squadron, of the 19th Bombardment Group]. Contains a brief history of the unit by Lt. Walter H. Johnson and impressions and records of personal experience by Squadron members.

5. Interviews

(*Note:* Ranks are given as of the date of the most recent interview. In most cases the units with which the subject served and his rank on December 8, 1941, or when he first entered the Southwest Pacific Area or first appears in this narrative, are included.)

Sergeant Walter N. Alexander (*see* Bolitho).

Short Title

Andrews
Lieutenant Colonel E. D. Andrews
(Maj.; CO 6th Squadron, Philippine Army Air Corps.)
Interviewed by W. D. Edmonds at Manila, P. I.,
June 3, 1945.

Avery
Major Stuart B. Avery
(1st Lt.; Hq Battery, 26th Field Artillery.)
Interviewed by T/Sgt. G. A. McCulloch at Morotai,
1944.

Backes
Colonel Charles Backes
(CO Philippine Army Air Corps.)
A-2 Library File: US 9000 Interviews.

Barden
Colonel Richard A. Barden
(1st Lt.; 3rd Bombardment Group [L]; CO Base Unit,
Port Moresby.)
Interviewed by W. D. Edmonds at AAFTAC, Or-
lando, Florida, August 6, 1945.
Master Sergeant J. H. Bean (*see* Kezar).

Bean
Captain Joe M. Bean
(2nd Lt.; 14th Squadron, 19th Bombardment Group.)
Interviewed by Sgt. E. R. Emmett and W. D. Edmonds at Drew Field, Tampa, Florida, March 1,
1945.
Colonel A. J. Beavers (*see* Fitzgerald).

Beezeley
Major Wilbur B. Beezeley
(2nd Lt.; 435th Squadron, 19th Bombardment Group.)
Interviewed by T/Sgt. G. A. McCulloch at Hollandia,
New Guinea, October 13, 1944.

Bennett
Major Bruce M. Bennett, M.C.
(2nd Lt.; 36th Squadron, 8th Fighter Group.)
Interviewed by W. D. Edmonds at Fort George
Wright, Spokane, Washington, July 31, 1945.

Bohnaker
Captain William J. Bohnaker
(1st Lt.; 93rd Squadron, 19th Bombardment Group.)
Interviewed at San Francisco, March 27, 1942.
A-2 Library File: US 9000 Interviews.

Bolitho
Staff Sergeant Hayes H. Bolitho
(Pfc.; 5th Air Base Squadron), and
Sergeant Walter N. Alexander
(Pvt.; 440th Ordnance Company, Bombardment).
Interviewed by W. D. Edmonds at Geiger Field, Spo-
kane, Washington, April 4, 1945.

Short Title

Bostrom   Lieutenant Colonel Frank P. Bostrom
         (1st Lt.; 435th Squadron, 19th Bombardment Group.)
         Interviewed by T/Sgt. G. A. McCulloch at AAB,
         Almogordo, New Mexico (no date given).
         (*See also* Carmichael.)

Bostwick   Captain William E. Bostwick
         (T/Sgt.; 22nd Squadron, 7th Bombardment Group;
         93rd Squadron, 19th Bombardment Group.)
         Interviewed by W. D. Edmonds at Peterson Field,
         Colorado Springs, Colorado, April 11, 1945.

Bradford   Lieutenant Colonel William R. Bradford
         (Capt.; Air Service Command—P. I.)
         Interviewed by T/Sgt. G. A. McCulloch at Hondo
         AAB, Hondo, Texas (no date given).

Broadhurst   Colonel Edwin B. Broadhurst
         (Capt.; 30th Squadron, 19th Bombardment Group.)
         Interviewed by T/Sgt. G. A. McCulloch at Washington, D. C., January 15, 1945.

Brownwell   Lieutenant Colonel John L. Brownwell
         (1st Lt.; 17th Squadron, 24th Pursuit Group.)
         Interviewed by W. D. Edmonds at Manila, P. I.,
         June 2, 1945.
         Master Sergeant William P. Campbell (*see* Carmichael).

Carlisle   Lieutenant Colonel Richard T. Carlisle
         (1st Lt.; 14th Squadron, 19th Bombardment Group.)
         Interviewed by Sgt. E. R. Emmett and W. D. Edmonds at AAFTAC, Orlando, Florida, February 27, 1945.

Carmichael   Lieutenant Colonel Richard H. Carmichael
         (Maj.; CO 88th Reconnaissance Squadron, 7th Bombardment Group; CO 40th Reconnaissance Squadron; CO 19th Bombardment Group, July 10 to December 20, 1942.) A group interview before General Arnold and Staff Members at Washington, D. C., December 5, 1942, including the following 19th Group personnel:
         Major Frank P. Bostrom
         (Executive Officer, 435th Squadron),
         Master Sergeant William P. Campbell
         (Armament Technician, 93rd Squadron),

Short Title

Major John E. Dougherty
  (Group Operations Officer),
Captain Fred C. Eaton, Jr.
  (435th Squadron),
Master Sergeant Durward W. Fesmire
  (Lead Bombardier, 93rd Squadron),
Captain Jacob Gottlieb
  (Group Flight Surgeon),
Major Felix M. Hardison
  (CO 93rd Squadron),
Staff Sergeant Orville Kiger
  (Lower turret gunner, 93rd Squadron),
Lieutenant Albert T. Nice
  (Lead Navigator, 93rd Squadron),
Captain Carey L. O'Bryan
  (Group Intelligence Officer),
Captain Vincent L. Snyder
  (Engineer Officer, 93rd Squadron),
Major Edward C. Teats
  (Group Plans and Training Officer).
A-2 Library File: US 9000 Interviews.

Carpenter   Colonel John W. Carpenter III
  (1st Lt.; 93rd Squadron, 19th Bombardment Group.)
  Interviewed by W. D. Edmonds at the Pentagon,
    Washington, D. C., March 9 and April 25, 1945.
1st Lieutenant William M. Carrithers (*see* Rowan).
(*See also* Preston.)

Cheatham   Master Sergeant C. W. Cheatham
  (1st Sgt.; 11th Squadron, 7th Bombardment Group;
    28th Squadron, 19th Bombardment Group.)
  Interviewed by T/Sgt. G. A. McCulloch at OWI,
    Washington, D. C. (no date given).

Chesson   Master Sergeant John B. Chesson
  (Sgt.; 90th Squadron, 3rd Bombardment Group.)
  Interviewed by W. D. Edmonds at Hq 2nd Air
    Force, Colorado Springs, Colorado, April 10, 1945.

Clark   Major Charles L. Clark
  (Hq and Hq Squadron, 8th Air Base Group.)
  Interviewed by Capt. E. A. Holt, FEASC Historian
    (no date given).

Short Title

Coats   Captain Lee B. Coats
                                      (1st Lt.; 30th Squadron, 19th Bombardment Group.)
                                      Interviewed April 3, 1942.
                                      A-2 Library File: US 9000 Interviews.

Combs   Colonel Cecil E. Combs
                                      (Capt.; CO 93rd Squadron; CO 19th Bombardment
                                         Group, Air Echelon, December 31, 1941, to February
                                         24, 1942.)
                                      Interviewed by W. D. Edmonds at the Pentagon,
                                         Washington, D. C., April 25, 1945.

Connally   Colonel James T. Connally
                                           (1st Lt.; 93rd Squadron; CO 19th Bombardment
                                         Group, Air Echelon, February 24 to March 14,
                                         1942; CO of the Group, May 1 to July 10, 1942.)
                                      Interviewed by W. D. Edmonds, Tinian, May 20, 1945.

Cosgrove   Colonel Cornelius B. Cosgrove
                                         (Capt.; S-1, 19th Bombardment Group; 5th Bomber
                                         Command.)
                                      Interviewed by W. D. Edmonds at the Pentagon,
                                      Washington, D. C., April 25, 1945.

Cottage   Captain Stanley Cottage
                                         (2nd Lt.; 14th Squadron, 19th Bombardment Group.)
                                         (No date given.)
                                      A-2 Library File: US 9000 Interviews.

Crimmins   Lieutenant Colonel Fred T. Crimmins, Jr.
                                         (1st Lt.; 93rd Squadron, 19th Bombardment Group.)
                                      Interviewed by W. D. Edmonds at Drew Field,
                                      Tampa, Florida, March 1, 1945.

Dale   Lieutenant Colonel Jack D. Dale
                                         (2nd Lt.; 17th Squadron, 24th Pursuit Group; 17th
                                         Pursuit Squadron, Provisional.)
                                      Interviewed by T/Sgt. G. A. McCulloch at AAFTAC,
                                      Orlando, Florida, November 24, 1944.

                                   Major Richard P. Davidson, C.E.
                                           (46th Engineers Construction Battalion, 6th Army.)
                                         Interviewed by T/Sgt. G. A. McCulloch and Lucien
                                         Hubbard at Tacloban Air Strip, Leyte, P. I., October
                                         27, 1944.

Davies   Brigadier General John H. Davies
                                         (Maj.; CO 27th Bombardment Group; CO 3rd Bom-
                                         bardment Group.)

Short Title

	Interviewed by W. D. Edmonds at Tinian, May 20, 1945.
Davies II	(The same, then Colonel.)
	Interviewed December 9, 1942.
	A-2 Library File: US 9000 Interviews.
Davis	Major Donald D. Davis, M.C.

Davies II   (The same, then Colonel.)

Interviewed by W. D. Edmonds at Tinian, May 20, 1945.

Davies II (The same, then Colonel.)
Interviewed December 9, 1942.
A-2 Library File: US 9000 Interviews.

Davis Major Donald D. Davis, M.C.
(1st Lt.; 30th Squadron, 19th Bombardment Group.)
Interviewed by W. D. Edmonds at Fort George Wright, Spokane, Washington, April 5, 1945.

DeWold Lieutenant William P. DeWold
(Sgt.; 11th Squadron, 7th Bombardment Group; 28th Squadron, 19th Bombardment Group), and
Master Sergeant Claude J. Fraley
(Pfc.; 11th Squadron, 7th Bombardment Group; 28th Squadron, 19th Bombardment Group).
Interviewed by W. D. Edmonds at Peterson Field, Colorado Springs, Colorado, April 11, 1945.

Diller Brigadier General LeGrande A. Diller
Interviewed by W. D. Edmonds at Hq USAFFE, Manila, P. I., May 22, 1945.

Dix Lieutenant Gerald J. Dix
2nd Lt.; 13th Pursuit Squadron, Provisional.)
Interviewed December 22, 1942.
A-2 Library File: US 9000 Interviews.
Sergeant Jack N. Donohoe (*see* Grashio).

Dougherty Colonel John E. Dougherty
(1st Lt.; 11th Squadron, 7th Bombardment Group; 28th Squadron, 19th Bombardment Group.)
Interviewed by W. D. Edmonds at Saipan, May 20, 1945.
(*See also* Carmichael.)
Staff Sergeant Arthur S. Downham (*see* Kasten).

Eads Colonel Harold E. Eads, C.E.
(Capt.; 5th Interceptor Command.)
Interviewed by W. D. Edmonds at MacDill Field, Tampa, Florida, August 7, 1945.
Captain Fred C. Eaton, Jr. (*see* Carmichael).
Major Dill Ellis
(408th Squadron, 22nd Bombardment Group.)
Interviewed May 22, 1943.
A-2 Library File: US 9000 Interviews.

Short Title

Elsmore

Colonel Raymond T. Elsmore
(Maj.; CO 5th Airbase Group.)
Interviewed by W. D. Edmonds at Hollandia, New Guinea, June 2, 1945.

Master Sergeant T. W. Epperson (*see* Kezar).

Eubank

Major General Eugene L. Eubank
(Lt. Col.; CO 19th Bombardment Group; CO 5th Bomber Command.)
Interviewed by W. D. Edmonds at the Pentagon, Washington, D. C., November 29, 1945.

Eubank II

(The same, then Colonel.)
Interviewed July 2, 1942.
A-2 Library File: US 9000 Interviews.

Feallock

Lieutenant Colonel William J. Feallock
(1st Lt.; 17th Squadron, 24th Pursuit Group.)
Interviewed by W. D. Edmonds, at Hq 5th Air Force, Fort Stotsenburg, P. I., May 30, 1945.

Master Sergeant Durward W. Fesmire (*see* Carmichael).

Fisher

Major William P. Fisher
(Maj.; 14th Squadron; CO 28th Squadron, 19th Bombardment Group; CO Interceptor Control, Soerabaja, Java.) (No date given; interview received May 27, 1942.)
A-2 Library File: US 9000 Interviews.

Fitzgerald

Colonel Wayne A. Fitzgerald, Q.M.C., with note by Colonel A. J. Beavers, M.C.
Interviewed by W. D. Edmonds at Hq 5th Air Force, Fort Stotsenburg, P. I., May 30, 1945.

Master Sergeant Claude J. Fraley (*see* DeWold).

Funk

Captain Ben I. Funk
(1st Lt.; Ferry Command.)
Interviewed April 1, 1942.
A-2 Library File: US 9000 Interviews.

Gammon

Major E. G. Gammon, Jr.
(2nd Lt.; 33rd Squadron, 22nd Bombardment Group.)
Interviewed by W. D. Edmonds at Mitchel Field, Long Island, N. Y., August 15, 1945.

Gause

Captain Damon J. Gause
(2nd Lt.; 17th Squadron, 27th Bombardment Group.)
Interviewed October 30, 1942.
A-2 Library File: US 9000 Interviews.

Short Title

Gideon   Colonel F. C. Gideon
                        (1st Lt.; 33rd Squadron, 22nd Bombardment Group;
                            Operations Officer, 7-Mile Airdrome, Port Moresby.)
                        Interviewed by W. D. Edmonds at Hq FEAF, Fort
                            McKinley, P. I., June 30, 1945.

Godman   Lieutenant Colonel Henry C. Godman
                        (1st Lt.; 14th Squadron, 19th Bombardment Group.)
                        Interviewed by T/Sgt. G. A. McCulloch at Hollandia,
                            New Guinea, October 13, 1944.

Gowen   Colonel John K. Gowen, Jr.
                        (Lt. Col.; G-2 for US Army Forces in Australia, and
                            simultaneously A-2 for US Air Forces in Australia.)
                        Interviewed October 22, 1942.
                        A-2 Library File: US 9000 Interviews.
                        Captain Jacob Gottlieb (*see* Carmichael).
                        Staff Sergeant Kenneth A. Gradle
                        (Cpl.; 435th Squadron, 19th Bombardment Group.)
                        Interviewed by T/Sgt. G. A. McCulloch at Pyote,
                            Texas (no date given).

Graf   Master Sergeant George R. Graf
                        (Pfc.; 435th Squadron, 19th Bombardment Group.)
                        Interviewed by T/Sgt. G. A. McCulloch at Hollandia,
                            New Guinea, October 13, 1944.

Grashio   Major Samuel C. Grashio
                        (2nd Lt.; 21st Squadron, 24th Pursuit Group), and
                        Sergeant Jack N. Donohoe
                        (Pvt.; 21st Squadron, 24th Pursuit Group).
                        Interviewed by W. D. Edmonds at Geiger Field, Spo-
                            kane, Washington, April 2, April 3-4, April 7,
                            1945.

Grashio II   (Then Captain Grashio.)
                        Interviewed by Lt. Col. S. M. Avery, November 30,
                            1943.
                        A-2 Library File—US Possessions—Philippine Islands—
                            9185.

Green   Captain Edwin S. Green
                        (1st Lt.; 30th Squadron, 19th Bombardment Group.)
                        Interviewed April 4, 1942.
                        A-2 Library File: US 9000 Interviews.

Gunn   Colonel Paul I. Gunn
                        (Capt.; Air Service Command; later, CO Air Trans-
                            port Command, Australia.)

Short Title

Interviewed by W. D. Edmonds at DeWitt General
Hospital, Auburn, California, August 2, 1945.

Hall   Colonel D. P. Hall
            (Capt.; 89th Squadron, 3rd Bombardment Group.)
            Interviewed by W. D. Edmonds at Hq 5th Air Force,
            Fort Stotsenburg, P. I., May 30, 1945.

            Major Felix M. Hardison (*see* Carmichael).

Hayes   Major Henry Hayes
            (T/Sgt.; 19th Bombardment Group.)
            Interviewed by W. D. Edmonds at Manila, P. I.,
            June 30, 1945.

Heiberg   Colonel E. R. Heiberg, C.E.
            Interviewed by W. D. Edmonds at the Pentagon,
            Washington, D. C., April 24, 1945.

Henebry   Colonel John P. Henebry
            (13th Squadron, 90th Squadron, 3rd Bombardment
            Group.)
            Interviewed by W. D. Edmonds at Nadzab, New
            Guinea, June 13, 1945.

Hickman   Technical Sergeant Furman M. Hickman
            (11th Squadron, 7th Bombardment Group; 28th
            Squadron, 19th Bombardment Group.)
            Interviewed by T/Sgt. G. A. McCulloch at AAB,
            Clovis, New Mexico (no date given).

Hill   Major John Hill
            (2nd Lt.; 8th Squadron, 3rd Bombardment Group.)
            Interviewed by W. D. Edmonds at Mitchel Field,
            Long Island, N. Y., May 1, 1945.

Hoffman   Lieutenant Colonel Arthur E. Hoffman
            (2nd Lt.; 93rd Squadron, 19th Bombardment Group.)
            Interviewed by W. D. Edmonds at AAFTAC, Or-
            lando, Florida, March 6, August 7, 1945.

            Staff Sergeant Russell G. Hollister (*see* Staley).

Hoover   Colonel Edward F. Hoover
            (1st Lt.; Hq Squadron, 13th Squadron, 3rd Bombard-
            ment Group.)
            Interviewed by W. D. Edmonds at AAFTAC, Or-
            lando, Florida, August 8, 1945.

Hornbeck   Lieutenant H. C. Hornbeck
            (1st Lt.; 435th Squadron, 19th Bombardment Group.)
            Interviewed February 23, 1943.
            A-2 Library File: US 9000 Interviews.

Short Title

Hubbard
: Captain Ronald D. Hubbard
(1st Lt.; Hq, then 16th Squadron, 27th Bombardment Group; 90th Squadron, 3rd Bombardment Group.)
Interviewed by T/Sgt. G. A. McCulloch at OWI, Washington, D. C. (no date given).

Huffsmith
: Colonel Victor C. Huffsmith, Ordnance Department
(Maj.; 440th Ordnance Company, Bombardment.)
Interviewed by W. D. Edmonds at the Pentagon, Washington, D. C., August 13, 1945.

Hunt
: Captain Gray Hunt
(Pvt.; 21st Squadron, 24th Pursuit Group.)
Interviewed by W. D. Edmonds at Manila, P. I., June 3, 1945.

Kasten
: Master Sergeant Hall E. Kasten,
Staff Sergeant Arthur S. Downham,
Technical Sergeant Lewis B. Thompson, and
Staff Sergeant James E. Knowlton
(All of the 8th Photo Reconnaissance Squadron.)
Joint interview by W. D. Edmonds at Hq 5th Air Force, Fort Stotsenburg, P. I., May 29, 1945.

Kennard
: Colonel William J. Kennard, M.C.
(Maj.; Senior Flight Surgeon, AC, in the Philippines.)
Interviewed by W. D. Edmonds at Fort George Wright, Spokane, Washington, April 3, and July 29, 30, 31, and August 1, 1945.

Kezar
: CWO Dalys C. Kezar
(1st Sgt.; 22nd Squadron, 7th Bombardment Group; 435th Squadron, 19th Bombardment Group) with
Master Sergeant T. W. Epperson, and
Master Sergeant J. H. Bean
(435th Squadron, 19th Bombardment Group.)
Joint interview by W. D. Edmonds at Hq 2nd Air Force, Colorado Springs, Colorado, April 10, 1945.

Kezar II
: (Then WOJG Kezar.)
Interviewed by T/Sgt. G. A. McCulloch at Colorado Springs (no date given).

Staff Sergeant Orville Kiger (*see* Carmichael).
Technical Sergeant James E. Knowlton (*see* Kasten).
Master Sergeant Russell G. Knudsen (*see* Staley).

Kreps
: Colonel Kenneth R. Kreps
(1st Lt.; Hq Squadron, 19th Bombardment Group.)

Short Title

Interviewed by T/Sgt. G. A. McCulloch at Washington, D. C., January 17, 1945.

Krieger   Lieutenant Colonel Andrew E. Krieger
(2nd Lt.; 3rd Squadron, 24th Pursuit Group.)
Interviewed by Sgt. E. R. Emmett and W. D. Edmonds at AAFTAC, Orlando, Florida, February 21 and 27, 1945.

Krieger II   (The same.)
Interviewed by T/Sgt. G. A. McCulloch at Orlando, January 22, 1945.

Lawrence   2nd Lieutenant Frank F. Lawrence
(A/C; 7th Bombardment Group.)
Interviewed April 3, 1942.
A-2 Library File: US 9000 Interviews.

Lnenicka   Sergeant Irving W. Lnenicka
(Cpl.; 91st Squadron, 27th Bombardment Group.)
Interviewed by T/Sgt. G. A. McCulloch at Hollandia, New Guinea, October 14, 1944.

Luther   Master Sergeant Martin Luther
(48th Matériel Squadron.)
Interviewed by Sgt. E. R. Emmett and W. D. Edmonds at AAFTAC, Orlando, Florida, February 23, 1945.

Captain Finley MacGillivray (*see* Walker).

Maiersperger   Major W. P. Maiersperger
(19th Squadron, 22nd Bombardment Group.)
Interviewed by Capt. E. A. Holt, FEASC Historian (no date given).

Marburg   Captain Charles L. Marburg
(Acting Adjutant and Executive Officer, Port Moresby, May-August, 1942.)
Interviewed October 6, 1942.
A-2 Library File: US 9000 Interviews.

Matthews   Colonel A. G. Matthews, C.E.
Interviewed by W. D. Edmonds, Washington, D. C., April 26, 1942.
Lieutenant R. B. Matthews
(Air Service Command.)
Interviewed by W. D. Edmonds at Eagle Farms, Brisbane, Australia, June 18, 1945.

Short Title

McDonald   Colonel William E. McDonald
                  (Capt.; Hq Squadron, 19th Bombardment Group.)
                  Interviewed by T/Sgt. G. A. McCulloch at Washing-
                  ton, D. C., January 18, 1945.

McMicking   Lieutenant Colonel Joseph R. McMicking
                  (1st Lt.; Philippine Army Air Corps; Asst. A-2,
                  FEAF; Asst. G-2, GHQ.)
                  Interviewed by W. D. Edmonds at Manila, P. I.,
                  June 5, 1945.

McTague   Lieutenant Colonel Hugh McTague
                  (1st Lt.; 9th Squadron, 7th Bombardment Group;
                  93rd Squadron, 19th Bombardment Group.)
                  Interviewed by W. D. Edmonds at the Pentagon,
                  Washington, D. C., April 24, 1945.

Morhouse   Colonel Charles H. Morhouse, M.C.
                  (Lt. Col.; Surgeon, First Provisional Air Corps Regi-
                  ment.)
                  Interviewed by W. D. Edmonds at Mitchel Field, Long
                  Island, N. Y., May 1, 1945.

Nanney   Major Stancill M. Nanney
                  (1st Lt.; Communications Officer, 19th Bombardment
                  Group.)
                  Interviewed by W. D. Edmonds at Guam, May 19,
                  1945.

Nanney II   (The same.)
                  Interviewed by T/Sgt. G. A. McCulloch at Colorado
                  Springs, Colorado (no date given).
                  Lieutenant Albert T. Nice (*see* Carmichael).

Nicholson   Sergeant Joseph L. Nicholson
                  (Pvt.; Armed Guard on the *Seawitch*.)
                  Interviewed by T/Sgt. G. A. McCulloch at OWI,
                  Washington, D. C. (no date given).

Norgaard   Technical Sergeant Arthur E. Norgaard
                  (Pfc.; 93rd Squadron, 19th Bombardment Group.)
                  Interviewed by Sgt. E. R. Emmett and W. D. Edmonds
                  at AAFTAC, Orlando, Florida, March 2, 1945.

O'Bryan   Lieutenant Colonel Carey L. O'Bryan
                  (2nd Lt.; 93rd Squadron, 19th Bombardment Group.)
                  Interviewed by Sgt. E. R. Emmett and W. D. Edmonds
                  at AAFTAC, Orlando, Florida, March 5, 1945.
                  (*See also* Carmichael.)

Short Title

Interviewed by W. D. Edmonds at Adv. Hq FEASC,
   Manila, P. I., May 26, 1945.

Smelser   Captain H. C. Smelser
                        (1st Lt.; 9th Squadron, 7th Bombardment Group.)
                        Synthesis of four detailed interviews dated April 6,
                           April 8, April 9, 1942, and one undated.
                        A-2 Library File: US 9000 Interviews.

A. W. Smith   Colonel Andrew W. Smith, M.C.
                        Interviewed by W. D. Edmonds at Hamilton Field,
                           California, May 13, 1945—including notes from
                           personal diary dated October 27-December 14, 1941,
                           describing 19th Group flight, Hawaii to Clark Field,
                           P. I.

F. H. Smith   Brigadier General Fred H. Smith
                        (Lt. Col.; CO 8th Fighter Group; 5th Fighter Com-
                           mand.)
                        Interviewed by W. D. Edmonds at Hq 5th Air Force,
                           Fort Stotsenburg, P. I., May 31, 1945.

J. P. Smith   2nd Lieutenant J. P. Smith
                        (19th Bombardment Group; also 2nd Squadron, 22nd
                           Bombardment Group.)
                        Interviewed July 22, 1943.
                        A-2 Library File: US 9000 Interviews.

Snyder   Major Vincent L. Snyder
                        (2nd Lt.; 93rd Squadron, 19th Bombardment Group.)
                        Interviewed by W. D. Edmonds at Hamilton Field,
                           California, May 14, 1945.
                        (*See also* Carmichael.)

Staley   Lieutenant Colonel Harry A. Staley
                        (Hq Squadron, 19th Bombardment Group),
                     Technical Sergeant Walter B. Williams
                        (Hq Squadron, 19th Bombardment Group),
                     Master Sergeant Russell G. Knudsen
                        (435th Squadron, 19th Bombardment Group), and
                     Staff Sergeant Gary C. Hollister
                        (30th Squadron, 19th Bombardment Group).
                        Joint interview by W. D. Edmonds at Hq 5th Air
                           Force, Fort Stotsenburg, P. I., May 31, 1945.

Stevens   Technical Sergeant E. P. Stevens
                        (63rd Squadron, 43rd Bombardment Group.)

Short Title

	Interviewed by W. D. Edmonds at Hq 5th Air Force, Fort Stotsenburg, P. I., May 29, 1945.
Sutherland	Lieutenant General Richard K. Sutherland
	Interviewed by W. D. Edmonds at GHQ, Manila, P. I., June 4, 1945.
Taggart	Major William C. Taggart
	(1st Lt.; Chaplain 7th Bombardment Group, later of 19th Bombardment Group.)
	Interviewed by W. D. Edmonds at Washington, D. C., March 23, 1945.
Tash	Lieutenant Colonel Earl R. Tash
	(1st Lt.; 93rd Squadron, 19th Bombardment Group.)
	Interviewed by Sgt. E. R. Emmett and W. D. Edmonds at AAFTAC, Orlando, Florida, February 26, 1945.
	Major Edward C. Teats (*see* Carmichael).
	Technical Sergeant Lewis B. Thompson (*see* Kasten).
Thompson	Sergeant Russell C. Thompson
	(93rd Squadron, 19th Bombardment Group.)
	Interviewed by T/Sgt. G. A. McCulloch at Hollandia, October 13, 1944.
Trenkle	Lieutenant Robert A. Trenkle
	(2nd Lt.; 11th Squadron, 7th Bombardment Group.)
	Interviewed April 7, 1942.
	A-2 Library File: US 9000 Interviews.
Tull	Captain James E. Tull
	(Adjutant, Hq Squadron, 7th Bombardment Group.)
	Interviewed by Sgt. G. A. McCulloch (no date, no place given).
Vandevanter	Lieutenant Elliott Vandevanter
	(1st Lt.; 93rd Squadron, 19th Bombardment Group.)
	Interviewed April 16, 1942.
	A-2 Library File: US 9000 Interviews.
	(*See also* Preston.)
Wagner	Lieutenant Colonel Boyd D. Wagner
	(1st Lt.; CO 17th Squadron, 24th Pursuit Group; CO 13th Pursuit Squadron, Provisional; Director of Pursuit, Port Moresby Area.)
	Interviewed by Roosevelt Der Tatevasion (no date, no place given).

Short Title

Walker   Lieutenant Colonel Leland A. Walker, Jr.
(2nd Lt.; 17th Squadron, 27th Bombardment Group; 13th Squadron, 3rd Bombardment Group), and Captain Finley MacGilllivray
(2nd Lt.; 17th Squadron, 27th Bombardment Group; 8th Squadron, 3rd Bombardment Group).
Interviewed by W. D. Edmonds at the Pentagon, Washington, D. C., April 27, 1945.

Wells   Colonel Harold R. Wells
(Air Service Command.)
Interviewed May 21, 1943.
A-2 Library File: US 9000 Interviews.

Wheatley   Staff Sergeant Herbert M. Wheatley
(Pfc.; 435th Squadron, 19th Bombardment Group.)
Interviewed by T/Sgt. G. A. McCulloch at Hamilton Field, California (no date given).

Wheless   Captain Hewitt T. Wheless
(1st Lt.; 30th Squadron, 19th Bombardment Group.)
Interviewed March or April, 1942.
A-2 Library File: US 9000 Interviews.

Wheless II   (The same, then Lieutenant Colonel)
Interviewed by T/Sgt. G. A. McCulloch at Hq 2nd Air Force, Colorado Springs, Colorado (no date given).

Whitcomb   Captain Edgar D. Whitcomb
(2nd Lt.; Hq Squadron, 19th Bombardment Group.)
Interviewed by Sgt. E. R. Emmett at Newcastle AAB, Wilmington, Delaware, March 20, 1945.

Whitehead   Major General Ennis C. Whitehead
(Brig. Gen.; CO Advanced Hq 5th Air Force, Port Moresby.)
Interviewed by W. D. Edmonds at Hq 5th Air Force, Fort Stotsenburg, P. I., May 30, 1945.

Wiecks   Major Max R. Wiecks
(2nd Lt.; 33rd Pursuit Squadron, Provisional.)
Interviewed by T/Sgt. G. A. McCulloch at Noemfoor, New Guinea, October 11, 1944.

Technical Sergeant Walter B. Williams (*see* Staley).

Wurtsmith   Major General Paul C. Wurtsmith
(Lt. Col.; CO 49th Fighter Group.)
Interviewed by W. D. Edmonds at Hq 13th Air Force, Leyte, P. I., June 28, 1945.

Short Title

Young   Colonel Sig R. Young
                           (1st Lt.; 30th Squadron, 19th Bombardment Group),
                           and
                         Lieutenant Colonel Ignatius B. Sargent
                           (1st Lt.; 28th Squadron, 19th Bombardment Group).
                           Interviewed by W. D. Edmonds at AAB Topeka,
                           Kansas, May 8-9, 1945.

6. Statements

Blanton   Statement by Major N. A. Blanton
  Statement   (2nd Lt.; 17th Squadron, 24th Pursuit Group; 17th
                           Pursuit Squadron, Provisional.)
Brown   Statement by Captain Ben S. Brown
  Statement   (1st Lt.; 34th Squadron, 24th Pursuit Group.)
Cobb   Statement by Major James O. Cobb
  Statement   (Personal experience in the air transport of the 32nd
                           Division Australia to New Guinea and subsequent
                           air transport operations.)
Dockstader   Statement by Captain Robert Dockstader
  Statement   (2nd Lt.; 17th Pursuit Squadron, Provisional) with
                           footnote by Lt. Col. James B. Morehead.
Elsmore   Statement by Lieutenant Colonel Raymond T. Elsmore
  Statement   (Maj.; CO 5th Air Base Group, Mindanao, P. I.)
Fellows   Major Richard W. Fellows
  Report   (Capt.; ASC, CO Philippine Air Depot.)
                         Report—Subject: Philippine Air Depot (dated May
                           18, 1943), together with covering letters to W. D.
                           Edmonds dated December 12, 1946, and January
                           14, 1947, and sketch maps of airfields on Bataan
                           and Corregidor and of the Bataan Field set up in
                           detail.
Kizer   Statement by Major George Kizer
  Statement   (2nd Lt.; 17th Squadron, 24th Pursuit Group, 17th
                           Pursuit Squadron, Provisional.)
Obert   Major David L. Obert
  Report   (2nd Lt.; 17th Squadron, 24th Pursuit Group.)
                         "Activities of Fighter Units in the Philippines."
Robb   Statement by Major Stewart W. Robb
  Statement   (2nd Lt.; 34th Squadron, 24th Pursuit Group.)

Short Title

Rowe

Captain William M. Rowe
(2nd Lt.; 17th Squadron, 24th Pursuit Group.)
"Combat Reports, 10 Dec. 41—29 April 42."
A-2 Library File: US 9000 Interviews.

Sheppard
Statement

Statement by Lieutenant Colonel William A. Sheppard
(1st Lt.; 17th Squadron, 24th Pursuit Group; 17th
Pursuit Squadron, Provisional), and by
Major Edwin B. Gilmore
(2nd Lt.; 20th Squadron, 24th Pursuit Group; 17th
Pursuit Squadron, Provisional).

7. Diaries and Personal Narratives

Ammons
Diary

Diary of 1st Lieutenant V. G. Ammons
(22nd Bombardment Group.)
April through August, 1942, Australia and New
Guinea.

Anonymous
Diary

Diary of personal experience, bombardment operations,
Philippines, Java, Australia.

Cool
Diary

Diary of Major Paul E. Cool
(1st Lt.; 19th Bombardment Group.)
January 19—December 10, 1942, Java, Australia, last
flight to Mindanao.

Gambonini
Diary

Diary of Major Paul B. Gambonini
(2nd Lt.; 20th, later 17th Pursuit Squadron, Provisional.)
January, February, March, 1942, Australia and Java.

Gerhard
Diary

Diary of Edward Ashley Gerhard, Jr., Ensign, USNR,
Corregidor, prisoner of war experiences.

Gowen
Diary

"Gowen's Log"—Diary of Lieutenant Colonel John
Knowles Gowen, G-2 USAFIA, January through
April, 1942, Australia.

Hickman
Diary

Diary of Sergeant Furman M. Hickman
(11th Squadron, 7th Bombardment Group; 28th
Squadron, 19th Bombardment Group.)
December 7, 1941, through April 1942; ground crew
activities, Australia, Java, Australia.

Knudsen
Diary

Diary of Captain Cecil E. Knudsen
(1st Lt.; 9th Squadron, 7th Bombardment Group;
28th Squadron, 19th Bombardment Group.)

Short Title

January 1—November 7, 1942, Java, Australia, New Guinea.

Krieger Personal record of Lieutenant A. E. Krieger
Narrative (3rd Squadron, 24th Pursuit Group.)
  Activities on Luzon and Bataan, set down in the form of a letter to his father, no date given, but written in 1942.

McAfee Diary of Lieutenant Colonel James B. McAfee
Diary (1st Lt.; 16th Squadron, 27th Bombardment Group; A-2 and A-3, 3rd Bombardment Group.)
  November 2, 1941—October 5, 1942, Philippines, Java, Australia, New Guinea.

Robenson's Personal record of Colonel John A. Robenson
Story Chapter IV through VII used here, dealing primarily with his activities December 1941 through February 1942 as Commanding Officer at Port Darwin and as Chief of the mission to supply the Philippine garrison from Java.

Rouse Diary of Lieutenant Colonel John A. Rouse
Diary (1st Lt.; 7th Bombardment Group; 93rd Squadron, 19th Bombardment Group.)
  December 7, 1941—November 16, 1942, Java, Australia, New Guinea.

Thorne Personal record of Colonel Henry G. Thorne, Jr.
Narrative (1st Lt.; CO 3rd Squadron, 24th Pursuit Group.)
  Activities on Luzon and Bataan, undated, but dictated in 1942 immediately after his return to the United States.

List of Abbreviations

AAF	American Air Force
ABDACOM	American, British, Dutch, and Australian Command
ABDAFLOAT	American, British, Dutch, and Australian Navy
ABDAIR	American, British, Dutch, and Australian Air Force
ABDARM	American, British, Dutch, and Australian Army
AIF	Australian Imperial Forces
ASC	Air Service Command
ATC	Air Transport Command
ATIS	Allied Translator and Intelligence Service
AVG	American Volunteer Group
FEAF	Far East Air Force
FEASC	Far East Air Service Command
PAAC	Philippine Army Air Corps
QUANTAS	Queensland and Northern Territory Air Service
RAAF	Royal Australian Air Force
RAF	Royal Air Force
USAF	United States Air Force
USAFFE	United States Army Forces in the Far East
USAFIA	United States Army Forces in Australia
USFIA	United States Forces in Australia
WPO	War Plan Orange

Acknowledgments

My work on this book began in February 1945 at the invitation of Colonel Hans C. Adamson, then Chief of the Personnel Narratives Office. This organization had been set up within the Office of the Chief of Air Staff to implement General Arnold's wish that a series of histories be written of Air Force activities in the various theaters of war from the point of view of the men in the field. Within the year, through illness resulting from active service, Colonel Adamson was forced to relinquish his post; but he has never lost touch with the work he set in motion, and, while both of us have been disappointed at the time it has taken to produce this first volume, I have always been aware of his interest and support.

The Personnel Narratives Office went through various changes, shifting first to the Office of Information and then, with a much smaller staff, becoming the New York City Field Office of the Director of Information, Hq AAF, and finally in March 1948 suffering a complete liquidation. But throughout its career its staff have helped me in every way within their power and I am happy to acknowledge my indebtedness to, in their various capacities: Lieutenant Colonel Bernard A. Bergman; Lieutenant Colonel Thorne Deuel; Major Norman S. Weiser; Major Edwin L. Wilber; Major Russell R. Singer; Lieutenant Robert C. Jackson; Technical Sergeant James E. Pitt; Sergeant E. Ralph Emmett; Mr. Murray Green, Mr. Roosevelt Der Tatevasion, Mr. Sid L. Schwartz; Miss Isabel McCollester; and Mr. Lucien Hubbard and Technical Sergeant George A. McCulloch, who, as stated in the Foreword, did valuable preliminary work on this assignment.

In accumulating the information and interviews on which the narrative is based, I have incurred so many debts and received so many kindnesses from Air Force and Army personnel that I cannot hope to acknowledge all.

The Historical Division, AAF, were uniformly co-operative in providing source material on the early period of the war in the Southwest Pacific Area, but my special thanks are due Major W. F. Craven, and particularly Major Richard C. Watson, author of the chapters of the Official Air Force History, THE ARMY AIR FORCES IN WORLD WAR II, covering the same period, who was kind enough to let me read preliminary drafts of his work on the Australian and early New Guinea phases.

Without the co-operation of General Curtis E. LeMay's Headquarters, 20th Air Force, in the Marianas; General MacArthur's General Headquarters in Manila; and General George C. Kenney's Far East Air Force Headquarters at Fort McKinley, it would have been impossible for me to interview many key figures in this story or trace actions which had already become history in the spring of 1945 over the seas, islands, and terrain on which they were enacted.

For special assistance, courtesies, or hospitality, I am under obligation to Brigadier General Martin F. Schneider, Deputy AAF Air Inspector; to Brigadier General Jack Upston; Major General Robert B. Williams, Colonel E. W. Gardiner, and Captain Jack Ginter, Hq 2nd Air Force; Major General Edwin J. House, Major General Donald Wilson, Colonel Thomas K. Fisher, Colonel H. B. Marks, AAFTAC, Orlando; to Colonel W. L. Kennard; to Major E. G. Gammon, Jr.; to Major Samuel C. Grashio; to Lieutenant Herbert Agoos; to Warrant Officer Dalys C. Kezar; to Colonel Sig R. Young; to Colonel John E. Dougherty; to Major M. C. Rowan; to Lieutenant Colonel Robert H. McCutcheon; to Major General Ennis C. Whitehead, Colonel A. J. Beavers, Major R. W. Schmidt (Historical Section), and Lieutenant C. O. Lacy (PRO), Hq 5th Air Force, Fort Stotsenburg, P. I., and to Sergeant A. C. Shraver of the 30th Air Service Squadron, 5th AF, at Clark Field; to Captain John E. Fagg and Captain Robert C. Futrell (Historical Section), to Major Rodney Southwick and Captain Richard Krolik (PRO), Hq FEAF, Fort McKinley, P. I.; to 2nd Lieutenant R. F. Vose and Sergeant J. B. Martin, Hq Squadron, FEAF; to Colonel Raymond T. Elsmore; to Major General Clements McMullen, Lieutenant Walter T. Cowan (PRO), and particularly to Captain E. A. Holt (Historical Section), Hq FEASC, Hollandia; to Colonel B. A. Shriever, Adv Hq, FEASC, Manila;

to Major Herbert Sapper and Captain J. C. Tillman; to Brigadier General LeGrande A. Diller, GHQ, Manila, and to Private Edward Kurelo, Hq Bn Co D, GHQ; to Major José Francisco, PAAC; to Colonel John P. Henebry, and to Captain Robert M. Irwin, Lieutenant John D. Gholson, Sergeant Willard Haas, and Corporal Kenneth M. Horne, 360th Service Group, at Nadzab; to Major General William E. Lynd, Colonel George C. Cressey, Colonel John Paul Ryan, and Lieutenant Colonel A. L. Erickson, Air Evaluation Board, Brisbane; and to Lieutenant L. M. Moore, Captain A. Cummings, Sergeant C. H. Holt, and Sergeant F. E. Ives, 1557th Bn ATC, Brisbane; to Colonel George K. Markell and Major M. J. Galer, 49th Air Depot Group, FEASC, Darwin; to Wing Commander R. H. Wreford, Hq RAAF, Brisbane; to Captain Fred V. Bell, CO 322nd Wing Detachment, Biak; to Major General Paul C. Wurtsmith (since lost in a tragic air accident) and Lieutenant Colonel J. C. Stehlin, Hq 13th Air Force, Leyte, P. I.; and to Lieutenant Colonel Van Sickle, 1st Infantry Regiment, 1st Battalion, 6th Division, whose hospitality to Lieutenant Colonel Hoffman and myself on Bataan is pleasantly remembered.

But in the matter of source material, my greatest debt is to the Air Force men of all ranks who generously gave their time in interviews and often shared their quarters, provided narratives copied from their personal records and in many cases have followed up our first encounter with correspondence correcting errors or offering additional material. I shall not list them here; their names are all included in the list of sources. It is enough to say that without their co-operation this book could not have been written. But I should like to thank here the following non-Air Force officers for their assistance in clearing up disputed details of the Japanese landings on the west coast of Bataan at the end of January, 1942: Brigadier General William T. Clement, USMC; and Brigadier General Clinton A. Pierce, Colonel Gilmer A. Bell, Colonel Donald B. Hilton, Colonel Clyde A. Sellecks, and Colonel Delbert Ausmus, all of the U. S. Army.

I owe special thanks, for their critical reading of this manuscript, to Major General Eugene L. Eubank, Colonel Orrin L. Grover, Colonel Reginald F. C. Vance, Colonel William L. Kennard, Colonel Lawrence S. Churchill, Colonel Walter B. Putnam, Colonel William J. Bohnaker,

Colonel Edward N. Backus; and also to George Weller and the Editors of MILITARY AFFAIRS for their generous permission to quote from the former's invaluable account of early fighter activities in Australia and in Java, "Luck to the Fighters."

Finally this book would be incomplete without acknowledging my lasting obligation to Lieutenant Colonel Arthur E. Hoffman for expediting my trip through the Pacific theaters in every possible way, for running down tactical personnel whom I might otherwise have missed, for monitoring the manuscript after the expiration of the Personnel Narratives Office, and for his at all times completely objective interest in its completion.

—WALTER D. EDMONDS

INDEX

Index

Note: Ranks given here in general conform to subject's rank during the period covered by the text.